Plan, Activity, and Intent Recognition

Plan, Activity, and Intent Recognition
Theory and Practice

Edited by

Gita Sukthankar

Robert P. Goldman

Christopher Geib

David V. Pynadath

Hung Hai Bui

AMSTERDAM • BOSTON • HEIDELBERG • LONDON
NEW YORK • OXFORD • PARIS • SAN DIEGO
SAN FRANCISCO • SINGAPORE • SYDNEY • TOKYO
Morgan Kaufmann is an imprint of Elsevier

Acquiring Editor: *Todd Green*
Editorial Project Manager: *Lindsay Lawrence*
Project Manager: *Punithavathy Govindaradjane*
Designer: *Russell Purdy*

Morgan Kaufmann is an imprint of Elsevier
225 Wyman Street, Waltham, MA 02451, USA

Library of Congress Cataloging-in-Publication Data
Plan, activity, and intent recognition / Gita Sukthankar, Robert P. Goldman, Christopher Geib, David V. Pynadath, Hung Hai Bui.
    pages cm.
 ISBN 978-0-12-398532-3
1. Human activity recognition. 2. Artificial intelligence. 3. Pattern perception. 4. Intention. I. Sukthankar, Gita, editor of compilation.
 TK7882.P7P57 2014
 006.3--dc23

                              2013050370

British Library Cataloguing-in-Publication Data
A catalogue record for this book is available from the British Library

ISBN: 978-0-12-398532-3

Printed and bound in the United States of America

14 15 16 17 18   10 9 8 7 6 5 4 3 2 1

Working together
to grow libraries in
developing countries

www.elsevier.com • www.bookaid.org

For information on all MK publications visit our website at *www.mkp.com*

Contents

PART 4 MULTIAGENT SYSTEMS

PART 5 APPLICATIONS

Contents   ix

About the Editors

Dr. Gita Sukthankar is an Associate Professor and Charles N. Millican Faculty Fellow in the Department of Electrical Engineering and Computer Science at the University of Central Florida, and an affiliate faculty member at UCF's Institute for Simulation and Training. She received her Ph.D. from the Robotics Institute at Carnegie Mellon, where she researched multiagent plan recognition algorithms. In 2009, Dr. Sukthankar was selected for an Air Force Young Investigator award, the DARPA Computer Science Study Panel, and an NSF CAREER award. Gita Sukthankar's research focuses on multiagent systems and computational social models.

Robert P. Goldman is a Staff Scientist at SIFT, LLC, specializing in Artificial Intelligence. Dr. Goldman received his Ph.D. in Computer Science from Brown University, where he worked on the first Bayesian model for plan recognition. Prior to joining SIFT, he was an Assistant Professor of computer science at Tulane University, and then Principal Research Scientist at Honeywell Labs. Dr. Goldman's research interests involve plan recognition; the intersection between planning, control theory, and formal methods; computer security; and reasoning under uncertainty.

Christopher Geib is an Associate Professor in the College of Computing and Informatics at Drexel University. Before joining Drexel, Professor Geib's career has spanned a number of academic and industrial posts including being a Research Fellow in the School of Informatics at the University of Edinburgh, a Principal Research Scientist working at Honeywell Labs, and a Postdoctoral Fellow at the University of British Columbia in the Laboratory for Computational Intelligence. He received his Ph.D. in computer science from the University of Pennsylvania and has worked on plan recognition and planning for more than 20 years.

Dr. David V. Pynadath is a Research Scientist at the University of Southern California's Institute for Creative Technologies. He received his Ph.D. in computer science from the University of Michigan in Ann Arbor, where he studied probabilistic grammars for plan recognition. He was subsequently a Research Scientist at the USC Information Sciences Institute and is currently a member of the Social Simulation Lab at USC ICT, where he conducts research in multiagent decision–theoretic methods for social reasoning.

Dr. Hung Hai Bui is a Principal Research Scientist at the Laboratory for Natural Language Understanding, Nuance in Sunnyvale, CA. His main research interests include probabilistic reasoning and machine learning and their application in plan and activity recognition. Before joining Nuance, he spent nine years as a Senior Computer Scientist at SRI International, where he led several multi-institutional research teams developing probabilistic inference technologies for understanding human activities and building personal intelligent assistants. He received his Ph.D. in computer science in 1998 from Curtin University in Western Australia.

List of Contributors

Noa Agmon
Bar Ilan University, Ramat Gan, Israel

James Allen
Florida Institute for Human and Machine Cognition, Pensacola, FL, USA

Amol Ambardekar
University of Nevada, Reno, NV, USA

Dorit Avrahami-Zilberbrand
Bar Ilan University, Ramat Gan, Israel

Chris L. Baker
Massachusetts Institute of Technology, Cambridge, MA, USA

Nate Blaylock
Nuance Communications, Montreal, QC, Canada

Prashant Doshi
University of Georgia, Athens, GA, USA

Katie Genter
University of Texas at Austin, Austin, TX, USA

Adam Goodie
University of Georgia, Athens, GA, USA

Sunil Gupta
Deakin University, Waurn Ponds, VIC, Australia

Eun Y. Ha
North Carolina State University, Raleigh, NC, USA

Jerry Hobbs
USC/ISI, Marina del Rey, CA, USA

Naoya Inoue
Tohoku University, Sendai, Japan

Kentaro Inui
Tohoku University, Sendai, Japan

Gal A. Kaminka
Bar Ilan University, Ramat Gan, Israel

Richard Kelley
University of Nevada, Reno, NV, USA

Christopher King
University of Nevada, Reno, NV, USA

Kennard R. Laviers
Air Force Institute of Technology, Wright Patterson AFB, OH, USA

James C. Lester
North Carolina State University, Raleigh, NC, USA

Felipe Meneguzzi
Pontifical Catholic University of Rio Grande do Sul, Porto Alegre, Brazil

Raymond J. Mooney
University of Texas at Austin, Austin, TX, USA

Bradford W. Mott
North Carolina State University, Raleigh, NC, USA

Thuong Nguyen
Deakin University, Waurn Ponds, VIC, Australia

Mircea Nicolescu
University of Nevada, Reno, NV, USA

Monica Nicolescu
University of Nevada, Reno, NV, USA

Jean Oh
Carnegie Mellon University, Pittsburgh, PA, USA

Ekaterina Ovchinnikova
USC/ISI, Marina del Rey, CA, USA

Dinh Phung
Deakin University, Waurn Ponds, VIC, Australia

Xia Qu
University of Georgia, Athens, GA, USA

Sindhu Raghavan
University of Texas at Austin, Austin, TX, USA

Parisa Rashidi
University of Florida, Gainesville, FL, USA

Jonathan P. Rowe
North Carolina State University, Raleigh, NC, USA

Parag Singla
Indian Institute of Technology Delhi, Hauz Khas, DL, India

Peter Stone
University of Texas at Austin, Austin, TX, USA

Gita Sukthankar
University of Central Florida, Orlando, FL, USA

Katia Sycara
Carnegie Mellon University, Pittsburgh, PA, USA

Alireza Tavakkoli
University of Nevada, Reno, NV, USA

Joshua B. Tenenbaum
Massachusetts Institute of Technology, Cambridge, MA, USA

Svetha Venkatesh
Deakin University, Waurn Ponds, VIC, Australia

Liesl Wigand
University of Nevada, Reno, NV, USA

Hankz Hankui Zhuo
Sun Yat-sen University, Guangzhou, China

Preface

The diversity of applications and disciplines encompassed by the subfield of plan, intent, and activity recognition, while producing a wealth of ideas and results, has unfortunately contributed to fragmentation in the area because researchers present relevant results in a broad spectrum of journals and at conferences. This book serves to provide a coherent snapshot of the exciting developments in the field enabled by improved sensors, increased computational power, and new application areas. While the individual chapters are motivated by different applications and employ diverse technical approaches, they are unified by the ultimate task of understanding another agent's behaviors.

As there is not yet a single common conference for this growing field, we hope that this book will serve as a valuable resource for researchers interested in learning about work originating from other communities. The editors have organized workshops in this topic area at the following artificial intelligence conferences since 2004:

- *Modeling Other Agents From Observations (MOO 2004)* at the International Conference on Autonomous Agents and Multi-agent Systems, AAMAS-2004, organized by Gal Kaminka, Piotr Gmytrasiewicz, David Pynadath, and Mathias Bauer
- *Modeling Other Agents From Observations (MOO 2005)* at the International Joint Conference on Artificial Intelligence, IJCAI-2005, organized by Gal Kaminka, David Pynadath, and Christopher Geib
- *Modeling Other Agents From Observations (MOO 2006)* at the National Conference on Artificial Intelligence, AAAI-2006, organized by Gal Kaminka, David Pynadath, and Christopher Geib
- *Plan, Activity, and Intent Recognition (PAIR 2007)* at the National Conference on Artificial Intelligence, AAAI-2007, organized by Christopher Geib and David Pynadath
- *Plan, Activity, and Intent Recognition (PAIR 2009)* at the International Joint Conference on Artificial Intelligence, IJCAI-2009, organized by Christopher Geib, David Pynadath, Hung Bui, and Gita Sukthankar
- *Plan, Activity, and Intent Recognition (PAIR 2010)* at the National Conference on Artificial Intelligence, AAAI-2010, organized by Gita Sukthankar, Christopher Geib, David Pynadath, and Hung Bui
- *Plan, Activity, and Intent Recognition (PAIR 2011)* at the National Conference on Artificial Intelligence, AAAI-2011, organized by Gita Sukthankar, Hung Bui, Christopher Geib, and David Pynadath
- *Dagstuhl Seminar on Plan Recognition* in Dagstuhl, Germany, organized by Tanim Asfour, Christopher Geib, Robert Goldman, and Henry Kautz
- *Plan, Activity, and Intent Recognition (PAIR 2013)* at the National Conference on Artificial Intelligence, AAAI-2013, organized by Hung Bui, Gita Sukthankar, Christopher Geib, and David Pynadath

The editors and many of the authors gathered together at the 2013 PAIR workshop to put the finishing touches on this book, which contains some of the best contributions from the community. We thank all of the people who have participated in these events over the years for their interesting research presentations, exciting intellectual discussions, and great workshop dinners (see Figure P.1).

abduction **activity** **agent** approach based
behavior data demonstration detecting domains
framework goal hierarchical **human** imitation
intent learning markov **modeling**
multiagent **networks** observing opponent personal
plan probabilistic programming
recognition recognizing study
suspicious systems **team** tracking user

FIGURE P.1

Tag cloud created from the titles of papers that have appeared at the workshops in this series.

Introduction

Overview

The ability to recognize the plans and goals of other agents enables humans to reason about what other people are doing, why they are doing it, and what they will do next. This fundamental cognitive capability is also critical to interpersonal interactions because human communications presuppose an ability to understand the motivations of the participants and subjects of the discussion. As the complexity of human–machine interactions increases and automated systems become more intelligent, we strive to provide computers with comparable intent-recognition capabilities.

Research addressing this area is variously referred to as plan recognition, activity recognition, goal recognition, and intent recognition. This synergistic research area combines techniques from user modeling, computer vision, natural language understanding, probabilistic reasoning, and machine learning. Plan-recognition algorithms play a crucial role in a wide variety of applications including smart homes, intelligent user interfaces, personal agent assistants, human–robot interaction, and video surveillance.

Plan-recognition research in computer science dates back at least 35 years; it was initially defined in a paper by Schmidt, Sridharan, and Goodson [64]. In the last ten years, significant advances have been made on this subject by researchers in artificial intelligence (AI) and related areas. These advances have been driven by three primary factors: (1) the pressing need for sophisticated and efficient plan-recognition systems for a wide variety of applications; (2) the development of new algorithmic techniques in probabilistic modeling, machine learning, and optimization (combined with more powerful computers to use these techniques); and (3) our increased ability to gather data about human activities.

Recent research in the field is often divided into two subareas. Activity recognition focuses on the problem of dealing directly with noisy low-level data gathered by physical sensors such as cameras, wearable sensors, and instrumented user interfaces. The primary task in this space is to discover and extract interesting patterns in noisy sensory data that can be interpreted as meaningful activities. For example, an activity-recognition system processing a sequence of video frames might start by extracting a series of motions and then will attempt to verify that they are all part of the activity of filling a tea kettle. Plan and intent recognition concentrates on identifying high-level complex goals and intents by exploiting relationships between primitive action steps that are elements of the plan. Relationships that have been investigated include causality, temporal ordering, coordination among multiple subplans (possibly involving multiple actors), and social convention.

A Brief History

The earliest work in plan recognition was rule based [63,64,77], following the dominant early paradigm in artificial intelligence. Researchers attempted to create inference rules that would capture the nature of plan recognition. Over time, it became clear that without an underlying theory to give them structure and coherence, such rule sets are difficult to maintain and do not scale well.

In 1986, Kautz and Allen published an article, Generalized Plan Recognition [35] that has provided the conceptual framework for much of the work in plan recognition to date. They defined the problem of plan recognition as identifying a minimal set of *top-level actions* sufficient to explain the set of observed actions. Plans were represented in a plan graph, with top-level actions as root nodes and expansions of these actions as unordered sets of child actions representing plan decomposition.

To a first approximation, the problem of plan recognition was then one of graph covering. Kautz and Allen formalized this view of plan recognition in terms of McCarthy's circumscription. Kautz [34] presented an approximate implementation of this approach that recast the problem as one of computing vertex covers of the plan graph. These early techniques are not able to take into account differences in the a priori likelihood of different goals. Observing an agent going to the airport, this algorithm views "air travel" and "terrorist attack" as equally likely explanations because they explain (cover) the observations equally well.

To the best of our knowledge, Charniak was the first to argue that plan recognition was best understood as a specific case of the general problem of *abduction* [11]. Abduction, a term originally defined by the philosopher C. S. Peirce, is reasoning to the best explanation: the general pattern being "if *A* causes *B* and we observe *B*, we may postulate *A* as the explanation." In the case of plan recognition, this pattern is specialized to "if an agent pursuing plan/goal *P* would perform the sequence of actions *S* and we observe *S*, we may postulate that the agent is executing plan *P*." Understanding plan recognition as a form of abductive reasoning is important to the development of the field because it enables clear computational formulations and facilitates connections to areas such as diagnosis and probabilistic inference.

One of the earliest explicitly abductive approaches to plan recognition was that of Hobbs et al. [27]. In this work, they defined a method for abduction as a process of cost-limited theorem-proving [65]. They used this cost-based theorem-proving to find "proofs" for the elements of a narrative, where the assumptions underlying these proofs constitute the interpretation of the narrative—in much the same way a medical diagnosis system would "prove" the set of symptoms in the process identifying the underlying disease. Later developments would show that this kind of theorem-proving is equivalent to a form of probabilistic reasoning [12].

Charniak and Goldman [9] argued that if plan recognition is a problem of abduction, it can best be done as Bayesian (probabilistic) inference. Bayesian inference supports the preference for minimal explanations in the case of equally likely hypotheses, but it also correctly handles explanations of the same complexity but different likelihoods. For example, if a set of observations could be equally well explained by three hypotheses—going to the store to shop *and* to shoplift, being one, and going to the store only to shop or going to the store only to shoplift being the others—simple probability theory (with some minor assumptions) will tell us that the simpler hypotheses are more likely. On the other hand, if as in the preceding, the two hypotheses were "air travel" and "terrorist attack," and each explained the observations equally well, then the prior probabilities will dominate and air travel will be seen to be the most likely explanation.

As one example of the unifying force of the abductive paradigm, Charniak and Shimony showed that Hobbs and Stickel's cost-based abductive approach could be given probabilistic semantics [12] and be viewed as search for the most likely a posteriori explanation for the observed actions. While the Bayesian approach to plan recognition was initially quite controversial, probabilistic inference, in one form or another, has since become the mainstream approach to plan recognition.

Another broad area of attack to the problem of plan recognition has been to reformulate it as a parsing problem (e.g., Vilain [74]) based on the observation that reasoning from actions to plans taken from a plan hierarchy was analogous to reasoning from sentences to parse trees taken from a grammar. Early work on parsing-based approaches to plan recognition promised greater efficiency than other approaches, but at the cost of making strong assumptions about the ordering of plan steps. The major weakness of early work using parsing as a model of plan recognition is that it did not treat partially ordered plans or interleaved plans well. Recent approaches that use statistical parsing [55,19,20] combine parsing and Bayesian approaches and are beginning to address the problems of partially ordered and interleaved plans.

Finally, substantial work has been done using extensions of Hidden Markov Models (HMMs) [6], techniques that came to prominence in signal-processing applications, including speech recognition. They offer many of the efficiency advantages of parsing approaches, but with the additional advantages of incorporating likelihood information and of supporting machine learning to automatically acquire plan models. Standard HMMs are nevertheless not expressive enough to sufficiently capture goal-directed behavior. As a result, a number of researchers have extended them to hierarchical formulations that can capture more complicated hierarchical plans and intentions [6,5].

Much of this latter work has been done under the rubric of *activity recognition* [15]. The early research in this area very carefully chose the term *activity* or *behavior recognition* to distinguish it from plan recognition. The distinction to be made between activity recognition and plan recognition is the difference between recognizing a single (possibly complex) activity and recognizing the relationships between a set of such activities that result in a complete plan.

Activity-recognition algorithms discretize a sequence of possibly noisy and intermittent low-level sensor readings into coherent actions that could be taken as input by a plan-recognition system. The steady decline in sensor costs has made placing instruments in smart spaces practical and brought activity recognition to the forefront of research in the computer vision and pervasive computing communities. In activity recognition, researchers have to work directly with sensor data extracted from video, accelerometers, motion capture data, RFID sensors, smart badges, and Bluetooth. Bridging the gap between noisy, low-level data and high-level activity models is a core challenge of research in this area.

As data becomes more readily available, the role of machine learning and data mining to filter out noise and abstract away from the low-level signals rises in importance. As in other machine learning tasks, activity recognition can be viewed as a supervised [57] or an unsupervised [78] learning task, depending on the availability of labeled activity traces. Alternatively, it can be treated as a problem of hidden state estimation and tackled with techniques such as hierarchical hidden (semi)-Markov models [47,15], dynamic Bayesian networks [39], and conditional random fields [79,73,40].

A specialized subfield of "action recognition" is dedicated to the problem of robustly recognizing short spatiotemporally localized actions or events in video with cluttered backgrounds (see Poppe [53] for a survey); generally, activity recognition carries the connotation that the activity recognized is a more complex sequence of behavior. For instance, "throwing a punch" is an example of an action that could be recognized by analyzing the pixels within a small area of an image and a short duration of time. In contrast, "having a fight" is a complex multiperson activity that could only be recognized by analyzing a large set of spatiotemporal volumes over a longer duration.

Several researchers have been interested in extending plan recognition to multiagent settings [62] and using it to improve team coordination [29,33]. If agents in a team can recognize what their teammates are doing, then they can better cooperate and coordinate. They may also be able to learn something about their shared environment. For example, a member of a military squad who sees another soldier ducking for cover may infer that there is a threat and therefore take precautions.

In domains with explicit teamwork (e.g., military operations or sports), it can be assumed that all the agents have a joint, persistent commitment to execute a goal, share a utility function, and have access to a common plan library grounded in shared training experiences. This facilitates the recognition process such that in the easiest case it is possible to assume that all the actions are being driven by one centralized system with multiple "actuators." For simpler formulations of the multiagent plan recognition (MAPR) problem, recognition can be performed in polynomial time [4]. In the more complex case of dynamic

FIGURE I.1

A mind map of research directions, methods, and applications in plan, activity, and intent recognition.

teams, team membership changes over time and accurate plan recognition requires identifying groupings among agents, in addition to classifying behaviors [67]. Grouping agents in the unconstrained case becomes a set partition problem, and the number of potential allocations rises rapidly, even for a small number of agents. Prior work on MAPR has looked at both extending single-agent formalisms for the multiagent recognition process [62,41,60] and creating specialized models and recognition techniques for agent teams [66,3].

Thus, we see how far the field has evolved, from the genesis of plan recognition as a subproblem within classical AI to a vibrant field of research that stands on its own. Figure I.1 illustrates the diversity of concepts, methods, and applications that now drive advances across plan, activity, and intent recognition. This book provides a comprehensive introduction to these fields by offering representative examples across this diversity.

Chapter Map

The collection of chapters in this book is divided into four parts: (1) classic plan- and goal-recognition approaches; (2) activity discovery from sensory data; (3) modeling human cognitive processes; (4) multiagent systems; and (5) applications of plan, activity, and intent recognition. We discuss each of these areas and the chapters we have grouped under the part headings next.

Classic Plan and Goal Recognition

The book begins with chapters that address modern plan-recognition problems through the same abductive perspective that characterized the seminal work in the field. The Chapter 1 addresses two important challenges in modern plan recognition. The questions are: How much recognition is actually needed to perform useful inference? Can we perform a more limited, but still useful, inference problem more efficiently? Blaylock and Allen, in "Hierarchical Goal Recognition" argue that in many cases we can, and propose to solve the simpler problem of *goal recognition*. They also address a second challenge: evaluating plan-recognition techniques, proposing to use synthetic corpora of plans to avoid the problems of acquiring human goal-directed action sequences annotated with "ground truth" motivation.

Blaylock and Allen's chapter provides a definition of goal recognition as a proper subset of plan recognition. In *goal recognition* all we are interested in is the top-level goal of the agent, while in *plan recognition* we also ask the system to produce a hypothesis about the plan being followed by the agent, and answer questions about the state of plan execution (e.g., "How much of the plan is completed?" and "What roles do particular actions play in the plan?") Blaylock and Allen present an approach to goal recognition based on Cascading Hidden Markov Models.

As plan recognition is maturing, it is moving away from exploratory engineering of proof-of-concept plan-recognition algorithms. However, it is difficult to do "apples-to-apples" comparisons of different techniques without shared datasets. The Monroe Corpus of plans and observation traces created by Blaylock for his Ph.D. dissertation was one of the first publicly available corpora for training and testing plan-recognition systems. It has been a significant resource for the plan recognition community because it attempts to move from an exploratory to a more empirical foundation. This chapter introduces the Monroe Corpus, describes the synthetic generation approach for creating the corpus, and then uses it to evaluate the accuracy and performance of Blaylock and Allen's goal–recognition system.

The next chapter "Weighted Abduction for Discourse Processing Based on Integer Linear Programming" by Inoue et al., represents two important threads in the history of plan recognition: the use of plan recognition in the service of language understanding and the theoretical development of plan recognition in terms of abduction. Some of the earliest work in plan recognition was done in the service of understanding natural language, both in comprehending the motivations and actions of characters in stories [63,10,11] and in order to identify the interests of participants in discourse [13,52,77].

Work by both Charniak's group at Brown and Hobbs's group (originally at SRI) went further, integrating language processing and deeper interpretation in ways that fed backward and forward, such that information about plans could be used to resolve semantic ambiguity in text interpretation. Inoue et al. describe an application to discourse processing, evaluating their work by measuring accuracy in recognizing textual entailment (RTE). RTE is the problem of determining whether particular hypotheses are entailed by the combination of explicit and implicit content of text. In RTE identifying the implicit content of text requires combining explicit content with commonsense background knowledge, including plan recognition.

Inoue et al. further develop Hobbs and Stickel's cost-based approach to abduction. They review the concepts of weighted abduction and describe an enhancement of these methods that uses integer linear programming (ILP) as a method for the cost-based reasoning. They show that this method can speed up the interpretation process by allowing them to exploit both highly optimized ILP solvers and machine learning methods for automatically tuning the cost parameters. They experimentally compare the technique with other methods for plan recognition and show that their wholly automated approach is more accurate than manually tuned plan-recognition methods.

The next chapter "Plan Recognition Using Statistical–Relational Models" by Raghavan et al. is also heavily influenced by an abductive view of the problem of plan recognition. Here, abductive reasoning is formulated in the framework of *statistical relational learning* (SRL) [22]. This framework unifies logical and probabilistic representation and provides expressive relational models that support efficient probabilistic reasoning and statistical parameter estimation from data.

Structured models have long been a challenge for plan-recognition techniques, especially those using probabilistic methods. Traditionally probabilistic models have had very simple structures. Handling more complex structures, including nesting (for subplans), inheritance, and coreference constraints (when shopping, the thing purchased is typically the same as the thing taken from the shelf) was a primary challenge to the development of the first Bayesian methods for plan recognition [9,24]. The early work combined logical and probabilistic *inference* techniques but had no means to perform efficient approximate inference, or to *learn* the required parameters of the models.

In Chapter 3, Raghavan et al. apply *Markov Logic Networks* (MLNs) [59] and *Bayesian Logic Programs* (BLPs) [36] to the problem of plan recognition. To do so, they extend both of these modeling frameworks. MLNs are a very general modeling framework. For MLNs, they provide a number of alternate encodings of abductive reasoning problems. BLPs are theoretically less general but can exploit directionality in the underlying probabilistic graphical model to encode causal relationships. Raghavan et al. develop an extension of BLPs called Bayesian *Abductive* Logic Programs (BALPs). They compare the performance of these techniques on plan-recognition benchmarks, showing that BALPs combine efficient inference with good quality results, outperforming the more general MLNs.

This part of the book then pivots to consider the particularly challenging problem of adversarial plan recognition. In the case of adversarial agents, we cannot expect the observed agents to obligingly provide us with their plan libraries, and they may attempt to evade our observational apparatus, or mislead our plan recognition through stealth or feints. In the chapter "Keyhole Adversarial Plan Recognition for Recognition of Suspicious and Anomalous Behavior," Avrahami-Zilberbrand and Kaminka describe a hybrid plan-recognition system that employs both standard plan recognition and *anomaly detection* to improve recognition in adversarial scenarios. The anomaly detection subsystem complements recognition of known suspicious behavior by detecting behaviors that are not known to be benign. This chapter also investigates the use of utility reasoning in conjunction with likelihood reasoning in plan recognition. Instead of simply identifying the most likely plan for a set of actions, their system also identifies hypotheses that might be less likely but have a larger impact on the system's utility function; in this context, these are more threatening hypotheses.

Activity Discovery and Recognition

An important precursor to the task of activity recognition is the discovery phase—identifying and modeling important and frequently repeated event patterns [43]. Two chapters in the book focus on this emerging research area: Rashidi's chapter on "Stream Sequence Mining and Human Activity Discovery" and "Learning Latent Activities from Social Signals with Hierarchical Dirichlet Processes" by Phung et al. Rashidi's chapter discusses the problem of analyzing activity sequences in smart homes. Smart homes are dwellings equipped with an array of sensors and actuators that monitor and adjust home control system settings to improve the safety and comfort of the inhabitants. Key advances in this area have been driven by several research groups who have made activities of daily living (ADL) datasets publicly available [48,71,70]. Rashidi's work was conducted using data from the CASAS testbed at Washington State [56]; examples of other smart environment projects include Georgia Tech's Aware Home [1] and MIT's House_n [68].

Smart environments pose a challenging data-analysis problem because they output nonstationary streams of data; new elements are continuously generated and patterns can change over time. Many activity discovery approaches (e.g., Minnen et al. [43] and Vahdatpour et al. [72]) use time-series *motif detection*, the unsupervised identification of frequently repeated subsequences, as an element in the discovery process. The term "motif" originated from the bioinformatics community in which it is used to describe recurring patterns in DNA and proteins. Even though these techniques are unsupervised, they make the implicit assumption that it is possible to characterize the user's activity with one dataset sampled from a fixed period of time. Problems arise when the action distribution describing the user's past activity differs from the distribution used to generate future activity due to changes in the user's habits. Thus, it can be beneficial to continue updating the library of activity models, both to add emerging patterns and to discard obsolete ones.

Rashidi proposes that activity discovery can be modeled as a *datastream processing* problem in which patterns are constantly added, modified, and deleted as new data arrives. Patterns are difficult to discover when they are discontinuous because of interruptions by other events, and also when they appear in varied order. Rashidi's approach, STREAMCom, combines a tilted-time window data representation with pruning strategies to discover discontinuous patterns that occur across multiple time scales and sensors. In a fixed-time window, older data are forgotten once they fall outside the window of interest;

however, with the tilted-time representation, the older data are retained at a coarser level. During the pruning phase, infrequent or highly discontinuous patterns are periodically discarded based on a compression objective that accounts for the pattern's ability to compress the dataset. The chapter presents an evaluation of STREAMCom's performance on discovering patterns from several months of data generated by sensors within two smart apartments.

The second chapter in this part by Phung et al., describes a method for analyzing data generated from personal devices (e.g., mobile phones [37], sociometric badges [49], and wearable RFID readers [18]). Wearable RFID readers, such as Intel's iBracelet and iGlove, are well suited for reliably detecting the user's interactions with objects in the environment, which can be highly predictive of many ADL [51]. Sociometric badges are wearable electronic devices designed to measure body movement and physical proximity to nearby badge wearers. The badges can be used to collect data on interpersonal interactions and study community dynamics in the workplace. Two datasets of particular importance, Reality Mining [16] and Badge [49], were released by the MIT Human Dynamics lab to facilitate the study of social signal processing [50].

Phung et al. describe how a Bayesian nonparametric method, the hierarchical Dirichlet process [69], can be used to infer latent activities (e.g., driving, playing games, and working on the computer). The strength of this type of approach is twofold: (1) the set of activity patterns (including its cardinality) can be inferred directly from the data and (2) statistical signals from personal data generated by different individuals can be combined for more robust estimation using a principled hierarchical Bayesian framework. The authors also show how their method can be used to extract social patterns such as community membership from the Bluetooth data that captures colocation of users in the Reality Mining dataset. The activity discovery techniques described in these two chapters will be of interest to readers working with large quantities of data who are seeking to model unconstrained human activities using both personal and environmental sensors.

Modeling Human Cognition

Much of this book presents computational mechanisms that try to recognize a human being's plans, activities, or intentions. This part, in contrast, examines the human brain's own mechanisms for performing such recognition in everyday social interaction. These mechanisms include a *Theory of Mind* (ToM) [75,76] that allows people to attribute to others the same kind of mental states and processes that they possess themselves.

Empirical studies have shown that people typically ascribe goals and beliefs to the observed behavior of others using a causal model informed by their own decision making [26]. This causal model often includes the observed agent's own ToM, leading to recursive levels of recognition [7]. Researchers have sought to build computational models that capture this naturally occurring theory of mind by combining models of rational decision making with reasoning from observed behavior to underlying beliefs and utilities. Such quantitative representations of uncertainty and preferences have provided a rich language for capturing human decision making, and the chapters in this section are emblematic of a growing number of human-inspired approaches to plan recognition [54,58].

This part's first chapter,"Modeling Human Plan Recognition Using Bayesian Theory of Mind," presents a framework for ToM that, like many computational approaches to plan recognition, starts with a generative model of decision making and then uses that model for abductive reasoning. Baker and

Tenenbaum frame a person's decision as a *partially observable Markov decision problem* (POMDP), representing uncertain beliefs as a probability distribution and preferences as a reward function. The POMDP also captures the effects of the person's action choices, supporting domain-independent algorithms that compute a value function over those action choices. These algorithms operate on the assumption that the choices that generate the highest expected reward will have the highest value to the decision maker. By inverting this value function, an observer can perform Bayesian inference to reconstruct the observed person's belief state and reward function, conditional on the observed behavior. The chapter presents empirical evidence showing that this Bayesian theory of mind is an accurate predictor of human judgments when performing plan recognition in experimental settings.

This part's second chapter, "Decision–Theoretic Planning in Multiagent Settings with Application to Behavioral Modeling," similarly uses POMDPs as a basis for abductive reasoning about human behavior. However, just as human ToM operates within the context of social interaction, Doshi et al. place POMDP models of others within the context of the observing agent's own decision making. In particular, their *interactive* POMDPs (I-POMDPs) use nested POMDPs to model an observing agent's decision making while also ascribing ToM in a recursive fashion to the observed agent. Thus, the I-POMDP framework supports plan recognition when observing the behavior of people, who may also be performing plan recognition of people, who may also be performing plan recognition, and so on. Although this recursion may be arbitrarily deep in theory, the chapter also presents a technique by which I-POMDPs of fixed nesting depth can fit data gathered from human behavior when reasoning about others.

Multiagent Systems

Plan- and activity-recognition formalisms generally assume that there is only one person or agent of interest; however, in many real-world deployment scenarios, multiple people are simultaneously performing actions in the same area or cooperating to perform a group task. The presence of multiple agents can lead to action interdependencies that need to be accounted for in order to perform accurate recognition.

The last chapter in this section "Multiagent Plan Recognition from Partially Observed Team Traces," frames the multiagent plan recognition (MAPR) process as a weighted maximum satisfiability (MAX-SAT) problem rather than treating it as abduction or inference, as was presented in the early chapters. In a weighted MAX-SAT problem, the aim is to determine the maximum number of clauses in a Boolean formula that can be satisfied by a variable assignment. Zhuo outlines two representation options: (1) team plans expressed as a set of matrices or (2) a set of action models and goals in the STRIPS planning language. Assuming the existence of a plan library, Zhuo's multiagent recognition system (MARS) finds candidate occurrences of team plans in the observed trace and generates constraints, based on this candidate set, that are used by the solver. In the case in which no plan library exists, Zhuo's alternate framework domain-based multiagent recognition (DARE) identifies plans constructed using the predefined action models that explain all observed activities and have the highest likelihood of achieving the goal, as measured by a combination of coordination costs and plan length. Both frameworks are reasonably robust to increases in the number of agents and the number of missing observations.

This section's second chapter, "Role-Based Ad Hoc Teamwork," moves from plan recognition in STRIPS' domains to examining movement-oriented team tasks (e.g., foraging and capture the flag). Motivated by pick-up soccer games, Genter et al.'s objective is to develop agents capable of participating in *ad hoc* teams. To be an effective participant, these agents adaptively decide on future actions after assessing their teammates' current play. In the Genter et al. approach, team activities are expressed as sets of roles filled by the different players. Assuming that it is possible to accurately recognize the roles of the other players, the agent joining the ad hoc team performs marginal utility calculations to select the best role to fill gaps in the current team's strategy. Analyzing multiagent activities is an area of ongoing research, and the two chapters in this section show the breadth of work in this area.

Applications

This part of the book presents work on the practical application of plan and activity-recognition techniques. The core plan-recognition algorithms are both versatile and broadly applicable to any application that involves human interaction. However, specialized customization, or "secret sauce," is often required to make systems with different types of input data—video [28], natural language [8], or user-interface events [38]—perform well and to adapt general-purpose heuristics to specific situations. These chapters discuss how the recognition process should interface with other system components, rather than focusing on algorithmic improvements to activity and plan recognition.

The first chapter in this part, "Probabilistic Plan Recognition for Proactive Assistant Agents" by Oh et al., illustrates one of the most common applications of plan- and activity-recognition techniques: automated systems that assist human users. To be able to choose the best assistance to provide, such systems must be able to infer the users' current tasks and goals, as well as anticipate their future needs. Oh et al. pay special attention to the need to be *proactive* in providing assistance when the users are under heavy cognitive load, as in emergency response domains. They apply probabilistic plan-recognition algorithms that use a generative *Markov decision problem* (MDP) model of the domain as the basis for the agent's inference of the users' goals. The agent can then use that inference to generate predictions of the users' chosen course of action and to inform its own planning process in assisting that course of action. The chapter illustrates the successful application of this general approach within the specific domains of military peacekeeping operations and emergency response.

Another application area of particular interest is the use of plan/activity recognition as a tool for modeling players in computer games and virtual worlds. Player modeling differs from other types of user-modeling problems because much of the user experience is driven by players' interpretation of virtual world events, rather than being limited to their interactions with menus, the mouse, and the keyboard. The human user simultaneously occupies multiple roles: software customer; inhabitant of the virtual world; and, in serious games, student seeking to perfect skills. Yet people's activities in virtual worlds are more structured than their real-world behavior due to the limited vocabulary of actions and the presence of artificial winning conditions. Also, data collection is easier in virtual environments due to the lack of sensor noise. Thus, human behavior recognition in computer games offers more complexity than other user modeling problems with fewer deployment issues than analyzing data from smart environments.

A popular game format is to provide players with quests that can be completed for character advancement; this style of game supports a nonlinear narrative structure, offers limited freedom to the players to select quest options, and easy extensibility for the game designers. Researchers modeling player behavior in games can assume that all the players' actions are performed in the service of completing quests and formalize the problem as one of goal recognition. Albrecht et al. implemented the earliest demonstration of online goal recognition for text-based computer adventure games using dynamic Bayesian networks to recognize quest goals and to predict future player actions [2]. Adding more game context information to the model has been shown to be helpful for identifying transitions between goals. For example, Gold's system [23] employs low-level inputs in conjunction with input–output HMMs.

The chapter by Ha et al., "Recognizing Player Goals in Open-Ended Digital Games with Markov Logic Networks," describes research done on one of the most famous testbeds, Crystal Island, a game-based learning environment in which the students solve a science mystery [42]. Crystal Island has been used as a testbed for both pedagogical research and earlier studies on performing goal recognition using Bayes nets and scalable n-gram models [45]. In this chapter, Ha et al. describe how Markov logic networks (discussed in Chapter 3 by Raghavan et al.) improve on the previous n-gram model. The authors show that a major advantage of their factored MLN model is that it can leverage associations between successive goals rather than treating the goals individually.

Good player modeling is an important stepping stone toward the creation of player-adaptive games that automatically adjust gameplay to enhance user enjoyment. For instance, dynamic difficulty adjustment games modify the challenge level of the scenario by changing the number, health, and firing accuracy of the opposing forces [30]. Previous work in this area has concentrated on simple numeric attribute adjustments or scenario modifications [32] rather than changing the action choices of the automated opponents.

The chapter, "Using Opponent Modeling to Adapt Team Play in American Football," tackles the problem of creating player-adaptive sports games that learn new strategies for countering the player's actions. Football plays are similar to conditional plans and generate consistent spatiotemporal patterns; the authors demonstrate that it is possible to recognize plays at an early execution stage using a set of supervised classifiers. This differs from prior work on camera-based football recognition systems in which the emphasis has been on recognizing completed plays rather than partial ones (e.g., Intille and Bobick [31]). Play recognition is used in multiple ways: (1) to learn an offline play book designed to be challenging for a specific player and (2) to make online repairs to currently executing plays. With the rapid expansion of game telemetry systems that collect massive amounts of data about players' online experience, it is likely that future game systems will increase their usage of machine learning for player modeling [17].

The last chapter in this part, "Intent Recognition for Human–Robot Interaction" by Kelley et al., addresses human–robot interaction. Many people dream of the day when a "robot butler" will be able to do all the boring, repetitive tasks that we wish we didn't have to do. However, creating a robot that can perform the tasks is only half the battle; it is equally important that the user's interactions with the system be effortless and pleasant. Ultimately, we want household assistants that can anticipate our intentions and plans and act in accordance with them. As discussed in many chapters of this book, building proactive assistant systems (e.g., a robot butler) requires plan recognition.

General-purpose autonomous, physically embodied systems, like the robot butler, rely on the successful integration of a large number of technologies. The system described in this chapter provides a good example that involves the integration of research in vision, planning, plan recognition, robotics, and natural language processing.

Highly integrated systems like this one provide many opportunities to test our research systems. First, and most obviously, they provide us with an opportunity to explore the limits of algorithms when they are taken out of the controlled conditions of the lab. Since plan recognition must share a limited pool of computational resources with other tasks, the real-time requirements in such "embodied" systems are often more demanding than in other application domains. For example, given how much time it takes to plan and execute a response, how much time can we spend on plan recognition?

Second, integration into whole real-world systems can give us much needed perspective on the challenging parts of our respective research questions when applied to actual problems rather than to theoretical cases. For example, what quality and detail can we expect from action observations that come from actual vision or sensor systems?

Finally, highly integrated applications provide us with opportunities to learn from the solutions of others. It exposes us to approaches that researchers in other subareas have employed to address problems that may be similar to ours. For example, can we use knowledge from language to form context structures to help disambiguate plans?

This final chapter illustrates all these issues, and shows us some of the first steps that plan-recognition algorithms are taking to help create applications that will be indispensable in the future.

Future Directions

The immediate future holds many exciting opportunities as well as challenges for the field. The new wave of user-centric and context-aware applications—for example, personal assistants, customized recommendations and content delivery, personalized health- and elder-care assistants, smart and interactive spaces, and human–robot interaction—all share one essential requirement: to accurately capture and track the current user's activities. The continued growth of such applications ensures that plan and activity recognition will receive increased attention from academia and industry. Thanks to the efforts of many research groups, there has been a democratization of recognition techniques in which more software developers are creating and deploying systems that use limited forms of plan and intent recognition. Software toolkits, such as the Google Activity Recognition API [25], have made common algorithms freely accessible for mobile phone platforms.

Yet important unsolved research questions remain and new challenges abound. Interestingly, prominent application areas of today have conflicting requirements for plan recognition. Big data and cloud computing drive the demand for large-scale analysis of data using vast computing power. On the other hand, personal assistants and robotic systems typically contend with resource-constrained mobile platforms. In many cases, we want to handle more complex activities by larger groups of users over extended time periods.

Since the conception of the field, researchers have grappled with a fundamental question: What are the suitable computational models and structures for representing plans, activities, and intents that also facilitate efficient and robust learning and recognition algorithms? Early work in the field mostly employed representations based on predicate or first-order logic, which are convenient for representing the kind of structures often encountered in a plan (e.g., preconditions, postconditions, subgoals). As the need to work with sensor data and events became more acute, recent work has made heavy use of probabilistic and statistical models. In doing so, researchers trade expressivity for robustness against noise, a necessity in real-world applications. As the type of activities and intents we consider increases in complexity, the question about suitable representation structure becomes the focus once more.

For more ambitious applications, we require (1) a rich structure for representing high-level plans and intentions and (2) a mechanism for scoring and ranking the different structures beyond what logical inference can offer. Recent statistical–relational learning frameworks that combine first-order logic, probabilistic reasoning, and statistical estimation promise to satisfy both of these requirements. New work, [46,61,44] including the chapter by Raghavan et al. in this book, has already started to explore this important direction, but much more needs to be done.

More efficient and scalable recognition methods will continue to be a key research theme in theoretical and algorithmic development in the field. We expect that the development of new techniques in machine learning, probabilistic inference, and optimization will serve as the foundation for advancing plan- and activity-recognition algorithms. A relatively unexplored direction is parallelization [21] and leveraging cloud computing resources. On a local scale, these could make our plan-recognition algorithms more responsive, and more globally, they could yield algorithms that can operate at the big data scale.

Automatic creation of models and plan libraries through activity discovery remains a significant problem. The exploding use of personal mobile devices, and location-based social media apps, has led to an increase in the amount of data available about human activities that can be leveraged by activity discovery algorithms. Wearable devices and sensors represent another potentially very large source of data of a different modality. It is clear that, in many domains, to author a large enough set of plans and activities to describe all the possibilities is impractical; therefore, discovering and estimating personalized models from this mostly unlabeled and multimodal data is important. It is also desirable for developers to be able to contribute their domain knowledge by authoring plan models, while not inhibiting the model discovery process.

An issue of growing importance will be protecting the individual's need for privacy in environments where sensors are more common and potentially intrusive. Creating opt-in policies, allowing users greater freedom to protect their data, is a first step toward addressing this issue. Proactive assistant agents and intelligent user interfaces have the potential to provide valuable services to users who choose to expose data to the application. For instance, many users opt to let their mobile phone apps use their GPS data because of the growing number of context-sensitive apps. Ultimately, we hope to see privacy-aware techniques for learning personalized models while allowing trade-offs between maintaining privacy and statistical estimation efficiency [14].

The combination of exciting research problems driven by high-impact, real-world applications, and the exponential growth of user data, will ensure that the field of plan, activity, and intent recognition continues to be an important and fruitful area for researchers and developers in the future.

References

[1] Abowd G, Mynatt E. Designing for the human experience in smart environments. In: Cook D, Das S, editors. Smart environments: technology, protocols, and applications. Wiley; 2004. p. 153–74.

[2] Albrecht A, Zukerman I, Nicholson A. Bayesian models for keyhole plan recognition in an adventure game. J User Modeling User-Adapted Interact 1998;9:5–47.

[3] Avrahami-Zilberbrand D, Kaminka G. Towards dynamic tracking of multi-agents teams: an initial report. In: Proceedings of the workshop on plan, activity, and intent recognition; 2007. p. 17–22.

[4] Banerjee B, Kraemer L, Lyle J. Multi-agent plan recognition: formalization and algorithms. In: Proceedings of the national conference on artificial intelligence; 2010. p. 1059–64.

[5] Bui HH, Phung DQ, Venkatesh S. Hierarchical Hidden Markov models with general state hierarchy. In: Proceedings of the 19th national conference on artificial intelligence; 2004. p. 324–29.

[6] Bui Hung H, Venkatesh Svetha, West Geoff. Policy recognition in the abstract Hidden Markov model. J Artif Intell Res 2002;17:451–99.

[7] Camerer C, Ho TH, Chong JK. A cognitive hierarchy model of games. Quart J Econom 2004;119:861–98.

[8] Carberry S. Plan recognition in natural language dialogue. MIT Press; 1990.

[9] Charniak E, Goldman RP. A Bayesian model of plan recognition. Artif Intell 1993;64(1):53–79.

[10] Charniak Eugene. A common representation for problem solving and language comprehension information. Artif Intell 1981;16:225–55.

[11] Charniak Eugene, McDermott Drew. Introduction to artificial intelligence. Addison-Wesley; 1985.

[12] Charniak Eugene, Eyal Shimony Solomon. Cost-based abduction and MAP explanation. Artif Intell 1994;66(2):345–74.

[13] Cohen Philip R, Raymond Perrault C. Elements of a plan-based theory of speech acts. Cogn Sci 1979;3:177–212.

[14] Duchi John C, Jordan Michael I, Wainwright Martin. Privacy aware learning. In: Neural information processing systems; 2012. p. 1439–47.

[15] Duong TV, Bui HH, Phung DQ, Venkatesh S. Activity recognition and abnormality detection with the switching Hidden semi-Markov model. In: Proceedings of the IEEE computer society conference on computer vision and pattern recognition; 2005. p. 838–45.

[16] Eagle N, Pentland A. Reality mining: sensing complex social systems. J Personal Ubiquitous Comput 2006;10(4):255–68.

[17] El-Nasr M, Drachen A, Canossa A, editors. Game analytics: maximizing the value of player data. Springer; 2013.

[18] Fishkin K, Philipose M, Rea A. Hands-on RFID: wireless wearables for detecting use of objects. In: Proceedings of the IEEE international symposium on wearable computers; 2005. p. 38–41.

[19] Geib Christopher W. Delaying commitment in probabilistic plan recognition using combinatory categorial grammars. In: Proceedings of the international joint conference on artificial intelligence; 2009. p. 1702–7.

[20] Geib Christopher W, Goldman Robert P. A probabilistic plan recognition algorithm based on plan tree grammars. Artif Intell 2009;173(11):1101–32.

[21] Geib Christopher W, Swetenham Christopher E. Parallelizing plan recognition. In: Workshop on plan activity and intent recognition at the twenty-seventh AAAI conference on artificial intelligence; 2013. p. 10–6.

[22] Getoor Lise, Taskar Ben. Introduction to statistical relational learning (Adaptive computation and machine learning). MIT Press; 2007.

[23] Gold Kevin. Training goal recognition online from low-level inputs in an action-adventure game. In: Proceddings of the AAAI conference on artificial intelligence and interactive digital entertainment; 2010. p. 21–6.

[24] Goldman RP, Charniak E. Probabilistic text understanding. Statist Comput 1992;2:105–14.

[25] Google. Activity recognition API. <http://developer.android.com/reference/com/google/android/gms/location/ActivityRecognitionClient.html>.

[26] Alison Gopnik, Meltzoff Andrew N. Words, thoughts, and theories. MIT Press; 1997.

[27] Hobbs Jerry, Stickel Mark, Appelt Douglas, Martin Paul. Interpretation as abduction. Artif Intell 1993;63:69–142.

[28] Hoogs A, Perera A. Video activity recognition in the real world. In: Proceedings of national conference on artificial intelligence; 2008. p. 1551–4.

[29] Huber M, Durfee E, Wellman M. The automated mapping of plans for plan recognition. In: Procceedings of the uncertainty in artifcial intelligence; 1994. p. 344–51.

[30] Hunicke R, Chapman V. AI for dynamic difficulty adjustment in games. In: Proceedings of the AAAI workshop on challenges in game artificial intelligence; 2004. p. 91–6.

[31] Intille S, Bobick A. A framework for recognizing multi-agent action from visual evidence. In: Proceedings of the national conference on artificial intelligence; 1999. p. 518–25.

[32] Jennings-Teats M, Smith G, Wardrip-Fruin N. Polymorph: dynamic difficulty adjustment through level generation. In: Proceedings of the FDG workshop on procedural content generation in games; 2010.

[33] Kaminka G, Bowling M. Towards robust teams with many agents. In: Proceedings of the international conference on autonmous agents and multi-agent systems; 2002. p. 729–36.

[34] Kautz H. A formal theory of plan recognition [Ph.D. thesis]. University of Rochester; 1987.

[35] Kautz Henry, Allen James F. Generalized plan recognition. In: Proceedings of the fifth national conference on artificial intelligence; 1986. p. 32–8.

[36] Kersting Kristian, De Raedt Luc. Bayesian logic programming: theory and tool. In: Getoor Lise, Taskar Ben, editors. Statistical relational learning. MIT Press; 2007.

[37] Lane N, Miluzzo E, Lu H, Peebles D, Choudhury T, Campbell A. A survey of mobile phone sensing. IEEE Commun 2010;49(9):140–50.

[38] Lesh N, Rich C, Sidner C. Using plan recognition in human-computer collaboration technical report TR98-23. Mitsubishi Electric Research Laboratories; 1998.

[39] Liao L, Fox D, Kautz H. Learning and inferring transportation routines. In: Proceedings of the national conference on artificial intelligence; 2004. p. 348–53.

[40] Liao Lin, Fox Dieter, Kautz Henry. Extracting places and activities from GPS traces using hierarchical conditional random fields. Int J Robot Res 2007;26(1):119–34.

[41] Masato Daniele, Norman Timothy, Vasconcelos Wamberto, Sycara Katia. Agent-oriented incremental team and activity recognition. In: Proceedings of the international joint conference on artificial intelligence; 2011. p. 1402–7.

[42] McQuiggan S, Rowe J, Lee S, Lester J. Story-based learning: the impact of narrative on learning experiences and outcomes. In: Proceedings of the international conference on intelligent tutoring systems; 2008. p. 530–9.

[43] Minnen D, Starner T, Essa I, Isbell C. Discovering characteristic actions from on-body sensor data. In: Proceedings of the IEEE international symposium on wearable computers; 2006. p. 11–8.

[44] Morariu Vlad I, Davis Larry S. Multi-agent event recognition in structured scenarios. In: Proceedings of the IEE conference on computer vision and pattern recognition; 2011. p. 3289–96.

[45] Mott B, Lee S, Lester J. Probabilistic goal recognition in interactive narrative environments. In: Proceedings of the national conference on artificial intelligence; 2006. p. 187–92.

[46] Natarajan Sriraam, Bui Hung, Tadepalli Prasad, Kersting Kristian, Wong Weng-Keen. Logical hierarchical Hidden Markov models for modeling user activities. In: Proceedings of the international conference on inductive logic programming; 2008. p. 192–209.

[47] Nguyen N, Phun D, Venkatesh S, Bui H. Learning and detecting activities from movement trajectories using hierarchical Hidden Markov models. In: Proceedings of the computer vision and pattern recognition; 2005. p. 955–60.

[48] Carnegie Mellon University. Quality of life technology center. Grand challenge data collection. <http://kitchen.cs.cmu.edu/>.

[49] Olguin D, Waber B, Kim T, Mohan A, Ara K, Pentland A. Sensible organizations: technology and methodology for automatically measuring organizational behavior. IEEE Trans Syst Man Cybernet: Part B 2009;39(1):43–55.

[50] Pentland A. Honest signals: how they shape our world. MIT Press; 2008.

[51] Pentney W, Popescu A, Wang S, Kautz H, Philipose M. Sensor-based understanding of daily life via large-scale use of common sense. In: Proceedings of the national conference on artificial intelligence; 2006. p. 906–12.

[52] Raymond Perrault C, Allen James F. A plan-based analysis of indirect speech acts. Am J Comput Linguist 1980;6(3–4):167–82.

[53] Poppe Ronald. A survey on vision-based human action recognition. J Image Vis Compu 2010;28(6):976–90.

[54] Pynadath David V, Marsella Stacy C. PsychSim: modeling theory of mind with decision-theoretic agents. In: Proceedings of the international joint conference on artificial intelligence; 2005. p. 1181–6.

[55] Pynadath David V, Wellman Michael P. Accounting for context in plan recognition with application to traffic monitoring. In: Proceedings of uncertainty in artificial intelligence; 1995. p. 472–81.

[56] Rashidi P, Cook D. The resident in the loop: adapting the smart home to the user. IEEE Trans Syst Man Cybernet (Part A) 2009;39(5):949–59.

[57] Ravi N, Dandekar N, Mysore P, Littman M. Activity recognition from accelerometer data. In: Proceedings of the national conference on innovative applications of artificial intelligence; 2005. p. 1541–46.

[58] Ray D, King-Casas B, Montague PR, Dayan P. Bayesian model of behavior in economic games. In: Advances in neural information processing systems 21; 2008. p. 1345–52.

[59] Richardson Matt, Domingos Pedro. Markov logic networks. Mach Learn 2006;62:107–36.

[60] Sadilek Adam, Kautz Henry. Location-based reasoning about complex multi-agent behavior. J Artif Intell Res 2012;43:87–133.

[61] Sadilek Adam, Kautz Henry A. Recognizing multi-agent activities from GPS data. In: Proceedings of the national conference on artificial intelligence; 2010. p. 1134–9.

[62] Saria S, Mahadevan S. Probabilistic plan recognition in multiagent systems. In: Proceedings of the international conference on automated planning and scheduling; 2004. p. 287–96.

[63] Schank Roger C, Abelson Robert P. Scripts, plans, goals, and understanding. Lawrence Erlbaum Associates; 1977.

[64] Schmidt CF, Sridharan NS, Goodson JL. The plan recognition problem: an intersection of psychology and artificial intelligence. Artif Intell 1978;11:45–83.

[65] Stickel Mark E. A Prolog-like inference system for computing minimum-cost abductive explanations in natural-language interpretation technical report. Artificial Intelligence Center, SRI International; 1988.

[66] Sukthankar Gita, Sycara Katia. Simultaneous team assignment and behavior recognition from spatio-temporal agent traces. In: Proceedings of the AAAI conference on artificial intelligence; 2006. p. 716–21.

[67] Sukthankar Gita, Sycara Katia. Activity recognition for dynamic multi-agent teams. ACM Trans Intell Syst Technol 2011;3(1):18:1–18:24.

[68] Tapia EM, Intille S, Larson K. Activity recognition in the home using simple and ubiquitous sensors. In: Proceedings of the international conference on pervasive computing; 2004. p. 158–75.

[69] Teh Yee Whye, Jordan Michael I, Beal Matthew J, Blei David M. Hierarchical Dirichlet processes. J Am Statist Assoc 2006;101(476).

[70] University of Rochester, activities of daily living dataset. <http://www.cs.rochester.edu/~rmessing/uradl/>.

[71] University of Washington Lahar Project. RFID data. <http://lahar.cs.washington.edu/displayPage.php?path=./content/Download/RFIDData/rfidData.html>.

[72] Vahdatpour A, Amini N, Sarrafzadeh M. Toward unsupervised activity discovery using multi-dimensional motif detection in time series. In: Proceedings of the international joint conference on artificial intelligence (IJCAI); 2009. p. 1261–6.

[73] Vail D, Lafferty J, Veloso M. Conditional random fields for activity recognition. In: Proceedings of the international conference on autonmous agents and multi-agent systems; 2007. p. 1326–33.

[74] Vilain M. Getting serious about parsing plans: a grammatical analysis of plan recognition. In: Proceedings of the national conference on artificial intelligence; 1990. p. 190–7.

[75] Wellman HM. The child's theory of mind. MIT Press; 1990.

[76] Andrew Whiten, editor. Natural theories of mind. Basil Blackwell; 1991.

[77] Wilensky Robert. Why John married Mary: understanding stories involving recurring goals. Cogn Sci 1978;2(3):235–66.

[78] Wyatt D, Philipose M, Choudhury T. Unsupervised activity recognition using automatically mined common sense. In: Proceedings of the national conference on artificial intelligence; 2005. p. 21–7.

[79] Zhao Liyue, Wang Xi, Sukthankar Gita, Sukthankar Rahul. Motif discovery and feature selection for CRF-based activity recognition. In: Proceedings of the IAPR/IEEE international conference on pattern recognition; 2010. p. 3826–9.

Plan and Goal Recognition

Hierarchical Goal Recognition

Nate Blaylock[a] and James Allen[b]

[a]*Nuance Communications, Montreal, QC, Canada*
[b]*Florida Institute for Human and Machine Cognition, Pensacola, FL, USA*

1.1 Introduction

Much work has been done over the years in *plan recognition* which is the task of inferring an agent's goal and plan based on observed actions. *Goal recognition* is a special case of plan recognition in which only the goal is recognized. Goal and plan recognition have been used in a variety of applications including intelligent user interfaces [6,18,20], traffic monitoring [26], and dialog systems [13].

For most applications, several properties are required in order for goal recognition to be useful, as follows:

Speed: Most applications use goal recognition "online," meaning they need recognition results before the observed agent has completed its activity. Ideally, goal recognition should take a fraction of the time it takes for the observed agent to execute its next action.

Precision and recall: We want the predictions to be correct (precision), and we want to make correct predictions at every opportunity (recall).

Early prediction: Applications need accurate plan prediction as early as possible in the observed agent's task execution (i.e., after the fewest number of observed actions). Even if a recognizer is fast computationally, if it is unable to predict the plan until after it has seen the last action in the agent's task, it will not be suitable for online applications; those need recognition results *during* task execution. For example, a helpful assistant application needs to recognize a user's goal early to be able to help. Similarly, an adversarial agent needs to recognize an adversary's goal early in order to help thwart its completion.

Partial prediction: If full recognition is not immediately available, applications often can make use of partial information. For example, if the parameter values are not known, just knowing the goal schema may be enough for an application to notice that a hacker is trying to break into a network. Also, even though the agent's top-level goal (e.g., steal trade secrets) may not be known, knowing a subgoal (e.g., gain root access to server 1) may be enough for the application to act. (Our approach enables both types of partial prediction.)

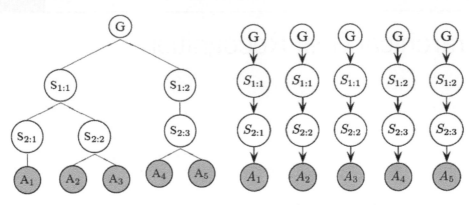

FIGURE 1.1

A hierarchical plan and corresponding goal chains.

In our work, we model goals, subgoals, and actions as parameterized action schemas from the SHOP2 HTN planner [23]. With this formalism, we can distinguish between recognition of a goal *schema* and its corresponding *parameter values*. The term *instantiated goal recognition* means the recognition of a goal schema together with its parameter values. Additionally, we consider the task of *hierarchical goal recognition*, which is the recognition of the chain of the agent's currently active top-level goal and subgoals within a hierarchical plan. As an illustration, consider Figure 1.1; it shows a hierarchical plan tree and a corresponding set of goal chains for left-to-right execution.

Here, the root of the tree (G) is the agent's top-level goal. Leaves of the tree (A_1-A_5) represent the atomic actions executed by the agent. Nodes in the middle of the tree represent the agent's various subgoals within the plan. For each executed atomic action, we can define a *goal chain* which is the subgoals that were active at the time it was executed. This is the path that leads from the atomic action to the top-level goal G. We cast hierarchical goal recognition as the recognition of the goal chain corresponding to the agent's last observed action.

Recognizing such goal chains can provide valuable information not available from a system that recognizes top-level goals only. First, though not full plan recognition, which recognizes the full plan tree, hierarchical goal recognition provides information about which goal an agent is pursuing as well as a partial description of *how* (through the subgoals).

Additionally, the prediction of subgoals can be seen as a type of partial prediction. As mentioned before, when a full prediction is not available, a recognizing agent can often make use of partial predictions. A hierarchical recognizer may be able to predict an agent's subgoals even when the top-level goal is still not clear. This can allow a recognizer to make predictions much earlier in an execution stream (i.e., after less observed actions).

The remainder of this chapter first discusses previous work in goal recognition. We then detail the need for annotated data for plan recognition and present a method for generating synthetic labeled data for training and testing plan recognizers. This is followed by a discussion of how best to measure plan recognition performance among a number of attributes. We then describe our own hierarchical goal recognizer and its performance. Finally, we conclude and discuss future directions.

1.2 **Previous Work**

We focus here exclusively on previous work on hierarchical goal recognition. For a good overview of plan recognition in general, see Carberry [14].

Pynadath and Wellman [27] use probabilistic state-dependent grammars (PSDGs) to do plan recognition. PSDGs are probabilistic context-free grammars (PCFGs) in which the probability of a production is a function of the current state. This allows, for example, the probability of a recipe (production) to become zero if one of its preconditions does not hold. Subgoals are modeled as nonterminals in the grammar, and recipes are productions that map those nonterminals into an ordered list of nonterminals or terminals. During recognition, the recognizer keeps track of the current productions and the state variables as a Dynamic Bayes Network (DBN) with a special update algorithm. The most likely string of current productions is predicted as the current hierarchical goal structure.

If the total state is observable, Pynadath and Wellman claim the complexity of the update algorithm to be linear in the size of the plan hierarchy (number of productions).[1] However, if the state is only partially observable, the runtime complexity is quadratic in the number of states consistent with observation, which grows exponentially with the number of unobservable state nodes.

Additionally, the recognizer only recognizes atomic goals and does not take parameters into account. Finally, although the PSDGs allow fine probability differences for productions depending on the state, it is unclear how such probability functions could be learned from a corpus because the state space can be quite large.

Bui [10] performs hierarchical recognition of Markov Decision Processes. He models these using an Abstract Hidden Markov Model (AHMM)—multilevel Hidden Markov Models where a policy at a higher level transfers control to a lower level until the lower level "terminates." The addition of memory to these models [11] makes them very similar to the PSDGs used by Pynadath in that each policy invokes a "recipe" of lower-level policy and does not continue until the lower level terminates.

Recognition is done using a DBN, but because this is intractable, Bui uses a method called Rao-Blackwellization (RB) to split network variables into two groups. The first group, which includes the state variables as well as a variable that describes the highest terminating state in the hierarchy, is estimated using sampling methods. Then, using those estimates, exact inference is performed on the second part—the policy variables. The separation is such that exact inference on the second group becomes tractable, given that the first group is known.

The recognizer was used in a system that tracked human behavior in an office building at three abstract levels, representing individual offices at the bottom level, then office groups, and then finally the entire building. Policies at each level were defined specific to each region—for example, the policy (behavior) of using the printer in the printer room. In this model, only certain policies are valid in a given state (location), which helps reduce the ambiguity. Typically, the domain is modeled such that lower-level policies become impossible as the agent moves to another room, which makes it fairly clear when they then terminate.

Although the algorithm was successful for this tracking task, it is unclear how effective estimation of policy termination would be in general (e.g., when most policies are valid in most states). Also, similar to Pynadath, this method only recognizes atomic goals and does not support parameters.

---

[1] This claim is disputed in Bui [10].

1.3 Data for Plan Recognition

Historically, work on plan recognition (under its many names and guises) has been quite fragmented, and, although statistical techniques have been used, the data-driven revolution, which has occurred in many AI fields, has lagged for plan recognition; in part this is because of a lack of common data sets and metrics that allow systems to be compared. This section discusses *plan corpora*: data appropriate for plan recognition. We first describe types and possible sources of plan corpora. We then detail a novel method for creating synthetic data and describe the Monroe Plan Corpus, which was created using this method and serves as the principal data set for the goal recognizer in this chapter.

1.3.1 Human Sources of Plan Corpora

In this section we mention several plausible ways of gathering plan corpora by observing humans. These can be divided into the kind of data that they make available: unlabeled, goal labeled, and plan labeled data. We describe each in turn and then discuss the general difficulties of gathering human data.

1.3.1.1 *Unlabeled data*

Several techniques are used in related fields for gathering unlabeled data, which could be useful for plan recognition.

A number of projects in ubiquitous computing [2,25,29] have gathered raw data of a user's state over time (location and speed from GPS data), which they use to predict user activity. These represent very low-level data, however, that is not immediately compatible with the intentional action streams that most plan recognizers take as input.

There have been several efforts to watch user behavior on a computer (e.g., mouse clicks, Unix commands) in order to recognize activity ([16,21], *inter alia*). It is unclear how useful such unlabeled data would be by itself for plan recognition (although Bauer [5], has done work on using such data to automatically construct recipe libraries).

1.3.1.2 *Goal-labeled data*

Much more useful to plan recognition are goal-labeled plan corpora, although such corpora are even more difficult to come by.

Albrecht et al. [1] extract a plan corpus from the logs of a Multi-User Dungeon (MUD) game. A log includes a sequence of both player location (within the game) and each command executed. In addition, the MUD records each successful quest completion, which can be used to automatically tag plan sessions with a top-level goal (as well as partial state with the user's location). Albrecht et al. report that the corpus data is quite noisy: first because of player errors and typos and then because players in MUDs often interleave social interaction and other activities. We should also note that the goals in the corpus are atomic, as opposed to being parameterized goal schemas.

More tightly controlled, goal-labeled corpora have been gathered through data collection efforts in Unix [19] and Linux[2] [7] domains. In these experiments, test subjects are given a specific goal (e.g., "find a file that ends in.tex") and their shell commands are recorded as they try to accomplish it. The

---

[2] www.cs.rochester.edu/research/cisd/resources/linux-plan/

subjects then report when they have successfully accomplished the goal because there is no way to easily compute this automatically.

In these controlled experiments, top-level goal labeling is much more reliable because it is assigned a priori. Of course, this work can still be noisy, as when the subject misunderstands the goal or incorrectly believes he has accomplished it. Also, this kind of data collection is expensive as compared to those mentioned earlier. The preceding data collections monitor the normal activity of subjects, whereas these types of collections require subjects to work on tasks specifically for the collection.

1.3.1.3 *Plan-labeled data*

Of course, the most useful type of plan corpus would include not only the top-level goal but also the plan and state of the world.

Bauer [4] records user action sequences (and corresponding system state) in an email program and uses a plan recognizer post hoc to label them with the appropriate goal and plan. This post hoc recognition can potentially be much more accurate than online prediction because it is able to look at the whole execution sequence. A potential problem we see with this approach is that, if the original plan recognizer consistently makes mistakes in predicting plans, these mistakes will be propagated in the corpus. This includes cases where the plan library does not cover extra or erroneous user actions.

1.3.1.4 *General challenges for human plan corpora*

In addition to the individual disadvantages mentioned, we see several shortcomings to this kind of human data collection for plan recognition.

First, this kind of data collection is most feasible in domains (e.g., operating systems) where higher-level user actions can be directly observed and automatically recorded (as opposed to low-level sensor readings). This, unfortunately, excludes most nonsoftware interaction domains. In fact, the only way we can envision to gather data for other domains would be to have it annotated by hand, which could be expensive and time consuming. Not to mention error-prone.

Finally, a major shortcoming of this work is that it is at most labeled with a top-level goal.[3] In most domains where plan recognition is used (e.g., natural language understanding), the system can benefit not only from the prediction of a top-level goal but also from partial results where a subgoal is predicted. This is especially true of domains with plans composed of large action sequences, where the top-level goal may not become apparent until very far into the plan's execution. We imagine that manual annotation of plan labeling would be quite tedious and error-prone.

1.3.2 **Artificial Corpus Generation**

In contrast to human data collection, we propose the use of an AI planner and Monte Carlo simulation to stochastically generate *synthetic* plan corpora [8]. This method can be used for any domain and provides a corpus accurately labeled with goal and hierarchical plan structure. It also provides an inexpensive way to produce the kind of large corpora needed for machine learning. The method is as follows:

1. Modify an AI planner to search for valid plans nondeterministically.
2. Model the desired domain for the planner.

---

[3]Except for Bauer [4], although, as we mentioned earlier, the corpus can be skewed by the original recognizer's mistakes.

3. The algorithm does the following to generate each item in the corpus:

    (a) Stochastically generates a goal.
    (b) Stochastically generates a start state.
    (c) Uses the planner to find a valid plan for the generated goal and start state.

Next, we first describe the modifications to an AI planner. Then we discuss issues of domain modeling and the stochastic generation of the goal and start state. Finally, we discuss the general characteristics of the corpora generated by this process and mention the Monroe Plan Corpus.

1.3.2.1 *Planner modification*

For plan recognition, we want to create corpora that allow for all possible plans in the domain. Typical AI planners do not support this, as they usually deterministically return the same plan for a given goal and start state. Many planners also try to optimize some plan property (e.g., length or cost) and therefore would never output longer, less optimal plans. We want to include all possible plans in our corpus to give us broad coverage.

We therefore modified the SHOP2 planner [23] to randomly generate one of the set of all possible plans for a given goal and start state.[4] We did this by identifying key decision points in the planner and randomizing the order that they were searched.

SHOP2 [23] is a sound and complete hierarchical transition network (HTN) planner. SHOP2 is novel in that it generates plan steps in the order they will be executed, which allows it to handle complex reasoning capabilities, such as axiomatic inference, and calls to external programs. It also allows partially ordered subtasks. The planning model in SHOP2 consists of *methods* (decomposable goals), *operators* (atomic actions), and *axioms* (facts about the state).

In searching the state space, there are three types of applicable decision points, which represent branches in the search space[5]:

- Which (sub) goal to work on next
- Which method to use for a goal
- Which value to bind to a parameter

To provide for completeness, SHOP2 keeps lists of all possibilities for a decision point so that it may backtrack if necessary. We modified the planner so that these lists are randomized after they are populated but before they are used. This one-time randomization guarantees that we search in a random order but also allows us to preserve the soundness and completeness of the algorithm. We believe the randomized version is equivalent to computing all valid plans and randomly choosing one.

1.3.2.2 *Domain modeling*

Each new domain must be modeled for the planner, just as it would if the intent were to use the planner for its usual purpose. As opposed to modeling for plan generation, however, care should be taken to model the domain such that it can encompass all anticipated user plans.

---

[4]In principle, the corpus-generation technique described here is possible using any planner. The only caveat is that the planner must be randomized, which may or may not be a straightforward thing to do. One of the reasons we chose SHOP2 was its small code base and a modular design that was amenable to randomization.

[5]There is also a fourth that deals with :immediate tasks, but that is beyond the scope of this chapter.

Usually the planning model must be written by hand, although work has been done on (semi-) automating the process (e.g., by Bauer [5]). Note that, in addition to the model of the plan library, which is also used in many plan recognizers, it is necessary to model state information for the planner.

1.3.2.3 *Goal generation*

We separate goal generation into two steps: generating the goal schema and generating parameter values for the schema.

Goal Schema Generation. In addition to the domain model for the planner, the domain modeler needs to provide a list of possible top-level goals in the domain, together with their a priori probability. A priori probabilities of goals are usually not known, but they could be estimated by the domain modeler's intuitions (or perhaps by a small human corpus). The algorithm uses this list to stochastically pick one of the goal schemas.

Goal Parameter Value Generation. In domains where goals are modeled with parameters, the values of the parameters also must be generated. Goal parameter values can be generated by using one of two techniques. For goal schemas where the parameter values are more or less independent, the domain modeler can give a list of possible parameter values for each slot, along with their a priori probabilities. For schemas where parameter values are not independent, each possible set of parameter values is given, along with their probabilities.

Once the goal schema has been chosen, the algorithm uses this list to stochastically generate values for each parameter in it. At this point, a fully instantiated goal has been generated.

1.3.2.4 *Start state generation*

In addition to a top-level goal, planners need to know the state of the world—the start state. To model agent behavior correctly, we need to stochastically generate start states, as this can have a big effect on the plan an agent chooses.

Generating the start state is not as straightforward as goal generation for several reasons. First, the domain must be structured such that we can generate start states with an accompanying a priori probability. Second, in order to make the planning fast, we need to generate a start state from which the generated goal is achievable. As a practical matter, most planners (including SHOP2) are **very slow** when given an impossible goal because they must search through all the search space before noticing that the goal is impossible.

For these reasons, only a start state that makes the generated goal achievable should be generated. Unfortunately, we know of no general way of doing this.[6] We do believe, however, that some general techniques can be used for start state generation. We discuss these next.

The approach we have chosen is to separate the state model into two parts: fixed and variable. In the *fixed* part, we represent all facts about the state that should be constant across sessions. This includes such things as fixed properties of objects and fixed facts about the state (e.g., the existence of certain objects, the location of cities).

The *variable* part of the state contains those facts that should be stochastically generated. Even with the fixed–variable separation, this part will probably not be a set of independent stochastically generated

---

[6]One possibility might be backchaining from the goal state, although we have not explored this.

Table 1.1 The Monroe Corpus	
Total sessions	5000
Goal schemas	10
Action schemas	30
Average actions/session	9.5
Subgoal schemas	28
Average subgoal depth	3.8
Maximum subgoal depth	9

facts. Instead, the domain modeler must come up with code to do this by taking into account, among other things, domain objects, their attributes, and other states of the world. It is likely that values of sets of facts will need to be decided simultaneously, especially in cases where they are mutually exclusive, or one implies another, and so forth. This will likely also need to be closely linked to the actual goal that has been generated to ensure achievability.

1.3.2.5 *The resulting synthetic corpus*

A corpus generated by the process described here will contain a complex distribution of plan sessions. This distribution results from the interaction between (1) the a priori probabilities of top-level goals, (2) the probabilities of top-level goal parameter values, (3) the algorithm for generating start states, and (4) information encoded in the plan library itself. Thus, although it cannot be used to compute the a priori probabilities of top-level goals and parameter values, which are given as input to the generator, it can be used to, for example, model the probabilities of subgoals and atomic actions in the domain. This is information that cannot be learned directly from the plan library, since the recipes and variable fillers used are also dependent on, for example, the start state.

1.3.2.6 *The Monroe Plan Corpus*

We used this process to create the Monroe Plan Corpus[7] for plans in an emergency response domain. In Monroe, we generated 5000 plans for 10 top-level goal schemas. Statistics about the Monroe Plan Corpus can be found in Table 1.1. For more details, see Blaylock and Allen [8]. This is the only plan-labeled corpus we are aware of.

1.4 Metrics for Plan Recognition

There are no agreed-on benchmarks and metrics for reporting results in the plan and goal recognition community. This, in addition to the lack of common datasets, makes it difficult if not impossible to compare performance across recognizers. This section discusses plan recognition metrics in general and then proposes several, which we use in our evaluations described later in the chapter.

To choose metrics, we need to look at the desiderata for plan recognition systems in general. We noted several of these in the introduction: speed, precision and recall, early prediction, and partial prediction.

---

[7]www.cs.rochester.edu/research/cisd/resources/monroe-plan/

While speed and precision and recall are quite obvious, the latter two (early and partial prediction) are often overlooked in the literature.

In reporting results for goal schema recognition, we use the following metrics:

Precision: the number of correct predictions divided by the total number of predictions made (*#correct/#predictions*).
Recall: the number of correct predictions divided by the total number of actions observed (*#correct/ #observations*).
Convergence: whether or not the final prediction was correct (i.e., whether the recognizer *finished* the session with the correct answer).
Convergence point: If the recognizer converged, at which point in the input it started giving only the correct answer. This is reported as a quotient of the action number (i.e., after observing x actions) over the total number of actions for that case.[8] This is similar to Lesh's measurement of work saved [19], which measures how many user actions are *saved* by the system recognizing the goal early.[9]

Precision and *recall* are used to measure overall accuracy of the recognizer, both in predicting and deciding when to predict. It is important to remember that here the predictions are "online" (i.e., that they occur after each observed action), and not post hoc after all observations have been seen.

Convergence and *convergence point* are an attempt to measure early prediction—that is, how far into the plan session does the recognizer zero in on the correct prediction. We use the term *convergence* here, as it is often the case that the recognizer is unsure at the start of a session, but that at some point it has seen enough evidence to converge on a particular prediction, which it then begins predicting, and predicts from that point on—compare to [1]. Note that, for the purposes of calculating the *convergence point* if the recognizer does not make a prediction (i.e., predicts "don't know"), it is considered an incorrect prediction and the convergence point is reset, even if the correct prediction was made before.

1.4.1 Example

To illustrate the metrics, we give a short (contrived) example here. Figure 1.2 shows the observed actions and resulting system prediction.

Each of the metrics for this example are shown in Figure 1.3. To calculate precision, we see that three predictions were made and two of them were correct, giving us 66.7%. For recall, we note there

Observed action	Prediction	Correct
pwd	*(no prediction)*	no
ls	know-usage	no
mv	move-file	yes
ls	move-file	yes

FIGURE 1.2

Example system performance.

---

[8]It is necessary to report the total number of actions as well. Because this statistic is only for the test cases that converged, it is possible that the average actions per session is different from that of the entire corpus.
[9]This measure assumes that goal recognition is being used in a helpful assistant and that, after recognition, the assistant can complete the rest of the task without any additional action from the user.

Precision	(2/3) 66.7%
Recall	(2/4) 50.0%
Convergence	yes
Convergence point	3.0/4.0

FIGURE 1.3

Evaluation metrics for example in Figure 1.2.

were four possible prediction points (one after each observed action), and again, two correct predictions were made, giving us 50.0%.

The example does converge since the last prediction was correct, therefore we can calculate a convergence point for it. After the third observed action, the recognizer made the right prediction, and it kept making this prediction throughout the rest of the plan session. Thus, we have a convergence point of 3.0 observed actions, over the total of 4.0 observed actions. Note that for a group of results, the denominator will be the average of total observed actions per each converged plan session.

1.4.2 Discussion

Plan recognition is almost never an end unto itself, but rather a component in a bigger system. However, this point is sometimes lost in the plan recognition field. It is important to use metrics beyond precision and recall to measure the behavior of systems to make sure that the systems we build can also handle early and partial predictions. Note that the general metrics described here do not cover partial prediction; however, we will introduce several metrics in the following for our formalism that do, by measuring performance at each level of the goal chain, as well as partial parameter prediction.

1.5 Hierarchical Goal Recognition

In this section, we discuss our system, which performs hierarchical recognition of both goal schemas and their parameters. We first describe the separate components: a goal schema recognizer and a goal parameter recognizer. We then discuss how these are put together to create a system that recognizes *instantiated* goals.

In most domains, goals are not monolithic entities; rather, they are *goal schemas* with instantiated parameters. Combining goal schema recognition with goal parameter recognition allows us to do *instantiated goal recognition*, which we will refer to here as simply *goal recognition*.

First we give some definitions that will be useful throughout the chapter. We then describe the recognition model and our most recent results.

1.5.1 Definitions

For a domain, we define a set of goal schemas, each taking q parameters, and a set of action schemas, each taking r parameters. If actual goal and action schemas do not have the same number of parameters as the others, we can easily pad them with "dummy" parameters, which always take the same value.[10]

---

[10]The requirement that goal and action schemas have the same number of parameters is for convenience in the mathematical analysis and is not a requirement of the algorithm itself.

Given an instantiated goal or schema, it is convenient to refer to the schema of which it is an instance as well as each of its individual parameter values. We define a function `Schema` that, for any instantiated action or goal, returns the corresponding schema. As a shorthand, we use $X^S \equiv \text{Schema}(X)$, where X is an instantiated action or goal.

To refer to parameter values, we define a function `Param`, which returns the value of the kth parameter of an instantiated goal or action. As a shorthand, we use $X^k \equiv \text{Param}(X, k)$, where X is again an instantiated action or goal.

As another shorthand, we refer to number sequences by their endpoints: $1, n \equiv 1, 2, \ldots, n$. Thus, $A_{1,n} \equiv A_1, A_2, \ldots, A_n$ and $A_{1,n}^{1,r} \equiv A_1^1, A_1^2, \ldots, A_1^r, A_2^1, A_2^2, \ldots, A_{n-1}^r, A_n^1, \ldots, A_n^r$.

1.5.2 **Problem Formulation**

We define goal recognition as the following: given an observed sequence of n instantiated actions observed thus far ($A_{1,n}$), find the most likely instantiated goal g:

$$g = \text{argmax}_G \, P(G|A_{1,n}) \tag{1.1}$$

If we expand the goal and actions into their schemas and parameters, this becomes[11]:

$$g = \text{argmax}_{G^S, G^{1,q}} \, P\left(G^S, G^{1,q} | A_{1,n}^S, A_{1,n}^{1,r}\right) \tag{1.2}$$

If we assume that goal parameters are independent of each other and that goal schemas are independent from action parameters (given their action schemas), this becomes:

$$g = \text{argmax} \, P\left(G^S | A_{1,n}^S\right) \prod_{j=1}^{q} P(G^j | G^S, A_{1,n}^S, A_{1,n}^{1,r}) \tag{1.3}$$

In Equation (1.3), the first term describes the probability of the goal schema, G^S, which we will use for goal schema recognition. The other terms describe the probability of each goal parameter, G^j. We discuss these both in this section.

1.5.3 **Goal Schema Recognition**

1.5.3.1 *Cascading Hidden Markov Models*

In our hierarchical schema recognizer, we use a *Cascading Hidden Markov Model (CHMM)*, which consists of D stacked state-emission HMMs ($H_{0,D-1}$). Each HMM (H_d) is defined by a 5-tuple $(\sigma_d, \kappa_d, \Pi_d, A_d, B_d)$, where σ_d is the set of possible hidden states; κ_d is the set of possible output states; $\Pi_d = \{\pi_{d:i}\}, i \in \sigma_d$ is the initial state probability distribution; $A_d = \{a_{d:ij}\}, i, j \in \sigma_d$ is the set of state transition probabilities; and $B_d = \{b_{d:ik}\}, i \in \sigma_d, k \in \kappa_d$ is the set of output probabilities.

The HMMs are stacked such that for each HMM (H_d), its output state is the hidden state of the HMM below it (H_{d+1}). For the lowest level (H_{D-1}), the output state is the actual observed output. In essence,

---

[11] From now on we drop the "argmax" subscript when the context makes it obvious.

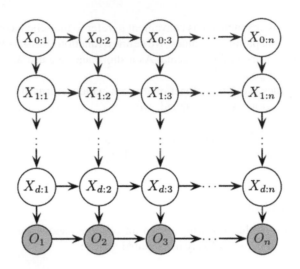

FIGURE 1.4

A Cascading Hidden Markov Model.

at each timestep t, we have a chain of hidden state variables $(X_{0,D-1:t})$ connected to a single observed output O_t at the bottom level. An example of a CHMM is shown in Figure 1.4. Here, the dth HMM (i.e., the HMM that starts with the hidden state $(X_{d:1})$ is a typical HMM with the output sequence $O_{1,n}$. As we go up the CHMM, the hidden level becomes the output level for the level above it, and so forth.

We will now describe the differences between CHMMs and other hierarchical HMMs. We then discuss how inference is done with CHMMs—in particular, how the forward probability is calculated, as this is a key part of our recognition algorithm.

Comparison to hierarchical HMMs

Hierarchical HMMs (HHMMs) [22] and the closely related Abstract HMMs (AHMMs) [12] also represent hierarchical information using a limited-depth stack of HMMs. In these models, an hidden state can output either a single observation or a string of observations. Each observation can also be associated with a hidden state at the next level down, which can also output observations, and so forth. In HHMMs, when a hidden state outputs an observation, control is transferred to that observation, which can also output and pass control. Control is only returned to the upper level (and the upper level moves to its next state) when the output observation has finished its output, which can take multiple timesteps.

In contrast, CHMMs are much simpler. Each hidden state can only output a single observation, thus keeping the HMMs at each level in lock-step. In other words, in CHMMs, each level transitions at each timestep, whereas only a subset transitions in HHMMs.

Next, we use CHMMs to represent an agent's execution of a hierarchical plan. As we discuss there, mapping a hierarchical plan onto a CHMM results in a loss of information that could be retained by using an HHMM—compare to [12]. This, however, is exactly what allows us to do tractable online inference, as we show later. Exact reasoning in HHMMs has been shown to be exponential in the number of possible states [22].

Computing the forward probability in CHMMs

An analysis of the various kinds of inference possible with CHMMs is beyond the scope of this chapter. Here we only focus on the forward algorithm [28], which is used in our recognition algorithm.[12]

In a typical HMM, the forward probability ($\alpha_i(t) = P(o_{1,t}, X_t = i | \Pi, A, B)$) describes the probability of the sequence of outputs observed up until time t ($o_{1,t}$) and that the current state X_t is i, given an HMM model (Π, A, B). The set of forward probabilities for a given timestep T, ($\alpha(T) = \{\alpha_i(T), i \in \sigma\}$), can be efficiently computed using the forward algorithm, which uses a state lattice (over time) to efficiently compute the forward probability of all intermediate states. We describe the forward algorithm here to allow us to more easily show how it is augmented for CHMMs.

First, $\alpha(0)$ is initialized with initial state probabilities (Π). Then, for each subsequent timestep t, individual forward probabilities are computed using the following formula:

$$\alpha_j(t) = \left[\sum_{i \in \sigma} \alpha_i(t-1) a_{ij} \right] b_{jo_t} \tag{1.4}$$

The complexity of computing the forward probabilities for a sequence of T observations is O $(|\sigma|^2 T)$, where σ is the set of possible hidden states. However, as we will use the forward probability in making online predictions in the next section, we are more interested in the complexity for *extending* the forward probabilities to a new timestep (i.e., calculating $\alpha(t+1)$ given $\alpha(t)$). For extending to a new timestep, the runtime complexity is O $(|\sigma|^2)$, or quadratic in the number of possible hidden states.

Algorithm overview

In a CHMM, we want to calculate the forward probabilities for each depth within a given timestep: $\alpha(t) = \{\alpha_d(t)\}, d \in 0, D-1$, where $\alpha_d(t) = \{\alpha_{d:i}(t)\}, i \in \sigma_d$. This can be done one timestep at a time, cascading results up from the lowest level ($D-1$).

Initialization of each level occurs as normal—as if it were a normal HMM—using the start state probabilities in Π_d. For each new observation o_t, the new forward probabilities for the chain are computed in a bottom-up fashion, starting with $\alpha_{D-1}(t)$. At this bottom level, the new forward probabilities are computed as for a normal HMM using Eq. (1.4).

We then move up the chain, computing one forward probability set at a time, using the results of the level below as observed output. However, we cannot use Eq. (1.4) to calculate these forward probability sets ($\alpha_d(t)$) because the forward algorithm assumes that output is observed with certainty. While this was the case for level $D-1$ (where the output variable is o_t), for all other levels, the output state is actually also a hidden state ($X_{d+1:t}$), and thus uncertain.

We overcome this by first observing that, although we do not know the value of $X_{d+1:t}$ with certainty, if we have the forward probability distribution for that node ($\alpha_{d+1}(t)$), we can use it as a probability distribution over possible values for the state. As discussed before, we can compute the forward probability set at the bottom level $\alpha_{D-1}(t)$, which gives us a probability distribution over possible values of $X_{D-1:t}$. To calculate the forward probability at the next level up $\alpha_{D-2}(t)$, as well as higher levels, we need to augment the forward algorithm to work for HMMs with uncertain output.

---

[12]The reader may wonder why we do not use the forward-backward algorithm; it is essentially for post hoc analysis. For goal recognition, we are interested in making "online" predictions (i.e., predictions after each observation) to which the forward-backward algorithm does not lend itself.

Changing the forward algorithm to handle uncertain output is straightforward, and needs only to include a weighted sum over output probabilities, as shown here:

$$\alpha_{d:j}(t) = \left[\sum_{i\in\sigma_d}\alpha_{d:i}(t-1)a_{ij}\right]\left[\sum_{k\in\sigma_{d+1}}\alpha_{d+1:k}(t)b_{jk}\right] \qquad (1.5)$$

Including this additional summation does not change the complexity of the forward algorithm. For updating each level, it remains quadratic in the number of hidden states $O(|\sigma_d|^2)$.

1.5.3.2 *Schema recognition algorithm*

From the previous discussion, it may be quite apparent where we are going with this. A quick comparison of the goal chains in Figure 1.1 and the CHMM in Figure 1.4 shows a remarkable resemblance. Our hierarchical goal schema recognizer models an agent's plan execution with a CHMM, with one level for each subgoal level in the hierarchical plan. The use of CHMMs requires having a plan tree of constant depth, which is not usually a valid assumption, including for the corpus we use later.

Given a variable depth corpus, we use a padding scheme to extend all leaves to the deepest level. To do this, we expand each leaf that is too shallow by copying the node that is its immediate parent and insert it between the parent and the leaf. We repeat this until the leaf node is at the proper depth. We refer to these copies of subgoals as *ghost* nodes.

After each observed action, predictions are made at each subgoal level using what we call *augmented forward probabilities*. Early experiments based purely on the CHMM forward probabilities gave only mediocre results. To improve performance, we added observation-level information to the calculations at each level by making both transition and output probabilities context-dependent on the current and last observed action (bigram). The idea was that this would tie upper-level predictions to possible signals present only in the actual actions executed, as opposed to just some higher-level, generic subgoal. This is similar to what is done in probabilistic parsing [15], where lexical items are included in production probabilities to provide better context.

The only change we made was to the transition probabilities (A_d) and output probabilities (B_d) at each level. Thus, instead of the transition probability $a_{d:ij}$ being $P(X_{d:t} = j|X_{d:t-1} = i)$, we expand it to be conditioned on the observed actions as well:

$$a_{d:ij} = P(X_{d:t} = j|X_{d:t-1} = i, O_t, O_{t-1})$$

Similarly, we added bigram information to the output probabilities ($b_{d:ik}$):

$$b_{d:ik} = P(X_{d:t} = i|X_{d+1:t} = k, O_t, O_{t-1})$$

We will now describe how the CHMM is trained, and then how predictions are made. We then analyze the runtime complexity of the recognition algorithm.

Training the CHMM

As a CHMM is really just a stack of HMMs, we need only to estimate the transition probabilities (A_d), output probabilities (B_d), and start state probabilities (Π_d) for each depth d. To estimate these, we need a plan-labeled corpus (as described before) that has a set of goals and associated plans. Each hierarchical plan in the corpus can be converted into a set of goal chains, which are used to estimate the different probability distributions.

Predictions

At the start of a recognition session, a CHMM for the domain is initialized with start state probabilities from the model. After observing a new action, we calculate the new forward probabilities for each depth using the CHMM forward algorithm.

Using the forward probabilities, n-best predictions are made separately for each level. The n most likely schemas are chosen, and their combined probability is compared against a confidence threshold τ. If the n-best probability is greater than τ, a prediction is made. Otherwise, the recognizer does not predict at that level for that timestep.

It is important to note that using this prediction algorithm means it is possible that, for a given timestep, subgoal schemas may not be predicted at all depths. It is even possible (and actually occurs in our experiments that follow) that the depths at which predictions occur can be discontinuous (i.e., a prediction could occur at levels 4, 3, and 1, but not 2 or 0). We believe this to be a valuable feature because subgoals at different levels may be more certain than others.

Complexity

The runtime complexity of the recognizer for each new observed timestep is the same as that of forward probability extension in the CHMM: $O(D|S|^2)$, where D is depth of the deepest possible goal chain in the domain (not including the observed action), and S is the set of possible subgoals (at any level). Thus, the algorithm is linear in the depth of the domain and quadratic in the number of possible subgoals in the domain.

1.5.4 Adding Parameter Recognition

The preceding system only recognizes *goal schemas*. To do full goal recognition, we also need to recognize the *parameter* values for each posited goal schema. Put more precisely, for each recognized goal schema, we need to recognize the value for each of its parameter slots.

First briefly describe the top-level parameter recognition algorithm and then describe how it can be augmented to support parameter recognition within a hierarchical instantiated goal recognizer.

1.5.4.1 *Top-level parameter recognition*

One straightforward way of doing parameter recognition would be to treat instantiated goal schemas as atomic goals and then use the goal schema recognition algorithm. However, this solution has several problems. First, it would result in an exponential increase in the number of goals, as we would have to consider all possible ground instances. This would seriously impact the speed of the algorithm. It would also affect data sparseness, as the likelihood of seeing an n-gram in the training data will decrease substantially.

Instead, we perform goal schema and parameter recognition separately, as described in Equation (1.3). From the last term of the equation, we get the following for a single parameter g^j:

$$g^j = \text{argmax } P(G^j | G^S, A_{1,n}^S, A_{1,n}^{1,r}) \tag{1.6}$$

We could estimate this with an n-gram assumption, as we did before. However, there are several problems here as well.

First, this would make updates at least linear in the number of objects in the world (the domain of g^j), which may be expensive in domains with many objects. Second, even without a large object space, we may run into data sparsity problems, since we are including both the action schemas and their parameter values.

This solution misses out on the generalization that, often, the *positions* of parameters are more important than their value. For example, in a Linux goal domain, the first parameter (i.e., the *source file*) of the action mv is often the $filename parameter of a goal to move a file of a certain name, whereas the second parameter (i.e., the *destination*) almost never is, regardless of the parameter's actual value. Our model learns probability distributions of equality over goal and action parameter positions. During recognition, we use these distributions along with a special, tractable case of Dempster-Shafer Theory to dynamically create a set of possible parameter values and our confidence in them, which we use to estimate Equation (1.6).

Formally, we want to learn the following probability distribution: $P((G^j = A_i^k)|G^S, A_i^S)$. This gives us the probability that the value of the kth parameter of action A_i is equal to the jth parameter of the goal G, given both the goal and action schemas as well as the two parameter positions. Note that the *value* of the parameter is not considered here, only the *position*. We can easily compute this conditional probability distribution from the training corpus.

To use this model to predict the value of each goal schema parameter as we make action observations, we need to be able to combine probabilities for each parameter in the observed action, as well as probabilities from action to action. For this we use the Dempster-Shafer Theory.

Dempster-Shafer Theory

Dempster-Shafer Theory (DST) [30] is a generalization of probability theory that allows for incomplete knowledge. Given a domain Ω, a probability mass is assigned to each subset of Ω, as opposed to each element, as in classical probability theory. Such an assignment is called a *basic probability assignment* (bpa).

Assigning a probability mass to a subset in a bpa means that we place that level of confidence in the subset but cannot be any more specific. For example, suppose we are considering the outcome of a die roll ($\Omega = \{1, 2, 3, 4, 5, 6\}$).[13] If we have no information, we have a bpa of $m(\Omega = 1)$ (i.e., all our probability mass is on Ω). This is because, although we have no information, we are 100% certain that *one* of the elements in Ω is the right answer; we just cannot be more specific.

Now suppose we are told that the answer is an even number. In this case, our bpa would be $m(\{2, 4, 6\}) = 1$; we have more information, but we still cannot distinguish between the even numbers. A bpa of $m(\{2, 4, 6\}) = 0.5$ and $m(\{1\}) = 0.5$ would intuitively mean that there is a 50% chance that the number is even, and a 50% chance that it is 1. The subsets of Ω that are assigned nonzero probability mass are called the *focal elements* of the bpa.

A problem with DST is that the number of possible focal elements of Ω is the number of its subsets, or $2^{|\Omega|}$. This is both a problem for storage and for time for bpa combination (as discussed later). For parameter recognition, we use a special case of DST that only allows focal elements to be singleton sets or Ω (the entire set). This, of course, means that the maximum number of focal elements is $O(|\Omega|)$. As we show

---

[13]Example taken from [3].

in the following, this significantly decreases the complexity of a bpa combination, allowing us to run in time linear with the number of actions observed so far, regardless of the number of objects in the domain.

Evidence combination

Two bpas, m and m', representing different evidence can be combined into a new bpa using Dempster's rule of combination:

$$(m \oplus m')(A) = \frac{\sum_{B \cap B' = A} m(B)m'(B')}{\sum_{B \cap B' \neq \emptyset} m(B)m'(B')} \tag{1.7}$$

The complexity of computing this is $O(l_m l_{m'} |\Omega|)$, where l_m and $l_{m'}$ are the number of focal elements in m and m', respectively. Basically, the algorithm does a set intersection (hence the $|\Omega|$ term) for combinations of focal elements.

As mentioned earlier, the complexity would be prohibitive if we allowed any subset of Ω to be a focal element. However, our special case of DST limits l_m and $l_{m'}$ to $|\Omega| + 1$. Also, because we only deal with singleton sets and Ω, we can do set intersections in constant time. Thus, for our special case of DST, the complexity of Dempster's rule of combination becomes $O(l_m l_{m'})$, or $O(|\Omega|^2)$ in the worst case.

As a final note, it can be easily shown that our special case of DST is closed under Dempster's rule of combination. We omit a formal proof, but it basically follows from the fact that the set intersection of any two arbitrary focal-element subsets from special-case bpas can only result in Ω—a singleton set, or the empty set. Thus, as we continue to combine evidence, we are guaranteed to still have a special-case bpa.

Representing the model with DST

As stated before, we estimate $P((G^j = A_i^k)|G^S, A_i^S)$ from the corpus. For a given goal schema G^S and the ith action schema A_i^S, we define a *local bpa* $m_{i,k}^j$ for each goal and action parameter positions j and k s.t. $m_{i,k}^j(\{A_i^k\}) = P((G^j = A_i^k)|G^S, A_i^S)$ and $m_{i,k}^j(\Omega) = P((G^j \neq A_i^k)|G^S, A_i^S)$. This local bpa intuitively describes the evidence of a single goal parameter value from looking at just one parameter position in just one observed action. The bpa has two focal elements: $\{A_i^k\}$, which is a singleton set of the actual action parameter value, and Ω. The probability mass of the singleton set describes our confidence that this value is the goal parameter value. The probability mass of Ω expresses our ignorance, as it did in the preceding die roll example.

To smooth the distribution, we always make sure that both elements (Ω and A_i^k) are given at least a little probability mass. If either one is 1, a very small value is taken from that and given to the other. Several things are worth noting here.

First, we assume here that we already know the goal schema G^S. This basically means that we have a two-step process with which we first recognize the goal schema and then use that to recognize the parameters. The following discusses how we can combine these processes in a more intelligent way.

Second, if a goal schema has more than one parameter, we keep track of these and make predictions about them separately. As we discuss next, it is possible that we will be more confident about one parameter and predict it, whereas we may not predict another parameter for the same goal schema. This allows us to make more fine-grained partial predictions. Finally, we do not need to represent, enumerate, or even *know* the elements of Ω. This means that we can handle domains where the set of possible values is very large, or in which values can be created or destroyed.

Combining evidence

As mentioned earlier, we maintain a separate *prediction bpa* m^j for each goal parameter position j. Each of these are initialized as $m^j(\Omega) = 1$, which indicates complete ignorance about the parameter values. As we observe actions, we combine evidence within a single action and then among single actions.

First, within a single action i, we combine each of the local bpas $m^j_{i,k}$ for each parameter position k, which gives us an *action bpa* m^j_i. This describes the evidence the entire action has given us. Then, we combine the evidence from each observed action to give us an overall *prediction bpa* that describes our confidence in goal parameter values given all observed actions so far. We then use this prediction bpa to make (or not make) predictions. When we observe an action $A_i(p_1, p_2, \ldots, p_r)$, we create local bpas for each action parameter position $m^j_{i,1} \ldots m^j_{i,r}$. The action bpa m^j_i is the combination of all these: $m^j_i = m^j_{i,1} \oplus m^j_{i,2} \oplus \ldots \oplus m^j_{i,r}$. The prediction bpa is similarly calculated from all action bpas from observed actions: $m^j = m^j_1 \oplus m^j_2 \oplus \ldots \oplus m^j_i$. However, we can calculate this incrementally by calculating $m'^j = m^j \oplus m^j_i$ at each action observation. This allows us to only do 1 action–bpa combination per observed action.

It is worth noting here that only values that we have seen as action parameter values will be part of the prediction bpa. Thus, the maximum number of focal elements for a bpa m^j will be the total number of unique action parameters seen, plus 1 (for Ω). As a corollary, this means that our method will not be able to correctly predict a goal parameter unless its value has been seen as an action parameter value during the current plan session.

In what follows, we report results of total recall and also "recall/feasible," which restricts recall to the prediction points at which the algorithm *had access to* the right answer. Admittedly, there are domains in which the correct parameter value could be learned directly from the training corpus without having been seen in the current session, although we do not believe it will be so in most cases.

Prediction

At some level, we are using the prediction bpa as an estimation of $P(G^j|G^S, A^S_{1,n}, A^{1,r}_{1,n})$ from Equation (1.6). However, because the bpa contains Ω, it is not a true probability distribution and cannot provide a direct estimation. Instead, we use Ω as a measure of confidence in deciding whether to make a prediction.

To make an n-best prediction, we take the n singleton sets with the highest probability mass and compare their combined mass with that of Ω. If their mass is greater, we make that prediction. If Ω has a greater mass, we are still too ignorant about the parameter value and hence therefore make no prediction.

Complexity

The other thing to mention is the computational complexity of updating the prediction bpa for a single goal parameter G^j. We first describe the complexity of computing the ith action bpa m^j_i and then the complexity of combining it with the previous prediction bpa m^j.

To compute m^j_i, we combine r 2-focal-element local bpas, one for each action parameter position. If we do a serial combination of the local bpas (i.e., $m^j_i = ((m^j_{i,1} \oplus m^j_{i,2}) \oplus m^j_{i,3}) \oplus \ldots \oplus m^j_{i,r})$, this results in $r - 1$ combinations, where the first bpa is an intermediate composite bpa $\hat{m}^j_i$ and the second is always a 2-element local bpa. Each combination (maximally) adds just 1 subset to $\hat{m}_i^j$ (the other subset is Ω which is always shared). The $(k-1)$th combination result $\hat{m}_{i,k-1}^j$ will have maximum length $k+1$. The combination of that with a local bpa is $(O2(k+1))$. Thus, the overall complexity of the combination of the action bpa is $\sum_{k=1}^{r-1} O(2(k+1)) \approx O(r^2)$.

The action bpa m_i^j is then combined with the previous prediction bpa, which has a maximum size of $r(i-1)+1$ (i.e., from the number of possible unique action parameter values seen). The combination of the two bpas is $O(ir^2)$, which, together with the complexity of the computation of the action bpa, becomes $O(ir^2 + r^2) \approx O(ir^2)$. Here, r is actually constant (and should be reasonably small), so we can treat it as a constant, in which case we get a complexity of $O(i)$. This is done for each of the q goal parameters, but q is also constant, so we still have $O(i)$. This gives us a fast parameter recognition algorithm that is not dependent on the number of objects in the domain.

1.5.4.2 *Hierarchical parameter recognition*

Application of this parameter recognition algorithm to the hierarchical case is not straightforward. For the rest of this section, we first describe our basic approach to hierarchical instantiated goal recognition and then discuss several problems (and their solutions) with incorporating the parameter recognizer.

The basic algorithm of the hierarchical instantiated goal recognizer is as follows: After observing a new action, we first run the hierarchical schema recognizer and use it to make preliminary predictions at each subgoal level. At each subgoal level, we associate a set of parameter recognizers, one for each possible goal schema, which are then updated in parallel. This is necessary because each parameter recognizer is predicated on a particular goal schema. Each parameter recognizer is then updated by the process described next to give a new prediction bpa for each goal parameter position. If the schema recognizer makes a prediction at that level (i.e., its prediction was above the threshold τ), we then use the parameter recognizers for the predicted goal schemas to predict parameter values in the same way just described. This is similar to the algorithm used by our instantiated top-level goal recognizer [9], and it combines the partial prediction capabilities of the schema and parameter recognizers to yield an instantiated goal recognizer.

Dealing with uncertain output

One problem when moving the parameter recognizer from a "flat" to a hierarchical setting is that, at higher subgoal levels, the hidden state (subgoal predictions) of the level below becomes the output action. This has two consequences: first, instead of the output being a single goal schema, it is now a probability distribution over possible goal schemas (computed by the schema recognizer at the lower level). Second, instead of having a single parameter value for each subgoal parameter position, we now have the prediction bpa from the parameter recognizer at the level below.

We solve both of these problems by weighting evidence by its associated probability. In general, a bpa in DST can be weighted using Wu's weighting formula [31]:

$$m'(A) = \begin{cases} wm(A) + 1 - w : A = \Omega \\ \quad\quad wm(A) : \text{otherwise}, \end{cases} \tag{1.8}$$

where m is the bpa to be weighted and w is the weight. This equation essentially weights each of the focal points of the bpa and redistributes lost probability to Ω, or the ignorance measure of the bpa.

To handle uncertain parameter values in the output level, we change the computation of local bpas. Here, we have an advantage because the uncertainty of parameter values at the lower level is actually itself represented as a bpa (the prediction bpa of the parameter recognizer at the lower level). We compute the local bpa by weighting that prediction bpa with the probability of positional equality computed from the corpus ($P((G^j = A_i^k)|G^S, A_i^S)$).

Using these local bpas, we can then calculate the action bpa (or evidence from a single action or subgoal) in the same way as the original parameter recognizer. However, we still have the lingering problem of having uncertain subgoal schemas at that level. Modifying the updated algorithm for this case follows the same principle we used in handling uncertain parameters.

To handle uncertain goal schemas, we compute an action bpa for each possible goal schema. We then introduce a new intermediate result called an *observation bpa*, which represents the evidence for a parameter position given an entire observation (i.e., a set of uncertain goal schemas each associated with uncertain parameter values). To compute the observation bpa, first each action bpa in the observation is weighted according to the probability of its goal schema (using Eq. (1.8)). The observation bpa is then computed as the combination of all action bpas. This effectively weights the contributed evidence of each uncertain goal schema according to its probability (as computed by the schema recognizer).

Uncertain transitions at the prediction level

In the original parameter recognizer, we assumed that the agent only had a single goal that needed to be recognized, thus we could assume that the evidence we saw was always for the same set of parameter values. However, in hierarchical recognition this is not the case because subgoals may change at arbitrary times throughout the observations (refer to Figure 1.1).

This is a problem because we need to separate evidence. In the example shown in Figure 1.1, subgoals $S_{2:1}$ and $S_{2:2}$ give us evidence for the parameter values of $S_{1:1}$ but presumably not (directly) $S_{1:2}$. Ideally, if we knew the start and end times of each subgoal, we could simply reset the prediction bpas in the parameter recognizers at that level after the third observation when the subgoal switched.

In hierarchical recognition, we do not know a priori when goal schemas begin or end. We can, however, provide a rough estimation by using the transition probabilities estimated for each HMM in the schema recognizer. We use this probability (i.e., the probability that a new schema does not begin at this timestep) to weight the prediction bpa at each new timestep.

Basically, this provides a type of decay function for evidence gathered from previous timesteps. Assuming we could perfectly predict schema start times, if a new schema started, we would have a 0 probability; thus, weighting would result in a reset prediction bpa. On the other hand, if a new subgoal did not start, then we would have a weight of 1 and thus use the evidence as it stands.

Uncertain transitions at the output level

A more subtle problem arises from the fact that subgoals at the output level may correspond to more than one timestep. As an example, consider again the goal chain sequence in Figure 1.1. At level 2, the subgoal $S_{2:2}$ is output for two timesteps by $S_{1:1}$. This becomes a problem because Dempster's rule of combination makes the assumption that combined evidence bpas represent independent observations. For the case in Figure 1.1, when predicting parameters for $S_{1:1}$, we would combine output evidence from $S_{2:2}$ two separate times (as two separate observation bpas), as if two separate events had occurred.

The predictions for $S_{2:2}$, of course, will likely be different at each of the timesteps, reflecting the progression of the recognizer at that level. However, instead of being two independent events, they actually reflect two estimates of the same event, with the last estimate presumably being the most accurate (because it has considered more evidence at the output level).

To reflect this, we also change the update algorithm to keep track of the prediction bpa formed with evidence from the last timestep of the most recently *ended* subgoal at the level below; this we call the *last subgoal prediction (lsp) bpa*. At a new timestep, the prediction bpa is formed by combining the observation bpa with this *lsp* bpa. If we knew the start and end times of subgoals, we could simply discard this prediction bpa if a subgoal had not yet ended, or make it the new lsp if it had. Not knowing schema start and end times gives us a similar problem at the output level. As we discussed, we need a way of distinguishing which observed output represents a new event versus which represents an updated view of the same event.

We handle this case in a similar way to that mentioned before. We calculate the probability that the new observation starts a new timestep by the weighted sum of all same transition probabilities at the level below. This estimate is then used to weight the prediction bpa from the last timestep and then combine it with the lsp bpa to form a new lsp bpa. In cases in which there is a high probability that a new subgoal was begun, the prediction bpa will have a large contribution to the lsp bpa, whereas it will not if the probability is low.

Complexity

First, we must analyze the complexity of the modified parameter recognizer, which deals with output with uncertain goal schemas. In this analysis, $|S|$ is the number of possible goal schemas, q is the maximum parameters for a goal schema, i is the current timestep, and D is the depth of the hierarchical plan.

The modified algorithm computes the observation bpa by combining (worst case) $|S|$ action bpas—each with a maximum size of iq. Thus, the total complexity for the update of a single parameter position is $O(|S|i^2q^3)$; for the parameter recognizer of a single goal schema (with q parameter positions), this becomes $O(|S|i^2q^4)$. As q is constant and likely small, we drop it, which gives us $O(|S|i^2)$.

The complexity of an update for the instantiated recognizer can be calculated from the runtime of the schema recognizer plus the runtime of each of the $D|S|$ parameter recognizers (one per each goal schema per level). Thus, the total runtime complexity is $O(D|S|^2 + D|S|^2i^2) = O(D|S|^2i^2)$, or quadratic in the number of possible goal schemas and the number of actions observed so far.

1.6 **System Evaluation**

We now report on our experiments: first on the parameter recognizer itself, and then on the hierarchical instantiated goal recognizer. For the experiments, we used 4500 plan sessions from the Monroe Plan Corpus (described earlier and in [8]) for training and the remaining 500 for testing. This is the same data used in the experiments on our instantiated top-goal recognizer [9] and allows us to make comparisons.

Before we describe the experiments and their results, however, we briefly discuss the metrics we use to report results.

1.6.1 **Metrics**

We report results for individual subgoal depths, as well as totals. For each depth, we use the same metrics described previously.

In reporting results for each level (and in the total), we *do not* count predictions when the correct answer was a "ghost" node; they, as we described, are used to pad the plan tree such that all leaves are at the same depth. Ghost node prediction tends to be correct, and thus resulted in heavily inflated results, especially at lower depths. Ghost nodes were only introduced to support use of CHMMs, so it is unfair to credit these as correct predictions.

In reporting results for parameter recognition, we additionally use *recall/feasible* and *convergence/feasible*, which measure recall and convergence for those cases in which it was possible for the parameter recognizer to get the right answer. As described earlier, our algorithm for parameter recognition can never predict a parameter that has not yet been seen as the parameter of an observed action.

In reporting results for instantiated recognition, *Parameter Percentage* ($p\%$) reports, for all correct predictions, the percentage of the goal parameters that were predicted. *Convergence Parameter Percentage* ($c/p\%$) reports the same for all sessions that converged. These are an attempt to measure the specificity of correct predictions made. For hierarchical recognition, we make a change to how convergence and convergence point are calculated. Some subgoals only span one timestep (e.g., they only result in one executed atomic action); in this case, it does not make sense to report convergence or a convergence point. For all levels, we only report convergence and convergence point for subgoals that correspond to at least two timesteps.

1.6.2 Schema Recognition Results

The results of the experiment are shown in Table 1.2. Overall, the results are very encouraging with 81.9% precision and 52.3% recall for 1-best prediction, which jumps to 94.9% precision and 71.4% recall for 2-best prediction. In the 2-best case, 95.7% of sessions converged on the right answer. On average, this was after a little more than half of the actions had been observed.

We now discuss the various levels in detail, first looking at the results for predicting top-level goal schemas (level 0) and then the other levels.

1.6.2.1 *Top-level results*

Results at the top level are also encouraging with 85.6% precision and 58.6% recall for 1-best prediction and 90.7% precision and 62.0% recall for 2-best. For comparison, we present the results of our top-level recognizer on the same dataset in Table 1.3.

For recall, convergence, and convergence point, the two recognizers' performance is fairly equivalent, both in 1-best and 2-best predictions. Precision, however, is markedly lower in the hierarchical recognizer for both the 1-best and 2-best cases. Whereas precision is 95.6% for 1-best in the flat recognizer, it drops to 85.7% for the hierarchical recognizer. A similar drop in precision from 99.4% to 91.5% is shown in the 2-best case.

Although there seem to be several factors involved in this drop, it is perhaps most important to mention two. First is the loss of true bigram information within the hierarchical recognizer. In the hierarchical recognizer, the top-level goal is predicted based on predictions at the next immediate subgoal level (level 1) as opposed to directly from the action observation level as is the top-level goal recognizer. Converting a plan tree into a sequence of goal chains loses explicit information about the actual previous subgoal.

Second, and most important, a direct comparison of algorithm performance is difficult because the hierarchical recognizer is doing much more than simple top-level goal classification, as was done in the top-level goal recognizer. Arguably, we could improve performance by using the hierarchical recognizer for the subgoal levels and then the flat recognizer for top-level recognition, although this then loses the generalization that the hierarchical recognizer can also handle cases where several top-level goals are pursued serially.

Table 1.2 Results of the Hierarchical Schema Recognition Experiment

Level	Prec.	Recall	Conv.	Conv. pt.
		1-best ($\tau = 0.7$)		
0	85.6%	58.6%	100%	5.2/10.2
1	84.3%	54.8%	71.8%	2.9/6.1
2	89.3%	46.3%	45.8%	3.4/4.7
3	74.8%	42.8%	41.2%	2.7/3.5
4	78.7%	53.5%	61.8%	3.3/3.7
5	59.3%	46.1%	6.2%	3.8/4.2
6	69.3%	69.3%	0.0%	N/A
7	95.2%	95.2%	N/A	N/A
8	100%	100%	N/A	N/A
Total	81.9%	52.3%	65.0%	3.8/6.8
		2-best ($\tau = 0.95$)		
0	90.7%	62.0%	100%	4.9/10.2
1	96.1%	77.3%	99.0%	2.3/5.6
2	93.0%	64.3%	84.4%	3.5/4.8
3	97.6%	80.1%	99.0%	3.5/4.5
4	97.0%	73.2%	100%	3.2/3.8
5	99.1%	77.1%	100%	2.0/3.9
6	100%	100%	100%	1.0/4.0
7	100%	100%	N/A	N/A
8	100%	100%	N/A	N/A
Total	94.9%	71.4%	95.7%	3.3/6.1

Table 1.3 Results of Top-level Goal Schema Recognition

Level	Prec.	Recall	Conv.	Conv. pt
		1-best ($\tau = 0.7$)		
top	95.6%	55.2%	96.4%	5.4/10.2
		2-best ($\tau = 0.95$)		
top	99.4%	58.7%	99.8%	5.4/10.3
Source: Adapted from [9]				

1.6.2.2 *Other levels*

Results at lower levels for 1-best prediction are on average not as good as those at the top level. The main reason is that there is actually more competition at lower levels, where more subgoals are possible, whereas only the 10 top-level schemas are possible at level 0. Also, there are several lower-level subgoals per level throughout a goal session. Only one top-level goal makes the transition probabilities much simpler at the top level as well; basically, transition probabilities are 1 between the same schemas and 0 between any others. This seems to especially account for the very low convergence numbers for levels 5 and 6 (6.2% and 0.0%, respectively), where there were only a few data points and these were fully recognized at the start of their interval, but not at the end. (In 2-best prediction both of these move to 100% convergence.)

That said, in the 1-best case, recognition results are fairly good for levels 1, 2, 7, and 8, although there is a trough between them. A partial explanation is that, at higher levels, there are less competitors. Thus, as we move to lower levels, things become more difficult to predict. At the same time, the lower we go, the closer to the observed output, and therefore the closer to certain information. Thus, the last two levels have very good precision and recall because they are so closely related to the observed action. (Levels 7 and 8 contained no subgoals that span more than one timestep, hence convergence and convergence point are not reported.)

It appears that in the middle (e.g., levels 3–6), the recognizer tends to not distinguish well among close competitors. That this is the case can be shown by looking at the 2-best case, where all levels move to the 90s or 100% for precision and also improve dramatically in recall.

1.6.3 Parameter Recognition Results

To test the parameter recognizer in its own right, we assumed perfect schema recognition—that is, for each new observation, we gave the parameter recognizer information about the chain of goal schemas at that time point, including information about which schemas began at that timestep. This perfect information about schema transitions meant that the parameter recognizer did not need to deal with (1) uncertain transitions at the prediction level and (2) uncertain schemas at the output level. Note that there was still uncertainty at the output level at higher levels because *parameter values* were still potentially uncertain, even though the schema was known (see Table 1.4).

1.6.3.1 *Top-level results*

To help interpret the results, we compare performance at the top level to that of the flat recognizer, which only made predictions at the top level. For convenience, the results of the flat parameter recognizer on the same dataset are shown in Table 1.5. The hierarchical parameter recognizer performed slightly better in both the 1-best and 2-best cases. In 1-best, precision moved from 94.3% to 98.6%, although there was a drop in recall from 27.8% to 25.8%. In the 2-best recognizer, results were slightly better all around (see Table 1.6).

The reason for the improvement in performance is likely attributable to the fact that (perfect) subgoal schema information was present in the hierarchical recognizer. This allowed parameter values to be considered given the immediate child subgoal, giving better context for predictions.

Table 1.4 Results of Parameter Recognition

Level	Prec.	Recall	Recall/Feas.	Conv.	Conv./Feas.	Conv. pt.
			1-best ($\psi = 2.0$)			
0	98.6%	25.8%	52.0%	44.7%	56.3%	5.0/9.9
1	99.7%	26.4%	52.0%	39.9%	55.2%	4.1/6.3
2	96.7%	53.0%	76.4%	51.6%	57.7%	2.5/4.8
3	98.7%	73.8%	89.4%	73.8%	74.1%	3.1/4.1
4	99.3%	80.0%	94.6%	80.9%	80.9%	3.3/3.8
5	97.5%	82.6%	91.1%	53.1%	53.1%	2.2/3.9
6	99.9%	98.3%	99.3%	50.0%	50.0%	2.0/4.0
7	100%	100%	100%	N/A	N/A	N/A
8	100%	100%	100%	N/A	N/A	N/A
Total	98.5%	51.7%	76.5%	51.6%	61.2%	3.5/5.7
			2-best ($\psi = 2.0$)			
0	97.7%	40.1%	80.8%	76.0%	95.8%	4.7/9.0
1	99.9%	41.3%	81.2%	63.6%	88.0%	3.5/5.7
2	99.6%	65.9%	95.1%	82.9%	92.8%	2.8/4.7
3	99.8%	81.0%	98.2%	97.6%	97.9%	3.4/4.5
4	100%	83.3%	98.5%	97.6%	97.6%	3.3/3.9
5	100%	89.7%	99.0%	93.0%	93.0%	2.5/3.9
6	100%	99.1%	100%	100%	100%	2.5/4.0
7	100%	100%	100%	N/A	N/A	N/A
8	100%	100%	100%	N/A	N/A	N/A
Total	99.5%	62.4%	92.4%	78.6%	93.2%	3.5/5.6

Table 1.5 Results of Flat Parameter Recognition

Level	Prec.	Recall	Recall/Feas.	Conv.	Conv./Feas.	Conv. pt.
			1-best ($\psi = 2.0$)			
top	94.3%	27.8%	55.9%	46.9%	59.1%	5.1/10.0
			2-best ($\psi = 2.0$)			
top	97.6%	39.2%	78.9%	76.2%	96.1%	4.8/9.0
Source: Adapted from [9]						

Table 1.6 Results of Instantiated Recognition

Level	Prec.	Recall	p%	Conv.	c/p%	Conv. pt.
			1-best ($\tau = 0.7$, $\psi = 2.0$)			
0	82.5%	56.4%	24.0%	90.8%	49.8%	5.6/10.3
1	81.3%	52.8%	23.5%	67.6%	26.5%	3.1/6.1
2	85.4%	44.3%	22.5%	45.8%	38.5%	3.4/4.7
3	72.9%	41.7%	82.4%	41.2%	90.6%	3.0/3.5
4	73.6%	50.0%	99.9%	61.8%	100%	3.7/3.7
5	58.8%	45.7%	100%	6.2%	100%	4.2/4.2
6	69.3%	69.3%	100%	0.0%	N/A	N/A
7	95.2%	95.2%	100%	N/A	N/A	N/A
8	100%	100%	100%	N/A	N/A	N/A
Total	79.0%	50.4%	44.1%	61.7%	46.4%	3.9/6.8
			2-best ($\tau = 0.95$, $\psi = 2.0$)			
0	88.2%	60.2%	23.2%	91.0%	49.9%	5.2/10.3
1	93.8%	75.4%	16.6%	94.8%	18.9%	2.4/5.6
2	89.7%	62.0%	42.1%	84.4%	45.2%	3.6/4.8
3	90.6%	74.4%	81.8%	99.0%	71.0%	3.9/4.5
4	90.8%	68.6%	96.5%	100%	80.9%	3.8/3.8
5	98.2%	76.4%	81.4%	100%	53.1%	2.0/3.9
6	98.3%	98.3%	99.2%	100%	50.0%	4.0/4.0
7	100%	100%	100%	N/A	N/A	N/A
8	100%	100%	100%	N/A	N/A	N/A
Total	91.3%	68.7%	47.2%	92.5%	43.7%	3.6/6.1

1.6.3.2 *Other levels*

The hierarchical parameter recognizer performed well at other levels too, with precision staying (for the 1-best case) in the high 90s and even up to 100% for levels 7 and 8. This performance inched up for the 2-best case (with 100% precision for levels 4–8).

It is interesting to note that recall begins quite low (25.8% for level 0) and then climbs as we go down levels, reaching 100% for levels 7 and 8. As mentioned earlier, high absolute recall is not to be expected in plan recognition, as ambiguity is almost always present. The closer we move to the actual observed action, however, the higher precision gets. This can be attributed to two factors.

First, subgoals at lower levels are closer to the observed input, and thus deal with less uncertainty about what the parameter values are. Second, and probably most important, lower-level subgoals span fewer timesteps than those at higher levels, meaning that, if parameter values are available, they will be seen after a shorter number of actions.

Table 1.7 Results of Flat Instantiated Recognition on the Monroe Corpus

Level	Prec.	Recall	p%	Conv.	c/p%	Con v. pt.
			1-best ($\tau = 0.7$, $\psi = 2.0$)			
top	93.1%	53.7%	20.6%	94.2%	40.6%	5.4/10.0
			2-best ($\tau = 0.95$, $\psi = 2.0$)			
top	95.8%	56.6%	21.8%	97.4%	41.1%	5.5/10.1
Note: Compare to [9].						

In the case of levels 7 and 8, all subgoals only spanned one timestep, and thus only had one chance to get the right parameter values. It turns out that parameter values at these levels always directly corresponded to the action parameters, which is why precision and recall reach 100% here.

Overall, the performance of the parameter recognizer was very encouraging, especially the performance at lower levels that had high recall. This is an important factor in our ability to do specific and accurate partial prediction in the instantiated goal recognizer, which we move to now.

1.6.4 Instantiated Recognition Results

Here we examine the results of experiments on the instantiated hierarchical goal recognizer, which combined both schema and parameter recognizers as described previously. We first look at the results at the top level (i.e., level 0) and then the other levels.

1.6.4.1 Top-level results

To help interpret the results, we compare performance at the top level to that of our "flat" goal recognizer, which only made predictions at the top level. For convenience, the results of the flat instantiated recognizer on the same dataset are shown in Table 1.7.

Hierarchical instantiated results at the top level closely mirror results of the hierarchical schema recognizer [9]. This also happened for the flat recognizer and is to be expected, as schema recognition performance limits performance of the instantiated recognizers. The addition of parameter predictions serves to degrade the precision and recall of schema recognition results.

In the 2-best case, precision decreased from 95.8% in the flat recognizer to 88.2% in the hierarchical recognizer. However, recall increased from 56.6% to 60.2% and parameter percentage from 21.8% to 23.2%. This difference was more stark in convergence parameter percentage, which rose from 41.1% to 49.9%.

Although moving to a hierarchical recognizer seemed to degrade performance at the top level, at least in precision, this may be somewhat misleading because of the relative short length 9.5 actions of plans in the Monroe domain. We believe that longer, more complex plans will make it much more difficult to predict the top-level goal early on, thus requiring partial recognition of subgoals. Of course, this remains to be tested.

1.6.5 Other Levels

Precision and recall at other levels also closely mirror the performance of the schema recognizer. Precision dips in the middle levels but levels out for 2-best prediction, which achieves precision ranging from the high 80s to 100% (with recall ranging in the 60s and 70s for high levels and high 90s and 100% for the lower levels).

For 1-best parameter prediction for levels 1 and 2, it remains in the 20s, with a sudden jump to 82.4% at level 3, 99.9% at level 4, and 100% for the lower levels. Note that the drop in parameter prediction at several levels in the 2-best case is a result of the fact that the recognizer gets more cases right (i.e., increases recall), but that many of the new correct predictions have less instantiated parameter values. Thus, the decrease in number reflects that the recognizer is getting more correct predictions, but it does not reflect a decrease in performance for the cases it got correct in the 1-best prediction.

1.7 Conclusion

In this chapter, we have formalized hierarchical goal recognition as the recognition of the chain of an agent's active subgoals given an observed action. We discussed needed metrics and data for plan recognition, and introduced a method for creating synthetic plan-labeled corpora using a randomized AI planner and Monte Carlo sampling, which was used to create the Monroe Plan Corpus. We also described a hierarchical goal recognition system that is able to recognize goal schemas and their parameters. We then showed its performance on the Monroe Plan Corpus.

We believe that an important area of future research will be the generalization of plan recognition to what we will call *problem-solving recognition*. Plan recognition is typically defined as the recognition of an agent's plan, given observed actions. This definition, however, implicitly makes the assumption that an agent first creates a plan and then executes it.

Of course this is not always the case, and we would argue that there are many domains in which this is usually *not* the case. We believe if we want to model real agents from observations, we need to recognize the agent's problem-solving activity itself. This would mean recognizing the agent's current problem-solving state, which could then change from timestep to timestep. There would no longer be a single *plan* data object attached to a plan session; rather, a post hoc view of a plan session would reveal a trace of the agent's problem-solving state over the session.

The agent may have had several (partial or full) plans over the session, which may have been expanded or revised (or scrapped) as time passed. This would also model shifts in execution of different plans for different objectives, and even phenomena such as goal abandonment. (It could be very useful to know when an agent has abandoned a goal without accomplishing it.) See Geib and Goldman [17] as an example of work on recognizing plan abandonment.

As this is a very new area, much work is needed here. However, as a possible extension to our work, we have considered the possibility of using an artificial agent to create a *problem-solving labeled corpus* which could then not only give us information about hierarchical goal structure over time but also could be used to train a recognizer to predict when phenomena (e.g., replanning or goal abandonment) has occurred. See Oliver et al. [24] for an example of using an agent to create synthetic data.

Acknowledgments

This material is based on work supported by a grant from DARPA under grant number F30602-98-2-0133, two grants from the National Science Foundation under grant numbers IIS-0328811 and E1A-0080124, ONR contract N00014-06-C-0032, and the EU-funded TALK project (IST-507802). Any opinions, findings, and conclusions or recommendations expressed in this material are those of the authors and do not necessarily reflect the views any of these organizations.

References

[1] Albrecht DW, Zukerman I, Nicholson AE. Bayesian models for keyhole plan recognition in an adventure game. User Model User-Adapted Interact 1998;8:5–47.

[2] Ashbrook D, Starner T. Using GPS to learn significant locations and predict movement across multiple users. Personal Ubiquitous Comput 2003;7(5):275–86.

[3] Bauer M. A Dempster-Shafer approach to modeling agent preferences for plan recognition. User Model User-Adapted Interact 1995;5:3–4.

[4] Bauer M. Acquisition of user preferences for plan recognition. In: Proceedings of the Fifth International Conference on User Modeling; 1996. p. 105–12.

[5] Bauer M. Acquisition of abstract plan descriptions for plan recognition. In: Proceedings of the 15th National Conference on Artificial Intelligence; 1998. p. 936–41.

[6] Bauer M, Paul G. Logic-based plan recognition for intelligent help systems. In: Bäckström C, Sandewall E, editors. Current trends in AI planning. EWSP '93—Second European workshop on planning. Frontiers in artificial intelligence and applications; 1993. p. 60–73 [see also DFKI Research, Report RR-93-43].

[7] Blaylock N, Allen J. Statistical goal parameter recognition. In: Zilberstein S, Koehler J, Koenig S, editors. Proceedings of the 14th International Conference on Automated Planning and Scheduling; 2004. p. 297–304.

[8] Blaylock N, Allen J. Generating artificial corpora for plan recognition. In: Ardissono L, Brna P, Mitrovic A, editors. User Modeling. Springer; 2005. p. 179–88.

[9] Blaylock N, Allen J. Recognizing instantiated goals using statistical methods. In: Kaminka G, editor. IJCAI workshop on modeling others from observations; 2005b. p. 79–86.

[10] Bui HH. Efficient approximate inference for online probabilistic plan recognition. Tech. Rep. 1/2002, School of Computing, Curtin University of Technology; 2002.

[11] Bui HH. A general model for online probabilistic plan recognition. In: Gottlob G, Walsh T, editors. Proceedings of the 18th International Joint Conference on Artificial Intelligence; 2003.

[12] Bui HH, Venkatesh S, West G. Policy recognition in the abstract hidden Markov model. J Artif Intell Res 2002;17.

[13] Carberry S. Plan recognition in natural language dialogue (ACL-MIT Press series on natural language processing). MIT Press; 1990.

[14] Carberry S. Techniques for plan recognition. User Model User-Adapted Interact 2001;11:31–48.

[15] Charniak E. Statistical techniques for natural language parsing. AI Mag 1997;18(4):33–43.

[16] Davison BD, Hirsh H. Predicting sequences of user actions. In: Notes of the AAAI/ICML. Workshop on predicting the future: AI approaches to time-series analysis; 1998. p. 5–12.

[17] Geib CW, Goldman RP. Recognizing plan/goal abandonment. In: Gottlob G, Walsh T, editors. Proceedings of the 18th International Joint Conference on Artificial Intelligence; 2003. p. 1515–7.

[18] Horvitz E, Paek T. A computational architecture for conversation. In: Proceedings of the Seventh International Conference on User Modeling; 1999. p. 201–10.

[19] Lesh N. Scalable and adaptive goal recognition. Ph.D. thesis, University of Washington; 1998.

[20] Lesh N, Rich C, Sidner CL. Using plan recognition in human-computer collaboration. In: Proceedings of the Seventh International Conference on User Modeling; 1999 [see also MERL Technical, Report TR98-23].

[21] Mitchell TM, Wang SH, Huang Y, Cheyer A. Extracting knowledge about users' activities from raw workstation contents. In: Proceedings of the 21st National Conference on Artificial Intelligence; 2006. p. 181–6.

[22] Murphy KP, Paskin MA. Linear time inference in hierarchical HMMs. In: Proceedings of Neural Information Processing Systems; 2001. p. 833–40.

[23] Nau D, Au T-C, Ilghami O, Kuter U, Murdock JW, Wu D, et al. SHOP2: an HTN planning system. J Artif Intell Res 2003;20:379–404.

[24] Oliver NM, Rosario B, Pentland A. Graphical models for recognizing human interactions. In: Proceedings of International Conference on Neural Information and Processing Systems; 1998. p. 924–30.

[25] Patterson DJ, Liao L, Fox D, Kautz H. Inferring high-level behavior from low-level sensors. In: Fifth Annual Conference on Ubiquitous Computing; 2003.

[26] Pynadath DV, Wellman MP. Accounting for context in plan recognition, with application to traffic monitoring. In: Proceedings of the 11th Conference on Uncertainty in Artificial Intelligence; 1995. p. 472–81.

[27] Pynadath DV, Wellman MP. Probabilistic state-dependent grammars for plan recognition. In: Proceedings of the 16th Conference on Uncertainty in Artificial Intelligence; 2000.

[28] Russell S, Norvig P. Artificial intelligence: a modern approach. 2nd ed. Pearson Education; 2003.

[29] Sadilek A, Kautz H. Location-based reasoning about complex multi-agent behavior. J Artif Intell Res 2012;43:87–133.

[30] Shafer G. A mathematical theory of evidence. Princeton University Press; 1976.

[31] Wu H. Sensor data fusion for context-aware computing using Dempster-Shafer theory. Ph.D. thesis, Carnegie-Mellon University, Robotics Institute; 2003.

Weighted Abduction for Discourse Processing Based on Integer Linear Programming

Naoya Inoue[a], Ekaterina Ovchinnikova[b], Kentaro Inui[a], and Jerry Hobbs[b]

[a]*Tohoku University, Sendai, Japan*
[b]*USC/ISI, Marina del Rey, CA, USA*

2.1 Introduction

Inference-based discourse processing was a thriving area of research during the 1970s and 1980s. But in spite of successful theoretical progress and small-scale systems, work on large-scale, "real-life" systems foundered on two main difficulties: (1) there was no sufficiently large knowledge base of the right sort for language processing and (2) reasoning procedures were not efficient enough.

In the last few years the situation has changed with respect to the available machine-readable knowledge and efficient reasoning. A number of resources have been developed that encode the kinds of knowledge needed for language processing [22,51,15,43]. In addition, progress has been made recently in efficient reasoning techniques [8,29]. Thus, it seems to be time to look again at the possibilities of inference-based discourse processing.

This chapter explores discourse processing based on a mode of inference called *abduction*, or inference to the best explanation. Abduction-based discourse processing was studied intensively during the 1980s and 1990s [11,28]. This framework is appealing because it is a realization of the observation that we understand new material by linking it with what we already know. It instantiates in natural language understanding the more general principle that we understand our environment by coming up with the best explanation for the observables in it. Hobbs et al. [28] show that the lowest-cost abductive proof provides the solution to a whole range of natural language pragmatics problems such as word sense disambiguation, anaphora and metonymy resolution, interpretation of noun compounds and prepositional phrases, and detection of discourse relations.

Previous experiments on applying abduction to large-scale discourse processing showed that existing implementations of abductive inference quickly become intractable given increased background knowledge [4,41]. We have developed a new efficient abductive inference framework based on the Integer Linear Programming (ILP) technique [29]. Our reasoning system converts a problem of abduction into an ILP problem, and it solves the problem by using efficient existing techniques developed by the ILP research community.

In this chapter, we describe experiments on applying ILP-based weighted abduction to two discourse-processing tasks: plan recognition and textual entailment recognition. The present study is the first attempt to apply abduction-based discourse processing in a realistic setting: (1) with a large knowledge base, (2) using a scalable inference engine, and (3) evaluated on large real-life discourse-processing problems. None of the previous studies on applying weighted abduction to plan recognition [46,54] or natural language understanding [4,41] have been done in a similar setting.

This chapter is organized as follows. Related work is described in Section 2.2. In Section 2.3, we present the weighted abduction framework. We describe the ILP-based implementation of weighted abduction in Section 2.4. Section 2.5 presents an experiment on plan recognition using the dataset originally developed for Ng and Mooney's system [39]. In Section 2.6, we introduce our discourse-processing pipeline based on the *Boxer* semantic parser [5] for converting text into a logical form and a large knowledge base of commonsense knowledge using two lexical semantic resources, WordNet [22] and FrameNet [51]. Section 2.7 presents an evaluation of our discourse-processing pipeline on a knowledge-intensive NLP task—recognizing textual entailment. Section 2.8 concludes the chapter.

2.2 Related Work

Previous work on abductive inference can be grouped into two categories in terms of the hypothesis evaluation measure: cost-based approaches and probabilistic approaches. In cost-based approaches [28,13], the system finds a hypothesis that has a minimum cost among other competing hypotheses, and identifies it as the best hypothesis. Weighted abduction [28], which we adopted, belongs to this group. Attempts to define probabilistic semantics to the cost-based approaches are discussed in Charniak and Shimony and Blythe et al. [12,4]. In probabilistic approaches [11,44,36,46,4], etc., the system identifies the highest probability hypothesis as the best hypothesis.

Regarding the inference engine, a number of methods for abduction have been proposed in the literature [52,33,45,1,14,25]. However, most of them focus on propositional logic-based abduction. One must thus transform knowledge bases written in first-order predicate logic to the propositional level (perform *grounding*) in order to employ these methods. Typically, grounding-based approaches generate a huge search space, and do not scale to larger problems as discussed in Section 2.4.

The closest approaches to the one presented in this chapter are implementations of weighted abduction described in Mulkar et al. [38] and Blythe et al. [4]. However, given the increasing size of observations and knowledge bases, these implementations immediately suffer from exponentially growing computational cost [4,41,40]. To avoid this problem, we adopted an ILP-based solution [29] inspired by Santos [52], where cost-based abduction was formalized as a linear constraint satisfaction problem, and efficiently obtained the best hypothesis by solving it with linear programming techniques.

A series of studies in machine reading [21] are aimed at recovering implicit information from texts. Although knowledge bases are acquired automatically, most of the machine reading applications to discourse are specifically designed for solving one particular discourse phenomenon; see, for example, Penas and Hovy [43]. In contrast, our framework is quite general and not tuned to a specific task. It can be modularized as a discourse-processing module for any NLP task. Different applications of weighted abduction to different discourse understanding problems are described, for example, in Ovchinnikova et al. and Ovchinnikova [41,40].

2.3 **Weighted Abduction**

Abduction is inference to the best explanation. Formally, logical abduction is defined as follows:

Given: Background knowledge B, observations O, where both B and O are sets of first-order logical formulas.

Find: A hypothesis H such that $H \cup B \models O$, $H \cup B \not\models \perp$, where H is a set of first-order logical formulas.

Typically, there exist several hypotheses H explaining O. Each of them is called a *candidate hypothesis*. To rank candidate hypotheses according to plausibility, we use the framework of weighted abduction as defined by Hobbs et al. [28].

In this framework, observation O is a conjunction of propositions existentially quantified with the widest possible scope. Each proposition has a positive real-valued cost. We use the notation $P^{\$c}$ to indicate that proposition P has cost c and $cost(P)$ to represent the cost of P. Observation costs imply the unequal treatment of atomic observations reflecting the demand for propositions to be proved. Those propositions that are the most likely to be proved are expensive to assume.

The background knowledge B is a set of first-order logic formulas of the form

$$P_1^{w_1} \wedge \ldots \wedge P_n^{w_n} \rightarrow Q_1 \wedge \ldots \wedge Q_m$$

All variables occurring in the antecedents of such axioms are universally quantified with the widest possible scope. Variables occurring in the consequent only are existentially quantified within the scope of the universal quantifiers. Propositions in the antecedents are assigned positive real-valued *weights*. We use the notation P^w to indicate that proposition P has weight w.

The two main inference operations in weighted abduction are backward chaining and unification. *Backward chaining* is the introduction of new assumptions given an observation and background knowledge. For example, given $O = q(A)^{\$10}$ and $B = \{\forall x(p(x)^{1.2} \rightarrow q(x))\}$, there are two candidate hypotheses: $H_1 = q(A)^{\$10}$ and $H_2 = p(A)^{\$12}$. We say that in H_2 $p(A)$ is *assumed* and it *explains* $q(A)$. A literal is assumed in a candidate hypothesis if it is included in a candidate hypothesis and not explained.

In weighted abduction, a *cost function* f is used to calculate assumption costs. The function takes two arguments: costs of the propositions backchained on and the weight of the assumption. Usually, a multiplication function is used i.e., $f(c, w) = c \cdot w$ (where c is the cost of the propositions backchained on and w is the weight of the corresponding assumption). For example, if $q(A)$ costs \$10 and w of p is 1.2 in the preceding example above, then assuming $p(A)$ in H_2 costs \$12.

Unification is the merging of propositions with the same predicate name by assuming that their arguments are the same and assigning the smallest cost to the result of the unification. For example, if $O = \exists x, y(p^{\$10}(x) \wedge p^{\$20}(y) \wedge q^{\$10}(y))$, then there is a candidate hypothesis $H = \exists x(p^{\$0}(x) \wedge p^{\$0}(y) \wedge q^{\$10}(y) \wedge x = y^{\$10})$. Note that the smallest cost \$10 $= min(cost(p(x), cost(p(y)))$ is assigned to the equality $x = y$ (the result of the unification) in H.

Both operations—backchaining and unification—can be applied as many times as possible to generate a possibly infinite set of hypotheses. The generation of the set of hypotheses $\mathcal{H}$ initialized as an empty set can be formalized as follows.

Backchaining

$$\frac{\bigwedge_{i=1}^{n} P_n \rightarrow \bigwedge_{j=1}^{m} Q_j \in B \quad and \quad \bigwedge_{j=1}^{m} Q_j \ occurs \ in \ O \wedge H, \ where \ H \in \mathcal{H}}{\mathcal{H} := \mathcal{H} \cup \{H \wedge \bigwedge_{i=1}^{n} P_n\}} \tag{2.1}$$

Unification

$$\frac{p(X) \wedge p(Y) \ occurs \ in \ O \wedge H, \ where \ H \in \mathcal{H}}{\mathcal{H} := \mathcal{H} \cup \{H \wedge X = Y\}} \tag{2.2}$$

Weighted abduction defines a *cost* of a candidate hypothesis H as

$$cost(H) = \sum_{h \in H} cost(h), \tag{2.3}$$

where h is an atomic conjunct in H also called an *elemental hypothesis* (e.g., $p(A)$ in the previous H_2).

In this framework, minimum-cost hypotheses are the best hypotheses. Given Eq. (2.3), weighting of the candidate hypotheses works as follows:

(1) Proofs with fewer assumptions are favored.
(2) Proofs are favored that exploit the implicit redundancy (unification of predicates with costs > 0 always reduces the overall cost of the hypothesis).
(3) Plausible axioms are favored over less plausible axioms.

Weighted abduction also solves the problem of where to stop drawing inferences, which could easily be unlimited in number; an inference is appropriate if it is part of the lowest-cost proof of the observation.

2.4 ILP-based Weighted Abduction

2.4.1 ILP Formulation of Weighted Abduction

Recently, we have developed an efficient implementation of weighted abduction based on Integer Linear Programming (ILP) [29,30]. The key idea of this implementation is that finding hypotheses in weighted abduction can be modeled as a constrained combinatorial optimization problem. This gives us three benefits. First, we reduce the search space of candidate hypotheses as compared to fully grounding approaches, because we represent the search space through the combination of literals and variable substitutions (see a detailed comparison later in this section). Second, we exploit the state-of-the-art combinatorial optimization technology developed in operations research. Specifically, our optimization problem can be naturally formulated as an ILP problem, which can be efficiently solved by existing ILP solvers. Third, the resulting framework is highly extensible; for example, we can easily incorporate linguistically motivated heuristics by simply adding some ILP variables and/or constraints to an optimization problem, keeping the overall framework unchanged.

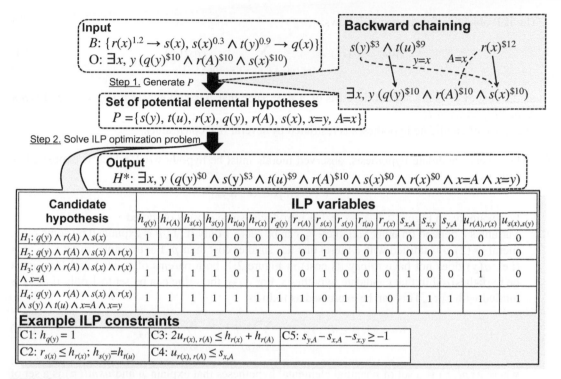

FIGURE 2.1

Illustration of our ILP-based reasoning procedure.

Let us give an informal description of the ILP-based implementation of weighted abduction (see Inoue and Inni [29] for more details). Figure 2.1 shows an example. Given an observation O and background knowledge B, the reasoner selects the best candidate hypothesis as follows. First, a set P of *potential elemental hypotheses* is constructed by applying backchaining and unification inference operations (step 1 in Figure 2.1). This procedure is called *search-space generation*.

Then, ILP variables and constraints are generated, which delimit the set of all possible candidate hypotheses (step 2 in Figure 2.1). The four main ILP variables are $h_p \in \{0, 1\}$, $r_p \in \{0, 1\}$, $u_{p,q} \in \{0, 1\}$, and $s_{x,y} \in \{0, 1\}$, where p, q are potential elemental hypotheses and x, y are first-order logical variables or constants used in P. h_p is used to represent whether p is hypothesized ($h_{p=1}$) or not ($h_{p=0}$).

A potential elemental hypothesis is *hypothesized* in a candidate hypothesis if it is assumed or explained in this candidate hypothesis. r_p is used to represent whether p pays its cost ($r_{p=0}$, i.e., it is assumed) or not ($r_{p=1}$, i.e., it is explained). For example, $r_{s(x)}$ in H_2 in Figure 2.1 is set to 1 since $s(x)$ is explained by $r(x)$. u and s are used to represent unification. When p and q are unified, $u_{p,q}$ is set to 1; 0 otherwise. $s_{x,y}$ is set to 1 if x and y are assumed equal (i.e., $x = y$). For instance, in H_3 in Figure 2.1, $u_{r(x),r(A)}$ and $s_{x,A}$ are set to 1, since $r(x)$ and $r(A)$ are unified and $x = A$ is assumed.

The ILP objective function is as follows:

$$\text{min. } cost(H) = \sum_{p \in \{p \mid p \in P, h_p = 1, r_p = 0\}} cost(p). \tag{2.4}$$

Thus, the cost of H is the sum of the costs of $p \in P$, such that p is hypothesized ($h_p = 1$) and is *not* explained ($r_p = 0$) in H.

The space of candidate hypotheses is restricted by several ILP constraints.

C1: For every candidate hypothesis, observed literals must be hypothesized, which is expressed as follows:

$$\text{for each } p \in O : h_{p=1} \tag{2.5}$$

For example, in Figure 2.1, $h_{q(y)} = 1$ is introduced since $q(y)$ is observed.

C2: Variables r depend on other variables. r_p can be set to 1 only if (1) p is explained by some other literal or (2) p is unified with a literal that has smaller cost than p. For example, to set $r_{q(y)} = 1$ (i.e., $q(y)$ does not have to pay its cost) in Figure 2.1, both parents of it, $s(y)$ and $t(u)$, must be hypothesized in that candidate hypothesis. For $r_{r(A)}$, the value can be set to 1 only if $r(A)$ is unified with $r(x)$. This can be expressed as follows:

$$\text{for each } p \in P : r_p \leq \sum_{e \in expl(p)} h_e + \sum_{q \in usml(p)} u_{p,q}, \tag{2.6}$$

where $expl(p)$ is a set of potential elemental hypotheses that explain p and $usml(p)$ is a set of potential elemental hypotheses that are unifiable with p and have smaller costs than p. In Figure 2.1, $r_{s(x)} \leq h_{r(x)}$ is introduced.

Furthermore, we use an additional constraint to link the variables for literals introduced by a conjunction (e.g., $s(y)$ and $t(u)$ in Figure 2.1) to be the same. We introduce the following equality:

$$\text{for each } p \in P : \sum_{a \in and(p)} h_a = h_p \cdot |and(p)|, \tag{2.7}$$

where $and(p)$ denotes a set of $a \in P$ such that a is conjoined with p by a conjunction. In Figure 2.1, $h_{s(y)} = h_{t(u)}$ is generated to represent that $s(y)$ is hypothesized if and only if $t(u)$ is hypothesized, and vice versa.

C3: Two elemental hypotheses p and q can be unified ($u_{p,q} = 1$) only if both are hypothesized, which is represented as $2u_{p,q} \leq h_p + h_q$. In Figure 2.1, for example, $2u_{r(x),r(A)} \leq h_{r(x)} + h_{r(A)}$ is introduced.

C4: Two literals $q(x_1, x_2, \ldots, x_n) \equiv q(X)$ and $q(y_1, y_2, \ldots, y_n) \equiv q(Y)$ can be unified (i.e., $u_{q(X),q(Y)} = 1$) only if their corresponding arguments are assumed to be equal (for all $i \in \{1, 2, \ldots, n\}$, $s_{x_i, y_i} = 1$). This can be expressed as follows:

$$n \cdot u_{q(\mathbf{x}),q(\mathbf{y})} \leq \sum_{i=1}^{n} s_{x_i, y_i} \tag{2.8}$$

In Figure 2.1, the constraint $u_{r(x),r(A)} \leq s_{x,A}$ is generated since $r(x)$ and $r(A)$ can be unified if x is substituted for A.

A second type of unification constraint is used for ensuring that the equality relation over s is transitive.

C5: s is transitive; namely, $s_{x,z}$ must be 1 if $s_{x,y} = 1$ and $s_{y,z} = 1$. This can be expressed as follows:

$$s_{x,z} - s_{x,y} - s_{y,z} \geq -1 \tag{2.9}$$

$$- s_{x,z} + s_{x,y} - s_{y,z} \geq -1 \tag{2.10}$$

$$- s_{x,z} - s_{x,y} + s_{y,z} \geq -1 \tag{2.11}$$

In practice, however, an exhaustive enumeration of potential elemental hypotheses is intractable. In the latter experiments, we use a simple heuristic approach to control the search by employing a depth parameter d, such that we stop backward chaining at depth d, that is, the longest inference chains have the length d.[1]

As mentioned in Section 2.2, our work is most similar to Santos's ILP-based formulation [52] of propositional logic-based abduction. There are two main differences between our approach and his [52].

The first difference is that we account for the specificity of explanations, which is important for abduction-based NLP as discussed in Hobbs et al. [28]. In Santos [52], most-specific explanations are favored. Suppose $O = \{p(A), q(A)\}$, and $B = \{r(x) \rightarrow p(x)\}$. There are two candidate hypotheses. The first one is $H_1 = \{p(A), q(A)\}$, which simply assumes observations, and it is $cost(p(A)) + cost(q(A))$ ($h_{p(A)} = 1, r_{p(A)} = 0, h_{q(A)} = 1, r_{q(A)} = 0$). Backward chaining on $p(A)$ results in the second hypothesis $H_2 = \{q(A), r(A)\}$, which is more specific than H_1.

The cost of H_2 is equal to $cost(q(A)) + cost(r(A))$ ($h_{p(A)} = 1, r_{p(A)} = 1, h_{q(A)} = 1, r_{q(A)} = 0, h_{r(A)} = 1, r_{r(A)} = 0$). Note that we do not count the cost of $p(A)$ because $p(A)$ is *not* assumed anymore. If $cost(r(A)) < cost(p(A))$, then the more specific hypothesis H_2 is selected as the best explanation; otherwise, the less specific hypothesis H_1 is selected as the best explanation. The choice is controlled by the ILP variables r and Constraint 2. To summarize, in our approach the choice of the best explanation is based on how well the explanation is supported by observations.

Another important difference is that our approach directly models abduction on first-order logic, while Santos [52] employs propositional logic using the grounding procedure of replacing variables with all possible constants. Suppose $B = \{q(x, y) \rightarrow p(x, y), r(x, y, z) \rightarrow q(x, y)\}$, $O = \{p(x, y)\}$ and all possible constants are $C = \{C_1, C_2, \ldots, C_n\}$. To ground this observation, we need to generate a disjunctive clause for $p(x, y)$, replacing x and y with all possible combinations from C, that is, $p(C_1, C_1) \vee p(C_1, C_2) \vee \ldots \vee p(C_n, C_n)$.

The problem arises in the search-space generation process: there are $O(n^2)$ potential elemental hypotheses ($p(C_i, C_j)$ for all $i, j \in \{1, 2, \ldots, n\}$) for the literal $p(x, y)$. In addition, backchaining on each $q(C_i, C_j)$ given $r(x, y, z) \rightarrow q(x, y)$ results in $O(n)$ potential elemental hypotheses ($r(C_i, C_j, C_k)$ for all $k \in \{1, 2, \ldots, n\}$). In contrast, we generate the set $\{p(x, y), q(x, y), r(x, y, u)\}$. Thus, our approach seems to be more robust to the domain size. In discourse processing, this robustness is important because natural language predicates usually have more than two arguments referring to participants of the same event.

---

[1]It is possible to develop smarter heuristics. For example, one can estimate in advance whether an axiom application can reduce the hypothesis cost or not to prune the search. We will address this problem in future work.

2.4.2 Handling Negation

The ILP-based framework described before does not provide full support for first-order linear programming (FOPL) since it cannot represent negation. Only axioms in the form of Horn clauses and positive literals in the observations are accepted. However, the capability to handle negation might be crucial for a wide range of reasoning tasks.

We extend ILP-based weighted abduction making it able to handle negated literals (e.g., $\neg p$) and inequality of variables (e.g., $x \neq y$); see Inoue and Inni [30] for more details. Given this extension, negated literals and variable inequalities are allowed both in observations and in background knowledge.

Additional unification constraints need to be introduced in order to handle negation. First, we consider the case where two propositions $p(x)$ and $\neg p(y)$ occur in set P of potential elemental hypotheses such that $p(x)$ and $p(y)$ are potentially unifiable. For example, we need to explain the observable $crane(A)$ given the axioms $bird(x) \rightarrow crane(x)$, $equipment(x) \rightarrow crane(x)$, $\neg bird(x) \rightarrow equipment(x)$. We want to prohibit the two propositions—$\neg bird(A)$ and $bird(A)$—from being hypothesized simultaneously. In other words, two propositions $q(x_1, x_2, \ldots, x_n) \equiv q(X)$ and $\neg q(y_1, y_2, \ldots, y_n) \equiv \neg q(Y)$ cannot both be hypothesized as ($h_{q(X)} = 1$ and $h_{\neg q(Y)} = 1$) if variable substitutions x_i/y_i are activated ($s_{x_i, y_i} = 1$) for all $i \in \{1, 2, \ldots, n\}$. This can be expressed as follows:

$$h_{q(X)} + h_{\neg q(Y)} + \sum_{i=1}^{n} s_{x_i, y_i} \leq 1 + n \tag{2.12}$$

Formulation of the ILP constraints corresponding to variable inequality is straightforward. For each pair of variables x and y such that $x \neq y \in P$, the following equality is introduced:

$$s_{x,y} = 0 \tag{2.13}$$

2.4.3 Cutting Plane Inference

The ILP-based reasoning framework generates $O(n^3)$ transitivity constraints (where n is the number of logical terms), making inference intractable in a large-scale setting. Our solution to this problem is based on the idea that there is no need to check all transitivity constraints at once. We gradually optimize and add transitivity constraints, if violated, in an iterative manner.

We employ Cutting Plane Inference (CPI), which is an iterative optimization strategy developed in operations research. It is an exact inference optimization technique originally developed for solving large linear programming problems [19]. CPI has been successfully applied to a wide range of constrained optimization problems [50,49,34,3].

We developed an algorithm called *CPI4CBA* that applies the CPI technique to our optimization problem. The pseudo-code of *CPI4CBA* is given in Algorithm 2.1. First, the algorithm creates an ILP optimization problem without any transitivity constraints (line 1). Ψ denotes a set of ILP variables, and I denotes a set of ILP constraints. Lines 2 through 12 describe the iteration process. The solution S is found for the current ILP optimization problem (line 3). Then, for each pair (x, y) of logical atomic terms unified in the solution S (line 4), find a logical term z that can be unified with x or y (line 5). If the transitive relation x, y with respect to z is violated (i.e., $s_{x,z} = 0 \wedge s_{y,z} = 1$ or $s_{x,z} = 1 \wedge s_{y,z} = 0$), then constraints for preventing this violation are generated and stored in set V (lines 6–8). Set I is extended with new constraints (line 11). The iteration terminates when no transitivity constraints are violated (line 12).

Algorithm 2.1 CPI4CBA(Background Knowledge **B**, Observation **O**)

1: $(\Psi, I) \leftarrow$ createBaseILP(B, O)

2: **repeat**

3:     $S \leftarrow$ solveILP(Ψ, I); $V \leftarrow \{\}$

4:     **for** $(x, y) \in$ unifiedTerms(S) **do**

5:       **for** $z \in$ termsUnifiableWith$(x) \cup$ termsUnifiableWith(y) **do**

6:         **if** $(s_{x,z} = 0$ and $s_{y,z} = 1)$ or $(s_{x,z} = 1$ or $s_{y,z} = 0)$ **then**

7:           $V \leftarrow V \cup \{-s_{x,y} - s_{x,z} + s_{y,z} \geq -1, -s_{x,y} + s_{x,z} - s_{y,z} \geq -1\}$

8:         **end if**

9:       **end for**

10:     **end for**

11:     $I \leftarrow I \cup V$

12: **until** $V \neq \phi$

The key advantage of *CPI4CBA* is that the algorithm reduces the time of search-space generation and the time of ILP optimization; see Inoue and Inni [30] for a theoretical proof and an empirical evaluation. *CPI4CBA* does not generate all transitivity constraints before starting optimization. In addition, optimization problems to be solved become smaller, as compared to the original problems, if not all transitivity constraints are to be considered.

2.5 **Weighted Abduction for Plan Recognition**

A *plan* is an agent's set of intentions and beliefs about achieving a goal. The task of plan recognition consists of inferring an agent's plan from observed actions or utterances. Recognizing plans is crucial for solving knowledge-intensive NLP tasks such as story understanding and dialogue planning. Since the task of plan recognition can be modeled as finding the best explanation (i.e., a plan) given an observation (i.e., utterances), most of the proposed methods have been based on abduction [11,39,54].

We tested the ILP-based abductive reasoner using a subset of the dataset originally developed for the evaluation of the abductive plan recognition system *ACCEL* [39]. We extracted 50 plan recognition problems and 107 background axioms from the dataset. The plan recognition problems represent an agent's actions as conjunctions of propositions. For example, problem *t2* consists of the following propositions:

$inst(get2, getting) \wedge agent\_get(get2, bob2) \wedge name(bob2, bob) \wedge$
$patient\_get(get2, get2) \wedge inst(get2, gun) \wedge precede(get2, getoff) \wedge$
$inst(getoff, getting\_off) \wedge agent\_get\_off(getoff, bob2) \wedge$
$patient\_get\_off(getoff, bus2) \wedge inst(bus2, bus) \wedge$
$place\_get\_off(getoff, ls2) \wedge inst(ls2, liquor\_store)$

Table 2.1 The Processing Time of Each System

System	d	% of solved	Time [sec.]	Precision	Recall	F-measure
ILPWA	1	100% (50/50)	0.03 (0.01/0.02)	0.57	0.69	0.62
	2	100% (50/50)	0.36 (0.06/0.30)	0.53	0.76	0.62
	3	100% (50/50)	0.96 (0.15/0.81)	0.52	0.77	0.62
M-TAC	1	28.0% (14/50)	8.3	0.43	0.61	0.50
	2	20.0% (10/50)	10.2	0.38	0.64	0.47
	3	20.0% (10/50)	10.1	0.38	0.64	0.47

This logical form represents the sequence of actions that can be described as follows: Bob got a gun; he got off the bus at the liquor store. The task is to infer Bob's plan given the preceding observations and background knowledge. For example, the dataset contains the following background axiom:

$$inst(R, robbing) \land get\_weapon\_step(R, G) \rightarrow inst(G, getting)$$

For each axiom, we set the sum of the assumption weights equal to 1.2 as a default, that is, $inst\_shopping(s)^{0.6} \land store(t, s)^{0.6} \rightarrow shopping\_place(t)$.

We first evaluate the processing time of our ILP-based reasoner. Table 2.1 shows the runtime of inference for different values of the depth parameter (d) that restricts the possible depth of the inference chains (system: ILPWA). For the sake of comparison, we present the performance of the state-of-the-art abductive reasoner *Mini-TACITUS*[2] [38] on the same dataset (system: M-TAC).

For all experiments, we restrict the maximum runtime of inference to 120 seconds. In the table, we show the percentage of the problems optimally solved by each reasoner within 120 seconds (% of solved) and the inference time averaged on such problems. For the ILP-based reasoner, we also show the runtime of each processing step (generation of ILP variables and constraints, ILP optimization).

To evaluate how well both systems do in plan recognition, we followed the evaluation strategy of Singla et al. [54] and focused on top-level plans and their role fillers (e.g., the agents, themes of plans). Top-level plans include *smarket_shopping, liqst_shopping, shopping, robbing, going_by_plane, going_by_bus, rest_dining, drinking, going_by_taxi, paying, jogging,* and *partying.* We used precision (the fraction of inferred literals that are correct), recall (the fraction of correct literals that are inferred by the system), and F-measure (the harmonic mean of precision and recall) as evaluation measures.

Table 2.1 shows that our reasoner can find optimal solutions for all problems within 120 seconds in all depths, while *Mini-TACITUS* cannot find optimal solutions for 72% of the problems (36/50) within 120 seconds even for depth 1. Given $d \geq 2$, 80% of the problems (40/50) could not be solved by *Mini-TACITUS* in 120 seconds. This indicates that *Mini-TACITUS* is sensitive to the depth parameter, which becomes a significant drawback for abductive inference using large-scale background knowledge.

Currently we are developing an automatic method for tuning the cost function in a supervised learning framework [32]. We report preliminary results of the learning procedure in the rest of this section

---

[2]www.rutumulkar.com/

Table 2.2 Results of Plan Recognition with Learned Parameters

	Precision	Recall	F-measure
Closed test	0.74	0.82	0.78
Open test	0.52	0.66	0.58

(see Inoue et al. [32] for more detail). In the learning framework, we model the cost function with a weighted linear model, and learn axiom weights with a Passive Aggressive algorithm [17]. This is a large-margin online learning algorithm for finding weight parameters that classifies given training examples and maximizes the margin (i.e., the minimal distance between the separating hyperplane and the examples). To make the predicates representing the top-level plans disjoint, we used 73 ILP constraints that represent disjointness of top-level plan predicates (e.g., $\forall x \, (robbing(x) \wedge shopping(x) \rightarrow \perp)$) in our experiment.[3]

Table 2.2 shows the results of plan recognition with learned parameters. In the "closed test" setting, we used the development set for both training and testing. In the "open test" setting, we used the development set for training and the test set for testing. The results show that our training procedure successfully learns the cost function from the dataset and has a generalization ability. We compare the results of the open test (0.58 F-score) with two existing systems: (1) the *ACCEL* system [39] and (2) a Markov Logic Networks-based (MLN-based) system [54].

Singla and Mooney [54] report that *ACCEL* achieves 0.89 F-score on the test set. However, the cost function of *ACCEL* (called *coherence* metric in Ng and Mooney [39]) is particularly tuned for the task of story understanding and is not trainable. Our system is more general and applicable to a wide range of tasks because of the learning framework. Singla and Mooney [54] also report that the MLN-based system achieves 0.72 F-score on the test set. The MLN-based system can learn the cost function as we do. However, it relies on manually initialized and tuned weights, while our weight vector is initialized with zeros in the experiment described.[4]

To summarize, the performance of our system is still not as good as the existing systems exploiting manually tuned weights. However, our system achieves 0.58 F-score, which is close to 0.62 of the logical abduction setting in Table 2.2, *without* any manual tuning of weights. It indicates that our learning framework is promising. In the future, we plan to evaluate the learning framework on a larger dataset and apply it to a wide range of discourse-processing tasks.

2.6 Weighted Abduction for Discourse Processing

This section describes how we apply weighted abduction to discourse processing. Our goal is to recover implicit information from natural language texts. The implicit information includes semantic relations

---

[3]For example, we use $h_{robbing(x)} + h_{shopping(y)} + s_{x,y} \leq 2$.

[4]For both systems, the results depend on how we initialize the weight values because the learning problem is a nonconvex optimization problem. In future work, we plan to investigate how the strategy of weight initialization affects the performance.

between discourse entities, anaphoric relations, character's intentions, and so on. These kinds of information have been shown to be useful in several NLP tasks such as question answering and recognizing textual entailment [26].

2.6.1 NL Pipeline

Our natural language pipeline produces interpretations of texts given a knowledge base. A text is first input to the English semantic parser *Boxer* [5]. For each segment, the parse produced by *Boxer* is a first-order fragment of the DRS language used in the Discourse Representation Theory [35]. An add-on to *Boxer* converts the DRS into a logical form (LF) in the style of Hobbs [27].

The LF is a conjunction of propositions, which have generalized eventuality arguments that can be used for showing relationships among the propositions. Hobbs [27] extends Davidson's approach [20] to all predications and posits that corresponding to any predication that can be made in natural language, there is an eventuality. Similarly, any predication in the logical notation has an extra argument, which refers to the "condition" of that predication being true. Thus, in the logical form $John(e_1, j) \wedge run(e_2, j)$ for the sentence *John runs*, e_2 is a running event by j and e_1 is a condition of j being named "John."

In terms of weighted abduction, logical forms represent observations, which need to be explained by background knowledge. In the context of discourse processing, we call a hypothesis explaining a logical form *an interpretation* of this LF. The interpretation of the text is carried out by the abductive system. The system tries to prove the logical form of the text, allowing assumptions whenever necessary. Where the system is able to prove parts of the LF, it is anchoring it in what is already known from the overall discourse or from a knowledge base. Where assumptions are necessary, it is gaining new information.

Let us illustrate the procedure with a simple example. Suppose we need to interpret the text fragment *"the Boston office secretary."* The logical form of this text fragment is as follows:

$$Boston(e_1, x_1) \wedge office(e_2, x_2) \wedge nn(e_3, x_1, x_2) \wedge secretary(e_4, x_3) \wedge nn(e_4, x_2, x_3)$$

Suppose our knowledge base contains the following axioms. Axioms 1 and 2 represent the facts that being in a location and working in a workspace can be expressed by a noun compound in English. Axioms 3, 4, and 5 say that Boston is a location, every secretary is a person, and every office is a workspace.

(1) $in(e_1, x, y) \wedge location(e_2, y) \rightarrow nn(e_3, y, x)$
(2) $work\_at(e_1, x, y) \wedge person(e_2, x) \wedge work\_space(e_3, y) \rightarrow nn(e_4, y, x)$
(3) $Boston(e_1, x) \rightarrow location(e_2, x)$
(4) $secretary(e_1, x) \rightarrow person(e_2, x)$
(5) $office(e_1, x) \rightarrow work\_space(e_2, x)$

Using these axioms, as illustrated in Figure 2.2, we can infer that the secretary works in the office located in Boston, which is an inference we can draw from the original text.

2.6.2 Knowledge Base

The proposed discourse-processing procedure is based on a knowledge base (KB) consisting of a set of axioms. To obtain a reliable KB with a large coverage we exploited existing lexical semantic resources.

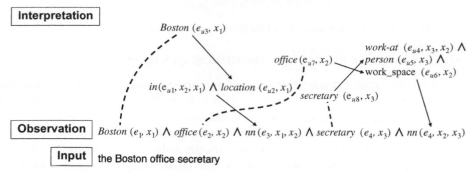

FIGURE 2.2

Weighted abduction for discourse processing.

First, we have extracted axioms from WordNet [22], version 3.0, which has already proved itself to be useful in knowledge-intensive NLP applications. The central entity in WordNet (WN) is called a *synset*. Synsets correspond to word senses, so that every lexeme can participate in several synsets. We used the lexeme-synset mapping for generating axioms. For example, in the next axioms, the verb *compose* is mapped to *synset-X*, which represents one of its senses.

$$synset - X(s, e) \rightarrow compose(e, x_1, x_2)$$

Moreover, we have converted the following WordNet relations defined on synsets and word senses into axioms: hypernymy (type-of), instantiation, entailment, similarity, causation, meronymy (part-of), and derivation. In total, 333,192 axioms have been generated from WordNet.

The second resource that we used as a source of axioms is FrameNet 1.5 [51]. FrameNet has a shorter history in NLP applications than WordNet, but lately more and more researchers have been demonstrating its potential to improve the quality of question answering [53] and recognizing textual entailment [7]. The lexical meaning of predicates in FrameNet is represented in terms of frames that describe prototypical situations spoken about in natural language. Every frame in FrameNet (FN) contains a set of roles corresponding to the participants of the described situation. Predicates with similar semantics are assigned to the same frame. For most of the lexemes, FrameNet provides syntactic patterns showing the surface realization of these lexemes and their arguments. We used the patterns for deriving axioms. For example, this axiom corresponds to phrases like *"John gave a book to Mary."*

$$\text{GIVING}(e_1, x_1, x_2, x_3) \land \text{DONOR}(e_1, x_1) \land \text{RECIPIENT}(e_1, x_2) \land \text{THEME}(e_1, x_3)$$
$$\rightarrow give(e_1, x_1, x_3) \land to(e_2, e_1, x_2)$$

FrameNet also introduces semantic relations defined on frames such as inheritance, causation, or precedence; for example, the GIVING and GETTING frames are connected with the causation relation. Roles of the connected frames are also linked (e.g., DONOR in GIVING is linked with SOURCE in GETTING). To generate corresponding axioms, we used the previous work on axiomatizing frame relations [42]. An example of an axiomatized relation follows. In total, 31,861 axioms have been extracted from FrameNet.

GIVING$(e_1, x_1, x_2, x_3) \land$ DONOR$(e_1, x_1) \land$ RECIPIENT$(e_1, x_2) \land$ THEME(e_1, x_3)

$\rightarrow$

GETTING$(e_2, x_2, x_3, x_1) \land$ SOURCE$(e_2, x_1) \land$ RECIPIENT$(e_2, x_2) \land$ THEME(e_2, x_3)

Axiom weights are calculated using frequency of the corresponding word senses in the annotated corpora. The information about frequency is provided both by WordNet and by FrameNet. In our framework, axioms of the type *species* → *genus* should have weights exceeding 1, which means that assuming *species* costs more than assuming *genus*, because there might be many possible *species* for the same *genus*. The weights of such axioms are heuristically defined as ranging from 1 to 2.

To assign a weight w_i to a sense i of a lexeme, we use information about the frequency f_i of the word sense in the annotated corpora. An obvious way of converting the frequency f_i to the weight w_i is the following equation:

$$w_i = 2 - \frac{f_i}{\sum_{f_n \in S} f_n}, \tag{2.14}$$

where S is a set of all senses of the lexeme.

2.6.3 Overmerging

Frequently, the lowest-cost interpretation results from unification (i.e., identifying two entities with each other) so that their common properties only need to be proved or assumed once. This is one of the principal methods by which coreference is resolved.

However, *overmerging*—unification of incompatible propositions—is quite a serious problem in large-scale processing. For example, given

$$O = \{animal(e_1, x) \land animal(e_2, y)\},$$

weighted abduction incorrectly assumes x equals y even when $dog(e_3, x)$ and $cat(e_4, y)$ are observed. For "*John runs and Bill runs,*" with the logical form

$$John(e_1, x) \land run(e_2, x) \land Bill(e_3, y) \land run(e_4, y),$$

weighted abduction assumes John and Bill are the same individual just because they are both running.

The problem we will address is this: If $p(x)$ and $p(y)$ both hold, how good is that as evidence that x and y are the same entity, given what else we know about x and y? To approach this problem, we adopt a solution of imposing constraints on unification based on linguistic observations.

2.6.3.1 *Argument constraints*

The rule for generating argument constraints can be formulated as follows: For each two propositions $p(e_1, x_1, \ldots, x_n)$ and $p(e_2, y_1, \ldots, y_n)$ if

- e_1 is not equal to e_2
- p is not a noun predicate
- $\exists i \in 1, \ldots, n$ such that x_i is not equal to y_i and both x_i and y_i occur as arguments of predicate q other than p

  then e_1 and e_2 cannot be unified.

This is expressed by the following ILP constraint:

$$n \cdot u_{p(e_1, x_1, x_2, \ldots x_n), p(e_2, y_1, y_2, \ldots y_n)} \leq \sum_{i=1}^{n} u_{q_i(\ldots, x_i, \ldots), q_i(\ldots, y_i, \ldots)} \tag{2.15}$$

This rule ensures that nouns can be unified without any restriction and other predicates can be merged only if all their arguments that are not first are equal (due to previous mergings) or uninstantiated. As seen from the preceding statements, the argument unification restriction concerns first arguments only. First arguments of all predicates in the logical forms are "handles" referring to conditions in which the predicate is true of its arguments (i.e., referring to the predication itself) rather than to its semantic arguments.

The proposed nonmerge rule is a heuristic, which corresponds to the intuition that it is unlikely that the same noun refers to different entities in a short discourse, while for other predicates this is possible. According to this rule, the two *run* propositions cannot be unified in logical form $John(e_1, x) \wedge run(e_2, x) \wedge Bill(e_3, y) \wedge run(e_4, y)$. At the same time, two *run* propositions in LF $John(e_1, x) \wedge run(e_2, x) \wedge man(e_3, y) \wedge run(e_4, y)$ can be unified given the axiom $John(e_1, x) \rightarrow man(e_2, x)$.

2.6.3.2 *Compatibility constraints*

We define sets of incompatible properties (e.g., *dog* and *cat*) and prohibit unification of two propositions if it implies unifying variables with incompatible properties. For example, we prohibit the unification $x = y$ if $dog(e_1, x)$ and $cat(e_2, y)$ are hypothesized. This kind of constraint can be formulated as the logical constraint $s_{x,y} = 1 \Rightarrow h_{p(e_1, x)} = 0 \vee h_{q(e_2, y)} = 0$, where p and q are predicates that have the property of exclusion. This can be expressed as the following ILP constraint: $h_{p(e_1, x)} + h_{q(e_2, y)} + s_{x,y} \leq 2$. One can reduce the number of the constraints by using ontological hierarchy information so that the constraints are introduced only for the most general classes. In the experiments described next, we set all antonym and sister terms in WordNet to be disjoint.

Another possible approach to overmerging is to evaluate the plausibility of the equality statements during inference [9, 10]. Charniak and Goldman [9, 10] perform first-order, logic-based plan recognition using Bayesian Networks (BNs). In the BN, each node represents the presence of an event or entity (e.g., (hang k1), (rope r2)) or an equality statement that means two entities are the same (e.g., (rope-of k1) = r2). Each edge connects causally related or implicationally related nodes (e.g., (hang k1) and (kill k1)).

Once the BN is constructed, plan recognition can be performed by Maximum a posteriori (MAP) inference over the BN given observed actions. In this framework, probabilities are defined over equality nodes. This direction is taken in Inoue et al. [31] and model the likelihood of equalities using a weighted linear feature function, such that parameters are discriminatively trained on a corpus with coreference annotations.

2.7 **Evaluation on Recognizing Textual Entailment**

The discourse interpretation procedure and the KB derived from WordNet and FrameNet are fairly general and not tuned for any particular type of inferences or tasks. We have performed an evaluation on the Recognizing Textual Entailment (RTE) task, which is a generic task that seems to capture major semantic inference needs across many NLP applications. In this task, the system is given a text (T) and a hypothesis (H) and must decide whether the hypothesis is entailed by the text plus commonsense knowledge. Suppose an RTE system gets the following input:

T: *John gave Mary a book.*
H1: *Mary got a book.*
H2: *Mary read a book.*

The task consists in predicting that T entails H1 but not H2. It was previously reported that inferring information implicit in the text and the hypothesis can improve the performance of an RTE system [26]. We intend to test whether implicit information produced by our system is helpful for solving the RTE task.

RTE has been previously approached by inference-based methods; see Riabinin and Dagan et al. [47,18] for overviews. Most of them are based on deductive reasoning. Deductive inference for RTE has a serious limitation: If some piece of knowledge required to infer H from T is missing from the KB, then the classic reasoner fails to find a proof and predicts "no entailment." To overcome this problem, deduction-based RTE systems employ two solutions.

Some systems introduce different heuristics and consider logical inference to be just one of the features used to classify T–H pairs as "entailment" or "no entailment" [6]. Other systems decompose logical forms into atomic propositions and measure whether each proposition from H is entailed by a proposition from T [2,23,55].

Abduction solves the problem of knowledge incompleteness by allowing assumptions. Attempts to use weighted abduction for RTE are presented in Blythe et al., Ovchinnikova et al., and Ovchinnikova [4,41,40]. Ovchinnikova et al. [41] employ the reasoning system *Mini-TACITUS* (mentioned in Section 2.5). Blythe et al. [4] implement weighted abduction as Markov Logic Networks [48]. Both systems suffer from the problem of computational inefficiency of inference that makes large-scale discourse processing intractable.

2.7.1 Weighted Abduction for Recognizing Textual Entailment

Our approach is to interpret both the text and the hypothesis using the abductive reasoner, and then to see whether adding information derived from the text to the knowledge base will reduce the cost of the best abductive proof of the hypothesis as compared to using the original knowledge base only. This idea is summarized in Figure 2.3.

To judge whether the hypothesis entails the text or not, we use Support Vector Machine (SVM) [56], a powerful and widely used binary classification algorithm, encoding the best proof as SVM features. This procedure can be summarized as follows:

1. Construct the best interpretation of the text $I(T)$.
2. Construct the best interpretation of the hypothesis $I(H)$.
3. Construct the best interpretation of the hypothesis given the best interpretation of the text $I(I(T) \wedge H)$.
4. For each entailment pair, extract the following features for SVM classification:

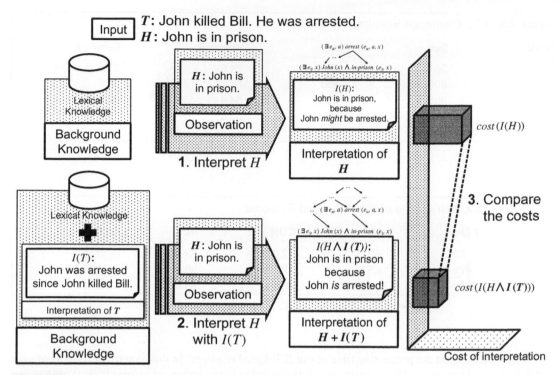

FIGURE 2.3

Weighted abduction for recognizing textual entailment.

- For each part of speech, number of proven/not proven propositions in H.
- For each part of speech, number of unified propositions in H.
- Number of proven/not proven *not* propositions in H (negation).

We used an RBF-kernel SVM classifier[5] classifying input T–H pairs as "entailment" or "no entailment."

2.7.2 **Experiment**

We evaluate our procedure on the RTE 1–5 Challenge datasets [18]. The evaluation measure in the RTE challenges is *accuracy* calculated as the percentage of correct judgments against the gold standard. The results for the corresponding datasets are presented in Table 2.3. For each challenge, the table shows the number of pairs in the development and test sets and the average accuracy achieved by the best runs of the original participants. We also replicate the results of Katrenko and Toledo [37] calculating the baseline on the basis of the lexical overlap between T and H by using a support vector classifier with the polynomial kernel.

---

[5]*libSVM*, www.csie.ntu.edu.tw/~cjlin/libsvm/

Table 2.3 RTE Challenge Results

RTE	Dev.	Test	Average	Baseline
1	567	800	54.6	53.6
2	800	800	60.3	59.2
3	800	800	54.4	62.8
4	–	1000	59.4	58.8
5	600	600	61.4	60.3

Table 2.4 Processing Time of the ILP-based Reasoner

D	PEH	VAR	CON	ALL	Time
1	89	3378	12,075	99.8%	0.33
2	479	12,534	22,094	98.4%	1.07
3	1171	32,941	58,612	95.8%	2.63

First, we evaluated the processing time of our ILP-based reasoner. In this experiment, we have used the RTE-2 development and test datasets and the knowledge base containing axioms from WordNet and FrameNet. In Table 2.4, we present the results for different values of the depth parameter (D) that restricts the possible depth of the inference chains. The table contains information about the average number of potential elemental hypotheses (PEH), ILP variables (VAR), and ILP constraints (CON) generated per sentence. The deeper the inference chains are, the more variables and constraints are generated, because more axioms can be applied on each inference step. The reasoner was given a 2-minute time limit to finish the inference. If all candidate hypotheses could not be evaluated by that time, the reasoner was requested to output the best solution found so far and terminate.

The column ALL in Table 2.4 shows data for how many sentences all hypotheses were evaluated in 2 minutes and what the average processing time was for such sentences (in seconds). Our reasoner is dramatically faster than the *Mini-TACITUS* system, which needed more than 30 minutes per sentence on average on the same dataset [41]. Blythe et al. [4] could run to completion only 28 of 100 selected RTE-2 problems with an average processing time of 7.5 minutes.

Then we performed five runs for each RTE dataset (N): without a KB (∅), with compatibility constraints (CC), with axioms from WordNet and compatibility constraints (WN), with axioms from FrameNet and compatibility constraints (FN), and with both axiom sets and compatibility constraints. The accuracy results are presented in Table 2.5. We also report how many original participants we out-perform in each challenge (Rank).[6] For RTE 1, 2, and 5 our system outperformed the baseline shown in Table 2.3. In addition, both WordNet and FrameNet helped entailment recognition for RTE 1, 2,

---

[6]X/Y means that we outperform X systems out of Y.

Table 2.5 Accuracy Results for RTE Challenge Datasets

N	∅	CC	WN	FN	WN,FN	Rank
1	53.2	51.3	53.3	51.3	**54.2**	5/15
2	59.4	60.8	60.3	60.7	**61.4**	14/19
3	**62.7**	59.4	62.2	59.4	61.4	12/26
4	56.5	56.0	56.0	56.1	**57.1**	8/19
5	**61.0**	55.0	56.6	55.5	56.6	10/23

and 4. However, for RTE 3 and 5, adding lexical-semantic knowledge was not helpful for predicting entailment, and our system could not beat the baseline.

We compare our results for RTE 2 with the results reported in Ovchinnikova et al. [41]. The developed compatibility constraints give an advantage over the empty KB setting in Ovchinnikova et al. [41] (i.e., 60.8% vs. 57%).[7] Our constraints preventing overmerging have been evaluated using a corpus annotated with coreference relations; see Inoue et al. [31] for a detailed description.

Obviously, WordNet and FrameNet alone are not enough to predict entailment. In the example that follows, our system inferred that *president* is related to *presidential*, Tehran is a part of Iran, *mayor* and *official* can refer to the same person, and *runoff* and *election* can mean the same by WN and WN relations. However, all this information does not help us to predict entailment.

T: *Iran will hold the first runoff presidential election in its history, between President Akbar Hashemi Rafsanjani and Tehran's hard-line mayor, election officials said Saturday.*

H: *Hashemi Rafsanjani will face Tehran's hard-line mayor in Iran's first runoff presidential election ever, officials said Saturday.*

The analysis of knowledge needed for RTE is given, for example, in Clark et al. [16] and Garoufi [24]. In both works, the conclusion is that lexical-semantic relations are just one type of knowledge required; thus, our knowledge base needs a significant extension. Moreover, a much more elaborate treatment of logical connectors and quantifiers, such as *if, not, or, all, each*, and others, is needed. In the next example, H is (lexically) fully contained in T, but there is still no entailment.

T: *Drew Walker, NHS Tayside's public health director, said: "It is important to stress that this is not a confirmed case of rabies."*

H: *A case of rabies was confirmed.*

2.8 Conclusion

In this chapter, we have explored the logical framework of weighted abduction as applied to discourse processing. We used a tractable implementation of weighted abduction based on Integer Linear Programming and a large knowledge base generated automatically.

---

[7]The accuracy results in Ovchinnikova et al. [41] are rounded to the nearest integer.

To the best of our knowledge, this is the first successful attempt to apply tractable inference to NLP on a large scale. We have shown that the proposed implementation of weighted abduction based on ILP is dramatically faster than previous implementations [4,41] evaluated on the same datasets.

Furthermore, the ILP-based implementation proved to be open to the introduction of linguistically motivated heuristics. For example, we have proposed a partial solution to the problem of coreference resolution as modeled in an abductive framework.

The inference procedure and the knowledge base are general and not tuned for a particular task. We performed evaluations on plan recognition and textual entailment recognition. The results obtained allow us to conclude that the proposed procedure showed performance comparable with those of the state-of-the-art systems. We consider the results of our experiments to be promising for many possible applications. In other papers, we describe evaluations of other knowledge-intensive natural language understanding tasks such as coreference resolution [31].

The experiments we have carried out have shown that there is still a lot of space for improving the procedure. In future work, we plan to investigate different strategies of weight initialization and evaluate our cost and weight learning framework on a larger dataset and apply it to a wide range of discourse processing tasks.

Another future work direction concerns the knowledge base. Lexical-semantic dictionaries offer an easily accessible source of inference rules. However, such resources have limited coverage and are difficult to update. For example, they systematically lack proper names. In the future, we would like to experiment with lexical-semantic resources automatically generated from large amounts of texts; see, for example, Penas and Hovy [43].

We also plan to elaborate our treatment of natural language expressions standing for logical connectors and quantifiers. This advance is needed in order to achieve more precise inferences, which are at the moment based on our approach to the unification of the core information content ("aboutness") of texts.

The ILP-based abductive reasoner is freely available for download at https://github.com/naoya-i/henry-n700/. The developed discourse processing pipeline is freely available for download at https://github.com/metaphor-adp/Metaphor-ADP.

Acknowledgments

This work was supported by Grant-in-Aid for JSPS Fellows (22-9719). We also would like to thank Johan Bos for making the *Boxer* parser available for our experiments.

References

[1] Abdelbar AM, Hefny M. An efficient LP-based admissible heuristic for cost-based abduction. JETAI 2005;17(3):297–303.

[2] Akhmatova E, Mollá D. Recognizing textual entailment via atomic propositions. In: Proceedings of the PASCAL Challenges Workshop on Recognizing Textual Entailment; 2005. p. 385–403.

[3] Berant J, Aviv T, Goldberger J. Global learning of typed entailment rules. In: ACL; 2008. p. 610–9.

[4] Blythe J, Hobbs JR, Domingos P, Kate RJ, Mooney RJ. Implementing weighted abduction in Markov logic. In: Proceedings of IWCS; 2011. p. 55–64.

[5] Bos J. Wide-coverage semantic analysis with Boxer. In: Bos J, Delmonte R, editors. Proceedings of STEP. Research in Computational Semantics. College Publications; 2008. p. 277–86.

[6] Bos J, Markert K. Recognizing textual entailment with logical inference. In: Proceedings of EMNLP; 2005. p. 628–35.

[7] Burchardt A, Pennacchiotti M, Thater S, Pinkal M. Assessing the impact of frame semantics on textual entailment. Nat Lang Eng 2009;15(4):527–50.

[8] Chalupsky H, MacGregor RM, Russ T. PowerLoom manual. Technical Report. University of Southern California; 2006. <www.isi.edu/isd/LOOM/PowerLoom/documentation/manual/manual.pdf>.

[9] Charniak E, Goldman RP. Plan recognition in stories and in life. In: Proceedings of the Fifth Annual Conference on Uncertainty in Artificial Intelligence; 1989. p. 343–52.

[10] Charniak E, Goldman RP. Plan recognition in stories and in life. In: Proceedings of the 11th International Joint Conference on Artificial Intelligence; 1989. p. 1074–9.

[11] Charniak E, Goldman RP. A probabilistic model of plan recognition. In: Proceedings of AAAI; 1991. p. 160–5.

[12] Charniak E, Shimony SE. Probabilistic semantics for cost based abduction. Proceedings of the Eighth National Conference on Artificial Intelligence, vol. 1; 1990. p. 106–11.

[13] Charniak E, Shimony SE. Cost-based abduction and MAP explanation. Artif Intell J 1994;66(2):345–74.

[14] Chivers ST, Tagliarini GA, Abdelbar AM. An evolutionary optimization approach to cost-based abduction, with comparison to PSO. In: IJCNN; 2007. p. 2926–30.

[15] Chklovski T, Pantel P. VerbOcean: mining the web for fine-grained semantic verb relations. In: Lin D, Wu D, editors. Proceedings of EMNLP; 2004. p. 33–40.

[16] Clark P, Murray W, Thompson J, Harrison P, Hobbs J, Fellbaum C. On the role of lexical and world knowledge in RTE3. In: Proceedings of the ACL-PASCAL Workshop on Textual Entailment and Paraphrasing; 2007. p. 54–9.

[17] Crammer K, Dekel O, Keshet J, Shalev-Shwartz SYS. Online passive-aggressive algorithms. J Mach Learn Res 2006;7:551–85.

[18] Dagan I, Dolan B, Magnini B, Roth D. Recognizing textual entailment: rational, evaluation and approaches—Erratum. Nat Lang Eng 2010;16(1):105.

[19] Dantzig GB, Fulkerson R, Johnson SM. Solution of a large-scale traveling salesman problem. Oper Res 1954;2(4):393–410.

[20] Davidson D. The logical form of action sentences. In: Rescher N, editor. The logic of decision and action. University of Pittsburgh Press; 1967. p. 81–120.

[21] Etzioni O, Banko M, Cafarella MJ. Machine reading. Proceedings of AAAI, vol. 6; 2006. p. 1517–9.

[22] Fellbaum C, editor. WordNet: an electronic lexical database. MIT Press; 1998.

[23] Fowler A, Hauser B, Hodges D, Niles I, Novischi A, Stephan J. Applying COGEX to recognize textual entailment. In: Proceedings of the PASCAL Challenges Workshop on Recognising Textual Entailment; 2005. p. 69–72.

[24] Garoufi K. Towards a better understanding of applied textual entailment: annotation and evaluation of the RTE-2 dataset. Master's thesis. Saarland University; 2007.

[25] Guinn C, Shipman W, Addison E. The parallelization of membrane computers to find near optimal solutions to cost-based abduction. In: GEM; 2008. p. 241–7.

[26] Hickl A, Bensley J. A discourse commitment-based framework for recognizing textual entailment. In: Proceedings of ACL-PASCAL Workshop on Textual Entailment and Paraphrasing; 2007. p. 171–6.

[27] Hobbs JR. Ontological promiscuity. In: Proceedings of ACL; 1985. p. 61–9.

[28] Hobbs JR, Stickel M, Martin P, Edwards D. Interpretation as abduction. Artif Intell 1993;63:69–142.

[29] Inoue N, Inui K. ILP-based reasoning for weighted abduction. In: Proceedings of AAAI Workshop on Plan, Activity and Intent Recognition; 2011. p. 25–32.

[30] Inoue N, Inui K. Large-scale cost-based abduction in full-fledged first-order predicate logic with cutting plane inference. In: Proceedings of the 13th European Conference on Logics in Artificial Intelligence; 2012. p. 281–93.

[31] Inoue N, Ovchinnikova E, Inui K, Hobbs JR. Coreference resolution with ILP-based weighted abduction. In: Proceedings of the 24th International Conference on Computational Linguistics; 2012. p. 1291–308.

[32] Inoue N, Yamamoto K, Watanabe Y, Okazaki N, Inui K. Online large-margin weight learning for first-order logic-based abduction. In: Proceedings of the 15th Information-based Induction Sciences Workshop, 2012. p. 143–50.

[33] Ishizuka M, Matsuo Y. SL Method for computing a near-optimal solution using linear and non-linear programming in cost-based hypothetical reasoning. In: PRCAI; 1998. p. 611–25.

[34] Joachims T, Finley T, Yu CJ. Cutting-plane training of structural SVMs. J Mach Learn 2009;77(1):27–59.

[35] Kamp H, Reyle U. From discourse to logic: introduction to model-theoretic semantics of natural language, formal logic and discourse representation theory. In: Studies in Linguistics and Philosophy. Kluwer; 1993.

[36] Kate RJ, Mooney RJ. Probabilistic abduction using Markov logic networks. In: Proceedings of the IJCAI-09 Workshop on Plan, Activity, and Intent Recognition; July 2009.

[37] Katrenko S, Toledo A. A comparison study of lexical and syntactic overlap for textual entailment recognition. In: Proceedings of BNAIC 2011; 2011.

[38] Mulkar R, Hobbs J, Hovy E. Learning from reading syntactically complex biology texts. In: Proceedings of the Eighth International Symposium on Logical Formalizations of Commonsense Reasoning; 2007.

[39] Ng HT, Mooney RJ. Abductive plan recognition and diagnosis: a comprehensive empirical evaluation. In: Proceedings of the Third International Conference on Principles of Knowledge Representation and Reasoning; October 1992. p. 499–508.

[40] Ovchinnikova E. Integration of world knowledge for natural language understanding. Atlantis Press, Springer; 2012.

[41] Ovchinnikova E, Montazeri N, Alexandrov T, Hobbs JR, McCord M, Mulkar-Mehta R. Abductive reasoning with a large knowledge base for discourse processing. In: Proceedings of IWCS; 2011. p. 225–34.

[42] Ovchinnikova E, Vieu L, Oltramari A, Borgo S, Alexandrov T. Data-driven and ontological analysis of FrameNet for natural language reasoning. In: Proceedings of LREC. European Language Resources Association; 2010. p. 3157–64.

[43] Penas A, Hovy E. Filling knowledge gaps in text for machine reading. In: Proceedings of COLING: Posters; 2010. p. 979–87.

[44] Poole D. Logic programming, abduction and probability: a top-down anytime algorithm for estimating prior and posterior probabilities. New Gen Comput July 1993;11(3–4):377–400.

[45] Prendinger H, Ishizuka M. First-order diagnosis by propositional reasoning: a representation based approach. In: Proceedings of the 10th International Workshop on Principles of Diagnosis; 1999. p. 220–5.

[46] Raghavan S, Mooney RJ. Abductive plan recognition by extending Bayesian logic programs. In: Proceedings of European Conference on Machine Learning and Principles and Practice of Knowledge Discovery in Databases; 2011. p. 629–44.

[47] Riabinin Y. Recognizing textual entailment using logical inference: a survey of the PASCAL RTE Challenge, 2008. http://www.yaroslavriabinin.com/CSC2519_Paper.pdf.

[48] Richardson M, Domingos P. Markov logic networks. Mach Learn 2006:107–36.

[49] Riedel S. Improving the accuracy and efficiency of MAP inference for Markov logic. In: UAI; 2008. p. 468–75.

[50] Riedel S, Clarke J. Incremental integer linear programming for non-projective dependency parsing. In: EMNLP; 2006. p. 129–37.

[51] Ruppenhofer J, Ellsworth M, Petruck M, Johnson C, Scheffczyk J. FrameNet II: extended theory and practice. Technical Report, Berkeley, CA. 2010.

[52] Santos E. Polynomial solvability of cost-based abduction. Artif Intell 1996;86:157–70.

[53] Shen D, Lapata M. Using semantic roles to improve question answering. In: Proceedings of EMNLP-CoNLL; 2007. p. 12–21.

[54] Singla P, Mooney R, Domingos P. Abductive Markov logic for plan recognition. In: Proceedings of AAAI-11; 2011. p. 1069–75.

[55] Tatu M, Moldovan D. A semantic approach to recognizing textual entailment. In: Proceedings of HLT and EMNLP; 2005. p. 371–8.

[56] Vapnik NN. The nature of statistical learning theory. Springer; 1995.

Plan Recognition Using Statistical–Relational Models

3

Sindhu Raghavan[a], **Parag Singla**[b], **and Raymond J. Mooney**[a]

[a]*University of Texas at Austin, Austin, TX, USA*
[b]*Indian Institute of Technology Delhi, Hauz Khas, DL, India*

3.1 Introduction

Plan recognition is the task of predicting an agent's top-level plans based on its observed actions. It is an abductive-reasoning task that involves inferring cause from effect [11]. Early approaches to plan recognition were based on first-order logic in which a knowledge base (KB) of plans and actions is developed for the domain and then default reasoning [31,30] or logical abduction [45] is used to predict the best plan based on the observed actions. Kautz and Allen [31] and Kautz [30] developed one of the first logical formalizations of plan recognition. They used nonmonotonic deductive inference to predict plans using observed actions, an action taxonomy, and a set of commonsense rules or constraints. The approach of Lesh and Etzioni [41] to goal recognition constructs a graph of goals, actions, and their schemas and prunes the network until the plans present in the network are consistent with the observed goals. The approach by Hong [21] also constructs a "goal graph" and analyzes the graph to identify goals consistent with observed actions. However, these approaches are unable to handle uncertainty in observations or background knowledge and are incapable of estimating the likelihood of different plans.

Another approach to plan recognition is to directly use probabilistic methods. Albrecht et al. [1] developed an approach based on dynamic Bayesian networks (DBN) to predict plans in an adventure game. Horvitz and Paek [22] developed an approach that uses Bayesian networks to recognize goals in an automated conversation system. Pynadath and Wellman [53] extended probabilistic context-free grammars to plan recognition. Kaminka et al. [28] developed an approach to multiagent plan recognition (MAPR) using DBNs to perform monitoring in distributed systems. Bui et al. [6] and Bui [5] used abstract hidden Markov models for hierarchical goal recognition. Saria and Mahadevan [59] extended the work by Bui [5] to MAPR. Blaylock and Allen [2] used statistical *n*-gram models for the task of instantiated goal recognition. Even though these approaches can handle uncertainty and can be trained effectively, they cannot handle the kind of structured relational data that can be represented in first-order predicate logic. Furthermore, it is difficult to incorporate planning domain knowledge in these approaches.

The third category of approaches use aspects of both logical and probabilistic reasoning. Hobbs et al. [20] attach weights or costs to predicates in the knowledge base and use these weights to guide the search for the best explanation. Goldman et al. [19] use the probabilistic Horn abduction [50] framework described by Poole to find the best set of plans that explain the observed actions. Several other approaches use Bayesian networks [9,8,23] to perform abductive inference. Based on the observed actions and a KB constructed for planning, Bayesian networks are automatically constructed using knowledge base model construction (KBMC) procedures. However, most of these approaches do not have the capabilities for learning the structure or the parameters. Another chapter by Inoue et al. [26] in this book explores the use of weighted abduction for large-scale discourse processing.

The last decade has seen a rapid growth in the area of *statistical–relational learning* (SRL) (e.g., see Getoor and Taskar [16]), which uses well-founded probabilistic methods while maintaining the representational power of first-order logic. Since these models combine the strengths of both first-order logic and probabilistic graphical models, we believe that they are well suited for solving problems like plan recognition. In this chapter, we explore the efficacy of different SRL models for the task of plan recognition. We focus on extending two specific SRL models—Markov Logic Networks (MLNs) [14], based on undirected probabilistic graphical models, and Bayesian logic programs (BLPs) [32], based on directed probabilistic graphical models—to the task of plan recognition.

MLNs attach real-valued weights to formulas in first-order logic in order to represent their certainty. They effectively use logic as a compact template for representing large, complex ground Markov networks. Since MLNs have been shown to formally subsume many other SRL models and have been successfully applied to many problems [14], we chose to explore their application to plan recognition. However, the representational power and flexibility offered by MLNs come at a cost in computational complexity. In particular, many problems result in exponentially large ground Markov networks, making learning and inference intractable in the general case.

Pearl [48] argued that causal relationships and abductive reasoning from effect to cause are best captured using directed graphical models (Bayesian networks). Since plan recognition is abductive in nature, this suggested that we also explore a formalism based on directed models. Therefore, we explored the application of BLPs, which combine first-order Horn logic and directed graphical models, to plan recognition. BLPs use SLD resolution to generate proof trees, which are then used to construct a ground Bayesian network for a given query. This approach to network construction is called knowledge base model construction. Similar to BLPs, prior approaches (i.e., Wellman et al. [66] and Ngo and Haddawy [46]) also employ the KBMC technique to construct ground Bayesian networks for inference.

Another approach, known as probabilistic Horn abduction (PHA) [50], performs abductive reasoning using first-order knowledge bases and Bayesian networks. However, since the BLP framework imposes fewer constraints on representation, both with respect to structure and parameters [33], and since it provides an integrated framework for both learning and inference, we decided to use BLPs as opposed to PHA or other similar formalisms.

Logical approaches to plan recognition, for example, those proposed by Kautz and Allen [31] and Ng and Mooney [45], typically assume a KB of plans and/or actions appropriate for planning, but not specifically designed for plan recognition. The advantage of this approach is that a single knowledge base is sufficient for both automated planning and plan recognition. Also, knowledge of plans and actions sufficient for planning is usually easier to develop than a knowledge base especially designed for plan recognition, which requires specific rules of the form: "If an agent performs action A, they may be executing plan P." Sadilek and Kautz's recent MLN-based approach to plan/activity recognition [58,57] requires such manually provided plan-recognition rules.

Our goal is to develop general-purpose SRL-based plan-recognition systems that only require the developer to provide a knowledge base of actions and plans sufficient for planning, without the need to engineer a KB specifically designed for plan recognition. Plan recognition using only planning knowledge generally requires *abductive* logical inference. BLPs use purely deductive logical inference as a preprocessing step to the full-blown probabilistic inference. Encoding planning knowledge directly into MLNs does not support abductive reasoning either. Further, using the standard semantics of MLNs of grounding the whole theory leads to a blowup for plan-recognition problems. Consequently, neither BLPs nor MLNs can be directly used in their current form for abductive plan recognition.

Therefore, this chapter describes reencoding strategies (for MLNs) as well as enhancements to both models that allow them to use logical abduction. Our other goal involves developing systems capable of learning the necessary parameters automatically from data. Since both BLPs and MLNs provide algorithms for learning both the structure and the parameters, we adapt them in our work to develop trainable systems for plan recognition. The main contributions of this chapter are as follows:

- Adapt SRL models, such as BLPs and MLNs, to plan recognition
- Introduce Bayesian Abductive Logic Programs (BALPs), an adaptation of BLPs that uses logical abduction
- Propose reencoding strategies for facilitating abductive reasoning in MLNs
- Introduce abductive Markov logic, an adaptation of MLNs that combines reencoding strategies with logical abduction to construct the ground Markov network
- Experimentally evaluate the relative performance of BALPs, abductive MLNs (i.e., using reencoding strategies and abductive model construction), traditional MLNs, and existing methods on three plan-recognition benchmarks

The rest of the chapter is organized as follows. First, we provide some background on logical abduction, BLPs, and MLNs in Section 3.2. Section 3.3 presents our extensions to both BLPs and MLNs to include logical abduction. Finally, we present an extensive evaluation of our approaches on three benchmark datasets for plan recognition, comparing them with the existing state-of-the-art for plan recognition, in Section 3.4.

3.2 Background

3.2.1 Logical Abduction

In a logical framework, abduction is usually defined as follows, according to Pople [52], Levesque [42], and Kakas et al. [27]:

Given: Background knowledge B and observations O, both represented as sets of formulae in first-order logic, where B is typically restricted to Horn clauses and O to ground literals
Find: A hypothesis H, also a set of logical formulae (typically ground literals), such that $B \cup H \not\models \bot$ and $B \cup H \models O$

Here, $\models$ represents logical entailment and $\bot$ represents false; that is, find a set of assumptions consistent with the background theory and explains the observations. There are generally many hypotheses H that explain a given set of observations O. Following Occam's Razor, the best hypothesis is typically defined as the one that minimizes the number of assumptions, $|H|$. Given a set of observations $O_1, O_2, \ldots, O_n$, the set of abductive proof trees is computed by recursively backchaining on each O_i until every literal in the proof is either proved or assumed. Logical abduction has been applied to tasks such as plan recognition and diagnosis by Ng and Mooney [45] and Peng and Reggia [49].

3.2.2 Bayesian Logic Programs

Bayesian logic programs (BLPs) [32] can be viewed as templates for constructing *directed* graphical models (Bayes nets). Given a knowledge base as a special kind of logic program, standard backward-chaining logical deduction (SLD resolution) is used to automatically construct a Bayes net on the same lines as KBMC (see, for example, Wellman et al. [66] and Breese et al. [4]). More specifically, given a set of facts and a query, all possible Horn-clause proofs of the query are constructed and used to build a Bayes net for answering the query. Standard probabilistic inference techniques are then used to compute the most probable answer.

More formally, a BLP consists of a set of *Bayesian clauses*, definite clauses of the form $A|A_1, A_2, A_3, \ldots, A_n$, where $n \geq 0$ and $A, A_1, A_2, A_3, \ldots, A_n$ are *Bayesian predicates* (defined in the next paragraph). A is called the head of the clause ($head(c)$) and ($A_1, A_2, A_3, \ldots, A_n$) is the body ($body(c)$). When $n = 0$, a Bayesian clause is a fact. Each Bayesian clause c is assumed to be universally quantified and range-restricted (i.e., $variables\{head\} \subseteq variables\{body\}$) and has an associated *conditional probability distribution*: $cpd(c) = P(head(c)|body(c))$.

A *Bayesian predicate* is a predicate with a finite domain, and each ground atom for a Bayesian predicate represents a random variable. Associated with each Bayesian predicate is a combining rule, such as *noisy-or* or *noisy-and*, that maps a finite set of *cpd*s into a single *cpd* [48]. Let A be a Bayesian predicate defined by two Bayesian clauses, $A|A_1, A_2, A_3, \ldots, A_n$ and $A|B_1, B_2, B_3, \ldots, B_n$, where cpd_1 and cpd_2 are their cpds. Let θ be a substitution that satisfies both clauses. Then, in the constructed Bayes net, directed edges are added from the nodes for each $A_i\theta$ and $B_i\theta$ to the node for $A\theta$. The combining rule for A is used to construct a single cpd for $A\theta$ from cpd_1 and cpd_2. The probability of a joint assignment of truth values to the final set of ground propositions is then defined in the standard way for a Bayes net: $P(X) = \prod_i P(X_i|Pa(X_i))$, where $X = X_1, X_2, \ldots, X_n$ represents the set of random variables in the network and $Pa(X_i)$ represents the parents of X_i.

Once a ground network is constructed, standard probabilistic inference methods can be used to answer various types of queries, as noted in Koller and Friedman [40]. Typically, we would like to compute the most probable explanation (MPE), which finds the joint assignment of values to unobserved nodes in the network that maximizes the posterior probability given the values of a set of observed nodes. This type of inference is also known as the Maximum a posteriori (MAP) assignment and may be used interchangeably in this book. We would also like to compute the marginal probabilities for the unobserved nodes given the values of observed nodes. The combining-rule parameters and cpd entries for a BLP can be learned automatically from data using techniques proposed by Kersting and De Raedt [34].

3.2.3 Markov Logic Networks

Markov logic (e.g., see Richardson and Domingos [55] and Domingos and Lowd [14]) is a framework for combining first-order logic and undirected probabilistic graphical models (Markov networks). A traditional first-order KB can be seen as a set of hard constraints on the set of possible worlds: if a world violates even one formula, its probability is 0. To soften these constraints, Markov logic attaches a weight to each formula in the knowledge base. A formula's weight reflects how strong a constraint it imposes on the set of possible worlds. Formally, an MLN is a set of pairs (F_i, w_i), where F_i is a first-order formula and w_i is a real number. A *hard clause* has an infinite weight and acts as a logical constraint; otherwise, it is a *soft clause*. Given a set of constants, an MLN defines a ground Markov network with a node in the network for each ground atom and a feature for each ground clause.

The joint probability distribution over a set of Boolean variables, $X = (X_1, X_2 \ldots)$, corresponding to the nodes in the ground Markov network (i.e., ground atoms) is defined as:

$$P(X = x) = \frac{1}{Z} exp \left(\sum_i w_i n_i(x) \right) \tag{3.1}$$

where $n_i(x)$ is the number of true groundings of F_i in x and Z is a normalization term obtained by summing $P(X = x)$ over all values of X. Therefore, a possible world becomes exponentially less likely as the total weight of the ground clauses it violates increases.

An MLN can be viewed as a set of templates for constructing ground Markov networks. Different sets of constants produce different Markov networks; however, there are certain regularities in their structure and parameters determined by the underlying first-order theory. Like in BLPs, once the ground network is constructed, standard probabilistic inference methods (i.e., MPE or marginal inference) can be used to answer queries. MLN weights can be learned by maximizing the conditional log-likelihood of training data supplied in the form of a database of true ground literals. A number of efficient inference and learning algorithms that exploit the structure of the network have also been proposed. Domingos and Lowd provide details on these and many other aspects of MLNs [14].

3.3 Adapting Bayesian Logic Programs

Bayesian Abductive Logic Programs are an adaptation of BLPs. In plan recognition, the known facts are insufficient to support the derivation of deductive proof trees for the requisite queries. By using *ab*duction, missing literals can be assumed in order to complete the proof trees needed to determine the structure of the ground network. We first describe the abductive inference procedure used in BALPs. Next, we describe how probabilistic parameters are specified and how probabilistic inference is performed. Finally, we discuss how parameters can be automatically learned from data.

3.3.1 Logical Abduction

Let $O_1, O_2, \ldots., O_n$ be the set of observations. We derive a set of most-specific abductive proof trees for these observations using the method originally proposed by Stickel [65]. The abductive proofs for each observation literal are computed by backchaining on each O_i until every literal in the proof is proved or assumed. A literal is said to be proved if it unifies with some fact or the head of some rule in the knowledge base; otherwise, it is said to be assumed. Since multiple plans/actions could generate the same observation, an observation literal could unify with the head of multiple rules in the KB. For such a literal, we compute alternative abductive proofs for each such rule. The resulting abductive proof trees are then used to build the structure of the Bayes net using the standard approach for BLPs.

The basic algorithm to construct abductive proofs is given in Algorithm 3.1. The algorithm takes as input a knowledge base in the form of Horn clauses and a set of observations as ground facts. It outputs a set of abductive proof trees by performing logical abduction on the observations. These proof trees are then used to construct the Bayesian network. For each observation O_i, AbductionBALP searches for rules with consequents that unify with O_i. For each such rule, it computes the substitution from the unification process and substitutes variables in the body of the rule with bindings from the substitution. The literals in the body now become new subgoals in the inference process. If these new subgoals cannot be proved (i.e., if they cannot unify with existing facts or with the consequent of any rule in the KB), then they are assumed. To minimize the number of assumptions, the assumed literals are first matched with existing assumptions. If no such assumption exists, then any unbound variables in the literal that are existentially quantified are replaced by Skolem constants.

Algorithm 3.1. AbductionBALP

Inputs: Background knowledge KB and observations O_1, O_2, O_3, ..., O_n both represented as sets of formulae in first-order logic, where KB is typically restricted to a set of Horn clauses and each O_i is a ground literal.

Output: Abductive proofs for all O_i

1: Let Q be a queue of unproven atoms, initialized with O_i
2: **while** Q not empty **do**
3:    $A_i \leftarrow$ Remove atom from Q
4:    **for** each rule R_i in KB **do**
5:       $consequent \leftarrow$ Head literal of R_i
6:       **if** A_i unifies with $consequent$ **then**
7:          $S_i \leftarrow$ unify A_i and $consequent$ and return substitution
8:          Replace variables in the body of R_i with bindings in S_i. Each literal in the body of R_i is a new subgoal.
9:          **for** each $literal_i$ in body of R_i **do**
10:            **if** $literal_i$ unifies with head of some rule R_j in KB **then**
11:               add $literal_i$ to Q
12:            **else if** $literal_i$ unifies with an existing fact **then**
13:               Unify and consider the literal to be proved
14:            **else**
15:               **if** $literal_i$ unifies with an existing assumption **then**
16:                  Unify and use the assumption
17:               **else**
18:                  Assume $literal_i$ by replacing any unbound variables that are existentially quantified in $literal_i$ with new Skolem constants.
19:               **end if**
20:            **end if**
21:          **end for**
22:       **end if**
23:    **end for**
24: **end while**

In SLD resolution, which is used in BLPs, if any subgoal literal cannot be proved, the proof fails. However, in BALPs, we assume such literals and allow proofs to proceed until completion. Note that there could be multiple existing assumptions that could unify with subgoals in Step 15. However, if we used all ground assumptions that could unify with a literal, then the size of the ground network would grow exponentially, making probabilistic inference intractable. To limit the size of the ground network, we unify subgoals with assumptions in a greedy manner (i.e., when multiple assumptions match a subgoal, we randomly pick one of them and do not pursue the others). We found that this approach worked well for our plan-recognition benchmarks. For other tasks, domain-specific heuristics could potentially be used to reduce the size of the network.

We now illustrate the abductive inference process with a simple example motivated by one of our evaluation benchmarks, the emergency response domain introduced by Blaylock and Allen [2] in the Monroe dataset described in Section 3.5.1. Consider the partial knowledge base and set of observations given in Figure 3.1(a) and Figure 3.1(b) respectively. The knowledge base consists of rules that give two explanations for a road being blocked at a location: (1) there has been heavy snow resulting in hazardous driving conditions and (2) there has been an accident and the crew is clearing the wreck. Given the observation that a road is blocked, the plan-recognition task involves abductively inferring one of these causes as the explanation.

For each observation literal in Figure 3.1(b), we recursively backchain to generate abductive proof trees. In the given example, we observe that the road is blocked at the location *plaza*. When we backchain on the literal blk_rd(plaza) using Rule 1, we obtain the subgoals hvy_snow(plaza) and drive_hzrd(plaza). These subgoals become assumptions since no observations or heads of clauses unify them. We then backchain on the literal blk_rd(plaza) using Rule 2 to obtain subgoals acdnt(plaza) and clr_wrk(Crew,plaza). Here again, we find that these subgoals have to be assumed since there are no facts or heads of clauses that unify them. We further notice

---

(**a**) Partial knowledge base with two rules for roadblock:

    1. blk_rd(Loc)|hvy_snow(Loc), drive_hzrd(Loc)
    2. blk_rd(Loc)|acdnt(Loc), clr_wrck(Crew, Loc)

(**b**) Observations:

    blk_rd(plaza)

(**c**) Ground abductive clauses:

    blk_rd(plaza)|hvy_snow(plaza), drive_hzrd(plaza)
    blk_rd(plaza)|acdnt(plaza), clr_wrck(a1, plaza)

FIGURE 3.1

Partial knowledge base and a set of observations. (a) A partial knowledge base from the emergency response domain in the Monroe dataset. All variables start with uppercase and constants with lowercase. (b) The logical representation of the observations. (c) The set of ground rules obtained from logical abduction.

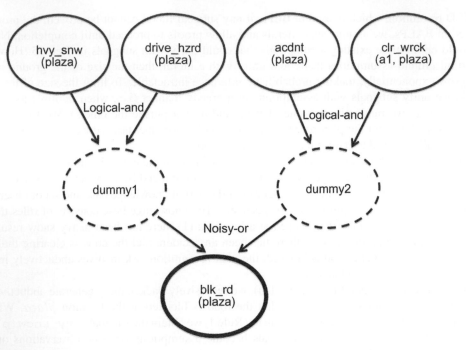

FIGURE 3.2

Bayesian network constructed for the example in Figure 3.1. *Note:* The nodes with *bold* borders represent observed actions, the nodes with *dotted* borders represent intermediate ones used to combine the conjuncts in the body of a clause, and the nodes with *thin* borders represent plan literals.

that `clr_wrk(Crew,plaza)` is not a fully ground instance. Since `Crew` is an existentially quantified variable, we replace it with a Skolem constant, $a1$, to get the ground assumption `clr_wrk (a1,plaza)`.

Figure 3.1(c) gives the final set of ground rules generated by abductive inference. After generating all abductive proofs for all observation literals, we construct a Bayesian network. Figure 3.2 shows the network constructed for the example in Figure 3.1. Note that since there are no observations and/or facts that unify the subgoals (i.e., `hvy_snow(plaza)`, `drive_hzrd(plaza)`, `acdnt(plaza)`, and `clr_wrk(Crew,plaza)`) generated during backchaining on observations, SLD resolution will fail to generate proofs. This is typical in plan recognition, and as a result, we cannot use BLPs for such tasks.

3.3.2 Probabilistic Modeling, Inference, and Learning

The only difference between BALPs and BLPs lies in the logical inference procedure used to construct proofs. Once abductive proofs are generated, BALPs use the same procedure as BLPs to construct the Bayesian network. Further, techniques developed for BLPs for learning parameters can also be used for BALPs.

We now discuss how parameters are specified in BALPs. We use *noisy/logical-and* and *noisy-or* models to specify the *cpd*s in the ground Bayesian network because these models compactly encode the *cpd* with fewer parameters (i.e., just one parameter for each parent node). Depending on the domain, we use either a strict *logical-and* or a softer *noisy-and* model to specify the *cpd* for combining evidence from the conjuncts in the body of a clause. We use a *noisy-or* model to specify the *cpd* for combining the disjunctive contributions from different ground clauses with the same head.

Figure 3.2 shows the *logical-and* and *noisy-or* nodes in the Bayesian network constructed for the example in Figure 3.1. Given the constructed Bayesian network and a set of observations, we determine the best explanation using the MPE inference [48]. We compute multiple alternative explanations using Nilsson's *k*-MPE algorithm [47], as implemented in the ELVIRA Elvira-Consortium [15] package.

Learning can be used to automatically set the *noisy-or* and *noisy-and* parameters in the model. In supervised training data for plan recognition, one typically has evidence for the observed actions and the top-level plans. However, we usually do not have evidence for network nodes corresponding to subgoals, *noisy-or*s, and *noisy/logical-and*s. As a result, there are a number of variables in the ground networks that are always hidden; thus, expectation-maximization (EM) is appropriate for learning the requisite parameters from the partially observed training data. We use the EM algorithm adapted for BLPs by Kersting and De Raedt [34]. We simplify the problem by learning only *noisy-or* parameters and using a deterministic *logical-and* model to combine evidence from the conjuncts in the body of a clause.

3.4 Adapting Markov Logic

As previously mentioned, encoding planning knowledge directly in MLNs does not support abductive reasoning. This is because of the deductive nature of the rules encoding the planning knowledge. In MLNs, the probability of a possible world increases with the total weight of the satisfied formulae. Since an implication is satisfied whenever its consequent is true, an MLN is unable to abductively infer the antecedent of a rule from its consequent. Given the rule $P \Rightarrow Q$ and the observation that Q is true, we would like to abduce P as a possible cause for Q. Since the consequent (Q) is true, the clause is trivially satisfied, independent of the value of the antecedent (P), and thus does not give any information about the truth value of the antecedent (P).

This section describes three key ideas for adapting MLNs with logical abductive reasoning, each one building on the previous. First, we describe the Pairwise Constraint (PC) model proposed by Kate and Mooney [29]. Next, we introduce the Hidden Cause (HC) model, which resolves some of the inefficiencies of the PC model. These two models offer strategies for the reencoding MLN rules but do not change the semantics of the traditional MLNs of Richardson and Domingos [55]. Next, we introduce an abductive model-construction procedure on top of the HC model that results in even simpler Markov networks. This gives us the formulation for abductive Markov logic. Our ground Markov network construction strategy is different from the one used in traditional MLNs; thus, our formulation results in different semantics.

We also describe an alternate approach to plan recognition in which the structure of the MLN is manually encoded to enable deductive inference of the top-level plans from observed actions. This allows us to compare abductive Markov logic to a manually encoded MLN for plan recognition.

3.4.1 Pairwise Constraint Model

Kate and Mooney [29] were the first to develop an approach to reencode MLNs with logical abductive reasoning, which we call the Pairwise Constraint model. We describe this approach here since it provides the context for understanding the more sophisticated models introduced in subsequent sections. The key idea is to introduce explicit reversals of the implications appearing in the original KB. Multiple possible explanations for the same observation are supported by having a disjunction of the potential explanations in the reverse implication. "Explaining away," according to Pearl [48] (inferring one cause eliminates the need for others) is achieved by introducing a mutual-exclusivity constraint between every pair of possible causes for an observation.

Given the set of Horn clauses (i.e., $P_1 \Rightarrow Q, P_2 \Rightarrow Q, \cdots P_n \Rightarrow Q$), a reverse implication (i.e., $Q \Rightarrow P_1 \vee P_2 \cdots \vee P_n$) and a set of mutual-exclusivity constraints (i.e., $Q \Rightarrow \neg P_1 \vee \neg P_2, \cdots Q \Rightarrow \neg P_{n-1} \vee \neg P_n$) for all pairs of explanations are introduced. The weights on these clauses control the strength of the abductive inference and the typical number of alternate explanations, respectively. We do not need to explicitly model these constraints in BLPs; this is because the underlying model is Bayesian networks, which capture the full CPD of each node given its parents and the mutual-exclusivity constraints are implicitly modeled in the conditional distribution. For first-order Horn clauses, all variables not appearing in the head of the clause become existentially quantified in the reverse implication. We refer the reader to Kate and Mooney for the details of the conversion process [29].

We now illustrate the PC model with the same example described in Section 3.3. It is an example from one of our evaluation benchmarks, the emergency response domain introduced by Blaylock and Allen [2]—all variables start with uppercase and constants with lowercase and by default variables are universally quantified:

```
hvy_snow(Loc) ∧ drive_hzrd(Loc) ⇒ blk_rd(Loc)
acdnt(Loc) ∧ clr_wrk(Crew,Loc) ⇒ blk_rd(Loc)
```

These rules give two explanations for a road being blocked at a location: (1) there has been heavy snow resulting in hazardous driving conditions and (2) there has been an accident and the crew is clearing the wreck. Given the observation that a road is blocked, the plan-recognition task involves abductively inferring one of these causes as the explanation. Using the PC model, we get the final combined reverse implication and PC clauses as follows:

```
blk_rd(Loc) ⇒ (hvy_snow(Loc) ∧ drive_hzrd(Loc)) ∨
  (∃Crew   acdnt(Loc) ∧   clr_wrk(Crew,Loc))
blk_rd(Loc) ⇒ ¬(hvy _snow(Loc) ∧ drive_hzrd(Loc)) ∨
  ¬(∃Crew   acdnt(Loc) ∧   clr_wrk(Crew,Loc))
```

The first rule introduces the two possible explanations and the second rule constrains them to be mutually exclusive.

The PC model can construct very complex networks because it includes multiple clause bodies in the reverse implication, making it very long. If there are n possible causes for an observation and each of the corresponding Horn clauses has k literals in its body, then the reverse implication has $O(nk)$ literals. This in turn results in cliques of size $O(nk)$ in the ground network. This significantly increases the computational complexity since probabilistic inference is *exponential* in the tree width of the graph, which in turn is at least the size of the maximum clique, as noted in Koller and Friedman [40]. The PC model also introduces $O(n^2)$ pairwise constraints, which can result in a large number of ground clauses. As a result, the PC model does not generally scale well to large domains.

3.4.2 Hidden Cause Model

The Hidden Cause model alleviates some of the inefficiencies of the PC model by introducing a hidden cause node for each possible explanation. The joint constraints can then be expressed in terms of these hidden causes, thereby reducing the size of the reverse implication (thus, the corresponding clique size) to $O(n)$. The need for the pairwise constraints is eliminated by specifying a low prior on all HCs. A low prior on the hidden causes indicates that they are most likely to be false, unless there is explicit evidence indicating their presence. Therefore, given an observation, inferring one cause obviates the need for the others.

We now describe the HC model more formally. We first consider the propositional case for the ease of explanation. It is extended to first-order Horn clauses in a straightforward manner. Consider the following set of rules describing the possible explanations for a predicate Q:

$$P_{i1} \wedge P_{i2} \wedge \cdots \wedge P_{ik_i} \Rightarrow Q, \forall i, (1 \leq i \leq n)$$

For each rule, we introduce a hidden cause C_i and add the following rules to the MLN:

1. $P_{i1} \wedge P_{i2} \wedge \cdots \wedge P_{ik_i} \Leftrightarrow C_i, \forall i, (1 \leq i \leq n)$ (soft)
2. $C_i \Rightarrow Q, \forall i, (1 \leq i \leq n)$ (hard)
3. $Q \Rightarrow C_1 \vee C_2 \cdots C_n$ (reverse implication, hard)
4. $\texttt{true} \Rightarrow C_i, \forall i, (1 \leq i \leq n)$ (negatively weighted, soft)

The first set of rules are soft clauses with high positive weights. This allows the antecedents to sometimes fail to cause the consequent (and vice versa). The next two sets of rules are hard clauses that implement a *deterministic-or* function between the consequent and the hidden causes. The last one is a soft rule and implements a low prior (by having a negative MLN weight) on the HCs. These low priors discourage inferring multiple hidden causes for the same consequent ("explaining way"), and the strength of the prior determines the degree to which multiple explanations are allowed.

Different sets of weights on the biconditional in the first set of rules implement different ways of combining multiple explanations. For example, a *noisy-or* model [48] can be implemented by modeling the implication from antecedents to the hidden cause as a soft constraint and the reverse direction as a hard constraint. The weight w_i for the soft constraint is set to $log[(1 - p_{f_i})/p_{f_i}]$, where p_{f_i} is the failure probability for cause i. This formulation is related to previous work done by Natarajan et al. [43] on combining functions in Markov logic; however, we focus on the use of such combining functions in the context of abductive reasoning. There has also been prior work on discovering hidden structure in a domain (e.g., Davis et al. [13] and Kok and Domingos [37]). However, in our case, since we know the structure of the hidden predicates in advance, there is no need to discover them using the preceding methods referenced.

We now describe how to extend this approach to first-order Horn clauses. For first-order Horn clauses, variables present in the antecedents, but not in the consequent, become existentially quantified in the reverse implication, as in the PC model. But unlike the PC model, the reverse implication expression is much simpler because it only involves one predicate (the hidden cause) for each rule implying the consequent. Let us revisit the example from the emergency-response domain. Based on the HC approach, we introduce two hidden causes (`rb_C1(Loc)` and `rb_C2(Loc)`) corresponding to the two (hard) rules:

```
hvy_snow(Loc) ∧ drive_hzrd(Loc) ⇔ rb_C1(Loc)
acdnt(Loc) ∧ clr_wrk(Crew,Loc) ⇔ rb_C2(Crew,Loc)
```

Note that each HC contains all variables present in the antecedent of the rule. These hidden causes are combined with the original consequent using the following (soft) rules:

rb_C1(Loc) ⇒ blk_rd(Loc)
rb_C2(Crew,Loc) ⇒ blk_rd(Loc)
blk_rd(Loc) ⇒ rb_C1(Loc) ∨ ∃Crew(rb_C2(Crew,Loc))

In addition, there are (soft) unit clauses specifying low priors on the hidden causes.

Figures 3.3 and 3.4 show the ground networks constructed by the PC and HC models, respectively, when loc is bound to Plaza and crew to Tcrew. The PC model results in a fully connected graph

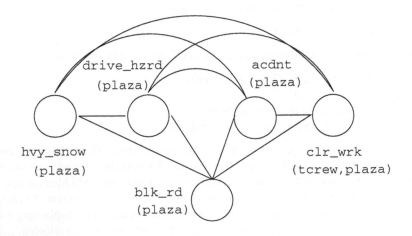

FIGURE 3.3

Ground network constructed by the PC model for the roadblock example.

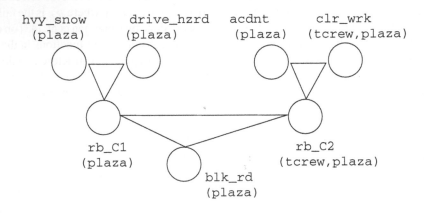

FIGURE 3.4

Ground network constructed by the HC model for the roadblock example.

(maximum clique size is 5), whereas the HC model is much sparser (maximum clique size is 3). Consequently, inference in the HC model is significantly more efficient.

Algorithm 3.2. GenReEncodedMLN (**KB**)

---

inputs: KB, background knowledge consisting of Horn clauses
output: M, set of rules in the reencoded MLN

1: $M \leftarrow \{\}$
2: **for all** $r \in$ **KB do**
3:     $A(r) \leftarrow$ antecedent in r
4:     $C(r) \leftarrow$ consequent in r
5:     $H(r) \leftarrow$ hidden cause for r
6:     $M \leftarrow M \cup \{A(r) \Leftrightarrow H(r)\}$
7:     $M \leftarrow M \cup \{H(r) \Rightarrow C(r)\}$
8: **end for**
9: Part(**KB**) $\leftarrow$ partition of **KB** into sets or rules with same
        (first-order) predicate in the consequent
10: **for all** set of rules $R \in$ Part(**KB**) **do**
11:     Let $R = \{r_1, r_2, \cdots r_m\}$
12:     $C(R) \leftarrow \bigcup_{i=1}^{m} \{C(r_i)\}$
13:     ($C(R)$ is set of unique consequents appearing in R)
14:     **for all** $c \in C(R)$ **do**
15:         $R_c \leftarrow \{r_i \in R \mid \exists \theta_i, c = C(r_i)\theta_i\}$
16:         (R_c is set of rules whose consequents subsume c)
17:         **for all** $r_i \in R_c$ **do**
18:             $H_{\theta_i}(r_i) \leftarrow H(r_i)\theta_i$
19:             $\{v_{i_1}, v_{i_2}, \cdots v_{i_k}\} \leftarrow$ variables appearing in
                    $H_{\theta_i}(r_i)$ but not in c
20:         **end for**
21:         $I_r(R_c) \leftarrow (c \Rightarrow \bigvee_{i=1}^{m} \exists v_{i_1}, v_{i_2}, \cdots v_{i_k} H_{\theta_i}(r_i))$
22:         $M \leftarrow M \cup \{I_r(R_c)\}$
23:     **end for**
24: **end for**
25: **for all** $r \in$ **KB do**
26:     $M \leftarrow M \cup \{\texttt{true} \Rightarrow H(r) \text{ (negatively weighted)} \}$
27: **end for**
28: **return** M

Algorithm 3.2 presents the pseudocode for constructing the reencoded MLN using the HC approach for a given Horn-clause KB. In lines 2 to 8, hidden causes are created for each possible explanation for each consequent (line 5). A biconditional is introduced between the hidden causes and the corresponding antecedents (line 6), which is modeled as a soft clause in the MLN. Each HC is also linked to the corresponding consequent via a hard clause (line 7).

The next part (lines 9 to 24) combines the hidden causes for each of the consequents into a single reverse implication. The rules are partitioned according to the first-order predicate appearing in the consequent (line 9). For each partition (line 10), each possible instantiation of the consequent predicate appearing in the underlying rule is considered (lines 11 to 13). For instance, given the rules $h_1 . X, Y/ \Rightarrow q.Y/$ and another, $h_2 . X, \text{const}/ \Rightarrow q.\text{const}/$, we need to consider each instantiation of $q(X)$ and $q(\text{const})$ separately. For each such instantiation c (line 14), we consider the rules that could result in the consequent c being true (line 15).

Technically, these are rules with consequents that subsume c (i.e., there exists a substitution θ_i such that $c = C(r_i)\theta_i$, where $C(r_i)$ is the consequent of rule r_i). These rules result in c when bound by the substitution θ_i. For each such rule r_i (line 17), substitution θ_i is applied to the corresponding hidden cause $H(r_i)$ (line 18). Then, the set of free variables in the HC (i.e., the variables not appearing in c) is extracted (line 19). These variables are existentially quantified in the reverse implication (next step). We then introduce a reverse implication to indicate that c implies at least one of the consequents among those that subsume c (line 21). This reverse implication is made a hard clause and added to the MLN (line 22). Finally, a low prior is introduced for each hidden cause (lines 25 to 27).

3.4.3 Abductive Model Construction

Abductive reasoning using MLNs consists of the following three steps:

1. Generate the reencoded MLN.
2. Construct the ground Markov network (model construction).
3. Perform learning/inference over the resulting ground network.

The standard MLN model-construction process uses the set of all possible ground atoms (the Herbrand base) and constructs the set of all possible ground clauses using these atoms.

Using logical rules to construct a graphical model is generally referred to as *knowledge-based model construction*, originally proposed by Wellman [66,4]. This idea was further used by Ngo and Haddawy [46] for answering queries from probabilistic knowledge bases. In abductive reasoning, we are looking for explanations for a given set of observations. In this task, the set of all possible ground atoms and ground clauses may not be needed to explain the observations. Considering the fully ground network leads to increased time and memory complexity for learning and inference. For instance, in the road-blocked example, if the observation of interest is `blk_rd(plaza)`, then we can ignore groundings when the location is not `plaza`.

We propose an alternative model-construction procedure that uses logical abduction to determine the set of *relevant* ground atoms. The procedure first constructs the set of abductive proof trees for the observations and then uses only the ground atoms in these proofs instead of the full Herbrand base for constructing the ground network. The ground Markov network is then constructed by instantiating the formulae in the abductive MLN using this reduced set of ground atoms. We refer to the set of ground atoms (Markov network) thus constructed as the abductive ground atoms (Markov network).

First, given a set of Horn rules and a set of observations, the rules for the abductive MLN are constructed using the HC model. Next, the set of most-specific abductive proof trees for the observations are computed using the method of Stickel [65]. The abductive inference process to get the set of most-specific abductive proofs was described earlier in Algorithm 3.1. The atoms in these proofs form the set of abductive ground atoms. For each formula in the abductive MLN, the set of all ground formulae with atoms that appear in the abductive ground atoms are added to the ground Markov network. While handling existentials, only those disjuncts that belong to the set of abductive ground atoms are used. Learning and inference are then performed over the resulting network.

In general, the abductive model-construction procedure results in a ground network that is substantially different (and usually much simpler) from the one constructed using the full Herbrand base. It also differs from the network constructed by starting KBMC from the query/observations (see Domingos and Lowd [14]) because of the use of backward-chaining and unification during the abductive model construction. Consequently, the probabilistic inferences supported by this model can be different from those of the traditional MLN model. This also makes the abductive process different from other preprocessing approaches, such as Shavlik and Natarajan [61], or existing lifted inference techniques, such as Singla and Domingos [63], both of which produce a network that is probabilistically equivalent to the original.

By focusing on the relevant ground atoms, abductive model construction significantly improves the performance of abductive MLNs *both* in terms of time and memory efficiency and predictive accuracy. Further, lifted inference could still be applied by constructing a lifted network over the nodes/clauses present in the abductive network. For consistency with Singla and Mooney [64], we will refer to abductive MLNs (using the HC model followed by abductive model construction) as MLN-HCAM.

Detailed experiments demonstrating significantly improved plan-recognition performance (with respect to both accuracy and efficiency) for the HC model and abductive model construction are presented by Singla and Mooney [64]. Therefore, we only compare with the MLN-HCAM approach in the experiments that follow.

3.4.4 Plan Recognition Using Manually Encoded MLNs

As discussed in the introduction, traditional (nonabductive) MLNs can be used for plan recognition if an appropriate set of clauses are manually provided that directly infer higher-level plans from primitive actions (e.g., Sadilek and Kautz [58, 57]). To compare to this approach, we developed an MLN approach that uses a manually engineered KB to perform deductive plan recognition.

The clauses for this manually encoded MLN were constructed as follows. For each top-level plan predicate, we identified any set of observations that uniquely identifies this plan. This implies that no other plan explains this set of observations. We then introduced a rule that infers this plan given these observations and we made it an HC in the MLN. If no such observations existed, we introduced a soft rule for each observation that could potentially indicate this plan. Hard mutual-exclusivity rules were included for plans when we knew only one of them could be true.

Alternatively, we gave a negative prior to all plan predicates as described in the MLN-HCAM model. Note that this approach does not include any predicates corresponding to subgoals that are never observed in the data. As a result, all variables in this model are fully observed during training, resulting in a less complex model for learning and inference. This way of encoding the domain knowledge avoids the automated machinery for introducing reverse implications and can potentially lead to a simpler knowledge base, which results in simpler ground networks. However, it requires a separate knowledge-engineering process that develops explicit plan-recognition rules for the domain, while the abductive approach only requires basic knowledge about plans and actions sufficient for planning. There are several ways in which such explicit plan-recognition KB can be manually engineered, and we have employed just one possible approach. Exploring alternative approaches is a direction for future work. Subsequently, we refer to this manually encoded traditional MLN model as "MLN-manual."

3.4.5 Probabilistic Modeling, Inference, and Learning

In MLN-HC and MLN-HCAM, we use the *noisy-or* model to combine multiple explanations. In all MLN models, we use the cutting-plane method of Riedel [56] for MPE inference and MC-SAT (see Poon and Domingos [51]) to compute marginal probabilities of plan instances. For learning weights of the clauses in MLN-HCAM, we use a version of gradient-based voted-perceptron algorithm of Singla and Domingos [62] modified for partially observed data as discussed in Chapter 20 (Section 3.3.1) of Koller and Friedman [40]. For the traditional MLN model, gradient-based voted-perceptron algorithm runs out of memory due to the size and complexity of the resulting ground networks. Therefore, we learned weights using the discriminative online learner proposed by Huynh and Mooney [24].[1] More details about various settings used in our experiments are described in the next section.

3.5 Experimental Evaluation

This section presents an extensive experimental evaluation of the performance of BALPs and MLNs on three plan-recognition datasets. Unfortunately, there have been very few rigorous empirical evaluations of plan-recognition systems, and there are no widely used benchmarks. Our experiments employ three extant datasets and compare them to the state-of-the-art results in order to demonstrate the advantages of SRL methods. In addition to presenting concrete results for BALPs and MLNs, we consider their relationship to other probabilistic logics, discussing the relative strengths and weaknesses of different SRL models for plan recognition.

3.5.1 Datasets

3.5.1.1 Story Understanding

We first used a small dataset previously employed to evaluate abductive Story Understanding systems (see Ng and Mooney [45] and Charniak and Goldman [8]).[2] In this task, characters' higher-level plans must be inferred from the actions described in a narrative text. A logical representation of the literal meaning of the text is given for each example. A sample story (in English) is: "Bill went to the liquor store. He pointed a gun at the owner." The plans in this dataset include shopping, robbing, restaurant dining, traveling in a vehicle (e.g., bus, taxi, or plane), partying, and jogging. Most narratives involve more than a single plan. This small dataset consists of 25 development examples and 25 test examples each containing an average of 12.6 literals. We used the planning background knowledge initially constructed for the ACCEL system of Ng and Mooney [45], which contains a total of 126 Horn rules.

---

[1] This is possible because the training data for this model is fully observed (i.e., there are no hidden nodes).
[2] Available at www.cs.utexas.edu/users/ml/accel.html

3.5.1.2 *Monroe*

We also used the Monroe dataset, an artificially generated plan-recognition dataset in the emergency-response domain by Blaylock and Allen [2]. This domain includes 10 top-level plans (e.g., setting up a temporary shelter, clearing a car wreck, and providing medical attention to victims). The task is to infer a single instantiated top-level plan based on a set of observed actions automatically generated by a *hierarchical transition network* (HTN) planner. We used the logical plan KB for this domain constructed by Raghavan and Mooney [54] which consists of 153 Horn clauses. We used 1000 artificially generated examples in our experiments. Each example instantiates one of the 10 top-level plans and contains an average of 10.19 ground literals describing a sample execution of this plan.

3.5.1.3 *Linux*

The Linux data is another plan-recognition dataset created by Blaylock and Allen [3]. Human users were asked to perform various tasks in Linux and their commands were recorded. The task is to predict the correct top-level plan from the sequence of executed commands. For example, one of the tasks involves finding all files with a given extension. The dataset contains 19 top-level plan schemas and 457 examples, with an average of 6.1 command literals per example. Here again, we used the plan KB constructed by Raghavan and Mooney [54] which consists of 50 Horn clauses.

Each of these datasets evaluates a distinct aspect of plan-recognition systems. Since the Monroe domain is quite large with numerous subgoals and entities, it tests the ability of a plan-recognition system to scale to large domains. On the other hand, the Linux dataset is not that large, but since the data comes from real human users, it is quite noisy. There are several sources of noise including cases in which users claim that they have successfully executed a top-level plan when actually they have not [2]. Therefore, this dataset tests the robustness of a plan-recognition system with noisy input. Monroe and Linux involve predicting a *single* top-level plan; however, in the Story Understanding domain, most examples have multiple top-level plans. Therefore, this dataset tests the ability of a plan-recognition system to identify multiple top-level plans.

3.5.2 Comparison of BALPs, MLNs, and Existing Approaches

This section presents experimental results comparing the performance of BALPs and MLNs to those of existing plan-recognition approaches (e.g., ACCEL [45]) and the system developed by Blaylock and Allen [2]. ACCEL is a purely logical abductive reasoning system that uses a variable evaluation metric to guide its search for the best explanation. It can use two different evaluation metrics: *simplicity*, which selects the explanation with the fewest assumptions, and *coherence*, which selects the explanation that maximally connects the input observations [10]. This second metric is specifically geared toward text interpretation by measuring *explanatory coherence* described by Ng and Mooney [44]. Currently, this bias has not been incorporated into either BALPs or any of the MLN approaches. Blaylock and Allen's system is a purely probabilistic system that learns statistical *n*-gram models to separately predict plan schemas (i.e., predicates) and their arguments.

Section 3.4 describes several variants of MLNs for plan recognition. All MLN models were implemented using Alchemy [39], an open-source software package for learning and inference in Markov logic. We used the logical abduction component developed for BALPs (see Algorithm 3.1) for abductive model construction in MLNs. Since this abductive Markov logic formulation (MLN-HCAM) performs better than simple reencodings of the traditional MLN, we restrict our comparative experiments to this approach. For more details on the experimental results comparing the different MLN enhancements, we refer the reader to Singla and Mooney [64]. For the Monroe and Linux datasets, we also compare with the traditional (nonabductive) MLN approach described in Section 3.4.4, referred to as "MLN-manual."

For BALPs, we learned the *noisy-or* parameters using the EM algorithm described in Section 3.3.2 whenever possible. Similarly, for both MLN-HCAM and MLN, we learned the parameters using the algorithms described in Section 3.4.5. For datasets that had multiple top plans as the explanation, we computed the MPE. For datasets that had a single correct top-level plan, we computed the marginal probability of plan instances and picked the one with the highest marginal probability. For both MLNs and BALPs, we used exact inference whenever feasible. However, when exact inference was intractable, we used approximate sampling to perform probabilistic inference—SampleSearch detailed by Gogate and Dechte [17] for BALPs and MC-SAT by Poon and Domingos [51] for MLNs. Both these techniques are approximate sampling algorithms designed for graphical models with deterministic constraints. Whenever we deviate from this standard methodology, we provide the specific details.

3.5.2.1 *Story Understanding*

This section provides information on the methodology and results for experiments on the Story Understanding dataset.

Parameter learning

For BALPs, we were unable to learn effective parameters from the mere 25 development examples. As a result, we set parameters manually in an attempt to maximize performance on the development set. A uniform value of 0.9 for all *noisy-or* parameters seemed to work well for this domain. The intuition behind our choice of *noisy-or* parameters is as follows: If a parent node is true, then with a probability of 0.9, the child node will be true. In other words, if a cause is true, then the effect is true with the probability of 0.9.

Using the deterministic *logical-and* model to combine evidence from conjuncts in the body of a clause did not yield high-quality results. Using *noisy-and* significantly improved the results; so we used *noisy-and*s with uniform parameters of 0.9. Here again, the intuition is that if a parent node is false or turned off, then the child node would also be false or turned off with a probability of 0.9. To disambiguate between conflicting plans, we set different priors for high-level plans to maximize performance on the development data. For MLN-HCAM, we were able to learn more effective weights from the examples in the development set using the learning algorithm described in Section 3.4.5.

Probabilistic inference

Since multiple plans are possible in this domain, we computed the MPE to infer the best set of plans. Since the resulting graphical models for this domain were not exceptionally large, we were able to apply exact, rather than approximate, inference algorithms. For BALPs, we used the k-MPE algorithm described by Nilsson [47] as implemented in ELVIRA [15]. For MLN-HCAM, we used the cutting-plane method, and its associated code, developed by Riedel [56].

Evaluation metrics

We compared BALPs and MLN-HCAM with ACCEL-Simplicity and ACCEL-Coherence. We compared the inferred plans with the ground truth to compute *precision* (percentage of the inferred plans

Table 3.1 Results for the Story Understanding Dataset

	Precision	Recall	*F*-measure
ACCEL-Simplicity	66.45	52.32	58.54
ACCEL-Coherence	89.39	89.39	89.39
BALPs	72.07	85.57	78.24
MLN-HCAM	69.13	75.32	72.10

that are correct), *recall* (percentage of the correct plans that were properly inferred), and *F-measure* (harmonic mean of precision and recall). Partial credit was given for predicting the correct plan predicate with some incorrect arguments. A point was rewarded for inferring the correct plan predicate, then, given the correct predicate, an additional point was rewarded for each correct argument. For example, if the correct plan was $plan_1(a_1, a_2)$ and the inferred plan was $plan_1(a_1, a_3)$, the score is 66.67%.

Results

Table 3.1 shows the results for Story Understanding. Both BALPs and MLN-HCAM perform better than ACCEL-Simplicity, demonstrating the advantage of SRL models over standard logical abduction. BALPs perform better than MLN-HCAM, demonstrating an advantage of a directed model for this task. However, ACCEL-Coherence still gives the best results. Since the coherence metric incorporates extra criteria specific to Story Understanding, this bias would need to be included in the probabilistic models to make them more competitive. Incorporating this bias into SRL models is difficult since it uses the graphical structure of the abductive proof to evaluate an explanation, which is not straightforward to include in a probabilistic model. It should be noted that the coherence metric is specific to narrative interpretation, since it assumes the observations are connected in a coherent "story," and this assumption is not generally applicable to other plan-recognition problems.

3.5.2.2 *Monroe and Linux*

This section provides information on the methodology and results for experiments on the Monroe and Linux datasets.

Parameter learning

For BALPs, we learned the *noisy-or* parameters automatically from data using the EM algorithm described in Section 3.3.2. We initially set all *noisy-or* parameters to 0.9, which gave reasonable performance in both domains. We picked a default value of 0.9 based on the intuition that if a parent node is true, then the child node is true with a probability 0.9. We then ran EM with two starting points: random weights and manual weights (0.9). We found that EM initialized with manual weights generally performed the best for both domains; thus, we used this approach for our comparisons. Even though EM is sensitive to its starting point, it outperformed other approaches even when initialized with random weights. For Monroe and Linux, initial experiments found no advantage to using *noisy-and* instead of *logical-and* in these domains, so we did not experiment with learning *noisy-and* parameters.

For MLN-HCAM, we learned the weights automatically from data using the methods described in Section 3.4.5. For MLN-manual, the online weight learner did not provide any improvement over default manually encoded weights (a weight of 1 for all the soft clauses and a weight of -0.5 on unit clauses for all plan predicates to specify a small prior for all plans). Therefore, we report results obtained using these manually encoded weights.

For Monroe, of the 1000 examples in our dataset we used the first 300 for training, the next 200 for validation, and the remaining 500 for tests. Blaylock and Allen learned their parameters on 4500 artificially generated examples. However, we found that using a large number of examples resulted in much longer training times and that 300 examples were sufficient to learn effective parameters for both BALPs and MLN-HCAM. For BALPs, we ran EM on the training set until we saw no further improvement in the performance on the validation set. For MLN-HCAM, the parameter learner was limited to training on at most 100 examples because learning on larger amounts of data ran out of memory. Therefore, we trained MLN-HCAM on three disjoint subsets of the training data and picked the best model using the validation set.

For Linux, we performed 10-fold cross-validation. For BALPs, we ran EM until convergence on the training set for each fold. For MLN-HCAM, within each training fold, we learned the parameters on disjoint subsets of data, each consisting of around 110 examples. As mentioned before for Monroe, the parameter learner did not scale to larger datasets. We then used the rest of the examples in each training fold for validation, picking the model that performed best on the validation set.

As discussed in Section 3.4.4, in the traditional MLN model, there are two ways to encode the bias that only a single plan is needed to explain a given action. The first approach is to include explicit hard mutual-exclusivity constraints between competing plans; the second approach involves setting a low prior on all plan predicates. While the former performed better on Monroe, the latter gave better results on Linux. We report the results of the best approach for each domain.

As noted, we had to adopt a slightly different training methodology for BALPs and MLN-HCAM because of computational limitations of MLN weight learning on large datasets. However, we used the exact same test sets for both systems on all datasets. Developing more scalable online methods for training MLNs on partially observable data is an important direction for future work.

Probabilistic inference

Both Monroe and Linux involve inferring a single top-level plan. Therefore, we computed the marginal probability of each plan instantiation and picked the most probable one. For BALPs, since exact inference was tractable on Linux, we used the exact inference algorithm implemented in Netica,[3] a commercial Bayes net software package. For Monroe, the complexity of the ground network made exact inference intractable and we used SampleSearch [17], an approximate sampling algorithm for graphical models with deterministic constraints. For both MLN approaches, we used MC-SAT [51] as implemented in the Alchemy system on both Monroe and Linux.

Evaluation metric

We compared the performance of BALPs, MLN-HCAM, and MLN with Blaylock and Allen's system using the *convergence score* as defined by them [2]. The convergence score measures the fraction of examples for which the correct plan predicate is inferred (ignoring the arguments) when given *all* of the

---

[3]www.norsys.com/

Table 3.2 Convergence Scores for Monroe and Linux Datasets

	Monroe	Linux
Blaylock	94.20	36.10
MLN-manual	90.80	16.19
MLN-HCAM	97.00	38.94
BALPs	98.40	46.60

observations. Use of the convergence score allowed for the fairest comparison to the original results on these datasets published by Blaylock and Allen.[4]

Results

Table 3.2 shows convergence scores for the Monroe and Linux datasets. Both BALPs and MLN-HCAM recognize plans in these domains more accurately than Blaylock and Allen's system. The performance of BALPs and MLN-HCAM are fairly comparable on Monroe; however, BALPs are significantly more accurate on Linux. The traditional MLN performs the worst and does particularly poorly on Linux. This demonstrates the value of the abductive approach as implemented in MLN-HCAM.

Partial observability results

The convergence score has the following limitations as a metric for evaluating the performance of plan recognition:

- It only accounts for predicting the correct plan predicate, ignoring the arguments. In most domains, it is important for a plan-recognition system to accurately predict arguments as well. For example, in the Linux domain, if the user is trying to move `test1.txt` to `test-dir`, it is not sufficient to just predict the move command; it is also important to predict the file (`test.txt`) and the destination directory (`test-dir`).
- It only evaluates plan prediction after the system has observed *all* of the executed actions. However, in most cases, we would like to be able to predict plans after observing as few actions as possible.

To evaluate the ability of BALPs and MLNs to infer plan arguments and to predict plans after observing only a partial execution, we conducted an additional set of experiments. Specifically, we performed plan recognition after observing the first 25%, 50%, 75%, and 100% of the executed actions. To measure performance, we compared the complete inferred plan (with arguments) to the gold standard to compute an overall *accuracy* score. As for Story Understanding, partial credit was given for predicting the correct plan predicate with only a subset of its correct arguments.

Table 3.3 shows the results for partial observability for the Monroe data. BALPs perform slightly better than MLN-HCAM on higher levels of observability, whereas MLN-HCAM tends to outperform BALPs on lower levels of observability. MLN-manual performs worst at higher levels of observability, but at 25% observability, it outperforms BALPs. Table 3.4 shows the results for partial observability on

---

[4]Blaylock and Allen also report results on predicting arguments, but using a methodology that makes a direct comparison difficult.

Table 3.3 Accuracy on Monroe Data for Varying Levels of Observability

	25%	50%	75%	100%
MLN-manual	10.63	13.23	37.00	67.13
MLN-HCAM	15.93	19.93	43.93	76.30
BALPs	7.33	20.26	44.63	79.16

Table 3.4 Accuracy on Linux Data for Varying Levels of Observability

	25%	50%	75%	100%
MLN-manual	10.61	10.72	10.61	10.61
MLN-HCAM	16.30	16.48	24.36	28.84
BALPs	19.83	25.45	34.06	36.32

the Linux data. Here, BALPs clearly outperform MLN-HCAM and traditional MLNs at all the levels of observability. The traditional MLN performs significantly worse than the other two models, especially at higher levels of observability. For Story Understanding, since the set of observed actions is already incomplete, we did not perform additional experiments for partial observability.

3.5.2.3 *Discussion*
We believe several aspects of SRL approaches led to their superior performance over existing approaches such as ACCEL and Blaylock and Allen's system. The ability of BALPs and MLN-HCAM to perform probabilistic reasoning most likely resulted in their improved performance over ACCEL-Simplicity, a standard logical abduction method. When Blaylock and Allen [2] perform instantiated plan recognition, it is done in a pipeline of two separate steps. The first step predicts the plan schema and the second step predicts the arguments given the schema. Unlike their approach, BALPs and MLN-HCAM are able to jointly predict both the plan schema and its arguments simultaneously.

We believe that this ability of SRL models to perform joint prediction of plans and their arguments is at least partially responsible for their superior performance. In addition, both BALPs and MLN-HCAM use prior planning knowledge encoded in the logical clauses given to the system, while Blaylock and Allen's system has no access to such planning knowledge. We believe that the ability of SRL models to incorporate such prior domain knowledge also contributes to their superior performance.

MLN-manual, although a joint model, cannot take advantage of all the domain knowledge in the planning KB available to BALPs and MLN-HCAM. Also, it does not have the advantages offered by the abductive model-construction process used in MLN-HCAM. This also makes it difficult to adequately learn the parameters for this model. We believe these factors led to its overall inferior performance compared to the other models.

For both the Monroe and Linux domains, the relative gap in the performance of MLN-manual model decreases with decreasing observability. This is particularly evident in Linux, where the performance stays almost constant with decreasing observability. We believe this is due to the model's ability to capitalize on even a small amount of information that deterministically predicts the top-level plan. Furthermore, at lower levels of observability, the ground networks are smaller and, therefore, approximate inference is more likely to be accurate.

Singla and Mooney [64] report that MLN-PC and MLN-HC models did not scale well enough to make them tractable for the Monroe and Linux domains. When compared to these models, MLN-manual has a substantial advantage; however, it still does not perform nearly as well as the MLN-HCAM model. This reemphasizes the importance of using a model that is constructed by focusing on both the query and the available evidence. Furthermore, the MLN-manual approach requires costly human labor to engineer the knowledge base. This is in contrast to the abductive MLN models that allow the same KB to be used for both planning *and* plan recognition.

Comparing BALPs and MLN-HCAM, BALPs generally performed better. We believe this difference is in part due to the advantages that directed graphical models have for abductive reasoning, as originally discussed by Pearl [48]. Note that MLN-HCAM already incorporates several ideas that originated with BALPs. By using hidden causes and *noisy-or* to combine evidence from multiple rules, and by using logical abduction to obtain a focused set of literals for the ground network, we improved the performance of MLNs by making them produce a graphical model that is more similar to the one produced by BALPs.

Although, in principle, any directed model can be reexpressed as an undirected model, the learning of parameters in the corresponding undirected model can be significantly more complex since there is no closed-form solution for the maximum-likelihood set of parameters, unlike in the case of directed models[5] [40]. Inaccurate learning of parameters can lead to potential loss of accuracy during final classification. Undirected models do have the advantage of representing cyclic dependencies (e.g., transitivity), which directed models cannot represent explicitly because of the acyclicity constraint. But we did not find it particularly useful for plan recognition since domain knowledge is expressed using rules that have inherent directional (causal) semantics. In addition, it is very difficult to develop a general MLN method that constructs a Markov net that is formally equivalent to the Bayes net constructed by a BALP given the same initial planning knowledge base.

In general, it took much more engineering time and effort to get MLNs to perform well on plan recognition compared to BLPs. Extending BLPs with logical abduction was straightforward. The main problem we encountered while adapting BLPs to work well on our plan-recognition benchmarks was finding an effective approximate inference algorithm that scaled well to the larger Monroe and Linux datasets. Once we switched to SampleSearch, which is designed to work well with the mix of soft and hard constraints present in networks, BALPs produced good results. However, getting competitive results with MLNs and scaling them to work with our larger datasets was significantly more difficult.

First, we needed to develop a method for properly introducing reverse clauses to allow MLNs to perform logical abduction. Next, we had to develop a method for introducing hidden causes to prevent the creation of networks with large cliques that made inference intractable. Finally, we had to develop an abductive model-construction process that used the ground literals constructed for BALPs to constrain the size and scope of the ground Markov net. Even after all these modifications, the weight learning algorithm did not scale to larger training sets, and the overall results are still not competitive with BALPs.

---

[5]In directed models, a closed-form solution exists for the case of full observability. This corresponds to the M step in EM when dealing with partial observability.

Some of the differences in the performance of BALPs and MLN-HCAM may also stem from the differences in the probabilistic inference and parameter learning algorithms employed. For instance, on the Linux dataset, we could run exact inference for BALPs; however, we had to resort to MC-SAT, an approximate sampling algorithm, for MLN-HCAM. On Monroe, even though we used approximate sampling algorithms for both BALPs and MLN-HCAM, it is unclear whether the performance of SampleSearch and MC-SAT are comparable. Furthermore, since probabilistic inference is used extensively during parameter learning, performance of the inference techniques could impact the quality of the learned weights/parameters.

In our preliminary work, we converted the *noisy-or* parameters learned using the EM algorithm for BALPs into weights in MLN-HCAM. When we performed plan recognition using these weights, we found that the performance of MLN-HCAM improved, demonstrating a lack of quality in the learned MLN weights. This could be due either to poor performance of probabilistic inference or to poor performance of the weight learner itself. Additional experiments that control for changes in the inference and learning algorithms are needed to further understand the effects of these differences.

3.5.3 Comparison of BALPs and MLNs to Other SRL Models

BLPs, BALPs, and MLNs are all languages for flexibly and compactly representing large, complex probabilistic graphical models. An alternative approach to SRL is to add a stochastic element to the deductive process of a logic program. ProbLog, described by Kimmig et al. [35], is the most recent and well developed of these approaches. ProbLog can be seen as extending and subsuming several previous models, such as Poole's Probabilistic Horn Abduction (PHA) [50] and PRISM described by Sato [60]. Finally, there is publicly available implementation of ProbLog[6] that exploits the latest inference techniques based on *binary decision diagrams* (BDDs) to provide scalability and efficiency.

Therefore, we attempted to also compare the performance of our models to ProbLog. It was relatively straightforward to develop a ProbLog program for plan recognition by appropriately formulating the planning KB used for both BLPs and abductive MLNs. However, our preliminary explorations with ProbLog revealed a serious limitation that prevented us from actually performing an experimental comparison on our plan-recognition datasets.

In a number of the planning axioms in our KBs, existentially quantified variables occur in the body of a clause that do not occur in the head. Representing these clauses in ProbLog requires binding such variables to all possible type-consistent constants in the domain. However, this results in the ProbLog inference engine attempting to construct an intractable number of explanations (i.e., proofs) due to the combinatorial number of possible combinations of the introduced constants. Therefore, it was intractable to run ProbLog on our datasets, preventing an empirical comparison. BALPs and MLN-HCAM use a greedy abductive proof-construction method described in Section 3.3.1 to prevent this combinatorial explosion. Therefore, we believe ProbLog would need a new approximate inference algorithm for this situation in order to be practically useful for plan recognition.

Abductive Stochastic Logic Programs (ASLPs), described by Chen et al. [12] are another SRL model that uses stochastic deduction and supports logical abduction and therefore could potentially be applied to plan recognition. However, we are unaware of a publicly available implementation of ASLPs that could be easily used for experimental comparisons.

---

[6]http://dtai.cs.kuleuven.be/problog/

3.6 **Future Work**

The research presented in this chapter could be extended in various ways. First, it would be good to evaluate the proposed plan-recognition systems on additional domains and applications. Unfortunately, there are very few publicly available datasets for plan recognition. Second, the existing SRL methods could be improved and extended in several productive directions.

Methods for lifted inference proposed by Singla and Domingos [63] could improve efficiency by allowing probabilistic inference to be performed without having to explicitly construct complete ground networks. In particular, the latest Probabilistic Theorem Proving (PTP) methods for lifted inference in MLNs, described by Gogate and Domingos [18], could be tried to improve the efficiency and accuracy of the MLN models.

Improved online weight learning algorithms could be developed to more efficiently train on large datasets and increase the accuracy of the learned models. In particular, discriminative rather than generative (i.e., EM) parameter learning for BALPs should be explored. Although discriminative learning is more difficult for directed graphical models than for undirected ones, Carvalho et al. [7] have made recent progress on this problem. Current discriminative online weight learners for MLNs, described by Huynh and Mooney [24], assume completely observable training data. These methods are not applicable to abductive MLNs, which contain unobserved subgoals and *noisy-or* nodes. Therefore, effective online methods for partially observed training data need to be developed.

With respect to the traditional MLN approach, better methods for manually engineering effective rules for deductive plan recognition could be developed. Alternatively, MLN structure learning (e.g., Kok and Domingos [36,38] and Huynh and Mooney [25]) could be used to automatically induce such rules from supervised training data. In addition, a similar approach could be developed for applying traditional (deductive) BLPs to plan recognition.

The current experimental comparisons should be extended to additional SRL models. As mentioned in Section 3.5.3, an improved approximate inference method is needed to make ProbLog tractable for our plan-recognition problems. Comparisons to other SRL models, such as Poole's Horn Abduction [50], PRISM [60], and Abductive Stochastic Logic Programs [12], are also indicated.

3.7 **Conclusion**

This chapter has introduced two new SRL approaches to plan recognition, one based on Bayesian Logic Programs and another on Markov Logic Networks. Both approaches combine the advantages of prior logical and probabilistic methods. We presented novel techniques for extending both MLNs and BLPs with logical abduction in order to allow for plan recognition given logical definitions of actions and plans as the only prior knowledge. Experimental evaluations on three benchmark datasets have shown that our approaches generally outperform other state-of-the-art plan-recognition methods. We believe their superior performance is due to the combination of logical abduction, joint probabilistic inference, and incorporation of planning domain knowledge. The results also indicate that the approach based on BLPs is generally more effective than the one based on MLNs.

Acknowledgments

We would like to thank Nate Blaylock for sharing the Linux and Monroe datasets and Vibhav Gogate for helping us modify SampleSearch for our experiments. We would also like to thank Luc De Raedt and Angelika Kimmig for their help in our attempt to run ProbLog on our plan-recognition datasets. This research was funded by MURI ARO Grant W911NF-08-1-0242 and U.S. Air Force Contract FA8750-09-C-0172 under the DARPA Machine Reading Program. Experiments were run on the Mastodon Cluster, provided by NSF Grant EIA-0303609. All views expressed are solely those of the authors and do not necessarily reflect the opinions of ARO, DARPA, NSF, or any other government agency.

References

[1] Albrecht DW, Zukerman I, Nicholson AE. Bayesian models for keyhole plan recognition in an adventure game. User Model User-Adap Intract 1998;8(1–2):5–47.

[2] Blaylock N, Allen J. Recognizing instantiated goals using statistical methods. In: Kaminka G, editor. Workshop on modeling others from observations; 2005. p. 79–86.

[3] Blaylock N, Allen JF. Statistical goal parameter recognition. In: Proceedings of the 14th International Conference on Automated Planning and Scheduling; 2004. p. 297–305.

[4] Breese JS, Goldman RP, Wellman MP. Introduction to the special section on knowledge-based construction of probabilistic and decision models. IEEE Trans Syst Man Cybern 1994;24(11):1577–9.

[5] Bui HH. A general model for online probabilistic plan recognition. In: Proceedings of the 18th International Joint Conference on Artificial Intelligence; 2003. p. 1309–15.

[6] Bui HH, Venkatesh S, West G. Policy recognition in abstract hidden Markov model. J Artif Intell Res 2002;17:451–99.

[7] Carvalho AM, Roos T, Oliveira AL, Myllymäki P. Discriminative learning of Bayesian networks via factorized conditional log-likelihood. J Mach Learn Res 2011;12:2181–210.

[8] Charniak E, Goldman R. A probabilistic model of plan recognition. In: Proceedings of the Ninth National Conference on Artificial Intelligence; 1991. p. 60–165.

[9] Charniak E, Goldman RP. A semantics for probabilistic quantifier-free first-order languages, with particular application to story understanding. In: Proceedings of the 11th International Joint Conference on Artificial Intelligence; 1989. p. 1074–9.

[10] Charniak E, Goldman RP. Plan recognition in stories and in life. In: Proceedings of the Fifth Annual Conference on Uncertainty in Artificial Intelligence; 1990. p. 343–52.

[11] Charniak E, McDermott D. Introduction to artificial intelligence. Addison-Wesley; 1985.

[12] Chen J, Muggleton S, Santos J. Learning probabilistic logic models from probabilistic examples. Mach Learn 2008;73(1):55–85.

[13] Davis J, Ong I, Struyf J, Costa VS, Burnside E, Page D. Change of representation for statistical relational learning. In: Proceedings of the 20th International Joint Conference on Artificial Intelligence; 2007. p. 2719–26.

[14] Domingos P, Lowd D. Markov logic: an interface layer for artificial intelligence. Morgan & Claypool; 2009.

[15] Elvira-Consortium. ELVIRA: an environment for probabilistic graphical models. In: Proceedings of the Workshop on Probabilistic Graphical Models; 2002. p. 222–30.

[16] Getoor L, Taskar B, editors. Introduction to statistical relational learning. MIT Press; 2007.

[17] Gogate V, Dechter R. Samplesearch: importance sampling in presence of determinism. Artif Intell 2011;175:694–729.

[18] Gogate V, Domingos P. Probabilistic theorem proving. In: Proceedings of the 27th Annual Conference on Uncertainty in Artificial Intelligence; 2011. p. 256–65.

[19] Goldman RP, Geib CW, Miller CA. A new model for plan recognition. In: Proceedings of the 15th Conference on Uncertainty in Artificial Intelligence; 1999. p. 245–54.

[20] Hobbs JR, Stickel ME, Martin P, Edwards D. Interpretation as abduction. In: Proceedings of the 26th Annual Meeting of the Association for Computational Linguistics; 1988. p. 95–103.

[21] Hong J. Goal recognition through goal graph analysis. J Artif Intell Res 2001;15:1–30.

[22] Horvitz E, Paek T. A computational architecture for conversation. In: Proceedings of the Seventh International Conference on User Modeling; 1999. p. 201–10.

[23] Huber MJ, Durfee EH, Wellman MP. The automated mapping of plans for plan recognition. In: Proceedings of the Tenth Conference on Uncertainty in Artificial Intelligence; 1994. p. 344–51.

[24] Huynh TN, Mooney RJ. Online max-margin weight learning for Markov logic networks. In: Proceedings of the 11th SIAM International Conference on Data Mining; 2011. p. 642–51.

[25] Huynh TN, Mooney RJ. Online structure learning for Markov Logic Networks. In: Proceedings of the European Conference on Machine Learning and Principles and Practice of Knowledge Discovery in Databases; 2011. p. 81–96.

[26] Inoue N, Ovchinnikova E, Inui K, Hobbs J. Weighted abduction for discourse processing based on integer linear programming. In: Sukthankar G, Goldman RP, Geib C, Pynadath DV, Bui HH, editors. Plan, activity, and intent recognition: theory and practice. Waltham, MA: Morgan Kaufmann Publishers; 2014. p. 33–56.

[27] Kakas AC, Kowalski RA, Toni F. Abductive logic programming. J Logic Comput 1993;2(6):719–70.

[28] Kaminka GA, Pynadath DV, Tambe M. Monitoring teams by overhearing: a mulit-agent plan-recognition approach. J Artif Intell Res 2002;17:83–135.

[29] Kate RJ, Mooney RJ. Probabilistic abduction using Markov logic networks. In: Proceedings of the Workshop on Plan, Activity, and Intent Recognition; 2009.

[30] Kautz HA. A formal theory of plan recognition. Ph.D. Thesis. Department of Computer Science. University of Rochester. Technical Report 215; 1987.

[31] Kautz HA, Allen JF. Generalized plan recognition. In: Proceedings of the Fifth National Conference on Artificial Intelligence; 1986. p. 32–7.

[32] Kersting K, De Raedt L. Towards combining inductive logic programming with Bayesian networks. In: Proceedings of the 11th International Conference on Inductive Logic Programming; 2001. p. 118–31.

[33] Kersting K, De Raedt L. Bayesian logic programming: Theory and tool. In: Getoor L, Taskar B, editors. Introduction to statistical relational learning. MIT Press; 2007.

[34] Kersting K, de Raedt L. Basic principles of learning Bayesian logic programs. In: De Raedt L, Frasconi P, Kersting K, Muggleton S, editors. Probabilistic inductive logic programming. Springer; 2008. p. 189–221.

[35] Kimmig A, Santos Costa V, Rocha R, Demoen B, De Raedt L. On the efficient execution of ProbLog programs. In: Proceedings of the 24th International Conference on Logic Programming; 2008. p. 175–89.

[36] Kok S, Domingos P. Learning the structure of Markov logic networks. In: Proceedings of 22nd International Conference on Machine Learning; 2005. p. 441–8.

[37] Kok S, Domingos P. Statistical predicate invention. In: Proceedings of 24th International Conference on Machine Learning; 2007. p. 433–40.

[38] Kok S, Domingos P. Learning Markov logic networks using structural motifs. In: Proceedings of the 27th International Conference on Machine Learning; 2010. p. 551–8.

[39] Kok S, Sumner M, Richardson M, Singla P, Poon H, Lowd D, et al. The alchemy system for statistical relational AI. University of Washington. Technical Report. Department of Computer Science and Engineering; 2010.

[40] Koller D, Friedman N. Probabilistic graphical models: principles and techniques. MIT Press; 2009.

[41] Lesh N, Etzioni O. A sound and fast goal recognizer. In: Proceedings of the 14th International Joint Conference on Artificial Intelligence; 1995. p. 1704–10.

[42] Levesque HJ. A knowledge-level account of abduction. In: Proceedings of the 11th International Joint Conference on Artificial Intelligence; 1989. p. 1061–7.

[43] Natarajan S, Khot T, Kersting K, Tadepalli P, Shavlik J. Exploiting causal independence in Markov logic networks: Combining undirected and directed models. In: Proceedings of the European Conference on Machine Learning and Principles and Practice of Knowledge Discovery in Databases; 2010. p. 434–50.

[44] Ng HT, Mooney RJ. The role of coherence in abductive explanation. In: Proceedings of the Eighth National Conference on Artificial Intelligence; 1990. p. 337–442.

[45] Ng HT, Mooney RJ. Abductive plan recognition and diagnosis: A comprehensive empirical evaluation. In: Proceedings of the Third International Conference on Principles of Knowledge Representation and Reasoning; 1992. p. 499–508.

[46] Ngo L, Haddawy P. Answering queries from context-sensitive probabilistic knowledge bases. Theor Comput Sci 1997;171:147–77.

[47] Nilsson D. An efficient algorithm for finding the M most probable configurations in probabilistic expert systems. Stat Comput 1998;8:159–73.

[48] Pearl J. Probabilistic reasoning in intelligent systems: networks of plausible inference. Morgan Kaufmann; 1988.

[49] Peng Y, Reggia JA. Abductive inference models for diagnostic problem-solving. Springer-Verlag; 1990.

[50] Poole D. Probabilistic Horn abduction and Bayesian networks. Artif Intell 1993;64:81–129.

[51] Poon H, Domingos P. Sound and efficient inference with probabilistic and deterministic dependencies. In: Proceedings of the 21st National Conference on Artificial Intelligence; 2006. p. 458–63.

[52] Pople HE. On the mechanization of abductive logic. In: Proceedings of the Third International Joint Conference on Artificial Intelligence; 1973. p. 147–52.

[53] Pynadath DV, Wellman MP. Probabilistic state-dependent grammars for plan recognition. In: Proceedings of the Conference on Uncertainty in Artificial Intelligence; 2000. p. 507–14.

[54] Raghavan S, Mooney RJ. Abductive plan recognition by extending Bayesian logic programs. In: Proceedings of the European Conference on Machine Learning and Principles and Practice of Knowledge Discovery in Databases; 2011. p. 629–44.

[55] Richardson M, Domingos P. Markov logic networks. Mach Learn 2006;62:107–36.

[56] Riedel S. Improving the accuracy and efficiency of MAP inference for Markov logic. In: Proceedings of 24th Conference on Uncertainty in Artificial Intelligence; 2008. p. 468–75.

[57] Sadilek A, Kautz H. Modeling and reasoning about success, failure, intent of multi-agent activities. In: Proceedings of the UbiComp Workshop on Mobile Context Awareness; 2010.

[58] Sadilek A, Kautz H. Recognizing multi-agent activities from GPS data. In: Proceedings of the 25th AAAI Conference on Artificial Intelligence; 2010. p. 1134–9.

[59] Saria S, Mahadevan S. Probabilistic plan recognition in multiagent systems. In: Proceedings of the International Conference on Automated Planning and Scheduling; 2004. p. 287–96.

[60] Sato T. A statistical learning method for logic programs with distribution semantics. In: Proceedings of the 12th International Conference on Logic Programming; 1995. p. 715–29.

[61] Shavlik J, Natarajan S. Speeding up inference in Markov logic networks by preprocessing to reduce the size of the resulting grounded network. In: Proceedings of the 21st International Joint Conference on Artificial Intelligence; 2009. p. 1951–6.

[62] Singla P, Domingos P. Discriminative training of Markov logic networks. In: Proceedings of the 20th National Conference on Artificial Intelligence; 2005. p. 868–73.

[63] Singla P, Domingos P. Lifted first-order belief propagation. In: Proceedings of the 23rd AAAI Conference on Artificial Intelligence; 2008. p. 1094–9.

[64] Singla P, Mooney R. Abductive Markov logic for plan recognition. In: Proceedings of the 25th National Conference on Artificial Intelligence; 2011. p. 1069–75.

[65] Stickel ME. A probLog-like inference system for computing minimum-cost abductive explanations in natural-language interpretation. Technical Note 451. SRI International; 1988.

[66] Wellman MP, Breese JS, Goldman RP. From knowledge bases to decision models. Knowl Eng Rev 1992;7(01):35–53.

Keyhole Adversarial Plan Recognition for Recognition of Suspicious and Anomalous Behavior

Dorit Avrahami-Zilberbrand and Gal A. Kaminka
Bar Ilan University, Ramat Gan, Israel

4.1 Introduction

Adversarial plan recognition is the use of plan recognition in settings where the observed agent is considered a potential adversary, having plans or goals that oppose those of the observer. The objective of adversarial plan recognition is to identify behavior that is potentially harmful, differentiating it from nonadversarial behavior, in time for the observer to decide on a reaction. Applications of adversarial plan recognition include computer intrusion detection [23], virtual training environments [56], in-office visual surveillance [10], and detection of anomalous activities [17,45,59]. Adversarial plan recognition faces several inherent challenges:

- First, often there are limited data from which to construct a plan library of the adversary's behavior. Unlike with most plan-recognition settings, we cannot assume knowledge of the complete set of plans an adversary may pursue. Thus, an adversarial plan-recognition system has to recognize anomalous plans—plans that are characterized simply by the fact that they are not known to the observing agent.
- Second, most nonadversarial plan-recognition systems ignore the expected impact of the explanations they generate on the observer. They generate a list of recognition hypotheses (typically ranked by decreasing likelihood). It is up to the observer's decision-making component to examine the hypotheses and draw a conclusion leading to taking action. But often adversarial plan hypotheses have low likelihoods because of their rarity. Thus, they must either be ignored for being too unlikely or they must be considered together with many other low-likelihood hypotheses, which may lead to many false positives.

For instance, suppose we observe a rare sequence of Unix commands that can be explained for some plan I or for a more common plan L. Most plan-recognition systems will prefer the most likely hypothesis L and ignore I. Yet, if the risk of I for the observer is high (e.g., if I is a plan to take down the computer system), then that hypothesis should be preferred *when trying to recognize suspicious behavior*. If I implies low risk (even if the observed sequence is malicious), or if the goal is not to recognize suspicious behavior, then L may be a better hypothesis.

This chapter describes a comprehensive system for adversarial plan recognition. The system is composed of a hybrid plan recognizer: A symbolic recognition system, Symbolic Behavior Recognition

(SBR) [3,4], is used to detect anomalous plans. Recognized nonanomalous plans are fed into an efficient utility-based plan-recognition (UPR) system [5], which reasons about the expected cost of hypotheses, recognizing suspicious plans even if their probability is low.

We evaluate the two components in extensive experiments using real-world and simulated activity data from a variety of sources. We show that the techniques are able to detect both anomalous and suspicious behavior while providing high levels of precision and recall (i.e., small numbers of false positives and false negatives).

4.2 Background: Adversarial Plan Recognition

Plan recognition is the task of inferring the intentions, plans, and/or goals of an agent based on observations of its actions and observable features. Other parts of this book provide an extensive survey of past and current approaches to plan recognition. We focus here on adversarial settings in which plan recognition is used to recognize plans, activities, or intentions of an adversary.

Applications of plan recognition to surveillance in particular, and adversarial plan recognition in general, began to appear shortly after the introduction of the basic probabilistic recognition methods (e.g., Hilary and Shaogang [26]) and continue to this day in studies done by various authors [10,15,17, 23,38,40,45,59]. We survey recent efforts in the following.

We limit ourselves to *keyhole* recognition, where the assumption is that the adversary is either not aware that it is being observed or does not care. Toward the end of this section, we discuss relaxing this assumption (i.e., allowing *intended* recognition, where the observed adversary possibly modifies its behavior because it knows it is being observed).

One key approach to adversarial plan recognition is *anomalous plan recognition*, based on anomaly detection (i.e., recognition of what is not normal). Here, the plan library is used in an inverse fashion; it is limited to accounting only for normal behavior. When a plan recognizer is unable to match observations against the library (or generates hypotheses with very low likelihood), an anomaly is announced.

The second key approach to adversarial plan recognition is *suspicious plan recognition*, based on directly detecting threatening plans or behavior. It operates under the assumption that a plan library is available that accounts for adversarial behavior; thus, recognition of hypotheses implying such behavior is treated no differently than recognition of hypotheses implying normal activity.

In both approaches, there is an assumption that the plan library is *complete*, in that it accounts for the full repertoire of expected normal behavior (in anomalous plan recognition) or adversarial behavior (in suspicious plan recognition). Likewise, a full set of observable features can be used for either approach: not only the type of observed action but also its duration and its effects; not only the identity of the agent being observed but also observable features that mark it in the environment (i.e., its velocity and heading, its visual appearance, etc.).

Superficially, therefore, a plan-recognition system intended for one approach is just as capable of being used for the other, as long as an appropriate plan library is used. However, this is not true in practice, because different approaches raise different challenges.

4.2.1 Different Queries

Fundamentally, the two approaches answer different queries about the observed agent's behavior.

The main query that an anomalous behavior-recognition system has to answer is a *set membership query*: "Is the observed behavior explained by the plan library?" If so, then no anomaly is declared. If not, then an anomaly is found. Thus, the relative likelihood of the hypothesized recognized plan, with respect to other hypotheses, is not important.[1]

In contrast, the main query that a suspicious behavior-recognition system has to answer is the *current state query*: "What is the preferred explanation for the observations at this point?" We use the term *preferred* because there are different ways of ranking plan-recognition hypotheses. The most popular one relies on probability theory to rank hypotheses based on their likelihood. But as we discuss later, this is only one way to rank hypotheses.

4.2.2 Origins of the Plan Library

The construction of a plan library for the two approaches, presumably by human experts or automated means, is based on knowledge sources that have different characteristics.

In many adversarial settings, knowledge of the adversarial behavior is clearly available. For instance, in applications of plan recognition in recognizing a fight between a small number of people, it is possible to imagine a specific set of recognition rules (e.g., accelerated limb motions, breaking of personal distances). If such knowledge exists, suspicious behavior recognition is more easily used.

However, in some settings, knowledge of specific adversarial plans is lacking and examples are rare. For instance, in surveillance for terrorist attacks in airport terminals, there are very few recorded examples, and certainly we cannot easily enumerate all possible ways in which the adversary might act prior to an attack. Here, the use of anomalous behavior recognition is more natural.

4.2.3 The Outcome from the Decision-Making Perspective

A challenge related to the different queries is the use of the output from the plan-recognition module as a basis for decision making. In suspicious plan recognition, the greater the match between the observations and the plan library (as measured by likelihood or another means), the greater the confidence in categorizing the behavior as suspicious. This can be used by a decision-making module to respond appropriately to different levels of suspiciousness (e.g., by actively taking actions to differentiate hypotheses or directly counter the implied threat).

But in the anomalous behavior-recognition case, the opposite is true. The *weaker* the match between the observations and the plan library, the greater the implied confidence in the anomaly. However, because in this case a sequence of observations is considered anomalous when it does not exist in the plan library, there is no universally accepted method for assessing confidence in the outcome. In other words, there is no universally correct method for measuring the degree to which the observations do *not* match the plan library.

We first discuss existing work using anomalous plan recognition. This approach has connections to machine learning (e.g., one-class learning for security) and monitoring (e.g., fault detection and diagnosis). The literature on anomaly detection within these areas is vast. However, much of it is only superficially related, in the sense that the overall goals may be the same, but the application domains

---

[1] Note that multiple levels of anomaly are built by using multiple plan libraries, where the membership query is applied to all, separately.

give rise to methods that are very data-oriented yet require little or no treatment of hierarchical states, interleaved activities, or future intentions. For instance, fingerprinting users from their characteristic behavior (e.g., see Lane and Brodley [37]) is a related task, but the focus is on supervised machine learning of mouse and keyboard events. Similarly, we will not address here related work done by various authors on anomaly detection in data signals. (e.g., [1,16,35]).

Within plan-recognition literature, Xiang and Gong [60] adopted dynamic Bayesian networks (DBNs) to model normal patterns of activity captured on video. An activity is identified as abnormal if the likelihood of it being generated by normal models is less then a threshold. Duong et al. [17] use Switching Semi-Markov Models to represent user activities that have a known duration (so an anomaly is detected if actions' durations deviate from normal). Marhasev et al. [43] look at low-likelihood hypotheses based on both duration and state in the context of a clinical diagnosis task.

Yin et al. [62] present a two-phase approach to detect anomalous behavior based on wireless sensors attached to the human body. This approach first uses Support Vector Machines (SVMs) that filter out the activities with a high probability of being normal, then derives from these an anomalous activity model. Here also the model is learned based on normal activities.

One key issue with all of these investigations is that they spend computational time on probabilistic reasoning that might not be necessary for a membership query. In contrast, we advocate an approach that uses symbolic behavior recognition, which can answer the membership query much more efficiently.

In particular, the SBR algorithms [3,4] advocated in this chapter provide extremely efficient membership query responses at the expense of recognition accuracy (since they cannot rank hypotheses based on likelihood). The SBR algorithms are most related to symbolic plan-recognition algorithms used to identify failures in teamwork. RESL [34], and later YOYO [30], are symbolic recognition algorithms for detecting disagreements among team members. Both RESL and YOYO exploit knowledge of the social structures of the team (called team hierarchy) to efficiently recognize splits in teams, where an agent is executing a different plan than agreed on with the rest of its team. Disagreements are therefore treated as recognition failures. Both algorithms ignore observation history in current state hypotheses in contrast to SBR. Moreover, these algorithms do not account for complex temporal reasoning (i.e., duration and interleaving), while SBR algorithms do.

We now turn to discussing work in suspicious behavior recognition. It operates under the assumption that the plan library directly covers the adversarial behavior to be recognized. Thus, recognition of hypotheses implying such behavior is treated no differently than recognition of hypotheses implying normal activity. Examples include systems that encode possible attacks in an intrusion-detection system, trying to predict whether an attack is performed [23]; systems that focus on recognizing specific suspicious behaviors in train stations [15] (e.g., fighting); systems with an a priori set of attack templates [29] that are compared with observations to infer whether a particular terrorist attack matches one or more templates; and models with representations of human activities based on tracked trajectories—for example, see Niu et al. [45].

Most suspicious behavior-recognition systems use probabilistic plan-recognition approaches. These focus on determining the most likely hypothesis, or set of hypotheses, as to the current and/or past states of the agent. Previous work in this area has focused on using specialized structures and techniques that allow more efficient recognition or more expressive forms of plan recognition.

Some of the early work applying plan recognition to visual surveillance applied belief (Bayesian) networks (e.g., see Hilary and Shaogang [26] and Hongeng et al. [27]). However, given the known computational hardness of exact and approximate reasoning in general belief networks [14] and general dynamic belief networks [8,36], more efficient models were needed. These typically trade expressiveness for runtime (e.g., by introducing a Markov assumption into the models).

Indeed, Hidden Markov Models (HMMs) and extensions have been explored extensively for plan recognition. These are special cases of dynamic belief networks, with much improved inference runtime (typically, polynomial), at the cost of introducing a Markovian assumption and restricting the set of variables. HMMs are widely used for recognition of simple activities (e.g., see Starner and Pentland [52] and Yamato et al. [61]). However, they do not allow for complex activities (e.g., interacting agents, hierarchical decomposition of the activities, or explicit temporal dependencies). *Coupled HMMs* [9] and *Factorial HMMs* [25] are extensions of the HMM with multiple hidden interacting chains (e.g., for modeling interactions between observed agents).

AHMMs [11], *HHMMs* [18], and *Layered HMMs* [47] are capable of handling activities that have hierarchical structures. These models are used in activity-recognition applications (e.g., learning and detecting activities from movement trajectories [44]) and inferring user's daily movements from raw GPS sensor data [38]. *Hidden Semi-Markov Models* (HSMMs) allow probabilistic constraints over the duration of plans [17]. Extensions to these can model dependencies on state durations [43]. More recent work has continued developing methods for greater expressiveness without sacrificing tractability. For example, Blaylock and Allen [7] provided a novel HMM-based model that allows efficient exact reasoning about hierarchical goals. Hu and Yang [28] model interacting and concurrent goals.

Recent work has moved beyond dynamic belief networks and Markov models to use *conditional random fields* [57], which allow for greater expressiveness. Bui et al. [12] introduce a Hidden Permutation model that can learn the partial ordering constraints in location-based activity recognition. There are also approaches to plan recognition based on parsing, in particular using *probabilistic grammars*, which allow for efficient exact inference (e.g., see the works of several authors [19–21,50,51]).

The key challenge to the use of probabilistic recognizers in suspicious behavior recognition is that most often adversarial behavior is not likely, typically because it is rare. Given a specific sequence of observations, if the adversarial hypothesis is the only explanation, then obviously it would be selected. But generally in plan recognition, there would be multiple hypotheses that match the observations and that have to be ranked in some fashion. In this general case, preferring the most likely hypothesis often means preferring the more common explanation rather than the rare explanation signifying adversarial intent.

In other words, the posterior likelihood of a hypothesis signifying adversarial behavior is very often low, given the observations. In the general case, it would be one hypothesis out of many. This leads to either of two cases: the observer has to always consider low-likelihood hypotheses (leading to many false alarms, i.e., false positives) or the observer sets a high threshold for likelihood, in which case she risks disregarding a suspicious behavior.

To address this, we posit that a system for suspicious plan recognition needs to reason about the *expected cost* to the observer, given that a hypothesis is correct. In other words, we argue that the observer ranks hypotheses based on their expected cost to itself rather than just based on their likelihood. This way, a low-likelihood hypothesis, which, if true, would signify large costs, may be preferred over a more likely hypothesis, which implies no risk. Put more generally, our work differs significantly from probabilistic approaches because we advocate reasoning about the expected utility of hypotheses rather than simply their likelihoods.

Essentially every probabilistic plan-recognition system can be used as the basis for expected cost computations. This can be done by taking the *entire* (ranked) set of hypotheses from the probabilistic recognizers and then externally associating each with costs to compute expected costs. Computationally, this can be very expensive because in addition to the plan-recognition computation, there would be more external computation of the expected costs. Note that the entire set of hypotheses must be processed, as a low-likelihood hypothesis (ranked low by the probabilistic recognizer) may end up implying a high expected utility.

The key to efficient computation of plan-recognition hypotheses, ranked by their expected costs, is the folding of the expected cost computation into the plan recognizer itself. The hypotheses would then be ranked directly, without the need for external computation.

We call this approach utility-based plan recognition (UPR); it is described fully in Avrahami-Zilberbrand [2] and Avrahami-Zilberbrand and Kaminka [5] and more briefly in this chapter. The origins of this approach come from a worst-case reasoning heuristic applied in Tambe and Rosenbloom's *RESC* algorithm [56]. RESC is a reactive plan-recognition system applied in simulated air-combat domains. Here, the observing agent may face ambiguous observations, where some hypotheses imply extreme danger (a missile being fired toward the observer) and other hypotheses imply gains (the opponent running away). RESC takes a heuristic approach that prefers hypotheses that imply significant costs to the observer (e.g., potential destruction). However, the relative likelihood of such hypotheses was ignored because RESC was a symbolic plan recognizer. While inspired by this work, we take a principled, decision–theoretic approach. In the algorithms we present, the likelihood of hypotheses is combined with their utilities to calculate the expected impact on the observer. Later we show that this subsumes the earlier heuristic work.

The UPR techniques described in this chapter use a technique for gaining the efficiency of symbolic plan recognition for recognizing anomalous plans, with a Markovian utility-based plan recognizer [5]. The Markovian assumption, which allows for efficient reasoning, comes at a cost of expressiveness. A more general UPR method, based on influence diagrams, is described in Avrahami-Zilberbrand [2]. It provides one way of extending the expressiveness of UPR but comes at a significant computational cost.

Recently, UPR has been extended in Kaluža et al. [53] to allow dynamic changes to the cost function, a specific extension that maintains the computational tractability while increasing the expressiveness of the original Markovian technique described in Avrahami-Zilberbrand and Kaminka [5] and in this chapter. This allows, for instance, expressing nonlinearly increasing costs for observing repeated occurrences of a suspicious event (e.g., repeatedly trying to avoid a cop whenever one passes by).

There have been related investigations of the use of utility and cost in plan recognition. However, these focused on modeling the expected utility of the observed agent, not of the observer. They therefore do not address the same challenge we do in recognizing suspicious plans. Indeed, it is arguable that modeling the utility of different plans to the observed agent is redundant, since a rational observed agent would be pursuing the plan with the highest expected utility; this would be reflected in the likelihood of the plan, as observed. Nevertheless, there are investigations of explicit modeling utilities of the observed agent, including Mao and Gratch [41,42], Suzic [55], Pynadath and Marsella [48,49], Baker [6], and Sukthankar and Sycara [54].

The techniques described in this chapter use a technique for gaining the efficiency of symbolic plan recognition for recognizing anomalous plans with a Markovian UPR [5]. Here, an underlying symbolic recognizer (SBR, described in Avrahami-Zilberbrand and Kaminka [3,4]) is used to efficiently filter inconsistent hypotheses, passing them to a probabilistic inference engine, which focuses on ranking recognition hypotheses using UPR principles.

There have been a number of other plan recognizers that use a hybrid approach, though of a different nature. Geib and Harp [24] developed PHATT, a hybrid symbolic/probabilistic recognizer, where a symbolic algorithm filters inconsistent hypotheses before they are considered probabilistically. PHATT assumes instantaneous, atomic actions. It takes the following approach: With each observation, the symbolic algorithm generates a *pending set* of possible expected observations, which are matched against the next observation to maintain correct state history hypotheses. The size of the pending set may grow exponentially [22].

In contrast, SBR decouples the current state and state history queries and incrementally maintains hypotheses implicitly, without predicting pending observations. Therefore hypotheses are computed only when needed (when, hopefully, many of them have been ruled out). PHATT does allow recognition of interleaved plans as well as some partial observability; however, the expected costs of plans are ignored.

YOYO* [33] is a hybrid symbolic/probabilistic plan-recognition algorithm for multiagent *overhearing* (recognition based on observed communication acts). The plan library used by YOYO* includes information about the average duration of plan steps, which is used to calculate the likelihood of an agent terminating one step and selecting another without being observed doing so. In this, YOYO* addresses missing observations (though their likelihood of becoming lost is assumed to be provided a priori). However, in contrast to our work, YOYO* does not address matching multifeature observations (where some features may be intermittently lost), nor does it allow for interleaved plans.

Quite recently, Lisy et al. have examined the problem of *intended* adversarial plan recognition [39], where the observed agent is actively attempting to prevent its plans from being recognized. They define the problem using game theory, where the observer and the observed play a game of selecting plans and actions for recognizing these plans. While the game tree grows very large for even moderate-sized problems, Lisy et al. show that its specialized structure lends itself to highly scalable algorithms for determining the Nash equilibrium solution. However, in contrast to the work described in this chapter and elsewhere in this book, the algorithms avoid any details of matching observations to plans, which is, from a computational standpoint, a key challenge in plan recognition.

4.3 An Efficient Hybrid System for Adversarial Plan Recognition

We present here a hybrid anomalous and suspicious adversarial plan-recognition system that uses efficient plan-recognition algorithms for detecting anomalous and suspicious behaviors. The system is composed from two modules: SBR, initially presented in Avrahami-Zilberbrand and Kaminka [3,4], and UPR, presented in Avrahami-Zilberbrand [2] and Avrahami-Zilberbrand and Kaminka [5].

The system uses a plan library, which encodes normal behavior including plans, that may or may not indicate a threat (i.e., may be suspicious). The SBR module extracts coherent hypotheses from the observation sequence. If the set of hypotheses is empty, it declares the observation sequence as anomalous. If the set is not empty, then the hypotheses are passed to the UPR module that computes the highest expected cost hypotheses. When the expected cost of the top-ranked hypothesis reaches a given threshold, the system declares that the observation sequence is suspicious. Figure 4.1 presents the

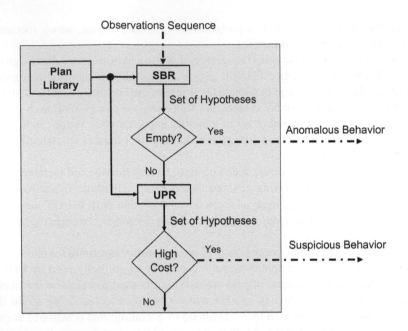

FIGURE 4.1

A hybrid adversarial plan-recognition system. *Note:* Inputs and outputs for the system shown with *dashed* arrows.

hybrid system. The input to the system is an observation sequence and the output is whether anomalous or suspicious behavior is detected.

We begin by considering recognition of anomalous behavior using the symbolic plan-recognition algorithm (see Section 4.3.1). Here, the plan library represents normal behavior; any activity that does not match the plan library is considered abnormal. This approach can be effective in applications in which we have few or no examples of suspicious behavior (which the system is to detect) but many examples of normal behavior (which the system should ignore). This is the case, for instance, in many vision-based surveillance systems in public places.

A symbolic plan-recognition system is useful for recognizing abnormal patterns such as walking in the wrong direction, taking more than the usual amount of time to get to the security check, and so on. The symbolic recognizer can efficiently match activities to the plan library and rule out hypotheses that do not match. When the resulting set of matching hypotheses is empty, the sequence of observations is flagged as anomalous. The symbolic algorithm is very fast, since it rejects or passes hypotheses without ranking them.

However, detection of abnormal behavior is not sufficient. There are cases where a normal behavior should be treated as suspicious. In such cases, we cannot remove the behavior from the plan library (so as to make its detection possible using the anomalous behavior-detection scheme previously outlined), and yet we expect the system to detect it and flag it.

Section 4.4.2 presents the use of UPR for recognizing suspicious behavior. Here the plan library explicitly encodes behavior to be recognized, alongside any costs associated with the recognition of this behavior. This allows the UPR system to rank hypotheses based on their expected cost to the observing agent. As we shall see, this leads to being able to recognize potentially dangerous situations despite their low likelihood.

4.3.1 Efficient Symbolic Plan Recognition

We propose an anomalous behavior-recognition system; the input of the system is an observation sequence. The system is composed of a Symbolic Behavior Recognition module, which extracts coherent hypotheses from the observation sequence. If the set of hypotheses is empty, it declares the observation sequence as anomalous.

The symbolic plan-recognition algorithm, briefly described in the following, is useful for recognizing abnormal behavior, since it is very fast (no need to rank hypotheses) and can handle key capabilities required by modern surveillance applications. The reader is referred to Avrahami-Zilberbrand and Kaminka [3,4] for details.

The SBR's plan library is a single-root directed graph, where vertices denote *plan steps* and edges can be of two types: decomposition edges decompose plan steps into substeps and sequential edges specify the temporal order of execution. The graph is acyclic along decomposition transitions.

Each plan has an associated set of conditions on observable features of the agent and its actions. When these conditions hold, the observations are said to match the plan. At any given time, the observed agent is assumed to be executing a *plan decomposition path*, root-to-leaf through decomposition edges. An observed agent is assumed to change its internal state in two ways. First, it may follow a sequential edge to the next plan step. Second, it may reactively interrupt plan execution at any time and select a new (first) plan. The recognizer operates as follows.

First, it matches observations to specific plan steps in the library according to the plan step's conditions. Then, after matching plan steps are found, they are tagged by the timestamp of the observation. These tags are then propagated up the plan library so that complete plan paths (root-to-leaf) are tagged to indicate that they constitute hypotheses as to the internal state of the observed agent when the observations were made. The propagation process tags paths along decomposition edges. However, the propagation process is not a simple matter of following from child to parent. A plan may match the current observation yet be *temporally inconsistent* when a history of observations is considered. SBR is able to quickly determine the temporal consistency of a hypothesized recognized plan [3].

At the end of the SBR process, we are left with a set of *current-state hypotheses* (i.e., a set of paths) through the hierarchy) that the observed agent may have executed at the time of the last observation.

The overall worst-case runtime complexity of this process is $O(LD)$ [3]. Here, L is the number of plan steps that directly match the observations; D is the maximum depth of the plan library. L is typically very small, which is the number of specific actions that can match a particular observation.

The preceding presented the basics of the symbolic plan-recognition model. Extensions to this model, discussed in Avrahami-Zilberbrand [2] and Avrahami-Zilberbrand and Kaminka [4], address several challenges:

1. Reducing space complexity of matching complex multifeatured observations to the plan library
2. Dealing with plan execution duration constraints
3. Handling lossy observations, where an observation is intermittently lost

4. Handling interleaved plans where an agent interrupts a plan for another, only to return to the first later.

4.3.2 Efficient Utility-based Plan Recognition

This section presents an efficient hybrid technique used for recognizing suspicious behavior. Utility-based plan recognition allows the observer to incorporate a utility function into the plan-recognition process. With every potential hypothesis, we associate a utility to the observer should the hypothesis be correct. In adversarial UPR, this utility is the cost incurred by the observer. This allows choosing recognition hypotheses based on their expected cost to the observer, even if their likelihood is low.

The highly efficient symbolic plan recognizer introduced in Section 4.3.1 is used to filter hypotheses, maintaining only those that are consistent with the observations (but not ranking the hypotheses in any way). We then add an expected utility aggregation layer, which is run on top of the symbolic recognizer.

We briefly describe the basics of the UPR recognizer in this section. Avrahami-Zilberbrand [2] presents a general UPR framework, using influence diagrams as the basis for reasoning. Unfortunately, such reasoning is computationally expensive. Relying on a Markovian assumption, a less expressive but much more efficient UPR technique is used here. For its details, consult Avrahami-Zilberbrand [2] and Avrahami-Zilberbrand and Kaminka [5].

After getting all *current-state hypotheses* from the symbolic recognizer, the next step is to compute the expected utility of each hypothesis. This is done by multiplying the posterior probability of a hypothesis by its utility to the observer. We follow in the footsteps of—and then extend—the *Hierarchical Hidden Markov Model* [18] in representing probabilistic information in the plan library. We denote plan steps in the plan library by q_i^d, where i is the plan-step index and d is its hierarchy depth, $1 \leq d \leq D$. For each plan step, there are three probabilities.

Sequential transition For each internal state q_i^d, there is a state-transition probability matrix denoted by $A^{q^d} = (a_{i,j}^{q^d})$, where $a_{i,j}^{q^d} = P(q_j^d | q_i^d)$ is the probability of making a sequential transition from the ith plan step to the jth plan step. Note that self-cycle transitions are also included in A^{q^d}.

Interruption We denote by $a_{i,end}^{q^d}$ a transition to a special plan step end^d, which signifies an interruption of the sequence of current plan step q_i^d and immediate return of control to its parent, q^{d-1}.

Decomposition transition When the observed agent first selects a decomposable plan step q_i^d, it must choose between its (first) children for execution. The decomposition transition probability is denoted $\Pi^{q^d} = \pi^{q^d}(q^{d+1}) = P(q_k^{d+1} | q_i^d)$, the probability that plan step q_i^d will initially activate plan step q_k^{d+1}.

Observation probabilities Each leaf has an output emission probability vector $B^{q^d} = (b^{q^d}(o))$. This is the probability of observing o when the observed agent is in plan step q^d. For presentation clarity, we treat observations as children of leaves and use the decomposition transition Π^{q^d} for the leaves as B^{q^d}.

In addition to transition and interruption probabilities, we add utility information onto the edges in the plan library. The utilities on the edges represent the cost or gains to the observer, given that the observed agent selects the edge. For the remainder of the chapter, we use the term *cost* to refer to a positive value associated with an edge or node. As in the probabilistic reasoning process, for each node we have three kinds of utilities: (1) E^{q^d} is the sequential-transition utility (cost) to the observer,

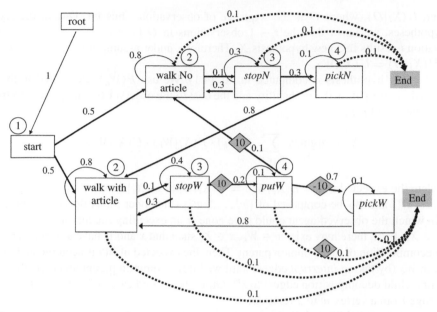

FIGURE 4.2

An example plan library. *Note:* Recognition timestamps (example in text) appear in *circles*. Costs appear in *diamonds*.

conditioned on the observed agent transitioning to the next plan step, paralleling A^{q^d}; (2) $e^{q^d}_{i,end}$ is the interruption utility; and (3) Ψ^{q^d} is the decomposition utility to the observer, paralleling Π^{q^d}.

Figure 4.2 shows a portion of the plan library of an agent walking with or without a suitcase in the airport, occasionally putting it down and picking it up again; this example is discussed later. Note the *end* plan step at each level, and the transition from each plan step to this end plan step. This edge represents the probability to interrupt. The utilities are shown in *diamonds* (0 utilities omitted, for clarity). The transitions allowing an agent to leave a suitcase without picking it up are associated with large positive costs, since they signify danger to the observer.

We use these probabilities and utilities to rank the hypotheses selected by the SBR. First, we determine all paths from each hypothesized leaf in timestamp $t-1$ to the leaf of each of the current-state hypotheses in timestamp t. Then, we traverse these paths, multiplying the transition probabilities on edges by the transition utilities and accumulating the utilities along the paths. If there is more than one way to get from the leaf of the previous hypothesis to the leaf of the current hypothesis, then it should be accounted for in the accumulation. Finally, we can determine the *most costly* current plan step (the current-state hypothesis with maximum expected cost). Identically, we can also find the *most likely* current plan step for comparison.

Formally, let us denote hypotheses at time $t-1$ (each a path from root-to-leaf) as $W = \{W_1, W_2, \ldots, W_r\}$ and the hypotheses at time t as $X = \{X_1, X_2, \ldots, X_l\}$. To calculate the maximum expected-utility (most costly) hypothesis, we need to calculate for each current hypothesis X_i its expected cost to the observer, $U(X_i|O)$, where O is the sequence of observations thus far. Due to the use of SBR to filter hypotheses, we know that the $t - 1$ observations in O have resulted in hypothesis W and that observation t results in a new hypothesis X. Therefore, under assumption of Markovian plan-step selection, $U(X_i|O) = U(X_i|W)$.

The most costly hypothesis is computed in Eq. (4.1). We use $P(W_k)$, calculated in the previous timestamp, and multiply it by the probability and the cost to the observer of taking the step from W_k to X_i. This is done for all i, k.

$$\hat{X}_i = \underset{X_i}{\operatorname{argmax}} \sum_{W_k \in W} P(W_k) \cdot P(X_i|W_k) \cdot U(X_i|W_k). \qquad (4.1)$$

To calculate the expected utility $E(X_i|W_k) = P(X_i|W_k) \cdot U(X_i|W_k)$, let X_i be composed of plan steps $\{x_i^1, \ldots, x_i^m\}$ and W_k be composed of $\{w_k^1, \ldots, w_k^n\}$ (the upper index denotes depth). There are two ways in which the observed agent could have gone from executing the leaf $w^n \in W_k$ to executing the leaf $x^m \in X_i$. First, there may exist $w \in W_k, x \in X_i$ such that x and w have a common parent and x is a direct decomposition of this common parent. Then, the expected utility is accumulated by climbing up vertices in W_k (by taking *interrupt* edges) until we hit the common parent and then climbing down (by taking first child decomposition edges) to x^m. Or, in the second case, x^m is reached by following a sequential edge from a vertex w to a vertex x.

In both cases, the probability of climbing up from a leaf w^n at depth n to a parent w^j, where $j < n$, is given by

$$\alpha_{w^n}^j = \prod_{d=n}^{j} a_{w,end}^d \qquad (4.2)$$

and the utility is given by

$$\gamma_{w^n}^j = \sum_{d=n}^{j} e_{w,end}^d. \qquad (4.3)$$

The probability of climbing down from a parent x^j to a leaf x^m is given by

$$\beta_{x^m}^j = \prod_{d=j}^{m} \pi^{x^d}(x^{d+1}) \qquad (4.4)$$

and the utility is given by

$$\delta_{x^m}^j = \sum_{d=j}^{m} \psi^{x^d}(x^{d+1}). \qquad (4.5)$$

Note that we omitted the plan-step index and left only the depth index for presentation clarity.

Using $\alpha_w^j, \beta_x^j, \gamma_w^j$, and δ_x^j, and summing over all possible j's, we can calculate the expected utility (Eq. (4.6)) for the two cases in which a move from w_n to x_m is possible:

$$E(X_i|W_k) = P(X_i|W_k) \times U(X_i|W_k)$$

$$= \sum_{j=n-1}^{1} [(\alpha_w^j \cdot \beta_x^j) \times (\gamma_w^j + \delta_x^j) \times \mathrm{Eq}(x^j, w^j)] \qquad (4.6)$$

$$+ \sum_{j=n-1}^{1} [\alpha_w^j \cdot a_{w,x}^j \cdot \beta_x^j] \times (\gamma_w^j + e_{w,x}^j + \delta_x^j).$$

The first term covers the first case (transition via interruption to a common parent). Let $\mathrm{Eq}(x^j, w^j)$ return 1 if $x^j = w^j$ and 0 otherwise. The summation over j accumulates the probability, multiplying the utility of all ways of interrupting a plan w^n, climbing up from w^n to the common parent $x^j = w^j$, and following decompositions down to x^m.

The second term covers the second case, where a sequential transition is taken. $a_{w,x}^j$ is the probability of taking a sequential edge from w^j to x^j, given that such an edge exists ($a_{w,x}^j > 0$) and that the observed agent is done in w_j. To calculate the expected utility, we first multiply the probability of climbing up to a plan step that has a sequential transition to a parent of x^m, then we multiply in the probability of taking the transition; after that we multiply in the probability of climbing down again to x^m. Then, we multiply in the utility summation along this path.

A naive algorithm for computing the expected costs of hypotheses at time t can be expensive to run. It would go over all leaves of the paths in $t - 1$ and for each traverse the plan library until getting to all leaves of the paths we got in timestamp t. The worst-case complexity of this process is $O(N^2 T)$, where N is the plan library size and T is the number of observations.

In Avrahami-Zilberbrand [2] we presented a set of efficient algorithms that calculate the expected utilities of hypotheses (Eq. (4.1)) in worst-case runtime complexity $O(NDT)$, where D is the depth of the plan library (N, T are as before). The reader is referred to Avrahami-Zilberbrand [2] for details.

4.4 Experiments to Detect Anomalous and Suspicious Behavior

This section evaluates the system that was described in Section 4.3 in realistic problems of recognizing both types of adversarial plans: anomalous and suspicious behaviors. We discuss recognition of anomalous behavior in Section 4.4.1. In Section 4.4.2, we turn to the use of UPR for recognizing suspicious behavior.

4.4.1 Detecting Anomalous Behavior

We evaluate the use of SBR for anomalous behavior recognition using real-world data from machine vision trackers, which track movements of people and report on their coordinate positions. We conduct our experiments in the context of a vision-based surveillance application. The plan library contains discretized trajectories that correspond to trajectories known to be valid. We use a specialized learning algorithm, described briefly in The learning algorithm subsection, to construct this plan library.

The Evaluation using CAVIAR data subsection describes in detail the experiments we conducted, along with their results on video clips and data from the CAVIAR project [13]. The AVNET consortium data subsection presents results from datasets gathered as part of our participation in a commercial R&D

consortium (AVNET), which developed technologies for detection of criminal, or otherwise suspicious, objects and suspects.

To evaluate the results of the SBR algorithms, we distinguish between two classes of observed trajectories: anomalous and nonanomalous. The true positives are the anomalous trajectories that were classified correctly. True negatives are, similarly, nonanomalous trajectories that were classified correctly. The false positives are the nonanomalous trajectories that were mistakenly classified as anomalous. The false negatives are the number of anomalous trajectories that were not classified as anomalous.

We use the *precision* and *recall* measures that are widely used in statistical classification. A perfect precision score of 1 means that every anomalous trajectory that was labeled as such was indeed anomalous (but this says nothing about anomalous trajectories that were classified as nonanomalous). A perfect recall score of 1 means that all anomalous trajectories were found (but says nothing about how many nonanomalous trajectories were also classified as anomalous). The reader is referred to [58] for a detailed description.

4.4.1.1 *The learning algorithm*

We use a simple learning algorithm that was developed for the purpose of building plan-recognition libraries based on examples of positive (valid) trajectories only. The learning algorithm is fully described in Avrahami-Zilberbrand [2] and Kaminka et al. [31,32]. We provide a description of its inputs and outputs next, as those are of interest here.

The learning algorithm L receives a *training set* that contains observation sequences, S. Each observation sequence $s \in S$ is one trajectory of an individual target composed of all observations (samples) o_i, where i is an ordering index within s. Each observation o_i is a tuple $\langle x_i, y_i, t_i \rangle$, where x_i, y_i are Cartesian coordinates of points within W and t is a time index.

The learning algorithm divides the work area W using a regular square-based grid. Each observation $\langle x_i, y_i, t_i \rangle$ is assigned a square that contains this point. For each trajectory of an individual target (s) in the *training set*, it creates a sequence of squares that represents that trajectory.

The output of the algorithm is a set K of discretized trajectories, each a sequence of grid cells that are used together as the plan library for the recognition algorithm. Figure 4.3 shows a work area that is divided into nine squares with one trajectory. The output of the algorithm is the sequence of squares that defines that trajectory (at *right* of figure).

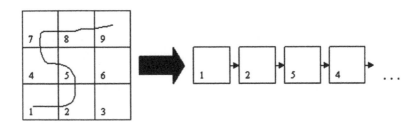

FIGURE 4.3

Result of running naive learning algorithm on one trajectory.

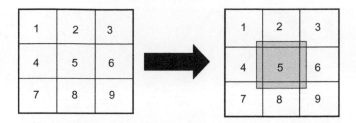

FIGURE 4.4

Demonstrating position overlap. *Note:* This shows the additional position overlap for square number 5.

The grid's square cell size is an input for the learning algorithm. By adjusting the size of the square, we can influence the relaxation of the model. By decreasing the size of the square, the learned library is more strict (i.e., there is less generalization); in contrast, too large a value would cause overgeneralization. Small square size may result in overfitting; a trajectory that is very similar to an already-seen trajectory but differs slightly will not fit the model. By increasing the size of the square, the model is more general and is less sensitive to noise, but trajectories that are not similar might fit.

People are rarely in the exact same position twice. As a result, the training set may contain many sample trajectories that differ by very small distances. Part of the challenge in addressing this lies in adjusting the square size, as described previously. However, often a part of a trajectory would fall just outside the cell that contains the other examples of the same trajectories.

To solve this, the learning algorithm has another input parameter called *position overlap size*. Position overlap prevents overfitting to the training data by expanding each square such that it overlaps with those around it (see Figure 4.4, where the position overlap is shown for square 5). Any point in a trajectory that lies in an overlapping area is defined to match both the overlapping square and the square within which it falls. Thus, for instance, a point within cell 3 in Figure 4.4 (i.e., *top right* corner within the darkened overlapping area of cell 5) would match cell 3 and 5, as well as 6 and 2 (since these cells also have their own overlapping areas). Essentially, this is analogous to having nonzero observation-emitting probabilities for the same observation from different states in a Hidden Markov Model.

4.4.1.2 *Evaluation using CAVIAR data*

We use two sets of real-world data to evaluate SBR's performance as an anomalous behavior recognizer. Experiments with the first set are described in this section. The second set is described in the next subsection.

The first set of experiments were conducted on video clips and data from the CAVIAR [13] project.[2] The CAVIAR project contains a number of video clips with different scenarios of interest: people walking alone, standing in one place and browsing, and so on. The videos are 384×288 pixels, 25 frames per second. Figure 4.5 shows a typical frame. Originally, the CAVIAR data were gathered to allow comparative evaluations of machine-vision tracking systems. To do this, the maintainers of the CAVIAR dataset determined the ground truth positions of subjects, in pixel coordinates, by hand labeling the images.

---

[2]EC-funded CAVIAR project/IST 2001 37540, can be found at http://homepages.inf.ed.ac.uk/rbf/CAVIAR/.

FIGURE 4.5

A typical frame of image sequence in the CAVIAR project.

We use the ground-truth data to simulate the output of realistic trackers at different levels of accuracy. To do this, each ground-truth position of a subject, in pixel coordinates, is converted by homography (a geometric transformation commonly used in machine vision) to a position in the 2D plane on which the subjects move (in centimeters). Then we add noise with normal distributions to simulate tracking errors. Higher variance simulates less accurate trackers, and low variance simulates more accurate trackers. In the experiments reported on in the following, we use a standard deviation of 11 cm diagonal (8 cm vertical and horizontal). The choice of noise model and parameters is based on information about state-of-the-art trackers (e.g., see McCall and Trivedi [46]).

To create a large set of data for the experiments, representing different tracking instances (i.e., the tracking results from many different video clips), we simulated multiple trajectories of different scenarios and trained the learning system on them to construct a plan library. This plan library was then used with different trajectories to test the ability of the algorithms to detect abnormal behavior.

In the first experiment, we tested simple abnormal behavior. We simulated three kinds of trajectories:

1. *Curved path A*. Taken from the first set in CAVIAR, titled *One person walking straight line and return*. In this video, a subject is shown walking along a path and then turning back. We took the first part, up to the turn back, as the basis for normal behavior in this trajectory.
2. *U-turn*. As in 1. but then including the movement back.
3. *Curved path B*. Taken from the CAVIAR set, titled *One person walking straight*, which is similar to 1. but curves differently toward the end. We use this to evaluate the system's ability to detect abnormal behavior (e.g., as compared to *Curved path A*).

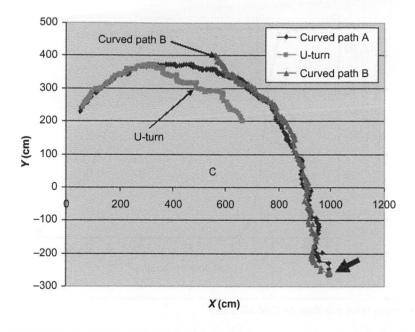

FIGURE 4.6

Three trajectories. Legal path (curved path A), suspicious path (curved path B), and return path (U-turn) from CAVIAR data. The *thick arrow* points at the starting point.

Figure 4.6 shows the three trajectories. The *arrow* shows the starting position of the trajectories. The endpoints lie at the other end (movement right to left).

We created 100 simulated trajectories of each type, for a total of 300 trajectories. We trained a model on 100 noisy trajectories from *Curved path A*, using the learning system described in The learning algorithm section. In this experiment, we fixed the grid cell size to 55 cm, and we vary the plan library relaxation parameter (called *position overlap size*). The cell size was chosen such that it covered the largest distance between two consecutive points in the training set trajectories.

Figure 4.7 shows the true positives versus false positives. The X-axis is the plan library relaxation, and the Y-axis is the number of trajectories (subjects). We can see that the system starts stabilizing in a plan library relaxation of 11 (number of false positives is 0), and after a plan library relaxation of 15, the system is too relaxed; the number of abnormal trajectories *not* detected slowly increases.

Figure 4.8 shows the precision and recall of the system. The X-axis is the plan library relaxation, and the Y-axis is the number of trajectories (subjects). The precision increases until a perfect score of 1 from relaxation 11. The recall starts with a perfect score of 1 and decreases slowly from relaxation 16. As in Figure 4.7, for values of plan library relaxation of 11 through 15, we get a perfect precision and a perfect recall of 1. Despite the optimistic picture that these results portray, it is important to remember that the results ignore the time for detection. However, in practice, the time for detection matters.

Figure 4.9 shows the time for detecting the abnormal behavior with standard deviation bars. The X-axis measures the plan library relaxation parameter range, and the Y-axis measures the time (in

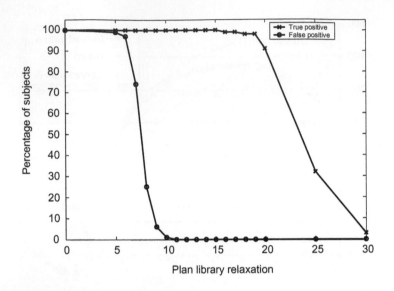

FIGURE 4.7

True positives versus false positives on CAVIAR data.

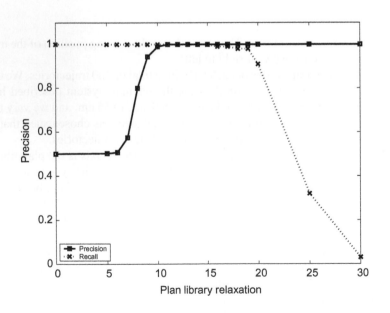

FIGURE 4.8

Precision and recall on CAVIAR data.

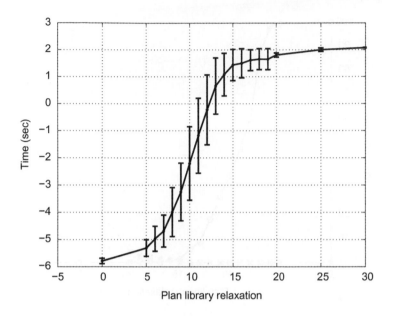

FIGURE 4.9

Time for detection of a suspicious path on CAVIAR data.

seconds) before passes until the detection of abnormal behavior. In this figure, we can see that before a relaxation of 12 cm, the time for detection is negative; this is because we detect too early (i.e., before the abnormal behavior takes place). Two seconds is the maximum of the graph, since this is the time when the scene was over; therefore detecting at 2 s is too late.

Figure 4.10 shows the trade-off between detecting too late and detecting too early as a function of plan library relaxation, where too early is before the split and too late is the end of the abnormal path. The X-axis is the plan library relaxation, and the Y-axis is the percentage of subjects detected too early or too late. We can see that a relaxation of 16 gives the best results of 1% too early and 1% too late. After a relaxation of 16, the percentage of trajectories that we detect too late slowly increases.

The recognition algorithm also is capable of detecting anomalous behavior in direction, not only in position. The following experiment demonstrates this capability; here, we evaluate the use of the system in identifying the U-turn trajectories in the dataset. We sampled 100 instances of the *U-turn* trajectory with Gaussian noise and checked the time for detection. We trained a model on the same 100 noisy trajectories from *curved path A* that we used in the first experiment.

We first examine the time to detect a U-turn as an abnormal behavior. Figure 4.11 shows the time for detecting abnormal behavior versus the plan library relaxation. The X-axis is the plan library relaxation, and the Y-axis is the time (sec) passed until detecting the U-turn. We can see that until plan library relaxation of about 10, the time for detection is negative, since we detect too early (i.e., before the U-turn behavior takes place), and the standard deviation is high. The maximum detection time is 2.5 s after the turn takes place. Figure 4.12 demonstrates the position on the trajectory 1 s after the turn, 2 s after the turn, and 10 s after the turn.

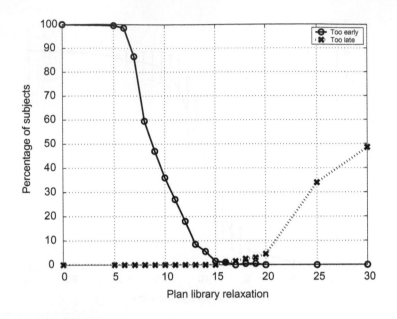

FIGURE 4.10

Too early detection and too late detection on CAVIAR data.

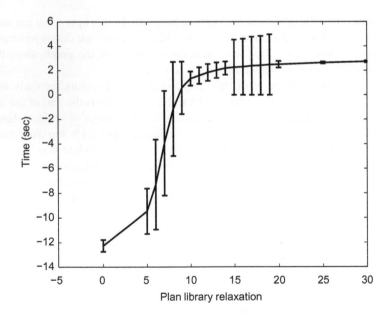

FIGURE 4.11

Time for detecting U-turn on CAVIAR data.

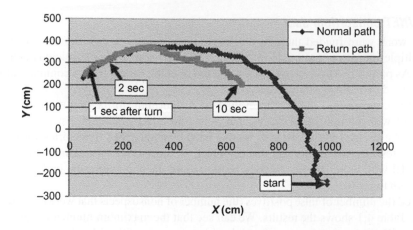

FIGURE 4.12

U-turn on CAVIAR data.

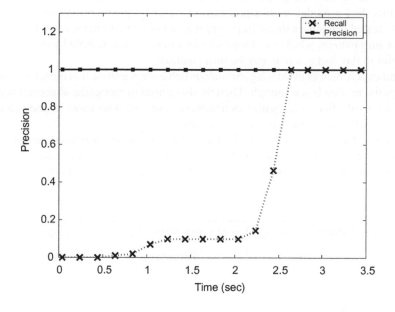

FIGURE 4.13

Precision and recall for U-turn versus time on CAVIAR data.

Figure 4.13 shows the precision and recall for the U-turn experiment as a function of the time. The plan library relaxation was set to 15, which is the best relaxation according to the first experiment. The precision has the perfect score of 1 for a plan relaxation of 15 (every suspect labeled as a suspect was indeed a suspect). The recall starts from score 0 and gradually increases, and after about 2.5 s it gets the perfect score of 1 (all suspects were found 2.5 s after the turn).

4.4.1.3 *AVNET consortium data*

Parts of our work were funded through the AVNET consortium, a government-funded project that includes multiple industrial and academic partners, for development of suspicious activity-detection capabilities. As part of this project, we were given the tracking results from a commercial vision-based tracker developed by consortium partners.

We used the consortium's datasets to evaluate our algorithm. In the first experiment, we got 164 trajectories, all with normal behavior. We ran a 10-fold cross-validation test on the dataset to test performance. We divided the 10 datasets so that each contained 148 trajectories for training and 16 trajectories for test (except the last test that contained 20 trajectories for test and 144 for training). We learned a model with its square size fixed to be the size of the maximum step in the data (31), and the *position overlap* to be 10.

We checked the number of false positives (the number of nonsuspects that were mistakenly classified as suspects). Table 4.1 shows the results. We can see that the maximum number of false positives is 1 out of 16 (6.25%). On average, across the trials, the percentage of the false positives is 2.375%.

The next two experiments evaluate the recognition of anomalous behavior using the AVNET dataset. In the first experiment, we were given data that consisted of 18 trajectories (432 single points). We learned from this data a model, with a grid size of 31 and a position overlap of 10, as in the first experiment. We tested it against a single trajectory with a U-turn pattern. Figure 4.14 shows all of the 18 trajectories; the turn pattern, which was found suspicious, is marked in bold by the recognition system. The arrows point to the start position and the turn position.

In the second experiment of evaluating anomalous behavior, we show that detecting abnormal behavior based on spatial motion is not enough. There is also a need to recognize abnormal behavior in time. For instance, we would like to recognize as abnormal someone who stays in one place an excessive amount of time or who moves too slowly or too quickly.

We were given a dataset consisting of 151 trajectories (a total of 4908 single points). In this experiment, we learned on this data a model, with grid size of 31 and position overlap of 10, as in the first experiment. We tested it against a single trajectory of standing in place for a long duration. Figure 4.15

Table 4.1 Percentage of False Positives in AVNET Data

Test Number	Percentage of False Positives
1	0
2	0
3	0
4	0
5	6.25%
6	6.25%
7	0
8	0
9	6.25%
10	5%

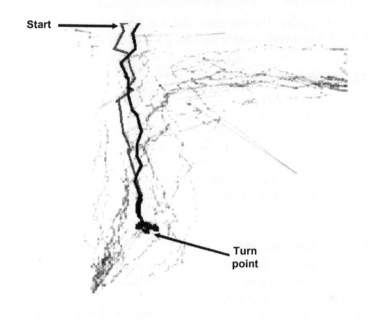

FIGURE 4.14

Detecting U-turn on AVNET data.

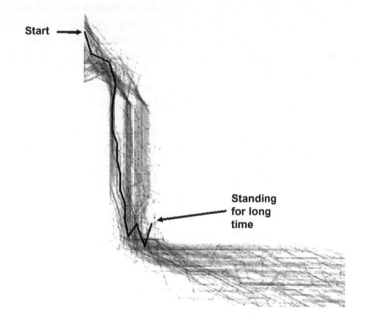

FIGURE 4.15

Detecting standing for long time on AVNET data.

shows all of the 151 trajectories. The trajectory that was detected as anomalous by the recognition system is shown in bold. The arrows point at the start position and the standing position.

4.4.2 Detecting Suspicious Behavior

To demonstrate the capabilities of UPR, and its efficient implementation as described in Section 4.3, we tested the capabilities of our system in three different recognition tasks. The domain for the first task consisted of recognizing passengers who leave articles unattended, as in the previous example. In the second task, we show how our algorithms can catch a dangerous driver who cuts between two lanes repeatedly. The last experiment's intent is to show how previous work, which has used costs heuristically [56], can now be recast in a principled manner. All of these examples show that we should not ignore observer biases, since the most probable hypothesis sometimes masks hypotheses that are important for the observer.

4.4.2.1 Leaving unattended articles

It is important to track a person who leaves her articles unattended in the airport. It is difficult, if not impossible, to catch this behavior using only probabilistically ranked hypotheses. We examine the instantaneous recognition of costly hypotheses.

We demonstrate the process using the plan library shown earlier in Figure 4.2. This plan library is used to track simulated passengers in an airport who walk about carrying articles, which they may put down and pick up again. The recognizer's task is to detect passengers who put something down and then continue to walk without it. Note that the task is difficult because the plan steps are hidden (e.g., we see a passenger bending but cannot decide whether she picks something up, puts something down, or neither); we cannot decide whether a person has an article when walking away.

For the purposes of a short example, suppose that in time $t = 2$ (see Figure 4.2), the SBR had returned that the two plan steps marked *walk* match the observations (*walkN* means walking with no article, *walkW* signifies walking with an article), in time $t = 3$ the two *stop* plan steps match (*stopN* and *stopW*), and in time $t = 4$ the plan steps *pickN* and *putW* match (e.g., we saw that the observed agent was bending).

The probability in $t = 4$ will be $P(putW|stopW) = 0.5 \times 0.2 = 0.1$ (the probability of *stopW* in previous timestamp is 0.5, then following sequential link to *putW*), and in the same way $P(pickN|stopN) = 0.5 \times 0.3 = 0.15$. Normalizing the probabilities for the current time $t = 4$, $P(putW|stopW) = 0.4$ and $P(pickN|stopN) = 0.6$. The expected utility in time $t = 4$ is $U(putW|stopW) = P(putW|stopW) \times E(putW|stopW) = 0.4 \times 10 = 4$. The expected utility of *pickN* is 0. The expected costs, rather than likelihoods, raise suspicions of a passenger putting down an article (perhaps not picking it up).

Let us examine a more detailed example. We generated the following observations based on the plan library shown in Figure 4.2: Suppose that in timestamps $t = \{1 - 5\}$ the passenger walks in an airport, but we cannot tell whether she has a dangerous article in her possession. In timestamps $t = \{6 - 7\}$ she stops, then at time $t = \{8\}$ we see her bending but cannot tell whether it is to put down or to pick up something. In timestamps $t = \{10 - 12\}$, she walks again.

Figure 4.16 shows the results from the recognition process for these observations. The X-axis measures the sequence of observations in time. The probability of different leaves (corresponding

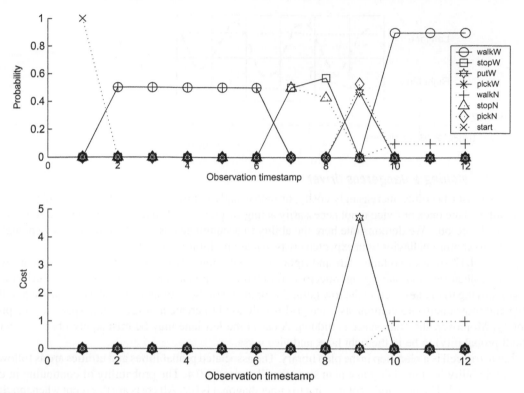

FIGURE 4.16

Leaving unattended articles: probabilities and costs.

to hypotheses) is shown on the *Y*-axis in the upper graph; expected costs are shown in the lower graph. In both, the top-ranking hypothesis (after each observation) is the one with a value on the *Y*-axis that is maximal for the observation.

In the probabilistic version (upper graph), we can see that the probabilities, in time $t = \{1-5\}$, are 0.5 since we have two possible hypotheses of walking, with or without an article (*walkW* and *walkN*). Later when the person stops, there are again two hypotheses, *stopW* and *stopN*. Then, in $t = \{7\}$ two plan steps match the observations: *pickW* and *putN*, where the prior probability of *pickN* is greater than *putN* (after all, most passengers do not leave items unattended). As a result, the most likely hypothesis for the remainder of the sequence is that the passenger is currently walking with her article in hand, *walkW*.

In the lower graph we can see a plot of the hypotheses, ranked by expected cost. At time $t = 8$ when the agent picks or puts something, the cost is high (equal to 5); then in timestamp $t = \{9 - 12\}$, the top-ranking hypothesis is *walkN*, signifying that the passenger might have left an article unattended. Note that the prior probabilities on the behavior of the passenger have not changed. What is different here is the importance (cost) we attribute to observed actions.

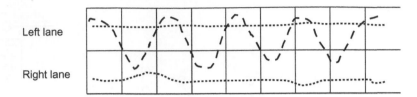

FIGURE 4.17

Simulated trajectories for drivers.

4.4.2.2 *Catching a dangerous driver*

Some behavior becomes increasingly costly, or increasingly gainful, if repeated. For example, a driver switching a lane once or twice is not necessarily acting suspiciously. But a driver zigzagging across two lanes is dangerous. We demonstrate here the ability to accumulate costs of the most costly hypotheses in order to capture behavior with expected costs that are prohibitive *over time*.

Figure 4.17 shows two lanes, left and right, in a continuous area divided by a grid. There are two straight trajectories and one zigzag trajectory from left to right lane. From each position, the driver can begin moving to the next cell in the row (straight) or to one of the diagonal cells. We emphasize that the area and movements are continuous—the grid is only used to create a discrete state space for the plan library. Moreover, the state space is hidden: A car in the left lane may be mistakenly observed (with small probability) to be in the right lane, and vice versa.

Each grid cell is a plan step in the plan library. The associated probabilities and utilities are as follows: The probability for remaining in a plan step (for all nodes) is 0.4. The probability of continuing in the same lane is 0.4. The probability of moving to either diagonal is 0.2. All costs are 0, except when moving diagonally, where the cost is 10. Observations are uncertain; with 0.1 probability, an observation would incorrectly report on the driver being in a given lane.

We generated 100 observation sequences (each of 20 observations) of a driver zigzagging and 100 sequences of a safe driver. The observations were sampled (with noise) from the trajectories (i.e., with observation uncertainty). For each sequence of observations, we accumulated the cost of the most costly hypothesis, along the 20 observations. We now have 100 samples of the accumulated costs for a dangerous driver and 100 samples of the costs for a safe driver. Depending on a chosen threshold value, a safe driver may be declared dangerous (if its accumulated cost is greater than the threshold) and a dangerous driver might be declared safe (if its accumulated cost is smaller than the threshold).

Figure 4.18 shows the confusion error rate as a function of the threshold. The error rate measures the percentage of cases (out of 100) incorrectly identified. The figure shows that a trade-off exists in setting the threshold in order to improve accuracy. Choosing a cost threshold at 50 results in high accuracy in this particular case: All dangerous drivers will be identified as dangerous, and yet 99% of safe drivers will be correctly identified as safe.

4.4.2.3 *Air-combat environment*

Tambe and Rosenbloom [56] used an example of agents in a simulated air-combat environment to demonstrate the RESC plan-recognition algorithm. RESC heuristically prefers a single worst-case hypothesis, since an opponent is likely to engage in the most harmful maneuver in an hostile environment.

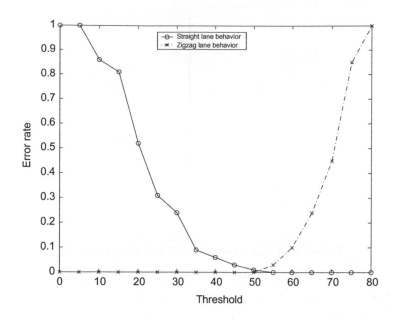

FIGURE 4.18

Confusion error rates for different thresholds for dangerous and safe drivers.

The authors [56] showed this heuristic in action in simulated air combat, where the turning actions of the opponent could be interpreted as either leading to it running away or to its shooting a missile.

RESC prefers the hypothesis that the opponent is shooting. However, unlike UPR, RESC will *always* prefer this hypothesis, regardless of its likelihood, and this has proved problematic [56]. Moreover, given several worst-case hypotheses, RESC will arbitrarily choose a single hypothesis to commit to, again regardless of its likelihood. Additional heuristics were therefore devised to control RESC's worst-case strategy [56].

We generalize this example to show UPR subsumes RESC's heuristic in a principled manner. For shooting a missile (which has infinite cost) versus running away, we consider hypotheses of *invading airspace* versus *runaway*, where invading the observer's airspace is costly but not fatal. Figure 4.19 shows models of two types of opponents: an aggressive one (*left* subfigure) who is more likely to shoot (0.8 a priori probability) than to run away (0.2), and a cowardly opponent (*right* subfigure) who is more likely to run away.

Note that these models are structurally the same; the assigned probabilities reflect the a priori preferences of the different opponent types. Thus, an observation matching both hypotheses will simply lead to both of them being possible, with different likelihoods. The maximum posterior hypothesis in the aggressive case will be that the opponent is trying to invade our airspace. In the cowardly case, it would be that the opponent is running away. RESC's heuristic would lead it to always select the aggressive case, regardless of the likelihood.

In contrast, UPR incorporates the biases of an *observing* pilot much more cleanly. Because it takes the likelihood of hypotheses into account in computing the expected cost, it can ignore sufficiently

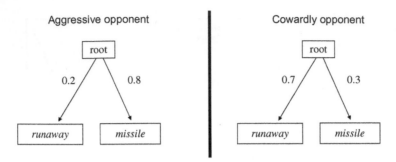

FIGURE 4.19

Air-combat environment: two types of opponents.

Table 4.2 Three Cases of Utilities for Figure 4.19

	Runaway	Missile
Case A	0	10
Case B	−10	10
Case C	10	10

Table 4.3 Aggressive Opponent: Result Utilities for Figure 4.19

	Runaway	Missile
Probabilistic	0.2	0.8
Cost A	0	8
Cost B	−2	8
Cost C	2	8

improbable (but still possible) worst-case hypotheses in a principled manner. Moreover, UPR also allows modeling optimistic observers, who prefer best-case hypotheses.

Table 4.2 presents three cost models. In the first case, the *runaway* plan step will get 0 cost and *invade* a high cost (10). This is an observer who is worried that his airspace is being invaded but not gaining anything from scaring the opponent away. In the second case, the *runaway* plan step will get negative cost (i.e., a gain for the observer). In the third case, the costs are the same. Tables 4.3 and 4.4 show the recognition results. The first row In Tables 4.3 and 4.4 shows the results of following only the probabilistic reasoning in each model. The next three rows show the hypothesis costs for each hypothesis in each of the three cases in Table 4.2.

Table 4.4 Cowardly Opponent: Result Utilities for Figure 4.19

	Runaway	Missile
Probabilistic	0.3	**0.7**
Cost A	0	3
Cost B	−7	3
Cost C	7	3

In the cases of the aggressive opponent, the most costly, or the most probable hypothesis, is the *invade* hypothesis. However, in the cowardly opponent case, the answer depends on the utility model. In cases A and B, where we gave a high cost for *missile*, the most probable hypothesis stays *runaway* but the costly hypothesis is *missile*. In the third case, C, since we gave neutral costs (same for the two plan steps), we got a result that is the same as in the probability model, meaning *runaway*. The conclusion is that the probabilistic model is not enough in case we want to incorporate biases of the observer, in this case that the *missile* plan step is harmful for the observer.

This generalization of the original example in Tambe and Rosenbloom [56] demonstrates that the heuristic worst-case preference of RESC is subsumed by the principled use of decision theoretic reasoning in our algorithms. In addition, the complexity analysis in earlier sections shows that such reasoning does not necessarily entail significant computational costs. RESC's runtime complexity is linear in the size of plan library; UPR's is polynomial.

4.5 Future Directions and Final Remarks

In this chapter, we concentrated on efficient hybrid adversarial plan-recognition algorithms (Section 4.3) and their contribution to the domain of detecting anomalous and suspicious behavior (Section 4.4). The two main contributions of this chapter are as follows:

- First, we presented an anomalous behavior recognition model using the Symbolic Behavior Recognizer (SBR) that is capable of answering the plan library membership query very efficiently [3,4]. Here, the plan library represents normal behavior; any activity that does not match the plan library is flagged as anomalous. We demonstrated its use in two sets of experiments with trajectories created by machine-vision systems.
- Second, we presented a suspicious behavior-recognition model using utility-based plan recognition (UPR) [2,5]. This is a general model of plan recognition that allows the observer to incorporate her own biases and preferences—in the form of a utility function—into the plan-recognition process. Here, the plan library explicitly represents suspicious behavior; any activity that matches the model will be assumed to be suspicious. We demonstrate the capabilities of the suspicious behavior-recognition model in three different domains and also its principled generalization of previous (heuristic) adversarial plan-recognition work [56].

The hybrid system presented is an instantiation of a more general approach to keyhole adversarial plan recognition, combining two approaches: one detecting anomalous behavior and the other detecting suspicious behavior. This approach leaves open many challenges, including:

- Formally defining multiagent plan recognition (MAPR) queries in adversarial settings, and exploring methods for anomalous and suspicious plan recognition in multiagent settings.
- Following up on Kaluža et al.[53], continuing to explore methods for UPR for suspicious plan recognition, which maintain computational tractability but with greater expressiveness.
- Most plan-recognition literature—and this chapter is no different—ignores *intended recognition*, where the adversary knows it is being observed and acts accordingly (for a recent exception see Lisy et al. [39]). In adversarial settings, assuming that the adversary knows it is being observed can cause a computational blow-up; this is because even when an another agent appears to not be suspicious, the system must necessarily assume it is only acting as such because it is being observed. Thus, pruning hypotheses is necessarily difficult.

Acknowledgments

We thank the anonymous reviewers and this book's editors for their very valuable and detailed comments on early drafts of this chapter. This research was carried out with partial support from the Israeli Ministry of Commerce's AVNET Consortium and the Israel Science Foundation, Grant #1511/12. As always, thanks to K. Ushi.

References

[1] Adams JA. Human management of a hierarchical system for the control of multiple mobile robots. PhD thesis, University of Pennsylvania; 1995.
[2] Avrahami-Zilberbrand D. Efficient hybrid algorithms for plan recognition and detection of suspicious and anomalous behavior. PhD thesis, Bar Ilan University; 2009.
[3] Avrahami-Zilberbrand D, Kaminka GA. Fast and complete symbolic plan recognition. In: Proceedings of the International Joint Conference on Artificial Intelligence; 2005. p. 653–8.
[4] Avrahami-Zilberbrand D, Kaminka GA. Fast and complete symbolic plan recognition. In: IJCAI Workshop on Modeling Other Agents from Observations; 2005.
[5] Avrahami-Zilberbrand D, Kaminka GA. Incorporating observer biases in keyhole plan recognition (efficiently!). In: Proceedings of 22nd National Conference on Artificial Intelligence; 2007. p. 944–9.
[6] Baker C, Tenenbaum J. Modeling human plan recognition using Bayesian theory of mind. In: Sukthankar G, Goldman RP, Geib C, Pynadath DV, Bui HH, editors. Plan, activity, and intent recognition. Waltham, MA: Morgan Kaufmann Publishers; 2014. p. 177–206.
[7] Blaylock N, Allen J. Fast hierarchical goal schema recognition. In: Proceedings of the 21st National Conference on Artificial Intelligence; 2006. p. 796–801.
[8] Boyen X, Koller D. Tractable inference for complex stochastic processes. In: Proceedings of the 14th Annual Conference on Uncertainty in AI; 1998. p. 33–42.
[9] Brand M, Oliver N, Pentland A. Coupled hidden Markov models for complex action recognition. In: Proceedings of the 1997 Conference on Computer Vision and Pattern Recognition; 1997. p. 994.
[10] Bui H. A general model for online probabilistic plan recognition. In: Proceedings of the International Joint Conference on Artificial Intelligence; 2003.

[11] Bui H, Venkatesh S, West G. Policy recognition in the abstract hidden Markov models. J Art Intell Res 2002;17:451–99.

[12] Bui HH, Phung D, Venkatesh S, Phan H. The hidden permutation model and location-based activity recognition. In: Proceedings of 23rd National Conference on Artificial Intelligence; 2008.

[13] EC-funded CAVIAR project/IST 2001-37540, available at: <http://homepages.inf.ed.ac.uk/rbf/CAVIAR/>.

[14] Cooper GF. The computational complexity of probabilistic inference using Bayesian belief networks (research note). Art Intell 1990;42(2–3):393–405.

[15] Cupillard F, Avanzi Alberto, Bremond F, Thonnat M. Video understanding for Metro surveillance. In: Proceedings of the IEEE ICNSC 2004 Special Session on Intelligent Transportation Systems; 2004. p. 186–91.

[16] Doyle RJ. Determining the loci of anomalies using minimal causal models. In: Proceedings of the International Joint Conference on Artificial Intelligence; 1995. p. 1821–7.

[17] Duong TV, Bui HH, Phung DQ, Venkatesh S. Activity recognition and abnormality detection with the switching hidden semi-Markov models. In: IEEE International Conference on Computer Vision and Pattern Recognition; 2005. p. 838–45.

[18] Fine S, Singer Y, Tishby N. The hierarchical hidden Markov model: analysis and applications. Mach Learn 1998;32(1):41–62.

[19] Geib C. Delaying commitment in plan recognition using combinatory categorial grammars. In: International Joint Conference on Artificial Intelligence; 2009. p. 1702–7.

[20] Geib C, Goldman R. Recognizing plans with loops represented in a lexicalized grammar. In: Proceedings of the 25th AAAI Conference on Artificial Intelligence; 2011. p. 958–63.

[21] Geib C, Steedman M. On natural language processing and plan recognition. In: International Joint Conference on Artificial Intelligence; 2007. p. 1612–7.

[22] Geib CW. Assessing the complexity of plan recognition. In: Proceedings of the 19th National Conference on Artificial Intelligence; 2004. p. 507–12.

[23] Geib CW, Goldman RP. Plan recognition in intrusion detection systems. In: DARPA Information Survivability Conference and Exposition; 2001. p. 329–42.

[24] Geib CW, Harp SA. Empirical analysis of a probabilistic task tracking algorithm. In: AAMAS Workshop on Modeling Other Agents from Observations; 2004.

[25] Ghahramani Z, Jordan MI. Factorial hidden Markov models. In: Touretzky DS, Mozer MC, Hasselmo ME, editors. Proceedings of the Conference Advances in Neural Information Processing Systems; 1995. p. 472–8.

[26] Hilary B, Shaogang G. Advanced visual surveillance using Bayesian networks. In: International Conference on Computer Vision; 1995. p. 111–23.

[27] Hongeng S, Brémond F, Nevatia R. Bayesian framework for video surveillance application. Proceedings of the 15th International Conference on Pattern Recognition; 2000. p. 164–70.

[28] Hu DH, Yang Q. CIGAR: concurrent and interleaving goal and activity recognition. In: Proceedings of 23rd National Conference on Artificial Intelligence; 2008. p. 1363–8.

[29] Jarvis P, Lunt T, Myers K. Identifying terrorist activity with AI plan recognition technology. In: Proceedings of the Sixth Innovative Applications of Artificial Intelligence Conference; 2004. p. 858–63.

[30] Kaminka GA. Detecting disagreements in large-scale multi-agent teams. J Autonom Agents Mul-Agent Sys 2009;18(3):501–25.

[31] Kaminka GA, Merdler E, Avrahami D. Advanced unsupervised spatial learning algorithm for the AVNET37 consortium: final report (in hebrew). Technical Report MAVERICK 2006/01, Bar Ilan University, Computer Science Department, MAVERICK Group; 2006.

[32] Kaminka GA, Merdler E, Avrahami D. Advanced unsupervised spatial learning algorithm for the AVNET37 consortium: interim report (in Hebrew). Technical Report MAVERICK 2006/01, Bar Ilan University, Computer Science Department, MAVERICK Group; 2006.

[33] Kaminka GA, Pynadath DV, Tambe M. Monitoring teams by overhearing: a multi-agent plan recognition approach. J Art Intell Res 2002;17:83–135.

[34] Kaminka GA, Tambe M. Robust multi-agent teams via socially-attentive monitoring. J Art Intell Res 2000;12:105–47.

[35] Khalastchi E, Kalech M, Kaminka GA, Lin R. Online anomaly detection in unmanned vehicles. In: Proceedings of the 10th International Joint Conference on Autonomous Agents and Multi-Agent Systems; 2011. p. 115–22.

[36] Kjærulff U. A computational scheme for reasoning in dynamic probabilistic networks. In: Proceedings of the Conference on Uncertainty in Artificial Intelligence; 1992. p. 121–9.

[37] Lane T, Brodley CE. Temporal sequence learning and data reduction for anomaly detection. ACM Trans Inform Sys Sec 1999;2(3):295–331.

[38] Liao L, Fox D, Kautz HA. Learning and inferring transportation routines. In: Proceedings of the 19th National Conference on Artificial Intelligence; 2004. p. 348–53.

[39] Lisy V, Pibil R, Stiborek J, Bosansky B, Pechoucek M. Game-theoretic approach to adversarial plan recognition. In: de Raedt L, Bessiere C, Dubois D, Doherty P, Frasconi P, Heintz F, et al., editors. 20th European Conference on Artificial Intelligence. Frontiers in artificial intelligence and applications, vol. 242. IOS Press; 2012. p. 546–51.

[40] Mahajan D, Kwatra N, Jain S, Kalra P, Banerjee S. A framework for activity recognition and detection of unusual activities. In: ICVGIP; 2004. p. 15–21.

[41] Mao W, Gratch J. Decision-theoretic approaches to plan recognition. In USC/ICT Technical Report; 2004.

[42] Mao W, Gratch J. A utility-based approach to intention recognition. In: Proceedings of the AAMAS Workshop on Modeling Other Agents from Observations; 2004.

[43] Marhasev E, Hadad M, Kaminka GA, Feintuch U. The use of hidden semi-Markov models in clinical diagnosis maze tasks. Intell Data Anal 2009;13(6):943–67.

[44] Nguyen N, Phung D, Venkatesh S, Bui H. Learning and detecting activities from movement trajectories using the hierarchical hidden Markov model. In: IEEE International Conference on Computer Vision and Pattern Recognition; 2005. p. 955–60.

[45] Niu W, Long J, Han D, Wang Y-F. Human activity detection and recognition for video surveillance. In: Proceedings of the IEEE Multimedia and Expo Conference; 2004. p. 719–22.

[46] McCall Joel C, Trivedi Mohan M. Performance evaluation of a vision based lane tracker designed for driver assistance systems. IEEE intellient vehicles symposium 2005:153–8.

[47] Oliver N, Horvitz E, Garg A. Layered representations for human activity recognition. In: Proceedings of the Fourth IEEE International Conference on Multimodal Interfaces; 2002. p. 831–43.

[48] Pynadath DV, Marsella S. Psychsim: modeling theory of mind with decision-theoretic agents. In: Proceedings of the International Joint Conference on Artificial Intelligence; 2005. p. 1181–6.

[49] Pynadath DV, Marsella S. Minimal mental models. In: Proceedings of the 22nd National Conference on Artificial Intelligence; 2007. p. 1038–44.

[50] Pynadath DV, Wellman MP. Generalized queries on probabilistic context-free grammars. IEEE Trans Pattern Anal Mach Intell 1998;20(1):65–77.

[51] Pynadath DV, Wellman MP. Probabilistic state-dependent grammars for plan recognition. In: Proceedings of the 16th Annual Conference on Uncertainty in Artificial Intelligence; 2000. p. 507–14.

[52] Starner T, Pentland A. Real-time American Sign Language recognition from video using hidden Markov models. In: Proceedings of the International Symposium on Computer Vision (SCV); 1995. p. 265–70.

[53] Kaluža B, Kaminka GA, Tambe M. Detection of suspicious behavior from a sparse set of multiagent interactions. In: Proceedings of the 11th International Joint Conference on Autonomous Agents and Multi-Agent Systems; 2012.

[54] Sukthankar G, Sycara K. A cost minimization approach to human behavior recognition. In: Proceedings of the Fourth International Joint Conference on Autonomous Agents and Multi-Agent Systems; 2005. p. 1067–74.

[55] Suzic R. A generic model of tactical plan recognition for threat assessment. In: Dasarathy BV, editor. Proceedings of SPIE Multisensor, vol. 5813; 2005. p. 105–16.

[56] Tambe M, Rosenbloom PS. RESC: an approach to agent tracking in a real-time, dynamic environment. In: Proceedings of the International Joint Conference on Artificial Intelligence; 1995. p. 103–11.

[57] Vail DV, Veloso MM, Lafferty JD. Conditional random fields for activity recognition. In: Proceedings of the Sixth International Joint Conference on Autonomous Agents and Multi-Agent Systems; 2007. p. 1331–8.

[58] Wikipedia entry: Precision and recall; 2009, available at: <http://en.wikipedia.org/w/index.php?title= Precision_and_recall> [accessed 23 March 2009].

[59] Wu G, Wu Y, Jiao L, Wang Y-F, Chang EY. Multi-camera spatio-temporal fusion and biased sequence-data learning for security surveillance. In: Proceedings of the 11th ACM International Conference on Multimedia; 2003. p. 528–38.

[60] Xiang T, Gong S. Video behavior profiling for anomaly detection. IEEE Trans Pattern Anal Mach Intell 2008;30(5):893–908.

[61] Yamato J, Ohya J, Ishii K. Recognizing human action in time-sequential images using hidden Markov model. In: Proceedings of IEEE Computer Society Conference on Computer Vision and Pattern Recognition; 1992. p. 379–85.

[62] Yin J, Yang Q, Pan JJ. Sensor-based abnormal human-activity detection. IEEE Trans Knowledge Data Eng 2008;20(8):1082–90.

Activity Discovery and Recognition

Stream Sequence Mining for Human Activity Discovery

Parisa Rashidi
University of Florida, Gainesville, FL, USA

5.1 Introduction

Remarkable recent advancements in sensor technology and sensor networking are leading us into a world of ubiquitous computing. Many researchers are now working on smart environments that can respond to the needs of the residents in a context-aware manner by using sensor technology. Along with data mining and machine learning techniques [12]. For example, smart homes have proven to be of great value for monitoring physical and cognitive health through analysis of daily activities [54]. Besides health monitoring and assisted living, smart homes can be quite useful for providing more comfort, security, and automation for the residents. Some of the efforts for realizing the vision of smart homes have been demonstrated in the real-world testbeds such as CASAS [51], MavHome [14], DOMUS [7], iDorm [17], House_n [61], and Aware Home [1].

A smart environment typically contains many highly interactive devices, as well as different types of sensors. The data collected from these sensors is used by various data mining and machine learning techniques to discover residents' activity patterns and then to recognize such patterns later [28,31]. Recognizing activities allows the smart environment to respond in a context-aware way to the residents' needs [21,50,70,67].

Activity recognition is one of the most important components of many pervasive computing systems. Here, we define an *activity* as a sequence of steps performed by a human actor to achieve a certain goal. Each step should be measurable by a sensor state or a combination of sensor states. It should be noted that besides activities, we can recognize other types of concepts such as *situations* or *goals*. We define a *situation* as a snapshot of states at a specific time point in a physical or conceptual environment.

Unlike activities, situations try to model high-level interpretation of phenomena in an environment. An example of an activity would be pouring hot water into a cup, but making tea would constitute a situation, according to these definitions. Rather than trying to figure out the purpose of a user from sensor data, it is also possible to define *goals* for users (e.g., each goal is the objective realized by performing an activity). The boundaries between those concepts are often blurred in practice. This chapter focuses on the problem of activity recognition.

Data in a smart home are collected from different types of *ambient sensors*. For example, a Passive Infrared Sensor (PIR) can be used for detecting motion, and a contact switch sensor can be used for detecting the open/close status of doors and cabinets. Some of the most widely used smart home sensors are summarized in Table 5.1. Most of the ambient sensors, such as the PIR sensor or the contact switch sensor, provide a signal in the form of on/off activation states, as depicted in Figure 5.1.

Table 5.1 Ambient Sensors Used in Smart Environments

Sensor	Measurement	Data format
PIR[a]	Motion	Categorical
Active infrared	Motion/identification	Categorical
RFID[b]	Object information	Categorical
Pressure	Surface pressure	Numeric
Smart tile	Floor pressure	Numeric
Magnetic switch	Open/close	Categorical
Ultrasonic	Motion	Numeric
Camera	Activity	Image
Microphone	Activity	Sound

[a] *Passive Infrared Motion Sensor*
[b] *Radio Frequency Identification*

Note: The PIR sensor is one of the most popular sensors used by many researchers for detecting motion. Other options, such as ultrasonic sensors, might prove more accurate for detecting motion; however, they are typically more expensive.

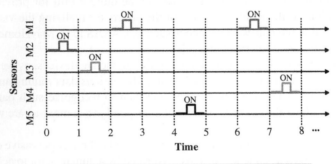

Observed data: M2 – M3 – M1 – M5 – M1 – M4 ...

FIGURE 5.1

A stream of sensor events. *Note:* Each one of the M1 through M5 symbols correspond to one sensor. For example, sensor M1 is activated during the third and seventh time intervals, and M5 is activated during the fifth time interval.

Before using sensor data in machine learning and data mining tasks, data are usually preprocessed into a higher-level format that is easier to interpret. For example, the signal levels are converted into categorical values, such as on/off binary values, in the case of PIR sensors. Table 5.2 shows an example format typically used in data mining and machine learning tasks.[1]

---

[1] Based on data collected from Center for Advanced Studies in Adaptive System (CASAS) testbeds [54].

Table 5.2 Example Sensor Data

Timestamp	Sensor ID	Label
7/17/2009 09:52:25	M3	Personal Hygiene
7/17/2009 09:56:55	M5	Personal Hygiene
7/17/2009 14:12:20	M4	None

As soon as data are collected from various sensors, they are passed to an *activity recognition* component. In supervised activity recognition methods, the algorithm is provided with the activity label of sensor event sequences. These labels are hand-done by a human annotator during the training phase of the system. Some researchers also have taken advantage of the crowdsourcing mechanism for labeling [72,59]. In Table 5.2, the first and the second sensor events are labeled *Personal Hygiene* activity. The ultimate goal is to predict the label of the future unseen activity patterns by generalizing based on the examples provided.

During the past decade, many supervised activity recognition algorithms have been proposed [8,61,65,13,31,47,57,39]. In real-world settings, using supervised methods is not practical because it requires labeled data for training. Manual labeling of human activity data is time consuming, laborious, and error-prone. Besides, one usually needs to deploy invasive devices in the environment during the data-collection phase to obtain reliable annotations. Another option is to ask the residents to report their activities. Asking residents to report their activities puts the burden on them, and in the case of the elderly with memory problems (e.g., dementia), it would be out the of question.

To address the annotation problem, recently a few unsupervised methods have been proposed for mining human activity data [23,44,51,58,54]. However, none of these mining approaches take into account the streaming nature of data or the possibility that patterns might change over time. In a real-world smart environment, we have to deal with a potentially infinite and unbounded flow of data. In addition, the discovered activity patterns can change from time to time. Mining the stream of data over time not only allows us to find new emerging patterns in the data, but it also allows us to detect changes in the patterns, which can be beneficial for many applications. For example, a caregiver can look at the pattern trends and spot any suspicious changes immediately.

Based on these insights, we extend a well-known stream mining method [20] in order to discover activity pattern sequences over time. Our activity discovery method allows us to find discontinuous varied-order patterns in streaming, nontransactional sensor data over time. The details of the model will be discussed in Section 5.3.[2]

5.2 **Related Work**

The following subsections provide a literature overview of several subjects. First we discuss the general activity recognition problem. Then, we describe various sequence mining and stream mining methods. Finally, we review activity discovery methods based on data mining approaches in more detail.

---

[2]A preliminary version of this method appeared in the 2010 ICDM Proceedings; see Rashid and Cook [53].

5.2.1 Activity Recognition

In recent years, many approaches have been proposed for activity recognition in different settings such as methods for recognizing nurses' activities in hospitals [57], recognizing quality inspection activities during car production [41], monitoring elderly adults' activities [13], studying athletic performance [4,40], gait analysis in diseases (e.g., Parkinson's [56,45,33], emergency response [34], and monitoring unattended patients [15]. Activity discovery and recognition approaches not only differ according to the deployed environment but also with respect to the type of activity data collected, the model used for learning the activity patterns, and the method used for annotating the sample data. The following subsections explain each aspect in more detail.

5.2.1.1 *Activity data*

Activity data in smart environments can be captured using different media depending on the target environment and also target activities. Activity data at home can be collected with ambient sensors (e.g., infrared motion) to track the motion of residents around home [51]. Additional ambient sensors, such as temperature sensors, pressure sensors, contact switch sensors, water sensors, and smart power-meters, can provide other types of context information. For recognizing residents' interaction with key objects, some researchers have used object sensors (e.g., RFID tags) that can be placed on key items [61,47].

Another type of sensor used for recognizing activities are wearable sensors such as accelerometers [39,69]. More recent research uses mobile phones as carryable sensors [74]. The advantage of wearable and mobile sensors is their ability to capture activity data in both indoor and outdoor settings. Their main disadvantage is their obtrusiveness because the user is required to carry the sensor all the time.

Besides ambient sensors and wearable sensors, surveillance cameras and other types of image-capturing devices (e.g., thermographic cameras) have been used for activity recognition [60]. However, individuals are usually reluctant to use cameras for capturing activity data due to privacy concerns [29]. Another limitation for using cameras is that activity recognition methods based on video-processing techniques can be computationally expensive.

5.2.1.2 *Activity models*

The number of machine learning models that have been used for activity recognition varies almost as widely as the types of sensor data that have been obtained. Naive Bayes classifiers have been used with promising results for activity recognition [8,61,65]. Other methods, such as decision trees, Markov models, dynamic Bayes networks, and conditional random fields, have also been successfully employed [13,31,47,57,39]. There also have been a number of works in the activity discovery area using unsupervised methods—to be discussed in Section 5.2.4.

5.2.1.3 *Activity annotation*

Another aspect of activity recognition is the method for annotating the sample training data. Most of the researchers have published results of experiments in which the participants are required to manually note each activity they perform at the time they perform it [31,61,47]. In other cases, the experimenters told the participants which specific activities should be performed, so the correct activity labels were identified before sensor data were even collected [13,23,39]. In some cases, the experimenter manually inspects the raw sensor data in order to annotate it with a corresponding activity label [67]. Researchers have also used methods, such as experience sampling [61], where subjects carry a mobile device to use for self-reporting.

5.2.2 Sequence Mining

Sequence mining has already proven to be quite beneficial in many domains such as marketing analysis or Web click-stream analysis [19]. A sequence s is defined as a set of ordered items denoted by $\langle s_1, s_2, \cdots, s_n \rangle$. In activity recognition problems, the sequence is typically ordered using timestamps. The goal of sequence mining is to discover interesting patterns in data with respect to some subjective or objective measure of how interesting it is. Typically, this task involves discovering frequent sequential patterns with respect to a frequency support measure.

The task of discovering all the *frequent* sequences is not a trivial one. In fact, it can be quite challenging due to the combinatorial and exponential search space [19]. Over the past decade, a number of sequence mining methods have been proposed that handle the exponential search by using various heuristics. The first sequence mining algorithm was called GSP [3], which was based on the a priori approach for mining frequent itemsets [2]. GSP makes several passes over the database to count the support of each sequence and to generate candidates. Then, it prunes the sequences with a support count below the minimum support.

Many other algorithms have been proposed to extend the GSP algorithm. One example is the PSP algorithm, which uses a prefix-based tree to represent candidate patterns [38]. FREESPAN [26] and PREFIXSPAN [43] are among the first algorithms to consider a projection method for mining sequential patterns, by recursively projecting sequence databases into smaller projected databases. SPADE is another algorithm that needs only three passes over the database to discover sequential patterns [71]. SPAM was the first algorithm to use a vertical bitmap representation of a database [5]. Some other algorithms focus on discovering specific types of frequent patterns. For example, BIDE is an efficient algorithm for mining frequent closed sequences without candidate maintenance [66]; there are also methods for constraint-based sequential pattern mining [44].

5.2.3 Stream Mining

Compared to the classic problem of mining sequential patterns from a static database, mining sequential patterns over datastreams is far more challenging. In a datastream, new elements are generated continuously and no blocking operation can be performed on the data. Despite such challenges, with the rapid emergence of new application domains over the past few years, the stream mining problem has been studied in a wide range of application domains. A few such application domains include network traffic analysis, fraud detection, Web click-stream mining, power consumption measurements, and trend learning [11,19].

For finding patterns in a datastream, using approximation based on a relaxed support threshold is a key concept [9,36]. The first stream mining approach was based on using a landmark model and calculating the count of the patterns from the start of the stream [36]. Later, methods were proposed for incorporating the discovered patterns into a prefix tree [18]. More recent approaches have introduced methods for managing the history of items over time [20,62]. The main idea is that one usually is more interested in details of recent changes, while older changes are preferred in coarser granularity over the long term.

The preceding methods discover frequent *itemsets* in streaming data. There are also several other methods for finding *sequential* patterns over datastreams, including the SPEED algorithm [49],

(a)

Transaction ID	Items
1	{Milk, egg, bread}
2	{Bread, beer}
3	{Soap, milk, egg }

(b)

FIGURE 5.2

Boundary problem in transaction data versus sensor data. Each symbol in (b) corresponds to one sensor event, and a sequence of such sensor events might represent an activity. However, it would be difficult to estimate the boundaries of activities. (a) In transaction data, there is a clear boundary between consecutive transactions; (b) The sensor data have no boundaries separating different activities or episodes from each other.

approximate sequential pattern mining in Web usage [37], a data cubing algorithm [25], and mining multidimensional sequential patterns over datastreams [48].

All of the sequential stream mining approaches consider data to be in a transactional format. However, the input datastream in a smart environment is a continuous flow of unbounded data. The sensor data has no boundaries separating different activities or episodes from each other, and it is just a continuous stream of sensor events over time. Figure 5.2 depicts the difference between transaction data and sensor data. As can be seen in Figure 5.2(a), in transaction data, each single transaction is associated with a set of items and is identified by a transaction ID, making it clearly separated from the next transaction. The sensor data has no boundaries separating different activities or episodes from each other, and it is just a continuous stream of sensor events over time. This property makes it a unique, challenging stream mining problem. To deal with this, we use a compression-based approach to group together the cooccurring events into varied-order discontinuous activity patterns. The details will be explained in Section 5.3.

5.2.4 Data Mining for Activity Discovery

Unlike supervised methods, unsupervised methods do not require any labeled sensor data. Instead, they try to automatically find interesting activity patterns in unlabeled sensor data. A number of different unsupervised approaches have been proposed in the past for discovering activity patterns.

One popular approach is to extend current data mining techniques in the context of activity recognition tasks. These methods look for regularly occurring interactions, and discover significant patterns with respect to measures such as frequency or periodicity. For example, Heierman et al. [28] discovered subsequences, or episodes, that are closely related in time. These episodes may be partially ordered and are evaluated based on information theory principles.

Gu et al. [23] use a frequency measure to discover emerging patterns and use feature relevance to segment the boundary of any two adjacent activities. More recently, they have extended their model to recognize sequential, interleaved, and concurrent activities using changes between classes of data [22]. Previously, we also have proposed a method for simultaneous discovery of frequent and periodic patterns using the minimum description length principle [51].

Another approach to activity discovery relies on time series techniques, especially in the context of activity data collected from wearable sensors such as accelerometers. For example, Vahdatpour et al. [64] analyze multidimensional time series data by locating multidimensional motifs in time series. Similarly

Zhao [73] converts times series activity data into a set of motifs for each data dimension, where each motif represents an approximately repeated symbolic subsequence. These motifs serve as the basis for a large candidate set of features, which later is used for training a conditional random field model.

The problem of unsupervised activity recognition also has been explored using vision community to discover activities from a set of images or from videos. For example, Mahajan et al. [35] used a finite state machine network in an unsupervised mode that learns the usual patterns of activities in a scene over long periods of time. During the recognition phase, the usual activities are accepted as normal, and deviant activity patterns are flagged as abnormal.

Other unsupervised options for activity discovery include techniques such as mixture models and dimensionality reduction. Schiele et al. [58] detect activity structure using low-dimensional Eigenspaces, and Barger et al. [6] use mixture models to develop a probabilistic model of behavioral patterns. Huynh et al. [30] also use a combination of discriminative and generative methods to achieve reduced supervision for activity recognition. As described in another chapter in this book, Nguyen et al. [63] use hierarchical Dirichlet processes (HDP) as a Bayesian nonparametric method to infer atomic activity patterns without predefining the number of latent patterns. Their work focuses on using a nonparametric method to infer the latent patterns, while we explore the problem of inferring discontinuous and dynamic patterns from a datastream.

It is also possible to combine background knowledge with unsupervised activity discovery methods to aid the discovery process. For example, Dimitrov et al. [16] use background domain knowledge about user activities and the environment in combination with probabilistic reasoning methods to build a possible explanation of the observed stream of sensor events. Also, a number of methods mine activity definitions from the Web by treating it as a large repository of background knowledge.

Perkowitz et al. [46] mine definitions of activities in an unsupervised manner from the Web. Similarly, Wyatt et al. [68] view activity data as a set of natural language terms. Activity models are considered as mappings from such terms to activity names and are extracted from text corpora (e.g., the Web). Palmes et al. [42] also mine the Web to extract the most relevant objects according to their normalized usage frequency. They develop an algorithm for activity recognition and two algorithms for activity segmentation with linear time complexities.

Unfortunately, none of these activity discovery methods address the problem of streaming data, nor the fact that the patterns might change over time. We explain in Section 5.3 how such challenges can be addressed.

5.3 Proposed Model

Due to the special requirements of our application domain, we cannot directly use the tilted-time window model [20]. First of all, the tilted-time approach, as well as most other similar stream mining methods, was designed to find sequences or itemsets in transaction-based streams [10,37,49]. The data obtained in a smart environment are a continuous stream of unbounded sensor events with no boundary between episodes or activities (refer to Figure 5.2). Second, as discussed in [54], because of the complex and erratic nature of human activity, we need to consider an activity pattern as a sequence of events. In such a sequence, the patterns might be interrupted by irrelevant events (called a discontinuous pattern). Also the order of events in the sequence might change from occurrence to occurrence (called a varied-order pattern).

Finding variations of a general pattern and determining their relative importance can be beneficial in many applications. For example, a study by Hayes et al. found that variation in the overall activity performance at home was correlated with mild cognitive impairment [27]. This highlights the fact that it is important to recognize and monitor all activities and the variations that occur regularly in an individual's daily environment.

Third, we also need to address the problem of varying frequencies for activities performed in different regions of a home. A person might spend the majority of his or her time in the living room during the day and only go to the bedroom for sleeping. We still need to discover the sleep pattern though its sensor support count might be substantially less than that found by the sensors in the living room.

Our previously introduced sequence mining methods, DVSM [54] and COM [52], do not take into account the streaming nature of data, nor the possibility that the patterns might change over time. In addition, an activity recognition system based on supervised methods, once trained, will not be able to adapt to any changes in the underlying stream. In a real-world situation, we have to deal with a potentially infinite and unbounded flow of data. The discovered activity patterns can also change over time, and algorithms need to detect and respond to such changes. Figure 5.3 better depicts the comparison of supervised, sequence mining, and stream mining approaches. Note that *activity discovery* and *activity*

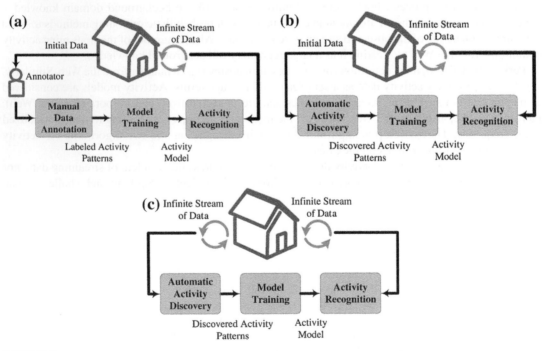

FIGURE 5.3

Comparing different approaches to activity recognition. (a) Supervised; (b) Sequence mining; (c) Stream mining.

annotation in sequence mining and supervised approaches are one-time events, while in the stream mining approach, the patterns are discovered and updated in a continuous manner.

To address these issues, we extended the tilted-time window approach [20] to discover activity patterns over time. An extended method, called StreamCOM, allows us to find discontinuous varied-order patterns in *streaming* sensor data *over time*. To the best of our knowledge, StreamCOM represents the first reported stream mining method for discovering human activity patterns in sensor data over time [53].

5.3.1 Tilted-Time Window Model

The tilted-time window model allows for managing the history of items over time [20]. It plays an important role in our stream mining model, therefore we explain it in more detail. This approach finds the frequent itemsets using a set of tilted-time windows, such that the frequency of the item is kept at a finer level for recent time frames and at a coarser level for older time frames. Such an approach can be quite useful for human activity pattern discovery. For example, a caregiver is usually interested in the recent changes of the patient at a finer level, and in the older patterns (e.g., from three months ago) at a coarser level.

Figure 5.4 shows an example of a natural tilted-time window, where the frequency of the most recent item is kept with an initial precision granularity of an hour, in another level of granularity in the last 24 h, and then again at another level in the last 30 days. As new data items arrive over time, the history of items will be shifted back in the tilted-time window.

It should be noted that the frequency of a pattern cannot be deterministically determined in the case of streaming data because data is observed only up to a certain point; consequently, the item frequencies reflect the computed frequencies up to that point. This also means that we will have computed frequency (observed frequency computed up to this point) in addition to the actual frequency (which we are unable to observe). Therefore, a pattern that is currently frequent might later become infrequent. Similarly, an infrequent pattern might later turn out to be frequent. Therefore, a relaxed threshold is used to find patterns.

Definition 5.1. Let the minimum support be denoted by σ, and the maximum support error be denoted by ϵ. An itemset I is said to be frequent if its support is no less than σ. If support of I is less than σ, but no less than $\sigma - \epsilon$, it is subfrequent; otherwise, it is considered to be infrequent.

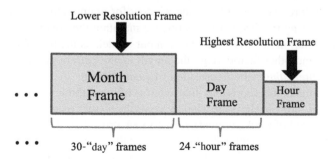

FIGURE 5.4

Natural tilted-time window.

The support of an itemset in this definition is defined as the proportion of transactions (events) in the observed dataset that contain the itemset. This definition defines subfrequent patterns (i.e., those patterns of which we are not yet certain about their frequency). Using the approximation approach for frequencies allows for the subfrequent patterns to become frequent later, while discarding infrequent patterns.

To reduce the number of frequency records in the tilted-time windows, the old frequency records of an itemset I are pruned. Let $\bar{f}_j(I)$ denote the computed frequency of I in time unit j, and let N_j denote the number of transactions received within time unit j. Also let τ refer to the most recent time point. For some m, where $1 \leq m \leq \tau$, the frequency records $\bar{f}_1(I), ..., \bar{f}_m(I)$ are pruned if both Equation 5.1 and Equation 5.2 hold.

$$\exists n \leq \tau, \ \forall i, 1 \leq i \leq n, \ \bar{f}_i(I) < \sigma N_i \tag{5.1}$$

$$\forall l, 1 \leq l \leq m \leq n, \ \sum_{j=1}^{l} \bar{f}_j(I) < (\sigma - \epsilon) \sum_{j=1}^{l} N_i \tag{5.2}$$

Equation 5.1 finds a point n in the stream such that before that point the computed frequency of the itemset I is always less than the minimum frequency required. Equation 5.2 finds a point m, where $1 \leq m \leq n$, such that before that point the sum of the computed support of I is always less than the relaxed minimum support threshold. In this case the frequency records of I from 1 to m are considered unpromising and are pruned. This type of pruning is referred to as *tail pruning* [20]. In our model, we extend the preceding defections and pruning techniques for discontinuous, varied order patterns.

5.3.2 Tilted-Time Window Model in Current System

The input data in our model are an unbounded stream of sensor events, each in the form of $e = \langle s, t \rangle$, where s refers to a sensor ID and t refers to the timestamp when sensor s has been activated. We define an activity instance as a sequence of n sensor events $\langle e_1, e_2, \ldots, e_n \rangle$. Note that in our notation an activity instance is considered as a sequence of sensor events, not a set of unordered events. We are assuming that the sensors capture binary status change events; that is, a sensor can be either on or off.

We assume that the input data are broken into batches $B_{a_1}^{b_1} \ldots B_{a_n}^{b_n}$, where each $B_{a_i}^{b_i}$ is associated with a time period $[a_i \ldots b_i]$, and the most recent batch is denoted by $B_{a_\tau}^{b_\tau}$ or for short as B_τ. Each batch $B_{a_i}^{b_i}$ contains a number of sensor events, denoted by $|B_{a_i}^{b_i}|$.

As we mentioned before, we use a tilted-time window for maintaining the history of patterns over time. Instead of maintaining the frequency records, we maintain the *compression* records, which will be explained in more detail in Section 5.3.3. Also, in our model, as the frequency of an item is not the single deciding factor and other factors (e.g., the length of the pattern and its continuity) also play a role. We use the term *interesting* pattern instead of *frequent* pattern.

The original tilted-time model represents data in terms of logarithmic windows [20]. Our tilted-time window is depicted in Figure 5.5. Here, the window keeps the history records of a pattern during the past four weeks at the finer level of week granularity. History records older than four weeks are only kept at the month granularity. In our application domain, we use a different tilted-time window format that is a more natural representation versus a logarithmic tilted-time window. For example, it would be it easier for a nurse or caregiver to interpret the pattern trend using a natural representation. Second, as we don't expect the activity patterns to change substantially over a very short period of time, we omit the day and

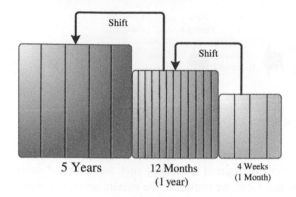

FIGURE 5.5

Our tilted-time window.

hour information for the sake of a more efficient representation. For example, in the case of dementia patients, it takes weeks and/or months to see some changes develop in their daily activity patterns.

Using such a schema, we only need to maintain 15 compression records instead of $365 \times 24 \times 4$ records in a normal natural tilted-time window. Note that we chose such a representation in this study for the reasons mentioned before. However, if necessary, one can adopt other tilted-window models (e.g., the logarithmic windows) as the choice of tilted-time window has no effect on the model except for efficiency.

To update the tilted-time window, whenever a new batch of data arrives, we replace the compression values at the finest level of time granularity and shift back to the next level of finest time granularity. During shifting, we check whether the intermediate window is full. If so, the window is shifted back even more; otherwise, the shifting stops.

5.3.3 Mining Activity Patterns

Our goal is to develop a method that can automatically discover resident activity patterns over time from streaming sensor data. This is so even if the patterns are somehow discontinuous or have different event orders across their instances. Both situations happen quite frequently when dealing with human activity data. For example, consider the *meal preparation* activity. Most people will not perform this activity in exactly the same way each time, rather, some of the steps or the order of the steps might be changed (variations). In addition, the activity might be interrupted by irrelevant events such as answering the phone (discontinuous). Our DVSM and COM methods find such patterns in a static dataset [54]. For example, the pattern $\langle a, b \rangle$ can be discovered from instances $\{b, x, c, a\}$, $\{a, b, q\}$, and $\{a, u, b\}$, despite the fact that the events are discontinuous and have varied orders.

We discover sequential patterns from current data batch B_τ using an extended version of COM that is able to handle streaming data. After finding patterns in current data batch B_τ, we update the tilted-time windows and prune any pattern that seems to be unpromising. Figure 5.6 depicts the steps of our activity pattern mining process better.

To find patterns in data, first a reduced batch B_τ^r is created from the current data batch B_τ. The reduced batch contains only frequent and subfrequent sensor events, which will be used for constructing longer

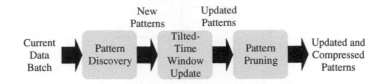

FIGURE 5.6

The activity pattern mining steps.

patterns. A minimum support is required to identify such frequent and subfrequent events. COM only identifies the frequent events. Here, we introduce the maximum sensor support error ϵ_s to allow for the subfrequent patterns to be discovered also. In addition, automatically derive multiple minimum support values corresponding to different regions of the space.

In mining real-life activity patterns, the frequency of sensor events can vary across different regions of the home or another space. If the differences in sensor event frequencies across different regions of the space are not taken into account, the patterns that occur in less frequently used areas of the space might be ignored. For example, if the resident spends most of his or her time in the living room during the day and only goes to the bedroom for sleeping, then the sensors will be triggered more frequently in the living room than in the bedroom. Therefore, when looking for frequent patterns, the sensor events in the bedroom might be ignored and consequently the sleep pattern might not be discovered. The same problem happens with different types of sensors, as usually the motion sensors are triggered much more frequently than another type of sensor such as cabinet sensors. This problem is known as the *rare item* problem in market-basket analysis and is usually addressed by providing multiple minimum support values [32].

We automatically derive multiple minimum sensor support values across space and over time. To do this, we identify different regions of the space using location tags l, corresponding to the functional areas such as bedroom, bathroom, and so on. Also different types of sensors might exhibit varying frequencies. In our experiments, we categorized the sensors into motion sensors and interaction-based sensors. The motion sensors are those sensors tracking the motion of a person around a home (e.g., infrared motion sensors). Interaction-based sensors, which we call *key sensors*, are the non-motion-tracking sensors (e.g., cabinet or RFID tags on items). Based on observing and analyzing sensor frequencies in multiple smart homes, we found that a motion sensor has a higher false positive rate than a key sensor in some other regions. Thus, we derive separate minimum sensor supports for different sensor categories.

For the current data batch B_τ, we compute the minimum regional support for different categories of sensors as in Equation 5.3. Here l refers to a specific location, c refers to the sensor's category, and $\mathcal{S}_c$ refers to the set of sensors in category c. Also $f_T(s)$ refers to the frequency of a sensor s over a time period T.

$$\sigma_T^c(l) = 1/\sum_{s \in \mathcal{S}_c^l}^{|\mathcal{S}_c^l|} f_T(s) \quad s.t. \quad \mathcal{S}_c^l = \{s | s \in l \wedge s \in \mathcal{S}_c\} \tag{5.3}$$

As an illustrative example, Figure 5.7 shows the computed minimum regional sensor support values for the smart home used in our experiments.

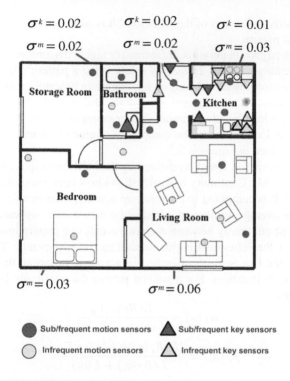

$\sigma^k = 0.02$ $\sigma^k = 0.02$ $\sigma^k = 0.01$

$\sigma^m = 0.02$ $\sigma^m = 0.02$ $\sigma^m = 0.03$

$\sigma^m = 0.03$ $\sigma^m = 0.06$

● Sub/frequent motion sensors   ▲ Sub/frequent key sensors

○ Infrequent motion sensors   △ Infrequent key sensors

FIGURE 5.7

The frequent/subfrequent sensors are selected based on the minimum regional support, instead of a global support.

Using the minimum regional sensor frequencies, frequent and subfrequent sensors are defined as follows.

Definition 5.2. Let s be a sensor of category c located in location l. The frequency of s over a time period T, denoted by $f_T(s)$, is the number of times in time period T in which s occurs. The support of s in location l and over time period T is $f_T(S)$ divided by the total number of sensor events of the same category occurring in L during T. Let ϵ_s be the maximum sensor support error. Sensor s is said to be frequent if its support is no less than $\sigma_T^c(l)$. It is subfrequent if its support is less than $\sigma_T^c(l)$, but no less than $\sigma_T^c(l) - \epsilon_s$; otherwise, it is infrequent.

Only the sensor events from the frequent and subfrequent sensors are added to the reduced batch B_τ^r, which is then used for constructing longer sequences. We use a pattern growth method that grows a pattern by its prefix and suffix [51]. To account for the variations in the patterns, the concept of a general pattern is introduced. A *general pattern* is a set of all the variations that have a similar structure in terms of comprising sensor events but have different event orders [54].

During pattern growth, if an already-discovered variation matches a newly discovered pattern, its frequency and continuity information are updated. If the newly discovered pattern matches the general pattern, but does not exactly match any of the variations, it is added as a new variation. Otherwise, it is considered a new general pattern.

At the end of each pattern growth iteration, infrequent or highly discontinuous patterns and variations are discarded as uninteresting patterns. Instead of solely using a pattern's frequency as a measure of interest, we use a compression objective based on the minimum description length (MDL) [55]. Using a compression objective allows us to take into account the ability of the pattern to compress a dataset with respect to the pattern's length and continuity. The compression value of a general pattern a over a time period T is defined in Equation 5.4. The compression value of a variation a_i of a general pattern over a time period T is defined in Equation 5.5.

Here, L refers to the description length as defined by the MDL principle, and Γ refers to continuity as defined in Rashidi et al. [54]. Continuity basically shows how contiguous the component events of a pattern or a variation are. It is computed in a bottom-up manner, such that for the variation continuity is defined in terms of the average number of infrequent sensor events separating each two successive events of the variation. The continuity between each two events of a pattern instance is defined in terms of the average number of the infrequent events separating the two events. The more the separation between the two events, the less is the continuity. For a pattern variation, the continuity is based on the average continuity of its instances. For a general pattern the continuity is defined as the average continuity of its variations.

$$\alpha_T(a) = \frac{L(B_T) * \Gamma_a}{L(a) + L(B_T|a)} \tag{5.4}$$

$$\beta_T(a_i) = \frac{(L(B_T|a) + L(a)) * \Gamma_{a_i}}{L(B_T|a_i) + L(a_i)} \tag{5.5}$$

Variation compression measures the capability of a variation to compress a general pattern compared to the other variations. Compression of a general pattern shows the overall capability of it to compress the dataset with respect to its length and continuity. Based on using the compression values and by using a maximum compression error, we define interesting, subinteresting, and uninteresting patterns and variations.

Definition 5.3. Let the compression of a general pattern a be defined as in Equation 5.4 over a time period T. Also let σ_g and ϵ_g denote the minimum compression and maximum compression error. The general pattern a is said to be interesting if its compression α is no less than σ_g. It is subinteresting if its compression is less than σ_g, but no less than $\sigma_g - \epsilon_g$; otherwise, it is uninteresting.

We also give a similar definition for identifying interesting/subinteresting variations of a pattern. Let the average variation compression of all variations of a general pattern a over a time period T be defined as in Equation 5.6. Here, the number of variations of a general pattern is denoted by n_a.

$$\tilde{\beta}_T(a) = \frac{1}{n_a} * \sum_{i=1}^{n_a} \frac{(L(B_T|a) + L(a)) * \Gamma_{a_i}}{L(B_T|a_i) + L(a_i)} \tag{5.6}$$

Definition 5.4. Let the compression of a variation a_i of a general pattern a be defined as in Equation 5.5 over a time period T. Also let ϵ_v denote the maximum variation compression error. A variation a_i is said to be interesting over a time period T if its compression $\beta_T(a_i)$ is no less than $\tilde{\beta}(a)_T$. It is subinteresting if its compression is less than $\tilde{\beta}(a)_T$, but no less than $\tilde{\beta}(a)_T - \epsilon_v$; otherwise, it is uninteresting.

During each pattern-growth iteration, based on the previous definitions, the uninteresting patterns and variations, that is, those that are either highly discontinuous or infrequent (with respect to their length) are pruned. We also prune redundant nonmaximal general patterns, that is, those patterns that are totally contained in another larger pattern. To only maintain the very relevant variations of a pattern, irrelevant variations of a pattern also are discarded based on using mutual information [24] as in Equation 5.7. It allows us to find core sensors for each general pattern a.

Finding the set of core sensors allows us to prune the irrelevant variations of a pattern that does not contain the core sensors. Here, $P(s, a)$ is the joint probability distribution of a sensor s and general pattern a, while $P(s)$ and $P(a)$ are the marginal probability distributions. A high mutual information value indicates that the sensor is a core sensor.

$$MI(s, a) = P(s, a) * \log \frac{P(s, a)}{P(s)P(a)} \tag{5.7}$$

We continue extending the patterns by prefix and suffix at each iteration until no more interesting patterns are found. A postprocessing step records attributes of the patterns (e.g., event durations and start times). We refer to the pruning process performed during the pattern growth on the current data batch as normal pruning. Note that it is different from the tail-pruning process performed on the tilted-time window to discard the unpromising patterns over time.

In the following subsection we describe how the tilted-time window is updated after discovering patterns of the current data batch.

5.3.4 Updating the Tilted-Time Window

After discovering the patterns in the current data batch as described in the previous subsection, the tilted-time window will be updated; each general pattern is associated with it. The tilted-time window keeps track of the general pattern's history as well as its variations. Whenever a new batch arrives, after discovering its interesting general patterns, we replace the compressions at the finest level of granularity with the recently computed compressions. If a variation of a general pattern is not observed in the current batch, we set its recent compression to 0. If none of the variations of a general pattern are perceived in the current batch, then the general pattern's recent compression is also set to 0.

To reduce the number of maintained records and to remove unpromising general patterns, we use the following tail-pruning mechanisms as an extension of the original tail-pruning method in [20]. Let $\alpha_j(a)$ denote the computed compression of general pattern a in time unit j. Also let τ refer to the most recent time point. For some m, where $1 \leq m \leq \tau$, the compression records $\alpha_1(a), ..., \alpha_m(a)$ are pruned if Equations 5.8 and 5.9 hold.

$$\exists n \leq \tau, \ \forall i, 1 \leq i \leq n, \ \alpha_i(a) < \sigma_g \tag{5.8}$$

$$\forall l, 1 \leq l \leq m \leq n, \ \sum_{j=1}^{l} \alpha_j(a) < l*(\sigma_g - \epsilon_g) \tag{5.9}$$

Equation 5.8 finds a point n in the stream, such that before that point the computed compression of the general pattern a is always less than the minimum compression required. Equation 5.9 computes the time unit m, where $1 \leq m \leq n$, such that before that point the sum of the computed compression of a is always less than the relaxed minimum compression threshold. In this case, the compression records of a from 1 to m are considered unpromising and are pruned.

We define a similar procedure for pruning the variations of a general pattern. We prune a variation a_k if the conditions in Equations 5.10 and 5.11 hold.

$$\exists n \leq \tau, \ \forall i, 1 \leq i \leq n, \ \beta_i(a_k) < \tilde{\beta}_i(a) \tag{5.10}$$

$$\forall l, 1 \leq l \leq m \leq n, \ \sum_{j=1}^{l} \beta_j(a_k) < l*(\tilde{\beta}_l(a) - \epsilon_v) \tag{5.11}$$

Equation 5.10 finds a point in time where the computed compression of a variation is less than the average computed compression of all variations in that time unit. Equation 5.11 computes the time unit m, where $1 \leq m \leq n$, such that before that point the sum of the computed compression of a_i is always less than the relaxed minimum support threshold. In this case, the compression records of a_i from 1 to m are considered unpromising and are pruned.

5.4 Experiments

The performance of the system was evaluated on the data collected from two smart apartments. The layout of the apartments including sensor placement and location tags, as well as the activity diagrams, are shown in Figure 5.8. We refer to the apartments in Figures 5.8a and 5.8b as Apartment 1 and Apartment 2. The apartments were equipped with infrared motion sensors installed on ceilings, infrared area sensors installed on the walls, and switch contact sensors to detect the open/close status of the doors and cabinets. The data were collected during 17 weeks for Apartment 1 and 19 weeks for Apartment 2.

During the data-collection period, the resident of Apartment 2 was away for approximately 20 days, once during day 12 and once during day 17. Also the last week of data collection in both apartments does not include a full cycle. In our experiments, we constrain each batch to contain approximately one week of data. In our experiments, we set the maximum errors ϵ_s, ϵ_g, and ϵ_v to 0.1, as suggested in the literature [20]. Also σ_g was set to 0.75 based on several runs of experiments.

To be able to evaluate the results of our algorithms based on a ground truth, each one of the datasets was annotated with activities of interest. A total of 10 activities were noted for each apartment, including bathing, bed-toilet transition, eating, leave home/enter home, housekeeping, meal preparation (cooking), personal hygiene, sleeping in bed, sleeping not in bed (relaxing), and taking medicine. Note that in our annotated datasets, each sensor event has an activity label as part of it. The activity label also can be "None," if a sensor event does not belong to any of the preceding activities.

To validate the results, we consider each discovered pattern by our system as representing one activity; therefore, all of its sensor events, or at least a high proportion of them, should have homogenous activity labels according to the ground truth annotations. In practice, if a certain percentage of the sensor events (e.g., 90%) have the same activity label l, we can say that our system has recovered the pattern l.

Apartment 1 includes 193,592 sensor events and 3384 annotated activity instances. Apartment 2 includes 132,550 sensor events and 2602 annotated activity instances. Figures 5.9a and 5.9b show the

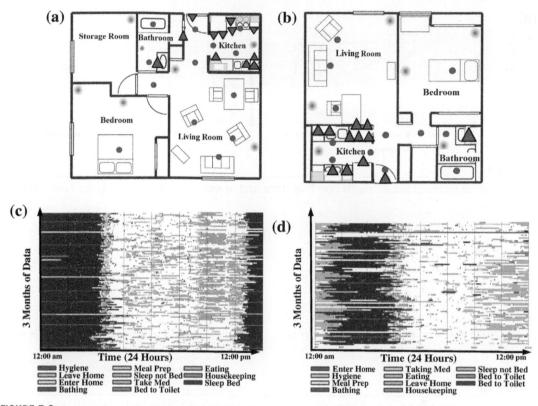

FIGURE 5.8

Sensor map and location tags for each apartment. On the map, circles show motion sensors while triangles show switch contact sensors. (a) Apartment 1 layout; (b) Apartment 2 layout; (c) Apartment 1 activity diagram; (d) Apartment 2 activity diagram.

number of recorded sensor events over time. As we mentioned, the resident of Apartment 2 was not at home during two different time periods; thus, we can see the gaps in Figure 5.9b.

We ran our algorithms on both apartments' datasets. Figures 5.10a and 5.10b show the number of distinct discovered patterns over time based on using a global support (the approach used by DVSM) versus using multiple regional support (the approach used by Stream/COM). The results show that by using multiple regional support, we are able to detect a higher percentage of interesting patterns. Some of the patterns that have not been discovered are indeed quite difficult to spot and in some cases also less frequent. For example, the housekeeping activity happens every 2 to 4 weeks and is not associated with any specific sensor. Also some of the similar patterns are merged together, as they use the same set of sensors (e.g., eating and relaxing activities).

It should be noted that some of the activities are discovered multiple times in the form of different patterns, as the activity might be performed with a different motion trajectory using different sensors.

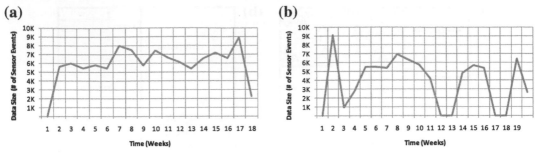

FIGURE 5.9

Total number of recorded sensor events over time (time unit = weeks). (a) Apartment 1; (b) Apartment 2.

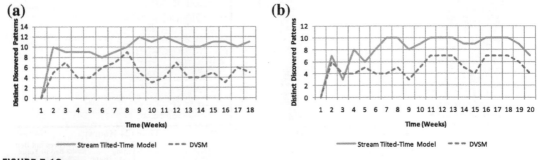

FIGURE 5.10

Total number of distinct discovered patterns over time. (a) Apartment 1 (time unit = weeks); (b) Apartment 2 (time unit = weeks).

One also can see that the number of discovered patterns increases at the beginning and then is adjusted over time depending on the perceived patterns in the data. The number of discovered patterns depends on perceived patterns in the current data batch and previous batches, as well as the compression of patterns in tilted-time window records. Therefore, some of the patterns might disappear and reappear over time, showing how consistently the resident performs those activities.

To reduce the number of discovered patterns over time, our algorithm performs two types of pruning. The first type, normal pruning, prunes patterns and variations while processing the current data batch. The second type, tail pruning, discards unpromising patterns and variations stored in all tilted-time windows. Figures 5.11a and 5.11b show the results of both types of pruning on the first dataset. Figures 5.11d and 5.11e show the results of both types of pruning on the second dataset. Figures 5.11c and 5.11f show the tail-pruning results in the tilted-time window over time. Note that the gaps for Apartment 2 results are due to the 20 days when the resident was away. Also, Figures 5.11b and 5.11e show the declining trend of number of pruned patterns over time, as the straight trend line indicates.

By comparing the results of normal pruning in Figures 5.11a and 5.11d against the number of recorded sensors in Figures 5.9a and 5.9b, one can see that the normal pruning somehow follows the pattern

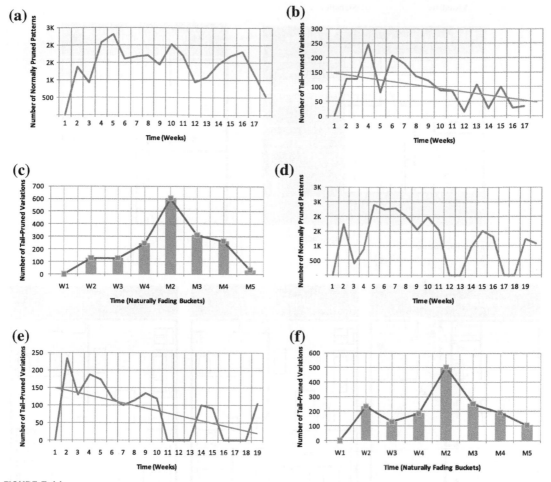

FIGURE 5.11

Total number of tail-pruned variations and normally pruned patterns over time. For the bar charts, W1–W4 refer to weeks 1 through 4, and M2–M5 refer to months 2 through 5. (a) Apartment 1 (time unit = weeks); (b) Apartment 1 (time unit = weeks); (c) Apartment 1 (time unit = tilted-time frame); (d) Apartment 1 (time unit = weeks); (e) Apartment 2 (time unit = weeks); (f) Apartment 2 (time unit = tilted-time frame).

of recorded sensors. If more sensor events were available, more patterns would be obtained and more patterns would be pruned. For the tail-pruning results, depicted in Figures 5.11b, 5.11e, 5.11c, and 5.11f, the number of tail-pruned patterns at first increases in order to discard the many unpromising patterns at the beginning. Then the number of tail-pruned patterns decreases over time as the algorithm stabilizes.

We have developed a visualization software that allows us to visualize the patterns and variations along with their statistics, as depicted in Figure 5.12. Figure 5.12b shows a *taking medication* activity in Apartment 1 that was pruned at the third week due to its low compression. Figure 5.12c shows

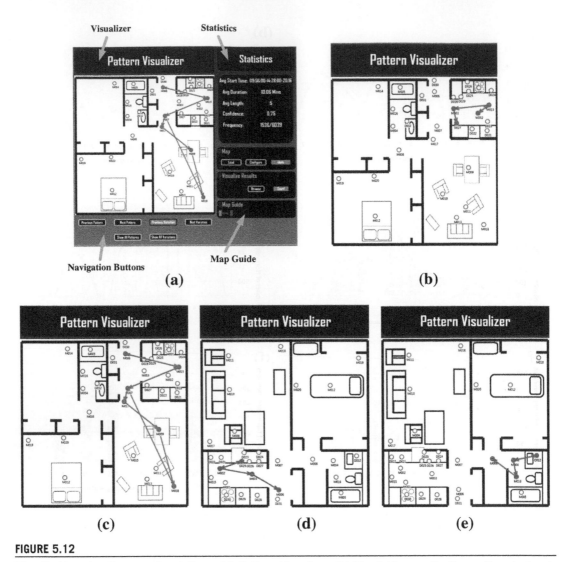

FIGURE 5.12

Visualization of patterns and variations. (a) Pattern Visualizer; (b) The *taking medication* pattern in Apartment 1; (c) Two variations of the *leave home* pattern in Apartment 1; (d) The *meal preparation* pattern in Apartment 2; (e) The *personal hygiene* pattern in Apartment 2.

two variations of the *leave home* activity pattern in Apartment 2. Note that we use color coding to differentiate between different variations if multiple variations are shown simultaneously. Figure 5.12e shows the *meal preparation* pattern in Apartment 2.

To illustrate the changes of a specific pattern over time, we show the results of our algorithm for the *taking medication* activity over time. Figure 5.13a shows the number of discovered variations over time for the *taking medication* activity. Figure 5.13b shows the same results in the tilted-time window

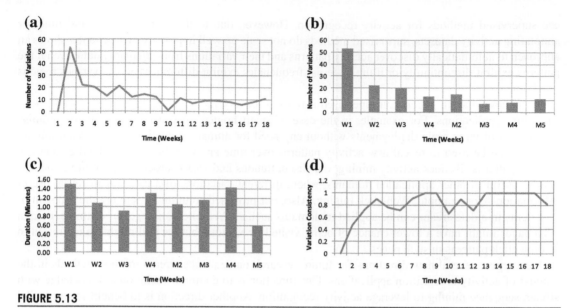

FIGURE 5.13

Number of discovered variations, duration, and consistency for the *taking medication* activity pattern over time. (a) Number of discovered variations (time unit = weeks); (b) Number of discovered variations (time unit = tilted-time frame); (c) Duration (time unit = weeks); (d) Variation consistency (time unit = weeks).

over time. We can clearly see that the number of discovered variations quickly drops due to the tail-pruning process. This shows that despite the fact that we are maintaining time records over time for all variations, many of the uninteresting, unpromising, and irrelevant variations are pruned over time, making our algorithm more efficient in practice.

We also show how the average duration of the *taking medication* pattern changes over time in Figure 5.13c. Presenting such information can be informative to caregivers to detect any anomalous events in the patterns. Figure 5.13d shows the consistency of the *taking medication* variations over time. Similar to the results obtained for the average variation consistency of all patterns, we see that the variation consistency increased and then stabilized quickly.

In summary, the results of our experiments confirm that we can find sequential patterns from a steam of sensor data over time. It also shows that using two types of pruning techniques allows for a large number of unpromising, uninteresting, and irrelevant patterns and variations to be discarded to achieve a more efficient solution that can be used in practice.

5.5 Conclusion

This chapter reviewed the state-of-the-art unsupervised methods for activity recognition. In particular, we described a scalable activity discovery and recognition method for complex large real-world datasets based on sequential data mining and stream data mining methods. Most current approaches use supervised methods for activity recognition. However, due to the required effort and time for annotating activity datasets, supervised methods do not scale up well in practice. This chapter shows an approach to automatically discover activity patterns and their variations from *streaming* data, even if the patterns exhibit discontinuity or if the patterns' frequencies exhibit differences across various regions in a home.

We believe that, in general, unsupervised activity discovery methods can have many implications for future applications. For example, in the case of smart homes, stream mining methods promise automation of large-scale deployments without any need for human annotation. Also, stream mining methods can be used to reveal new activity patterns over time and to help us understand changes in activity patterns. Besides activity mining, our discontinuous and varied-order stream mining method can be useful in other application domains, where different variations of a pattern can reveal useful information—for example, Web-click mining. Also, our proposed solution for solving the problem of rare items in a datastream can be applied to domains such as Web-click mining. For example, certain Web pages might have a lower chance of being visited by visitors, but we still might be interested in finding click patterns in such pages.

We suggest several new directions for future research on sequence stream mining methods in the context of activity recognition applications. One direction is to combine background knowledge with stream sequence mining to leverage activity recognition. Another direction is to benefit from parallel and distributed implementation in order to speed up the algorithms. Finally, we envision that progress in sensor development will allow us to fuse activity knowledge with many other types of information such as health-related data or environmental information. This ultimately will allow us to model our surroundings more accurately in an autonomous manner.

References

[1] Abowd G, Mynatt E. Designing for the human experience in smart environments. In: Cook DJ, Das SK, editors. Smart environments: technology, protocols, and applications. Wiley; 2004. p. 153–74.

[2] Agrawal R, Imieliński T, Swami A. Mining association rules between sets of items in large databases. In: Proceedings of the ACM SIGMOD International Conference on Management of Data; 1993. p. 207–16. Available from: http://dx.doi.org/10.1145/170035.170072.

[3] Agrawal R, Srikant R. Mining sequential patterns. In: ICDE '95: Proceedings of the 11th International Conference on Data Engineering; 1995. p. 3–14.

[4] Ahmadi A, Rowlands D, James D. Investigating the translational and rotational motion of the swing using accelerometers for athlete skill assessment. In: IEEE Conference on Sensors; 2006. p. 980–3.

[5] Ayres J, Flannick J, Gehrke J, Yiu T. Sequential pattern mining using a bitmap representation. In: Proceedings of the Eighth ACM SIGKDD International Conference on Knowledge Discovery and Data Mining; 2002. p. 429–35. Available from: http://dx.doi.org/10.1145/775047.775109.

[6] Barger T, Brown D, Alwan M. Health-status monitoring through analysis of behavioral patterns. IEEE Trans Syst Man Cybern Part A: Syst Hum 2005;35(1):22–7.

[7] Bouchard B, Giroux S, Bouzouane A. A keyhole plan recognition model for Alzheimer patients: first results. Appl Artif Intell 2007;21:623–58.

[8] Brdiczka O, Maisonnasse J, Reignier P. Automatic detection of interaction groups. In: Proceedings of the Seventh International Conference on Multimodal Interfaces; 2005. p. 32–6.

[9] Chang JH, Lee WS. Finding recent frequent itemsets adaptively over online data streams. In: Proceedings of the Ninth ACM SIGKDD International Conference on Knowledge Discovery and Data Mining; 2003. p. 487–92.

[10] Chen G, Wu X, Zhu X. Sequential pattern mining in multiple streams. In: ICDM '05: Proceedings of the Fifth IEEE International Conference on Data Mining; 2005. p. 585–8.

[11] Cheng J, Ke Y, Ng W. A survey on algorithms for mining frequent itemsets over data streams. Knowl Inform Syst 2008;16(1):1–27.

[12] Cook D, Das S. Smart environments: technology, protocols and applications. Wiley series on parallel and distributed computing. Wiley-Interscience; 2004.

[13] Cook D, Schmitter-Edgecombe M. Assessing the quality of activities in a smart environment. Method Inform Med 2009;48(05):480–5.

[14] Cook D, Youngblood M, Heierman EOI, Gopalratnam K, Rao S, Litvin A. Mavhome: an agent-based smart home. In: IEEE International Conference on Pervasive Computing and Communications; 2003. p. 521–4.

[15] Curtis DW, Pino EJ, Bailey JM, Shih EI, Waterman J, Vinterbo SA, et al. Smart: an integrated wireless system for monitoring unattended patients. J Am Med Inform Assoc 2008;15(1):44–53.

[16] Dimitrov T, Pauli J, Naroska E. Unsupervised recognition of ADLs. In: Konstantopoulos S, Perantonis S, Karkaletsis V, Spyropoulos C, Vouros G, editors. Artificial intelligence: theories, models and applications. Lecture notes in computer science, vol. 6040. Springer; 2010. p. 71–80.

[17] Doctor F, Hagras H, Callaghan V. A fuzzy embedded agent-based approach for realizing ambient intelligence in intelligent inhabited environments. IEEE Trans Syst Man Cybern Syst Hum 2005;35(1):55–65.

[18] Fu Li H, Yin Lee S, Kwan Shan M. An efficient algorithm for mining frequent itemsets over the entire history of data streams. In: First International Workshop on Knowledge Discovery in Data Streams; 2004. p. 45–55.

[19] Garofalakis M, Gehrke J, Rastogi R. Querying and mining data streams: you only get one look a tutorial. In: Proceedings of the ACM SIGMOD International Conference on Management of Data; 2002. p. 635.

[20] Giannella C, Han J, Pei J, Yan X, Yu P. Mining frequent patterns in data streams at multiple time granularities. Next Gen Data Min 2003;212:191–212.

[21] Gopalratnam K, Cook DJ. Online sequential prediction via incremental parsing: the active LeZi algorithm. IEEE Intell Syst 2007;22(1):52–8.

[22] Gu T, Wang L, Wu Z, Tao X, Lu J. A pattern mining approach to sensor-based human activity recognition. IEEE Trans Knowl Data Eng 2011:1.

[23] Gu T, Wu Z, Tao X, Pung H, Lu J. Epsicar: an emerging patterns based approach to sequential, interleaved and concurrent activity recognition. In: International Conference on Pervasive Computing and Communication; 2009. p. 1–9.

[24] Guyon I, Elisseeff A. An introduction to variable and feature selection. Mach Learn Res 2003;3:1157–82.

[25] Han J, Chen Y, Dong G, Pei J, Wah BW, Wang J. Stream cube: an architecture for multi-dimensional analysis of data streams. Distrib Parall Dat 2005;18(2):173–97.

[26] Han J, Pei J, Mortazavi-Asl B, Chen Q, Dayal U, Hsu M-C. Freespan: frequent pattern-projected sequential pattern mining. In: Proceedings of the Sixth ACM SIGKDD International Conference on Knowledge Discovery and Data Mining; 2000. p. 355–9. Available from: http://dx.doi.org/10.1145/347090.347167.

[27] Hayes TL, Pavel M, Larimer N, Tsay IA, Nutt J, Adami AG. Distributed healthcare: simultaneous assessment of multiple individuals. IEEE Pervas Comput 2007;6(1):36–43.

[28] Heierman III EO, Cook DJ. Improving home automation by discovering regularly occurring device usage patterns. In: ICDM '03: Proceedings of the Third IEEE International Conference on Data Mining; 2003. p. 537.

[29] Hensel B, Demiris G, Courtney K. Defining obtrusiveness in home telehealth technologies: a conceptual framework. J Am Med Inform Assoc 2006;13(4):428–31.

[30] Huynh T, Schiele B. Towards less supervision in activity recognition from wearable sensors. In: Proceedings of the 10th IEEE International Symposium on Wearable Computers; 2006. p. 3–10.

[31] Liao L, Fox D, Kautz H. Location-based activity recognition using relational Markov networks. In: Proceedings of the International Joint Conference on Artificial Intelligence; 2005. p. 773–8.

[32] Liu B, Hsu W, Ma Y. Mining association rules with multiple minimum supports. In: Proceedings of the Fifth ACM SIGKDD International Conference on Knowledge Discovery and Data Mining; 1999. p. 337–41.

[33] Lorincz K, Chen B-R, Challen GW, Chowdhury AR, Patel S, Bonato P. Mercury: a wearable sensor network platform for high-fidelity motion analysis. In: ACM Conference on Embedded Networked Sensor Systems; 2009. p. 183–96.

[34] Lorincz K, Malan DJ, Fulford-Jones TRF, Nawoj A, Clavel A, Shnayder V, et al. Sensor networks for emergency response: challenges and opportunities. IEEE Pervas Comput 2004;3(4):16–23.

[35] Mahajan D, Kwatra N, Jain S, Kalra P, Banerjee S. A framework for activity recognition and detection of unusual activities. In: Indian Conference on Computer Vision, Graphics and Image Processing; 2004. p. 15–21.

[36] Manku GS, Motwani R. Approximate frequency counts over data streams. In: Proceedings of the 28th International Conference on Very Large Data Bases; 2002. p. 346–57.

[37] Marascu A, Masseglia F. Mining sequential patterns from data streams: a centroid approach. J Intell Inform Syst 2006;27(3):291–307.

[38] Masseglia F, Cathala F, Poncelet P. The PSP approach for mining sequential patterns. In: Proceedings of the Second European Symposium on Principles of Data Mining and Knowledge Discovery; 1998. p. 176–84.

[39] Maurer U, Smailagic A, Siewiorek D, Deisher M. Activity recognition and monitoring using multiple sensors on different body positions. In: International Workshop on Wearable and Implantable Body Sensor Networks; 2006. p. 4–116.

[40] Michahelles F, Schiele B. Sensing and monitoring professional skiers. IEEE Pervas Comput 2005;4(3):40–6.

[41] Ogris G, Stiefmeier T, Lukowicz P, Troster G. Using a complex multi-modal on-body sensor system for activity spotting. In: IEEE International Symposium on Wearable Computers; 2008. p. 55–62.

[42] Palmes P, Pung HK, Gu T, Xue W, Chen S. Object relevance weight pattern mining for activity recognition and segmentation. Pervas Mob Comput 2010;6:43–57. Available from: http://dx.doi.org/10.1016/j.pmcj.2009.10.004.

[43] Pei J, Han J, Mortazavi-Asl B, Pinto H, Chen Q, Dayal U. Prefixspan: mining sequential patterns by prefix-projected growth. In: Proceedings of the 17th International Conference on Data Engineering; 2001. p. 215–24.

[44] Pei J, Han J, Wang W. Constraint-based sequential pattern mining: the pattern-growth methods. J Intell Inform Syst 2007;28(2):133–60.

[45] Pentland AS. Healthwear: medical technology becomes wearable. Computer 2004;37(5):42–9.

[46] Perkowitz M, Philipose M, Fishkin K, Patterson DJ. Mining models of human activities from the web. In: Proceedings of the 13th International Conference on World Wide Web; 2004. p. 573–82. Available from: http://dx.doi.org/10.1145/988672.988750.

[47] Philipose M, Fishkin KP, Perkowitz M, Patterson DJ, Fox D, Kautz H. Inferring activities from interactions with objects. IEEE Pervas Comput 2004;3(4):50–7.

[48] Raïssi C, Plantevit M. Mining multidimensional sequential patterns over data streams. In: DaWaK '08: Proceedings of the 10th International Conference on Data Warehousing and Knowledge Discovery; 2008. p. 263–72.

[49] Raïssi C, Poncelet P, Teisseire M. Need for speed: mining sequential pattens in data streams. In: BDA05: Actes des 21iemes Journees Bases de Donnees Avancees; 2005. p. 1–11.

[50] Rashidi P, Cook DJ. Adapting to resident preferences in smart environments. In: AAAI Workshop on Preference Handling; 2008. p. 78–84.

[51] Rashidi P, Cook DJ. The resident in the loop: adapting the smart home to the user. IEEE Trans Syst Man Cybern J, Part A 2009;39(5):949–59.

[52] Rashidi P, Cook DJ. Mining and monitoring patterns of daily routines for assisted living in real world settings. In: Proceedings of the First ACM International Health Informatics Symposium; 2010. p. 336–45. Available from: http://dx.doi.org/10.1145/1882992.1883040.

[53] Rashidi P, Cook DJ. Mining sensor streams for discovering human activity patterns over time. IEEE International Conference on Data Mining 2010:431–40.

[54] Rashidi P, Cook DJ, Holder LB, Schmitter-Edgecombe M. Discovering activities to recognize and track in a smart environment. IEEE Trans Knowl Data Eng 2010;23(4):527–39.

[55] Rissanen J. Modeling by shortest data description. Automatica 1978;14:465–71.

[56] Salarian A, Russmann H, Vingerhoets F, Dehollain C, Blanc Y, Burkhard P. Gait assessment in Parkinson's disease: Toward an ambulatory system for long-term monitoring. IEEE Trans Biomed Eng 2004;51(8):1434–43.

[57] Sánchez D, Tentori M, Favela J. Activity recognition for the smart hospital. IEEE Intell Syst 2008;23(2):50–7.

[58] Schiele B. Unsupervised discovery of structure in activity data using multiple eigenspaces. In: Second International Workshop on Location and Context Awareness; 2006. p. 151–67.

[59] Song Y, Lasecki W, Bigham J, Kautz H. Training activity recognition systems online using real-time crowd-sourcing. In: UbiComp; 2012. p. 1–2.

[60] Stauffer C, Grimson W. Learning patterns of activity using real-time tracking. IEEE Trans Pattern Anal Mach Intell 2000;22(8):747–57.

[61] Tapia EM, Intille SS, Larson K. Activity recognition in the home using simple and ubiquitous sensors. Pervas Comput 2004;3001:158–75.

[62] Teng W-G, Chen M-S, Yu PS. A regression-based temporal pattern mining scheme for data streams. In: Proceedings of the 29th International Conference on Very Large Data Bases; 2003. p. 93–104.

[63] Nguyen T, Phung D, Gupta S, Venkatesh S. Extraction of latent patterns and contexts from social honest signals using hierarchical Dirichlet processes. In: PerCom; 2013. p. 47–55.

[64] Vahdatpour A, Amini N, Sarrafzadeh M. Toward unsupervised activity discovery using multi-dimensional motif detection in time series. In: Proceedings of the 21st International Joint Conference on Artificial Intelligence; 2009. p. 1261–6.

[65] van Kasteren T, Krose B. Bayesian activity recognition in residence for elders. In: Third IET International Conference on Intelligent Environments; 2007. p. 209–12.

[66] Wang J, Han J. Bide: efficient mining of frequent closed sequences. In: Proceedings of the 20th International Conference on Data Engineering; 2004. p. 79.

[67] Wren C, Munguia-Tapia E. Toward scalable activity recognition for sensor networks. In: Proceedings of the Workshop on Location and Context-Awareness; 2006. p. 218–35.

[68] Wyatt D, Philipose M, Choudhury T. Unsupervised activity recognition using automatically mined common sense. In: Proceedings of the 20th National Conference on Artificial Intelligence, Vol. 1; 2005. p. 21–7.

[69] Yin J, Yang Q, Pan JJ. Sensor-based abnormal human-activity detection. IEEE Trans Knowl Data Eng 2008;20(8):1082–90.

[70] Yiping T, Shunjing J, Zhongyuan Y, Sisi Y. Detection elder abnormal activities by using omni-directional vision sensor: activity data collection and modeling. In: SICE-ICASE: Proceedings of the International Joint Conference; 2006. p. 3850–3.

[71] Zaki MJ. Spade: an efficient algorithm for mining frequent sequences. Mach Learn 2001;42:31–60. Available from: <http://portal.acm.org/citation.cfm?id=370660.370671>.

[72] Zhao L, Sukthankar G, Sukthankar R. Incremental relabeling for active learning with noisy crowdsourced annotations. In: Privacy, Security, Risk and Trust (Passat)—Third International Conference on IEEE Third International Conference on Social Computing; 2011. p. 728–33.

[73] Zhao L, Wang X, Sukthankar G, Sukthankar R. Motif discovery and feature selection for crf-based activity recognition. In: Proceedings of the 20th International Conference on Pattern Recognition; 2010. p. 3826–9. Available from: http://dx.doi.org/10.1109/ICPR.2010.932.

[74] Zheng VW, Zheng Y, Xie X, Yang Q. Collaborative location and activity recommendations with GPS history data. In: Proceedings of the 19th International Conference on World Wide Web; 2010. p. 1029–38.

Learning Latent Activities from Social Signals with Hierarchical Dirichlet Processes

Dinh Phung, Thuong Nguyen, Sunil Gupta, and Svetha Venkatesh

Deakin University, Waurn Ponds, VIC, Australia

6.1 Introduction

The proliferation of pervasive sensing platforms for human computing and healthcare has deeply transformed our lives. Building scalable activity-aware applications that can learn, act, and behave intelligently has increasingly become an important research topic. The ability to discover meaningful and measurable activities are crucial to this endeavor. Extracting and using simple forms of activity, such as spatial whereabouts or radio frequency identification (RFID) triggers of entering a building, have remained the focus of much existing work in context-aware applications (e.g, see a recent survey in Bettini et al. [5] and Dey [16]). In most cases, these activities can be readily derived from the recorded raw signals—geolocation from GPS, colocation with known people from Bluetooth, or the presence/absence of someone from a meeting room using RFID tags, though they might be susceptible to changes without careful data cleaning and processing when data grows [5].

Beyond these simple forms of activity, learning *latent* activities that are more semantically interpretable, which *cannot* be trivially derived from the signals, remains a challenging problem. We call these *latent activities*. For example, instead of using raw (x, y, z) coordinate readings from the accelerometer sensor, we consider the user's movement status such as walking or running; or instead of using GPS longitude/latitude readings, one may want to learn high-level daily rhythms from the GPS data [52].

Inferring latent activities is a challenging task that has received little research attention. Most of the existing approaches have used parametric methods from machine learning and data mining. Standard supervised learning and unsupervised learning techniques are the most popular ones used. These include Support Vector Machines (SVMs), Naive Bayes, and hidden Markov models (HMM), to name a few. Typical unsupervised learning methods include Gaussian mixture models (GMM), *K*-means, and latent Dirichlet allocation (LDA) (see Section 6.2). These methods are parametric models in the sense that, once models are learned from a particular dataset, they are fixed and unable to grow or expand as the data grow.

A more severe drawback of these methods is the need to specify the number of latent activities in advance, thus limiting the model to a predefined set of activities. For example, one needs to specify the number of clusters for GMM, the number of states for HMM, or the number of topics for LDA. It is often difficult in practice to specify these parameters in the first place. A common strategy is to perform model selection, searching through the parameter space to pick the best performance on a held-out dataset, which can be cumbersome, computationally inefficient, and sensitive to the held-out dataset. These parametric methods are potentially unsuitable for ubiquitous applications, such as in pervasive health, as the data are typically growing over time and have "no clear beginning and ending" [1].

This chapter addresses these problems by proposing the use of Bayesian nonparametric (BNP) methods, a recent data modeling paradigm in machine learning, to infer latent activities from sensor data acquired in a pervasive setting with an emphasis on social signals. These Bayesian models specify a nonparametric prior on the data-generative process; as such, they allow the number of latent activities to be learned automatically and grow with the data, thus overcoming the fundamental difficulty of model selection encountered in the aforementioned parametric models.

In particular, we employ the hierarchical Dirichlet process (HDP) [62], a recent BNP model designed for modeling grouped data (e.g., a collection of documents, images, or signals) represented in appropriate form. Similar to other Bayesian nonparametric models, HDP automatically infers the number of latent topics—equivalent to our latent activities—from data and assigns each data point to a topic; thus, HDP simultaneously discovers latent activities and assigns a mixture proportion to each document (or a group of signals), which can be used as a latent feature representation for users' activities for additional tasks such as classification or clustering.

We demonstrate the framework on the collection of social signals, a new type of data-sensing paradigm and network science pioneered at the MIT Media Lab [50]. We experiment with two datasets. The first was collected in our lab using sociometric badges provided by Sociometric Solutions.[1] The second one is the well-known Reality Mining dataset [20]. For the sociometric data, we report two experiments: discovering latent *movement* activities derived from accelerometer data and *colocation* activities from Bluetooth data.

To demonstrate the feasibility of the framework in a larger setting, we experiment with the Reality Mining dataset and discover the *interaction* activities from this data. In all cases, to demonstrate the strength of Bayesian nonparametric frameworks, we also compare our results with activities discovered by latent Dirichlet allocation [7]—a widely acknowledged state-of-the-art parametric model for topic modeling. We derive the similarity between subjects in our study using latent activities discovered, then feed the similarity to a clustering algorithm and compare the performance between the two approaches. We quantitatively judge the clustering performance on four metrics commonly used in information retrieval and data mining: F-measure, Rand index, purity, and normalized mutual information (NMI). Without the need of searching over the parameter space, HDP consistently delivers results comparable with the best performance of LDA, up to 0.9 in F-measure and NMI in some cases.

6.2 Related Work

We briefly describe a typical activity recognition system in this section before surveying work on sensor-based activity recognition using wearable sensors. Background related to Bayesian nonparametric models is deferred to the next section.

---

[1]www.sociometricsolutions.com/

6.2.1 Activity Recognition Systems

A typical activity-recognition system contains three components: a sensor infrastructure, a feature extraction component, and a learning module for recognizing known activities to be used for future prediction.

The *sensor infrastructure* uses relevant sensors to collect data from the environment and/or people. A wide range of sensor types have been used during the past decade. Early work in activity recognition has mainly focused on using static cameras (e.g., see Chellappa [11], Duong et al. [18,19]) or circuits embedded indoors [64,65]. However, these types of sensors are limited to some fixed location and only provide the ability to classify activities that have occurred previously. Often they cannot be used to predict future activities, which is more important, especially in healthcare assistance systems.

Much of the recent work has shifted focus to wearable sensors due to their convenience and ease of use. Typical sensing types include GPS [40], accelerometers [24,30,36,38,46,57], gyroscopes [24,38], galvanic skin response (GSR) sensors, and electrocardiogram (ECG) sensors [33,38] to detect body movement and physical states. These sensors have been integrated into pervasive commercial wearable devices such as Sociometric Badge [47][2] or SHIMMER [10].[3] These types of sensors and signals are becoming more and more prevalent, creating new opportunities and challenges in activity-recognition research.

The purpose of the *feature extraction* component is to extract the most relevant and informative features from the raw signals. For example, in vision-based recognition, popular features include scale-invariant feature transform (SIFT) descriptors, silhouettes, contours, edges, pose estimates, velocities, and optical flow. For temporal signals, such as those collected from accelerometers or gyroscopes, one might use basic descriptive statistics derived from each window (e.g., mean, variance, standard deviation, energy, entropy, FFT, and wavelet coefficients) [2,57,59]. Those features might be processed further to remove noise or reduce the dimensionality of the data using machine learning techniques, such as Principal Component Analysis (PCA) [31] or Kernel PCA [66,68], to provide a better description of the data.

The third and perhaps the most important component of an activity-recognition system is the *learning module.* This module learns predefined activities from training data with labels to be used for future activity prediction. Activity labels are often manually annotated during the training phase and supplied to a supervised learning method of choice. Once trained, the system can start to predict the activity label based on acquired signals. However, manually annotating activity labels is a time-consuming process. In addition, the activity patterns may grow and change over time, and this traditional method of supervised training might fail to address real-world problems. Our work presents an effort to address this problem.

A relevant chapter in this book by Rashidi [56] also recognizes this challenge and proposes a sequential data mining framework for human activity discovery. However, Rashidi's work focuses on discovering dynamic activities from raw signals collected from a data stream, whereas by using Bayesian nonparametric models, our work aims to discover higher-order latent activities such as *sitting*, *walking*, and *people gathering*, referred to as *situations* or *goals* in Rashidi's chapter.

---

[2]www.sociometricsolutions.com/
[3]www.shimmer-research.com/

6.2.2 **Pervasive Sensor-Based Activity Recognition**

As mentioned earlier, much of the recent work has shifted focus to sensor-based approaches because of the rapid growth of wearable devices. In particular, accelerometer signals have been exploited in pervasive computing research (e.g., see Kwapisz et al. [36], Olguin and Pentland [46], Ravi et al. [57], and Bui et al. [9]). Ravi et al. [57] experimented with a single three-axis accelerometer worn near the pelvic region and attempted to classify a set of eight different activities. Olguin and Pentland [46] defined and classified eight different activities using data generated by three accelerometers placed on right wrist, left hip, and chest using the HMM. Kwapisz et al. [36] used accelerometer data from cell phones of 29 users to recognize various activities and gestures. Unlike our work in this chapter, a common theme of these approaches is that they employ supervised learning, which requires labeled data.

Another thread of work relevant to ours uses wearable signals to assess energy expenditure (e.g., Fortune et al. [24]). The atomic activity patterns derived in our work might have implications in this line of research. In contrast to Fortune et al., our results on body movement pattern extraction do not require any supervision. In addition to accelerometer data, signals from a multisensor model have also been investigated. Choudhury et al. [12] constructed a sensing platform that includes six types of sensors for activity recognition; again with a supervised learning setting, they report good results when accelerometer data is combined with microphone data. Notably, Lorincz et al. [38] introduced a platform, called Mercury, to integrate a wearable sensor network into a unified system to collect and transfer data in real time or near real time. These types of platforms are complementary to the methods proposed in this chapter for extracting richer contexts and patterns.

6.2.3 **Pervasive Sensors for Healthcare Monitoring**

Pervasive sensors have been popularly used in much of the recent research in healthcare. This research can be classified into three categories: anomaly detection in activity, physical disease detection, and mental disease detection. *Anomaly* in human activity might include falls by elderly or disabled patients or changes in muscle/motion function; detection of those anomalies can be performed using accelerometers [14, 60, 63], wearable cameras [60], barometric pressure sensors [63], or passive infrared motion sensors [67]. Real-time management of *physical diseases* (e.g., cardiac or respiratory disease) can improve the diagnosis and treatment.

Much of the recent research uses wearable electrocardiogram (ECG) sensors [4, 13] or electromagnetic generators [48]. However, in our opinion, the most difficult and challenging research problem related to healthcare is *mental problem detection*. Mental problems might include emotions, mood, stress, depression, or shock. Much recent work has focused on using physiological signals such as ECG [26] or galvanic skin response (GSR) [39, 55]. Some other researchers also have examined the utility of audio signals [39] to detect stress, and this problem remains challenging due to the lack of psychoacoustic understanding of the signals.

6.2.4 **Human Dynamics and Social Interaction**

Understanding human dynamics and social interaction from a network science perspective presents another line of related work. Previous research on discovery of human dynamics and social interaction can be broadly classified into two groups based on the signal used: base-station signal and pairwise signal.

In the first group, the signal is collected by wearable devices to extract its relative position to some base stations with known positions. This approach might be used to perform indoor positioning [3,28,34]. The work of Mortaza et al. [3] employs this approach and introduces the Context Management Frame infrastructure, in which the Bluetooth fingerprint is constructed by received signal strength indication (RSSI) and response rate (RR) to base stations. This requires some training data with the location-labeled fingerprint in order to extract the location of new fingerprint data. Kondragunta [34] built an infrastructure system with some fixed base stations to detect wearable Bluetooth devices. They used the particle filtering method to keep track of people and detect the location contexts. However, these approaches share the same drawback because they require some infrastructure to be installed in advance to fixed locations and cannot be easily extended to new locations. Our early work [51–53] attempted to model high-level routine activities from GPS and WiFi signals but remains limited to a parametric setting.

Some recent work has attempted to extract high-level activities and perform latent context inference (e.g., Huynh et al. [30] and Kim et al. [33]). The authors in Huynh et al. applied LDA to extract daily routine. They used a supervised learning step to recognize activity patterns from data generated by two accelerometers and then applied a topic model on discovered activity patterns to recognize daily routines. An unsupervised clustering algorithm (K-means) was used to cluster sensor data into K clusters and use them as the vocabulary for topic modeling.

Kim et al. [33] attempted to extract high-level descriptions of physical activities from ECG and accelerometer data using latent Dirichlet allocation. These approaches are parametric in nature, requiring many key parameters (e.g., the number of topics or the size of vocabulary) to be specified in advance. In fact, methods presented in our work can be seen as a natural progression of the work of Huynh et al. [30] and Kim et al. [33] in which they overcame the aforementioned drawbacks.

The second related line of work is detecting colocation context based on pairwise Bluetooth signals. In this approach, each user wears a device that can detect other surrounding devices within a short distance. From this type of signal, a pairwise colocation network can be constructed and we can use a graph-based algorithm to extract subcommunities from this network. A suitable method is *k-clique* proposed by Derenyi et al. [15] and Palla et al. [49]. This method attempts to extract *k-cliques*—subgraphs of k fully connected nodes—from the network. The *k-clique* in this approach might be seen as a colocation context in our approach.

Kumpula et al. [35] proposed a sequential method for this approach. However, to be able to use these methods, we have to generate a pairwise colocation network and the corresponding weights. Instead of a graph-based approach [8,21,42,44], use the signal directly to detect colocation groups. Nicolai and Kenn [44] collected proximity data via Bluetooth of a mobile phone during the Ubicomp conference in 2005. They counted the number of familiar and unfamiliar people and computed the dynamic of the familiar and unfamiliar group. These dynamic metrics reflected the events during the conference. They have not proposed a method to detect typical colocation groups.

Eagle et al. [21] use the Reality Mining dataset [20] to analyze users' daily behaviors using a factor analysis technique, where the behavior data of each user in a day can be approximated by weighted sum of some basic behavioral factors named eigenbehaviors. They employ this method, which is a parametric model with a different number of factors, and run it in a batch setting.

Dong et al. [17] use the Markov jump process to infer the relationships between survey questions and sensor data on a dataset collected using mobile phones. Their work includes two aspects: predicting relations (friendship) from sensor data and predicting sensor data from the survey questions.

6.3 Bayesian Nonparametric Approach to Inferring Latent Activities

In this section, we first briefly discuss probabilistic mixture models to motivate the need of the Dirichlet process to specify infinite mixture modeling. The Dirichlet process mixture (DPM) model is then described followed by the hierarchical Dirichlet process.

6.3.1 Bayesian Mixture Modeling with Dirichlet Processes

Mixture modeling is a probabilistic approach to model the existence of latent subpopulations in the data. A mixture component k is represented by a cluster-specific[4] probability density $f_k(\cdot \mid \phi_k)$, where ϕ_k parametrizes the cluster distribution. For a data point x, its subpopulation is assumed to be unknown thus the generative likelihood is modeled as a mixture from K subpopulations:

$$p(x \mid \pi, \phi_{1:K}) = \sum_{k=1}^{K} \pi_k f(x \mid \phi_k), \tag{6.1}$$

where π_k is the probability that x belongs to the kth subpopulation and $\sum_{k=1}^{K} \pi_k = 1$. This is the parametric and frequentist approach to mixture modeling. The expectation-maximization (EM) algorithm is typically employed to estimate the parameters π and ϕ_k (s) from the data.

Under a Bayesian setting, the parameters π and ϕ_k(s) are further endowed with prior distributions. Typically a symmetric Dirichlet distribution $\mathrm{Dir}(\gamma)$ is used as the prior of π, and the prior distributions for ϕ_k are model-specific depending on the form of the likelihood distribution F. Conjugate priors are preferable; for example, if F is a Bernoulli distribution, then conjugate prior distribution H is a Beta distribution. Given the prior specification and defining f as the density function for F, Bayesian mixture models specify the generative likelihood for x as:

$$p(x \mid \gamma, H) = \int_{\pi} \int_{\phi_{1:K}} \sum_{k=1}^{K} \pi_k f(x \mid \phi_k) dP(\pi) dP(\phi_{1:K}) \tag{6.2}$$

Under this formalism, inference is required to derive the posterior distribution for π and ϕ_k (s), which is often intractable. Markov Chain Monte Carlo methods, such as Gibbs sampling, are common approaches for the task. A latent indicator variable z_i is introduced for each data point x_i to specify its mixture component. Conditional on this latent variable, the distribution for x_i is simplified to:

$$p(x_i \mid z_i = k, \phi_{1:K}, \pi) = \pi_k f(x_i \mid \phi_k), \tag{6.3}$$

where $\mathrm{Pr}\,(z_i = k) = \pi_k$. Full Gibbs sampling for posterior inference becomes straightforward by iteratively sampling the conditional distributions among the latent variable π, z_i (s), and ϕ_k (s); that is,

$$p(z_i \mid z_{-i}, x_{1:n}, \pi, \phi_{1:K}) \propto p(x_i \mid z_i) = f(x_i \mid \phi_{z_i}) \tag{6.4}$$

---

[4]We also use the term "probability density" to imply a "probability mass function" when the data domain is discrete.

$$p(\boldsymbol{\pi} \mid z_{1:n}, x_{1:n}, \phi_{1:K}) \propto p(z_{1:n} \mid \boldsymbol{\pi}) \, p(\boldsymbol{\pi}) \tag{6.5}$$

$$p(\phi_k \mid z_{1:n}, x_{1:n}, \boldsymbol{\pi}, \phi_{-k}) \propto \prod_{x \in \{x_i : z_i = k, i = 1, \dots n\}} p(x \mid \phi_k) \, p(\phi_k) \tag{6.6}$$

It is not difficult to recognize that the posterior for $\boldsymbol{\pi}$ is again a Dirichlet, and with a conjugate prior, the posterior for ϕ_k also remains in the same form; thus, they are straightforward to sample.[5] A collapsed Gibbs inference scheme can also be developed to improve the variance of the estimators by integrating out $\boldsymbol{\pi}$ and ϕ_k (s), leaving out only the following conditional to sample from:

$$p(z_i = k \mid z_{-i}, x_{1:n}, \Psi)$$
$$\propto (\alpha + n_k^{-i}) \int_{\phi_k} p(x_i \mid \phi_k) \, p\left(\phi_k \mid \{x_j : j \neq i, z_j = k\}, \Psi\right) d\phi_k, \tag{6.7}$$

where $n_k^{-i} = \sum_{j=1, j \neq i}^{n} \mathbf{1}\{z_j = k\}$ is the number of assignments to cluster k, excluding position i, and α is the hyperparameter for $\boldsymbol{\pi}$, assumed to be a symmetric Dirichlet distribution. The second term involves an integration that can easily be recognized as the predictive likelihood under a posterior distribution for ϕ_k. For conjugate prior, this expression can be analytically evaluated. Several results can readily be found in many standard Bayesian textbooks such as Gelman et al. [27].

A key theoretical limitation in the parametric Bayesian mixture model described so far is the assumption that the number of subpopulations in the data is known. In the realm of activity recognition, given the observed signals x_i (s), each subpopulation can be interpreted as one class of activity, and it is desirable to infer the number of classes automatically. Model-selection methods such as cross-validation, Akaike information criterion (AIC), or Bayesian information criterion (BIC) can be used to estimate K. However, these methods are still sensitive to held-out data. Moreover, it is expensive and difficult to reselect the model when new data arrives.

Recent advances in Bayesian nonparametric modeling provide a principled alternative to overcome these problems by introducing a nonparametric prior distribution on the parameters, thus allowing a countably infinite number of subpopulations, leading to an *infinite mixture* formulation for data likelihood (compare to Eq. (6.1))

$$p(x \mid \cdot) = \sum_{k=1}^{\infty} \pi_k f(x \mid \phi_k) \tag{6.8}$$

It is then natural to ask what would be a suitable prior distribution for infinite-dimensional objects that arise in the preceding equation. The answer to this is the Dirichlet process [23]. One way to motivate the arrival of the Bayesian nonparametric setting is to reconsider the mixture likelihood in Eq. (6.1). As usual, let $(\pi_1, \dots, \pi_K) \sim \text{Dir}(\gamma)$, ϕ_k iid H, $k = 1, \dots, K$, then construct a new discrete measure:

$$G = \sum_{k=1}^{K} \pi_k \delta_{\phi_k}, \tag{6.9}$$

---

[5]Here we assume we are observing n data points $x_{1:n}$ and we write z_{-i} to imply the set of all z (s) except z_i (i.e., $z_{-i} = \{z_1, \dots, z_{i-1}, z_{i+1}, \dots, z_n\}$); a similar convention is applied for ϕ_{-k}.

where δ_{ϕ_k} denotes the atomic probability measure placing its mass at ϕ_k. The generative likelihood for data x can be equivalently expressed as: $x \mid \phi \sim F(x \mid \phi)$ where $\phi \mid G \sim G$.

To see why, we express the conditional distribution for x given G as

$$p(x \mid G) = \int_\phi f(x \mid \phi) dG(\phi) = \int_\phi f(x \mid \phi) \sum_{k=1}^{K} \pi_k \delta_{\phi_k} d\phi \qquad (6.10)$$

$$= \sum_{k=1}^{K} \pi_k \int_\phi f(x \mid \phi) \delta_{\phi_k} d\phi = \sum_{k=1}^{K} \pi_k f(x \mid \phi_k), \qquad (6.11)$$

which identically recovers the likelihood form in Eq. (6.1). Therefore, one sensible approach to move from a finite mixture representation in Eq. (6.1) to an infinite mixture in Eq. (6.8) is to define a discrete probability measure constructed from an infinite collection of atoms ϕ_k (s) sampled iid from the base measure H and the weight π_k (s):

$$G = \sum_{k=1}^{\infty} \pi_k \delta_{\phi_k} \qquad (6.12)$$

Since both ϕ_k (s) and π_k (s) are random, G is also a random probability measure. It turns out that random discrete probability measures constructed in this way follow a Dirichlet process (DP).

Briefly, a Dirichlet process (γ, H) is a distribution over random probability measure G on the parameter space Ω and is specified by two parameters: $\gamma > 0$ is the *concentration* parameter and H is base measure [23]. The terms "Dirichlet" and "base measure" come from the fact that for any finite partition of the measurable space Ω, the random vector obtained by applying G on this partition will distribute according to a Dirichlet distribution with parameters obtained from γH. Alternatively, the nonparametric object G in Eq. (6.12) can be viewed as a limiting form of the parametric G in Eq. (6.9) when $K \to \infty$ and weights π_k (s) are drawn from a symmetric Dirichlet $\pi \sim \text{Dir}(\frac{\gamma}{K}, \dots, \frac{\gamma}{K})$ [62]. Using G as a nonparametric prior distribution, the data-generative process for infinite mixture models can be summarized as follows:

$$G \sim \text{DP}(\gamma, H) \qquad (6.13)$$

$$\theta_i \sim G, \text{ for } i = 1, \dots, n \qquad (6.14)$$

$$x_i \sim F(\cdot \mid \theta_i) \qquad (6.15)$$

The representation for G in Eq. (6.12) is known as the *stick-breaking* representation, taking the form $G = \sum_{k=1}^{\infty} \pi_k \delta_{\phi_k}$, where ϕ_k iid H, $k = 1, \dots, \infty$ and $\pi = (\pi_k)_{k=1}^{\infty}$ are the weights constructed through a stick-breaking process $\pi_k = v_k \prod_{s<k} (1 - v_s)$ with v_k iid $\text{Beta}(1, \gamma)$, $k = 1, \dots, \infty$ [58]. It can be shown that $\sum_{k=1}^{\infty} \pi_k = 1$ with probability one, and we denote this process as $(\pi_1, \pi_2, \dots) \sim \text{GEM}(\gamma)$. A recent book by Hjort et al. [29] provides an excellent account on theory and applications of DP.

Inference in the DPM can be carried out under a Gibbs sampling scheme using the Polya urn characterization of the Dirichlet process [6]—also known as the Chinese restaurant process [54]. Again, let z_i be the cluster indicator variable for x_i, the collapsed Gibbs inference reduces to [43]:

$$p(z_i = k \mid z_{-i}, \boldsymbol{x}_{1:N}, \gamma) \propto \begin{cases} (n_k^{-i}) f_k^{-x_i}(x_i) & \text{if } k \text{ previously used} \\ \gamma f_{k_{\text{new}}}^{-x_i}(x_i) & \text{if } k \text{ takes on a new value,} \end{cases} \qquad (6.16)$$

where n_k^{-i} denotes the number of times the k cluster has been used excluding position i and $f_k^{-x_i}(x_i) = \int_{\phi_k} p(x_i \mid \phi_k) p(\phi_k \mid \{x_j : z_j = k, j \neq i\}) d\phi_k$ is the predictive likelihood of observing x_i under the kth mixture, which can be evaluated analytically thanks to the conjugacy between H and F. The expression in Eq. (6.16) illustrates the *clustering property* induced by DPM: a future data observation is more likely to return to an existing cluster with a probability proportional to its popularity n_k^{-i}; however, it is also flexible enough to pick on a new value if needed as data grows beyond the complexity that the current model can explain. Furthermore, the number of clusters grow at $O(n \log \gamma)$ under the Dirichlet process prior.

6.3.2 Hierarchical Dirichlet Process

Activity-recognition problems typically involve multiple sources of information either from an egocentric or device-centric point of view. In the former, the individual user acquires user-specific datasets, whereas in the later different sensors collect their own observations. Nonetheless, these data sources are often correlated by an underlying and hidden process that dictates how the data is observed. It is desirable to build a hierarchical model to learn activities from these multiple sources jointly by leveraging mutual statistical strength across datasets. This is known as the *shrinkage* effect in Bayesian analysis.

The Dirichlet process mixture model described in the previous section is suitable for analyzing a single data group, such as data that comes from an individual user or a single device. Moreover, the Dirichlet process can also be utilized as a nonparametric prior for modeling grouped data. Under this setting, each group is modeled as a DPM and these models are "linked" together to reflect the dependency among them.

One particularly attractive formalism is the hierarchical Dirichlet process [61,62], which posits the dependency among the group-level DPM by another Dirichlet process. Due to the discreteness property of the DP, mixture components are naturally shared across groups. Specifically, let J be the number of groups and $\{x_{j1}, \ldots, x_{jN_j}\}$ be N_j observations associated with the group j, which are assumed to be exchangeable within the group. Under the HDP framework, each group j is endowed with a random group-specific mixture distribution G_j, which is hierarchically linked by another DP with a measure G_0 that itself is a draw from another DP:

$$G_j \mid \alpha, G_0 \underset{\sim}{\text{iid}} \text{DP}(\alpha, G_0), \quad j = 1, \ldots, J \tag{6.17}$$

$$G_0 \mid \gamma, H \sim \text{DP}(\gamma, H) \tag{6.18}$$

The stick-breaking construction for HDP makes it clear how mixture components are shared across groups:

$$G_0 = \sum_{k=1}^{\infty} \beta_k \delta_{\phi_k} \text{ where } (\beta_1, \beta_2, \ldots) \sim \text{GEM}(\gamma), \quad \phi_k \underset{\sim}{\text{iid}} H \tag{6.19}$$

$$G_j = \sum_{k=1}^{\infty} \pi'_{jk} \delta_{\psi_k} \text{ where } (\pi'_{j1}, \pi'_{j2}, \ldots) \sim \text{GEM}(\alpha), \quad \psi_k \underset{\sim}{\text{iid}} G_0 \tag{6.20}$$

Since G_0 is discrete, taking the support on $\{\phi_1, \phi_2, \ldots\}$, G_j can equivalently be expressed [62] as:

$$G_j = \sum_{k=1}^{\infty} \pi_{jk} \delta_{\phi_k} \text{ where } \pi_j \mid \alpha, \beta \sim \text{DP}(\alpha, \beta) \tag{6.21}$$

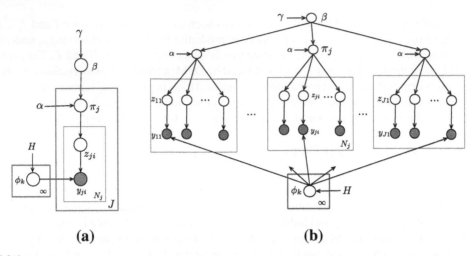

(a) **(b)**

FIGURE 6.1

Generative model for Hierarchical Dirichlet Process. (a) Stick-breaking graphical model representation for HDP in plate notation. (b) Expanded graphical model representation over groups. Each box represents one group of data (e.g., document) with observed data points that are shaded. Unshaded nodes are latent variables. Each observed data point x_{ji} is assigned to a latent mixture indicator variable z_{ji}; γ and α are the concentration parameters and H is the base measure. Each group of data possesses a separate mixture proportion vector π_j of latent topics ϕ_k (s).

Recall that x_{ji} and $x_{ji'}$ belong to the same mixture component if they are generated from the sample component parameter (i.e., $\theta_{ji} = \theta_{ji'}$). Equations (6.19) and (6.21) immediately reveal that θ_{ji} (s) share the same discrete support $\{\phi_1, \phi_2, \ldots\}$, thus mixture components are shared across groups.

Integrating out the random measures G_j (s) and G_0, the posterior for θ_{ji} (s) has been shown to follow a Chinese Restaurant Franchise process that can be used to develop an inference algorithm based on Gibbs sampling, and we refer to Teh et al. [62] for details. Alternatively, an auxiliary variable collapsed Gibbs sampling can be developed based on the stick-breaking representation by integrating out group-specific stick-breaking weights π_{jk} (s) and the atomic atoms ϕ_k (s) *but* explicitly sampling the stick weights β_k (s) at the higher level as described in Teh et al. [62].

Assume L is the number of clusters that have been created, but only $K < L$ components are active, which means the cluster indicator is limited within K clusters $z_{ji} \in \{1, \ldots, K\}$. There are $(L - K)$ inactive components, which we shall cluster together and represent by k_{new}. Therefore, using the additive property of Dirichlet distribution, $(\beta_1, \ldots, \beta_K, \beta_{K+1}, \ldots, \beta_L) \sim \text{Dir}(\frac{\gamma}{L}, \ldots, \frac{\gamma}{L})$ can now be written as $(\beta_1, \ldots, \beta_K, \beta_{\text{new}}) \sim \text{Dir}(\gamma_1, \ldots, \gamma_K, \gamma_{\text{new}})$, where $\gamma_k = \frac{\gamma}{L}$ for $k = 1, \ldots, K$ and $\gamma_{\text{new}} = \frac{(L-K)\gamma}{L}$. Integrating out $\pi_{1:J}$ and ϕ_k (s) our Gibbs sampling state space is $\{z, \beta_{1:K}, \beta_{\text{new}}\}$.

To sample z_{ji}, since there are only K current active components, we can work out the conditional distribution for z by discarding inactive components β_{new} and integrating out π_j within each group j where we note that $\pi_j \sim \text{Dir}(\alpha\beta_1, \ldots, \alpha\beta_K)$; thus, we apply the marginal likelihood result for the

Multinomial-Dirichlet conjugacy:

$$p(z \mid \beta_{1:L}) = p\left(z \mid \beta_{1:K}\right) = \prod_{j=1}^{J} \left[p\left(z_j \mid \beta_{1:K}\right) \right] \tag{6.22}$$

$$= \prod_{j=1}^{J} \int_{\pi_j} p(z_j \mid \pi_j) \, p\left(\pi_j \mid \beta_{1:K}\right) d\pi_j \tag{6.23}$$

$$= \prod_{j=1}^{J} \frac{\Gamma(\alpha)}{\Gamma(\alpha + N_j)} \prod_{k=1}^{K} \frac{\Gamma(\alpha\beta_k + n_{jk})}{\Gamma(\alpha\beta_k)} \tag{6.24}$$

With some further simple manipulations, we get $p\left(z_{ji} = k \mid z^{-ji}, \beta_{1:K}\right) \propto (\alpha\beta_k + n_k^{-ij})$. Therefore, together with the data x_{ji} (s), the Gibbs sampling equation for z_{ji} can be established:

$$p(z_{ji} = k \mid z^{-ji}, \beta_{1:K}, \mathbf{x}) \propto p(z_{ji} = k \mid z^{-ji}, \beta_{1:K})$$
$$\times \int_{\phi_k} p\left(x_{ji} \mid \phi_k\right) \, p\left(\phi_k \mid \left\{x_{j'i'} : z_{j'i'} = k, (j', i') \neq (j, i)\right\}\right) d\phi_k \tag{6.25}$$

$$\propto (\alpha\beta_k + n_k^{-ji}) f^{-ji}(x_{ji}) \tag{6.26}$$

Again the last term is a form of predictive likelihood for x_{ji} under a standard Bayesian setting. It is model-specific but can be evaluated analytically when H is conjugate to F. Note that when resampling z_{ji} we have to consider the case that it may take on a new value k_{new}. If $z_{ji} = k_{\text{new}}$ introduces a new active cluster, we then need to update as follows: $K \leftarrow K + 1, z_{ji} = K, \phi_{K+1} = \phi_{\text{new}}, \beta_K \leftarrow \epsilon\beta_{\text{new}}$, $\beta_{\text{new}} \leftarrow (1 - \epsilon)\beta_{\text{new}}$ where $\epsilon \sim \text{Beta}(1, \gamma)$, where the splitting step for β_K and β_{new} is justified by the splitting property of the Dirichlet distribution [62].

To sample $\{\beta_{1:K}, \beta_{\text{new}}\}$, we express their conditional distribution, which turns out to be the ratio of two Gamma functions; therefore, as shown in Teh et al. [62], we sample them together with an auxiliary variable m_{jk} in which we note that conditional on m, β follows a Dirichlet distribution:

$$q(m_{jk} = m \mid z, m^{-jk}, \beta) \propto s(n_{jk}, m)(\alpha\beta_k)^m \tag{6.27}$$

$$q(\beta_{1:K}, \beta_{\text{new}} \mid z, m) \propto \beta_{\text{new}}^{\gamma-1} \prod_{k=1}^{K} \beta_k^{\sum_j m_{jk} - 1} \tag{6.28}$$

The hyperparameters α and γ can also be resampled by further endowing them with Gamma distributions and following the methods described in [22]. In this work, these hyperparameters are always resampled together with the main parameters. Lastly, assuming that the size of each group is roughly the same at $O(N)$, as shown in Teh and Jordan [61], the number of mixture components grows at $O\left(\gamma \log \frac{\alpha}{\gamma} + \gamma \log J + \gamma \log \log \frac{N}{\alpha}\right)$, which is doubly logarithmically in N and logarithmically in J.

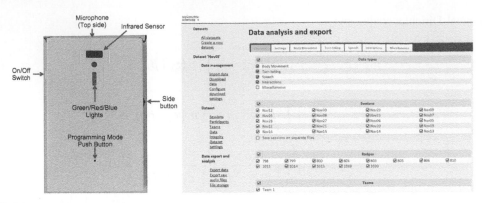

FIGURE 6.2

The front appearance of the sociometric badge (*left*) and its software user interface (*right*).

6.4 Experiments

Two datasets are used: the first collected in our lab using *sociometric badges* provided by Sociometric Solutions[6] and the second is the well-known public Reality Mining data [20].

6.4.1 Sociometric Data

Sociometric badges were invented by the MIT Media Lab [47] and have been used in various applications. Figure 6.2 shows the front of a badge with the infrared sensor, the top-side microphone,[7] and the programming mode button. These badges record a rich set of data, including anonymized *speech* features (e.g., volume, tone of voice, speaking time), *body movement* features derived from accelerometer sensors (e.g., energy and consistency), information of *people nearby* and *face-to-face interaction* with those who are also wearing a sociometric badge, the presence and signal strength of *Bluetooth-enabled device*s, and approximate *location information*. We briefly explain these features next.

Body movement. Each badge has a three-axis accelerometer, set at a sampling rate of every 50 ms. For our data collection, a window frame of 10 s was used and the data were averaged within each window to construct one data point. We record the coordinate (x, y, z) and two derived features: *energy* and *consistency*. Energy is simply the mean of three-axis signals $\sqrt{x^2 + y^2 + z^2}$, and the consistency attempts to capture the stability or consistency of the body movement computed as $1 - \alpha$, where α is

---

[6]www.sociometricsolutions.com/

[7]The purpose of the top-side microphone is to detect the speech by the user wearing the badge. Full descriptions of these badges can be obtained from the company website at: www.sociometricsolutions.com/

the standard deviation of the $\sqrt{x^2 + y^2 + z^2}$ values. These two features have been used in experiments previously with sociometric badges and are reported to be good features [45].

Proximity and people nearby.   The badge has the capacity to record the opportunistic devices with Bluetooth enabled. It can detect the devices' MAC addresses as well as the received signal strength indicators (RSSI).

We ordered 20 sociometric badges from Sociometric Solutions^{TM}, collecting data for three weeks on every working day, five days a week. However, due to some inconsistency in the way members of the lab were carrying and collecting data at the initial phase, we cleaned up and reported data from only 11 subjects in this chapter. We focus on two types of data here: accelerometer data and Bluetooth data. We refer to the accelerometer data as *activity data* and the Bluetooth data as *colocation data*.

6.4.1.1 *Activity data*

The sociometric badges record activity data from a three-axis accelerometer. We used the *consistency* measure [45] as the activity data representing the body movement. A consistency value closer to 1 indicates less movement and closer to 0 if more movement was detected. We aim to extract basis latent activities from these signals, which might be used to build healthcare applications such as monitoring users with obesity or stress. Using Bayesian nonparametric approach, we treat each data point as a random draw from a univariate Gaussian with unknown mean (μ) and unknown precision τ:

$$p(x \mid \mu, \sigma^2) = \mathbf{N}\left(x \mid \mu, \tau^{-1}\right) = \left(\frac{\tau}{2\pi}\right)^{1/2} \exp\left\{-\frac{\tau}{2}(x - \mu)^2\right\} \qquad (6.29)$$

Each Gaussian, parametrized by (μ, τ), represents *one latent activity*. We further specify the conjugate prior distribution for (μ, τ), which is a product of Gaussian-Gamma:

$$p(\tau \mid \alpha_0, \beta_0) = \text{Gamma}(\tau \mid \alpha_0, \beta_0) \qquad (6.30)$$

$$p(\mu \mid \mu_0, s_0, \tau) = \mathbf{N}\left(\mu \mid \mu_0, (s_0\tau)^{-1}\right), \qquad (6.31)$$

where μ_0, α_0, β_0, and s_0 are hyperparameters for the prior distribution in a standard Bayesian setting. These hyperparameters express the prior belief on the distribution of the parameter space and only need to be specified roughly [27]. A widely used approach is to carry out an empirical Bayes step using observed data to infer these parameters before running Gibbs. We adapt this strategy in this chapter.

For the activity data, values of a user on a day are grouped into a document, where each data point is the consistency value in a 10-second interval during the collection time. We run Gibbs sampling for 250 iterations with a burn-in period of 50 samples. The concentration parameters γ and α are also resampled according to a Gamma distribution as described in Teh et al. [62]. Figure 6.3(a) plots the value α for each Gibbs iteration, settling at around 1.2. Figure 6.3(b) shows the posterior distribution over the number of latent activities K with a mode that is 4, and Figure 6.3(c) plots the estimated value of K together with its mode as we run the Gibbs sampler. In this case, the model has inferred $K = 4$ latent activity; each is represented by a univariate Gaussian distribution. These four activities are shown on the left side of Figure 6.4, which can be seen to be separated and captures the activity level well.

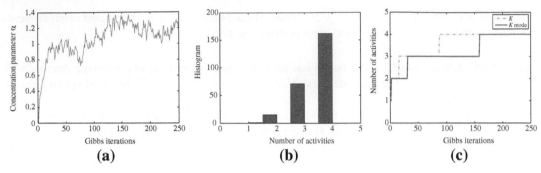

FIGURE 6.3

HDP results run for activity data acquired from sociometric badges from 11 subjects. (a) shows the concentration parameter α being sampled at each Gibbs iteration, which tends to settle down around 1.2; (b) illustrates the empirical posterior distribution for the number of latent activities inferred; and (c) is a plot of the detailed value of K and its mode tracked from the posterior distribution as Gibbs was run.

The right side of Figure 6.4 illustrates an example of consistency signal from Subject 3 with his annotated activity.

6.4.1.2 *Colocation data*

The sociometric badge regularly scans for surrounding Bluetooth devices including other badges. Therefore, we can derive the colocation information of the badge user. We used a window of 30 seconds to construct data in the form of count vectors. In each time interval, a data point is constructed for each user whose badge detects other badges. There are $V = 11$ valid subjects in our sociometric dataset. Thus each data point is an 11-dimensional vector. With an element that represents the corresponding presence status of the subject, the owner of the data point is always present. Data from each day of a user is grouped into one document. All documents from all subjects are collected together to form a corpus to be used with the HDP (thus, each subject may correspond to multiple documents).

We model the observation probability as a multinomial distribution (the distribution F in our description in Section 6.3.1) with a conjugate prior that is the Dirichlet (the base measure H). Thus, a latent colocation activity is described by a discrete distribution $\phi = (\phi_1, \ldots, \phi_V)$ over the set $\{1, 2, \ldots, V = 11\}$ satisfying $\sum_{v=1}^{V} \phi_v = 1$ and can be interpreted as follows: the higher probability of an entry represents the higher chance of its colocation with others. For example, $\phi_1 = \phi_2 = 0.5$ and $\phi_v = 0$ everywhere else indicate a strong colocation activity of Subjects 1 and 2.

Figure 6.6 plots various statistics from our Gibbs inference, which shows that our model has inferred five latent colocation activities from the data as shown in Figure 6.5. These activities are interpretable by inspecting against the ground truth from the lab. For example, the first activity represents the colocation of PhD students because they share the same room; the second captures only two subjects who happen to be two research fellows sharing the same room.

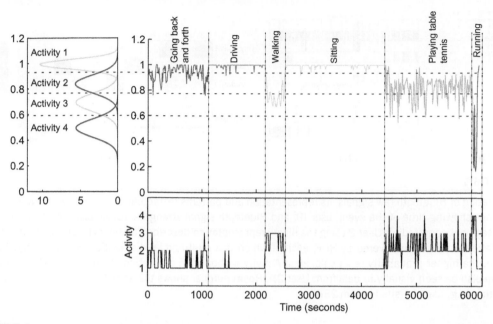

FIGURE 6.4

An illustration of accelerometer signals for different activity types. LHS: our model has learned four latent activities, each of which is represented by a univariate Gaussian: $\mu_1 = 0.992, \sigma_1^2 = 0.0015; \mu_2 = 0.837, \sigma_2^2 = 0.0049; \mu_3 = 0.693, \sigma_3^2 = 0.0050; \mu_4 = 0.493, \sigma_4^2 = 0.0051$. y-axis represents the consistency value derived from the (x, y, z) accelerometer sensor described in Section 6.4.1. A learned latent activity implies a moving status of the subject. For example, Activity 1 has a mean close to 1, which represents the state of nonmovement (e.g., sitting). RHS: An example of consistency signal from Subject 3 with annotated activities. The decoded sequence of states is also plotted underneath. This decoded sequence was computed using the MAP estimation from the Gibbs samples; each state assumes a value in the set {1,2,3,4} corresponding to four latent activities discovered by HDP.

To further quantify the results from our model and demonstrate its strength over existing parametric models, we compare it to latent Dirichlet allocation [7], which has been used regularly as the state-of-the-art method for activity profiling and modeling in pervasive settings [30,51,53]. For each subject, we derive an average mixture proportion of latent activities (topics) from π_j (s) vectors learned from the data for that subject. We then use Jensen-Shannon divergence to compute the distance between each pair of subjects. The Jensen-Shannon divergence for two discrete distribution p and q is defined as:

$$JS(p, q) = \frac{1}{2}KL(p||m) + \frac{1}{2}KL(q||m), \tag{6.32}$$

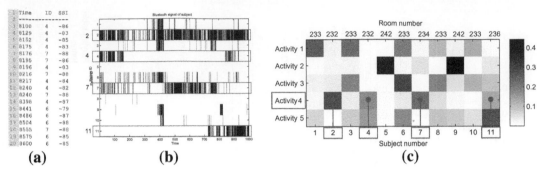

(a)   (b)   (c)

FIGURE 6.5

Illustration of Bluetooth raw signals, its representation and patterns extracted. (a) Examples of raw Bluetooth readings showing time of the event, user ID, and Bluetooth signal strengths. (b) An example of a Bluetooth data segment acquired for User 2 using the binary representation described in the text. (c) Five atomic latent colocation activities discovered by HDP, each of which is a multinomial distribution over 11 subjects (the darker, the higher probability (e.g., colocation Activity 4 shows the colocation of Subjects 2, 4, 7, and 11, as can also be seen visually in data from User 2)). Room number shows the actual room where each subject is sitting (e.g, user 11 sits in room 236).

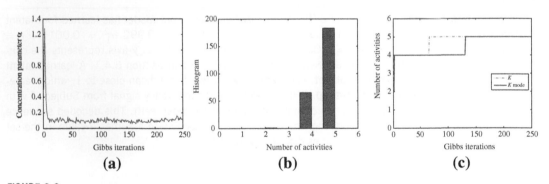

(a)   (b)   (c)

FIGURE 6.6

HDP results on colocation data collected from sociometric badges. (a) The concentration parameter α, settling at around 0.2, (b) the posterior distribution on the number of latent activities, and (c) the estimated number of activity K for each Gibbs and its mode tracked over time.

where $m = \frac{1}{2}(p+q)$ and $KL(p||m) = \sum_i p_i \log \frac{p_i}{m_i}$ is the Kullback-Leibler divergence. The similarity between two subjects i and j is then defined as:

$$similarity(i, j) = e^{-JS(\pi_i, \pi_j)}, \tag{6.33}$$

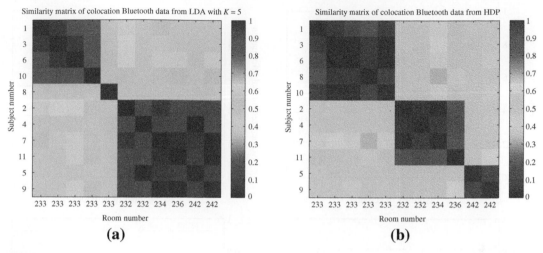

FIGURE 6.7

Similarity matrix obtained for 11 subjects using colocation Bluetooth data from sociometric badge dataset. (a) Using LDA for five activities and (b) using HDP. Similarity is computed for each pair of users using the Jensen-Shannon divergence between mixture proportions of activities being used by the two subjects.

where, with a little abuse of notation, π_i and π_j are the average mixture proportion for Subjects i and j, respectively.

Figure 6.7 represents the similarity matrix obtained from the HDP, which automatically infers the number of activities, and the LDA, which prespecifies the number of activities to 5. Visual inspection shows a clear separation in the result from the HDP compared to LDA.

To further substantiate and understand the proposed framework, we run LDA for various predefined values of K and construct a gross ground truth by dividing 11 subjects into four groups according to the room they share: the first includes 5 PhD students and the next 6 users are divided into 3 groups (2 subjects in one room, except Subjects 7 and 11, who are in two adjacent rooms). We then use the Affinity Propagation (AP) algorithm [25] to perform a clustering. AP uses the similarity matrix as input and Figure 6.8 reports the clustering results using popular performance metrics in clustering and data mining literature, which includes *F-measure*, *cluster purity*, *Rand index*, and *normalized mutual information* (NMI); further details can be found in Jiawei and Kamber [32] and Manning et al. [41]. As can be clearly seen, HDP achieves the best result without the need for specifying the number of activities (topics) in advance, whereas LDA results are sensitive and dictated by this model specification. HDP has achieved a reasonably high performance: an F-measure and a NMI close to 0.9 and Rand index of more than 0.9.

6.4.2 Reality Mining Data

Reality Mining [20] is a well-known mobile phone dataset collected at the MIT Media Lab involving 100 users over 9 months; a wide range of information from each phone was recorded (see appendix

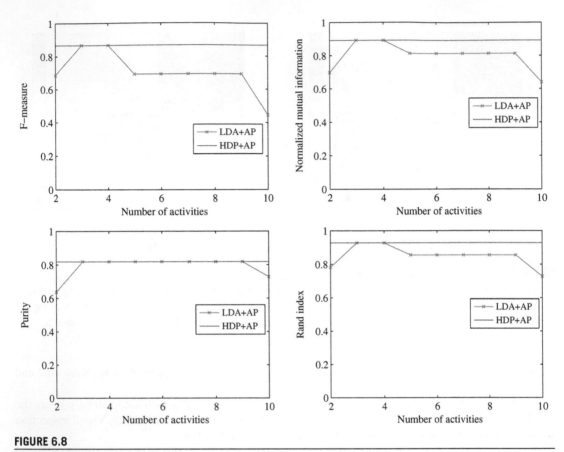

FIGURE 6.8

Performance of LDA + AP and HDP + AP on colocation data. Since HDP automatically learns the number of activities (5 in this case), we repeat this result for HDP over the horizontal axis for easy comparison with LDA.

of Lambert [37] for a full description of the database schema). To demonstrate the feasibility of our proposed framework, we focus on the Bluetooth events. Using Bluetooth-recoded events as colocation information, our goal is to automatically learn activity of subject colocation in this dataset.

Using this information, we further compute the similarity between subjects and group them into clusters. The affiliation information recorded in the database is used as the ground truth in which subjects can be roughly divided into labeled groups (e.g., staff, master frosh, professor, Sloan Business School students). Removing groups of less than 2 members and users whose affiliations are missing, we ended up with a total of $V = 69$ subjects divided into 8 groups in our dataset. For each subject, we construct 1 data point for every 10 minutes of recording. Each data point is a 69-dimensional vector with an element that is set to 1 if the corresponding subject is present and 0 otherwise (self-presence

Table 6.1 Visualization for Nine Latent Activities Learned by HDP

Activity	Tag cloud (person ID)	Tag cloud (group name)
1	6 11 13 · 22 28 39 51 · 56 58 · 61 · 68	– – new-grad – · student
2	3 9 14 15 17 18 23 25 26 27 30 33 34 35 49 50 52 54 59 65	new-grad sloan student
3	· · · 21 40 · ·	masfrosh – student
4	· · · 18 · 36 37 44 48 · 60 63 68	1styear-grad – – ML-grad new-grad – – –
5	· · 7 12 16 · · 36 37 · 43 · · 48 · 65 · 60 63 64 · 67 · ·	1styear-grad – ML-grad new-grad student
6	1 · · · 18 · 22 · · 45 · 53 · · 57 · 64 47 · 58	ML-grad new-grad sloan · student
7	1 · · 12 · 16 · 31 · 43 · 63 55 57 · 60 · 64 67 69	– – ML-grad new-grad – student
8	· 6 · · · · 51 37 · 44 48 · · · 58 60 · 63 · · · ·	– – ML-grad new-grad – –
9	1 · 6 12 · · · · · · 55 · · 64 47 · ·	ML-grad new-grad · student

Note: Each is a discrete distribution over the set of V = 69 subjects in the Reality Mining data. Each number corresponds to an index of a subject and its size is proportional to the probability within that activity. The tag cloud column visualizes the tag cloud of affiliation labels for each activity.

is always set to 1). All data points for each subject are treated as one collection of data, analogous to a document or a group in our HDP description.

Similar to colocation data from sociometric badges, each latent topic is a multinomial distribution over the set of users $\{1, 2, \ldots, V = 69\}$. In this case, nine activities have been discovered and visualized in Table 6.1. Visual inspection reveals some interesting activities: Activity 3, for example, shows a strong colocation of only Subjects 21 and 40; Activity 9 shows that Subject 55 mostly works alone; Activity 2 shows a typical colocation of Sloan Business School students; and so on.

Figure 6.9 attempts to construct a clustering structure directly by using the mixture probability of latent activities assigned for each user. This colocation network is generated by thresholding the (topic, user) mixture matrix learned from HDP. The resultant matrix is then used as the adjacency matrix. In this network, the Sloan Business School students and the master frosh students are usually colocated with

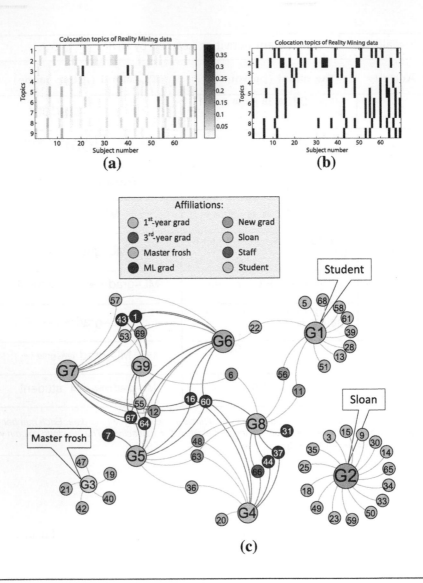

FIGURE 6.9

A clustering structure constructed using the mixture probability of latent activities. (a) The matrix represents the probability of latent activities (topics) given subjects (69 from Reality Mining data) and (b) after applying a hard-threshold to convert it to a binary adjacency matrix. (c) Graphic visualization based on adjacency matrix inferred from latent activities with the node colors representing the affiliation labels from the ground truth.

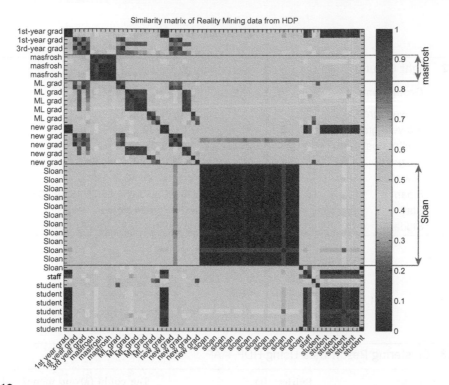

FIGURE 6.10

Similarity matrix for 69 subjects from Reality Mining data using the results from HDP.

other members of the same group. On the other hand, members of the Media Lab might be colocated with members of other affiliation groups.

To further demonstrate the strength of the Bayesian nonparametric approach, we again perform a clustering experiment similar to the setting reported for colocation data in the Colocation data section and compared against LDA. We use the mixture proportion of activity and Jensen-Shannon divergence to compute the distance between users and similarity measures in Eq. (6.33). Figure 6.10 shows the similarity matrix for Reality Mining data. It can be clearly seen that Sloan Business School students and master frosh students are in two separate groups. This is because the Sloan students are physically adjacent to the Media Lab, while master frosh students only join the lab at particular times. Table 6.2 shows ground truth groups in Reality Mining data and Table 6.3 presents the clustering result using HDP and AP. Figure 6.11 further shows the performance comparison of HDP against LDA (run for various values of K). Again HDP consistently delivers a performance comparable to the best performance of LDA, which requires searching over the parameter space.

Table 6.2 Eight Ground Truth Groups in Reality Mining Data

Group	Group name	Subject ID
1	1st-year grad	8 20 36 51
2	3rd-year grad	32 66
3	master frosh	2 19 21 40 42 47
4	ML grad	1 7 16 31 37 43 44 60 64 67
5	new grad	4 6 11 12 46 48 56 63 69
6	Sloan	3 9 14 15 17 18 23 25 26 27 29 30 33 34 35 38 45 49 50 52 54 57 59 65
7	Staff	10 24 62
8	Student	5 13 22 28 39 41 53 55 58 61 68

Table 6.3 Clustering Result Data Using HDP + AP

Cluster	Subject ID	Tag could (group name)
1	1 15	ML–grad student
2	5 8 10 11 13 22 24 28 39 41 51 56 58 61 68	1styear–grad new–grad staff student
3	3 9 14 15 17 18 23 25 26 27 29 30 33 34 35 38 45 49 50 52 54 59 65	Sloan
4	7 12 32 36 46 63 66	1styear–grad 3rdyear–grad ML–grad new–grad
5	2 19 21 40 42 47	masfrosh
6	4 16 20 31 43 64 67 69	1styear–grad ML–grad new–grad
7	37 44 48	ML–grad new–grad
8	53 57	Sloan student
9	6 60 62	ML–grad new–grad staff

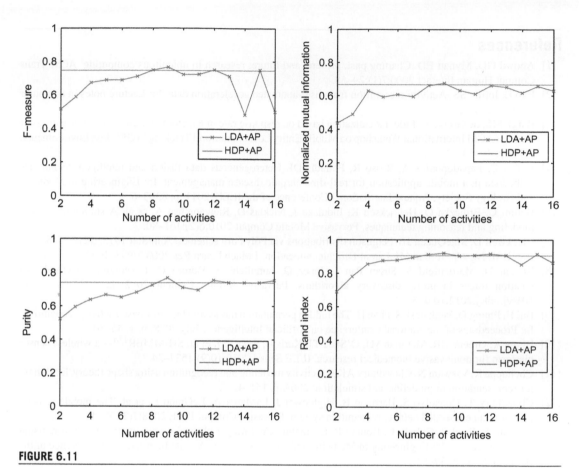

FIGURE 6.11

Performance of LDA + AP and HDP + AP on Reality Mining data.

6.5 Conclusion

Learning latent activities that are nontrivially present in the raw sensor data is important to many activity-aware applications, and this chapter has explored the use of Bayesian nonparametric models for this task. In particular, we make use of the hierarchical Dirichlet process to discover movement and colocation activities from social signals. The key advantage of this approach is its ability to learn the number of latent activities automatically and grow with the data, thus completely bypassing the fundamental difficulty of model selection encountered in parametric models. We use data collected by sociometric badges in the lab as well as the public Reality Mining dataset. In all cases, we have demonstrated how the framework can be used, illustrated insights in the activities discovered, and used them for clustering tasks. To demonstrate the strengths and key advantages of the framework, we have rigorously compared the performance against state-of-the-art existing models and demonstrated that high performance is consistently achieved.

References

[1] Abowd GD, Mynatt ED. Charting past, present, and future: research in ubiquitous computing. ACM Trans Comput Human Interact 2000;7(1):29–58.

[2] Bao L, Intille SS. Activity recognition from user-annotated acceleration data. In: Lecture notes in computer science; 2004. p. 1–17.

[3] Bargh MS, de Groote R. Indoor localization based on response rate of Bluetooth inquiries. In: Proceedings of the First ACM International Workshop on Mobile Entity Localization and Tracking in GPS-less Environments; 2008. p. 49–54.

[4] Bellos C, Papadopoulos A, Rosso R, Fotiadis DI. Heterogeneous data fusion and intelligent techniques embedded in a mobile application for real-time chronic disease management. In: Engineering in Medicine and Biology Society, Annual International Conference of the IEEE; 2011. p. 8303–6.

[5] Bettini C, Brdiczka O, Henricksen K, Indulska J, Nicklas D, Ranganathan A, et al. A survey of context modeling and reasoning techniques. Pervasive Mobile Comput 2010;6(2):161–80.

[6] Blackwell D, MacQueen JB. Ferguson distributions via Pólya urn schemes. Ann Stat 1973;1(2):353–5.

[7] Blei DM, Ng AY, Jordan MI. Latent Dirichlet allocation. J Mach Learn Res 2003;3:993–1022.

[8] Boston D, Mardenfeld S, Susan Pan J, Jones Q, Iamnitchi A, Borcea C. Leveraging Bluetooth co-location traces in group discovery algorithms. Pervasive Mobile Comput 2012. http://dx.doi.org/10.1016/j.pmcj.2012.10.003.

[9] Bui H, Phung D, Venkatesh S, Phan H. The hidden permutation model and location-based activity recognition. In: Proceedings of the National Conference on Artificial Intelligence; July 2008. p. 1345–50.

[10] Burns A, Greene BR, McGrath MJ, O'Shea TJ, Kuris B, Ayer SM, et al. SHIMMER^{TM}—a wireless sensor platform for noninvasive biomedical research. IEEE Sens J 2010;10(9):1527–34.

[11] Chellappa R, Vaswani N, Chowdhury AKR. Activity modeling and recognition using shape theory. In: Behavior representation in modeling and simulation; 2003. p. 151–4.

[12] Choudhury T, Consolvo S, Harrison B, Hightower J, LaMarca A, LeGrand L, et al. The mobile sensing platform: an embedded activity recognition system. Pervasive Comput IEEE 2008;7(2):32–41.

[13] Del Din S, Patel S, Cobelli C, Bonato P. Estimating Fugl-Meyer clinical scores in stroke survivors using wearable sensors. In: Engineering in Medicine and Biology Society, Annual International Conference of the IEEE; 2011. p. 5839–42.

[14] Della Toffola L, Patel S, Chen B, Ozsecen YM, Puiatti A, Bonato P. Development of a platform to combine sensor networks and home robots to improve fall detection in the home environment. In: Engineering in Medicine and Biology Society, Annual International Conference of the IEEE; 2011. p. 5331–4.

[15] Derényi I, Palla G, Vicsek T. Clique percolation in random networks. Phys Rev Lett 2005;94(16):160202.

[16] Dey AK. Understanding and using context. Personal Ubiquitous Comput 2001;5(1):4–7.

[17] Dong W, Lepri B, Pentland AS. Modeling the co-evolution of behaviors and social relationships using mobile phone data. In: Proceedings of the Tenth International Conference on Mobile and Ubiquitous Multimedia; 2011. p. 134–43.

[18] Duong T, Phung D, Bui H, Venkatesh S. Human behavior recognition with generic exponential family duration modeling in the hidden semi-Markov model. International Conference on Pattern Recognition, vol. 3; 2006. p. 202–7.

[19] Duong T, Phung D, Bui H, Venkatesh S. Efficient duration and hierarchical modeling for human activity recognition. Artif Intell 2009;173(7–8):830–56.

[20] Eagle N, Pentland A. Reality mining: sensing complex social systems. Personal Ubiquitous Comput 2006;10(4):255–68.

[21] Eagle N, Pentland AS. Eigenbehaviors: identifying structure in routine. Behav Ecol Sociobiol 2009;63(7):1057–66.

[22] Escobar MD, West M. Bayesian density estimation and inference using mixtures. J Am Stat Assoc 1995;90(430):577–88.

[23] Ferguson TS. A Bayesian analysis of some nonparametric problems. Ann Stat 1973;1(2):209–30.

[24] Fortune E, Tierney M, Scanaill CN, Bourke A, Kennedy N, Nelson J. Activity level classification algorithm using SHIMMER^{TM} wearable sensors for individuals with rheumatoid arthritis. In: Annual International Conference of the IEEE Engineering in Medicine and Biology Society; 2011. p. 3059–62.

[25] Frey BJ, Dueck D. Clustering by passing messages between data points. Science 2007;315:972–6.

[26] Gaggioli A, Pioggia G, Tartarisco G, Baldus G, Corda D, Cipresso P, et al. A mobile data collection platform for mental health research. Personal Ubiquitous Comput 2013;17(2):241–51.

[27] Gelman A, Carlin JB, Stern HS, Rubin DB. Bayesian data analysis. Chapman & Hall/CRC; 2003.

[28] Hay S, Harle R. Bluetooth tracking without discoverability. In: Location and context awareness. Springer; 2009. p. 120–37.

[29] Hjort NL, Holmes C, Müller P, Walker SG. Bayesian nonparametrics. Cambridge University Press; 2010.

[30] Huynh T, Fritz M, Schiele B. Discovery of activity patterns using topic models. In: Proceedings of the Tenth International Conference on Ubiquitous Computing; 2008. p. 10–9.

[31] Huynh T, Schiele Bv. Unsupervised discovery of structure in activity data using multiple eigenspaces. In: Hazas M, Krumm J, Strang T, editors. Location and context awareness. Springer; 2006. p. 151–67.

[32] Jiawei H, Kamber M. Data mining: concepts and techniques. Morgan Kaufmann; 2001.

[33] Kim S, Li M, Lee S, Mitra U, Emken A, Spruijt-Metz D, et al. Modeling high-level descriptions of real-life physical activities using latent topic modeling of multimodal sensor signals. In: Engineering in Medicine and Biology Society, Annual International Conference of the IEEE; 2011. p. 6033–6.

[34] Kondragunta J. Building a context aware infrastructure using Bluetooth. PhD thesis, University of California, Irvine; 2009.

[35] Kumpula JM, Kivelä M, Kaski K, Saramäki J. Sequential algorithm for fast clique percolation. Phys Rev E 2008;78(2):026109.

[36] Kwapisz JR, Weiss GM, Moore SA. Activity recognition using cell phone accelerometers. ACM SIGKDD Exploration Newsl 2011;12(2):74–82.

[37] Lambert MJ. Visualizing and analyzing human-centered data streams. PhD thesis, Massachusetts Institute of Technology; 2005.

[38] Lorincz K, Chen B, Challen GW, Chowdhury AR, Patel S, Bonato P, et al. Mercury: a wearable sensor network platform for high-fidelity motionanalysis. In: Proceedings of the Seventh ACM Conference on Embedded Networked Sensor Systems; 2009. p. 183–96.

[39] Lu H, Frauendorfer D, Rabbi M, Schmid Mast M, Chittaranjan GT, Campbell AT, et al. StressSense: detecting stress in unconstrained acoustic environments using smartphones. In: Proceedings of the ACM Conference on Ubiquitous Computing; 2012. p. 351–60.

[40] Lu H, Yang J, Liu Z, Lane ND, Choudhury T, Campbell AT. The jigsaw continuous sensing engine for mobile phone applications. In: Proceedings of the Eighth ACM Conference on Embedded Networked Sensor Systems; 2010. p. 71–84.

[41] Manning CD, Raghavan P, Schütze H. Introduction to information retrieval, vol. 1. Cambridge University Press; 2008.

[42] Mardenfeld S, Boston D, Juan Pan S, Jones Q, Iamntichi A, Borcea C. GDC: group discovery using co-location traces. In: IEEE Second International Conference on Social Computing; 2010. p. 641–8.

[43] Neal RM. Markov chain sampling methods for Dirichlet process mixture models. J Comput Graphical Stat 2000;9:249–65.

[44] Nicolai T, Kenn H. Towards detecting social situations with Bluetooth. In: Adjunct Proceedings Ubicomp; 2006.

[45] Olguín DO. Sociometric badges: wearable technology for measuring human behavior. PhD thesis, Massachusetts Institute of Technology; 2007.

[46] Olguín DO, Pentland AS. Human activity recognition: accuracy across common locations for wearable sensors. Citeseer; 2006.

[47] Olguín DO, Pentland AS. Social sensors for automatic data collection. In: Americas conference on information systems; 2008. p. 171.

[48] Padasdao B, Boric-Lubecke O. Respiratory rate detection using a wearable electromagnetic generator. In: Engineering in Medicine and Biology Society, EMBC, 2011 Annual International Conference of the IEEE; 2011. p. 3217–20.

[49] Palla G, Derényi I, Farkas I, Vicsek T. Uncovering the overlapping community structure of complex networks in nature and society. Nature 2005;435(7043):814–8.

[50] Pentland AS. Honest signals: how they shape our world. The MIT Press; 2008.

[51] Phung D, Adams B, Tran K, Venkatesh S, Kumar M. High accuracy context recovery using clustering mechanisms. In: Proceedings of the IEEE International Conference on Pervasive Computing and Communications; March 2009. p. 1–9.

[52] Phung D, Adams B, Venkatesh S. Computable social patterns from sparse sensor data. In: First international workshop on location and the web, in conjunction with the world wide web conference; 2008. p. 69–72.

[53] Phung D, Adams B, Venkatesh S, Kumar M. Unsupervised context detection using wireless signals. Pervasive Mobile Comput 2009;5(6):714–33.

[54] Pitman J. Combinatorial stochastic processes. Lecture notes in mathematics, vol. 1875. Springer-Verlag; 2006. p. 7–24. [Lectures from the 32nd summer school on probability theory, Saint-Flour, 2002, with a foreword by Jean Picard].

[55] Puiatti A, Mudda S, Giordano S, Mayora O. Smartphone-centred wearable sensors network for monitoring patients with bipolar disorder. In: Engineering in Medicine and Biology Society, Annual International Conference of the IEEE; 2011. p. 3644–7.

[56] Rashidi P. Stream sequence mining for human activity discovery. In: Sukthankar G, Goldman RP, Geib C, Pynadath DV, Bui HH, editors. Plan, activity, and intent recognition. Waltham, MA: Morgan Kaufmann Publishers; 2014. p. 123–48.

[57] Ravi N, Dandekar N, Mysore P, Littman ML. Activity recognition from accelerometer data . In: Proceedings of the National Conference on Artificial Intelligence,;vol. 20; 2005. p. 1541–6.

[58] Sethuraman J. A constructive definition of Dirichlet priors. Statistica Sinica 1994;4(2):639–50.

[59] Munguia Tapia E. Activity recognition in the home setting using simple and ubiquitous sensors. PhD thesis, Massachusetts Institute of Technology; 2003.

[60] Tasoulis SK, Doukas CN, Maglogiannis I, Plagianakos VP. Statistical data mining of streaming motion data for fall detection in assistive environments. In: Engineering in Medicine and Biology Society, Annual International Conference of the IEEE; 2011. p. 3720–3.

[61] Teh YW, Jordan MI. Hierarchical Bayesian nonparametric models with applications. In: Hjort N, Holmes C, Müller P, Walker S, editors. Bayesian nonparametrics: principles and practice. Cambridge University Press; 2009. p. 158.

[62] Teh YW, Jordan MI, Beal MJ, Blei DM. Hierarchical Dirichlet processes. J Am Stat Assoc 2006;101(476):1566–81.

[63] Tolkiehn M, Atallah L, Lo B, Yang GZ. Direction sensitive fall detection using a triaxial accelerometer and a barometric pressure sensor. In: Engineering in Medicine and Biology Society, Annual International Conference of the IEEE; 2011. p. 369–72.

[64] Valtonen M, Maentausta J, Vanhala J. Tiletrack: capacitive human tracking using floor tiles. In: IEEE International Conference on Pervasive Computing and Communications; 2009. p. 1–10.

[65] Valtonen M, Vanhala J. Human tracking using electric fields. In: IEEE International Conference on Pervasive Computing and Communications; 2009. p. 1–3.

[66] Wang L, Suter D. Recognizing human activities from silhouettes: motion subspace and factorial discriminative graphical model. In: IEEE Conference on Computer Vision and Pattern Recognition; 2007. p. 1–8.

[67] Zhang Z, Kapoor U, Narayanan M, Lovell NH, Redmond SJ. Design of an unobtrusive wireless sensor network for nighttime falls detection. In: Engineering in Medicine and Biology Society, International Conference of the IEEE; 2011. p. 5275–8.

[68] Zheng H, Wang H, Black N. Human activity detection in smart home environment with self-adaptive neural networks. In: IEEE International Conference on Networking, Sensing and Control; 2008. p. 1505–10.

Modeling Human Cognition

Modeling Human Plan Recognition Using Bayesian Theory of Mind

Chris L. Baker and Joshua B. Tenenbaum

Massachusetts Institute of Technology, Cambridge, MA, USA

7.1 Introduction

Among the many impressive cognitive endowments of the human species, our physical intelligence and our social intelligence are two of the most essential for our success. Human physical intelligence uses intuitive theories of the physical laws of the world to maintain accurate representations of the state of the environment; analogously, human social intelligence uses folk–psychological theories to reason about other agents' state of mind. For example, to drive safely we must reason about the acceleration and deceleration of massive objects (physical intelligence), but more subtly, we must reason about the state of mind of other drivers (social intelligence). Consider the situation in Figure 7.1, in which an oncoming car is approaching an intersection with its left turn signal on. To safely pass through this intersection in the opposite direction, a driver must quickly judge whether the driver of the oncoming car knows he is there. If yes, he can safely proceed through the intersection without slowing; if not, he should slow down to avoid a collision as the other car turns left in front of him. That these judgments go beyond simple, programmatic rules of thumb (e.g., "use caution at two-way intersections when oncoming car signals left") is evident from the flexibility with which they apply. If eye contact is made with the oncoming driver, one can be more certain that she will wait; if there is glare on the windshield, the opposite is the case. Other contexts engage analogous cognitive processes; for example, there is always the risk that an oncoming car will turn left without signaling, which is more likely when the driver is on the phone, when visibility is poor, at intersections where left turns are prohibited and so on.

These kinds of nuanced, context-sensitive inferences are ubiquitous in human social intelligence, but virtually absent from even the most advanced artificial intelligence (AI) and robotic systems. To return to our driving example, the recent successes in self-driving cars [127], though impressive, are more the result of advances in machine vision and AI planning than social intelligence; even the most advanced, lifelike robots cannot reason about the beliefs, desires, and intentions of other agents. Machines lack a theory of mind (ToM): the intuitive grasp that humans have of our own and other people's mental states—how they are structured, how they relate to the world, and how they cause behavior. Humans understand that others use their observations to maintain accurate representations of the state and structure of the world; that they have desires for the world to be a certain way; and that these mental states guide their actions in predictable ways, favoring the means most likely to achieve their desires according to their beliefs.

An influential view among developmental psychologists and philosophers is that ToM is constructed around an intuitive causal schema, sketched in Figure 7.1(b), in which beliefs and desires generate

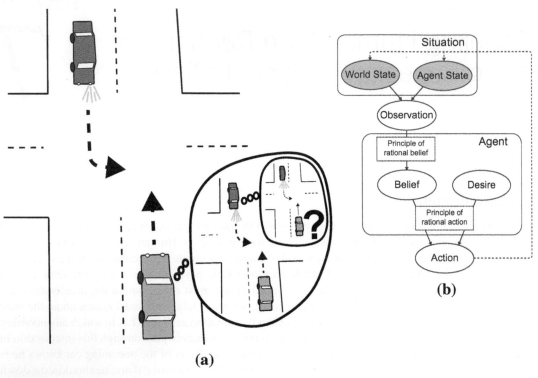

FIGURE 7.1

Commonsense theory of mind reasoning. (**a**) Safely crossing an intersection opposite a car signaling left requires us to represent the other driver's beliefs about the situation: Does the driver of the oncoming car believe the way is clear? (**b**) Causal schema for ToM. Traditional accounts of ToM (e.g., Dennett [38], Wellman [136], and Gopnik and Meltzoff [57]) have proposed informal versions of this schema, characterizing the content and causal relations of ToM in commonsense terms; e.g., "seeing is believing" for the principle of rational belief, or "get what you desire" for the principle of rational action.

actions via abstract causal laws [57,137,138,91]. These causal models allow us to perform mental simulations of others' situation-dependent thought processes and actions, and also to reason backward to infer what others are thinking, given their behavior. A growing body of evidence has shown that simple forms of these representations are present even in young infants, who by 6 months of age have the capacity to attribute goals or desires on the basis of others' reaching movements [142], or to infer whether one agent intends to help or hinder another based on their actions and the context in which they are performed [63]. These abilities rapidly increase in sophistication; by as early as 10 months of age, infants represent agents' beliefs and use them to predict their behavior [90,99] and attribute goals to agents who act rationally in pursuit of those goals, but not to agents who act irrationally [50,35].

Based on this evidence, Gergely et al. [50] have proposed that infants' precocious social reasoning abilities rely on an early-emerging version of the "intentional stance" [38]: the assumption that agents will have sensible beliefs about the world and their situation, and will act rationally to achieve their desires; these functional relationships are illustrated by the "principle of rational belief" and "principle of rational action" boxes in Figure 7.1(b), respectively. Although this perspective provides a unifying account of the developmental data, its insights are restricted to qualitative phenomena—it does not explain quantitative variation in human reasoning as a function of actions, situations, or prior expectations of plausible mental states. Furthermore, generating empirical predictions from nonformal accounts involves introspecting on our own intuitive psychological knowledge—a circular reliance on the very intuitions theories of ToM must ultimately explain.

To go beyond these limitations, we propose to "reverse-engineer" the core representations and mechanisms of human ToM using cognitively inspired computational modeling. This allows us to test competing hypotheses about the nature of human ToM by comparing the ability of computational models defined over different knowledge representations—different priors over the kinds of mental states and the relations among them—to quantitatively fit human judgments into controlled behavioral experiments. We ground our modeling within the large body of research on plan, activity, and intent recognition (PAIR) to highlight its potential to scale to real-world action understanding problems of the kind that solve humans effortlessly, an essential property that computational theories of human ToM must capture.

Our proposed framework, called Bayesian theory of mind (BToM), formalizes ToM as a theory-based Bayesian model [126]. BToM formalizes the core principles of human ToM proposed by classic accounts—that others' behavior is generated by approximately rational belief- and desire[1]-dependent planning—in terms of maximization of expected gains and minimization of expected losses within partially observable Markov decision processes (POMDPs) [76]. This casts ToM as a kind of "intuitive economics"—a folk analog of utility theory used for understanding everyday behavior. Importantly, this does not assume that humans necessarily plan or act rationally in all circumstances. Rather, we tacitly expect others to behave rationally (or approximately so) in particular situations, and perform "explanation by rationalization" by attributing the mental states that make their behavior appear the most rational within the present context. For a given situational context, these principles are applied by running an approximate planning mechanism, which takes the situation and the agents' hypothesized beliefs and desires as input and produces a probability distribution over actions as output. Today, many off-the-shelf software packages are available that can provide this planning mechanism within BToM for modestly sized problems.

Our knowledge of others' mental states is fundamentally uncertain, both due to the inability to observe them directly and due to the unpredictability of how someone with a particular mental state will behave; many different mental states could produce the same action, and the same mental state could produce many different actions. The probabilistic, causal models generated by the planning mechanism within BToM capture these properties, supporting prediction of agents' noisy behavior, given their beliefs and desires, but also the reverse—"inverting" models of planning to perform causal inference of beliefs and desires, given observed behavior. We express "inverse planning" as a Bayesian inference, scoring

---

[1] These are the so-called "propositional attitudes" central to classic discussions of ToM and "folk–psychology" (e.g., see Wimmer and Perner [140], Dennett [38] and Churchland [30]). This chapter focuses on beliefs and desires; in general, ToM may encompass a broader class of mental states (e.g., including emotions), although the extent to which the propositional content of these may be reducible to beliefs and desires is debatable (e.g., see Searle [117]).

candidate belief–desire hypotheses by the probability they could have generated the observed behavior, weighted by the prior.

These probabilistic inferences are inspired by techniques long employed within the PAIR literature; however, PAIR research has primarily focused on inference of "motivational" states (e.g., desires, goals, intentions or plans), rather than "epistemic" states (e.g., beliefs or knowledge). Traditionally, PAIR models also have not embedded probabilistic representations of behavior within top-down theories of rational planning, though this is now changing in the field [103, 107, 108, 40, 39] and in the work we describe here. These aspects of BToM are inspired by classic philosophical and psychological accounts of human ToM. Explicit representation of a theory of utility–theoretic planning is the key to integrating these two sources of inspiration, and highlights the inextricable coupling of belief and desire attributions—expected utility is a function of both beliefs and desires, with beliefs modulating the degree to which different desires influence any particular decision. In most situations, other agents' beliefs are only partially known (as in our driving example), but when inferred jointly with desires, they can often be plainly determined.

We describe an experimental paradigm designed to evoke quantitatively varying judgments in situations that reflect the naturalistic contexts in which ToM is commonly used. For this, we created a "foraging" scenario in which observers (human subjects and computational models) are given a birds-eye view of individual agents walking around a campus environment to eat lunch at one of several "food trucks" (see Figure 7.2). Agents can desire to eat at particular trucks, but be uncertain about the trucks' locations, requiring careful consideration of where to walk based on these desires and beliefs. Over a number of trials, the task is to infer the agent's degree of desire for each truck and belief about each truck's location, based on observing a single trajectory. This induces a rich set of joint attributions, ranging from totally uncertain beliefs and ambivalent desires to sharply peaked beliefs and strongly ordered

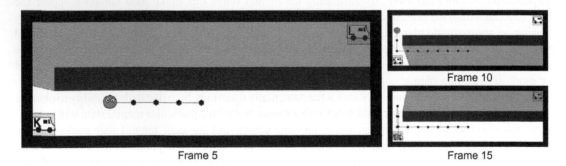

Frame 5   Frame 10   Frame 15

FIGURE 7.2

Example experimental scenario. The small sprite represents the location of the agent and the black trail with arrows superimposed records the agent's movement history. Two shaded cells in opposite corners of the environment represent spots where trucks can park and each contains a different truck. The shaded area of each frame represents the area that is outside of the agent's current view. This figure shows actual frames from an experimental stimulus. (For color version of this figure, the reader is referred to the online version of this chapter.)

desires. We analyze the output of BToM, as well as several alternative models, when given the same time-series input presented to human subjects, then compare the fit of each model to the human data. Accurately predicting people's judgments across all conditions is a challenging task, and it provides a strong basis for identifying the best model of human ToM knowledge and reasoning.

The remainder of this chapter is organized as follows. First, Section 7.2 begins with an informal description of the BToM framework to convey the main intuitions behind our modeling, expressed in terms of the food-truck domain of our experiments for clarity. We then provide the formal, mathematical details of BToM. We also formulate several alternative models as simplified versions of the full belief–desire inference model; these serve to test the level of representational complexity necessary to capture human ToM reasoning. We then relate our models to proposals from the large literature on PAIR, and discuss the connections between AI and psychology that have been made within this field. Section 7.3 describes a domain and methodology for testing computational models of ToM behaviorally, showing the output of our models over a selection of key scenarios, then comparing these predictions with human behavioral judgments. Section 7.4 describes several extensions of the BToM modeling and experiments presented here to give a sense of the generality of our approach. We also discuss limitations of the framework, and open questions for future research to address. Section 7.5 summarizes our main findings and contributions to PAIR, AI, and cognitive science.

7.2 Computational Framework

Bayesian theory of mind (BToM) is a theory-based Bayesian (TBB) framework [126], which models the structured knowledge of human ToM at multiple levels of abstraction, representing the ontology and principles of the theory at an abstract level and mapping these concepts to particular domains and contexts to generate specific predictions and inferences. The TBB approach divides the world into domain-specific theories, with each theory applying its own set of abstract principles to organize the phenomena within its domain. Often these principles consist of sophisticated mechanisms or models, analogous to the principles posited by scientific theories, e.g., a physics engine for intuitive physical reasoning [65], genetic and ecological networks for intuitive biology [120], or rational planning for intuitive psychology [8,130,6]). Theories bridge different levels of abstraction, applying their mechanisms within a specific context (e.g., running a physical simulation that takes the present scene as input) and grounding the output of these mechanisms in the observed data (i.e., establishing the meaning and referents of the theory). TBB analysis has been applied in Cognitive Science [126,59,80] to formulate "rational" [4], "computational-level" [92] or "ideal-observer" [48,81] models of human cognition. This approach can be used to evaluate how closely human judgments approach the ideal Bayesian inferences, but it can also serve to identify which structured representations best explain human judgments under hypothetically unbounded computational resources. Here, we study the representational content of ToM, aiming to show that human inferences closely approach the Bayesian ideal under plausible representational assumptions.

7.2.1 Informal Sketch

BToM represents an *observer* using a theory of mind to understand the actions of an individual *agent* within some environmental context. This corresponds to the setting of "keyhole plan recognition" [31] in the PAIR literature. For concreteness, we use as a running example a simple spatial context (e.g., a college campus or urban landscape) defined by buildings and perceptually distinct objects, with agents' actions corresponding to movement, although in general BToM can be defined over arbitrary state and action spaces (e.g., a card game where the state describes players' hands and actions include draw or fold). Figure 7.2 shows an example condition from our behavioral experiment. The world is characterized by the campus size, the location and size of buildings, and the location of several different goal objects, here food trucks. The agent is a hungry graduate student leaving his office and walking around campus in search of satisfying lunch food. There are three trucks that visit campus: Korean (K), Lebanese (L) and Mexican (M), but only two parking spots where trucks are allowed to park, indicated in Figure 7.2 by the shaded cells in which K and L are parked. The area of the environment that is not visible from the student's location is shaded in gray.

Given the information provided by the context, the state space for planning is constructed by enumerating the set of all possible configurations of the dynamic aspects of the world. In our spatial contexts, we decompose the state representation into the world state, which represents the location of all dynamic objects (here, arrangement of trucks in parking spaces), and the agent state, which specifies the objective, physical properties of the agent (e.g., its current location in space, which is assumed to occupy a discrete grid in our experiment). The action space represents the set of actions available to the agent, and the state-transition distribution is constructed to capture the (possibly stochastic) effects of these actions on the world and agent state. In a spatial domain, the actions consist of moving in a particular direction (e.g., North, South, East, West). The state-transition distribution represents the movement that results from attempting these actions from each state, integrating the spatial relations, (e.g., adjacency), and constraints (e.g., walls or obstacles) defined by the environment. Here we assume for simplicity that the world state remains constant across each observed episode.

The observation space represents the set of possible sensory signals an agent can receive, and the observation distribution expresses the observations generated by each state. In a spatial setting, observations depend on the agent's 360-degree field of view, illustrated by the unshaded regions in Figure 7.2. As an example, in Frames 5 and 15, the agent can observe that K is in the Southwest parking spot but cannot see which truck is in the Northeast parking spot; only in Frame 10 does the observation uniquely identify the world as containing K in the Southwest parking spot and L in the Northeast parking spot. To capture the possibility of failing to see a truck that is actually there, we assume that with a small probability, an agent can mistakenly observe a spot to be empty. This captures the inference, for example, in Figure 7.2 that the agent really *did* want L but didn't notice that the truck was in fact parked in the Northeast spot.

The hallmark of ToM is an awareness that others have representational mental states that can differ from our own. The representations we have described so far are assumed to be shared by both the agent and the observer, but the BToM observer also maintains representations of the agent's representational mental states—beliefs about the agent's beliefs and desires. The content of the agent's desire consists of objects or events in the world. The agent's degree of desire is represented in terms of the subjective reward received for taking actions in certain states (e.g., acting to attain a goal while in close proximity to the goal object). The agent can also act to change its own position (or the state of the world) at a certain cost (e.g., navigating to reach a goal may incur a small cost at each step). Like desires, beliefs are defined by both their content and the strength or degree with which they are held. The content of a belief is a representation corresponding to a possible world. For instance, if the agent is unsure about the location of a particular object, its belief contents are worlds in which the object is in different locations. The agent's degree of belief reflects the subjective probability it assigns to each possible world.

The principles governing the relation between the world and the agent's beliefs, desires, and actions can be naturally expressed within partially observable Markov decision processes (POMDPs) [76]. POMDPs capture the causal relationship between beliefs and the world using the principle of rational belief, which formalizes how the agent's belief is affected by observations in terms of Bayesian belief updating. Given an observation, the agent updates its degree of belief in a particular world based on the likelihood of receiving that observation in that world. POMDPs represent how beliefs and desires cause actions using the principle of rational action, or rational planning. Intuitively, rational POMDP planning provides a predictive model of an agent optimizing the trade-off between exploring the environment to discover the greatest rewards and exploiting known rewards to minimize costs incurred.

On observing an agent's behavior within an environment, the beliefs and desires that caused the agent to generate this behavior are inferred using Bayesian inference. The observer maintains a hypothesis space of joint beliefs and desires, which represent the agent's initial beliefs about the world state and the agent's static desires for different goals. For each hypothesis, the observer evaluates the likelihood of generating the observed behavior given the hypothesized belief and desire. The observer integrates this likelihood with the prior over mental states to infer the agent's joint belief and desire.

As an example of how this works, consider the scenario shown in Figure 7.2. At first, the agent can only see where K, but not L, is parked. Because he can see K, he knows that the spot behind the building either holds L, M, or is empty. By Frame 10, the agent has passed K, indicating that he either wants L or M (or both) and believes that the desired truck is likely to be behind the building—or else he would have gone straight to K under the principle of rational action. After Frame 10, the agent discovers that L is behind the building and turns back to K. Obviously, the agent desires K more than L, but more subtly, it also seems likely that he wants M more than either K or L; this attribution is made without explicit observation of the choice for M–even without M being present in the scene. BToM captures this inference by resolving the desire for L or M over K in favor of M after the agent rejects L. In other words, BToM infers the best explanation for the observed behavior—the only consistent desire that could lead the agent to act the way he did.

7.2.2 **Formal Modeling**

This section provides mathematical details of the BToM framework sketched previously; this can be skipped by the casual reader. First, we describe the construction of the state space, action space, state-transition distribution, observation space, and observation distribution used for POMDP planning. We then derive the formation and dynamics of the BToM representation of agents' beliefs and desires. Finally, we derive the Bayesian computations that support joint belief and desire inference, then explain how model predictions are generated for our experiment.

In the food-truck domain, the agent occupies a discrete state space S of points in a 2D grid. The world state space W is the set of possible assignments of the K, L, and M trucks to parking spots (consisting of 13 configurations in total). For simplicity, we assume that the world is static (i.e., that the locations of the trucks do not change over the course of a episode), although the extension to dynamic worlds is straigntforward (e.g., allowing trucks to arrive, depart, or move). The action space A includes actions North, South, East, West, Stay, and Eat. The state-transition distribution $P(s_t \mid s_{t-1}, a_{t-1}, w)$ represents the conditional probability of transitioning to agent state $s_t \in S$ at time t, given the world $w \in W$, the agent state $s_{t-1} \in S$, and action $a_{t-1} \in A$ at time $t-1$. Valid movement actions are assumed to yield their intended transition with probability $1 - \epsilon$ and to do nothing otherwise; invalid actions (e.g., moving into walls) have no effect on the state. The Eat action is assumed to lead to a special "Finished" state if selected when the agent is at the location of a food truck and to have no effect on the state otherwise.

The agent's visual observations are represented by the isovist from its present location: a polygonal region containing all points of the environment within a 360-degree field of view [36,94]. Example isovists from different locations in one environment are shown in Figure 7.2. The observation distribution $P(o_t \mid s_t, w)$ is constructed by first computing the isovist for every agent and world state pair in $(s, w) \in \mathcal{S} \times \mathcal{W}$. Then, for each agent state $s \in \mathcal{S}$, the isovists for all worlds $w \in \mathcal{W}$ are compared to establish which sets of worlds are perceptually distinguishable from that agent state. In the food-truck domain, worlds are distinguished by the locations of the food trucks.

We assume that the probability of observing which truck is in a parking spot is proportional to the area of that grid cell contained within the isovist. We model observation noise with the simple assumption that with probability v, the agent can fail to notice a truck's presence in a parking spot, mistakenly observing the symbol that "nothing" is there instead. From a given agent state, all perceptually distinguishable worlds are assumed to generate different observation symbols; worlds that are indistinguishable will emit the same observation symbol. For example, in Figure 7.2, Frames 5 and 15, the observation symbol will be consistent with only worlds containing the Korean truck in the Southwest parking spot and either the Lebanese truck, Mexican truck, or nothing in the Northeast parking spot. The observation symbol in Frame 10 will uniquely identify the state of the world.

Students are assumed to know their own location $s \in \mathcal{S}$ (and the location of all buildings and parking spots) but can be uncertain about the state of the world $w \in \mathcal{W}$ (i.e., the truck locations); technically, this induces a particular kind of POMDP called a mixed-observability MDP [98]. The observer represents the agent's belief as a probability distribution over $\mathcal{W}$; for $w \in \mathcal{W}$, $B(w)$ denotes the agent's degree of belief that w is the true world state. In the food-truck domain, B represents students' beliefs about which trucks are where. As agents receive observations, they are assumed to perform Bayesian belief updating to integrate $b_{t-1}(w)$, the probability their belief assigns to world w at time $t - 1$ with two likelihood functions[2]: $P(s_t \mid s_{t-1}, a_{t-1}, w)$, the probability of making the observed transition from s_{t-1} to s_t given action a_{t-1} in world w; and $P(o_t \mid s_t, w)$, the likelihood of generating observation o_t, given the agent state S_t and world w:

$$b_t(w) \propto P(o_t \mid s_t, w) P(s_t \mid s_{t-1}, a_{t-1}, w) b_{t-1}(w). \tag{7.1}$$

From the agent's perspective, given o_t and s_t, the belief update at time t is a deterministic function of the prior belief b_{t-1}, the action a_{t-1}, and the previous agent state s_{t-1}. As a shorthand for this deterministic computation, we write:

$$b_t \leftarrow \text{BeliefUpdate}(o_t, s_t, s_{t-1}, a_{t-1}, b_{t-1}). \tag{7.2}$$

BToM assumes that agents' desires are defined over classes of states, actions and "events" (state transitions), and that each desire has an associated "degree" or strength. In the food-truck domain,

---

[2]The first of these is necessary to capture belief updating on the basis of worlds with different dynamics. For example, suppose the agent is at a parking spot, and believes a truck to be there. If the agent does not transition to the "Finished" state on choosing the "Eat" action, it can instantly deduce that no truck is there, even without receiving the corresponding observation signal (assuming "Finished" state transitions are deterministic when trucks are present).

agents' desires correspond to eating at one of several food trucks, but their degree of desire for each truck is unknown. Within the POMDP model, eating events are represented as state transitions from a truck location to the "Finished" state. The degree of desire for each truck is embedded within the agent's reward function $R(s_t, s_{t-1}, w, a_{t-1})$, where $s_t =$ "Finished", s_{t-1} is the location of a truck in world w, and $a_{t-1} =$ "Eat". This reward represents the subjective utility the agent receives for eating at the truck located at s_{t-1}. The reward function also represents the costs (negative rewards) the agent incurs for movement actions, which are each assumed to have a cost of 1. Once the student has eaten (i.e., transitioned to the absorbing "Finished" state), all rewards and costs cease, implying that rational agents should optimize the trade-off between the distance traveled versus the reward obtained, choosing which truck to visit based on its desirability, the probability that it will be present, and the total cost to reach its location.

The representations defined so far provide the input to the POMDP planning mechanism of BToM. The output of the POMDP solver is the value function $V(b, s)$, where b is the agent's $|\mathcal{W}|$-dimensional belief vector and s is an agent state. Given V, the agent's *policy* is computed, which represents the probability distribution over the agent's actions, given its beliefs and location. First, the lookahead state–action value function [70] $Q^{LA}(b, s, a)$ is computed to integrate the expected immediate cost of action a with the expected discounted future value of taking that action:

$$Q^{LA}(b, s, a) = \sum_w b(w) \sum_{s'} P(s' \mid s, w, a)$$

$$\times \left(R(s', s, w, a) + \gamma \sum_o P(o \mid s', w) V(\text{BeliefUpdate}(o, s', s, a, b), s') \right) \quad (7.3)$$

The agent's policy $P(a \mid b, s)$ is assumed to stochastically maximize the lookahead state–action value function using the softmax function:

$$P(a \mid b, s) \propto \exp\left(\beta Q^{LA}(b, s, a)\right) \quad (7.4)$$

The β parameter establishes the degree of determinism with which the agent executes its policy, capturing the intuition that agents tend to, but do not always, follow the optimal policy.

A wealth of algorithms and off-the-shelf solvers are applicable to the (relatively simple) POMDPs of our food-truck domain. Because many of the probabilistic computations involved in solving these POMDPs are shared with the inferential component of BToM, we implement one of the simplest approximate POMDP solvers, based on discretizing the real-valued belief space with a set of belief points drawn from a regular grid, and applying the value iteration algorithm to these points [88]. The value of arbitrary beliefs is then obtained by linearly interpolating between the values at the neighboring grid points; this provides a piecewise-linear upper bound to the optimal value function.

Together, the state-transition distribution and the agent's policy, belief updating function, and observation distribution comprise the BToM observer's predictive model of the agent's behavior and mental states. These representations are composed to form the structured probabilistic model in Figure 7.3, which takes the form of a dynamic Bayesian network (DBN) described by Murphy [95]. The most basic computation the DBN model supports is forward-sampling: given initial belief b_0, desire d, world state w, and agent state s_1, drawing samples from the joint distribution over all variables in the network

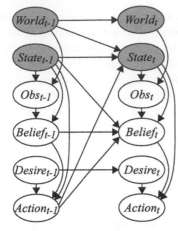

$$
\begin{aligned}
B_0 &\sim \text{BeliefPrior}(\alpha) \\
D_0 &\sim \text{DesirePrior}()
\end{aligned}
$$

$$
\begin{aligned}
W_t &\leftarrow W_{t-1} \\
S_t &\sim P(\cdot|S_{t-1}, A_{t-1}, W_{t-1}, \epsilon) \\
O_t &\sim P(\cdot|S_t, W_t, \nu) \\
B_t &\leftarrow \text{BeliefUpdate}(O_t, S_t, S_{t-1}, A_{t-1}, B_{t-1}) \\
D_t &\leftarrow D_{t-1} \\
A_t &\sim P(\cdot|B_t, D_t, S_t, \beta)
\end{aligned}
$$

FIGURE 7.3

Observer's grounding of the theory as a dynamic Bayes net. Variables in the DBN are abbreviated by their first letter, the "$\sim$" symbol denotes "is distributed as," and the "$\leftarrow$" symbol denotes deterministic assignment. The DBN encodes the observer's joint distribution over an agent's beliefs $B_{1:T}$ and desires $D_{1:T}$ over time, given the agent's physical state sequence $s_{1:T}$ in world w. For simplicity, we assume that the world W and the agent's desire D remain constant over the course of an episode.

involves sequentially sampling from the conditional distributions in Figure 7.3. This is the process by which the BToM observer assumes an agent's trajectory to have been generated, only with initial beliefs b_0 and desires d that are unknown to the observer and must be inferred.

Bayesian inference of an agent's beliefs $b_{0:t}$ and desires d, given its observed trajectory $s_{1:t}$ in world w, requires prior probability distributions over the agent's initial beliefs and desires to be specified. To tractably represent these priors over the multidimensional, continuous space of beliefs, we discretize the belief simplex $\Delta^{|\mathcal{W}|-1}$ using the Freudenthal triangulation [88] of resolution μ to generate $m(0) = \binom{|\mathcal{W}|-1+\mu}{|\mathcal{W}|-1}$ initial belief points $b_0^{1:m(0)}$. Each initial belief point b_0^i is assigned prior probability proportional to the density of $\text{BeliefPrior}(\alpha)$ at b_0^i, assumed to be a $|\mathcal{W}|$-dimensional symmetric Dirichlet distribution with parameter α. Similarly, in our scenarios, the agent's actions depend on its desires for the three different food trucks, and we generate a regular 3D grid with resolution η to represent $n = \eta^3$ hypotheses $d^{1:n}$ about the agent's joint desires for each truck. For simplicity, we assume a uniform prior over the space of desires, denoted $\text{DesirePrior}()$.

Given the agent's state sequence $s_{1:T}$ in world w, reasoning about the agent's beliefs and desires over time is performed using the belief-propagation algorithm, a standard approach to inference in DBNs. For clarity, we describe belief–desire inference in BToM by analogy to the forward–backward algorithm for inference in hidden Markov models (HMMs) [105], a well-known special case of belief propagation. At each timestep, given the set of belief points $b_{t-1}^{1:m(t-1)}$ at the previous timestep, a new set of $m(t)$ belief points, $b_t^{1:m(t)}$ is generated by applying the $\text{BeliefUpdate}()$ function to each pair of possible actions and observations $(a_{t-1}, o_t) \in \mathcal{A} \times \mathcal{O}$ of the agent. To determine the probability of transitioning from each b_{t-1}^j to each b_t^i (given desire hypothesis d^k), we compute a belief- and desire-transition matrix Z_t^i, summing over all actions a_{t-1} and observations o_t that could yield the transition:

$$Z_t^{ijk} = \sum_{a_{t-1}, o_t} P(o_t \mid s_t) P(s_t \mid s_{t-1}, a_{t-1}) P(a_{t-1} \mid b_{t-1}^j, s_{t-1}, d^k)$$

$$\times \delta(b_t^i, \text{BeliefUpdate}(o_t, s_t, s_{t-1}, a_{t-1}, b_{t-1}^j)), \tag{7.5}$$

where the δ-function equals 1 when $b_t^i = \text{BeliefUpdate}(o_t, s_t, s_{t-1}, a_{t-1}, b_{t-1}^j)$ and 0 otherwise. This ensures that only prior beliefs b_{t-1}^j, observations o_t, and actions a_{t-1} that produce the belief update b_t^i enter into the summation.

As in HMMs, an online estimate of the state of the system—in this case, the beliefs and desires that constitute the agent's mental state—is given by the *forward* distribution:

$$P(b_t^i, d^k \mid s_{1:t}, w) \propto \sum_{j=1:m(t-1)} Z_t^{ijk} \cdot P(b_{t-1}^j, d^k \mid s_{1:t-1}, w). \tag{7.6}$$

This provides the marginal posterior distribution over the agent's beliefs and desires, given all the information provided by the agent's trajectory up to time t. The recursive matrix multiplication in Eq. 7.6 resembles the filtering computation within HMMs, but with a nonstationary, context-dependent transition matrix defined over two jointly distributed variables. It is also related to the algorithm for filtering over infinitely nested beliefs proposed by Zettlemoyer et al. [146]; here, we consider a special case with only one agent, but extend their algorithm to jointly infer desires in addition to beliefs.

Next, we define the *backward* distribution, which recursively propagates information backward in time to give the marginal likelihood of the agent's future trajectory up to time T, given its mental state at some past time point t:

$$P(s_{t+1:T} \mid b_t^i, d^k, w) \propto \sum_{i=1:m(t+1)} Z_{t+1}^{jik} \cdot P(s_{t+2:T} \mid b_{t+1}^j, d^k, w). \tag{7.7}$$

Together, the forward and backward distributions allow us to compute the joint posterior marginal over the agent's beliefs and desires at time t, given the state sequence until $T \geq t$. This is given by the product of the forward and backward distributions, called the *smoothing* distribution:

$$P(b_t^i, d^k \mid s_{1:T}, w) = P(b_t^i, d^k \mid s_{1:t}, w) P(s_{t+1:T} \mid b_t^i, d^k, w). \tag{7.8}$$

This computation is analogous to the forward–backward algorithm in HMMs. Equation 7.8 provides the basis for model predictions of people's joint desire and retrospective belief inferences in our experiment.

7.2.3 Alternative Models

To test whether the full representational capacity of BToM is necessary to understand people's mental state attributions, we formulate two alternative models as special cases of our joint inference model. Each alternative model "lesions" a central component of the full model's representation of beliefs, and tests whether it is possible to explain people's inferences about agents' desires in our experiment without appeal to a full-fledged ToM.

Our first alternative model is called *TrueBelief*. This model assumes that the true world state is fully observable to the agent, implying that the agent has true beliefs about the location of every truck and plans to go directly to the truck that will provide the maximum reward while incurring the least cost. Technically, TrueBelief uses an MDP generative model of the agent's behavior, instead of the more complex, more computationally intensive POMDP model used by BToM. We formulate the TrueBelief model by modifying the agent's beliefs (i.e., the `BeliefPrior ()` distribution and `BeliefUpdate ()` function) to assign probability 1 to the true world state w:

$$B_t^{\text{TrueBelief}}(w) \leftarrow 1 \qquad (7.9)$$

We hypothesized that TrueBelief would correlate moderately well with people's desire judgments because of the statistical association between desired objects and actions. In addition, if people's belief attributions are highly influenced by the true state of the world in each condition, their belief judgments should correlate strongly with the TrueBelief model predictions.

Our second alternative model is called *NoObs*. In this model, the agent's initial belief about the world state is generated from the `BeliefPrior(α)` distribution in the same manner as in BToM (see Figure 7.3), but the `BeliefUpdate ()` function is modified so that the initially sampled belief remains fixed throughout the trial (as if the agent was "blindfolded," or otherwise unable to observe the world state):

$$B_t^{\text{NoObs}} \leftarrow B_{t-1}^{\text{NoObs}} \qquad (7.10)$$

We hypothesized that this model might fit people's belief and desire inferences in situations where the agent appears to move toward the same truck throughout the entire trial, but that for actions that require belief updating or exploration to explain, for instance, when the agent begins by exploring the world, then changes direction based on observation of the world state (e.g., Figure 7.2), NoObs would be a poor fit.

7.2.4 AI and ToM

The long association between psychology and PAIR research in AI provides important touchstones for our work. From the perspective of this chapter, the key threads running through research on understanding agents and actions in philosophy, psychology, linguistics, and AI are:

1. Modeling others as intentional agents with representational mental states such as beliefs and desires
2. Framing PAIR as a problem of probabilistic inference over generative models of behavior.

Both of these assumptions are fundamental to our work here.

An explicit connection with "commonsense psychology" was made by the earliest literature on plan recognition [111,113,139], which arose from multiple fertile collaborations between AI and social psychology researchers. Plan recognition also became an important component within models of pragmatics and discourse understanding in linguistics [102,3,60,86,32]. Inspired by speech-act theory [5,116] and Gricean pragmatics [58], these approaches assume that speakers have a representation of listeners' knowledge, beliefs, desires, and intentions (expressed in modal or first-order logic), and use these representations to plan utterances to influence interlocutors' mental states and behavior [33].[3]

---

[3] Analyses based on sophisticated notions of *common knowledge* described by Lewis [84] and Fagin et al. [42] and *joint intention* described by Searle [118] and Grosz and Sidner [61], are outside of the scope of this chapter.

Classical accounts of plan recognition were motivated conceptually in terms of reasoning about intentional action—the first key thread identified above—but in practice inference in these models typically involved heuristic, rule-based reasoning about the speaker's beliefs, desires, intentions, and planning process [111,102,3]. Although general algorithmic approaches to inference about classical planning agents were later developed by Kautz and Allen [79,78], logical approaches to plan recognition remained limited by the difficulty of capturing naturalistic behaviors in purely logical terms, and by the inability of logical inferences to capture the gradedness and ambiguity inherent in human mental state attributions.

A subsequent generation of models picked up the second key thread, formulating PAIR as a problem of probabilistic inference over context-dependent, generative models of actions [27,2,53,104,20,47]. However, unlike the previous generation of plan-recognition approaches, these models do not explicitly employ planning algorithms to generate models of agents' actions. Instead, they either assume that probability distributions over intention- or goal-dependent actions are specified a priori [27,53,104,20, 47], or that they are learned from a corpus of previously observed behavior [2]. Given observed actions, the plan, goal, or intention most likely to have generated them can be inferred using Bayes' rule.

Recent approaches have also applied discriminative probabilistic models to PAIR [85,131], directly learning the structure and parameters of the conditional distribution over activities and goals, given behavioral observations. These probabilistic PAIR techniques perform graded inferences, and given sufficient data, they can learn the appropriate probability distributions over real-world behavior. They can also achieve generalization to new contexts and activities using abstract, structured representations of environments, actions, and goals. However, without explicit representations of intent- or goal-directed planning—the purposeful, adaptive processes captured by classic accounts of PAIR—these models' generalization beyond the realm of previous experience is fundamentally limited.

Recent work across a number of fields has begun to tie together the two key threads running through previous PAIR research. Within the field of economics, the seminal "Bayesian games" framework of Harsanyi [67–69] and research in behavioral economics and behavioral game theory [122,72,21,22] have modeled the degree to which people represent and reason about other players' *types*, encompassing information about their utility functions, knowledge, and strategic reasoning processes. Research in the fields of multiagent systems and human–computer interaction has also explored these issues [52,93, 44,51,45,40], modeling agents' recursive reasoning about each others' utility functions, strategies, and plans and recently framing these representations in terms of ToM [103,121,39]. Although these approaches focus on the need for recursive representations of intentional agents in interactive contexts (rather than on PAIR per se), the probabilistic inferences over models of intentional agents' planning they perform integrate the key threads of both classic and probabilistic PAIR models.

Within the field of machine learning, Ng and Russell [97] formulated the problem of inferring an agent's utility function to explain its behavior in terms of "inverse reinforcement learning" (IRL; also see Chajewska and Koller [25]). Reinforcement learning describes the problem facing an agent figuring out how to act to maximize reward in an unknown environment [124]. Inverse reinforcement learning is the opposite problem: given data on how an agent behaves, determine the unknown reward function it is maximizing. In recent years, IRL (also known as "inverse optimal control") has seen increasing interest in Machine Learning, yielding an expanding number of theoretical and applied results [26,1,106,96,41,147,135,28].

In the field of cognitive science, a rapidly growing body of research, complementing game–theoretic and IRL-based approaches to PAIR, has suggested that human judgments about intentional agents' mental states (i.e., goals, intentions, preferences, desires) can be modeled as probabilistic inverse planning, or inverse decision making–Bayesian inferences over predictive models of rational, intentional behavior [9,133,54,10,7,143,8,55,89,130,16,144,125,74,75,73,123]. Closely related to, but preceding these approaches, models of motor control have been applied to capture the understanding and imitation of physical movement [141,100,109]. Recent research has also begun to develop probabilistic versions of the ideas from pragmatics and discourse understanding previously discussed in similar terms [43,56], and similar models of intentional communication have been effective in modeling pedagogy as well [119].[4]

An array of alternative approaches to modeling ToM have been proposed in cognitive science as well. Logical frameworks analogous to classical PAIR models have been formulated in terms of rule-based schemas [112,115,134], and more recently expressed in the cognitive architecture Polyscheme [23] to capture the dynamics of cognitive processing during ToM reasoning [14,15,13,12]. Accounts analogous to discriminative probabilistic models have been expressed both as connectionist models [132,17], and in terms of low-level motion cue-based action categorization [18,11,145]. Elsewhere, we have compared the ability of heuristic or cue-based versus inverse-planning accounts to quantitatively fit human judgments [7,8,130,73], arguing that models of planning, rather than simple heuristics or low-level cues, are core mental representations of ToM.

7.3 Comparing the Model to Human Judgments

Given the diverse range of AI and cognitive models relating to human ToM, how can we evaluate these models, both in terms of their quantitative fit to human behavior, and in terms of their real-world practicality and performance? Here we describe a range of scenarios, set within our food-truck domain, that can be presented to both human subjects and computational models. These scenarios systematically vary the observed actions, the environmental constraints, the truck locations, and the costs incurred for executing a particular trajectory. This establishes a natural setting for ToM reasoning, involving agents with varying beliefs and desires, whose actions depend on these factors as well as the structure of environment.

As illustrated earlier in Figure 7.2, these food-truck scenarios can be presented to human subjects as animated 2D displays of agents navigating through simple "grid-world" contexts. In Figure 7.2, the agent and trucks' locations are marked by small sprites, buildings are marked by black grid squares, and potential parking spaces are marked by shaded grid squares. These details determine the agent's line-of-sight visibility, which is illustrated by the unshaded region of space surrounding the agent. Similar 2D animations have been shown to evoke strong impressions of agency and intentionality in infant [50,64] and adult [71,128,129] observers, and have been employed in several computational studies of human-action understanding [8] and social goal inference [18,130]. They are also known to recruit brain regions that have been implicated in the perception of animacy and biological motion [114,24,83,46].

People's intuitive judgments on viewing these animated stimuli can be elicited behaviorally using psychophysical methods. In the food-truck context, people can report their desire attributions by rating

---

[4]These frameworks depart from the keyhole plan-recognition setting considered here, instead performing *intended* plan recognition.

how much the student liked each truck, and their belief attributions by retrospectively rating the student's degree of belief in each possible world—Lebanese truck (L), Mexican truck (M), or nothing (N) parked in the Northeast spot—before they set off along their path, based on the information from their subsequently observed trajectory. Both kinds of ratings can be expressed using a 7-point Likert scales.

Applying BToM to our food-truck scenarios requires specifying a number of settings and parameters. We select resolutions $\mu, \eta = 7$ for discretizing the belief and desire spaces, respectively. This directly corresponds to the 7-point psychological scale for human ratings, providing sufficient resolution to represent the joint probabilistic dependencies between beliefs and desires and allowing inference to be performed relatively tractably. The range of reward values is calibrated to the spatial scale of our environments, taking values $-20, 0, \ldots, 100$ to represent desires ranging from aversion, to ambivalence, to a strong desire for each truck. These desires trade off against the relative cost of movements, assumed to be equal to 1 for each step, with 15 steps required to cross the environment from East–West and 5 steps required to cross from South–North.

Model predictions are based on the student's expected reward value for each truck (K, L, M) and the expected degree of belief in each possible world (L, M, N) for each trial, where the expectation is taken over the posterior marginal distribution in Eq. 7.8. Two free parameters are fit for the BToM model: β, which specifies the agent's degree of determinism in selecting the best action, and ν, which specifies the agent's level of observation noise. Only the determinism parameter β is relevant for the *TrueBelief* and *NoObs* models and is set for them as well. Parameter fits are not meant to be precise; we report the best values found among several drawn from a coarse grid. The remaining parameters, α, the Dirichlet hyperparameter for the `BeliefPrior`(α) distribution, and ϵ, the movement noise in the state-transition distribution, are set to default values: $\alpha = 0$ to produce a uniform prior over beliefs, and $\epsilon = 0.01$ to reflect a very small probability of the agent's intended movements failing.

Next, we provide a detailed demonstration of some of the rich dynamical inferences made by BToM, using the food-truck scenario shown in Figure 7.2. Initially, the agent can see that the Korean (K) truck is in the Southwest parking spot, but the Northeast parking spot is not visible from its location—it may believe that either the Lebanese (L) truck, the Mexican (M) truck, or Nothing (N) is parked there, or be uncertain which of these possibilities is the case. At first, the agent heads in the direction of the Korean truck, which is also the shortest route to reach the Northeast parking spot or to see what is there. The agent then passes the Korean truck, rounds the corner to see the Northeast parking spot, sees that the Lebanese truck is parked there, and turns back to eat at the Korean truck.

Over the course of this simple scenario, BToM performs a range of nuanced, but intuitive, types of temporal inferences, all of which can be expressed as different queries over Eq. 7.8. Figure 7.4 plots examples of several of these types of mental state reasoning over time. The most straightforward inferences are those about an agent's current mental state, given its actions up to the present time, referred to as *online* inferences. For example, the annotated stimulus in Figure 7.4(a) illustrates online inference of the agent's mental state at time 10, given its movements up to that point. More conceptually challenging are *retrospective* inferences, shown in Figure 7.4(b), which are about the agent's beliefs at some past moment, given its trajectory prior and subsequent to that moment. The annotated stimulus in Figure 7.4(b) depicts retrospective inference of the agent's initial mental state at time 1, given its full trajectory up to Step 15, once it has arrived at K.

BToM's online desire and belief inferences plotted in Figure 7.4(a) correspond closely to the intuitive mentalistic description of the scenario given in Section 7.2.1. The model initially infers that the agent

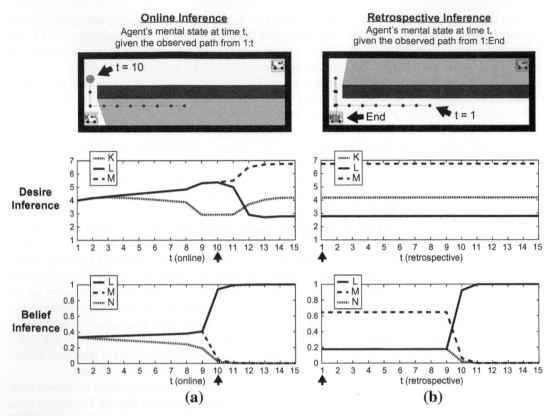

FIGURE 7.4

Online and retrospective desire and belief inferences in BToM. In each stimulus panel, the marked path up to the position of the agent indicates the portion of the trajectory observed: in (a), up to $t = 10$; in (b), up to $t = 15$. The *arrow* in each stimulus panel indicates the point in time at which the agent's mental state is queried: in (a) at $t = 10$; in (b) at $t = 1$. For each plot of the model inferences, the arrows along the X axis indicate the timestep shown in the annotated example stimulus. (**a**) Online inference of the agent's desires and beliefs, given its partial trajectory. (**b**) Retrospective inference of the agent's desires and beliefs at each frame, given its entire trajectory.

desires K, L, and M equally, and believes that L, M, or N are equally likely to be in the Northeast parking spot. Gradually, BToM infers that the agent desires L and M over K and desires L and M equally. The model also gradually infers that the agent believes that either L or M is more likely to be in the Northeast parking spot than N. By Frame 10, the inferred desire for L or M over K has strengthened after the agent passes K. Once the agent gains line-of-sight visual access to the Northeast parking spot, the model strongly infers that the agent's belief resolves toward L—the true state of the world. At Frame 11, the agent pauses in the same position for one timestep, which causes the model's desire attributions for M and L to begin to diverge; by Frame 12, the agent's full desire ordering has been inferred: M is desired over K and both M and K are desired over L.

These online inferences are intuitive and demonstrate the potential for ToM reasoning to go beyond the data given, but the retrospective inferences made by BToM go further still. BToM retrospectively explains the agent's entire trajectory by inferring the agent's full sequence of mental states—its desires and beliefs at each point in time, how they caused its actions, and how they were affected by its observations. Earlier in Figure 7.4(b), BToM retrospectively attributes that the agent had a strong *false* belief before Frame 10 that M was in the Northeast parking spot. Contrast this with the online inference, shown in Figure 7.4(a), which infers the agent's belief at each frame based only on the information available up to that point, and thus cannot distinguish whether the agent believes L or M to be more likely. After frame 10, the online and retrospective inferences match—because the agent has observed the Northeast parking spot, both models attribute the true belief that L is there, and no further changes occur. BToM retrospectively attributes an intense desire for M, a weak desire for K, and almost no desire for L. Note that the retrospective desire inference matches the online inference in Figure 7.4(a) at the last timestep because both reflect the agent's entire movement history, and the inferred desire is assumed to be constant over the agent's trajectory.

So far we have shown that BToM makes rich, intuitive predictions about the patterns of mental state inferences induced by our food-truck scenarios. Now we test how accurately these predictions, as well as those of our alternative models, fit human behavioral judgments. Figure 7.5 presents revealing comparisons of human judgments with model predictions in several specific cases. Example A compares behavioral and modeling results for our running example scenario introduced in Figure 7.2, and analyzed with BToM in Figure 7.4. For both desire and belief inferences, people's judgments in Condition A closely match the predictions of BToM but not those of the two alternative models. In this condition, both humans and BToM infer that the agent desires M most, K second most, and L least, while *NoObs* and *TrueBelief* incorrectly infer that K is most strongly desired because, superficially, it is the agent's eventual destination. Humans and BToM attribute the false belief to the agent that M is most likely to be in the Northeast parking spot, which (necessarily) differs from the TrueBelief inference, but also that of NoObs, which makes no specific prediction in this case.

Further examples of the close correspondence between human judgments and BToM predictions are shown in Conditions B, C, and D of Figure 7.5. The simplest example is Condition B in which the agent moves directly to K without first checking the contents of the Northeast parking spot. People and all models correctly attribute a strong desire for K, and infer that L and M are probably desired equally. BToM and NoObs match people's judgment that the agent's belief is ambiguous between all possible worlds because the strong desire inferred for K renders this belief irrelevant to the agent's behavior.

In Condition C, the agent's path initially overlaps with that of Condition A, but once the Northeast parking spot is in view, the agent continues onward to reach the L truck. Here, humans, BToM, and TrueBelief infer that L is desired most, M second most, and K least. BToM also predicts people's belief attributions, with L being most likely, M second most likely, and N least likely. However, NoObs does not distinguish between L or M for either desires or beliefs. The explanation for the maximal desire and belief ratings for L is straightforward, but the systematically elevated desire and belief ratings for M are more subtle and interesting. For these ratings, BToM infers that the agent may have desired *both* L and M over K, and initially believed M to be in the Northeast parking spot. Indeed, this hypothesis could also explain the observed trajectory, but the evidence for it is weak and indirect, which is reflected in the relatively weaker ratings for M than L.

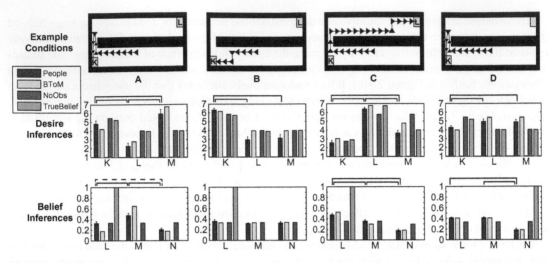

FIGURE 7.5

Four representative conditions from the experiment, illustrating experimental stimuli, and corresponding mean human desire and belief judgments alongside BToM, NoObs, and TrueBelief model predictions. Desire attributions were performed for trucks K, L, or M, rated on a scale of 1 to 7, and belief attributions were made about the agents' initial beliefs about the contents of the Northeast parking spot—either truck L or M or no truck (N)—rated on a 1 to 7 scale, and normalized to a probability scale from 0 to 1. Error bars show standard error (n = 16). *Solid* brackets indicate differences between pairs of human ratings that were predicted by the model. The bracket in example Condition A between L and N indicates the sole difference that the model did not predict.

Condition D is similar to Condition A but with an empty Northeast parking spot. As in Condition A, only BToM predicts the pattern of people's inferences for desires and beliefs. Here, it is ambiguous whether the agent most desires L or M, or which one it believes to be present, and people's judgments reflect this, with their desire ratings for L and M greater than for K, and their belief ratings for L and M greater than for N. In this case, NoObs and TrueBelief make desire attributions that are identical to those made in Condition A because both are unable to reason about the role of the agent's beliefs and observations in determining its behavior.

Finally, we analyze the overall quantitative fit between people's judgments and our three models. Over 54 conditions in total, BToM predicted people's judgments about agents' desires closely ($r = 0.86$), and less well, but still reasonably for judgments about agents' initial beliefs ($r = 0.72$). NoObs and TrueBelief fit substantially worse than BToM for desire judgments ($r = 0.58$ and $r = 0.69$, respectively), suggesting that joint reasoning over desires and beliefs is essential for explaining people's desire attributions. The NoObs model can in principle infer agents' beliefs but without a theory of how beliefs are updated from observations, it must posit highly implausible initial beliefs that correlate poorly with subjects' judgments over the whole set of experimental conditions ($r = 0.39$). TrueBelief's belief predictions are based on the actual state of the world in each trial; the poor correlation with people's judgments ($r = 0.12$) demonstrates that they did not simply refer to the true world state in their belief attributions.

7.4 Discussion

This chapter described a model of human theory of mind inspired by techniques in plan, activity, and intent recognition and artificial intelligence. We argued that the central representations of ToM can be understood as intuitive versions of the formal models of intelligent agents developed by AI researchers and economists, supporting rich, context-sensitive simulations of the thoughts and plans of others. Our Bayesian ToM model formulated reasoning about others' mental states as probabilistic inference over these intuitive models, yielding rich attributions of beliefs and desires from sparsely observed behavior. To test these models, we proposed an approach to rigorously evaluating computational models of ToM against fine-grained human judgments, which showed a strong quantitative correspondence between BToM and human inferences.

Although this chapter has focused on reasoning about the activities of individual agents within simple spatial situations, in related work we have extended our models to multiagent situations involving competitive or cooperative interactions, e.g., chasing and fleeing [7] or helping and hindering [130,62]. In these domains, our generative models of agents' interactive behavior take the form of Markov games [87] (see Gmytrasiewicz and Doshi [51] and Doshi et al. [39] (this book) for related multiagent planning formalisms). Inference is performed over agents' social goals, beliefs, and other mental states using Bayesian computations similar to those described in this chapter. For example, Figure 7.6 compares human inferences with theory- and heuristic-based model inferences of whether each of two agents is "chasing" or "fleeing" the other across three simple environmental contexts. At a coarse level, people's judgments are sensitive to the agents' relative movements (i.e., "toward" or "away" from the other agent), which both the theory- and heuristic-based models capture, but they also exhibit fine-grained variation as a function of the environment, which only the theory-based model is able to explain by reasoning about the agents' context- and goal-dependent planning.

Generally speaking, AI models of (approximately) rational planning, including MDPs, POMDPs, and multiagent extensions such as Markov games [87], interactive POMDPs [51], and partially observable stochastic games [66] are becoming increasingly practical for real-world applications. As algorithms for solving these problems improve, so will the ability of our computational models to perform forward-simulation of agents' mental state-dependent behaviors in realistic contexts. As described here, the inverse inference problems involved in ToM are strictly more difficult than the forward-planning problems; however, tractable optimization- and search-based algorithms for solving the inverse problems have been the focus of promising ongoing research [97,1,96,147,41,28]. Thus, although the BToM framework can surely be generalized outside of the spatial situations presented in this chapter, its capacity to quantitatively predict human reasoning beyond our examples remains an open question for future research.

Another open question concerns whether alternative models can explain human ToM judgments with accuracy and precision comparable to BToM. Here, we tested two simplified alternatives to BToM, and other work [8,130,73,101] has considered several models based on discriminative or generative statistical inference (prominent theoretical alternatives discussed in Section 7.2.4 [18,145,2]). In the

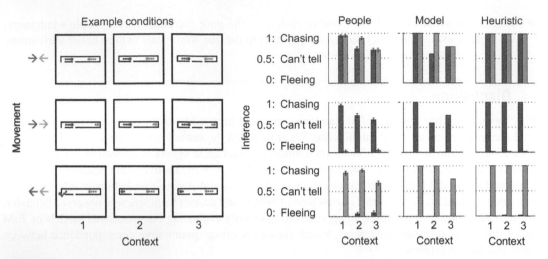

FIGURE 7.6

Example stimuli and results from an experiment on inferring "chasing" or "fleeing." Stimuli consist of a dark agent and light agent occupying a discrete grid world, with obstacles and boundaries marked by black grid squares. The different agents occupy opposite sides of a long enclosing "room," with their location indicated by large dots, and their path history illustrated by the *dotted* trail extending behind them. A 3 × 3 subset of the experimental design is shown, with three different environmental contexts and three different relative movement patterns. The three contexts differ in the exits available at each side of the room, and the three relative movement patterns are "dark moves toward light and light moves toward dark," "dark moves toward light and light moves away from dark," and "dark moves away from light and light moves toward dark." Experimental subjects inferred whether each agent was "chasing" or "fleeing" the other. Two models were compared with human judgments: a theory-based model, which assumed that agents use representations of each others' goals to plan actions to achieve their own goals, and a heuristic-based model, which used minimizing or maximizing geodesic distance as correlates of chasing and fleeing, respectively. Both models capture the coarse structure of people's judgments, which reflects the agents' relative movements, but only the theory-based model captures the fine-grained, joint dependence of people's inferences on both the agents' movements and the environmental context.

settings we have tested, variants of BToM uniformly outperform these alternative models, but it is possible that PAIR is supported by different mechanisms in other settings, in particular, those in which strict notions of rationality are ill-defined [101].

From a practical standpoint, the suitability of BToM for engineering PAIR systems depends on two factors: whether AI models of intentional agents are actually the correct generative models of naturalistic behavior within a given setting and whether the Bayesian computations BToM requires can be tractably approximated. In domains similar to the present experimental setting, it is plausible that these conditions are satisfied. Foraging and spatial navigation, as instantiated within our food-truck scenario, are very natural tasks even for infants; they are evolutionarily ancient and necessary for the survival of our species [34,19,11,82], and we can gain volumes of experience performing and observing others perform them throughout the lifespan. Therefore, it is plausible that humans behave near rationally, have finely tuned expectations that others will behave near rationally, and perform reasoning in ways that come impressively close to the optimal Bayesian inferences within these domains.

Of course, none would argue that human behavior is strictly rational under all circumstances [77]–is BToM simply inapplicable to these situations? In fact, Saxe's "argument from error" cites a body of research showing a systematic dissociation between people's expectations that others will behave rationally, and the behavior that others actually produce, as evidence for a rationality-based ToM [110]. Although overattribution of rationality constitutes a departure from ideal observer or rational inference in the sense defined earlier, an advantage of predictive models of rational planning is their ability to generalize to novel contexts, allowing behavior to be understood far outside of the familiar situations encountered in everyday life. Furthermore, the rationality assumption may provide a general space of prior models that is refined as more data from others' or even one's own behavior are observed. Additional data could even be "simulated" offline using neural mechanisms for decision making; these possibilities highlight the prospect of a hybrid account combining the strengths of planning- and statistically-based mechanisms within the BToM framework. Elucidating the role of these and other mechanisms within a range of contexts by comparing actual behavior, predicted behavior, and interpreted behavior is a promising next step within the BToM research program defined in this chapter.

Under circumstances where BToM and human inferences diverge, this may be because people's expectations are sensitive to others' systematic deviations from strict rationality in ways that our present models do not capture. Developing formal models of the complex psychological factors influencing real-world decision making is the goal of the burgeoning fields of behavioral economics [21] and neuroeconomics [37]; as research in these fields produces more realistic models of human behavior, integrating these models within theory-based Bayesian models of ToM will be a promising avenue for improving PAIR systems, perhaps bringing them more in line with human intuitions as well. In other cases, discrepancies between BToM and people could result from fundamental human processing constraints, in the spirit of Chomsky's "competence-versus-performance" distinction [29]. Understanding people's approximate inference strategies at the algorithmic [92] or process [4] levels is essential for identifying these cases and could suggest adaptive, resource-constrained algorithms for AI systems to emulate. On the other hand, these areas provide opportunities where computational social intelligence may eventually surpass and augment human intelligence.

Our experimental finding that people's inferences about agents' desires are more robust than their inferences about beliefs, and more consistent with our Bayesian model's predictions, is intriguingly consistent with classic asymmetries between these two kinds of mental state attributions in the ToM literature. Intentional actions are the joint consequence of an agent's beliefs and desires, but inferences from actions back to beliefs are frequently more difficult and indirect than inferences about desires. Actions often point with salient perceptual cues directly toward an agent's goal or desired state. When a person wants to take a drink, her hand moves clearly *toward* the full glass of water on the table. In contrast, no motion so directly indicates what she believes to be inside the glass. Infants as young as five months old can infer agents' goals from their actions [49], while inferences about representational beliefs seem to be present only in rudimentary forms by one year of age [99] and in more robust forms only by age four [137]. Whether these differences are best explained at the competence level, in terms of modifications to the theory of belief-dependent planning described here or at the performance level, in terms of fundamental cognitive processing constraints, is a crucial question for future study.

7.5 Conclusion

Research on plan recognition began with the idea that AI models of planning can be used in reverse to understand as well as generate behavior. This chapter identified a strong connection between this classic AI idea and human social intelligence, modeling human ToM within a theory-based Bayesian framework inspired by work in AI, PAIR, and machine learning. It is fascinating to find such close parallels between AI and human cognition, but perhaps it should not be too surprising. AI modeling has always been informed by introspection on human intelligence, and cognitive science has always looked to AI for representations and algorithms to explain the abstract computations performed in the human mind and brain. It makes good sense that formal theories of planning should mirror our intuitive theories of what it means to be an intelligent agent because their design has been guided by ToM in the minds of AI researchers.

In the real world, humans still far surpass even the most advanced artificial social intelligence. We believe that engineering PAIR systems with humanlike ToM, using the same kinds of probabilistic models and action representations that support social reasoning in humans, will help to narrow this gap, while also advancing our basic scientific understanding of human social cognition. While psychologists have long studied ToM and action understanding using behavioral experiments, they did not have rigorous computational models of these capacities, framed in the same terms used to engineer AI systems. That is changing as modern PAIR research (and AI more broadly) offers tools to recast the relevant areas of psychological and behavioral science as engineering (or more accurately, "reverse engineering") disciplines. Engineering large-scale PAIR systems that integrate models of ToM will provide the most challenging test yet of these models' adequacy and, if successful, demonstrate the need for continual exchange of ideas and techniques between AI and cognitive science.

References

[1] Abbeel P, Ng AY. Apprenticeship learning via inverse reinforcement learning. In: Proceedings of the 21st International Conference on Machine Learning; 2004.

[2] Albrecht DW, Zukerman I, Nicholson AE. Bayesian models for keyhole plan recognition in an adventure game. User Model User-Adapt Interact 1998;8(1–2):5–47.

[3] Allen JF, Perrault CR. Analyzing intention in utterances. Artif Intell 1980;15:143–78.

[4] Anderson JR. The adaptive character of thought. Lawrence Erlbaum Associates; 1990.

[5] Austin JL. How to do things with words. Clarendon Press; 1962.

[6] Baker CL. Bayesian theory of mind: modeling human reasoning about beliefs, desires, goals and social relations. Unpublished doctoral dissertation, Massachusetts Institute of Technology, Cambridge, MA, 2012.

[7] Baker CL, Goodman ND, Tenenbaum JB. Theory-based social goal inference. In: Proceedings of the 13th Annual Conference of the Cognitive Science Society; 2008. p. 1447–55.

[8] Baker CL, Saxe R, Tenenbaum JB. Action understanding as inverse planning. Cognition 2009;113:329–49.

[9] Baker CL, Tenenbaum JB, Saxe RR. Bayesian models of human action understanding. In: Advances in neural information processing systems, vol. 18; 2006. p. 99–106.

[10] Baker CL, Tenenbaum JB, Saxe RR. Goal inference as inverse planning. In: Proceedings of the 29th Annual Conference of the Cognitive Science Society; 2007. p. 779–87.

[11] Barrett H, Todd PM, Miller G, Blythe P. Accurate judgments of intention from motion cues alone: a cross-cultural study. Evol Human Behav 2005;26(4):313–31.

[12] Bello P. Shared representations of belief and their effects on action selection: a preliminary computational cognitive model. In: Proceedings of the 33rd Annual Conference of the Cognitive Science Society; 2011. p. 2997–3002.

[13] Bello P, Bignoli P, Cassimatis NL. Attention and association explain the emergence of reasoning about false beliefs in young children. In: Proceedings of the Eighth International Conference on Cognitive Modeling; 2007. p. 169–74.

[14] Bello P, Cassimatis NL. Developmental accounts of theory-of-mind acquisition: achieving clarity via computational cognitive modeling. In: Proceedings of the 28th Annual Conference of the Cognitive Science Society; 2006. p. 1014–9.

[15] Bello P, Cassimatis NL. Some unifying principles for computational models of theory-of-mind. In: Proceedings of the Seventh International Conference on Cognitive Modeling; 2006.

[16] Bergen L, Evans OR, Tenenbaum JB. Learning structured preferences. In: Proceedings of the 32nd Annual Conference of the Cognitive Science Society; 2010.

[17] Berthiaume VG, Shultz TR, Onishi KH. A constructivist connectionist model of developmental transitions on false-belief tasks. Cognition 2013;126(3):441–58.

[18] Blythe PW, Todd PM, Miller GF. How motion reveals intention: categorizing social interactions. In: Todd PM, Gigerenzer G, The ABC Research Group, editors. Simple heuristics that make us smart. Oxford University Press; 1999. p. 257–86.

[19] Bogdan RJ. Interpreting minds. Bradford Books, MIT Press; 1997.

[20] Bui H, Venkatesh S, West G. Policy recognition in the abstract hidden Markov model. J Artif Intell Res 2002;17:451–99.

[21] Camerer CF. Behavioral game theory: experiments in strategic interaction. Princeton University Press; 2003.

[22] Camerer CF, Ho T-H, Chong J-K. A cognitive hierarchy model of games. Quart J Econom 2004;119(3):861–98.

[23] Cassimatis NL. Integrating cognitive models based on different computational methods. In: Proceedings of the 27th Annual Conference of the Cognitive Science Society; 2005.

[24] Castelli F, Happe F, Frith U, Frith C. Movement and mind: a functional imaging study of perception and interpretation of complex intentional movement patterns. Neuroimage 2000;12(3):314–25.

[25] Chajewska U, Koller D. Utilities as random variables: density estimation and structure discovery. In: Proceedings of the 16th Annual Conference on Uncertainty in Artificial Intelligence; 2000. p. 63–71.

[26] Chajewska U, Koller D, Ormoneit D. Learning an agent's utility function by observing behavior. In: Proceedings of the 18th International Conference on Machine Learning; 2001. p. 35–42.

[27] Charniak E, Goldman RP. A Bayesian model of plan recognition. Artif Intell 1993;64:53–79.

[28] Choi J, Kim K-E. Inverse reinforcement learning in partially observable environments. J Mach Learning Res 2011;12:691–730.

[29] Chomsky N. Aspects of the theory of syntax. MIT Press; 1965.

[30] Churchland PM. Eliminative materialism and the propositional attitudes. J Philos 1981;78(2):67–90.

[31] Cohen P, Perrault R, Allen J. Beyond question answering. In: Lehnart W, Ringle M, editors. Strategies for natural language processing. Lawrence Erlbaum Associates; 1981. p. 245–74.

[32] Cohen PR, Morgan J, Pollack ME, editors. Intentions in communication. MIT Press; 1990.

[33] Cohen PR, Perrault CR. Elements of a plan-based theory of speech acts. Cognitive Sci 1979;3:177–212.

[34] Cosmides L, Tooby J. Cognitive adaptations for social exchange. In: Barkow J, Cosmides L, Tooby J, editors. The adapted mind: evolutionary psychology and the generation of culture. Oxford University Press; 1992.

[35] Csibra G, Biró S, Koós O, Gergely G. One-year-old infants use teleological representations of actions productively. Cognitive Sci 2003;27:111–33.

[36] Davis LS, Benedikt ML. Computational models of space: Isovists and isovist fields. Comput Graph Image Processing 1979;11:49–72.

[37] Dayan P, Daw ND. Decision theory, reinforcement learning, and the brain. Cognitive Affective Behav Neurosci 2008;8(4):429–53.

[38] Dennett DC. The intentional stance. MIT Press; 1987.

[39] Doshi P, Qu X, Goodie A. Decision-theoretic planning in multiagent settings with application to behavioral modeling. In: Sukthankar G, Goldman RP, Geib C, Pynadath DV, Bui HH, editors. Plan, activity, and intent recognition. Waltham, MA: Morgan Kaufmann Publishers; 2014. p. 205–26.

[40] Doshi P, Qu X, Goodie A, Young D. Modeling recursive reasoning by humans using empirically informed interactive POMDPs. In: Proceedings of the Ninth International Conference on Autonomous Agents and Multiagent Systems; 2010.

[41] Dvijotham K, Todorov E. Inverse optimal control with linearly-solvable MDPs. In: Proceedings of the 27th International Conference on Machine Learning; 2010. p. 335–42.

[42] Fagin R, Halpern JY, Moses Y, Vardi MY. Reasoning about knowledge. MIT Press; 1995.

[43] Frank MC, Goodman ND, Lai P, Tenenbaum JB. Informative communication in word production and word learning. In: Proceedings of the 31st Annual Conference of the Cognitive Science Society; 2009.

[44] Gal Y, Pfeffer A. Reasoning about rationality and beliefs. In: Proceedings of the Third International Conference on Autonomous Agents and Multiagent Systems; 2004.

[45] Gal Y, Pfeffer A. Networks of influence diagrams: a formalism for representing agents beliefs and decision-making processes. J Artif Intell Res 2008;33:109–47.

[46] Gao T, Scholl BJ, McCarthy G. Dissociating the detection of intentionality from animacy in the right posterior superior temporal sulcus. J Neurosci 2012;32(41):14276–80.

[47] Geib CW, Goldman RP. A probabilistic plan recognition algorithm based on plan tree grammars. Artif Intell 2009;173(11):1101–32.

[48] Geisler WS. Sequential ideal-observer analysis of visual discrimination. Psychol Rev 1989;96:267–314.

[49] Gergely G, Csibra G. Teleological reasoning in infancy: the naïve theory of rational action teleological reasoning in infancy: the naïve theory of rational action. Trends Cognitive Sci 2003;7(7):287–92.

[50] Gergely G, Nádasdy Z, Csibra G, Biró S. Taking the intentional stance at 12 months of age. Cognition 1995;56:165–93.

[51] Gmytrasiewicz PJ, Doshi P. A framework for sequential planning in multi-agent settings a framework for sequential planning in multi-agent settings. J Artif Intell Res 2005;24:49–79.

[52] Gmytrasiewicz PJ, Durfee EH. A rigorous, operational formalization of recursive modeling. In: Proceedings of the First International Conference on Multi-agent Systems; 1995.

[53] Goldman RP, Geib CW, Miller CA. A new model of plan recognition. In: Proceedings of the 15th Conference on Uncertainty in Artificial Intelligence; 1999. p. 245–54.

[54] Goodman ND, Baker CL, Bonawitz EB, Mansinghka VK, Gopnik A, Wellman H. Intuitive theories of mind: a rational approach to false belief. In: Proceedings of the 28th Annual Conference of the Cognitive Science Society; 2006. p. 1382–90.

[55] Goodman ND, Baker CL, Tenenbaum JB. Cause and intent: social reasoning in causal learning. In: Proceedings of the 21st Annual Conference of the Cognitive Science Society; 2009. p. 2759–64.

[56] Goodman ND, Stuhlmüller A. Knowledge and implicature: modeling language understanding as social cognition. Top Cognitive Sci 2013;5:173–84.

[57] Gopnik A, Meltzoff AN. Words, thoughts, and theories. MIT Press; 1997.

[58] Grice P. Studies in the way of words. Harvard University Press; 1989.

[59] Griffiths TL, Tenenbaum JB. Theory-based causal induction. Psychol Rev 2009;116:661–716.

[60] Grosz BJ, Sidner CL. Attention, intentions, and the structure of discourse. Comput Linguist 1986;12:175–204.

[61] Grosz BJ, Sidner CL. Plans for discourse. In: Cohen PR, Morgan J, Pollack ME, editors. Intentions in communication. MIT Press; 1990. p. 417–44.

[62] Hamlin JK, Ullman TD, Tenenbaum JB, Goodman ND, Baker CL. The mentalistic basis of core social cognition: experiments in preverbal infants and a computational model. Develop Sci 2013;16(2): 209–26.

[63] Hamlin JK, Wynn K. Young infants prefer prosocial to antisocial others. Cognitive Develop 2011;26(1):30–9.

[64] Hamlin JK, Wynn K, Bloom P. Social evaluation by preverbal infants. Nature 2007;450:557–60.

[65] Hamrick JB, Battaglia PW, Tenenbaum JB. Internal physics models guide probabilistic judgments about object dynamics. In: Proceedings of the 33rd Annual Conference of the Cognitive Science Society; 2011.

[66] Hansen EA, Bernstein DS, Zilberstein S. Dynamic programming for partially observable stochastic games. In: Proceedings of the 19th National Conference on Artificial Intelligence; 2004.

[67] Harsanyi JC. Games with incomplete information played by Bayesian players: Part I. the basic model. Manage Sci 1967;14(3):159–82.

[68] Harsanyi JC. Games with incomplete information played by Bayesian players: Part II Bayesian equilibrium points. Manage Sci 1968;14(5):320–34.

[69] Harsanyi JC. Games with incomplete information played by Bayesian players: Part III. The basic probability distribution of the game. Management Sci 1968;14(7):486–502.

[70] Hauskrecht M. Value-function approximations for partially observable Markov decision processes. J Artif Intell Res 2000;13:33–94.

[71] Heider F, Simmel MA. An experimental study of apparent behavior An experimental study of apparent behavior. Am J Psychol 1944;57:243–9.

[72] Ho TH, Camerer C, Weigelt K. Iterated dominance and iterated best response in experimental p-beauty contests. AmEconom Rev 1998;88:947–69.

[73] Jara-Ettinger J, Baker CL, Tenenbaum JB. Learning what is where from social observations. In: Proceedings of the 34th Annual Conference of the Cognitive Science Society; 2012. p. 515–20.

[74] Jern A, Kemp C. Capturing mental state reasoning with influence diagrams. In: Proceedings of the 33rd Annual Conference of the Cognitive Science Society; 2011.

[75] Jern A, Lucas CG, Kemp C. Evaluating the inverse decision-making approach to preference learning. In: Advances in neural information processing systems; 2011.

[76] Kaelbling LP, Littman ML, Cassandra AR. Planning and acting in partially observable stochastic domains planning and acting in partially observable stochastic domains. Artif Intell 1998;101:99–134.

[77] Kahneman D, Slovic P, Tversky A, editors. Judgment under uncertainty: heuristics and biases. Cambridge University Press; 1982.

[78] Kautz, H. A Formal Theory of Plan Recognition A formal theory of plan recognition. Unpublished doctoral dissertation, University of Rochester, Rochester, NY; 1987.

[79] Kautz H, Allen J. Generalized plan recognition. In: Proceedings of the Fifth National Conference on Artificial Intelligence; 1986. p. 32–7.

[80] Kemp C, Tenenbaum JB. Structured statistical models of inductive reasoning. Psychol Rev 2009;116(1):20–58.

[81] Knill D, Richards W. Perception as Bayesian inference. Cambridge University Press; 1996.

[82] Krasnow MM, Truxaw D, Gaulin SJC, New J, Ozono H, Uono S, et al. Cognitive adaptations for gathering-related navigation in humans. Evol Human Behav 2011;32:1–12.

[83] Lee SM, Gao T, McCarthy G. Attributing intentions to random motion engages the posterior superior temporal sulcus. Soc Cogn Affect Neurosci 2014;9(1):81–7.

[84] Lewis D. Convention: a philosophical study. Harvard University Press; 1969.

[85] Liao L, Fox D, Kautz H. Learning and inferring transportation routines. In: Proceedings of the 19th National Conference on Artificial Intelligence; 2004. p. 348–53.

[86] Litman DJ, Allen JF. A plan recognition model for subdialogues in conversations. Cognitive Sci 1987;11:163–200.

[87] Littman ML. Markov games as a framework for multi-agent reinforcement learning. In: Proceedings of the 11th International Conference on Machine Learning; 1994. p. 157–63.

[88] Lovejoy WS. Computationally feasible bounds for partially observed Markov decision processes. Oper Res 1991;39(1):162–75.

[89] Lucas C, Griffiths TL, Xu F, Fawcett C. A rational model of preference learning and choice prediction by children. In: Advances in neural information processing systems 21; 2009.

[90] Luo Y. Three-month-old infants attribute goals to a non-human agent. Develop Sci 2011;14(2):453–60.

[91] Luo Y, Baillargeon R. Toward a mentalistic account of early psychological reasoning. Curr Direct Psychol Sci 2010;19(5):301–7.

[92] Marr D. Vision. Freeman Publishers; 1982.

[93] Milch B, Koller D. Probabilistic models for agents' beliefs and decisions. In: Proceedings of the 16th Conference on Uncertainty in Artificial Intelligence; 2000. p. 389–96.

[94] Morariu VI, Prasad VSN, Davis LS. Human activity understanding using visibility context. IEEE/RSJ IROS workshop: from sensors to human spatial concepts; 2007.

[95] Murphy, KP. Dynamic Bayesian Networks: Representation, Inference and Learning. Unpublished doctoral dissertation, Massachusetts Institute of Technology; 2002.

[96] Neu G, Szepesvári C. Apprenticeship learning using inverse reinforcement learning and gradient methods. In: Proceedings of the 23rd Conference on Uncertainty in Artificial Intelligence; 2007.

[97] Ng AY, Russell S. Algorithms for inverse reinforcement learning. In: Proceedings of the 17th International Conference on Machine Learning; 2000. p. 663–70.

[98] Ong SCW, Png SW, Hsu D, Lee WS. POMDPs for robotic tasks with mixed observability. Robotics: Sci Syst 2009;5.

[99] Onishi KH, Baillargeon R. Do 15-month-old infants understand false beliefs? Science 2005;308(5719):255–8.

[100] Oztop E, Wolpert D, Kawato M. Mental state inference using visual control parameters. Cognitive Brain Res 2005;22:129–51.

[101] Pantelis PC, Baker CL, Cholewiak SA, Sanik K, Weinstein A, Wu C, et al. Inferring the intentional states of autonomous virtual agents. Cognition 2014;130:360–79.

[102] Perrault CR, Allen JF. A plan-based analysis of indirect speech acts. Comput Linguist 1980;6(3–4):167–82.

[103] Pynadath DV, Marsella SC. Psychsim: modeling theory of mind with decision-theoretic agents. In: Proceedings of the 21st International Joint Conference on Artificial Intelligence; 2005.

[104] Pynadath DV, Wellman MP. Probabilistic state-dependent grammars for plan recognition. In: Proceedings of the 16th Conference on Uncertainty in Artificial Intelligence; 2000.

[105] Rabiner LR. A tutorial on hidden Markov models and selected applications in speech recognition. Proc IEEE 1989;77(2):257–86.

[106] Ramachandran D, Amir E. Bayesian inverse reinforcement learning. In: Proceedings of the 20th International Joint Conference on Artificial Intelligence; 2007.

[107] Ramirez M, Geffner H. Probabilistic plan recognition using off-the-shelf classical planners. In: Proceedings of the 25th National Conference on Artificial Intelligence; 2010.

[108] Ramirez M, Geffner H. Goal recognition over POMDPs: inferring the intention of a POMDP agent. In: Proceedings of the 27th International Joint Conference on Artificial Intelligence; 2011.

[109] Rao RPN, Shon AP, Meltzoff AN. A Bayesian model of imitation in infants and robots. In: Dautenhahn K, Nehaniv C C, editors. Imitation and social learning in robots, humans, and animals. Cambridge University Press; 2007.

[110] Saxe R. Against simulation: the argument from error. Trends Cognitive Sci 2005;94.

[111] Schank RC, Abelson RP. Scripts, plans, goals, and understanding: an inquiry into human knowledge structures. Lawrence Erlbaum Associates; 1977.

[112] Schmidt CF, Marsella SC. Planning and plan recognition from a computational point of view. In: Whiten A, editor. Natural theories of mind: evolution, development, and simulation of everyday mindreading. Basil Blackwell; 1991. p. 109–26.

[113] Schmidt CF, Sridharan NS, Goodson JL. The plan recognition problem: an intersection of psychology and artificial intelligence. Artif Intell 1978;11:45–83.

[114] Schultz J, Friston K, Wolpert DM, Frith CD. Activation in posterior superior temporal sulcus parallels parameter inducing the percept of animacy. Neuron 2005;45:625–35.

[115] Schultz TR. From agency to intention: a rule-based, computational approach. In: Whiten A, editor. Natural theories of mind: evolution, development, and simulation of everyday mindreading. Basil Blackwell; 1991. p. 79–95.

[116] Searle JR. Speech acts: an essay in the philosophy of language. Cambridge University Press; 1969.

[117] Searle JR. Intentionality: an essay in the philosophy of mind. Cambridge University Press; 1983.

[118] Searle JR. Collective intentions and actions. In: Cohen PR, Morgan J, Pollack ME, editors. Intentions in communication. MIT Press; 1990. p. 401–15.

[119] Shafto P, Goodman ND. Teaching games: statistical sampling assumptions for learning in pedagogical situations. In: Proceedings of the 30th Annual Conference of the Cognitive Science Society; 2008.

[120] Shafto P, Kemp C, Bonawitz EB, Coley JD, Tenenbaum JB. Inductive reasoning about causally transmitted properties. Cognition 2008;109:175–92.

[121] Si M, Marsella SC, Pynadath DV. Modeling appraisal in theory of mind reasoning. J Autonomous Agents Multi Agent Syst 2010;20(1):14–31.

[122] Stahl DO, Wilson PW. On players models of other players: theory and experimental evidence. Games Econom Behav 1995;10:218–54.

[123] Stuhlmüller A, Goodman ND. Reasoning about reasoning by nested conditioning: modeling theory of mind with probabilistic programs. J Cognitive Syst Res 2013.

[124] Sutton RS, Barto AG. Reinforcement learning: an introduction. MIT Press; 1998.

[125] Tauber S, Steyvers M. Using inverse planning and theory of mind for social goal inference. In: Proceedings of the 33rd Annual Conference of the Cognitive Science Society; 2011.

[126] Tenenbaum JB, Griffiths TL, Kemp C. Theory-based Bayesian models of inductive learning and reasoning. Trends Cognitive Sci 2006;10(7):309–18.

[127] Thrun S, Montemerlo M, Dahlkamp H, Stavens D, Aron A, Diebel J, et al. Stanley: the robot that won the DARPA grand challenge. J Field Robot 2006;23(9):661–92.

[128] Tremoulet PD, Feldman J. Perception of animacy from the motion of a single object. Perception 2000;29:943–51.

[129] Tremoulet PD, Feldman J. The influence of spatial context and the role of intentionality in the interpretation of animacy from motion. Percept Psychophys 2006;29:943–51.

[130] Ullman TD, Baker CL, Macindoe O, Evans O, Goodman ND, Tenenbaum JB. Help or hinder. In: Advances in neural information processing systems 22; 2009. p. 1874–82.

[131] Vail DL, Veloso MM, Lafferty JD. Conditional random fields for activity recognition conditional random fields for activity recognition. In: Proceedings of the Sixth International Conference on Autonomous Agents and Multiagent Systems; 2007.

[132] Van Overwalle F. Infants' teleological and belief inference: a recurrent connectionist approach to their minimal representational and computational requirements. Neuroimage 2010;52:1095–108.

[133] Verma D, Rao R. Goal-based imitation as probabilistic inference over graphical models. In: Advances in neural information processing systems, vol. 18; 2006. p. 1393–400.

[134] Wahl S, Spada H. Children's reasoning about intentions, beliefs and behaviour. Cognitive Sci Quart 2000: 15–34.

[135] Waugh K, Ziebart BD, Bagnell JA. Computational rationalization: the inverse equilibrium problem. In: Proceedings of the 28th International Conference on Machine Learning; 2011.

[136] Wellman HM. The child's theory of mind. MIT Press; 1990.

[137] Wellman HM, Bartsch K. Young children's reasoning about beliefs. Cognition 1988;30:239–77.

[138] Wellman HM, Gelman SA. Cognitive development: foundational theories of core domains. Annu Rev Psychol 1992;43:337–75.

[139] Whiten A, editor. Natural theories of mind: evolution, development, and simulation of everyday mindreading. Basil Blackwell; 1991.

[140] Wimmer H, Perner J. Beliefs about beliefs: representation and constraining function of wrong beliefs in young children's understanding of deception. Cognition 1983;13(1):103–28.

[141] Wolpert DM, Doya K, Kawato M. A unifying computational framework for motor control and social interaction. Philos Trans R Soc Lond B 2003;358:593–602.

[142] Woodward AL. Infants selectively encode the goal object of an actor's reach. Cognition 1998;69:1–34.

[143] Yoshida W, Dolan RJ, Friston KJ. Game theory of mind. PLoS Comput Biol 2008;4(12):1–14.

[144] Yoshida W, Seymour B, J Friston K, Dolan RJ. Neural mechanisms of belief inference during cooperative games. J Neurosci 2010;30(32):10744–51.

[145] Zacks JM. Using movement and intentions to understand simple events. Cognitive Sci 2004;28:979–1008.

[146] Zettlemoyer LS, Milch B, Kaelbling LP. Multi-agent filtering with infinitely nested beliefs. Advances in neural information processing systems, 21; 2009.

[147] Ziebart BD, Bagnell JA, Dey AK. Modeling interaction via the principle of maximum causal entropy. In: Proceedings of the 27th International Conference on Machine Learning; 2010.

Decision-Theoretic Planning in Multiagent Settings with Application to Behavioral Modeling

8

Prashant Doshi, Xia Qu, and Adam Goodie
University of Georgia, Athens, GA, USA

8.1 Introduction

Partially observable Markov decision processes (POMDP) [28,44] offer a formal approach for decision–theoretic planning in contexts that are uncertain. This type of planning involves deciding on a sequence of actions that is expected to be optimal under the uncertainty. In particular, the framework is appropriate for planning given uncertainty about the physical state and action outcomes, using observations that reveal partial information about the current state. Consequently, a decision–theoretic "universal plan," also called a *policy*, is typically a mapping from a sequence of observations of increasing length to the optimal action.

Although a policy is similar in its representation to a contingent plan for classical nondeterministic domains [27], it is usually associated with a guarantee of optimality while the contingent plans are often outcomes of fast heuristic search. Because observation sequences could become very long with time, POMDPs usually maintain probability distributions over the state space called beliefs, which are sufficient statistics for the observation history and provide for a compact policy representation. Littman [30] provides a generally accessible tutorial on POMDPs for obtaining a detailed background.

The basic formulation of POMDPs may not be adequate if the context also includes other interacting agents that observe and act. This is because others' actions may disturb the plan in various ways. We could include a fixed marginal distribution over others' actions within the POMDP as a way of anticipating how others act. However, this form of implicit modeling would be naive because other agents' behaviors often evolve with time. Consequently, more sophisticated generalizations that provide explicit support for modeling other agents are needed for decision–theoretic planning in multiagent settings.

A framework that generalizes POMDPs to multiagent settings is the decentralized POMDP (Dec-POMDP) [4]. This framework provides a vector of decision–theoretic plans—one for each agent—in a cooperative setting. Another generalization is the interactive POMDP (I-POMDP) framework [22], which generalizes the state space of the problem to include behavioral models of the other agents; these are updated over time and a plan is formulated in response to these models' distribution.

The interaction context in a multiagent setting may range from complete cooperation among the agents to strict competition. As we may include computable models of any type in the state space, the I-POMDP framework has the attractive property of being applicable in situations where agents may have identical or conflicting objectives, thereby modeling interaction contexts that are varied compared to the common rewards in Dec-POMDPs [14].

In this chapter, we focus on the I-POMDP framework because of its relevance to the topics covered in this book. The key difference from a POMDP is that I-POMDPs define an *interactive state space*, which combines the traditional physical state space with explicit models of other agents sharing the environment in order to predict their behavior. Inspired in part by Dennett's intentional stance [13], the framework categorizes models into those that are intentional and others that are subintentional. Intentional models ascribe beliefs, capabilities, and preferences to others, assuming that the agent is Bayesian and rational, and could themselves be I-POMDPs. Examples of subintentional models include probability distributions and finite-state controllers.

The notion of learning the models of other agents in an I-POMDP is generally similar to Bayesian approaches for probabilistic plan recognition, especially those that perform weighted model counting [19]. Early implementations of plan recognition inferred the likelihood of the models from observing the other agents' actions directly. We may also use general-purpose Bayesian networks for plan recognition [10,11], which allows for inference over the models using observations of the effect that others' actions may have on the subject agent's state. Such inferential modeling is an integral part of I-POMDPs, making the framework an appropriate choice for this problem and its subsequent use for planning. Furthermore, I-POMDPs account for agents' nested modeling of others as intentional agents.

Investigations reveal that human recursive thinking of the sort, *what do you think that I think that you think*, often vital to recognizing intent, tends to be shallow by default [9,17,26]. Camerer et al. [9], for example, concludes that typical recursive reasoning could go no deeper than two or even one level. However, recent experiments [23,33] show that human recursive thinking could generally go deeper than previously thought in competitive situations. Because I-POMDPs consider recursive beliefs, they are a natural choice as a point of departure for computationally modeling the behavioral data collected in the experiments.

We apply them augmented with well-known human learning and behavioral models in order to model human data that are consistent with *three* levels of recursive reasoning in fixed-sum games. We compare the performance of the I-POMDP-based models to the use of weighted fictitious play [12] for modeling the data. Instead of ascertaining the opponent's mental models, weighted fictitious play relies exclusively on past patterns of the opponent's actions. In the broader context, Camerer [8] provides a detailed survey of behavioral experiments in strategic settings and the implications for game theory.

The remainder of the chapter is structured as follows. We describe in detail the I-POMDP framework and its finitely nested approximation in Section 8.2. In this section, we outline its formal definition and discuss the key steps involving the belief update and value iteration that underpin the solution of I-POMDPs. Next, in Section 8.3, we focus on an application of I-POMDPs to modeling human behavior in games of strategy. We briefly describe the study and the data that we seek to model; subsequently, we explore multiple computational models of the behavioral data, two of which are based on I-POMDPs. We end this chapter with a brief summary discussion in Section 8.4.

8.2 The Interactive POMDP Framework

The presence of other agents in a shared environment complicates planning because other agents' actions may impact the state of the planning problem as well. Although the planning process could remain oblivious of others, this would likely make the policy suboptimal. Therefore interactive POMDPs generalize POMDPs to multiagent settings by explicitly including models of the other agents as part of the state space [22]. For clarity, we focus on a setting shared by two agents, i and j, although the framework naturally extends to multiple agents.

The I-POMDP for an agent, i, in a setting with one other agent, j, is mathematically defined as:

$$\text{I-POMDP}_i = \langle IS_i, A, \Omega_i, T_i, O_i, R_i, OC_i \rangle,$$

where

IS_i is the set of *interactive states* defined as $IS_i = S \times M_j$. Here, S is the set of physical states and M_j is the set of computable models of the other agent, j.

$A = A_i \times A_j$ is the set of joint actions of the agents.

Ω_i is the set of observations of agent i.

T_i models the probabilistic transitions between the physical states. Mathematically, T_i is a function that maps each transition between states on performing a joint action to its probability, $T_i : S \times A \times S \rightarrow [0, 1]$. Notice that we do not include transitions between models because we assume that actions do not manipulate the (mental) models directly.

O_i represents the observational capabilities of the agent and is a function that maps observations in a state resulting from joint actions to a probability distribution, $O_i : S \times A \times \Omega_i \rightarrow [0, 1]$. We assume that models may not be observed directly and therefore do not include them in O_i.

$R_i : S \times A \rightarrow [0, 1]$ gives the immediate reward obtained by agent i conditioned on the physical state and the joint action. Another interpretation of R_i is that it models the preferences of agent i.

OC_i is the criterion under which the reward is optimized. This is often an optimization of the summed reward over a finite set of timesteps, or of the summation of the geometrically discounted reward over an infinite set of timesteps in the limit.

We subdivide the set of computable models of the other agent, M_j, into those that are intentional, and the remaining are subintentional. Intentional models, denoted by Θ_j, are analogous to *types* as in game theory [25] and ascribe beliefs, capabilities, and preferences to the other agent. These are abstractions that constitute Dennett's intentional stance [13] and allow for a reasoned prediction of the other agent's behavior using well-studied mental constructs.

An intentional model of agent j, $\theta_j = \langle b_j, \hat{\theta}_j \rangle$, consists of j's belief, $b_j \in \Delta(IS_j)$, and j's frame, $\hat{\theta}_j = \langle A, \Omega_j, T_j, O_j, R_j, OC_j \rangle$, where the parameters of agent j are defined analogously to the preceding. Because j could be modeling agent i intentionally, the belief could be infinitely nested. Subintentional models, on the other hand, include finite-state automatons and probability distributions over the agent's actions, and scant attention is paid to how we arrive at such models.

8.2.1 Finitely Nested I-POMDP

Infinitely nested beliefs pose challenges for making the framework operational. An obvious challenge is that of noncomputability of the belief system; other challenges include some impossible belief systems that could arise in infinitely nested beliefs, as noted by Binmore [5] and Brandenburger [6]. A natural way to enable computability is to truncate the beliefs to finite levels by defining level 0 beliefs. Finite nestings, additionally, avoid the impossible beliefs. This leads to a finitely nested framework, I-POMDP$_{i,l}$, with l denoting the level, which approximates the original I-POMDP outlined in the previous section.

Such beliefs are similar to the hierarchical belief systems discussed in game theory in order to define universal type spaces [7,35] and formalize interactive epistemology [1,2]. Specifically, level 0 interactive states are just the physical states and level 0 beliefs are probability distributions over the level 0 states. Subsequently, level 0 models contain level 0 intentional models—each of which consists of a level 0 belief and the frame—and subintentional models. Level 1 interactive states are combinations of the physical states and level 0 models of the other agent. Level 1 beliefs are distributions over the level 1 interactive states, and level 1 models contain level 1 intentional models and level 0 models.

We construct higher levels analogously:

$$IS_{i,0} = S, \qquad \Theta_{j,0} = \{\langle b_{j,0}, \widehat{\theta_j} \rangle : b_{j,0} \in \Delta(IS_{j,0})\}, \quad M_{j,0} = \Theta_{j,0} \cup SM_j;$$
$$IS_{i,1} = S \times M_{j,0}, \quad \Theta_{j,1} = \{\langle b_{j,1}, \widehat{\theta_j} \rangle : b_{j,1} \in \Delta(IS_{j,1})\}, \quad M_{j,1} = \Theta_{j,1} \cup M_{j,0};$$

$$\qquad \qquad \vdots \qquad \qquad \qquad \vdots$$

$$IS_{i,l} = S \times M_{j,l-1}, \quad \Theta_{j,l} = \{\langle b_{j,l}, \widehat{\theta_j} \rangle : b_{j,l} \in \Delta(IS_{j,l})\}.$$

Notice that the level l interactive state space contains models of all levels up to $l - 1$. A common simplifying approximation, which we adopt from here onward, is to consider models of the previous level only.

8.2.2 Bayesian Belief Update

Because of partial observability, the solution approach maintains a belief over the interactive states, which is a sufficient statistic fully summarizing the observation history. Beliefs are updated after the subject agent's action and observation using Bayes rule, and a key step involves inferring the other agents' models from observations, which has similarities with Bayesian plan recognition.

Two differences complicate the belief update in multiagent settings. First, because the state of the physical environment depends on the actions performed by all agents, the prediction of how it changes has to be made based on the probabilities of various actions of the other agent. Probabilities of the other's actions are obtained by solving its models. Agents attempt to infer which actions other agents have performed by sensing their results on the environment. Second, and of greater interest in the context of this book, changes in the subject agent's belief over the models and changes in the models themselves have to be included in the update. The latter changes reflect the other's observations and, if it is modeled intentionally, the update of the other agent's beliefs is the result of its actions and observations. In this case, the agent has to update its beliefs about the other agent based on which models support its observations and on what it anticipates the other agent may observe and how it updates.

To facilitate understanding, we may decompose the belief update, denoted using $SE(b_{i,l}^{t-1}, a_i^{t-1}, o_i^t)$, into the two steps of prediction and correction, analogously to POMDPs. Gmytrasiewicz and Doshi [22] provide a formal derivation of the update from first principles. In the first step (Eq. 8.1), the distribution over the interactive state is updated given the joint action of the agents and the previous belief. We predict the probability of the other agent's action using its models and revise its intentional models by updating the belief contained in each of them using the action and its possible observations:

$$b_{i,l}'(is_{i,l}^t | a_i^{t-1}, a_j^{t-1}, b_{i,l}^{t-1}) = \sum_{is_{i,l}^{t-1}:\widehat{\theta}_j^{t-1}=\widehat{\theta}_j^t} b_i^{t-1}(is_{i,l}^{t-1}) Pr(a_j^{t-1} | \theta_{j,l-1}^{t-1}) T_i(s^{t-1}, a_i^{t-1},$$

$$a_j^{t-1}, s^t) \sum_{o_j^t} O_j(s^t, a_i^{t-1}, a_j^{t-1}, o_j^t) \delta_K(SE(b_{j,l-1}^{t-1}, a_j^{t-1}, o_j^t) - b_{j,l-1}^t), \tag{8.1}$$

where

$is_{i,l}^t = \langle s^t, \langle b_{j,l-1}^t, \hat{\theta}_j \rangle \rangle$.

$Pr(a_j^{t-1}|\theta_{j,l-1}^{t-1})$ is the distribution over j's actions obtained by solving the intentional model.

δ_K is the Kronecker delta function, which is 1 when its argument vanishes and 0 otherwise.

$SE(b_{j,l-1}^{t-1}, a_j^{t-1}, o_j^t)$ is the update of the other agent's belief in its model, $\theta_{j,l-1}^{t-1}$.

The rest of the functions were defined previously.

Because the other agent's action is not directly observed, beliefs obtained after prediction are averaged over the other agent's action and weighted based on the likelihood of the observation, o_i^t, that i receives:

$$b_{i,l}^t(is_{i,l}^t|o_i^t, a_i^{t-1}, b_{i,l}^{t-1}) = \beta \sum_{a_j^{t-1}} O_i(a_i^{t-1}, a_j^{t-1}, s^t, o_i^t) b_{i,l}'(is_{i,l}^t|a_i^{t-1}, a_j^{t-1}, b_{i,l}^{t-1}), \tag{8.2}$$

where

β is the normalization constant.

$b_{i,l}'(is_{i,l}^t|a_i^{t-1}, a_j^{t-1}, b_{i,l}^{t-1})$ is defined in Eq. 8.1.

O_i is as defined previously.

While the belief update just presented is for intentional models, it is performed analogously when the model is subintentional, with the main difference being that j's belief and its update are not explicitly considered. Equations 8.1 and 8.2 together formalize a key inferential step of modeling others within the belief update. This involves updating the subject agent's belief over the models and updating the models themselves, both of which facilitate dynamic plan recognition under uncertainty.

8.2.3 Solution Using Value Iteration

Analogous to a POMDP, we associate a value with each belief, which represents the discounted, long-term expected reward that would be obtained by starting at that belief and following the optimal policy from there onward. Formally,

$$V(\langle b_{i,l}, \hat{\theta}_i \rangle) = \max_{a_i \in A_i} \rho(b_{i,l}, a_i) + \gamma \sum_{o_i \in \Omega_i} Pr(o_i|a_i, b_{i,l}) V(\langle SE(b_{i,l}, a_i, o_i), \hat{\theta}_i \rangle),$$

where $\rho(b_{i,l}, a_i) = \sum_{is \in IS_{i,l}} b_{i,l}(is) \sum_{a_j \in A_j} R_i(s, a_i, a_j) Pr(a_j|m_{j,l-1})$ and $\gamma \in [0, 1)$ discounts the value of the future expected reward. Because the belief space is continuous, we may not iteratively compute the value of each belief. Instead, we compute the value of each interactive state (i.e., corners of the belief simplex) and obtain the value for each belief by performing an inner product between the vector of values for the interactive states and the belief vector. However, notice that the space of interactive states itself may be very large but is countable[1] and may be abstracted to permit solutions [39].

---

[1] Mathematically, the space is continuous because it includes probability distributions, but limiting the models to those that are computable makes it countable.

While the asymptotic complexity of finitely nested I-POMDPs has not been formally established as yet, it is possible that they are at least as difficult to solve as decentralized POMDPs. In particular, they may involve solving an exponential number of POMDPs with given beliefs, in the worst case.

8.3 Modeling Deep, Strategic Reasoning by Humans Using I-POMDPs

A general approach for recognizing the intent and plans of another agent in strategic contexts involves modeling its strategic reasoning. An important aspect of strategic reasoning is the *depth* to which one thinks about others' thinking about others in order to decide on an action. Investigations in the context of human recursive reasoning [9,17,26,45] reveal a pessimistic outlook: in general-sum games, humans think about others' strategies but usually do not ascribe further recursive thinking to others. When humans repeatedly experience games where others do reason about others' actions to decide on their own, humans learn to reason about others' reasoning; however, the learning in general tends to be slow, requiring many experiences, and incomplete—a significant population continues to exhibit shallow thinking.

Recently though, Goodie et al. [23] reported that in fixed-sum, *competitive* games human behavior is generally consistent with deeper levels of recursive reasoning. In games designed to test two and three levels of recursive reasoning, the observed actions were broadly consistent with the deeper levels by default. On experiencing these games repeatedly, the proportion of participants exhibiting the deeper thinking, leading to rational behavior in those games, increased even further, which is indicative of learning.

We apply I-POMDPs to model human judgment and behavioral data, reported by Goodie et al. [23], that is consistent with *three* levels of recursive reasoning in the context of fixed-sum games. In doing so, we investigate principled modeling of aggregate behavioral data consistent with levels rarely observed before and provide insights on how humans model another's planning. Previously, Doshi et al. [15] used an *empirically informed* I-POMDP, simplified and augmented with psychologically plausible learning and choice models, to computationally model data pertaining to recursive reasoning up to the second level. Data from both general- and fixed-sum games, providing evidence of predominantly level 1 and 2 reasoning, respectively, were successfully modeled.

An I-POMDP is particularly appropriate because of its use of intentional modeling, which elegantly integrates modeling others and others' modeling of others in the subject agent's decision-making process. Furthermore, intentional models are directly amenable to descriptively modeling human behavior. An important outcome of this application of I-POMDPs is that it contributes specific insights on how people perform plan recognition in strategic contexts involving extended interactions.

We investigate the performance of three candidate models on previously unmodeled behavioral data. Our first model is the previous I-POMDP-based model, which uses underweighted belief learning, parameterized by γ, and a quantal-response choice model [31] for the subject agent, parameterized by λ. This choice model is based on the broad empirical finding that rather than always choosing the optimal action that maximizes the expected utility, individuals are known to select actions that are proportional to their utilities. The quantal-response model assigns a probability of choosing an action as a sigmoidal function of how close to optimal is the action:

$$Pr(a) = \frac{e^{\lambda \cdot EU(a)}}{\sum_{a \in A} e^{\lambda \cdot EU(a)}}, \tag{8.3}$$

where a is an action of the subject agent belonging to the set, A, and $EU(a)$ is the expected utility of this action. Choice models (e.g., the quantal response), which permit multiple actions, serve a dual purpose of allowing for choices that reasoning may not have modeled accurately. We extend the I-POMDP-based model to make it applicable to games, evaluating up to level 3 reasoning.

Although the preceding model employs an empirically supported choice model for the subject agent, it does not ascribe plausible choice models to the opponent in the experiments who is also projected as being human. We *hypothesize* that an informed-choice model for the opponent supports more nuanced explanations for observed opponent actions. This provides greater flexibility to the model, thereby leading to improved performance. Thus, our second candidate model generalizes the previous by intuitively using a quantal-response choice model for selecting the opponent's actions at level 2.

Finally, our third candidate model deviates from using I-POMDPs by using weighted fictitious play [12], which predominantly relies on the past pattern of the opponent's observed actions to form a judgment about what the opponent will do next. We couple it with a quantal-response choice model to generate the decisions for the games. This model differs from the previous two in that it does not seek to ascertain the mental models of the opponent but instead bases itself on the observed frequency of empirical play.

Other decision–theoretic approaches exist that model reasoning about others. A Bayesian model [3,24] attributes representational beliefs and desires to others; it captures these attributions as Bayesian inference in a POMDP that does rational planning and belief updating. Baker et al. [3] employed this approach in controlled spatial scenarios to infer participants' judgment about the initial beliefs and desires of another agent from observed data. In particular, the experiments demonstrated that the full representational capacity of POMDPs was needed to explain human judgments about both beliefs and desires of others, which may change in the scenarios.

PsychSim [38], a social simulation tool, employs a formal decision–theoretic approach using recursive modeling to provide a computational model of how agents influence each other's beliefs. PsychSim was used to analyze toy school bully scenarios and deployed in training software for teaching cross-cultural skills (e.g., language and negotiation) for modeling urban stabilization and health interventions. Another POMDP-based model [40] used beliefs based on the well-known cognitive hierarchy [9] combined with an inequity-aversion-based utility function, leading to a generative model to classify different types of subjects engaged in multiround investor–trustee games. In these studies, belief attributions play a key role in the modeling of reasoning about others' actions in the context of human social interactions. Similarly, beliefs generalized recursively are integral to I-POMDPs and our modeling of data.

8.3.1 Background: Level 3 Recursive Reasoning

The experiments used a two-player, alternate-move game of complete and perfect information. The game and its tree are depicted in Figure 8.1. It starts at state A, where player I may choose to *move* or *stay*. If I chooses to move, the game goes to state B, where player II needs to decide between moving or staying. If a move is taken, the game proceeds to the next state and the other player takes her or his turn to choose. The game continues up to two moves of II. An action of *stay* by either player also terminates the game. In the study, the focus is on how player I plays the game when it starts at A.

Outcomes of staying or when the game terminates at E are probabilities of winning in a different task for each player. The rational action is the one that maximizes the probability of winning. To decide whether to move or stay at state A, a rational player I must reason about whether player II will choose

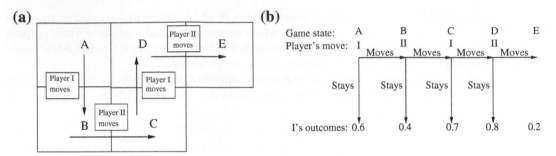

FIGURE 8.1

A four-stage, fixed-sum sequential game in (**a**) grid and (**b**) tree form. The probabilities are for player I. While the structure is similar to Rosenthal's Centipede game [41], the fixed-sum payoffs differ. The sum of the players' payoffs in Rosenthal's version grow as the game progresses ("the pie grows"); they remain fixed at 1 in this game.

to move or stay at B. A rational player *II*'s choice in turn depends on whether player *I* will move or stay at C, and a rational player *I*'s choice in turn depends on whether player *II* will move or stay at D. Thus, the game lends itself naturally to recursive reasoning, and the level of reasoning is governed by the height of the game tree.

8.3.1.1 *Methodology*

To test up to the third level of recursive reasoning, Goodie et al. designed the computer opponent (player *II*), projected as a human player, to play a game in three ways if player *I* chooses to move and the game proceeds to state B:

1. Player *II* decides on an action by simply choosing rationally between the outcomes of default staying at states B and C in Figure 8.1; *II* is a zero-level player and is called *myopic*.
2. *II* reasons that player *I* will choose rationally between the outcomes of stay at C and move followed by default stay at D, and based on this action, *II* selects an action that maximizes its outcomes; *II* is a first-level player who explicitly reasons about *I*'s subsequent choice and is called *predictive*.
3. *II* reasons that player *I* is predictive and will act rationally at C, reasoning about *II*'s rational action at D; *II* is a second-level player who explicitly reasons about *I*'s subsequent choice, which is decided by rationally thinking about *II*'s subsequent action at D. We call this type of *II* a *super-predictive*.

Therefore, if player *I* thinks that *II* is super-predictive, then *I* is reasoning extensively to the third level.

To illustrate, if player *I* in Figure 8.1 chooses to move, then she thinks that a myopic player *II* will stay to obtain a payoff of 0.6 at B compared to move, which will obtain 0.3 at C. She thinks that a predictive *II* thinking that *I* being myopic will move to D, thereby obtaining 0.8 instead of staying at C, and will decide to move, thinking that he can later move from D to E, which gives *II* an outcome of 0.8. A super-predictive *II* knows that *I* is predictive, expecting that if *I* moves from C to D then *II* will move to E, which gives *I* only 0.2; thus, *I* will choose to stay at C and, therefore, *II* will stay at B.

The rational choice of players depends on the preferential ordering of states of the game rather than specific probabilities. Because we cannot find a single preference ordering that distinguishes between the actions of the three opponent reasoning types, Goodie et al. [23] employed a combination of two differently ordered games to diagnose each level of reasoning from the other two.

8.3.1.2 *Results*

Participants were assigned randomly to different groups that played against a myopic, predictive, or super-predictive opponent. Each person participated in 30 trials, with each trial consisting of two games with payoff orderings that were diagnostic and a "catch" trial controlling for inattention. For convenience of presentation, the 30 trials were grouped into 6 blocks of 5 trials each.

From the participants' data in each of the three types of opponent groups, Goodie et al. measured an *achievement score*, which is the proportion of trials in a block in which the participants played the conditionally rational action (best response) given the opponent's level of reasoning. They also reported a *prediction score*, which is the proportion of trials in which the participants' expectation about the opponent's action was correct given the opponent type. This score provides a measure of successful plan recognition. The *rationality error* measured the proportion of trials in which participants' actions were not consistent with their expectations of the opponent's actions.

In Figure 8.2(**a**), we show the mean achievement scores across all participants for each of the three opponent groups. Goodie et al. define a metric, L, as the trial after which performance over the most

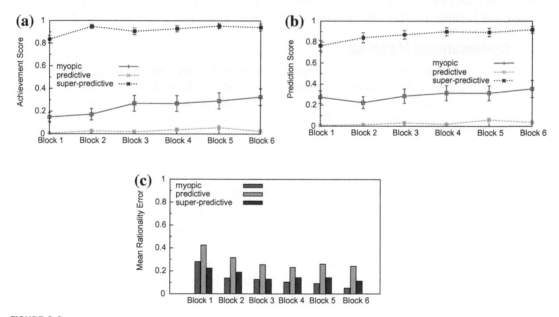

FIGURE 8.2

(**a**) Mean achievement and (**b**) mean prediction scores of participants for the different opponent groups across test blocks. (**c**) Mean rationality errors. Comparatively low achievement scores for the myopic opponent group are due to a large proportion of participants in that group reasoning at the deepest level of 3, but this proportion gradually reduces due to learning.

recent 10 trials never failed to achieve statistical significance (cumulative binomial probability < 0.05). This implies making no more than one incorrect choice in any window of 10 trials. For participants who never permanently achieved statistical significance, L was assigned a value of 30. We observe that participants in the super-predictive opponent group had the highest overall achievement score, with an average L score of 11.3, followed by those in myopic opponent group with L score of 27.2. These L scores are consistent with the observations that achievement scores in these two groups are increasing.

We further investigated the achievement scores for the myopic opponent group by computing the mean achievement scores for just this group given the three types of opponents. We observed that the achievement scores of this group, given a super-predictive opponent, are high, indicating that a large proportion of participants are reasoning at the deepest level of 3; however, this proportion gradually reduces as a result of learning. Participants in the predictive opponent group had an achievement score close to 0 and an L score of 30, which means they never truly achieved a corresponding strategy. Similar to the mean achievement score, participants in the super-predictive opponent group exhibited the highest prediction scores while those in the predictive opponent group had the lowest scores; see Figure 8.2(**b**).

The high achievement scores for the super-predictive group in combination with the low achievement scores for the other groups validate the study's hypothesis that participants generally engage in third-level reasoning by default in enabling scenarios. A secondary hypothesis was that participants' reasoning level will change from the default as the games progress. This is evident from the significantly increasing achievement scores for the super-predictive and myopic groups, thereby providing evidence of learning. However, participants for whom first-level reasoning is optimal learned slowly and incompletely.

8.3.2 Computational Modeling

We seek process-oriented and principled computational models with predictions that are consistent with the observed data of the previous subsection. These models differ from statistical curve fitting by providing some insights into the cognitive processes of judgment and decision making that possibly led to the observed data. To computationally model the results, a multiagent framework that integrates recursive reasoning in the decision process is needed. Finitely nested I-POMDPs described in Section 8.2 represent a choice that meets the requirements of explicit consideration of recursive beliefs and decision making based on such beliefs.

8.3.2.1 *Simplified and empirically informed I-POMDP*

Doshi et al. [15] modeled the shorter three-stage games using I-POMDP$_{i,2}$. We extend this modeling to the four-stage games considered here. These games challenge modeling by being larger; allow for a deeper level of reasoning; and, as mentioned in Section 8.3.1, permit additional plausible models that could be ascribed to the opponent. As Doshi et al. noted, the lookahead in the game is naturally modeled recursively rather than sequentially, and we model the four-stage game using I-POMDP$_{i,3}$.

Physical state space, $S = \{A, B, C, D, E\}$, is perfectly observable though the interactive space is not; i's actions, $A_i = \{stay, move\}$ are deterministic and j has similar actions; i observes other's actions, $\Omega_i = \{stay, move\}$; T_i is not needed; O_i deterministically indicates j's action given i's observations; and R_i captures the diagnostic preferential ordering of the states contingent on which of the three games in a trial is being considered.

Because the opponent is thought to be human and guided by payoffs, we focus on intentional models only. Given that expectations about the opponent's action by the participants showed consistency with the opponent types used in the experimentation, intuitively, model set $\Theta_j = \{\theta_{j,0}^B, \theta_{j,1}^B, \theta_{j,2}^B\}$, where $\theta_{j,0}^B$ is the level 0 (myopic) model of the opponent, $\theta_{j,1}^B$ is the level 1 (predictive) model, and $\theta_{j,2}^B$ is the level 2 (super-predictive) model—all of which model j's action at the superscripted state B. Parameters of these models are analogous to the I-POMDP for agent i, except for R_j, which reflects the preferential ordering of the states for the opponent.

The super-predictive model, $\theta_{j,2}^B$, includes the level 1 model of i, $\theta_{i,1}^C$, which includes the level 0 model of j, $\theta_{j,0}^D$, in its interactive state space. Agent i's initial belief, $b_{i,3}$, assigns a probability distribution to j's models based on the game being modeled. This belief will reflect the general, de facto thinking of the participants about their opponents. It also assigns a marginal probability 1 to state A, indicating that i decides at that state. Beliefs $b_{j,0}$, $b_{j,1}$, and $b_{j,2}$ that are part of j's three models, respectively, assign a marginal probability 1 to B, indicating that j acts at that state. Belief $b_{i,1}$, which is part of $\theta_{i,1}^C$, assigns a probability of 1 to state C. Additionally, belief $b_{j,0}$, which is part of $\theta_{j,0}^D$, assigns a marginal probability of 1 to state D.

Previous investigations of strategic behavior in games, including Trust [29] and Rosenthal's Centipede games, have attributed social models (e.g., reciprocity and altruistic behavior) to others [18, 32,40]. Although it may not be possible to completely eliminate such social factors and others (e.g., inequality aversion) from influencing participants' choices, Goodie et al. sought to design the game to minimize their effects and isolate the level of recursive thinking as the variable. Reciprocity motivates participants to reward kind actions and punish unkind ones.

Altruism and reciprocity are usually observed when the sum of payoffs for both players has a potential to increase through altruistic actions, as in both the Trust and Rosenthal's Centipede games. However, the setting of fixed-sum with no increase in total payoffs at any stage makes the games we consider competitive and discourages these models. Nevertheless, participants may choose to alternate between staying and providing an opportunity to the opponent by moving at state A. Such play is weakly reflective of altruism and is also optimal given the opponent types of myopic and predictive in our games. Consequently, it should result in high achievement scores for these groups. Figure 8.2 shows low achievement scores for these groups and high achievement scores for the super-predictive group that requires the participant to stay at each game, both of which point to minimal evidence of such alternating play.

Another social process that could explain some of the participants' behavior is a desire for inequality aversion [16], which would motivate participants to choose an action that leads to similar chances of winning for both players. For example, such a desire should cause participants to move proportionately more if the chance of winning at state A is 0.6 and this chance is preferentially in the middle, than say, when the chance at A is between 0.45 and 0.55. However, participants displayed a lower move rate of about 12% in the former case compared to a move rate of 14.5% in the latter case. Thus, we believe that inequality aversion did not play a significant role in motivating participants, and we do not model it. Finally, Goodie et al. [23] report on an additional experiment, which measured for the effect of uncertainty (risk) aversion on choices, and concluded that it did not offer an alternative explanation for the observed data.

8.3.2.2 *Learning and decision models*

From Figures 8.2(**a,b**) and our analysis, notice that some of the participants learn about the opponent model as they continue to play. However, in general, the rate of learning is slow. This is indicative of the cognitive phenomenon that the participants could be underweighting the evidence they observe. We may model this by making the observations slightly noisy in O_i and augmenting normative Bayesian learning in the following way:

$$b'_{i,l}(s, \theta_{j,l-1}|o_i; \gamma) = \alpha b_{i,l}(s, \theta_{j,l-1}) \left\{ \sum_{a_j} O_i(o_i|a_i, a_j, s') Pr(a_j|\theta_{j,l-1}) \right\}^{\gamma}, \qquad (8.4)$$

where α is the normalization factor; $l - 1$ is the nested level of the model; state s corresponds to A and s' to B; action a_i is to move; and if $\gamma < 1$, then the evidence $o_i \in \Omega_i$ is underweighted while updating the belief over j's models.

In Figure 8.2(**c**), we observe significant rationality errors in the participants' decision making. Such "noisy" play was also observed by McKelvey and Palfrey [32] and included in the model for their data. We use the *quantal-response* model [31] described previously in Eq. 8.3 to simulate human nonnormative choice. Although the quantal response has broad empirical support, it may not correctly model the reasons behind nonnormative choice in this context. Nevertheless, its inclusive property provides our modeling with a general capability to account for observed actions that are not rational.

Doshi et al. [15] augmented I-POMDPs with both these models to simulate human recursive reasoning up to level 2. As they continue to apply to our data, we extend the I-POMDP model to the longer games and label it as I-POMDP$_{i,3}^{\gamma,\lambda}$.

The methodology for the experiments reveals that the participants are deceived into thinking that the opponent is human. *Therefore, participants may justify observed actions of the opponent that are not rational given the attributed type as errors in their decision making rather than due to their level of reasoning.* Thus, we generalize the previous model by attributing quantal-response choice to opponent's action selection as well. We clarify that our use of quantal response here provides a way for our model to account for nonnormative choices by others. Let λ_1 be the quantal-response parameter for the participant and λ_2 be the parameter for the opponent's action. Then,

$$Q(a_i^*; \gamma, \lambda_1, \lambda_2) = \frac{e^{\lambda_1 \cdot EU(b'_{i,3}, a_i^*; \gamma, \lambda_2)}}{\sum_{a_i \in A_i} e^{\lambda_1 \cdot EU(b'_{i,3}, a_i; \gamma, \lambda_2)}} \qquad (8.5)$$

parameters, $\lambda_1, \lambda_2 \in [-\infty, \infty]$; a_i^* is the participant's action and $Q(a_i^*)$ is the probability assigned by the model. $EU(b'_{i,3}, a_i; \gamma, \lambda_2)$ is the expected utility for i on performing action a_i, given its updated belief, $b'_{i,3}$, for the game, with λ_2 parameterizing j's action probabilities, $Pr(a_j|\theta_{j,l-1})$, present in Eq. 8.4 and in computation of the utility. We label this new model as I-POMDP$_{i,3}^{\gamma,\lambda_1,\lambda_2}$.

8.3.2.3 *Weighted fictitious play*

A different reason for participant behavior that relies more heavily on past patterns of observed actions of the opponent, instead of ascertaining the mental models of the opponent as in the previous I-POMDP-based models, is applicable. A well-known learning model in this regard is weighted (generalized) fictitious play [12]. To apply this model, we first transform the game of Figure 8.1 into its equivalent normal form.

Let $E_i(a_j)$ be the observed frequency of opponent's action, $a_j \in A_j$. We update this as:

$$E_i^t(a_j; \phi) = I(a_j, o_i) + \phi E_i^{t-1}(a_j)t = 1, 2, \ldots, \qquad (8.6)$$

where parameter $\phi \in [0, 1]$ is the weight put on the past observations; $I(a_j, o_i)$ is an indicator function that is 1 when j's action in consideration is identical to the currently observed j's action, o_i, and 0 otherwise. We point out that when $\phi = 0$, the model collapses into the Cournot dynamics that involves responding to the opponent's action in the previous time step only. When $\phi = 1$, it assumes the form of the original fictitious play. We may initialize $E_i^0(\cdot; \phi)$ to 1 for all actions. The weighted frequency, when normalized, is deemed to be representative of agent i's belief of what j will do in the next game in the trials.

Due to the presence of rationality errors in the data, we combine the belief update of Eq. 8.6 with quantal response:

$$Q(a_i^*; \phi, \lambda) = \frac{e^{\lambda \cdot \sum_{a_j} \bar{E}_i(a_j; \phi) R_i(a_i^*, a_j)}}{\sum_{a_i \in A_i} e^{\lambda \cdot \sum_{a_j} \bar{E}_i(a_j; \phi) R_i(a_i, a_j)}} \tag{8.7}$$

Here, $\bar{E}_i$ is the normalized frequency (belief) as obtained from Eq. 8.6 and $\lambda \in [-\infty, +\infty]$. We label this model as $\text{wFP}_i^{\phi, \lambda}$.

8.3.3 Evaluation

We evaluate the comparative fitness of the different generative models to the data and visually compare the experiment's data with model simulations. We begin by discussing our technique for learning the parameters of the models from the data.

8.3.3.1 *Learning parameters from data*

In I-POMDP$_{i,3}^{\gamma, \lambda_1, \lambda_2}$, three parameters are involved: γ representing participants' learning rate, λ_1 and λ_2 representing nonnormative actions of the participant and her opponent, respectively. The empirically informed I-POMDP model gives a likelihood of the experiment data given specific values of the three parameters.

We begin by learning λ_2. Because this parameter characterizes expected opponent behavior, we use the participants' expectations of their opponent's action in each game, denoted as a_{ij}, as the data. Denoting this set of expectations as $\mathcal{P}$, the likelihood of $\mathcal{P}$ is obtained by taking the product of $Q(a_{ij}^*; \lambda_2)$ over G games and N participants because the probability is hypothesized to be conditionally independent between games given the model and is independent between participants.

$$L(\mathcal{P}; \lambda_2) = \prod_{i=1}^{N} \prod_{g=1}^{G} Q(a_{ij}^*; \lambda_2)$$

Here, a_{ij}^* is the observed expectation of j's action in game g, and $Q(a_{ij}^*; \lambda_2)$ is the probability assigned by the model to the action, with a computation that is analogous to Eq. 8.5 except that j's lower-level belief replaces i's belief and j does not ascribe nonnormative choice to its opponent.

To learn parameters γ and λ_1 (or γ and λ in I-POMDP$_{i,3}^{\gamma, \lambda}$), we use the participants' actions at state A. Data consisting of these actions are denoted as $\mathcal{D}$. The likelihood of this data is given by the probability of the observed actions of participant i as assigned by our model over all games and participants.

$$L(\mathcal{D}; \gamma, \lambda_1, \lambda_2) = \prod_{i=1}^{N} \prod_{g=1}^{G} Q(a_i^*; \gamma, \lambda_1, \lambda_2)$$

$$= \prod_{i=1}^{N} \prod_{g=1}^{G} \frac{e^{\lambda_1 \cdot U(b_{i,3}^g, a_i^*; \gamma, \lambda_2)}}{\sum_{a_i \in A_i} e^{\lambda_1 \cdot U(b_{i,3}^g, a_i; \gamma, \lambda_2)}} \text{(from Eq. 8.5)}$$

We may simplify the computation of the likelihoods by taking its log. To estimate the values of the three parameters $(\gamma, \lambda_1, \lambda_2)$, we maximize the log likelihoods using the Nelder–Mead simplex method [36]. Notice that the ideal Q functions will assign a probability of 1 to the observed actions, resulting in a log likelihood of 0; otherwise, the likelihoods are negative.

Parameters for $wFP_i^{\phi,\lambda}$ are learned by maximizing the log likelihood of the data, $\mathcal{D}$, in which the quantal-response function is as shown in Eq. 8.7. In this regard, we note that the experiment's data include actions performed by the participants at states A and C, and programmed opponent actions at states B and D, if the game progressed to those states.

8.3.3.2 *Model performance*

We use stratified, fivefold cross-validation to learn the parameters and evaluate the models.

To learn λ_2, we use the expectations data of the catch games only. This is because no matter the type of the opponent, the rational action for the opponent in catch games is to move. Thus, expectations of *stay* by the participants in the catch trials would signal a nonnormative action selection by the opponent. This also permits learning a single λ_2 value across the three groups. However, this is not the case for the other parameters.

In Figure 8.2, we observe that for different opponents, the learning rate, L, is different. Also, in Figure 8.2(**c**), we observe that the rationality errors differ considerably between the opponent groups. Therefore, we learn parameters, γ and λ_1 given the value of λ_2 (and λ in I-POMDP$_{i,3}^{\gamma,\lambda}$), separately from each group's diagnostic games. Analogously, we learn ϕ and λ for $wFP_i^{\phi,\lambda}$ from the diagnostic games. We report the learned parameters averaged over the training folds in Table 8.1.

From Table 8.1, we see that γ for the predictive opponent group is close to 0. This is consistent with the observation that participants in this group did not make much progress in learning the opponent's type. Consequently, we focus our analysis on the myopic and super-predictive opponent groups from here onward. Furthermore, note the dichotomy in the value of ϕ between the myopic and super-predictive opponent groups. A value closer to 0 for the super-predictive group indicates that the previously observed action is mostly sufficient to predict the opponent's action in the next game. However, ϕ's value close to 1 is indicative of the past pattern of observed actions, not helping much in modeling the behavior of the other groups.

We show the log likelihoods of the different models, including a random one that predicts the other's actions randomly and chooses its own actions randomly, in Table 8.2. The random model serves as our null hypothesis. We point out that I-POMDP$_{i,3}^{\gamma,\lambda_1,\lambda_2}$ has the highest likelihood in the myopic context, although the likelihood of the other I-POMDP-based model is slightly better for the super-predictive group. The difference for the myopic context is significant, with a log likelihood ratio test yielding $p < 0.001$, while the difference for the super-predictive context is not significant.

Table 8.1 Average Parameter Values Learned from the Training Folds

Model	Parameter	Myopic	Predictive	Super-predictive
I-POMDP$_{i,3}^{\gamma,\lambda_1,\lambda_2}$	λ_2		1.959	
	γ	0.164	0.049	0.221
	λ_1	3.259	3.906	3.768
I-POMDP$_{i,3}^{\gamma,\lambda}$	γ	0.232	0.079	0.357
	λ	2.985	3.826	3.667
wFP$_i^{\phi,\lambda}$	ϕ	0.999	0.999	0.150
	λ	2.127	3.107	3.165

Note: Data for the experiment are for the three candidate models.

Table 8.2 Log Likelihood of the Different Models Evaluated on the Test Folds

Model	Log likelihood	
	Myopic	Super-predictive
Random	−1455.605	−1414.017
I-POMDP$_{i,3}^{\gamma,\lambda_1,\lambda_2}$	−522.3421	−339.8796
I-POMDP$_{i,3}^{\gamma,\lambda}$	−548.0494	−337.4591
wFP$_i^{\phi,\lambda}$	−1288.06	−775.96

Note: This table uses the parameters shown in Table 8.1. The difference between the I-POMDP-based models for the myopic group is significant.

On the other hand, wFP$_i^{\phi,\lambda}$ exhibits a vast difference in the log likelihoods between groups, with the low likelihood for the myopic group—though still better than that for the random model—indicating a poor fit. As we see next, this is a result of the potentially poor descriptive prediction of the opponent's actions by relying solely on observed empirical play.

We use the learned values in Table 8.1 to parameterize the underweighting and quantal responses within the I-POMDP-based models and fictitious play. We cross-validated the models on the test folds. Using a participant's actions in the first 5 trials, we initialized the prior belief distribution over the opponent types. The average simulation performance of the I-POMDP$_{i,3}^{\gamma,\lambda_1,\lambda_2}$ model is displayed in Figure 8.3. We do not show the simulation performance of other models due to lack of space. Notice that I-POMDP$_{i,3}^{\gamma,\lambda_1,\lambda_2}$-based achievement and prediction scores have values and trends similar to the experimental data. However, there is some discrepancy in the first block caused by the difficulty in determining an accurate measure of the participant's initial beliefs as she or he starts the experiment. Each model data point is the average of 500 simulation runs.

We also measure the goodness of the fit by computing the mean squared error (MSE) of the output by the models—I-POMDP$_{i,3}^{\gamma,\lambda}$, I-POMDP$_{i,3}^{\gamma,\lambda_1,\lambda_2}$, and wFP$_i^{\phi,\lambda}$—and compare it to those of the random

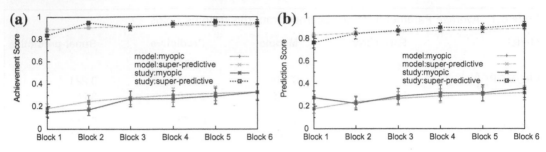

FIGURE 8.3

Comparison of I-POMDP$_{i,3}^{\gamma,\lambda_1,\lambda_2}$-based Simulations with Actual Data in Test Folds (**a**) mean achievement scores and (**b**) mean prediction scores. The model-based scores exhibit values and trends similar to the experimental data, albeit the larger discrepancy in the first block. Additionally, the trend in the model-based scores appears smoother compared to the actual data, possibly because of the large number of simulation runs.

Table 8.3 MSE of the Different Models Comparison with the Experiment's Data

	Mean Squared Error			
Opponent type	**Achievement score**		**Prediction score**	
	Myopic	**Super-predictive**	**Myopic**	**Super-predictive**
Random	0.0041	0.4502	0.0035	0.3807
I-POMDP$_{i,3}^{\gamma,\lambda_1,\lambda_2}$	0.0014	0.0009	0.0020	0.0010
I-POMDP$_{i,3}^{\gamma,\lambda}$	0.0025	0.0008	0.0016	0.0014
wFP$_i^{\phi,\lambda}$	0.0123	0.0082	0.0103	0.0120
Note: The difference in MSE of the achievement score for the myopic group between the two I-POMDP models is significant.				

model (null hypothesis) for significance. We show the MSE for the achievement and prediction scores based on the models in Table 8.3.

Notice from the table that both I-POMDP-based models have MSEs that are significantly lower than the random model. Recall that the log likelihood of I-POMDP$_{i,3}^{\gamma,\lambda_1,\lambda_2}$ is higher than I-POMDP$_{i,3}^{\gamma,\lambda}$ for the myopic opponent (refer to Table 8.2). This is reflected in the difference in MSE of the achievement score for the myopic group between the two that is significant (Student's paired t-test: $p = 0.015$). However, other MSE differences between the two models are insignificant and do not distinguish one model over the other across the scores and groups. A large MSE of wFP$_i^{\phi,\lambda}$ reflects its weak simulation performance, although it does improve on the par *set* by random model for the super-predictive group.

Although attributing nonnormative action selection to the opponent did not result in significantly more accurate expectations for any group, we think that it allowed the model to generate actions for agent i that fit the data better by supporting an additional account of j's (surprising) myopic behavior. This provides preliminary evidence that humans could be attributing the same error in choice that they themselves make to others. Of course, this positive result should be placed in the context of the increased expense of learning an additional parameter, λ_2.

8.4 Discussion

Recent applications of I-POMDPs testify to the significance and growing appeal of intent-recognition and decision–theoretic planning in multiagent settings. They are being used to explore strategies for countering money laundering by terrorists [34,37] and enhanced to include trust levels for facilitating defense simulations [42,43]. They have been used to produce winning strategies for playing the lemonade stand game [47], explored for use in playing Kriegspiel [20,21], and even discussed as a suitable framework for a robot learning a task interactively from a human teacher [46].

Real-world applications of planning often involve *mixed* settings populated by humans and human-controlled agents. Examples of such applications include UAV reconnaissance in an urban operating theater and online negotiations involving humans. The optimality of an agent's decisions as prescribed by frameworks, such as I-POMDPs, in these settings depends on how accurately the agent models the strategic reasoning of others and, subsequently, on their plans. Consequently, I-POMDPs have been modified to include empirical models for simulating human behavioral data pertaining to strategic thought and action [15], an application that we explored in detail earlier in this chapter. Successfully modeling deep-recursive reasoning is indicative that multiagent decision–theoretic models can be descriptively expressive and can provide a principled alternative to ad hoc modeling.

Additionally, parameterized and procedural modeling contributes valuable insights on how people engage in recognizing others' strategic plans. For example, the substantial mean prediction scores observed for the super-predictive and myopic groups (refer to Figure 8.2) imply that participants in our context generally predict that others are using the optimal strategy and—with less success—the simple strategy of relying on just immediate rewards. This implies that people are capable of thorough thinking about others' plans in motivating scenarios. As they experience more games, which provides an opportunity for learning others' plans, the general level of success improves, though slowly, and remains incomplete. Finally, the modeling points toward people attributing the possibility of nonnormative action selection to others.

Although the simplicity of our particular game setting did not require the full use of the I-POMDP machinery, it does provide a principled "top-down" point of departure for building computational models. Of course, the alternative would be to build new models from scratch, "bottom-up," which may not generalize. I-POMDPs bring with themselves a probabilistic representation and belief-based learning, both of which are key to this behavioral modeling application. Even though we did not show modeling results for the predictive opponent group in order to promote clarity, the I-POMDP-based models simulated the low scores closely.

Despite the good descriptive validity, I-POMDP models should not be viewed as being uniquely competent for modeling data. Nor should they preclude exploring opponent modeling along different dimensions. For example, our use of the quantal-response choice model characterizes the probability of selecting actions as being proportional to their expected utilities. While this model is indeed plausible, a simpler choice model, which suggests performing the optimal action with probability ϵ and $1 - \epsilon$ uniformly distributed over the remaining actions, could be plausible as well.

As applications emerge for I-POMDPs, approaches that allow their solutions to scale become crucial. Consequently, developing approximations that trade solution optimality for efficiency is a fruitful line of investigation for decision–theoretic planning in multiagent settings.

8.5 Conclusion

Decision-theoretic planning in multiagent settings as formalized using the I-POMDP framework combines inferential reasoning over agent models with decision-theoretic planning in partially observable environments. If the models are intentional, reasoning on a nested hierarchy of models is performed. We explored an application of this framework appropriately generalized with cognitive models of choice and belief update toward modeling behavioral data on human recursive thinking in competitive games. Empirical results demonstrate that humans could be attributing the same errors in choice that they themselves make to others in order to explain non-normative behavior of others. This finding improves our understanding of the theory of mind and adversarial intent.

Acknowledgments

We acknowledge grant support from the U.S. Air Force, #FA9550-08-1-0429, and from the National Science Foundation, CAREER #IIS-0845036. All opinions expressed in this article are those of the authors alone and do not reflect on the funding agencies in any way.

References

[1] Aumann RJ, Brandenburger A. Epistemic conditions for Nash equilibirum. Econometrica 1995;63:1161–80.

[2] Aumann RJ. Interactive epistemology II: probability. Int J Game Theor 1999;28:301–14.

[3] Baker C, Saxe R, Tenenbaum J. Bayesian theory of mind: modeling joint belief-desire attribution. In: Conference of Cognitive Science Society; 2011. p. 2469–74.

[4] Bernstein DS, Givan R, Immerman N, Zilberstein S. The complexity of decentralized control of Markov decision processes. Math Oper Res 2002;27:819–40.

[5] Binmore K. Essays on foundations of game theory. Pittman; 1982.

[6] Brandenburger A. The power of paradox: some recent developments in interactive epistemology. Int J Game Theor 2007;35:465–92.

[7] Brandenburger A, Dekel E. Hierarchies of beliefs and common knowledge. J Economic Theor 1993;59:189–98.

[8] Camerer C. Behavioral game theory: experiments in strategic interaction. Princeton University Press; 2003.

[9] Camerer C, Ho T-H, Chong J-K. A cognitive hierarchy model of games. Quart J Econom 2004;119:861–98.

[10] Charniak E, Goldman R. A probabilistic model for plan recognition. In: Proceedings AAAI; 1991. p. 160–5.

[11] Charniak E, Goldman R. A Bayesian model of plan recognition. Artifi Intell 1993;64:53–79.

[12] Cheung Y-W, Friedman D. Individual learning in normal-form games. Games Econom Behav 1997;19:46–76.

[13] Dennett D. Intentional systems. Brainstorms. MIT Press; 1986.

[14] Doshi P. Decision making in complex multiagent settings: a tale of two frameworks. AI Mag 2012;33:82–95.

[15] Doshi P, Qu X, Goodie A, Young D. Modeling human recursive reasoning using empirically informed interactive POMDPs. IEEE Trans Syst Man Cybern A: Syst Humans 2012;42(6):1529–42.

[16] Fehr E, Schmidt K. A theory of fairness, competition and cooperation. Quart J Econom 1999;114:817–68.

[17] Ficici S, Pfeffer A. Modeling how humans reason about others with partial information. In: International Conference on Autonomous Agents and Multiagent Systems; 2008. p. 315–22.

[18] Gal Y, Pfeffer A. Modeling reciprocal behavior in human bilateral negotiation. In: Twenty-Second Conference on Artificial Intelligence; 2007. p. 815–20.

[19] Geib CW, Goldman RP. Recognizing plan/goal abandonment. In: Eighteenth International Joint Conference on Artificial Intelligence; 2003. p. 1515–7.

[20] Giudice AD, Gmytrasiewicz P. Towards strategic Kriegspiel play with opponent modeling. In: Game Theoretic and Decision-Theoretic Agents, AAAI Spring Symposium; 2007. p. 17–22.

[21] Giudice AD, Gmytrasiewicz P. Towards strategic Kriegspiel play with opponent modeling (extended abstract). In: Autonomous Agents and Multiagent Systems Conference; 2009. p. 1265–6.

[22] Gmytrasiewicz PJ, Doshi P. A framework for sequential planning in multiagent settings. J Artif Intell Res 2005;24:49–79.

[23] Goodie AS, Doshi P, Young DL. Levels of theory-of-mind reasoning in competitive games. J Behav Decis Making 2012;24:95–108.

[24] Goodman N, Baker C, Tenebaum J. Cause and intent: social reasoning in causal learning. In: Conference of Cognitive Science Society; 2009. p. 2759–64.

[25] Harsanyi JC. Games with incomplete information played by Bayesian players. Manage Sci 1967;14:159–82.

[26] Hedden T, Zhang J. What do you think I think you think? Strategic reasoning in matrix games. Cognition 2002;85:1–36.

[27] Hoffmann J, Brafman RI. Contingent planning via heuristic forward search with implicit belief states. In: International Conference on Artificial Planning Systems; 2005. p. 71–80.

[28] Kaelbling L, Littman M, Cassandra A. Planning and acting in partially observable stochastic domains. Artif Intell 1998;101:99–134.

[29] King-Casas B, Tomlin D, Anen C, Camerer C, Quartz S, Montague P. Getting to know you: reputation and trust in a two-person economic exchange. Science 2005;308:78–83.

[30] Littman M. A tutorial on partially observable Markov decision processes. J Math Psychol 2009;53:119–25.

[31] McKelvey R, Palfrey T. Quantal response equilibria for normal form games. Games Econom Behav 1995;10:6–38.

[32] McKelvey RD, Palfrey TR. An experimental study of the centipede game. Econometrica 1992;60:803–36.

[33] Meijering B, Rijn HV, Taatgen N, Verbrugge R. I do know what you think I think: second-order theory of mind in strategic games is not that difficult. In: Cognitive Science; 2011. p. 2486–91.

[34] Meissner C. A complex game of cat and mouse. Lawrence Livermore Natl Labor Sci Technol Rev 2011:18–21.

[35] Mertens J, Zamir S. Formulation of Bayesian analysis for games with incomplete information. Int J Game Theor 1985;14:1–29.

[36] Nelder JA, Mead R. A simplex method for function minimization. Comput J 1965;7:308–13.

[37] Ng B, Meyers C, Boakye K, Nitao J. Towards applying interactive POMDPs to real-world adversary modeling. In: Innovative Applications in Artificial Intelligence; 2010. p. 1814–20.

[38] Pynadath D, Marsella S. Psychsim: modeling theory of mind with decision-theoretic agents. In: International Joint Conference on Artificial Intelligence; 2005. p. 1181–6.

[39] Rathnasabapathy B, Doshi P, Gmytrasiewicz PJ. Exact solutions to interactive POMDPs using behavioral equivalence. In: Autonomous Agents and Multi-Agent Systems Conference; 2006. p. 1025–32.

[40] Ray D, King-Casas B, Montague PR, Dayan P. Bayesian model of behavior in economic games. In: Neural information processing systems; 2008. p. 1345–52.

[41] Rosenthal R. Games of perfect information, predatory pricing and the chain store paradox. J Econom Theor 1981;25:92–100.

[42] Seymour R, Peterson GL. Responding to sneaky agents in multi-agent domains. In: Florida Artificial Intelligence Research Society Conference; 2009. p. 99–104.

[43] Seymour R, Peterson GL. A trust-based multiagent system. In: IEEE International Conference on Computational Science and Engineering; 2009. p. 109–16.

[44] Smallwood R, Sondik E. The optimal control of partially observable Markov decision processes over a finite horizon. Oper Res 1973;21:1071–88.

[45] Stahl D, Wilson P. On player's models of other players: theory and experimental evidence. Games Econom Behav 1995;10:218–54.

[46] Woodward, MP, Wood, RJ. Learning from humans as an I-POMDP. Position paper, Harvard University; 2010.

[47] Wunder M, Kaisers M, Yaros J, Littman M. Using iterated reasoning to predict opponent strategies. In: International Conference on Autonomous Agents and Multi-Agent Systems; 2011. p. 593–600.

Multiagent Systems

PART

4

Multiagent Systems

Multiagent Plan Recognition from Partially Observed Team Traces

9

Hankz Hankui Zhuo
Sun Yat-sen University, Guangzhou, China

9.1 Introduction

Plan recognition [14], as an inverse problem of plan synthesis, can be used for a variety of applications including natural language pragmatics [18], story understanding [30], psychological modeling [24], intelligent computer system interfaces [11], and report-based monitoring [13]. The plan-recognition problem has been addressed by many algorithms. For example, Kautz proposed an approach to recognize plans based on parsing viewed actions as sequences of subactions and essentially model this knowledge as a context-free rule in an "action grammar" [15]. Bui et al. presented approaches to probabilistic plan-recognition problems [7,10]. Instead of using a library of plans, Ramirez and Geffner proposed an approach to solving the plan-recognition problem using slightly modified planning algorithms [20]. These systems all focus on single-agent plan recognition.

Multiagent plan recognition (MAPR) seeks an explanation of observed team-action traces. From the set of team traces of a set of agents, MAPR aims to identify the team structures and behaviors of agents that are probably changing over time [29]. Many approaches have been proposed in the past to automatically recognize team plans given an observed team trace as input. For example, Avrahami-Zilberbrand and Kaminka presented a Dynamic Hierarchical Group Model (DHGM), which indicated the connection between agents and tracked the dynamically changed structures of groups of agents [2]. Banerjee et al. [4] proposed to formalize MAPR with a new model. This algorithm solved MAPR problems using a first-cut approach, provided that a *fully* observed team trace and a library of *full* team plans were given as input. Furthermore, to consider the relationship between activities, Banerjee and Kraemer [3] introduced a *branch and price* approach to solve multiagent plan recognition problems that accommodated activity interleaving and plan abandonment given a library of plan graphs.

These systems function well by assuming that team traces and team plans are *complete* (or fully observed); that is, missing values (denoted by *null*, indicating activities that are not observed) are not allowed. In many real-world applications, however, it is often difficult to observe full team traces or to collect full team plans because of environmental or resource limitations. For example, in military operations, it may be difficult to observe every activity of teammates, since they sometimes need to hide when their enemies are attacking. As another example, in teamwork at a company, there may not be sufficient sensors to set in every possible place to observe all activities of teammates. Thus, it is important to design a novel approach to solving the problem so that team traces (and team plans) can be fully observed.

We are aware of systems that are capable of recognizing multiagent plans from noisy observations (i.e., observations may be incorrect or missing), such as STABR [26,28] and the system proposed by Sadilek and Kautz [22]. These systems exploit *data mining*-based techniques (e.g., classification) provided a set of "numerical" data are available; however, in this chapter we focus on a *symbolic relation* (e.g., STRIPS [8]) technique that assumes numerical data are not available. To the best of our knowledge, there is no previous work using the *symbolic relation* scenario—that is, where missing values are allowed in the observed team traces when numerical data are unavailable.

This chapter addresses the new MAPR problem that allows team traces to be partially observed (i.e., there are *missing values* in them). We introduce two algorithm frameworks to solve this problem with different types of auxiliary input knowledge (i.e., a library of partial team plans and a set of action models, respectively). The first algorithm, called MARS [33], which stands for MultiAgent plan Recognition System, takes a library of partial team plans as the auxiliary input knowledge. The second algorithm, called DARE [35], which stands for Domain model-based multiAgent REcognition, takes a set of Stanford Research Institute Problem Solver (STRIPS) [8] action models as the auxiliary input knowledge. Note that action models can be created by experts or learned by previous systems such as ARMS [31] and LAMP [34]. Our approaches can be applied to domains (e.g., military operations, virtual laboratories [1], and other similar applications), where we assume activities are modeled with preconditions and effects (i.e., action models described by a formal language such as STRIPS [8], by domain experts, or by state-of-the-art learners).

To solve the MAPR problem, both algorithms take advantage of the maximum satisfiability (MAX-SAT) framework [5, 16, 32]. Specifically, MARS first builds a set of *candidate occurrences* (i.e., a possible case that a team plan occurs in the team trace). After that, it generates sets of *soft* constraints and *hard* constraints based on candidate occurrences. Finally, it solves all these constraints using a state-of-the-art weighted MAX-SAT solver, such as MaxSatz [16], and converts the output of the solver to the solution of our MAPR problem.

Likewise for DARE, it first builds a set of *hard* constraints that encode the correctness property of the team plans and a set of *soft* constraints that encode the optimal utility property of team plans based on the input team trace and action models. After that, it solves all these constraints using a state-of-the-art weighted MAX-SAT solver, such as MaxSatz [16], and converts the solution to a set of team plans as output.

The rest of the chapter is organized as follows. In Section 9.2, we first introduce preliminaries related to weighted MAX-SAT problems and multiagent plan STRIPS-based planning. Then in Section 9.3 we discuss the recognition problem and details of the MARS algorithm. After that we introduce the details of DARE in Section 9.4. We show the experimental results and present related work in Sections 9.5 and 9.6, respectively. Finally, we conclude the chapter with discussion on future work.

9.2 Preliminaries

This section introduces preliminaries related to our problems—that is, the MAX-SAT problem and multiagent STRIPS-based planning.

9.2.1 MAX-SAT Problem

In computer science, satisfiability (often abbreviated SAT) is the problem of determining whether there exists an interpretation that satisfies the formula. In other words, it establishes whether the variables of a given Boolean formula can be assigned in such a way as to make the formula evaluate to *true*. Equally important is to determine whether no such assignments exist, which would imply that the function expressed by the formula is identically *false* for all possible variable assignments. In this latter case, we would say that the function is unsatisfiable; otherwise, it is satisfiable. To emphasize the binary nature of this problem, it is often referred to as Boolean or propositional satisfiability.

SAT is known to be NP-complete [9], but the flip side is that it is very powerful in its representational ability: any propositional logic formula can be rewritten as a conjunctive normal form (CNF) formula. A CNF formula f is a conjunction of clauses. A clause is a disjunction of literals. A literal l_i is a variable x_i or its negation $\neg x_i$. A variable x_i may take values 0 (for false) or 1 (for true). The length of a clause is the number of its literals. The size of f, denoted by $|f|$, is the sum of the length of all its clauses. An assignment of truth values to the variables satisfies a literal x_i if x_i takes the value 1, satisfies a literal $\neg x_i$ if x_i takes the value 0, satisfies a clause if it satisfies at least one literal of the clause, and satisfies a CNF formula if it satisfies all the clauses of the formula. An empty clause contains no literals and cannot be satisfied. An assignment for a CNF formula f is complete if all the variables occurring in f have been assigned; otherwise, it is partial.

The MAX-SAT problem for a CNF formula f is the problem of finding an assignment of values to variables that minimizes the number of unsatisfied clauses (or equivalently, that maximizes the number of satisfied clauses). Two CNF formulas, f_1 and f_2, are equivalent if f_1 and f_2 have the same number of unsatisfied clauses for every complete assignment of f_1 and f_2. There are many solvers for MAX-SAT problems (e.g., MaxSatz [17]); we used the weighted version of MaxSatz[1] in our implementation.

9.2.2 Multiagent STRIPS-Based Planning

In artificial intelligence (AI), STRIPS was developed by Richard Fikes and Nils Nilsson [8]. This language is the basis for most of the languages for expressing automated planning problem instances in use today; such languages are commonly known as action languages. A STRIPS action model is a quadruple $\langle a, Pre, Add, Del \rangle$, where a is an action name with 0 or more parameters, *Pre* is a list of preconditions specifying the conditions that should be satisfied when applying action a, *Add* is a list of adding effects specifying the propositions added after applying action a, and *Del* is a list of deleting effects specifying the propositions deleted after applying action a. An example STRIPS action model *pickup* is as follows:

> Name: (*pickup ?x - block*)
> Pre: (*ontable ?x*) (*handempty*) (*clear ?x*)
> Add: (*holding ?x*)
> Del: (*ontable ?x*) (*handempty*) (*clear ?x*)

A STRIPS problem is composed of a triple $\langle A, I, G \rangle$, where A a set of STRIPS action models, I is an initial state that is composed of a set of propositions, G is a goal state that is also composed of a set of propositions. A solution (or a plan) to the problem is a sequence of actions.

---

[1]www.laria.u-picardie.fr/~cli/EnglishPage.html

An expressible problem in an MA-extension of the STRIPS language is called MA-STRIPS. Formally, an MA-STRIPS planning problem for a system of agents $\Phi = \{\phi_i\}_{i=1}^k$ is given by a quadruple $\Pi = \langle P, \{A_i\}_{i=1}^k, s_0, g \rangle$ [6], where

- P is a finite set of atoms (also called propositions), $s_0 \subseteq P$ encodes the initial situation, and $g \subseteq P$ encodes the goal conditions.
- For $1 \leq i \leq k$, A_i is the set of action models that the agent ϕ_i is capable of performing. Each action model in A, where $A = \bigcup A_i$, has the standard STRIPS syntax and semantics; that is, each action model is composed of $\langle a, Pre, Add, Del \rangle$.

A solution to an MA-STRIPS problem is a *plan* that is composed of a sequence of ordered actions $\langle a_1, \ldots, a_m \rangle$. These actions are executed by different agents to project the initial state s_0 to the goal g.

9.3 Multiagent Plan Recognition with Plan Library

This section introduces the first algorithm, MARS, which takes as input a library of team plans. We will first describe the formulation of the recognition problem and then present the details of the MARS algorithm.

9.3.1 Problem Formulation

Considering a set of agents $A = \{\alpha_1, \alpha_2, \ldots, \alpha_n\}$, a library of team plans $\mathcal{P}$ of agents A is defined as a set of matrices. Specifically, each team plan[2] $p \in \mathcal{P}(p = [p_{ij}])$ is an $r \times c$ matrix, where $0 < r \leq T, 1 < c \leq n$, and T is the number of total timesteps. p_{ij} is an activity that is expected to be executed at time i by agent j, where $i = \{1, 2, \ldots, c\}$ and $j = \{1, 2, \ldots, r\}$. The value of each team plan p is associated with a utility function $\mu(p)$.

An observed team trace $\mathcal{O}$ executed by agents A is a matrix $\mathcal{O} = [o_{tj}]$. o_{tj} is the observed activity executed by agent j at timestep t, where $0 < t \leq T$ and $0 < j \leq n$. A team trace $\mathcal{O}$ is *partial* if some elements in $\mathcal{O}$ are empty (denoted by *null*) (i.e., there are missing values in $\mathcal{O}$). We define *occurrence* (we slightly revised the original definition given by Benerje et al. [4]) as follows:

Definition 9.1 (Occurrence).   A team plan (submatrix) $p = [p_{ij}]_{r \times c}$ is said to occur in a matrix $\mathcal{O}$ if r contiguous rows $(t_1, \ldots, t_r, t_i = t_{i-1} + 1)$ and c columns (say $k_1, \ldots, k_c$, a c-selection in any order from n agent indices) can be found in $\mathcal{O}$ such that

$$o_{t_i k_j} = \text{null} \vee p_{ij} = \text{null} \vee p_{ij} = o_{t_i k_j},$$

where $i = 1, \ldots, r, j = 1, \ldots, c$, and $o_{t_i k_j}$ is the observed activity of row t_i and column k_j in $\mathcal{O}$.

We denote an occurrence by $(t_1, p, \langle \alpha_{k_1}, \alpha_{k_2}, \ldots, \alpha_{k_c} \rangle)$, where t_1 is the start position of the occurrence in $\mathcal{O}$, p is a team plan *id*, and $\langle \alpha_{k_1}, \alpha_{k_2}, \ldots, \alpha_{k_c} \rangle$ is the agent sequence as is described in Definition 9.1.

Our MAPR problem can be defined as follows: Given as input a team trace and a library of team plans, both of which may have missing values, our algorithm outputs a set of occurrences $\mathcal{C}^{sol}$ that

---

[2]Note that we do not allow AND/OR cases in the team plan description (i.e., there are no AND/OR branches in the team plan). We assume that plans with AND/OR branches have been compiled into multiple different team plans.

Input: a team trace				
t	α_1	α_2	α_3	α_4
1	a	d	*null*	a
2	a	b	c	*null*
3	*null*	*null*	c	e
4	b	e	b	*null*

Input: a library of team plans

p_1		p_2	
null	*null*	a	d
a	c	b	b
b	b		

	p_4	
	b	c

p_3		
e	a	
	a	*null*

output: $\{(2, p_1, <\alpha_1, \alpha_3>), (1, p_2, <\alpha_4, \alpha_2>), (1, p_3, <\alpha_3, \alpha_1>),$
$(3, p_3, <\alpha_4, \alpha_2>), (4, p_3, <\alpha_2, \alpha_4>)\}$

FIGURE 9.1

An example of our recognition problem.

satisfies the following conditions C1 through C3:

C1: All occurrences in $\mathcal{C}^{sol}$ occur in the team trace.
C2: For each activity o_{ij} in $\mathcal{O}$, o_{ij} occurs in *exactly* one occurrence in $\mathcal{C}^{sol}$.
C3: The total utility of $\mathcal{C}^{sol}$ is optimal; that is, $\sum_{p \in \mathcal{C}^{sol}} \mu(p)$ is the maximal utility that can be obtained.

We show an example of our recognition problem in Figure 9.1. In the team trace, $\alpha_1, \alpha_2, \alpha_3,$ and α_4 are agents. t is a timestep $((1 \leq t \leq 4))$. $a, b, c, d,$ and e are activities. *null* indicates the activity that is missing (note that we do not allow noisy activities in the team trace). $p_1, p_2, p_3,$ and p_4 are four team plans that compose a library. In the output, there are five occurrences that exactly cover the team trace that is input.

9.3.2 The MARS Algorithm

An overview of the MARS algorithm is shown in Algorithm 9.1. We will present each step of the algorithm in detail in Sections 9.3.3 through 9.3.6.

Algorithm 9.1. An overview of the MARS algorithm

---

input: a library of team plans $\mathcal{P}$ and a team trace $\mathcal{O}$
outputs: a set of occurrences $\mathcal{C}^{sol}$ that cover $\mathcal{O}$

  1: create a set of candidate occurrences in $\mathcal{O}$:
     $\mathcal{C}^{cand} = create\text{-}candidate(\mathcal{P}, \mathcal{O})$
  2: generate a set of *soft* constraints SC
  3: generate a set of *hard* constraints HC
  4: solving all the constraints using a weighted MAX-SAT solver
  5: convert the solving result to $\mathcal{C}^{sol}$
  6: **return** $\mathcal{C}^{sol}$

9.3.3 Creating Candidate Occurrences

In Step 1 of Algorithm 9.1, we first create a set of *candidate* occurrences, denoted by C^{cand}, by scanning all the team plans in $\mathcal{P}$. Each candidate occurrence $c \in C^{cand}$ is probably an occurrence that composes the final solution to the MAPR problem (i.e., $c \in C^{sol}$ probably holds). We call a candidate occurrence c a *solution occurrence* if $c \in C^{sol}$. We describe the creation process in Algorithm 9.2.

Algorithm 9.2. $C^{cand} = create\_candidate(\mathcal{P}, \mathcal{O})$

---

input: a library of team plans $\mathcal{P}$ and a team trace $\mathcal{O}$
output: a set of candidate occurrences C^{cand}

1: $C^{cand} = \emptyset$
2: **for** $t = 1$ to T **do**
3:   **for** each $p \in \mathcal{P}$ **do**
4:     **for** each c-selection $\langle \alpha_{k_1}, \alpha_{k_2}, \ldots, \alpha_{k_c} \rangle$, such that p occurs in $\mathcal{O}$ starting at position t in $\mathcal{O}$ **do**
5:       $C^{cand} = \{(t, p, \langle \alpha_{k_1}, \alpha_{k_2}, \ldots, \alpha_{k_c} \rangle)\} \cup C^{cand}$
6:     **end for**
7:   **end for**
8: **end for**
9: **return** C^{cand}

In Step 4 of Algorithm 9.2, $\langle \alpha_{k_1}, \alpha_{k_2}, \ldots, \alpha_{k_c} \rangle$ is a c-selection in any order from n agent indices (c is the number of columns in p), as is described in Definition 9.1. Note that since there may be different c-selections, such that p occurs in $\mathcal{O}$ (because there may be different columns with the same values), we need to search all the possible c-selections to create all possible candidate occurrences. *For instance, in Figure 9.1, there are two possible c-selections $\langle 3, 1 \rangle$ and $\langle 3, 4 \rangle$ (or equivalently, $\langle \alpha_3, \alpha_1 \rangle$ and $\langle \alpha_3, \alpha_4 \rangle$) for p_3 starting at the $t = 1$ position in $\mathcal{O}$. As a result, we can build all the candidate occurrences C^{cand}, as is shown in Table 9.1, with inputs given by Figure 9.1.*

9.3.4 Generate Soft Constraints

For each candidate occurrence $c_i \in C^{cand}$, we conjecture that it could be possibly one of the final set of solution occurrences C^{sol}. In other words, for each candidate occurrence c_i, the following constraint

---

Table 9.1 An Example of Candidate Occurrences C^{cand} That Can Be Created by Algorithm 9.2

$C^{cand} = \{(1, p_2, \langle \alpha_4, \alpha_2 \rangle), (1, p_3, \langle \alpha_3, \alpha_1 \rangle),$
$(1, p_3, \langle \alpha_3, \alpha_4 \rangle), (2, p_1, \langle \alpha_1, \alpha_3 \rangle), (2, p_3, \langle \alpha_4, \alpha_1 \rangle),$
$(2, p_4, \langle \alpha_2, \alpha_3 \rangle), (3, p_3, \langle \alpha_1, \alpha_2 \rangle), (3, p_3, \langle \alpha_2, \alpha_1 \rangle),$
$(3, p_3, \langle \alpha_4, \alpha_1 \rangle), (3, p_3, \langle \alpha_4, \alpha_2 \rangle), (4, p_3, \langle \alpha_2, \alpha_4 \rangle)\}$

could possibly hold: $c_i \in C^{sol}$. We associate this constraint with weight w_i to specify that it is not to be 100% *true*. We call these kind of constraints *soft constraints* (denoted by SC).

We calculate weight w_i of candidate occurrence c_i with the following equation:

$$w_i = \lambda(c_i) \times \mu(p_i), \tag{9.1}$$

where the first term $\lambda(c_i)$ is the observing rate (defined later), describing the degree of *confidence* we have on the candidate occurrence c_i. Generally, we assume that the more activities being observed, the more confidence we have in the happening of c_i. The second term $\mu(p_i)$ is the utility of p_i that needs to be considered as an impact factor in order to maximize the total utility. Note that p_i is the team plan *id* in c_i. The observing rate $\lambda(c_i)$ is defined by

$$\lambda(c_i) = \frac{2|p_i| - |\{null_{p_i}\}| - |\{null_O\}|}{2|p_i|},$$

where $|p_i|$ is the total number of actions of team plan p_i, $|\{null_O\}|$ is the number of *null* in the scope of $\mathcal{O}$ restricted by c_i, and $|\{null_{p_i}\}|$ is the number of *null* in p_i.

For example, consider the occurrence $(2, p_1, \langle \alpha_1, \alpha_3 \rangle)$ *that is shown earlier in Figure 9.1. The number of* p_1 *is 6 (i.e.,* $|p_1| = 6$*). The number of null is 1, corresponding to the occurrence in the observed team trace (i.e.,* $|\{null_O\}| = 1$*). The number of null in* p_1 *is 2 (i.e.,* $|\{null_{p_1}\}| = 2$*). Thus, we have*

$$\lambda(p_1) = \frac{2 \times 6 - 2 - 1}{2 \times 6} = \frac{3}{4}.$$

It is easy to find that $\lambda(c_i)$ is equivalent to 0 when $|\{null\}| = |p_i|$, resulting in $w_i = 0$. This suggests that the occurrence c_i cannot be a solution occurrence if none of its actions are observed. This is not true according to our MAPR problem definition. Thus, we relax this constraint by revising $\lambda(c_i)$ as follows:

$$\lambda(c_i) = \frac{2|p_i| - |\{null_{p_i}\}| - |\{null_O\}| + 1}{2|p_i| + 1}, \tag{9.2}$$

where "1" can be interpreted as if there is a *virtual* action (that makes the occurrence c_i happen) that can always be observed.

9.3.5 Generating Hard Constraints

According to condition C2, each element of $\mathcal{O}$ should be covered by *exactly* one solution occurrence. In this step, we seek to build *hard* constraints to satisfy this condition. To do this, we first collect an occurrence subset of C^{cand} for each element $o_{ij} \in \mathcal{O}$, such that o_{ij} is covered by all the occurrences in the subset. We use S_{ij} to denote this subset and $\mathbb{S}$ to denote the collection of all the subsets with respect to different elements of $\mathcal{O}$; thst is, $\mathbb{S} = \{S_{ij}|o_{ij} \in \mathcal{O}\}$. The detailed description can be found from Algorithm 9.3. Note that collection $\mathbb{S}$ has different elements, which is guaranteed by the union operator in Step 10 of Algorithm 9.3.

Algorithm 9.3. Build a collection of subsets of candidate occurrences in $\mathcal{C}^{cand}$

---

input: The team trace $\mathcal{O}$ and candidate occurrences $\mathcal{C}^{cand}$
output: A collection $\mathbb{S}$ of subsets of occurrences in $\mathcal{C}^{cand}$

 1: $\mathbb{S} = \emptyset$
 2: **for** each element $o_{ij} \in \mathcal{O}$ **do**
 3:     $S = \emptyset$
 4:     **for** each candidate occurrence c in $\mathcal{C}^{cand}$ **do**
 5:         **if** o_{ij} is covered by c **then**
 6:             $S = S \cup \{c\}$
 7:         **end if**
 8:     **end for**
 9:     **if** $S \neq \emptyset$ **then**
10:         $\mathbb{S} = \mathbb{S} \cup \{S\}$
11:     **end if**
12: **end for**
13: **return** $\mathbb{S}$

With $\mathbb{S}$, we generate hard constraints to guarantee condition C2 as follows. For each subset $S \in \mathbb{S}$, there is only one occurrence $c \in S$ that belongs to $\mathcal{C}^{sol}$; that is, the proposition variable "$c \in \mathcal{C}^{sol}$" is assigned to be *true*. Formally, we have the following constraints:

$$\bigvee_{c \in S} (c \in \mathcal{C}^{sol} \wedge \bigwedge_{c' \in S - \{c\}} c' \notin \mathcal{C}^{sol}),$$

where the term $\bigwedge_{c' \in S - \{c\}} c' \notin \mathcal{C}^{sol}$ indicates all occurrences, which are different from c, do not belong to $\mathcal{C}^{sol}$. Furthermore, we have the following constraints with respect to $\mathbb{S}$:

$$\bigwedge_{S \in \mathbb{S}} \{ \bigvee_{c \in S} (c \in \mathcal{C}^{sol} \wedge \bigwedge_{c' \in S - \{c\}} c' \notin \mathcal{C}^{sol}) \}. \tag{9.3}$$

We set the weights for this kind of constraint, denoted by HC, with "high" enough values to guarantee the constraints are *hard*. We empirically choose the sum of the weights of soft constraints as this "high" value.

9.3.6 Solving Constraints

With Steps 2 and 3 of Algorithm 9.1, we have two kinds of weighted constraints (i.e., soft constraints, SC, and hard constraints, HC). In this step, we put SC and HC together and solve them using a weighted MAX-SAT solver. In the experiment, we would like to test two different cases using, or not using, the observing rate function $\lambda(c_i)$.

We introduce a new parameter, $\rho \in \{0, 1\}$, and revise Eq. 9.1 to a new equation as follows:

$$w_i = \lambda^\rho(c_i) \times \mu(p_i). \tag{9.4}$$

If ρ is 1, Eq. 9.4 is reduced to Eq. 9.1; otherwise, Eq. 9.4 is reduced to $w_i = \mu(p_i)$. Our evaluation shows that $\lambda(c_i)$ is helpful in improving the recognizing accuracy in the experiment section.

The solving result of the weighted MAX-SAT solver is a set of assignments (*true* or *false*) to proposition variables, such that

$$\{c_i \in \mathcal{C}^{sol} | \text{for all } c_i \in \mathcal{C}^{cand}\}.$$

If a proposition variable "$c_i \in \mathcal{C}^{sol}$" is assigned to be *true*, c_i is one of the solution occurrences output by MARS; otherwise, c_i is not output by MARS.

9.3.7 Discussion

In this section, we discuss the properties of our MARS algorithm related to *completeness* and *soundness*.

Property 9.1 (Completeness).   *The completeness of* MARS *depends only on the completeness of the weighted MAX-SAT solver (i.e., given an MAPR problem that is solvable).* MARS *can output a solution to this problem if the weighted MAX-SAT solver is complete.*

The sketch of the proof can be presented as follows. For each solvable MAPR problem, we can encode the problem with constraints SC and HC in polynomial time using Steps 1 though 3 of Algorithm 9.1. Furthermore, if the weighted MAX-SAT solver is complete, it can successfully solve these constraints (by Step 4) and output a solving result, which can be converted to the solution to the MAPR problem in polynomial time (by Step 5). □

Property 9.2 (Soundness).   *Given an MAPR problem, if the ρ is set to be 0 in Eq. 9.4, the output of* MARS *is the solution to the MAPR problem.*

The sketch of the proof can be described as follows. From Step 1 of Algorithm 9.1, we can see that the candidate occurrences $\mathcal{C}^{cand}$, covered by the observed team trace, are all from the library of team plans, which satisfies the first condition, C1. From Step 2, if ρ is set to be 0, the weights of soft constraints are determined by the utility function μ. Furthermore, the solution output by the weighted MAX-SAT solver maximizes the total weights (i.e., done by Step 4), which suggests the second condition, C3, is also satisfied. Finally, the third condition, C3, is satisfied by the hard constraints established by Step 3. Thus, the output of MARS satisfies C1 through C3, which means it is the solution to the MAPR problem. □

9.4 Multiagent Plan Recognition with Action Models

The MARS algorithm assumes that a library of team plans has been collected beforehand and provided as input. However, there are many applications where collecting and maintaining a library of team plans is difficult and costly. For example, in military operations, it is difficult and expensive to collect team plans, since activities of teammates may consume lots of resources (e.g., ammunition and human labor). Collecting a smaller library is not an option because it is not feasible to recognize team plans if they are not covered by the library. Thus it is useful to design approaches for solving the MAPR problem where we do not require libraries of team plans to be known. This section introduces the DARE algorithm that takes as input a set of action models instead of a library of team plans. We first define the input and output of the recognition problem and then present the details of DARE.

9.4.1 Problem Formulation

We first define an action model in the MA-STRIPS language [6], as is described in Section 9.2.2. An action model is a tuple $\langle a, \text{Pre}(a), \text{Add}(a), \text{Del}(a) \rangle$, where a is an action name with 0 or more parameters, $\text{Pre}(a)$ is a list of preconditions of a, $\text{Add}(a)$ is a list of add effects, and $\text{Del}(a)$ is a list of deleting effects. A set of action models is denoted by $\mathcal{A}$. An action name with 0 or more parameters is called an *activity*. An observed activity o_{tj} in a partial team trace $\mathcal{O}$ is either an instantiated action of $\mathcal{A}$ or *noop* or *null*, where *noop* is an empty activity that does nothing.

An initial state s_0 is a set of propositions that describes a *closed* world state from which the team trace $\mathcal{O}$ starts to be observed. In other words, activities at timestep $t = 0$ can be *applied* in the initial state s_0. When we say an activity can be applied in a state, we mean the activity's preconditions are satisfied by the state. A set of goals G, each of which is a set of propositions, describes the probable targets of any team trace. We assume s_0 and G can both be observed by sensing devices.

A team is composed of a subset of agents $\Phi' = \{\phi_{j_1}, \phi_{j_2}, \ldots, \phi_{j_m}\}$. A team plan is defined as

$$p = [a_{tk}]_{0 < t \leq T}^{0 < k \leq m},$$

where $m \leq n$ and a_{tk} is an activity or *noop*. A set of *correct* team plans P is required to have properties P1 through P5.

P1: P is a partition of the team trace $\mathcal{O}$; that is, each element of $\mathcal{O}$ should be in exactly one p of P and each activity of p should be an element of $\mathcal{O}$.

P2: P should cover all the observed activities; that is, for each $p \in P$ and $0 < t \leq T$ and $0 < k \leq m$, if $o_{tj_k} \neq null$, then $a_{tk} = o_{tj_k}$, where $a_{tk} \in p$ and $o_{tj_k} \in \mathcal{O}$.

P3: P is executable starting from s_0 and achieves some goal $g \in G$; that is, a_{t*} is executable in state s_{t-1} for all $0 < t \leq T$ and achieves g after Step T, where $a_{t*} = \langle a_{t1}, a_{t2}, \ldots, a_{tm} \rangle$.

P4: Each team plan $p \in P$ is associated with a likelihood $\mu(p) : P \mapsto R^+$. $\mu(p)$ specifies the likelihood of recognizing team plan p and can be affected by many factors, including the number of agents in the team, the cost of executing p, and so on. The value of $\mu(p)$ is composed of two parts, $\mu_1(\mathcal{N}_{activity}(p))$ and $\mu_2(\mathcal{N}_{agent}(p))$; that is,

$$\mu(p) = \frac{1}{\mu_1(\mathcal{N}_{activity}(p)) + \mu_2(\mathcal{N}_{agent}(p))},$$

where $\mu_1(\mathcal{N}_{activity}(p))$ depends on $\mathcal{N}_{activity}(p)$, the number of activities of p, and $\mu_2(\mathcal{N}_{agent}(p))$ depends on $\mathcal{N}_{agent}(p)$, the number of agents (i.e., teammates) of p. Generally, $\mu_1(\mathcal{N}_{activity}(p))$ (or $\mu_2(\mathcal{N}_{agent}(p))$) becomes larger when $\mathcal{N}_{activity}(p)$ (or $\mathcal{N}_{agent}(p)$) increases. Note that more agents would have a smaller likelihood (or larger cost) of coordinating these agents in order to successfully execute p. Thus, we require that μ_2 should satisfy this condition:

$$\mu_2(n_1 + n_2) > \mu_2(n_1) + \mu_2(n_2).$$

For each goal $g \in G$, the output plan P should have the largest likelihood; that is,

$$P = \arg\max_{P'} \sum_{p \in P'} \mu(p),$$

where P' is a team-plan set that achieves g. Note that we presume that teams are (usually) organized with the largest likelihood.

P5: Any pair of interacting agents must belong to the same team plan. In other words, if agent ϕ_i interacts with another agent ϕ_j (i.e., ϕ_i provides or deletes some conditions of ϕ_j), then ϕ_i and ϕ_j should be in the same team, and activities of agents in the same team compose a team plan. Agents exist in *exactly* one team plan; that is, team plans do not share any common agents.

Our multiagent plan recognition problem can be stated as: *Given a partially observed team trace $\mathcal{O}$, a set of action models $\mathcal{A}$, an initial state s_0, and a set of goals G, the recognition algorithm must output a set of team plans P with the maximal likelihood of achieving some goal $g \in G$, where P satisfies the properties* P1 *through* P5.

Figures 9.2 and 9.3 show example input and output of our MAPR problem from *blocks*.[3] In part (a) of Figure 9.2, the first column indicates the timesteps from 1 to 5. $h_1, \ldots, h_5$ are five *hoist* agents. The value *null* suggests the missing observation, and *noop* suggests the empty activity. We assume μ_1 and μ_2 are defined by $\mu_1(k) = k$ and $\mu_2(k) = k^2$. Based on μ_1 and μ_2, the corresponding output is shown in Figure 9.3, which is the set of two team plans $\{p_1, p_2\}$.

9.4.2 The DARE Algorithm

Algorithm 9.4 describes the plan-recognition process in DARE. In the subsequent subsections, we describe each step of this algorithm in detail.

T	h1	h2	h3	h4	h5
1	a1	a3	a0	*null*	a7
2	a0	*null*	*null*	*null*	a0
3	*null*	*null*	a2	a6	*null*
4	a4	a5	*null*	a0	a0
5	a0	*null*	a0	a0	*null*

null: missing value; a0: no operator; a1: unstack(C B);
a2: stack(B A); a3: unstack(E D); a4: stack (C B);
a5: stack(F D); a6: putdown(D); a7: pickup(G);

(a) Team trace

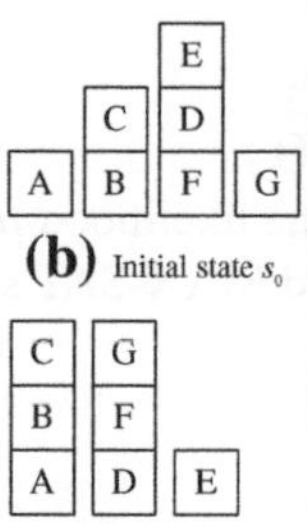

(b) Initial state s_0

(c) Goals $\{g\}$

```
pickup(?x – block)
precondition: (handempty)(clear ?x)(ontable ?x)
effect: (holding ?x)(not (handempty))
        (not (clear ?x))(not (ontable))
putdown(?x – block)
precondition: (holding ?x)
effect: (clear ?x) (ontable ?x)(handempty)
        (not (holding ?x))
unstack(?x – block ?y – block)
precondition: (on ?x ?y) (clear ?x) (handempty)
effect: (holding ?x)(clear ?y)(not (clear ?x))
        (not (handempty))(not (on ?x ?y))
stack(?x – block ?y – block)
precondition: (holding ?x) (clear ?y)
effect: (not (holding ?x))(not (clear ?y))(clear ?x)
        (handempty) (on ?x ?y)
```

(d) Action models

FIGURE 9.2

An example of the input for MAPR problem from the *blocks* domain. *Note:* (a) is an observed team trace, (b) is a set of propositions: {(ontable A)(ontable B)(ontable F)(ontable G)(on C B)(on D F)(on E D)(clear A)(clear C)(clear E)(clear G)(handempty)}, (c) is a goal set composed of one goal g, and g is composed of propositions: {(ontable A)(ontable D)(ontable E)(on B A)(on C B)(on F D)(on G F)(clear C)(clear G)(clear E)}, and (d) is a set of action models.

[3]www.cs.toronto.edu/aips2000/

(a)   **(b)**

T	h1	h3
1	a1	a0
2	a0	a8
3	a0	a2
4	a4	a0
5	a0	a0

T	h2	h4	h5
1	a3	a0	a7
2	a10	a9	a0
3	a11	a6	a0
4	a5	a0	a0
5	a0	a0	a12

a0: no operator;
a1: unstack(C B);
a2: stack(B A);
a3: unstack(E D);
a4: stack (C B);
a5: stack(F D);
a6: putdown(D);
a7: pickup(G);
a8: pickup(B);
a9: unstack(D F);
a10: putdown(E);
a11: pickup(F);
a12: stack(G F);

FIGURE 9.3

An example of the output of the MAPR problem from the *blocks* domain. Note that this is a set of team plans $\{p_1, p_2\}$ (a) team plan p_1 and (b) team plan p_2.

Algorithm 9.4. An overview of our algorithm framework

input: a partial team trace $\mathcal{O}$, an initial state s_0, a set of goals G, and a set of
      action models $\mathcal{A}$;
output: a set of team plans P ;

1:   $max = 0$;
2:   **for each** $g \in G$ **do**
3:      build a set of candidate activities Θ ;
4:      build a set of hard constraints based on Θ ;
5:      build a set of soft constraints based on the likelihood μ ;
6:      solve all the constraints using a weighted MAX-SAT solver, with $\langle max', sol \rangle$
       as output ;
7:      **if** $max' > max$ **then**
8:        $max = max'$;
9:        convert the solution sol to a set of team plans P', and let $P = P'$;
10:     **end if**
11: **end for**
12: **return** P ;

9.4.3 Candidate Activities

In Step 3 of Algorithm 9.4, we build a set of *candidate activities* Θ by instantiating each parameter of action models in $\mathcal{A}$ with all objects in the initial state s_0, team trace $\mathcal{O}$, and goal g. We perform the following phases. First, we scan each parameter of propositions (or activities) in s_0, $\mathcal{O}$, and g and collect sets of different objects. Note that each set of objects corresponds to a *type* (e.g., there is a *type* "block" in the *blocks* domain). Second, we substitute each parameter of each action model in $\mathcal{A}$ with its corresponding objects—the correspondence relationship is reflected by *type* (i.e., the parameters of action models and objects should belong to the same *type*); this results in a set of different activities, called *candidate activities* Θ. Note that we also add a *noop* activity in Θ.

For example, there are seven objects {A, B, C, D, E, F, G} corresponding to type "block" in Figure 9.2. The set of candidate activities Θ is: {noop, pickup(A), pickup(B), pickup(C), pickup(D), pickup(E), pickup(F), pickup(G), ...}, where the "dots" suggest other activities that are generated by instantiating parameters of actions "putdown, stack, unstack."

9.4.4 Hard Constraints

With the set of candidate activities Θ, we build a set of hard constraints to ensure the properties P1 to P3 in Step 4 of Algorithm 9.4. We associate each element $o_{tj} \in \mathcal{O}$ with a *variable* v_{tj}; that is, we have a set of variables, such that

$$V = [v_{tj}]_{0<t\leq T}^{0<j\leq n},$$

which is also called a *variable matrix*. Each variable in the matrix will be assigned a specific activity in candidate activities Θ, and we partition these variables to attain a set of team plans that have the properties P1 through P5 based on the assignments. According to properties P2 and P3, we build two kinds of hard constraints: *observation constraints* and *causal-link constraints*. Note that P1 is guaranteed since the set of team plans output is a partition of the team trace.

Observation constraints: For P2— given a team plan $p = [a_{tk}]_{0<t\leq T}^{0<k\leq m}$ composed of agents $\Phi' = \{\phi_{j_1}, \phi_{j_2}, \ldots, \phi_{j_m}\}$, if $o_{tj_k} \neq null$, then $a_{tk} = o_{tj_k}$. This suggests v_{tj_k} should have the same activity of o_{tj_k} if $o_{tj_k} \neq null$, since the team plan p is a partition of V and a_{tk} is an element of of p. Thus, we build hard constraints as follows. For each $0 < t \leq T$ and $0 < j \leq n$, we have

$$(o_{tj} \neq null) \rightarrow (v_{tj} = o_{tj}).$$

We call this kind of hard constraints the *observation constraints*, since they are built based on the partially observed activities of $\mathcal{O}$.

Causal-link constraints: For P3—each team plan p should be executable starting from the initial state s_0, suggesting that each row of variables $\langle v_{t1}, v_{t2}, \ldots, v_{tn} \rangle$ should be executable, where $0 < t \leq T$. Note that "executable" suggests that the preconditions of v_{tj} should be satisfied. This means, for each $0 < t \leq T$ and $0 < j \leq n$, the following constraints should be satisfied:

- Each precondition of v_{tj} either exists in the initial state s_0 or is added by $v_{t'j'}$ and is not deleted by any activity between t' and t, where $t' < t$ and $0 < j' \leq n$.
- Likewise, each proposition in goal g either exists in the initial state s_0 or is added by $v_{t'j'}$ and is not deleted by any activity between t' and T, where $t' < T$ and $0 < j' \leq n$.

We call this kind of hard constraints *causal-link constraints*, since they are created according to the causal-link requirement of executable plans.

9.4.5 Soft Constraints

In Step 5 of Algorithm 9.4, we build a set of soft constraints based on the likelihood function μ. Each variable in V can be assigned any element of the candidate activities Θ. We require that all variables in

V be assigned exactly one activity from Θ. For each $\langle a_1, a_2, \ldots, a_{|V|} \rangle \in \Theta \times \ldots \times \Theta$, we have

$$\bigwedge_{0 < i \leq |V|} (v_i = a_i).$$

We calculate the weights of these constraints by the following phases. First, we partition the variable matrix V based on property P5 into a set of team plans P; that is, agent ϕ_i provides or deletes some conditions of ϕ_j, then ϕ_i and ϕ_j should be in the same team, and activities of agents in the same team compose a team plan. Second, for all team plans, we calculate the total likelihood $\mu(P)$; that is,

$$\mu(P) = \sum_{p \in P} \mu(p) = \sum_{p \in P} \frac{1}{\mu_1(\mathcal{N}_{activity}(p)) + \mu_2(\mathcal{N}_{agent}(p))}$$

and let $\mu(P)$ be the weight of the soft constraints. Note that we aim to maximize the total likelihood when solving these constraints (together with hard constraints) with a weighted MAX-SAT solver.

9.4.6 Solving Constraints

In Step 6 of Algorithm 9.4, we put both hard and soft constraints together and solve these constraints using MaxSatz [16], a MAX-SAT solver. The solution *sol* is an assignment for all variables in V, and *max'* is the total weight of the satisfied constraints corresponding to the solution *sol*. In Step 8 of Algorithm 9.4, we partition V into a set of team plans P based on P5.

As an example, earlier in part (a) of Figure 9.2, the team trace's corresponding variable in V is assigned activities, which means the *null* values in Figure 9.2(a) are replaced with the corresponding assigned activities in V. According to property P5, we can simply partition the team trace into two team plans, as was shown before in Figure 9.3, by checking preconditions and effects of activities in the team trace.

In MAX-SAT, a proposition variable x_i may take values *false* or *true*. A literal l_i is either a variable x_i or its negation $\bar{x}_i$. A clause is a disjunction of literals, and a CNF formula ϕ is a conjunction of clauses. An assignment of truth values to the propositional variables satisfies a literal x_i if x_i takes the value *true* and satisfies a literal $\bar{x}_i$ if x_i takes the value *false*. An assignment satisfies a clause if it satisfies at least one literal of the clause, and it satisfies a CNF formula if it satisfies all the clauses of the formula. An assignment for a CNF formula ϕ is complete if all the variables occurring in ϕ have been assigned; otherwise, it is partial.

The MAX-SAT problem for a CNF formula ϕ is the problem of finding an assignment of values to propositional variables that minimizes the number of unsatisfied clauses (or equivalently, that maximizes the number of satisfied clauses). The MAX-SAT problem is NP-hard, since the Boolean satisfiability problem, which is NP-complete, can be easily reduced into MAX-SAT.

One extension to MAX-SAT is weighted MAX-SAT, which asks for the maximum weight that can be satisfied by any assignment given a set of weighted clauses. There have been many approaches that solve weighted MAX-SAT problems, such as MaxSatz [16,17], which implements a lower-bound computation method that consists of incrementing the lower bound by one for every disjoint inconsistent subset that can be detected by unit propagation.

9.4.7 Properties of DARE

DARE can be shown to have the following properties:

Theorem 9.1 (Conditional Soundness). *If the weighted MAX-SAT solver is powerful enough to optimally solve all solvable SAT problems,* DARE *is sound.*

Theorem 9.2 (Conditional Completeness). *If the weighted MAX-SAT solver we exploit in* DARE *is complete,* DARE *is also complete.*

For Theorem 9.1, we only need to check that the solutions output by DARE satisfy P1 through P5. P2 and P3 are guaranteed by observation constraints and causal-link constraints; P4 is guaranteed by the soft constraints built in Section 9.4.5 and the MAX-SAT solver; P1 and P5 are both guaranteed by the partition step in Section 9.4.6 (i.e., partitioning the variable matrix into a set of team plans); that is to say, the conditional soundness property holds.

For Theorem 9.2, since all steps in Algorithm 9.4, except Step 6 that calls for a weighted MAX-SAT solver, can be executed in finite time, the completeness property only depends on the weighted MAX-SAT solver; this means that the conditional completeness property holds.

9.5 Experiment

In this section we first evaluate MARS in different settings. After that, we compare MARS and DARE with respect to a different number of agents and a different percentage of *null* values.

9.5.1 Evaluation of MARS

We follow the experimental method prescribed by Banerjee et al. [4] to generate a set of multiagent plan recognition problems. For generating an MAPR problem, we first generate a random team trace with dimensions 100×50 (i.e., 100 timesteps and 50 agents). Each element of the team trace belongs to a set of activities A with $|A| = 20$. We randomly partition the team trace into a set of team plans that initiate the members of the library of team plans $\mathcal{P}$. This guarantees there is a solution to the MAPR problem. We generate a set of such problems $\mathbb{R}$, where $|\mathbb{R}| = 3000$. After that we add M random team plans to library $\mathcal{P}$ of each MAPR problem to enlarge the library. We test different values of M from $\{20, 40, 60, 80\}$ to vary the size of the library. We also test different percentages ξ of random missing values from $\{0\%, 10\%, 20\%, 30\%, 40\%, 50\%\}$ for each team trace and team plan. Note that "$\xi = 10\%$" indicates that there are randomly 10% of values that are missing in each team trace and team plan, likewise for other ξ. To define the utility function of team plans, we associate each team plan with a random utility value.

To evaluate MARS, we define a recognizing accuracy $Acc(\xi, M)$ as follows. For each MAPR problem $R \in \mathbb{R}$ with a specific M value and $\xi = 0\%$ (without any missing values), we solve the problem using MARS and denote the solution by $\mathcal{C}$. After that, we revise the problem R by setting ξ to another percentage to get a new problem R'. We solve R' and get a solution $\mathcal{C}'$. If $\mathcal{C}'$ is the same as $\mathcal{C}$, the function $\theta_R(\xi, M)$ with respect to R is set to be 1; otherwise, $\theta_R(\xi, M)$ is set to be 0. The recognizing accuracy with respect to ξ and M can be defined as follows:

$$Acc(\xi, M) = \frac{\sum_{R \in \mathbb{R}} \theta_R(\xi, M)}{|\mathbb{R}|}. \tag{9.5}$$

As a special case, $Acc(\xi, M) = 1$ when ξ is 0%.

9.5.1.1 *Experimental results*

We would like to test the following four aspects of MARS:

1. The recognizing accuracy with respect to different percentages of missing values.
2. The recognizing accuracy with respect to different numbers of randomly added team plans (referred to as "team plans" for simplicity).
3. The number of generated clauses with respect to each percentage.
4. The running time with respect to different percentages of missing values.

We present the experiment results in these aspects next.

Varying the percentage of missing values

To evaluate that MARS functions well in missing-value problems, we set the number of team plans M to be 80 and vary the percentage of missing values ξ from $\{0\%, 10\%, 20\%, 30\%, 40\%, 50\%\}$ to see the recognizing accuracy Acc defined earlier by Eq. 9.5. For each ξ, we run five random selections to calculate an average accuracy. The results are shown in Figure 9.4, where the curve denoted by $\rho = 1$ indicates the result obtained by setting $\rho = 1$ in Eq. 9.4, likewise for the curve denoted by $\rho = 0$.

From Figure 9.4, we can see that the accuracy Acc generally decreases when the percentage increases, no matter whether ρ is 1 or not. This is expected because missing values can provide information that may be exploited to find accurate occurrences. The more values that are missing, the more information is lost. Considering the difference between two curves, we can find that the accuracy is generally larger when $\rho = 1$ than that when $\rho = 0$. The results are statistically significant; we performed the Student's t-test and the result is 0.0482, which indicates that the two curves are significantly different

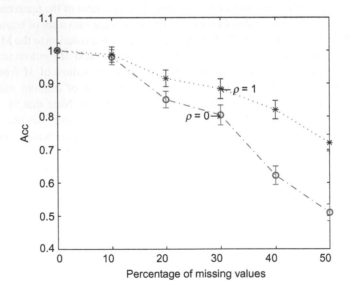

FIGURE 9.4

The recognizing accuracy with respect to different percentages of missing values (M is set to be 80).

at the 5% significance level. This suggests that the observing rate function λ is helpful in improving the accuracy. We can also find that the difference becomes larger when more values are missing, which indicates that λ is more significant then. By observation, MARS generally functions well in handling missing values when less than 30% of values are missing, where there is no less than an accuracy of ~ 0.9 by setting $\rho = 1$.

Varying the number of team plans

We now analyze the relationship between recognizing accuracy and the size of team plans. We set the percentage ξ to be 30% and vary the size of team plans M to see the change of accuracies. We show the results in Figure 9.5. From the curves, we can see that the accuracy is generally reduced when the number of team plans increases. This is consistent with our intuition, since more "uncertain" information is introduced as more team plans are added (each has 30% of missing values that introduce uncertain information).

We also observe that the curve denoted by $\rho = 1$ is generally better than the one denoted by $\rho = 0$, and the difference between two curves becomes sharp as the size of team plans increases. This indicates that MARS exploits the observing rate function (corresponding to $\rho = 1$) and performs better than the one that does not exploit it, especially when the size of team plans is large.

From Figures 9.4 and 9.5, we can conclude that in order to improve the recognizing accuracy, we should better exploit the observing rate function to control weights of constraints as is given in Eq. 9.1, especially when the percentage of missing values and the size of team plans are large.

The generated clauses

We would like to verify that the generated constraints SC and HC would not increase too fast when the percentage of missing values increases. We record the total number of clauses, which correspond to

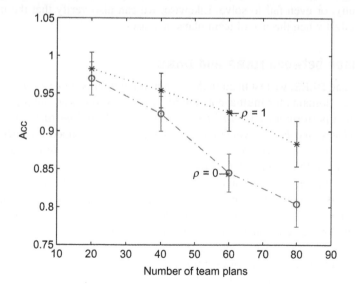

FIGURE 9.5

The recognizing accuracy with respect to different numbers of team plans (ξ is set to be 30%).

Table 9.2 Average Numbers of Clauses with Respect to Different Percentages of Missing Values

Number of team plans	Percentage of missing values					
	0%	**10%**	**20%**	**30%**	**40%**	**50%**
20	181	233	269	282	338	392
40	225	253	341	482	619	773
60	536	611	657	718	821	1059
80	692	785	843	929	983	1123

SC and HC, with respect to each percentage of missing values. Note that the clauses obtained from SC and HC are disjunctions of propositions that can be solved directly by a weighted MAX-SAT solver. The results are shown in Table 9.2, where the first column is the number of team plans and the other columns are numbers of clauses corresponding to each percentage of missing values. For instance, in the second row and the last column, "392" is the number of clauses generated from 20 team plans with 50% of missing values. Note that the numbers of clauses in the table are average results over 3000 MAPR problems. We observe that we can fit the performance curve with a polynomial of order 2.

As an example, we provide the polynomial for fitting the numbers of clauses of the last row in Table 9.2, which is $y = 0.0391x^2 + 6.1446x + 703.0357$, where x is the number of percentage points (e.g., $x = 50$ in the last column of the table) and y is the number of clauses. This suggests that MARS can handle MAPR problems with missing values well since the number of clauses would not increase too fast when missing values increase. Note that clauses increasing fast may make the weighted MAX-SAT solver have difficulty, or even fail to solve. Likewise, we can also verify that the number of clauses would not increase fast when the size of team plans increases.

9.5.2 Comparison between MARS and DARE

To compare MARS and DARE, we test them in three planning domains: *blocks*[3], *driverlog*[4] and *rovers*[4]. We modify the three domains for multiagent settings. In *blocks*, there are multiple *hoists*, which are viewed as agents that perform actions of *pickup*, *putdown*, *stack*, and *unstack*. In *driverlog*, there are multiple *trucks*, *drivers*, and *hoists*, which are agents that can be grouped together to form different teams (trucks and drivers can be on the same team, likewise for hoists). In *rovers*, there are multiple *rovers* that can be grouped together to form different teams.

For each domain, we set $T = 50$ and generate 50 team traces with the size of $T \times n$ for each $n \in \{20, 40, 60, 80, 100\}$. For each team trace, we have a set of optimal team plans—viewed as the *ground truth*—denoted by P_{true}, and its corresponding goal g_{true}, which best explains the team trace according to the likelihood function μ. We define the likelihood function by $\mu = \mu_1 + \mu_2$, where $\mu_1(k) = k$ and $\mu_2(k) = k^2$, as was presented at the end of the problem definition section.

We randomly delete a subset of activities from each team trace with respect to a specific percentage ξ. We test different ξ values with 0%, 10%, 20%, 30%, 40%, and 50%. As an example, $\xi = 10\%$

---

[4]http://planning.cis.strath.ac.uk/competition/

suggests there are 10 activities deleted from a team trace with 100 activities. We also randomly add 10 more goals, together with g_{true}, to form the goal set G, as was presented in the problem definition section. We define the accuracy λ as follows:

$$\lambda = \frac{\text{the number of correctly recognized team plan sets}}{\text{the total number of team traces}},$$

where "correctly recognized team plan sets" suggests the recognized team plan sets and goals are the same as the expected team plan sets $\{P_{true}\}$ and goals G.

We generate 100 team plans as the library as described by MARS [33] and compare the recognition results with MARS as a baseline.

9.5.2.1 *Experimental results*

We evaluate DARE in the following aspects:

1. Accuracy with respect to different number of agents.
2. Accuracy with respect to different percentages of *null* values.
3. Running time

Varying the number of agents

We would like to evaluate the change in accuracies when the number of agents increases. We set the percentage of *null* values to be 30% and also ran DARE five times to calculate an average of accuracies. The result is shown in Figure 9.6. From the figure, we found that the accuracies of both DARE and MARS generally decreased when the number of agents increased. This is because the problem space is enlarged when the number of agents increases, which decreases the available information compared to the large problem space and is not enough to attain high accuracies.

We also found that the accuracy of DARE was lower than MARS at the beginning and then became better than MARS as the number of agents became larger. This indicates that DARE performs better when

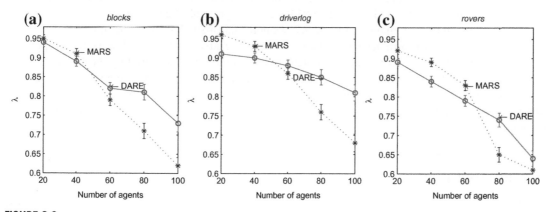

FIGURE 9.6

Accuracies with respect to different number of agents.

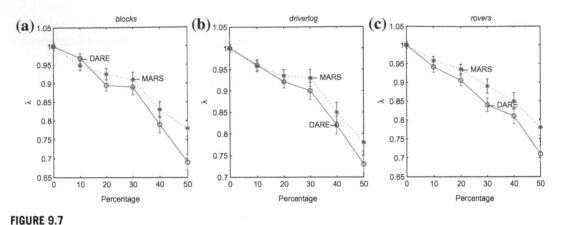

FIGURE 9.7

Accuracies with respect to different percentages of *null* values.

handling a large number of agents based on action models. This is because DARE builds the MAX-SAT problem space (described as proposition variables and constraints) based on model inferences (i.e., action models), while MARS is based on instances (i.e., plan library). When the number of agents is small, the problem space built by MARS is smaller than that built by DARE. In other words, when the number of agents becomes larger, the problem space built by MARS becomes larger than that built by DARE; the larger the problem space is, the more difficult it is for MAX-SAT to solve the problem; thus, DARE performs worse than MARS with less agents but better with more agents.

Varying the percentage of null values

We set the number of agents to be 60 and run DARE five times to calculate an average of accuracies with a percentage ξ of *null* values. We found both accuracies of DARE and MARS decreased when the percentage ξ increased as a result of less information being provided when the percentage increased. When the percentage is 0%, both DARE and MARS can recognize all the team traces successfully.

By observing all three domains in Figure 9.7, we note that DARE does not function as well as MARS when the percentage of incompleteness is large. This relative advantage for the library-based approach is due in large part to the fact that all team plans to be recognized are covered by the small library in the experiment, and the library of team plans helps reduce the recognition problem space compared to DARE. We conjecture that if the team plans to be recognized are not covered by the library (because of the library's size restrictions), DARE will perform better than MARS. In this case, MARS cannot successfully recognize some team plans.

9.6 Related Work

The plan-recognition problem has been addressed by many researchers. Except for the previous works [15,7,10,20] on the plan-recognition problem presented in the introduction section, Singla and Mooney proposed an approach to abductive reasoning using a first-order probabilistic logic to recognize plans

[25]. Amir and Gal addressed a plan-recognition approach to recognizing student behaviors using virtual science laboratories [1]. Ramirez and Geffner exploited off-the-shelf classic planners to recognize probabilistic plans [21]. Despite the success of these systems in solving the plan-recognition problem, a limitation is that they all focus only on single-agent plans; this is different from our problem setting that focuses on multiagent environments.

Different from the aforementioned single-agent work, there have been approaches related to the MAPR problem. For example, Saria and Mahadevan presented a hierarchical multiagent Markov process as a framework for hierarchical probabilistic plan recognition in cooperative multiagent systems [23]. Sukthankar and Sycara presented an approach that leveraged several types of agent resource dependencies and temporal ordering constraints to prune the size of the plan library considered for each observation trace [27]. Avrahami-Zilberbrand and Kaminka preferred a library of single-agent plans to team plans; however, they identified dynamic teams based on the assumption that all agents in a team are executing the same plan under the temporal constraints of that plan [2]. The constraint on activities of the agents that can form a team can be severely limiting when teammates can execute coordinated but different behaviors.

Instead of using the assumption that agents in the same team should execute a common activity, besides the approaches introduced in Section 9.1 [4,3,33], Sadilek and Kautz provided a unified framework to model and recognize activities that involved multiple related individuals playing a variety of roles with the help of GPS data [22]. In addition, Masato et al. proposed a probabilistic model based on conditional random fields to automatically recognize the composition of teams and team activities in relation to a plan [19]. In these systems, although coordinated activities can be recognized, they are applicable in scenarios where a set of real-world GPS data is available or team traces are fully observed. In contrast, we do not require GPS data and full team traces in both MARS and DARE.

9.7 Conclusion

This chapter presented two algorithms, MARS and DARE, to recognize multiagent plans from partially observed team traces. Given a partial team trace and a library of team plans, MARS builds a set of soft/hard constraints and solves them using a weighted MAX-SAT solver. The solution obtained is a set of occurrences that covers each element in the team trace exactly once. DARE takes a partial team trace and a set of action models as input. It first builds a set of candidate activities and then builds sets of hard and soft constraints to finally recognize team plans.

From MARS, we observed the following from our empirical evaluation:

1. Using the observing rate function can help improve the recognizing accuracy, especially when the percentage of missing values and the size of team plans are large.
2. The recognizing accuracy decreases with an increase in missing values or the size of the library.
3. The running time of our algorithm increases polynomially with the percentage of missing values increasing.

   From DARE, we show that it is effective in three benchmark domains compared to the state-of-the-art multiagent plan recognition system of MARS, which relies on a library of team plans. Thus, our approach is well suited for scenarios where collecting a library of team plans is not feasible before performing team plan-recognition tasks.

In the current work, we assume that the action models are *complete*. A more realistic assumption is to allow the models to be incomplete [12]. In future work, one promising direction is to extend our recognizing algorithms to work with incomplete action models. Another assumption in the current model is that it expects, as input, the alternative sets of goals, one of which the observed plan is expected to be targeting. Another direction therefore is to relax this so that these algorithms can take as input a set of potential goals, with the understanding that the observed plan is achieving a bounded subset of these goals. We believe that both these extensions can be easily incorporated into the MAX-SAT framework of the current algorithms.

Acknowledgment

Hankz Hankui Zhuo thanks Professor Subbarao Kambhampati for suggesting combining the MARS and DARE algorithms initially. Zhuo's research is supported in part by the National Natural Science Foundation of China (No. 61309011) and Research Fund for the Doctoral Program of Higher Education of China (No. 20110171120054), and Guangzhou Science and Technology Project (No. 2011J4300039).

References

[1] Amir O, Gal YK. Plan recognition in virtual laboratories. In: Proceedings of IJCAI; 2011. p. 2392–7.

[2] Avrahami-Zilberbrand D, Kaminka GA. Towards dynamic tracking of multi-agents teams: an initial report. In: Proceedings of the AAAI Workshop on Plan, Activity, and Intent Recognition; 2007.

[3] Banerjee B, Kraemer L. Branch and price for multi-agent plan recognition. In: Proceedings of AAAI; 2011. p. 601–7.

[4] Banerjee B, Kraemer L, Lyle J. Multi-agent plan recognition: formalization and algorithms. In: Proceedings of AAAI; 2010. p. 1059–64.

[5] Borchers B, Furman J. A two-phase exact algorithm for MAX-SAT and weighted MAX-SAT problems. J Comb Optim 1998;2(4):299–306.

[6] Brafman RI, Domshlak C. From one to many: planning for loosely coupled multi-agent systems. In: Proceedings of ICAPS; 2008. p. 28–35.

[7] Bui HH. A general model for online probabilistic plan recognition. In: Proceedings of IJCAI; 2003. p. 1309–18.

[8] Fikes R, Nilsson NJ. STRIPS: a new approach to the application of theorem proving to problem solving. Artif Intell J 1971:189–208.

[9] Garey MR, Johnson DS. Computers and intractability: a guide to the theory of NP-completeness. W. H. Freeman; 1979.

[10] Geib CW, Goldman RP. A probabilistic plan recognition algorithm based on plan tree grammars. Artif Intell 2009;173(11):1101–32.

[11] Goodman BA, Litman DJ. Plan recognition for intelligent interfaces. In: Proceedings of the Sixth Conference on Artificial Intelligence Applications; 1990. p. 297–303.

[12] Kambhampati S. Model-lite planning for the web age masses: the challenges of planning with incomplete and evolving domain theories. In: Proceedings of AAAI; 2007. p. 1601–5.

[13] Kaminka G, Pynadath DV, Tambe M. Monitoring teams by overhearing: a multiagent plan-recognition approach. J Artif Intell Res 2002;17:83–135.

[14] Kautz HA. A formal theory of plan recognition and its implementation. Morgan Kaufmann; 1991.

[15] Kautz HA, Allen JF. Generalized plan recognition. In: Proceedings of AAAI; 1986. p. 32–7.

[16] Li CM, Manya F, Mohamedou N, Planes J. Exploiting cycle structures in Max-SAT. In: Proceedings of Twelth International Conference on the Theory and Applications of Satisfiability Testing; 2009. p. 467–80.

[17] Li CM, Manya F, Planes J. New inference rules for MAX-SAT. J Artif Intell Res October 2007;30:321–59.

[18] Litman DJ, Allen JF. A plan recognition model for subdialogues in conversation. Cognitive Sci. 1987;11:163–200.

[19] Masato D, Norman TJ, Vasconcelos WW, Sycara K. Agent-oriented incremental team and activity recognition. In: Proceedings of IJCAI; 2011. p. 1402–7.

[20] Ramirez M, Geffner H. Plan recognition as planning. In: Proceedings of IJCAI; 2009. p. 1778–83.

[21] Ramirez M, Geffner H. Probabilistic plan recognition using off-the-shelf classical planners. In: Proceedings of AAAI; 2010. p. 1121–6.

[22] Sadilek A, Kautz H. Recognizing multi-agent activities from GPS data. In: Proceedings of AAAI; 2010. p. 1134–9.

[23] Saria S, Mahadevan S. Probabilistic plan recognition in multiagent systems. In: Proceedings of ICAPS; 2004. p. 287–96.

[24] Schmidt CF, Sridharan NS, Goodson JL. The plan recognition problem: an intersection of psychology and artificial intelligence. Artif Intell 1978;11(1–2):45–83.

[25] Singla P, Mooney R. Abductive Markov logic for plan recognition. In: Proceedings of AAAI; 2011. p. 1069–75.

[26] Sukthankar G, Sycara K. Simultaneous team assignment and behavior recognition from spatio-temporal agent traces. In: Proceedings of Twenty-First National Conference on Artificial Intelligence; 2006. p. 716–21.

[27] Sukthankar G, Sycara K. Hypothesis pruning and ranking for large plan recognition problems. In: Proceedings of AAAI; 2008. p. 998–1003.

[28] Sukthankar G, Sycara K. Activity recognition for dynamic multi-agent teams. ACM transactions on intelligent systems and technology 2011;3(1):18:1–18:24.

[29] Tambe M. Towards flexible teamwork. J Artif Intell Res 1997;7:83–124.

[30] Wilensky R. Planning and understanding. Addison-Wesley; 1983.

[31] Yang Q, Wu K, Jiang Y. Learning action models from plan examples using weighted MAX-SAT. Artif Intel J 2007;171:107–43.

[32] Zhang L, Bacchus F. Maxsat heuristics for cost optimal planning. In: Proceedings of AAAI; 2012. p. 1846–52.

[33] Zhuo HH, Li L. Multi-agent plan recognition with partial team traces and plan libraries. In: Proceedings of IJCAI; 2011. p. 484–9.

[34] Zhuo HH, Yang Q, Hu DH, Li L. Learning complex action models with quantifiers and implications. Artif Intell 2010;174(18):1540–69.

[35] Zhuo HH, Yang Q, Kambhampati S. Action-model based multi-agent plan recognition. In: Proceedings of NIPS; 2012. p. 377–85.

Role-Based Ad Hoc Teamwork

Katie Genter[a], **Noa Agmon**[b,1], **and Peter Stone**[a]

[a]*University of Texas at Austin, Austin, TX, USA*
[b]*Bar Ilan University, Ramat Gan, Israel*

10.1 Introduction

As software and robotic agents become increasingly common, there becomes a need for agents to collaborate with unfamiliar teammates. Consider a disaster situation where rescue robots from all around the world are brought in to assist with search and rescue. Ideally, these robots would be able to collaborate immediately—with little to no human assistance—to divide and conquer the necessary tasks according to their relative abilities. Some agents would locate victims, while other agents would lift fallen debris away from trapped victims. However, most existing agents are designed to only collaborate with known teammates that they were specifically preprogrammed to work with. As such, collaborating on the fly with unknown teammates is impossible for most current agents.

Ad hoc teamwork is a relatively new research area that examines this exact problem—how an agent ought to act when placed on a team with other agents such that there was no prior opportunity to coordinate behaviors. In ad hoc teamwork situations, several agents find themselves in a situation where they all have perfectly aligned goals, yet they have had no previous opportunity to coordinate their teamwork [1]. This problem arises quite often for humans who tend to solve the problem quite naturally. However, autonomous agents (e.g., robots and software agents) do not currently handle this problem as gracefully.

Consider briefly that you recently arrived in a foreign country where you do not speak the local language. Now assume that you come across a pickup soccer game. After watching the game for a few minutes, some of the players on one team motion you to join. Despite not being able to verbally communicate with any of your teammates, you can still contribute to the team and work as a cohesive unit with your teammates. Through observing your teammates, you can quickly make a rough analysis of their strengths and weaknesses and determine how you should play to best help the team.

Throughout this chapter we refer to the agents that make up a team as either *ad hoc agents* or *teammates*. Ad hoc agents are agents whose behavior we can control. Teammates, on the other hand, are agents that we have no control over, potentially because they were programmed by other groups or at different times such that future collaboration with our agents was unforeseeable.

In some team domains, such as search and rescue missions and many team sports, the team behavior can easily be broken down into *roles*. Under a *role-based approach* to ad hoc teamwork, each teammate

---

[1]This work was done while at the Learning Agents Research Group (LARG) at the University of Texas at Austin.

is inferred to be following a specialized role that accomplishes a specific task or exhibits a particular behavior. Using this information, an ad hoc agent's main task is to decide which role to assume such that the team's performance is maximized. This decision is situation-specific: it depends on the task the team performs, the environment in which it acts, the roles currently performed by the team members, and the capabilities of the team members.

One trivial approach is for an ad hoc agent to assume the role at which it is most *individually* capable. However, the choice of optimal role—one that results in highest *team* utility—depends not only on the ad hoc agent, but also on the ability and behavior of the other team members. Thus, an ad hoc agent will sometimes not adopt the role that it performs best if adopting a different role is optimal for the team. We examine the contribution of an ad hoc agent to the team by the measure of *marginal utility*, which is the increase in a team's utility when an ad hoc agent is added to the team and assumes a particular role. An *optimal mapping* of an ad hoc agent to a role is, therefore, one that maximizes the marginal utility, thus maximizing the contribution of the ad hoc agent to the team's utility.

This chapter presents a *role-based approach* for ad hoc teamwork. We begin by noting related work in Section 10.2. Section 10.3 formally defines the role-based ad hoc teamwork problem. In Section 10.4, we emphasize the importance of accurate role recognition. Section 10.5 defines several methods for modeling the marginal utility of an ad hoc agent's role selection as a function of the roles performed by the other teammates. Then we empirically show in a foraging domain that each method is appropriate for a different class of role-based tasks. In Section 10.6, we demonstrate that use of these methods can lead to efficient calculation of the role that yields maximal team utility. We then include an empirical examination in a more complex Pacman Capture-the-Flag domain of how to choose the best-suited method for role assignment in a complex environment where it is not trivial to determine the optimal role assignment. Finally, we show that the methods we describe have a predictive nature, meaning that once an appropriate assignment method is determined for a domain, it can be used successfully in new tasks that the team has not encountered before and for which only limited experience is available. Section 10.7 concludes the chapter and presents some avenues for future work.

Unlike much of the rest of the book, this chapter does not focus on methods of role recognition. Instead, it examines the question of how to use successful role recognition to assist in multiagent decision making. Indeed, this work contributes to answering the ad hoc teamwork challenge presented by Stone et al. [1]. Specifically, this ad hoc teamwork challenge is to *"create an autonomous agent that is able to efficiently and robustly collaborate with previously unknown teammates on tasks to which they are all individually capable of contributing as team members."* Stone et al. laid out three abstract technical challenges. This chapter presents an approach toward solving one of these challenges—finding theoretically optimal and/or empirically effective algorithms for behavior—in role-based ad hoc teamwork settings.

10.2 Related Work

Although there has been much work in the field of multiagent teamwork, there has been little work towards getting agents to collaborate to achieve a common goal without precoordination. In this section, we review some selected work that is related to the role-based ad hoc teamwork approach presented in this chapter. Specifically, we consider work related to multiagent teamwork, multiagent plan recognition, and our two experimental domains.

10.2.1 **Multiagent Teamwork**

Most prior multiagent teamwork research requires explicit coordination protocols or communication protocols. Three popular protocols for communication and coordination—SharedPlans [2], Shell for TEAMwork (STEAM) [3], and Generalized Partial Global Planning (GPGP) [4]—all provide collaborative planning or teamwork models to each team member. Each of these protocols works well when all agents know and follow the protocol. However, in ad hoc teamwork settings, we do not assume that any protocol is known by all agents, so protocols such as these cannot be successfully used.

Some multiagent teams are even designed to work specifically with their teammates in predefined ways such as via locker-room agreements [5]. Specifically, a locker-room agreement is formed when there is a team synchronization period during which a team can coordinate their teamwork structure and communication protocols. This work divides the task space via the use of roles like we do, but our work differs in that we do not assume the availability of a team synchronization period.

Liemhetcharat and Veloso formally defined a weighted synergy graph that models the capabilities of robots in different roles and how different role assignments affect the overall team value [6]. They presented a team formation algorithm that can approximate the optimal role assignment policy given a set of teammates to choose from and a task. They applied this algorithm to simulated robots in the RoboCup Rescue domain and to real robots in a foraging task, and found that the resulting role assignments outperformed other existing algorithms. This work determines how to best form a team when given many agents to choose from, while our work determines how a particular agent should behave to best assist a preexisting team.

Wu et al. present an online planning algorithm for ad hoc team settings [7]. Their algorithm constructs and solves a series of stage games, and then uses biased adaptive play to choose actions. They test their algorithm in three domains: cooperative box pushing, meeting in a 3×3 grid, and multichannel broadcast. In these tests, they show that they are able to perform well when paired with suboptimal teammates. Their work is different from ours in that we choose the best-suited role assignment method and then assign the ad hoc agent to perform a role using the chosen role assignment method, whereas in their work they optimize each individual action taken by the ad hoc agent.

Bowling and McCracken examined the concept of "pick-up" teams in simulated robot soccer [8]. Similar to us, they propose coordination techniques for a single agent that wants to join a previously unknown team of existing agents. However, they take a different approach to the problem in that they provide the single agent with a play book from which it selects the play most similar to the current behaviors of its teammates. The agent then selects a role to perform in the presumed current play.

Jones et al. perform an empirical study of dynamically formed teams of heterogeneous robots in a multirobot treasure hunt domain [9]. They assume that all the robots know they are working as a team and that all the robots can communicate with one another, whereas in our work we do not assume that the ad hoc agent and the teammates share a communication protocol.

Han, Li, and Guo study how one agent can influence the direction in which an entire flock of agents is moving [10]. They use soft control in a flocking model in which each agent follows a simple control rule based on its neighbors. They present a simple model that works well in cases where the agents reflexively determine their behaviors in response to a larger team. However, it is not clear how well this work would apply to more complex role-based tasks such as those studied and discussed in our work.

10.2.2 **Multiagent Plan Recognition**

An ad hoc team player must observe the actions of its teammates and determine what plan or policy its teammates are using before determining which behavior it should adopt. In this work, we assume that the ad hoc agent is given the policy of each teammate so as to focus on the role-selection problem. However, in many situations this is not a valid assumption, so recognizing the plan or policy of each teammate is an important part of solving the ad hoc teamwork challenge.

Barrett and Stone present an empirical evaluation of various ad hoc teamwork strategies [11]. In their work they show that efficient planning is possible using Monte Carlo Tree Search. Additionally, they show that an ad hoc agent can differentiate between its possible teammates on the fly when given a set of known starting models, even if these models are imperfect or incomplete. Finally, they show that models can be learned for previously unknown teammates. Unlike our work, theirs does not take a role-based approach to solving the ad hoc teamwork problem. Instead, they evaluate the ability of various algorithms to generate ad hoc agent behaviors in an online fashion.

Sukthankar and Sycara present two approaches for recognizing team policies from observation logs, where a team policy is a collection of individual agent policies along with an assignment of individual agents to policies [12]. Each of their approaches—one model-based and one data-driven—seem generally well suited for application to the ad hoc teamwork challenge. Specifically, their approaches would be best suited for ad hoc teamwork settings that (1) are turn-based tasks, (2) do not require analysis of observation logs in real time, and (3) do not require excessive amounts of training data to avoid overfitting.

Zhuo and Li provide a new approach for recognizing multiagent team plans from partial team traces and team plans [13]. Specifically, given a team trace and a library of team plans, their approach is to first create a set of constraints and then solve these constraints using a weighted MAX-SAT solver. The required library of team plans might be difficult to obtain in some ad hoc teamwork settings though, so this approach is not well suited for all ad hoc teamwork settings.

10.2.3 **Experimental Domains**

In this chapter we use two experimental domains: Capture-the-Flag and foraging. There has been previous research on multiagent teamwork in both the Capture-the-Flag domain and the foraging domain, and we discuss a few examples in this section. However, most of this work focuses on coordination between all teammates instead of coordination of one or more ad hoc agents with existing teammates; thus, this work does not address the ad hoc teamwork problem.

Blake et al. present their Capture-the-Flag domain, which they implemented both physically and in simulation [14]. In their work, the focus is on effective path planning for their robots as they navigate through a mazelike environment. Although similar to our Capture-the-Flag domain, their domain is different from ours because they assume that target coordinates will be communicated to the ground robots from an overhead flying robot. This communication might not be possible in an ad hoc teamwork setting because we cannot assume that the teammates and the ad hoc agent will be able to communicate and exchange data.

Sadilek and Kautz used a real-world game of Capture-the-Flag to validate their ability to understand human interactions, attempted interactions, and intentions from noisy sensor data in a well-defined multiagent setting [15]. Our work currently assumes that the actual behaviors of the teammates are provided to us, such that we can focus on determining the best behavior for the ad hoc agent. However, work like that of Sadilek and Kautz–which focuses on recognizing interactions and inferring their intentions–will be necessary to solve the complete ad hoc teamwork problem.

Mataric introduced the multiagent foraging domain and focused on teaching agents social behaviors in this domain [16]. Specifically, the foraging agents learned yielding and information sharing behaviors. In Mataric's work, she assumed that all the foraging robots are capable of communicating with each other. However, in our work we do not assume that the foraging robots share a communication protocol.

Lerman et al. considered the problem of dynamic task allocation in a multiagent foraging environment [17]. They designed a mathematical model of a general dynamic task-allocation mechanism. As long as all the agents use this mechanism, a desirable task division can be obtained in the absence of explicit communication and global knowledge. However, such an approach does not work in ad hoc teamwork settings because we cannot assume that the ad hoc agent will be able to use the same mechanism as its teammates.

10.3 **Problem Definition**

This chapter introduces the *role-based* ad hoc teamwork problem, which is one that requires or benefits from dividing the task at hand into roles. Throughout we refer to the agents that make up a team as either *ad hoc agents* or *teammates*. Ad hoc agents are ones whose behavior we can control. Teammates, on the other hand, are agents that we have no control over, potentially because they were programmed by other groups or at different times such that future collaboration with our agents was unforeseeable.

Under a role-based ad hoc teamwork approach, the ad hoc agent first must infer the role of each teammate and then decide which role to assume such that the team's performance is maximized. The teammates do not need to believe or understand that they are performing a role. Indeed, the classification of teammates into roles is merely done so that the ad hoc agent can determine the best role for itself. Using the pick-up soccer example presented in Section 10.2.1, under a role-based ad hoc teamwork approach you might determine which positions your teammates are playing and then adopt a position accordingly. You might adopt the most important position that is unfilled or the position you are best at that is unfilled—or more likely you would adopt a position based on a function of these two factors.

Each teammate's role will be readily apparent to the ad hoc agent in many domains. For example, the goalie in a pickup soccer game is immediately apparent due to her proximity to her team's goal. However, in some domains it may take more extended observations for the ad hoc agent to determine the actual role of each teammate. In such domains, the role of each teammate may be determined with increasing certainty as observations are made regarding the agent's behavior and the areas of the environment she explores.

We assume that different roles have different inherent values to the team, and that each agent has some ability to perform each role. As such, an ad hoc agent must take into account both the needs of the team and its own abilities when determining what role to adopt. A team receives a score when it performs a task. Therefore, the goal of an ad hoc agent is to choose a role that maximizes the team's score and therefore maximizes the marginal utility of adding itself to the team. Thus, an ad hoc agent will sometimes not adopt the role that it performs best if adopting a different role is optimal for the team. Using the pick-up soccer example, if your team is in dire need of a goalie, it may be best for the team if you play goalie even if you are better at another position.

10.3.1 Formal Problem Definition

In this section, we define our problem more formally and introduce the notation that we use throughout the chapter.

Let a task d be drawn from domain D, where task d has m roles $R(d) = \{r_0, \ldots, r_{m-1}\}$. Each role r_i has an associated relative importance value v_i, where r_x is more critical to team utility than r_y if $v_x > v_y$. Each v_i is constant for a particular task d and set of potential roles $R(d)$ but might change if d or $R(d)$ were different. Let $\mathbf{A} = \{a_0, \ldots, a_{n-1}\}$ be the set of ad hoc agents and $\mathbf{B} = \{b_0, \ldots, b_{k-1}\}$ be the set of teammates such that $T = A \cup B$ is the team that is to perform task d. Each agent $t_j \in T$ has a utility $u(t_j, r_i) \geq 0$ for performing each role $r_i \in R(d)$. This utility $u(t_j, r_i)$ represents player t_j's ability at role r_i in task d.

Using the pick-up soccer example, let domain $D = \{\text{soccer}\}$, task $d = \{\text{game against a local boys high school team}\}$, and $R(d) = \{\text{goalie, sweeper, stopper, outside back, center midfield, outside midfield, striker}\}$. If $A = \{\text{Katie}\}$ and $B = \{\text{Jake, Noa, Peter, Sam, Todd}\}$, then $T = A \cup B = \{\text{Jake, Katie, Noa, Peter, Sam, Todd}\}$.

Let mapping $\mathbf{P} : B \to R(d)$ be the mapping of the teammates in B to roles $\{r_0, \ldots, r_{m-1}\}$ such that the teammates associated with role r_i are B_i^P, where $|B_i^P| = m_i^P$ and $B_0^P \oplus B_1^P \oplus \ldots \oplus B_{m-1}^P = B$. Without loss of generality, the agents in each B_i^P are ordered such that $u(b_j, r_i) \geq u(b_{j+1}, r_i)$. In the pick-up soccer example, assume $B_0^P = \{\text{Todd}\}$, $B_4^P = \{\text{Sam, Jake}\}$, and $B_6^P = \{\text{Peter, Noa}\}$. This assumption means that Todd is playing goalie under mapping P, Sam and Jake are playing center midfield under mapping P (where Sam's utility for playing center midfield is greater than Jake's utility for playing center midfield), and Noa and Peter are playing striker under mapping P (where Peter's utility for playing striker is greater than Noa's utility for playing striker). Mapping P may be given fully or probabilistically, or it may need to be inferred via observation. However, it is important to note that ad hoc agents cannot alter P by commanding the teammates to perform particular roles. For simplicity, we assume in this work that the ad hoc agents have perfect knowledge of mapping P.

Let mapping $\mathbf{S} : A \to R(d)$ be the mapping of the ad hoc agents in A to roles $\{r_0, \ldots, r_{m-1}\}$ such that the ad hoc agents performing role r_i are A_i^S, where $|A_i^S| = m_i^S$ and $A_0^S \oplus A_1^S \oplus \ldots \oplus A_{m-1}^S = A$. In the pick-up soccer example, if $A_6^S = \{\text{Katie}\}$, then Katie is playing striker under mapping S. Additionally, let mapping $\mathbf{SP} : T \to R(d)$ be the combination of mappings S and P. As such, agents $T_i^{SP} = B_i^P \cup A_i^S$ are performing role r_i and $T_0^{SP} \oplus T_1^{SP} \oplus \ldots \oplus T_{m-1}^{SP} = T$. In other words, mapping SP is the association of *all* team members to the roles they are performing. Without loss of generality, the agents in each T_i^{SP} are ordered such that $u(t_j, r_i) \geq u(t_{j+1}, r_i)$. In the pick-up soccer example, if $T_6^{SP} = \{\text{Peter, Katie, Noa}\}$, then Peter, Katie, and Noa are all playing striker under mapping SP and Peter's utility for playing striker is greater than Katie's utility for playing striker, which is greater than Noa's utility for playing striker. A team score $U(W, d, T)$ results when the set of agents T perform a task d, with each $t_j \in T$ fulfilling some role $r_i \in R(d)$ under mapping W.

Team score U is a function of individual agent utilities, but its precise definition is tied to the particular domain D and the specific task $d \in D$. For example, in the pick-up soccer example, the team score might be the goal differential after 90 minutes of play. The marginal utility $MU(S, P)$ obtained by mapping S, assuming P is the mapping of the teammates in B to roles, is the score improvement obtained when each ad hoc agent $a_j \in A$ chooses role $r_S(a_j)$ under mapping S. Assuming that either B can perform the task or that $U(P, d, B) = 0$ when B cannot complete the task, marginal utility

$MU(S, P) = U(SP, d, T) - U(P, d, B).$[2] Going back to the pick-up soccer example, the marginal utility obtained by mapping S is the difference in the expected score differential when B mapped by P plays a local boys high school team and the expected score differential when T mapped by SP plays a local boys high school team.

Given that mapping P is fixed, the role-based ad hoc team problem is to find a mapping S that maximizes marginal utility. The preceding problem definition and notation provided are valid for any number of ad hoc team agents. Thus, although for the remainder of this chapter we focus our attention on the case in which there is only one ad hoc agent such that $A = \{a_0\}$, our general theoretical contributions can be applied to teams to which multiple ad hoc agents are added. For example, multiple ad hoc agents could coordinate and work together as a single "agent" and the theoretical results presented later would still hold. Note that multiple ad hoc agents could not each individually determine a mapping to a role that maximizes marginal utility using the approach presented in the following, since each ad hoc agent would merely choose the role that would be optimal were it the only ad hoc agent to join the team. These mappings would not be guaranteed to collectively maximize marginal utility.

10.4 **Importance of Role Recognition**

The work presented in this chapter concerns how an ad hoc agent should select a role in order to maximize the team's marginal utility. However, in order to do that using the role-based ad hoc teamwork we present, the roles of the teammates must be correctly identified. This need for accurate role recognition is what ties this chapter to the other chapters in this book.

We do not focus on how to do role recognition here. Indeed, we assume that the ad hoc agents have complete knowledge concerning the roles of the teammates. As such, accurate role recognition is an important prerequisite for our work. Role recognition might be easy in some situations but extremely difficult in others. However, role recognition always becomes easier as time passes and more experience is gained. For example, in the pick-up soccer example presented in Sections 10.2 and 10.3, it might be easy to recognize that a player positioned in the goal is playing the goalie role. However, a player positioned around midfield could be playing a variety of roles; one might be able to better determine his role as time passes and play continues.

If the ad hoc agents have imperfect or noisy knowledge of the mapping of teammates to roles—in other words, if role recognition is imperfect—the general processes presented in this chapter can still be useful. However, the resulting mapping of the ad hoc agents to roles may not maximize marginal utility when role recognition is imperfect. Such uncertainty can be dealt with formally if the agents have probabilistic knowledge of the mapping of the teammates to roles. Given a prior probability distribution over roles, a Bayesian approach could be used to modify the ad hoc agent's beliefs over time and to enable it to act optimally given its uncertain knowledge—including acting specifically so as to reduce uncertainty using a value of information approach.

In this work we assume that the roles of the agents remain fixed throughout the task. If the roles were to change, the ad hoc agent would first need a new process to identify such changes, perhaps by noticing that the teammates' observable behavior has changed. After detecting the change, the processes

---

[2] MU is actually a function of d, B, T, P, and S; however, throughout this chapter we use this more compact notation.

described in this chapter could be used to find a new mapping of the ad hoc agents to roles that maximizes marginal utility.

10.5 Models for Choosing a Role

The gold standard way for an ad hoc agent to determine the marginal utility from selecting a particular role, and thus determine its optimal role, is to determine $U(SP, d, T)$ for each possible role it could adopt. However, in practice, the ad hoc agent may only select *one* role to adopt. Therefore, the ad hoc agent must *predict* its marginal utility for all possible roles and then select just one role to adopt. This section lays out three possible models with which the ad hoc agent could do this prediction based on the roles its teammates are currently filling. We also empirically verify that each model is appropriate for a different class of role-based tasks in the multiagent foraging domain described next.

In this foraging domain, a team of agents is required to travel inside a given area, detecting targets and returning them to a preset station [16]. We use a 50×50 cell map in our experiments, but an example 10×10 cell map can be seen in Figure 10.1. Each target can be acquired by a single agent that enters the target's cell as long as the agent is not already carrying a target and has the capability to collect targets of that type. To avoid random wandering when no collectable targets are visible, we assume that each agent has perfect information regarding target locations. Additionally, we allow multiple agents and targets to occupy the same cell simultaneously.

The goal of each agent is for the team to collect as many targets as possible, as quickly as possible. We consider a special case of the foraging problem in which targets are divided into two groups: red targets to the North and blue targets to the South, where the blue targets are worth twice as much to the team as the red targets. As such, the blue targets and agents that collect blue targets are randomly initialized on the lower half of the map, while the red targets and agents that collect red targets are randomly initialized on the upper half of the map.

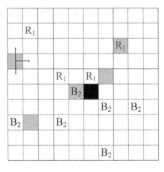

FIGURE 10.1

A sample 10×10 cell map of our foraging environment. Each target occupies one cell—blue targets are represented by B_2 and red targets are represented by R_1, where the subscript denotes the target's point value. Agents are represented by gray boxes, occupy only one cell at a time, and can move up, down, left, or right one cell each timestep (as long as the move does not carry them off the board). The station to which targets should be delivered is shown as a black box.

Table 10.1 Number of Statistically Significant Incorrect/Correct Decisions Made by an Ad Hoc Agent

Model	Task A	Task B	Task C	Task D
Unlimited	**0/36**	1/18	14/22	0/36
Limited	3/33	**1/26**	6/30	9/27
Incremental w/Logarithmic	0/36	1/19	**3/33**	8/27
Incremental w/Exponential	0/36	1/20	**2/34**	8/27
Incremental w/Sigmoidal	0/36	1/18	14/22	0/36

Note: These are for each model in the four different tasks presented throughout Section 10.5.

As each model is presented, we also describe a foraging task in which the model has been empirically shown to be most appropriate using the methods described later in this chapter. Results of each model on each task are presented in Table 10.1.

For all of the models, except the Unlimited Role Mapping model, we assume that the ad hoc agent a_0 knows the utilities $u(b_j, r_i)$, $\forall\, b_j \in B, r_i \in R(d)$ and the mapping $P : B \to R(d)$. Additionally, when considering the following three models, note that the marginal utility of agent a_j choosing to fulfill role r_i under mapping S is often given by an algorithm $\mathsf{MU} - \mathsf{X}$ (see Algorithms 10.1 and 10.2). In these cases, $\mathsf{MU} - \mathsf{X}(a_j, r_i, P) = U(SP, d, T_i^{SP}) - U(P, d, B_i^P)$.

10.5.1 Unlimited Role Mapping Model

Consider the multiagent foraging example just presented. Assume there are 100 red targets and 5000 blue targets in a constrained area with limited time (50 time steps) for the agents to collect targets. This example is Task A in Table 10.1. Due to the ample amount of valuable blue targets and the limited time, it would never be optimal for an agent to collect red targets instead of blue targets. The blue targets will be surrounding the base after the agent delivers its first target, and hence easy to collect and deliver quickly. On the other hand, the red targets will be less numerous and likely farther from the base and hence slower to collect and deliver. Therefore, in tasks such as this one, the benefit the team receives for an agent performing a role does *not* depend on the roles fulfilled by its teammates.

In such a case, the contribution to the team of an agent t_j performing role r_i is simply the agent's utility $u(t_j, r_i)$ at role r_i multiplied by the value of the role v_i. As such, the team utility can be modeled as

$$U(SP, d, T) = \sum_{i=0}^{m-1} rs_i * v_i \tag{10.1}$$

where

$$rs_i = \sum_{t_j \in T_i^{SP}} u(t_j, r_i) \tag{10.2}$$

Note that in this model, agent utility $u(t_j, r_i)$ for performing each role r_i and the importance v_i of each role r_i are parameters that can be tuned to match the characteristics of a particular task.

Theorem 10.1 describes the optimal role mapping under this model.

Theorem 10.1. *In Unlimited Role Mapping tasks, mapping S, under which a_0 chooses the role r_i that obtains* $\underset{0 \le i \le m-1}{\text{argmax}} (u(a_0, r_i)*v_i)$, *maximizes marginal utility such that* $\forall S' \ne S\ MU(S', P) \le MU(S, P)$.

10.5.2 Limited Role Mapping Model

Returning to the multiagent foraging example, assume that there are 1000 red targets and 5000 blue targets in a constrained environment with limited time (50 timesteps) for the agents to collect the targets. Also assume that there are rules prohibiting an agent from collecting the valuable blue targets if there is not at least one other agent also collecting blue targets or if more than three other agents are already collecting blue targets. This task is Task B in Table 10.1. Due to the ample amount of valuable blue targets, the ad hoc agent should collect blue targets if the conditions for being able to collect blue targets are satisfied. However, if the conditions are not satisfied, the ad hoc agent should default to collecting the less valuable red targets.

In tasks such as this, each role r_i has an associated r_i^{min} value and r_i^{max} value that represent the minimum and maximum number of agents that should perform role r_i. For all i, let $0 \le r_i^{min} \le r_i^{max} \le n$. If the number of agents performing role r_i is less than r_i^{min}, then the team gains no score from their actions. On the other hand, if the number of agents performing role r_i is greater than r_i^{max}, then only the r_i^{max} agents with highest utility, $T_i^{SP}[r_i^{max}]$, will be taken into account when calculating the team score. As such, the team utility for Limited Role Mapping tasks can be modeled as

$$U(SP, d, T) = \sum_{i=0}^{m-1} rs_i * v_i \tag{10.3}$$

where

$$rs_i = \begin{cases} \displaystyle\sum_{t_j \in T_i^{SP}} u(t_j, r_i) & \text{if } r_i^{min} \le m_i^{SP} \le r_i^{max} \\ \displaystyle\sum_{t_k \in T_i^{SP}[r_i^{max}]} u(t_k, r_i) & \text{if } m_i^{SP} > r_i^{max} \\ 0 & \text{if } m_i^{SP} < r_i^{min} \end{cases}$$

The function $\mathsf{MU} - 1(a_j, r_i, P)$ displayed in Algorithm 10.1 gives the marginal utility obtained from the ad hoc agent a_j choosing to perform role r_i, where the current mapping of teammates to roles is described by P. In this model, agent utility $u(t_j, r_i)$ for performing each role r_i, the importance v_i of each role r_i, and the minimum and maximum number of agents that should perform each role r_i are all tunable model parameters.

Function $\mathsf{MU} - 1(a_j, r_i, P)$ uses some special notation. Specifically, let $pos\,B(a_j, r_i)$ denote the 0-indexed position in T_i^{SP} that the ad hoc agent a_j occupies. Additionally, let $T_i^W(num)$ denote the agent that is performing role r_i under mapping W with the num highest utility on role r_i. For example, if agents $A, B, C,$ and D are performing role R under mapping Y with the following utilities for role $R : A = 1, B = 2, C = 3,$ and $D = 4$, then $T_R^T(0) = D, T_R^T(1) = C,$ and $T_R^T(2) = B$.

Algorithm 10.1 ($MU - 1(a_j, r_i, P)$)

1: **if** $m_i^P + 1 < r_i^{min}$ **then**
2:     **return** 0
3: **else**
4:     **if** $m_i^P + 1 = r_i^{min}$ **then**
5:         **return** $\displaystyle\sum_{t_j \in T_i^{SP}} u(t_j, r_i) * v_i$

6:     **else**
7:         **if** $r_i^{max} < m_i^P + 1$ **then**
8:             **if** $posB(a_j, r_i) \le r_i^{max}$ **then**
9:                 **return** $u(a_j, r_i) * v_i - u(T_i^P(r_i^{max}), r_i) * v_i$
10:             **else**
11:                 **return** 0
12:         **else**
13:             **return** $u(a_j, r_i) * v_i$

Theorem 10.2 describes the optimal role mapping for the ad hoc agent under this model.

Theorem 10.2. *In Limited Role Mapping tasks, mapping S, under which a_0 chooses the role r_i that obtains* $\underset{0 \le i \le m-1}{\operatorname{argmax}} MU - 1(a_0, r_i, P)$, *maximizes marginal utility such that* $\forall S' \ne S \; MU(S', P) \le MU(S, P)$.

10.5.3 Incremental Value Model

Continuing the multiagent foraging example, consider a task in which there are 500 blue targets and 5000 red targets in a constrained environment with limited time (50 timesteps) for the agents to collect the targets. This example is Task C in Table 10.1. Since the time to collect targets is limited and there are more red targets than blue targets, the optimal role will sometimes be one that collects less plentiful but more valuable blue targets and sometimes be one that collects less valuable but more plentiful red targets. Collecting the less valuable red targets may be optimal if there are many other agents collecting blue targets and few other agents collecting red targets. This is because if there are many other agents collecting blue targets, the blue targets close to the base will be quickly collected, which forces all the agents collecting blue targets to venture farther away from the base in order to collect blue targets. In such a case, collecting less valuable red targets may prove to be optimal since competition for them is less fierce and therefore they can be collected and returned to the station more frequently.

In tasks like this, the value added by agents performing a role may not be linearly correlated with the number of agents performing that role. As such, the team utility in incremental value tasks can be modeled as

$$U(SP, d, T) = \sum_{i=0}^{m-1} rs_i * v_i \tag{10.4}$$

where

$$rs_i = \sum_{t_j \in T_i^{SP}} u(t_j, r_i) * F(i, j) \tag{10.5}$$

In particular, we consider the following three functions F—each with two parameters that can be tuned to match the characteristics of a particular task—that describe how the value added to the team by each subsequent agent performing a role incrementally increases or decreases as more agents perform that role.

Logarithmic function $F(i, j) = \log_{j+1}(x_i) + k_i$, where k_i represents the amount added to the role score rs_i for each agent performing role r_i and x_i sets the pace at which the function decays for agents performing r_i.

Exponential function $F(i, j) = g_i^{(j/t_i)}$, where g_i is the growth factor and t_i is the time required for the value to decrease by a factor of g_i—both for each agent performing role r_i.

Sigmoidal function $F(i, j) = \frac{1}{1+e^{s_i*(j+b_i)}}$, where s_i determines the sharpness of the curve and b_i dictates the x-offset of the sigmoid from the origin for each agent performing role r_i.

The function $MU - 2(a_j, r_i, P)$ displayed in Algorithm 10.2 gives the marginal utility obtained when an ad hoc agent a_j chooses to perform role r_i, where the current mapping of teammates to roles is described by P. Remember from function $MU - 1(a_j, r_i, P)$ that $posB(a_j, r_i)$ denotes the 0-indexed position in T_i^{SP} that the ad hoc agent a_j occupies. In this model, agent utility $u(t_j, r_i)$ for performing each role r_i, the importance v_i of each role r_i, and the parameters used in function F are all tunable parameters. Note that although we generally assume benefit is obtained as additional agents join a team, our models can also handle the case in which additional agents add penalty as they join the team.

Algorithm 10.2 $(MU - 2(a_j, r_i, P))$

1: **if** $m_i^P = 0$ **then**
2:     **return** $v_i * (u(a_j, r_i) * F(j, 1))$
3: **else**
4:     **if** $posB(a_j, r_i) = m_i^P$ **then**
5:         **return** $v_i * u(a_j, r_i) * F(j, m_i^P + 1)$
6:     **else**

7:         **return** $v_i * u(a_j, r_i) * F(j, posB(a_j, r_i) + 1) - \sum_{y=b_{posB(a_j,r_i)}}^{m_i^P - 1} (u(b_y, r_i) * v_i *$

$$F(j, posB(b_y, r_i) + 1) - u(b_y, r_i) * v_i * F(j, posB(b_y, r_i) + 2))$$

Theorem 10.3 describes the optimal role mapping for the ad hoc agent under this model.

Theorem 10.3. *In Incremental Value tasks, mapping S, under which a_0 chooses the role r_i that obtains* $\underset{0 \le i \le m-1}{\mathrm{argmax}} MU - 2(a_0, r_i, P)$, *maximizes marginal utility such that $\forall S' \ne S\ MU(S', P) \le MU(S, P)$.*

10.5.4 Empirical Validation of Models

As each model was presented, a foraging task in which the model has been empirically shown to be most appropriate was also described. Results of each model on each task are presented in Table 10.1. Task D—a task with 5000 blue targets, 5000 red targets, limited time (50 timesteps), and crowding penalties that only let one agent move from each cell in a timestep—is also included to represent a case where the limited model and two of the incremental models do poorly.

Throughout this chapter, we evaluate models based on how often they lead an ad hoc agent to make the "correct" decision about which role to assume. An ad hoc agent's decision to perform role r_1 instead of r_2 is correct if empirical data shows that performing r_1 yields a team score that is better by a statistically significant margin than the team score obtained by performing r_2. Likewise, an ad hoc agent's decision to perform role r_1 instead of r_2 is "incorrect" if empirical data shows that performing r_1 yields a team score that is worse by a statistically significant margin than the team score obtained by performing r_2. If the margin is not statistically significant, then the decision is not counted as correct or incorrect. We determine statistical significance by running a two-tailed student's t-test assuming two-sample unequal variance.

As seen in Table 10.1, each model presented earlier in this section is indeed appropriate for some task. Interestingly enough, no model is best or worst for all tasks. In fact, each model performs poorly in at least one task. Thus, this experiment serves to show that each of the models presented is worth considering. Tasks C and D of this experiment also serve to highlight the differences between the incremental model with sigmoidal function and the incremental model with logarithmic and exponential functions.

10.6 Model Evaluation

The role-based ad hoc teamwork problem lies in determining which role an ad hoc agent should select when faced with a *novel* teamwork situation. Thus, the main questions in terms of role selection are: given a task in a particular environment, how should the correct model be selected? Additionally, once a model is selected, how should we determine reasonable parameters for the model given limited gold standard data? Answering these questions makes substantial progress toward solving the role-based ad hoc teamwork problem. Therefore, this section examines both questions in the Pacman Capture-the-Flag environment.

10.6.1 Pacman Capture-the-Flag Environment

We empirically examine each of the three models previously described in a Capture-the-Flag style variant of Pacman designed by John DeNero and Dan Klein [18]. The foraging domain used earlier in the chapter was a simple and easily configurable domain. However, we move to the Pacman domain now both as an example of a more complex domain and to validate that our approach works in multiple domains.

The Pacman map is divided into two halves and two teams compete by attempting to eat the food on the opponent's side of the map while defending the food on its side. A team wins by eating all but two of the food pellets on the opponent's side or by eating more pellets than the opponent before 3000 moves have been made. When a player is captured, it restarts at its starting point.

The result of each game is the difference between the number of pellets protected by the team and the number of pellets protected by the opponent—we refer to this as the *score differential*. Wins result in positive score differentials, ties result in zero score differentials, and losses result in negative score differentials. High positive score differentials indicate that the team dominated the opponent, while score differentials closer to zero indicate that the two teams were well matched. We mainly care whether we win or lose, so we transform each score differential using a sigmoid function in order to emphasize differences in score differentials close to zero. We input the score differential from each game into the sigmoid function $\frac{1}{1+e^{-0.13*\text{scoreDifferential}}}$ to obtain *gold standard* data. We examined different values for the multiplicand and found that 0.13 yielded the most representative score differential spreads in the three tasks presented in the following.

In each experiment, we consider two roles that could be performed: $R = \{\text{offense}, \text{defense}\}$. Offensive players move toward the closest food on the opponent's side, making no effort to avoid being captured. Defensive players wander randomly on their own side and chase any invaders they see. These offensive and defensive behaviors are deliberately suboptimal, as we focus solely on role decisions given whatever behaviors the agents execute when performing their roles.

We consider the opponents and map to be fixed and part of the environment for each experiment. Half of the opponents perform defensive behaviors and half perform offensive behaviors. Additionally, all the agents run either the offensive or defensive behavior just described. As such, all agents performing a particular role have the same ability to perform that role. In other words, for agents T_i^{SP} performing role r_i, $u(t_0, r_i) = \ldots = u(t_{m_i^P - 1}, r_i)$.

10.6.2 Determining the Best-Suited Model

We use three tasks to determine which of the models best represents the marginal utility of a role selection for the Pacman Capture-the-Flag environment. In particular, a *task* is defined by the number of opponents and the map. The first task "vs-2" is against two opponents on the "Basic" map shown in Figure 10.2(a), the second task "vs-6" is against six opponents on the "Basic" map, and the third task "vs-2-SmallDefense" is against two opponents on the "SmallDefense" map shown in Figure 10.2(b).

To decide which of the models is most representative of the marginal utility of a role selection in the Pacman Capture-the-Flag environment, we first gather full sets of gold standard data. In particular, in each task we gather scores over 1000 games for each team of 0 to 6 offensive agents and 0 to 6 defensive

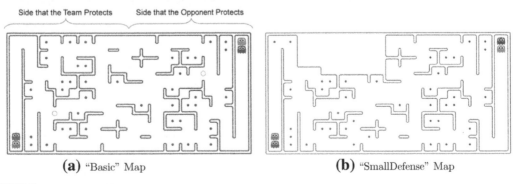

(a) "Basic" Map   (b) "SmallDefense" Map

FIGURE 10.2

Maps used to determine which model best represents the marginal utility of a role selection for the Pacman Capture-the-Flag environment.

agents (i.e., 49 teams). Then we calculate the gold standard data for each team by putting the score differential from each of the 1000 games through the sigmoidal function given before and then average the results. The gold standard data from the "vs-2" environment is shown in Table 10.2. Note that 0.09 is the worst possible gold standard performance and corresponds to obtaining 0 pellets and losing all 18 pellets to the opponent. Likewise, 0.88 is the best possible gold standard performance, and corresponds to obtaining 18 pellets and losing no pellets to the opponent.

We then use the gold standard data to determine the *gold standard decision* of whether an ad hoc agent should perform an offensive role or a defensive role on any team composed of 0 to 5 offensive agents and 0 to 5 defensive agents in each of the three tasks. To determine the gold standard decision of whether it is better for the ad hoc agent to perform an offensive or defensive role when added to a particular team, we look at whether the gold standard data is higher for the team with one extra defensive player or the team with one extra offensive player. If the gold standard data is higher for the team with one extra defensive player, then the gold standard decision is for the ad hoc agent to play defense. Likewise, if the gold standard data is higher for the team with one extra offensive player, then the gold standard decision is for the ad hoc agent to play offense. We determine whether a gold standard decision is statistically significant by running a two-tailed student's *t*-test assuming two-sample unequal variance.

As an example, consider the gold standard data from the "vs-2" environment shown in Table 10.2. The gold standard decision of whether an ad hoc agent should perform an offensive role or a defensive role on a team composed of two offensive agents and one defensive agent can be determined by considering whether the data for a team with two offensive agents and two defensive agents is greater than or less than the gold standard data for a team with three offensive agents and one defensive agent. By looking at the data from the "vs-2" environment shown in Table 10.2, we can see that the data for a team with two offensive agents and two defensive agents is 0.75, while the gold standard data for a team with three offensive agents and one defensive agent is 0.71. Since the data for a team with two offensive agents and two defensive agents is greater than the gold standard data for a team with three offensive agents and one defensive agent, the gold standard decision regarding a team composed of two offensive agents and one defensive agent is to perform a defensive role.

Table 10.2 Rounded Gold Standard Data and Decisions from the "vs-2" Environment

	0d	1d	2d	3d	4d	5d	6d
0o	0.09 (+o)	0.09 (+o)	0.09 (+o)	0.13 (+o)	0.23 (+o)	0.31 (+o)	0.36
1o	0.29 (+d)	0.49 (X)	0.64 (+o)	0.74 (+o)	0.79 (+o)	0.81 (+o)	0.82
2o	0.42 (+d)	0.63 (+d)	0.75 (+d)	0.81 (+d)	0.83 (X)	0.85 (X)	0.86
3o	0.54 (+d)	0.71 (+d)	0.80 (+d)	0.83 (+d)	0.85 (X)	0.85 (X)	0.86
4o	0.56 (+d)	0.74 (+d)	0.81 (+d)	0.84 (+d)	0.85 (+d)	0.87 (X)	0.87
5o	0.61 (+d)	0.75 (+d)	0.83 (+d)	0.84 (+d)	0.86 (X)	0.87 (+d)	0.88
6o	0.64	0.79	0.83	0.86	0.87	0.88	0.88

Note: The rows represent the 0...6 agents performing an offensive role, while the columns represent the 0...6 agents performing a defensive role. A '+o' ('+d') decision means that the ad hoc agent should adopt an offensive (defensive) role if added to a team with teammates performing the roles indicated by the row and column. An 'X' decision means that the decision of which role to perform was not statistically significant at p = 0.05.

Once we calculate the gold standard decisions for the ad hoc agent in each of the three tasks, we can determine which of the three models best captures the actual marginal utility of role selection in each task. First, we input the gold standard data and the model function into MATLAB's *lsqcurvefit* algorithm, which uses the trust region reflexive least squares curve-fitting algorithm, and obtain *fitted*

Table 10.3 Obtained Fitted Parameters for the Unlimited Role Mapping Model

Parameter	Initial	vs-2	vs-6	vs-2-SmallDefense
$u(*, offense)$	1	0.3456	0.2277	0.3508
$u(*, defense)$	1	0.3010	0.2918	0.2827
$v_{offense}$	1	0.3456	0.2277	0.3508
$v_{defense}$	1	0.3010	0.2918	0.2827

Table 10.4 Obtained Fitted Parameters for the Limited Role Mapping Model

Parameter	Initial	vs-2	vs-6	vs-2-SmallDefense
$u(*, offense)$	1	0.6764	0.2937	0.5437
$u(*, defense)$	1	0.2924	0.2926	0.2849
$v_{offense}$	1	0.6764	0.2937	0.5437
$v_{defense}$	1	0.2924	0.2926	0.2849
$r_{offense}^{min}$	1	1	1	1
$r_{defense}^{min}$	1	1	1	1
$r_{offense}^{max}$	3	1.2876	3.1476	2.0388
$r_{defense}^{max}$	3	3.3742	4.7504	3.2672

Table 10.5 Obtained Fitted Parameters for the Logarithmic Incremental Value Model

Parameter	Initial	vs-2	vs-6	vs-2-SmallDefense
$u(*, offense)$	1	0.5916	1.5926	0.4655
$u(*, defense)$	1	0.5650	0.5630	0.5164
$v_{offense}$	1	0.8081	0.1355	1.7277
$v_{defense}$	1	0.3675	0.1322	0.6257
$k_{offense}$	1	−0.5163	−0.3232	−0.1447
$k_{defense}$	1	−0.2510	0.4069	−0.0622
$x_{offense}$	1	2.4560	1.6866	1.7287
$x_{defense}$	1	1.9180	1.4599	1.3864

Table 10.6 Obtained Fitted Parameters for the Exponential Incremental Value Model

Parameter	Initial	vs-2	vs-6	vs-2-SmallDefense
$u(*, offense)$	1	1.1761	0.3837	1.0742
$u(*, defense)$	1	0.3398	0.8327	0.1804
$v_{offense}$	1	1.3387	0.4658	1.2690
$v_{defense}$	1	0.5712	0.1280	0.8254
$g_{offense}$	1	0.9123	0.6285	0.2809
$g_{defense}$	1	0.5510	0.8831	0.7534
$t_{offense}$	1	0.0706	0.9366	1.0924
$t_{defense}$	1	1.3116	1.1912	0.6606

Table 10.7 Obtained Fitted Parameters for the Sigmoidal Incremental Value Model

Parameter	Initial	vs-2	vs-6	vs-2-SmallDefense
$u(*, offense)$	1	1.8120	0.7068	1.9380
$u(*, defense)$	1	1.7941	0.5136	0.6841
$v_{offense}$	1	1.7544	0.6969	1.6301
$v_{defense}$	1	0.2533	0.4558	0.5369
$s_{offense}$	1	1.3934	0.5801	1.2311
$s_{defense}$	1	0.5263	0.1577	0.4917
$b_{offense}$	1	0.3318	1.1634	0.5131
$b_{defense}$	1	0.9327	1.3573	1.1455

parameters for the model function. The fitted parameters vary in type and number for each of the three models, but always include the role importance value v_i, the agent's utility $u(a_j, r_i)$ at performing role v_i, and parameters of the model function—all for each role $r_i \in R(d)$. The obtained fitted parameters for each of the models in the "vs-2", "vs-6", and "vs-2-SmallDefense" tasks can be found in Tables 10.3–10.7. We use the fitted parameters to calculate *fitted results* for teams of 0 to 6 offensive agents and 0 to 6 defensive agents. Lastly, we translate these fitted results into *fitted decisions* using the same methodology used to translate the gold standard score differentials into gold standard decisions.

Now that we have gold standard decisions for each of the three tasks and fitted decisions for all three models in the three tasks, we compare the number of times the gold standard decision (e.g., "+o") is statistically significant but does not match the fitted decision for a particular team arrangement (e.g., "+d")—in other words, the number of times the ad hoc agent made an *incorrect decision*.

As is apparent from Table 10.8, all three incremental model functions perform rather well. Unfortunately we have yet to discover any clear insight as to when each of the incremental model functions are most appropriate. Thus, for now, it seems to be something that must be determined empirically for each new domain using gold standard data.

Table 10.8 Number of Statistically Significant Incorrect/Correct Decisions Made by the Ad Hoc Agent

Model	vs-2	vs-6	vs-2-Small Defense
Unlimited Role Mapping	19/10	8/21	14/16
Limited Role Mapping	3/26	10/19	3/27
Logarithmic Incremental Value	3/26	2/27	1/29
Exponential Incremental Value	**1/28**	**1/28**	**1/29**
Sigmoidal Incremental Value	**0/29**	**1/28**	**2/28**

Note: The results here are for each of the three tasks. Fewer incorrect and greater correct decisions is desirable.

In the Pacman domain, as can be seen in Table 10.8, the exponential and sigmoidal functions of the incremental model make the fewest incorrect decisions across the three tasks. Thus, we conclude that in the Pacman Capture-the-Flag domain, at least on the maps and opponents we studied, the incremental model using either an exponential function or a sigmoidal function most accurately models team utility. However, to conclude this we generated a full set of gold standard data for each of the three tasks, amounting to 49,000 games per task, and used this data to fit the parameters of the model. Next we consider how to use the chosen model for predictive modeling when substantially less gold standard data is available.

10.6.3 Predictive Modeling

The main research problem in role-based ad hoc teamwork is how to choose a role for the ad hoc agent that maximizes marginal utility. This problem is particularly important when the ad hoc agent is placed in a situation it has never encountered before.

Once a model type has been selected for a domain, the ad hoc agent can use this model to *predict* the marginal utility of role selection on new tasks in this domain for which we have limited gold standard data. Essentially we want to be able to determine how the ad hoc agent should behave during a new task—including never seen before situations—without the expense of gathering substantial amounts of gold standard data for every scenario. We do this by choosing fitted parameters for the new task based on the data that is available. Remember that fitted parameters can be obtained by inputting the gold standard data and the chosen model function into MATLAB's *lsqcurvefit* algorithm, as this will fit the chosen model to the limited gold standard data using a least squares curve-fitting algorithm. Then these fitted parameters can be used to calculate fitted results and fitted decisions, which represent the decisions chosen by the agent given each possible set of teammates.

In the following we evaluate the accuracy of the incremental value model in our Pacman domain on multiple tasks when various amounts of randomly selected data are available for choosing fitted parameters. We use two new tasks in this section, both against two opponents. One task "vs-2-alley" is on the "AlleyDefense" map shown in Figure 10.3(a) and the other task "vs-2-33%" is on the "33%Defense" map shown in Figure 10.3(b). Both the "AlleyDefense" and "33%Defense" maps include a smaller defensive area than offensive area for the team to which the ad hoc agent is added. However, the alley in "AlleyDefense" calls for the ad hoc agent to behave very differently than in the "33%Defense" map,

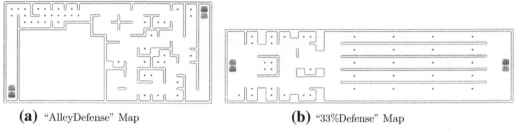

(a) "AlleyDefense" Map   **(b)** "33%Defense" Map

FIGURE 10.3

The maps used for the predictive modeling tasks.

where the opponent's food pellets are relatively easy for the ad hoc agent's team to capture. Specifically, in the "33%Defense" map it is desirable—up to a certain threshold—to add an offensive agent as long as there is at least one defensive agent, whereas in the "AlleyDefense" map it is desirable to have substantially more defensive agents than offensive agents as long as there is at least one offensive agent.

Consider the case in which the ad hoc team agent is given, either through experience or observation, randomly selected data points that represent some sparse experience in a task, where a data point consists of the number of agents fulfilling each role and the average gold standard data calculated over 25 games. We chose 25 games because this proved to be an appropriate trade-off between the time required to collect data and the value of minimizing incorrect predictions. However, in practice the agent will usually not get to determine how many games it receives information about, and instead must do the best it can with whatever experience it is given. Note that if only one data point is used to fit the model, then score differentials from 25 games are required. Likewise, use of 10 data points requires $250(10 \times 25)$ games. Even if all 49 data points are used, only $1225(49 \times 25)$ games are required. To put these game numbers in perspective, we can usually run 500 games on our high-throughput computing cluster in under five minutes.

We evaluate the prediction accuracy of each of the three function variations of the incremental value model on two tasks for which we have limited data ranging from 1 to 49 randomly selected data points. In this experiment, we endeavor to determine how many data points are needed to obtain reasonable prediction accuracy—in other words, we want to find the point at which it might not be worth obtaining additional data points. Note that since a data point cannot be selected more than once, all data points are being used when 49 data points are selected. Prediction accuracy is reported as the number of statistically significant incorrect predictions made by the model. Figure 10.4 shows the accuracy of each variation of the chosen model on the "vs-2-alley" task, while Figure 10.5 shows accuracy on the "vs-2-33%" task, both when given varying amounts of randomly selected data points calculated from 25 games.

As would be expected, the accuracy of each variation of the chosen model improves steadily in both tasks as additional data points are used to fit the model. Note that in both tasks, using as few as ten data points yields about as many incorrect predictions on average as using all forty-nine data points. One interesting result to note is that in the "vs-2-alley" task, the incremental model with the logarithmic function does the worst of the incremental models, whereas in the "vs-2-33%" task it does the best. This performance variability is acceptable; although the incremental model with either an exponential function or a sigmoidal function was shown in the previous section to be the best for the

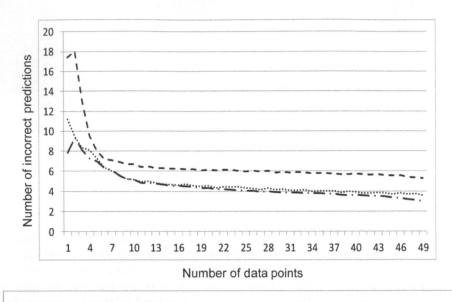

FIGURE 10.4

Accuracy of each variation of the incremental value model. *Note:* The data were averaged over 1000 trials using various amounts of randomly selected data points from 25 games in the "vs-2-alley" task.

Pacman Capture-the-Flag domain, it will not always be the absolute best. What is notable is that the chosen model—the incremental model with either an exponential function or a sigmoidal function in our domain—does the best or close to best in both tasks.

10.6.3.1 *Importance of Determining the Fitted Parameters*

In the previous section we presented the idea that once an ad hoc agent has chosen a model for a particular domain, it can use this chosen model to predict the marginal utility of role selection on new tasks in the same domain by using limited gold standard data to determine new fitted parameters for the model.

However, how important is it to use limited gold standard data to determine appropriate fitted parameters for the chosen model function in a new task? We found experimentally that if parameters fit onto one task are used on another task, the results can be quite poor. For example, using parameters fit for the "vs-6" task, which yield one incorrect decision on the "vs-6" task, yields 14 incorrect decisions on the "vs-2-33%" task. As such, it is almost always important and worthwhile to find new fitted parameters when a new task is encountered and there is opportunity to obtain *any* gold standard data.

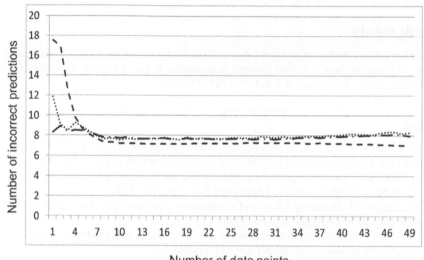

FIGURE 10.5

Accuracy of each variation of the incremental value model. *Note:* The data were averaged over 1000 trials using various amounts of randomly selected data points from 25 games in the "vs-2-33%" task.

10.7 **Conclusion and Future Work**

This chapter presented a formalization of role-based ad hoc teamwork settings, introduced several methods for modeling the marginal utility of an ad hoc agent's role selection, and empirically showed that each of these methods is appropriate for a different class of role-based tasks. We assume in this work that the roles of the teammates are known and that we know how well some team configurations do in a particular task. However, we do not know how much an ad hoc agent could help the team if added to each role. As such, we show that it is possible to use a particular functional form to model the marginal utility of a role selection in a variety of tasks. Additionally, we show that only a limited amount of data is needed on a new task in order to be able to fit the function such that it can be used as a predictive model to determine how an ad hoc agent should behave in situations involving a task that it has not previously encountered.

This research is among the first to study role-based ad hoc teams. As such, there are many potential directions for future work. One such direction would be to expand this work into more complicated environments with more than two potential roles to fulfill and more than one ad hoc agent. Another direction would be to consider the case in which the ad hoc agents encounter teammates that are running unfamiliar behaviors, as this would force the ad hoc agents to model their teammates.

Acknowledgments

This work has taken place in the Learning Agents Research Group (LARG) at the Artificial Intelligence Laboratory, The University of Texas at Austin. LARG research is supported in part by grants from the National Science Foundation (CNS-1330072, CNS-1305287) and ONR (21C184-01).

References

[1] Stone P, Kaminka GA, Kraus S, Rosenschein JS. Ad hoc autonomous agent teams: Collaboration without pre-coordination. In: Proceedings of the 24th Conference on Artificial Intelligence; 2010.

[2] Grosz BJ, Kraus S. Collaborative plans for complex group action. Artif Intell J 1996;86(2):269–357.

[3] Tambe M. Towards flexible teamwork. J Artif Intell Res 1997;7:83–124.

[4] Decker KS, Lesser VR. Designing a family of coordination algorithms. In: Proceedings of the First International Conference on Multi-Agent Systems; 1995.

[5] Stone P, Veloso M. Task decomposition, dynamic role assignment, and low-bandwidth communication for real-time strategic teamwork. Artif Intell J 1999;110(2):241–73.

[6] Liemhetcharat S, Veloso M. Weighted synergy graphs for role assignment in ad hoc heterogeneous robot teams. In: Proceedings of the IEEE/RSJ International Conference on Intelligent Robots and Systems; 2012.

[7] Wu F, Zilberstein S, Chen X. Online planning for ad hoc autonomous agent teams. In: Proceedings of the 22nd International Joint Conference on Artificial Intelligence; 2011.

[8] Bowling M, McCracken P. Coordination and adaptation in impromptu teams. In: Proceedings of the 20th Conference on Artificial Intelligence; 2005.

[9] Jones E, Browning B, Dias MB, Argall B, Veloso M, Stentz AT. Dynamically formed heterogeneous robot teams performing tightly-coordinated tasks. In: Proceedings of the International Conference on Robotics and Automation; 2006.

[10] Han J, Li M, Guo L. Soft control on collective behavior of a group of autonomous agents by a shill agent. J Syst Sci Complex 2006;19:54–62.

[11] Barrett S, Stone P, Kraus S. Empirical evaluation of ad hoc teamwork in the pursuit domain. In: Proceedings of 11th International Conference on Autonomous Agents and Multiagent Systems; 2011.

[12] Sukthankar G, Sycara K. Policy recognition for multi-player tactical scenarios. In: Proceedings of the Sixth International Conference on Autonomous Agents and Multiagent Systems; 2007.

[13] Zhuo HH, Li L. Multi-agent plan recognition with partial team traces and plan libraries. In: Proceedings of the Twenty-Second International Joint Conference on Artificial Intelligence; 2011.

[14] Blake M, Sorensen G, Archibald J, Beard R. Human assisted capture-the-flag in an urban environment. In: Proceedings of the International Conference on Robotics and Automation; 2004.

[15] Sadilek A, Kautz H. Modeling and reasoning about success, failure, and intent of multi-agent activities. In: Proceedings of the 12th International Conference on Ubiquitous Computing, Workshop on Mobile Context-Awareness; 2010.

[16] Mataric M. Learning to behave socially. In: Proceedings of From Animals to Animats 3. Proceedings of the Third International Conference on Simulation of Adaptive Behavior; 1994.

[17] Lerman K, Jones C, Galstyan A, Mataric M. Analysis of dynamic task allocation in multi-robot systems. Int J Robot Res 2006;25:225–42.

[18] DeNero J, Klein D. Teaching introductory artificial intelligence with Pac-Man. In: Proceedings of the First Symposium on Educational Advances in Artificial Intelligence; 2010.

Applications

Probabilistic Plan Recognition for Proactive Assistant Agents

Jean Oh[a], Felipe Meneguzzi[b], and Katia Sycara[a]

[a]*Carnegie Mellon University, Pittsburgh, PA, USA*
[b]*Pontifical Catholic University of Rio Grande do Sul, Porto Alegre, Brazil*

11.1 Introduction

Plan recognition, which refers to the task of identifying the user's high-level goals (or intentions) by observing the user's current activities, is a crucial capability for intelligent assistant systems that are intended to be incorporated into the user's computing environment.

This chapter discusses how we use plan recognition to develop a software agent that can proactively assist human users in time-stressed environments. Human users dealing with multiple objectives in a complex environment (e.g., military planners or emergency response operators) are subject to a high level of cognitive load. When this load is excessive, it can severely impair the quality of the plans that are created [28]. To help users focus on high-priority objectives, we develop a software assistant agent that can recognize the user's goals and plans in order to proactively assist with tedious and time-consuming tasks (e.g., anticipating information needs or reserving resources ahead of user need).

Plan-recognition algorithms generally center on a model that describes how a user behaves. Such a model can be built by collecting frequently observed sequences of user actions (e.g., as a plan library) [13,11,3]. By contrast, a generative approach can be taken to develop a user model to represent how a user makes decisions to solve a problem (e.g., as a planning process) [4,24,20,21]. Choosing the right approach requires an understanding of where the target problem's uncertainty originates. Whereas a plan library is suitable for representing a user's activities that may constitute multiple unrelated problems (i.e., uncertainty lies in a user's objectives), a planning process can succinctly represent a complex decision-making process that may result in a large number of various plans (i.e., uncertainty lies in an environment).

In this chapter, we focus on a case where a user is solving a domain-specific problem that deals with a high level of complexity and uncertainty (e.g., an emergency response system), where a flexible plan is made in advance but the actual course of action is dynamically determined during execution [7]. Thus, our discussion here focuses on the generative approach—using a planner to represent a user model—and how this model can be used in intelligent assistant systems.

The rest of this chapter is organized as follows. After discussing proactive assistant systems generally in Section 11.2, a generative plan-recognition algorithm is described in detail in Section 11.3, followed by a description of how the results of plan recognition are used within a proactive assistant architecture in Section 11.4. Section 11.5 presents two examples of fully implemented proactive assistant systems. Finally, the chapter is summarized in Section 11.6.

11.2 Proactive Assistant Agent

A software assistant system, like a human assistant, is expected to perform various tasks on behalf of a user. An assistant's role has a set of desired qualifications including the ability to learn a user's preferences [17,22], the ability to assess the current state and to make rational decisions in various situations [8], and the ability to speculate on a user's future activities so that time-consuming actions can be taken proactively [5]. Here, we focus on the assistant's ability to make proactive decisions where plan recognition is a crucial part.

The core componency of an intelligent assistant system is its decision-making module. For instance, an agent can make decisions according to a set of prescribed rules if complete information about its tasks is available a priori. An assistant's decision making can also be data-driven—that is, an action is executed whenever its preconditions are changed as new information is propagated (e.g., as with constraint-based planners) [2]. Alternatively, a decision–theoretic planner can be adopted; for example, the Electric Elves [8] uses a Markov decision process (MDP) to develop a personal assistant, known as Friday, which determines the optimal action given various states. For instance, given an invitation (to which a user is supposed to respond), Friday may wait a little until its user responds or take an action on behalf of the user according to the expected reward for each action.

To add the notion of plan recognition to an assistant's decision-making module, a partially observable MDP (POMDP) is generally used, where a user's goals (or intentions) are inserted as unobservable variables [10]. In this approach, plan recognition is tightly coupled with an assistant's action selection. That is, an assistant learns an optimal action to take in response to each user state without having a notion of its own (agent) goals or planning. In other words, traditional (PO)MDP approaches model immediate assistant actions in response to individual user actions, even if they implicitly consider the reward of future user actions for this action selection. This approach does not explicitly "look ahead" within a user's plan nor does it consider time constraints. For these reasons, the types of support that this approach can provide may be limited to atomic (or single) actions (e.g., opening a door for a user as in [10]) and may not be suitable for time-consuming actions, such as information prefetching, or more complex jobs that require the planning of multiple actions.

By contrast, the proactive assistant agent architecture, known here as Anytime Cognition (ANTICO[1]), separates plan recognition from the assistant's decision-making module [19]. Figure 11.1 illustrates an abstract view of the architecture. At this point, the user plan represents the assistant's estimation of how a user makes decisions. Based on this user plan, plan recognition is performed to generate sequences of expected actions. The proactive manager *evaluates* the predicted user plan to identify potential assistance needs. Here, the general purpose of the evaluation is to identify a set of unmet preconditions (or prerequisites) of predicted user actions, but the criteria for evaluating user plans is specific to each problem domain—for instance, identifying information needed to execute certain actions [19, 15] or detecting potential norm violations [21]. The set of identified assistance needs is labeled as new tasks for the assistant and is passed to the assistant's planning module.

The ANTICO architecture also supports the notion of an assistant's goals and planning similar to Friday's planner in Electric Elves [8]. Whereas Friday's actions are triggered on the receipt of a new request, ANTICO determines a set of assistive tasks according to its prediction of user needs.

---

[1]In earlier work, an instance of ANTICO is referred to as ANTicipatory Information and Planning Agent (ANTIPA).

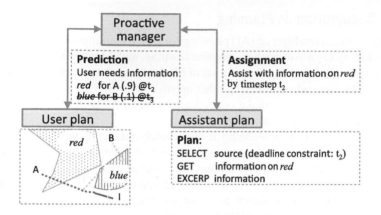

FIGURE 11.1

An abstract view of a proactive assistant agent architecture.

Figure 11.1 includes a simple example, which can be seen within the dotted lines. By evaluating the user plan, it is predicted with 0.9 probability that heading toward area *A* suggests information about the *red* zone is needed. The prediction also suggests information about the *blue* zone is needed, but the need has a low probability, so the requirement has been pruned. The proactive manager assigns the assistant a new goal of acquiring red zone information. Note that a deadline time constraint is imposed on this assignment because the user will need this information by timestep t_2.

The assistant plans and schedules necessary resources to acquire the needed information. For instance, the assistant first selects an information source from which the needed information can be retrieved before the deadline. After the assistant retrieves the information from the selected source, a data postprocessing action can be taken to excerpt the information for a user to parse quickly. The information that has been prepared is passed back to the proactive manager to be presented to the user when needed.

Disengaging an assistant's planning from its user's planning has several advantages over approaches based on tight coupling. First, the size of the state space is exponentially reduced as follows. Let us define a user's planning space in terms of a set of variables, where a subset of those variables can be delegated to an assistant. The size of the state space grows exponentially in the number of variables. Let u and a denote the number of user variables and assistant variables, respectively. Without loss of generality, we add two simplifying assumptions that user and agent variables are exclusive and that the domain size for all variables is a constant d. Then, the size of the state space where these variables are tightly coupled is d^{u+a}, whereas that of the detached approach is $d^u + d^a$.

The ANTICO architecture has been flexibly applied to two types of information assistants [19,15] and to an assistant that supports humans in complying with organizational norms [21], which will be described further in Section 11.5.

11.3 Probabilistic Plan Recognition

This section describes a generative approach to plan recognition [19] and discusses related work.

11.3.1 Plan Recognition as Planning

The idea of using artificial intelligence (AI) planning for plan recognition has been gaining attention in various fields including cognitive science, machine learning, and AI planning.

In cognitive science, Baker et al. [4] used a set of Markov decision processes to model how a human observer makes predictions when observing other agents' activities. Their results show that the MDP framework resembles how humans make predictions in experiments in which human subjects were asked to recognize the goal of an animated agent.

The idea of plan recognition as planning is also closely related to the notion of *inverse optimal control* in MDP-based planners [26]. Inverse optimal control, which refers to the task of recovering a cost function from observed optimal behavior, has been studied under various names including *inverse reinforcement learning* [18], *apprenticeship learning* [1], and *imitation learning* [29]. These algorithms focus on the learning of hidden cost functions (as opposed to using predetermined cost functions) and have been specifically designed for the MDP framework.

A series of studies by Ramírez and Geffner contributes to bridging AI planning and goal recognition, establishing the notion of plan recognition as planning. Because their main objective is to identify a user's goals, it is more appropriate to refer to their work as "goal recognition." Their initial work used classic planners for goal recognition [24]; in it goal prediction worked only when the observed actions precisely matched an expected sequence of actions. To overcome this drawback, they adopted a probabilistic model to address uncertainty [24]. This framework has also been applied to the partially observable MDP framework [25].

In the following subsections, we describe a probabilistic plan-recognition algorithm presented in Oh et al. [20,21].

11.3.2 Representing a User Plan as an MDP

We use an MDP [6] to represent a user's decision-making model. An MDP is a rich framework that can represent various real-life problems involving uncertainty.

The use of an MDP to represent a user plan is justified for the problem domain of our interest in which users are strongly motivated to accomplish a set of clearly defined goals. Thus, we can assume that a user is executing a sequence of planned actions; that is, the user has *planned* the observed actions. For instance, in emergency-response situations, every major governmental organization has a set of emergency operations plans (EOP) that has been created in advance. The EOP provides a foundation for the creation of specific plans to respond to the actual details of a particular event [7].

To model the user's planning process, we consider an AI planner so that we can generate a set of alternative plans by solving a user's planning problem. At the same time, we need a model that can capture the *nondeterministic* nature of real-life applications. Since an MDP is a stochastic planner, it suits both of our purposes.

Throughout the chapter we use Definition 11.1 to refer to an MDP. We note that the discount factor, γ, in the definition is an optional component used to ensure that the Bellman equations converge in infinite horizon. When the discount factor is not specified, it is assumed to be 1. Moreover, given the multiple equivalent ways to render the equations that solve MDPs, in this chapter we use the presentation style of Russell and Norvig (see Chapter 17) [27] for clarification.

Definition 11.1 (MDP).   A Markov decision process is represented as a tuple $\langle S, A, r, T, \gamma \rangle$, where S denotes a set of states; A, a set of actions; $r : S \times A \to \mathbb{R}$, a function specifying a reward of taking an action in a state; $T : S \times A \times S \to \mathbb{R}$, a state-transition function; and γ, a discount factor indicating that a reward received in the future is worth less than an immediate reward. Solving an MDP generally refers to a search for a *policy* that maps each state to an optimal action with respect to a discounted long-term expected reward.

Without loss of generality we assume that the reward function, $r(s)$, can be given such that each individual state yields a reward when the agent reaches it.[2] Although the MDP literature sometimes refers to a goal state as being an absorbing or terminal state; that is, a state s with $T(s'|s, a) = 0$ for all a and for all s' in S except the current state s (i.e., a state with no possibility of leaving), we mean a goal state to be a state with a positive reward (i.e., any state s with $r(s) > 0$). Note that satisfying time constraints is imperative in the target problem domain; that is, actions must be taken in a timely manner (e.g., in an emergency-response case). Here, discount factor γ is used to manage time constraints in a planner, specifying that a reward is decayed as a function of time.

Definition 11.2 (Value Iteration).   Given an MDP, denoted by a tuple $\langle S, A, r, T, \gamma \rangle$, the value of state s, denoted by $V(s)$, can be defined as the discounted long-term expected reward when starting from state s and taking the best action thereafter, which is known as the Bellman equation as follows:

$$V(s) = \max_{a \in A} \left[r(s, a) + \gamma \sum_{s' \in S} V(s')T(s'|s, a) \right].$$

The value iteration algorithm initializes the values of states with some value (e.g., an arbitrary constant) and iteratively updates values $V(s)$ for all states until they converge. The algorithm is guaranteed to converge when $0 < \gamma < 1$. Value iteration computes a deterministic policy by selecting an optimal action in each state as follows:

$$\pi(s) = \arg\max_{a \in A} \left[r(s, a) + \gamma \sum_{s' \in S} V(s')T(s'|s, a) \right].$$

In addition to optimal actions, there can be "good" actions with expected values that come close to the optimum. It would be too naive for an assistant to assume that a human user will always choose the optimal action. In Definition 11.3, instead of computing a deterministic policy as in Definition 11.2, we compute a stochastic policy that, instead of selecting an optimal action, ascribes probability $\pi(s, a)$ of selecting action a in state s according to the expected value of taking action a. This policy expresses the probability with which an imperfect decision maker selects an action based on the actual perfectly rational choice. This stochastic policy allows the assistant to prepare for a wider range of user actions that are likely to be chosen in reality. A similar idea of computing a stochastic policy from value iteration can be found in Zeibart et al. [29].

Definition 11.3 (Value Iteration for a Stochastic Policy).   Let $a \in A$ be an action and $s, s' \in S$ be states; we define a stochastic policy $\pi(s, a)$ denoting the probability of selecting action a in state s.

---

[2]It is trivial to see that $r(s, a) = \sum_{s'} T(s'|s, a)r(s')$.

This probability is computed as a proportion of the maximum expected reward of selecting action a in state s, such that:

$$\pi(s, a) \propto \left[r(s, a) + \gamma \sum_{s' \in S} V(s') T(s' | s, a) \right].$$

Algorithm 11.1. predictFuturePlan

---

input : a set of goals G, a set of policies Φ, a sequence of observations O
output: predicted planTree
planTree t ← createNewTree();
node n ← getRootNode(t);
state s ← getCurrentState();
foreach *goal* $g \in G$ **do**
  policy π_g ← getPolicyForGoal(Φ, g);
  weight w_g ← $p(g | O_t)$ /* Equation (1) */;
  buildPlanTree($t, n, \pi_g, s, w_g, 0$);

Let $\Phi = \langle S, A, r, T, \gamma \rangle$ denote an MDP representing the user's planning problem. The plan-recognition algorithm shown in Algorithm 11.1 is a two-step process. The agent first estimates which goals the user is trying to accomplish and then predicts a sequence of possible plan steps that the user is most likely to take to achieve those goals.

11.3.3 Goal Recognition

In the first step, the algorithm estimates a probability distribution over a set of possible goals. We use a Bayesian approach that assigns a probability mass to each goal according to how well a series of observed user actions is matched with the optimal plan toward the goal.

We define set G of possible goal states as all states with positive rewards such that $G \subseteq S$ and $r(g) > 0, \forall g \in G$. The algorithm initializes the probability distribution over the set G of possible goals, denoted by $p(g)$ for each goal g in G, proportionally to the reward $r(g)$, such that $\sum_{g \in G} p(g) = 1$ and $p(g) \propto r(g)$. The algorithm then computes an optimal policy, π_g, for every goal g in G, considering the positive reward only from the specified goal state g and 0 rewards from any other states $s \in S \wedge s \neq g$. We use the variation of the value iteration algorithm described in Definition 11.3 for computing an optimal policy.

For each potential goal $g \in G$, the algorithm computes a goal-specific policy, π_g, to achieve goal g. Following the assumption that the user acts more or less rationally, this policy can be computed by solving the MDP to maximize the long-term expected rewards. Instead of a deterministic policy that specifies only the best action that results in the maximum reward, we compute a stochastic policy, such that probability $p(a | s, g)$ of taking action a given state a when pursuing goal g is proportional to its long-term expected value $v(s, a, g)$:

$$p(a | s, g) \propto \beta v(s, a, g),$$

where β is a normalizing constant. Note that this step of computing optimal policies is performed only once and can be done offline, and the resulting policies are also used in the second step, as will be described in Section 11.3.4.

Let $O_t = s_1, a_1, s_2, a_2, \ldots, s_t$ denote a sequence of observed states and actions from timesteps 1 through t, where $s_{t'} \in S, a_{t'} \in A, \forall t' \in \{1, \ldots, t\}$. Here, the assistant agent must estimate the user's targeted goals.

After observing a sequence of user states and actions, the assistant agent updates the conditional probability, $p(g|O_t)$, that the user is pursuing goal g given the sequence of observations O_t. The conditional probability $p(g|O_t)$ can be rewritten using the Bayes rule as:

$$p(g|O_t) = \frac{p(s_1, a_1, \ldots, s_t|g) p(g)}{\sum_{g' \in G} p(s_1, a_1, \ldots, s_t|g') p(g')}. \tag{11.1}$$

By applying the chain rule, we can write the conditional probability of observing the sequence of states and actions given goal g as:

$$\begin{aligned} p(s_1, a_1, \ldots, s_t|g) &= p(s_1|g) p(a_1|s_1, g) p(s_2|s_1, a_1, g) \\ &\quad \ldots p(s_t|s_{t-1}, a_{t-1}, \ldots, s_1, g). \end{aligned}$$

By the MDP problem definition, the state-transition probability is independent of the goals. With the Markov assumption, the state-transition probability is also independent of any past states except the current state, and the user's action selection depends only on the current state and the specific goal. By using these conditional independence relationships, we get:

$$\begin{aligned} p(s_1, a_1, \ldots, s_t|g) &= p(s_1) p(a_1|s_1, g) p(s_2|s_1, a_1) \\ &\quad \ldots p(s_t|s_{t-1}, a_{t-1}), \end{aligned} \tag{11.2}$$

where the probability $p(a|s, g)$ represents the user's stochastic policy $\pi_g(s, a)$ for selecting action a from state s given goal g, which was computed during the initialization step.

By combining Eqs. 11.1 and 11.2, the conditional probability of a goal given a series of observations can be obtained. We use this conditional probability to assign weights when constructing a predicted plan-tree in the next step.

The algorithmic complexity of solving an MDP using value iteration is quadratic in the number of states and linear in the number of actions. Here, the optimal policies for candidate goals can be precomputed offline. Thus, the actual runtime complexity of our goal-recognition algorithm is linear in the number of candidate goals and the number of observations.

11.3.4 Plan Prediction

Based on the predicted goals from the first step, we now generate a set of possible scenarios that the user will follow. Recall that we solved the user's MDP Φ to get stochastic policies for each potential goal. The intuition for using a stochastic policy is to allow the agent to explore multiple likely plan paths in parallel, relaxing the assumption that the user always acts to maximize her or his expected reward.

Algorithm 11.2. buildPlanTree

---

input : planTree t, node n, policy π, state s, weight w, deadline d
output: predicted planTree
foreach action $a \in A$ **do**
> weight $w' \leftarrow \pi(s, a)w$;
> **if** $w' >$ threshold θ **then**
>> $s' \leftarrow$ sampleNextState (state s, action a);
>> node $n' \leftarrow$ createNewNode (s', w', d);
>> addChild (n, n');
>> buildPlanTree $(t, n', \pi, s', w', d + 1)$;

Using the MDP model and the set of stochastic policies, we *sample* a tree of the most likely sequences of user actions and resulting states from the user's current state, known here as a *plan-tree*. In a predicted plan-tree, a *node* contains the resulting state from taking a predicted user action, associated with the following two features: *priority* and *deadline*. We compute the *priority* of a node from the probability representing the agent's belief that the user will select the action in the future; that is, the agent assigns higher priorities to assist those actions that are more likely to be taken by the user. On the other hand, the *deadline* indicates the predicted timestep when the user will execute the action; that is, the agent must prepare assistance before a certain point in time by which the user will need help.

The algorithm builds a plan-tree by traversing the actions that, according to the policy generated from the MDP user model, the user is most likely to select from the current state. First, the algorithm creates a root node with probability 1 with no action attached. Then, according to the MDP policy, likely actions are sampled, such that the algorithm assigns higher priorities to those actions that lead to a better state with respect to the user's planning objective. Note that the algorithm adds a new node for an action only if the agent's belief about the user selecting the action is higher than some threshold θ; otherwise, actions are pruned. Note that the assistant may prepare for all possible outcomes if the problem space is manageably small; however, resources (e.g., time, CPU, and network bandwidth) are generally constrained and it is thus necessary to prioritize assistive tasks according to predicted needs.

The recursive process of predicting and constructing a plan-tree from a state is described in Algorithm 11.2. The algorithmic complexity of plan generation is linear in the number of actions. The resulting plan-tree represents a horizon of sampled actions and their resulting states for which the agent can prepare appropriate assistance.

11.4 Plan Recognition within a Proactive Assistant System

This section describes how the predicted plan-tree from Section 11.3 fits inside the ANTICO architecture shown earlier in Figure 11.1. ANTICO is a scalable model where the assistant agent dynamically plans and executes a series of actions to manage a set of current tasks as they arise.

11.4.1 **Evaluating Predicted User Plan**

After a user plan is predicted through a process of plan recognition, the proactive manager evaluates each node in a predicted plan-tree according to domain-specific criteria. For example, if a user is solving a maze game that requires a password to enter a certain room, the passwords in the predicted user path are identified as unmet requirements [19]. A user plan can also be evaluated according to a set of regulatory rules such as social norms. In this case, any potential norm violation in the predicted user plan gives rise to a need for assistance [21].

The evaluation of a user plan results in a set of new tasks for the assistant (e.g., acquiring necessary information or resolving norm violations) to restore normative states. Since the evaluation of the user plan is not the focus of this chapter, we refer readers to related work of Oh et al. for further details [21].

11.4.2 **Assistive Planning**

In ANTICO, the assistant is essentially a planning agent that can plan its actions to accomplish a specified goal. The proactive manager formulates an assistive task in terms of the assistant's initial state and its goal state.

The architecture is not bound to any specific type of planners (e.g., a classic planner may be used). Recall that a predicted user plan from the plan recognizer imposes deadline constraints (specified as the node depth) on the agent's planning. An MDP is a preferred choice not only because it is consistent with the user-plan model but also because the discount factor can be used to implement ad hoc deadline constraints. A deadline constraint is used to determine the horizon for an MDP plan solver, such that the agent planner can complete the task to satisfy the deadline. For more principled time-constraint management, integrated planning and resource scheduling can be considered.

The planning problem formulated by the proactive manager may not always be solvable; for instance, the goal state may only be accomplished by modifying those variables that the assistant cannot access, or none of the assistant's actions have affects that can lead to the specified goal state. In such cases, the assistant notifies the user immediately so that she can take appropriate action on her own. Otherwise, the assistant starts executing its actions according to the optimal policy until it reaches a goal state.

11.4.3 **Cognitively Aligned Plan Execution**

Execution of an agent action may change one or more variables. For each newly generated plan (or policy) from the planner module, an executor is created as a new thread. An executor *waits* for a signal from the *variable observer* that monitors changes in the environment variables to determine the agent's current state. When a new state is observed, the variable observer *notifies* the plan executor to wake up. The plan executor then selects an optimal action in the current state according to the policy and executes the action. After taking an action, the plan executor is required to wait for a new signal from the variable observer. If the observed state is an absorbing state, then plan execution is terminated; otherwise, an optimal action is executed from the new state.

The agent's plan can be updated during execution as more recent assessments of rewards arrive from the proactive manager, forcing the assistant to replan. Any plans that are inconsistent with the current assessment are aborted.

To handle unexpected exceptions during execution, an executable action has a timeout, such that when the execution of an action reaches its timeout the plan is aborted. When a plan is aborted, the specific goals of the plan are typically unmet. If the goals are still relevant to the user's current plan (according to a newly predicted user plan), then the proactive manager will generate them as new goals for the agent.

11.5 Applications

In this section, we study two examples of ANTICO implemented in practical problem domains, summarizing work presented in Oh et al. and Meneguzzi et al. [21,19,15].

11.5.1 Norm Assistance

In certain scenarios, human decision making is affected by policies, often represented by deontic concepts such as permissions, obligations, and prohibitions. Individual rules within a policy have been actively studied in the area of *normative reasoning* [14]. Norms generally define constraints that should be followed by the members in a society at particular points in time to ensure certain systemwide properties [12]. These constraints are generally specified by guarded logic rules of the form $v \leftarrow \phi$, which indicate that when the condition ϕ occurs, a norm v becomes activated, imposing a restriction on the set of desirable states in the domain. If v is an *obligation*, the norm defines a set of states through which an agent must pass; otherwise, if v is a *prohibition*, v the norm defines a set of states that must be avoided.

For example, in international peacekeeping operations, military planners must achieve their own unit's objectives while following standing policies that regulate how interaction and collaboration with non-governmental organizations (NGOs) ought to take place. Because the planners are cognitively overloaded with mission-specific objectives, such normative stipulations increase the complexity of planning to both accomplish goals and abide by the norms.

Although much of the research on normative reasoning focuses on deterministic environments populated by predictable agent decision making, such a model is not suitable for reasoning about human agents acting in the real world. By leveraging recent work on normative reasoning over MDPs [9], it is possible to reason about norm compliance in nondeterministic environments; however, the issue of nondeterminism in the decision maker has remained problematic. To address this problem, an instantiation of the proactive assistance architecture was created to provide prognostic reasoning support by designing the proactive manager to analyze user plans for normative violations [21] in the context of military escort requests for relief operations. An overview of this architecture is provided in Figure 11.2a, while a screenshot of the assistance application is shown in Figure 11.2b.

The normative assistant relies on a probabilistic plan recognizer to generate a tree of possible plan steps. The proactive manager evaluates a user plan through a norm reasoner, which analyzes the sequence of states induced by the predicted plan for norm violations. These predicted violations are the object of the agent planner, which tries to find the nearest norm-compliant states in order to recommend user actions that will ensure norm-compliant behavior. If compliant states are not achievable, for example, because some violations are unavoidable in the user's possible future state, or if the user has already violated certain norms, the agent can also suggest remedial actions to either comply with penalties or mitigate the effects of a violation (i.e., *contrary-to-duty obligations* [23]).

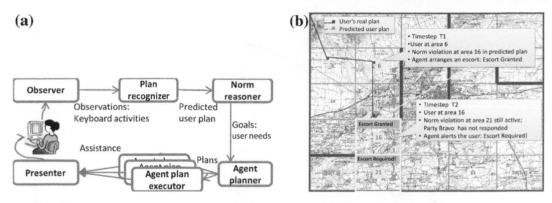

FIGURE 11.2

Norm assistance agent overview. (a) Agent architecture; (b) Application screenshot.

11.5.2 Emergency Response

ANTICO was applied in an emergency-response application assistant aimed at proactively supporting a manager responsible for responding to emergencies in civilian areas, including natural disasters or attacks on infrastructure [16]. The architecture customized for information assistant is shown in Figure 11.3a, and a screenshot of this application in emergency response is shown in Figure 11.3b. Given this application scenario, the adaptations deployed in ANTICO have two purposes. First, given the fluidity of an emergency situation, plan recognition should focus on providing assistance only to events in the near future with a high degree of confidence about the user's current activity. Second, given the structure of the emergency-response plans, assistance should follow the steps of these plans as closely as possible.

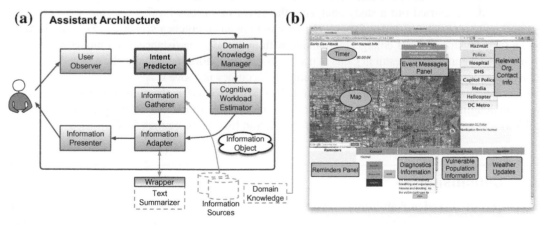

FIGURE 11.3

ANTICO overview. (a) Agent architecture; (b) Application screenshot.

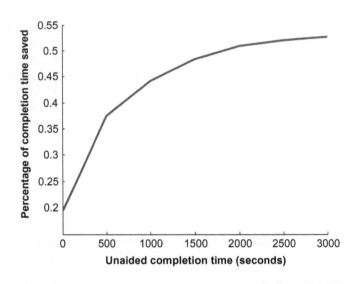

FIGURE 11.4

The amount of time saved with proactive agent assistance for problems with varying difficulty. *Note:* Problem difficulty is measured in terms of unaided completion time (*x*-axis).

The performance of proactive assistants depends on the accuracy of the plan-recognition algorithm, combined with seamless integration of the assistance provided to the user's regular workflow. On one extreme of the performance spectrum, a perfect assistance agent always recognizes user behavior correctly and provides assistance exactly when the user expects it; on the other extreme, the agent's predictions are never correct and the assistance provided is intrusive to the user, causing the user to waste time dealing with agent interventions. To assess the impact of prediction correctness on user performance, we carried out a study analyzing the effect of various levels of accuracy for the plan-recognition module on a simulated user's response time in an emergency scenario [15]. This study has shown that, for the selected emergency domain, with unobtrusive assistance, even moderate accuracy from plan recognition can result in gains in user performance. More specifically, the agent significantly reduces the completion time as long as its prediction accuracy is above 0.2.

Figure 11.4 shows that the amount of time reduced is increased as the human user's task becomes more challenging, thus requiring more time to finish unaided. For the most challenging category of the problem set, agent assistance reduced the job completion time by more than 50%.

11.6 Conclusion

This chapter discussed probabilistic plan recognition suitable for proactive assistant agents. We specifically focus on a class of problems in which a user faces a highly complex task of planning, executing, and replanning in a time-stressed environment. For example, an operator in an emergency response must react to high-risk and rare events by creating a specific plan from a set of predefined EOPs to deal with uncertainty in that specific event setting. Since the user's main activities form a planning process, this has led to a generative approach to probabilistic plan recognition that has been gaining attention within both the cognitive science and the AI communities. We described a generative plan-recognition algorithm that can predict a user's future plan steps with probabilities, such that the assistant's plan can be optimized with respect to expected user benefit. We developed an assistant agent framework using this plan-recognition algorithm and demonstrated two applications that have been implemented in practical problem domains.

Acknowledgment

The research for this chapter was sponsored by the U.S. Army Research Laboratory and was accomplished under Cooperative Agreement Number W911NF-09-2-0053. The views and conclusions contained in this document are those of the authors and should not be interpreted as representing the official policies, either expressed or implied, of the Army Research Laboratory or the U.S. government. The U.S. government is authorized to reproduce and distribute reprints for government purposes notwithstanding any copyright notation hereon.

References

[1] Abbeel P, Ng AY. Apprenticeship learning via inverse reinforcement learning. In: Proceedings of the 25th International Conference; 2004.

[2] Ambite JL, Barish G, Knoblock CA, Muslea M, Oh J, Minton S. Getting from here to there: interactive planning and agent execution for optimizing travel. In: Proceedings of the National Conference on Artificial Intelligence; 2002. p. 862–9.

[3] Armentano MG, Amandi A. Plan recognition for interface agents. Artif Intell Rev 2007;28(2):131–62.

[4] Baker CL, Saxe R, Tenenbaum JB. Action understanding as inverse planning. Cognition 2009;31:329–49.

[5] Barish G, Knoblock CA, et al. Speculative execution for information gathering plans. In: Proceedings of the 6th International Conference on AI Planning and Scheduling; 2002. p. 184–93.

[6] Bellman R. A Markovian decision process. Indiana Univ Math J 1957;6:679–84.

[7] Card AJ, Harrison H, Ward J, Clarkson PJ. Using prospective hazard analysis to assess an active shooter emergency operations plan. J Healthcare Risk Management 2012;31(3):34–40.

[8] Chalupsky H, Gil Y, Knoblock CA, Lerman K, Oh J, Pynadath DV, et al. Electric elves: applying agent technology to support human organizations. In: Proceedings of the 13th Conference on Innovative Applications of Artificial Intelligence; 2001. p. 51–8.

[9] Fagundes MS, Billhardt H, Ossowski S. Reasoning about norm compliance with rational agents. In: Helder Coelho, Rudi Studer, Michael Wooldridge, editors. Proceedings of the 19th European Conference on Artificial Intelligence. Frontiers in artificial intelligence and applications, vol. 215; 2010. p. 1027–8.

[10] Fern A, Natarajan S, Judah K, Tadepalli P. A decision-theoretic model of assistance. In: Veloso Manuela M, editor. Proceedings of the 20th International Joint Conference on Artificial Intelligence; 2007. p. 1879–84.

[11] Geib CW, Steedman M. On natural language processing and plan recognition. In: Proceedings of the 20th International Joint Conference on Artificial Intelligence; 2007. p. 1612–7.

[12] Jones AJI, Sergot M. On the characterisation of law and computer systems: the normative systems perspective. Deontic logic in computer science: normative system specification. Wiley; 1993. pp. 275–307.

[13] Kautz H, Allen JF. Generalized plan recognition. Proceeding of the AAAI, vol. 19; 1986. p. 86.

[14] Meneguzzi F, Luck M. Norm-based behaviour modification in BDI agents. In: Proceedings of the 8th International Conference on Autonomous Agents and Multiagent Systems; 2009. p. 177–84.

[15] Meneguzzi F, Mehrotra S, Tittle J, Oh J, Chakraborty N, Sycara K. A cognitive architecture for emergency response. In: Proceedings of the 11th International Conference on Autonomous Agents and Multiagent Systems; 2012. p. 1161–2.

[16] Meneguzzi F, Oh J, Chakraborty N, Sycara K, Mehrotra S, Lewis M. Anytime cognition: an information agent for emergency response. In: Proceedings of the 5th Annual Conference of the International Technology Alliance; 2011.

[17] Mitchell TM, Caruana R, Freitag D, McDermott J, Zabowski D, et al. Experience with a learning personal assistant. Comm ACM 1994;37(7):80–91.

[18] Ng AY, Russell S. Algorithms for inverse reinforcement learning. In: Proceedings of the 21st International Conference; 2000. p. 663–70.

[19] Oh J, Meneguzzi F, Sycara K. Probabilistic plan recognition for intelligent information agents: towards proactive software assistant agents. In: Proceedings of the 3rd International Conference on Agents and Artificial Intelligence; 2011. p. 281–7.

[20] Oh J, Meneguzzi F, Sycara KP. ANTIPA: an architecture for intelligent information assistance. In: Proceedings of the 19th European Conference on Artificial Intelligence; 2010. p. 1055–6.

[21] Oh J, Meneguzzi F, Sycara KP, Norman TJ. An agent architecture for prognostic reasoning assistance. In: Proceedings of the 22nd International Joint Conference on Artificial Intelligence; 2011. p. 2513–8.

[22] Oh J, Smith S. Learning user preferences in distributed calendar scheduling. Prac Theory Automated Timetabling V 2005:3–16.

[23] Prakken H, Sergot MJ. Contrary-to-duty obligations. Studia Logica 1996;57(1):91–115.

[24] Ramíez M, Geffner H. Probabilistic plan recognition using off-the-shelf classical planners. In: Proceedings of the 24th AAAI Conference on Artificial Intelligence; 2010.

[25] Ramírez M, Geffner H. Goal recognition over POMDPs: inferring the intention of a POMDP agent. In: Proceedings of the 22nd International Joint Conference on Artificial Intelligence; 2011.

[26] Ratliff N, Ziebart B, Peterson K, Bagnell JA, Hebert M, Dey A. Inverse optimal heuristic control for imitation learning. In: Proceedings of the 12th International Conference on Artificial Intelligence and Statistics; 2009.

[27] Russell Stuart, J, Norvig Peter. Artificial intelligence—a modern approach. 3rd ed. Pearson Education; 2010.

[28] Sycara K, Norman TJ, Giampapa JA, Kollingbaum MJ, Burnett C, Masato D, et al. Agent support for policy-driven collaborative mission planning. Computer J 2010;53(5):528–40.

[29] Ziebart BD, Maas A, Bagnell JA, Dey AK. Maximum entropy inverse reinforcement learning. In: Proceedings of the 22nd AAAI Conference on Artificial Intelligence; 2008. p. 1433–8.

Recognizing Player Goals in Open-Ended Digital Games with Markov Logic Networks

Eun Y. Ha, Jonathan P. Rowe, Bradford W. Mott, and James C. Lester

North Carolina State University, Raleigh, NC, USA

12.1 Introduction

Goal recognition, and its more general form of plan recognition, are classic problems in artificial intelligence [6,20,37]. Goal recognition is the process of identifying the high-level objective that an agent is trying to achieve based on an observed sequence of actions performed by the agent. It is a restricted form of plan recognition, a task that involves identifying both the agent's goal and the action sequence that will achieve that goal based on an observed sequence of actions. These tasks, plan recognition and goal recognition, are connected by their shared focus on recognizing patterns in action sequences, and they are widely regarded as key components of human intelligence.

The capacity to interpret patterns in others' actions is critical for navigating everyday situations, such as driving a car, holding a conversation, or playing a sport. Consequently, computational models of plan recognition are relevant to a broad range of applications. Plan- and goal-recognition models have been devised for story understanding systems [5], productivity software [16], intelligent tutoring systems [9], and dialogue systems [4]. More recently, related models for activity recognition have been used to create assistive technologies for the disabled [8] as well as aircraft-refueling recognizers that operate on video data [15]. An emerging, promising application area for goal-recognition systems is digital games [14,19,21,25,26]. Digital games vary considerably in genre and gameplay style, giving rise to many formulations of goal-recognition tasks.

Digital games continue to grow increasingly complex in their graphical presentations, interaction designs, and simulation capabilities. However, digital games rarely demonstrate capabilities for interpreting players' low-level actions at higher levels—in other words, recognizing patterns in player behavior—to dynamically adapt game events. A key example of this missing capability is games' inability to recognize players' goals. Recognizing a player's goals in a digital game involves identifying the concrete objectives that a player is attempting to achieve given a domain model and sequence of actions in the virtual environment. In theory, games have full access to fine-grained information about players' actions, and this data could be used by goal-recognition models to drive how games respond to players' behavior at runtime. Yet digital games have traditionally relied on comparatively unsophisticated methods, such as scripts, triggers, and state machine-driven approaches, for reacting to player behavior, leading to rigid and sometimes artificial results [40].

If adopted, goal-recognition models offer several prospective benefits to game creators. First, they expand the potential of *player-adaptive games*, which dynamically adapt game events in response to players' actions [31]. As an illustrative example, consider a game in which a player forms a goal to give some food, an apple, to a hungry villager. Later in the narrative, unbeknownst to the player, the apple will emerge as an important element of the game's narrative; the player will discover that the apple is transmitting an infectious disease that the player must diagnose. Giving the apple to the villager conflicts with this planned narrative. The player will not be able to later examine the apple if he has previously fed it to the hungry villager.

Without a goal-recognition model, the game is unable to interpret the player's actions as anything more than a sequence of movements, object manipulations, and conversations. A goal-recognition model enables the player-adaptive game to recognize the player's goal and subsequently infer that the goal conflicts with the planned narrative. Using knowledge about the player's goal, the player-adaptive game can dynamically augment the game experience, such as by directing the villager to refuse the apple.

Second, *game-based learning environments* stand to benefit from goal-recognition models. Interpreting players' goals and plans is valuable in assessment, particularly for subjects where the player is expected to demonstrate a problem-solving strategy or complex multistep skill in the virtual environment. More generally, goal-recognition models can inform intelligent tutoring systems embedded within game-based learning environments [18,22]. Accurately diagnosing students' problem-solving goals is essential for intelligent tutors to assess what concepts and skills a player understands, as well as possible misconceptions that she may possess. These capabilities enable intelligent tutoring systems to provide hints or remediation tailored to individual learners.

Third, goal recognizers can provide valuable information for *telemetry efforts* by game developers. Game telemetry involves remotely collecting, storing, and analyzing log data about player behaviors, yielding information about how players use digital games "in the wild" [41]. Over the past several years, telemetry has been the subject of growing interest as game developers seek information to inform future game designs, such as which items are most popular or which regions of virtual maps cause gameplay problems. Adding goal-recognition models to developers' suites of game telemetry tools facilitates high-level interpretations of players' raw interaction data. Goal-recognition models equip analysts with tools to identify players' intentions, determine which gameplay strategies are most successful, and adjust parts of the game that cause frustration or lead to players quitting.

While goal-recognition models show promise for a broad range of games, their potential for enriching open-ended (or "sandbox") games is especially notable. Open-ended games, such as the popular Elder Scroll series [3] and Minecraft [24], feature expansive environments and multiple paths for accomplishing in-game objectives [39]. In these immersive 3D games, players choose the goals they want to pursue, and they develop their own plans to achieve them. Goals can be formed in several ways in open-ended games: the software may explicitly present goals for the player to achieve, or the player may implicitly define the goals for herself during gameplay, effectively hiding the goals from the software.

In either of these cases, goals may be well defined (e.g., Retrieve the magical staff from the dragon's cave and return it to the magician) or they may be ill defined (e.g., Build a castle on the mountain). Players may perform actions in deliberate sequences in order to accomplish goals, or they may perform actions in an exploratory manner, inadvertently encountering or achieving goals. Successive goals within a game may be independent of one another, or they may have complex interrelationships defined by overarching narrative structures. Each of these variations introduces significant challenges for goal recognition.

Goal-recognition models in digital games must cope with several sources of inherent uncertainty. A single sequence of player actions is often explainable by multiple possible player goals, and a given goal can be achieved through a wide range of possible action sequences. Although logical representations enable concise encodings of structural relations in goal-recognition domains, they lack support for reasoning about uncertainty. Markov logic networks (MLNs) provide a formalism that unifies logical and probabilistic representations into a single framework, preserving the representational properties of first-order logic while supporting reasoning about uncertainty as made possible by probabilistic graphical models [30]. This chapter reports on an investigation of MLNs for recognizing player goals in an open-ended digital game environment with exploratory actions. Specifically, we evaluate the predictive accuracy of MLN-based goal-recognition models for a story-centric, game-based learning environment.

This chapter surveys prior work on player goal recognition in digital games. We also motivate our decision to use Markov logic networks for goal recognition, comparing our framework to other computational approaches for goal recognition in various domains, as well as recent work leveraging MLNs for related tasks. We describe a MLN goal-recognition model that was trained on a corpus collected from player interactions with an open-ended, game-based learning environment called CRYSTAL ISLAND. In CRYSTAL ISLAND, players are assigned a single high-level objective: solve a science mystery. Players interleave periods of exploration and deliberate problem solving in order to identify a spreading illness that is afflicting a research team stationed on the island. In this setting, goal recognition involves predicting the next-narrative subgoal that the player will complete as she solves the interactive mystery.

We present findings that suggest the MLN goal-recognition model yields significant accuracy gains beyond alternative probabilistic approaches for predicting player goals. We discuss the study's implications, both in terms of algorithmic techniques for goal recognition, as well as methodologies that leverage digital games for investigating goal-recognition models. We conclude with an examination of future directions.

12.2 Related Work

Recognizing players' goals and plans offers significant promise for increasing the effectiveness of digital game environments for education, training, and entertainment. Plan recognition, which seeks to infer agents' goals along with their plans for achieving them from sequences of observable actions, has been studied for tasks ranging from traffic monitoring [28] to operating system usage [4] to story understanding [7]. Plan recognition is inherently uncertain, and solutions supporting reasoning under uncertainty (e.g., Bayesian models [7], probabilistic grammars [28], and hidden Markov models [5]) have demonstrated strong empirical performance in a range of settings. In the restricted form of plan recognition that focuses on inferring users' goals without concern for identifying their plans or subplans, goal-recognition models have been automatically acquired using statistical corpus-based approaches without the need for hand-authored plan libraries [4].

The classic goal-recognition problem assumes that a single agent is pursuing a single goal using deterministic actions, and it assumes that a user's plan can be identified using a given plan library. A major focus of recent work on goal and plan recognition has been probabilistic approaches that relax several of these assumptions. For example, Ramirez and Geffner [29] describe a plan-recognition approach that does not require the provision of an explicit plan library. Hu and Yang [17] describe a two-level goal-recognition framework that uses conditional random fields and correlation graphs to support recognition of multiple concurrent and interleaving goals.

Geib and Goldman [11] have devised the PHATT algorithm, which is a Bayesian approach to plan recognition that focuses on plan execution. PHATT provides a unified framework that supports multiple concurrent goals, multiple instantiations of a single goal, and principled handling of unobserved actions. Geib and Goldman [12] also proposed a lexical parsing-based approach to plan recognition that supports plans with loops. While probabilistic approaches have achieved considerable success, the propositional nature of probabilistic graphical models introduces limitations in formalizing plan-recognition models.

Recent efforts have begun to focus on statistical relational learning frameworks for plan and activity recognition. Statistical relational learning techniques combine the representational strengths of logical formalisms and the capabilities for reasoning under uncertainty, which are often associated with probabilistic graphical models. Of particular note, Markov logic networks provide a single, unified formalism that supports structured representations and probabilistic reasoning. Sadilek and Kautz [36] used Markov logic to investigate activity recognition in a multiagent Capture the Flag game using GPS data. In their model, a MLN combines hard and soft constraints derived from Capture the Flag rules to de-noise and label GPS data in terms of "capture" events. Experiments demonstrated that the MLN model significantly outperforms alternate probabilistic and nonprobabilistic approaches, correctly identifying 90% of the capture events. Although they are related, our work differs from Sadilek and Kautz's in several ways: (1) our models encode minimal domain-specific knowledge (i.e., our constraints are not first-order encodings of game rules), (2) our focus is only on a single agent's behavior, and (3) our focus is on modeling goals, with cyclical relationships between goals and actions, rather than modeling players' activities.

Singla and Mooney [38] devised a method for constructing MLN-based plan-recognition models using abductive reasoning over planning domains. Their method is comprised of two parts: a Hidden Cause model, which augments Markov logic to support efficient abduction (inference from observations to explanations), and an abductive model construction procedure that reduces the number of atomic groundings considered while constructing ground Markov networks. Experiments found that Singla and Mooney's approach improved predictive accuracy over competing techniques. However, by framing the problem in terms of abductive inference, their approach requires that a formal description of the planning domain be available. In our work, goal recognition is conceptualized as a classification problem. Our approach does not directly perform abductive inference over the planning domain as in the approach of Singla and Mooney; therefore it does not require a planning domain to be explicitly provided.

There have been several studies of goal- and plan-recognition models in digital games. Kabanza and colleagues [19] explored challenges with behavior recognition in real-time strategy (RTS) games, which involve opposing armies battling for control of regions using complex tactics and units. Their work extended the Geib and Goldman PHATT algorithm [11] to perform intent recognition on the behaviors of RTS opponents. Preliminary experiments using game replays achieved 89% accuracy, although the authors assumed fully observable actions for the purposes of their initial evaluation.

In other work, Laviers and Sukthankar [21] combined plan-recognition and plan-repair models for real-time opponent modeling in a football videogame. Their approach used Upper Confidence bounds applied to Trees (UCT) in order to learn plan-repair policies in real time. The plan-repair policies enabled the offense to adjust its passing plan after recognizing the defense's play. In an empirical evaluation, the UCT approach outperformed baseline and heuristic-based plan-repair methods in terms of yardage gain metrics and reductions in interceptions thrown. It should be noted that while both of these studies focused on plan-recognition (and related) tasks in digital games, the tasks have major structural and application differences from our work involving exploratory actions in open-ended games.

More closely related to the study described in this chapter, Albrecht, Zukerman, and Nicholson [1] conducted an early examination of Bayesian networks for plan recognition in adventure games. The study compared several alternate Bayesian network structures for predicting players' quests, actions, and locations in a text-based multiuser dungeon adventure game. The evaluation found that network structures incorporating both action and location data outperformed ablated versions with reduced connectivity and variables. However, no comparisons to non-DBN baselines were performed.

More recently, Gold [14] investigated Input-Output Hidden Markov Models (IOHMM) for recognizing high-level player goals in a simple 2D action-adventure game. The IOHMM model, which used hand-engineered parameters as opposed to machine-learned parameters, was compared to a hand-authored finite state machine (FSM)—a common representational technique used in commercial games. A preliminary evaluation involving human subjects observed that the IOHMM model did outperform the FSM baseline. However, the generalizability of the findings was unclear due to the hand-authored nature of the model and baseline, as well as the relative simplicity of the application. The work also differed from our work in that it did not involve exploratory actions; player goals were directly presented to players in the upper left part of their screens.

Studies of *The Restaurant Game* [26] examined data-driven techniques for devising *plan networks* from thousands of user interactions with a simulated restaurant scenario. The plan networks encode common action sequences associated with customer–waiter interactions in a restaurant setting. An evaluation of the plan networks found they achieved high interrater reliability with human judges in assessing the "typicality" of observed restaurant sequences in the game environment. While work on The Restaurant Game is related to classic plan-recognition tasks, it has largely focused on different and, in some ways, simpler modeling tasks.

The work presented in this chapter investigates a Markov logic network goal-recognition framework for the CRYSTAL ISLAND open-ended educational game. CRYSTAL ISLAND shares several characteristics with adventure games (e.g., exploring a virtual environment, advancing an emerging narrative, and collecting and manipulating objects). Although several goal-recognition studies have been conducted using digital games, fundamental differences among the game genres and recognition tasks suggest that there is no established state-of-the-art performance level for this area. For this reason, we evaluate the efficacy of our approach by comparing it against techniques employed in prior goal-recognition work with an earlier version of our game environment.

12.3 Observation Corpus

To investigate goal recognition in an open-ended game environment involving many possible goals and user actions, data collected from player interactions with the CRYSTAL ISLAND learning environment

FIGURE 12.1

The CRYSTAL ISLAND virtual environment.

were used. CRYSTAL ISLAND (Figure 12.1) is a game-based learning environment for eighth-grade microbiology. It is built on Valve Software's Source™ engine—the 3D game platform for Half-Life 2.

The environment features a science mystery in which players attempt to discover the identity and source of an infectious disease that is plaguing a research team stationed on an island. Players adopt the role of a visitor who recently arrived in order to see her sick father, but they are promptly drawn into a mission to save the entire research team from the outbreak. Players explore the research camp from a first-person viewpoint and manipulate virtual objects, converse with characters, and use lab equipment and other resources to solve the mystery. Players choose among multiple paths to investigate the mystery, and they are free to identify and pursue goals in a range of different orders.

CRYSTAL ISLAND has been the subject of extensive empirical investigation and has been found to provide substantial learning and motivational benefits [35]. Players consistently demonstrate significant learning gains after using CRYSTAL ISLAND, and they report experiencing boredom less frequently than in alternative instructional software. The environment is also challenging for players, with less than 50% of players solving the mystery in under an hour. The current investigation of goal-recognition models is part of an overarching research agenda focused on AI techniques for dynamically shaping players' interactions with game-based learning environments. Prior work has focused on a range of computational modeling tasks, including probabilistic representations for user knowledge modeling [34] and machine learning frameworks for driving characters' affective behaviors [33].

The present work is most closely related to two prior investigations of user models with CRYSTAL ISLAND. The first is the Mott, Lee, and Lester [25] investigation of Bayesian networks and n-gram models for goal recognition (2006). Although we adopt and extend several ideas from that research, the present work uses a significantly modified version of CRYSTAL ISLAND, as well as a version that does not explicitly advise players about which goals to next achieve. The current version of CRYSTAL

ISLAND is substantially more open ended, as players are encouraged to identify and follow their own paths to solve the mystery.

The present work also complements a prior investigation of user knowledge modeling with dynamic Bayesian networks [34]. That work employed hand-engineered dynamic Bayesian networks to model player beliefs related to the narrative backstory, science curriculum, mystery solution, and gameplay mechanics. The current work models users' goals with a MLN, which leverages parameters (i.e., weights) induced from user-interaction data. The two categories of models are distinct but complementary, and in concert they could be used to drive decisions about how to dynamically tailor game events to individual players.

Player interactions with CRYSTAL ISLAND are comprised of a diverse set of actions occurring throughout the seven major locations of the island's research camp: an *infirmary*, a *dining hall*, a *laboratory*, a *living quarters*, the *lead scientist's quarters*, a *waterfall*, and a large *outdoor* region. Players can perform actions that include the following: *moving around the camp*, *picking up* and *dropping objects*, *using the laboratory's testing equipment*, *conversing with virtual characters*, *reading microbiology-themed books* and *posters*, *completing a diagnosis worksheet*, *labeling microscope slides*, and *taking notes*. Players advance through CRYSTAL ISLAND's nonlinear narrative by completing a partially ordered sequence of goals that comprise the scenario's plot. Seven narrative goals are considered in this work: *speaking with the camp nurse* about the spreading illness, *speaking with the camp's virus expert*, *speaking with the camp's bacteria expert*, *speaking with a sick patient*, *speaking with the camp's cook* about recently eaten food, *running laboratory tests on contaminated food*, and *submitting a complete diagnosis* to the camp nurse.

The following scenario illustrates a typical interaction with CRYSTAL ISLAND. (See Figure 12.2 for a related sequence of screenshots.) The scenario begins with the player's arrival at the research camp (Figure 12.3). The player approaches the first building, an infirmary, where several sick patients and a camp nurse are located. The player approaches the nurse and initiates a conversation with her. The nurse explains that an unidentified illness is spreading throughout the camp and asks for the player's help in determining a diagnosis. The conversation with the nurse takes place through a combination of multimodal character dialogue—spoken language, gesture, facial expression, and text—and player dialogue menu selections. All character dialogue is provided by voice actors and follows a deterministic branching structure.

After speaking with the nurse, the player has several options for investigating the illness. Inside the infirmary, the player can talk to sick patients lying on medical cots. Clues about the team members' symptoms and recent eating habits can be discussed and recorded using the in-game note-taking features. Alternatively, the player can move to the camp's dining hall to speak with the camp cook. The cook describes the types of food that the team has recently eaten and provides clues about which items warrant closer investigation. In addition to learning about the sick team members, the player has several options for gathering information about disease-causing agents. For example, the player can walk to the camp's living quarters where she will encounter a pair of virtual scientists who answer questions about viruses and bacteria. The player can also learn more about pathogens by viewing posters hanging inside of the camp's buildings or reading books located in a small library. In this way, the player can gather information about relevant microbiology concepts using resources presented in multiple formats.

Beyond gathering information from virtual scientists and other instructional resources, the player can conduct tests on food objects using the laboratory's testing equipment. The player encounters food items

1. Discussing outbreak with nurse.

2. Meeting cook in Dining Hall.

3. Reading book about influenza.

4. Running test in laboratory.

5. Discussing viruses with scientist.

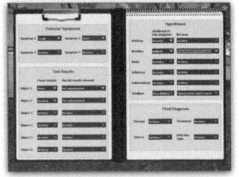

6. Recording findings in worksheet.

FIGURE 12.2

Sample events in the CRYSTAL ISLAND narrative.

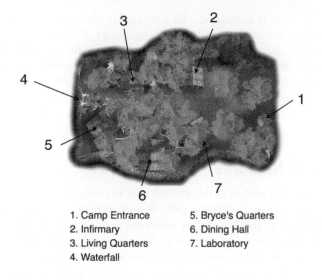

1. Camp Entrance
2. Infirmary
3. Living Quarters
4. Waterfall
5. Bryce's Quarters
6. Dining Hall
7. Laboratory

FIGURE 12.3

Map of the CRYSTAL ISLAND research camp.

in the dining hall and laboratory, and she can test them for pathogenic contaminants at any point during the learning interaction. A limited number of tests are allocated to the player at the start of the scenario, but additional tests can be earned by answering microbiology-themed multiple-choice questions posed by the camp nurse.

After running several tests, the player discovers that the sick team members have been consuming contaminated milk. Having arrived at this finding, the player is instructed to see the lab technician, Elise, for a closer look. The screen momentarily fades to black to indicate elapsing time, and Elise returns with an image of the contaminated specimen, which she explains was taken using a microscope. At this point, the player is presented with a labeling exercise during which she must identity the contamination as bacterial in nature. After successfully completing this activity, the player uses in-game resources to investigate bacterial diseases associated with symptoms matching those reported by the sick team members. Once she has narrowed down a diagnosis and a recommended treatment, she records them in a diagnosis worksheet and returns to the infirmary to inform the camp nurse. If the player's diagnosis worksheet contains errors, the nurse identifies the errors and recommends that the player keep working. If the player correctly diagnoses the illness and specifies an appropriate treatment, the mystery is solved.

The data used for investigating MLN goal-recognition models were collected from a study involving the eighth grade population of a public middle school. There were 153 participants in the study. Data for 16 of the participants was removed from the analysis due to incomplete data or prior experience with CRYSTAL ISLAND. Participants whose data was included had no prior experience with the software. All player actions were logged by the CRYSTAL ISLAND software and stored for later analysis. The log files were generated by a modified version of the Source^{TM} engine's built-in logging features, and they consist of chronological, flat sequences of time-stamped actions.

In the corpus, each student is associated with a single log file, except in cases of hardware and/or software crashes, which occasionally resulted in multiple logs. Examples of actions recorded in the log files include movements between locations, pickup object events, drop object events, conversation initiation events, dialogue turn events, read book events, and goal-achievement events. Additionally, the raw logs include records of players' positions and orientations, which are recorded several times per second, although the data are filtered out in the present analysis. Arguments for each action (e.g., the object that was dropped, the book that was read) are included in each entry of the logs.

12.4 Markov Logic Networks

The goal-recognition model described in this chapter uses the statistical relational learning framework provided by *Markov logic networks* (MLNs) [30]. Statistical relational learning frameworks support modeling complex phenomena for domains in which the assumption of *independent and identically distributed* data does not hold. This section provides a brief overview of MLNs.

An MLN is a knowledge base that consists of first-order logic formulae and a finite set of constants representing domain objects. In contrast to traditional first-order logic, in which logic formulae have binary values (i.e., *true* or *false*) and represent hard constraints, each formula in an MLN is associated with a weight that has a real number value and represents a soft constraint that is allowed to be violated. When the arguments of every predicate in the first-order knowledge base are replaced with all possible domain constants and a truth value is assigned to each ground predicate, it represents a possible world that can be constructed from the given knowledge base.

In traditional first-order logic, possible worlds have binary values: the value of a possible world is *true* when all the ground formulae in the knowledge base are true; otherwise, it is *false*. In contrast, an MLN defines a probability distribution over possible worlds in a continuous range. Weights of MLN formulae reflect the strength of the constraint that their associated logic formula imposes on the possible worlds. Table 12.1 shows an example of a simple MLN, which consists of two first-order logic formulae and associated weights.

Formally, an MLN is defined as a set of tuples (f_i, w_i) in which f_i is a first-order logic formula in the knowledge base and w_i is a real number. Grounded with domain constants $C = \{c_1, c_2, \ldots, c_{|c|}\}$, an

Table 12.1 Example MLN

First-Order Logic	Clausal Form	Weight
$\forall x\ Cold(x) \Rightarrow Coughs(x)$ If a person has a cold, then they cough.	$\neg Cold(x) \lor Coughs(x)$	1.5
$\forall x \forall y\ Family(x, y) \Rightarrow$ $(Cold(x) \Longleftrightarrow Cold(y))$ If two people are family, they both have colds or neither does.	$\neg Family(x, y) \lor Cold(x) \lor \neg Cold(y)$ $\neg Family(x, y) \lor \neg Cold(x) \lor Cold(y)$	1.1 1.1

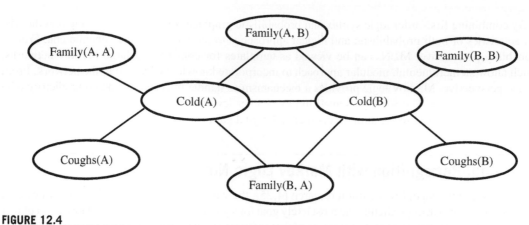

FIGURE 12.4

Graphical structure of MLN in Table 12.1.

MLN defines a *Markov network* (MN), also known as a *Markov random field*. An MN is an undirected probabilistic graphical model that defines a joint distribution of a set of random variables $X = (X_1, X_2, \ldots, X_n) \in X$ [27]. The MN defined by a ground MLN has a graph node for each ground predicate in the MLN. The value of the node is 1 if the corresponding ground predicate is *true* and 0 otherwise. Two nodes in the graph are connected by an edge if and only if their corresponding ground predicates appear together in at least one ground MLN formula. Thus, the MN has a unique feature (i.e., a clique in the graph) for each ground MLN formula.

Figure 12.4 depicts a graphical structure of a ground MLN, which is constructed by applying domain constants A and B to the MLN in Table 12.1. The value of the feature is 1 if the corresponding ground MLN formula is *true* and 0 otherwise. Features in MNs are assigned the same weights as their corresponding MLN formulae. The probability distribution over possible worlds for a ground MLN is defined by the following equation:

$$P(X = \alpha) = \frac{1}{z} \exp \left(\Sigma_{i=1}^{F} w_i n_i(\alpha) \right), \tag{12.1}$$

in which F represents the number of formulae in the MLN and $n_i(\alpha)$ is the number of groundings of a formula f_i that has *true* value in the given world α. Z is a normalization constant, which is computed as:

$$Z = \Sigma_x \exp \left(\Sigma_{i=1}^{F} w_i n_i(x) \right). \tag{12.2}$$

Cutting Plane Inference (CPI) provides an accurate and efficient Maximum a posteri (MAP) method for MLNs [32]. CPI is a meta-algorithm that instantiates a small fraction of a given complex MLN incrementally and solves it using a conventional MAP inference method such as MaxWalkSAT or integer linear programming. At each incremental step, the CPI refines a current solution by instantiating only those portions of the complete MN for which the current solution can be further optimized. CPI has been shown to improve the efficiency of MAP inference compared to conventional methods alone.

By combining first-order logic syntax and probabilistic graphical models, MLNs bring together the characteristics of both probabilistic and logical approaches to modeling complex phenomena. From a probability perspective, MLNs can be viewed as templates for constructing large Markov networks, which allow an incremental, modular approach to incorporate knowledge bases into the network. From a logic perspective, Markov logic provides a mechanism to handle uncertainty and contradictory data in a knowledge base. The work presented in this chapter leverages MLNs as a template language to construct a MN for goal recognition in open-ended digital games.

12.5 Goal Recognition with Markov Logic Networks

Drawing on previous goal-recognition research [4,25], the work presented in this chapter defines goal recognition as the task of predicting the most likely goal for a given sequence of observed low-level player behavior in the game environment. It is assumed that a given sequence of player behavior maps to a single goal, and no interleaving occurs between different goals. We attribute all actions leading up to a goal (and taking place after the previous goal was achieved) as part of the action sequence associated with that goal. In part, this assumption is due to the nature of our data; that is, during data collection, we could not directly observe students' intentions as they played CRYSTAL ISLAND. Therefore, we identified students' narrative goals during post hoc analysis. During data collection, students did not self-report their goals, nor did trained human experts provide judgments about students' intentions as they played CRYSTAL ISLAND. Although these techniques—student think-alouds and expert observational protocols—hold promise for yielding data that enable relaxation of single-goal assumptions, these efforts are reserved for future work.

Under the described conditions, goal recognition is cast as a classification problem in which a learned classifier predicts the most likely goal for the present observed player behavior. With the given task formulation, the current goal-recognition model leverages task structure in CRYSTAL ISLAND both at the local and global levels. That is, the local task structure is encoded as pairwise ordering patterns of goals, and the global task structure is incorporated by a special attribute that encodes the player's progress in solving the problem within the narrative scenario. The next subsection discusses the representation of player behavior used in our goal-recognition model, the motivation to use MLNs for goal recognition, and the MLN goal-recognition model.

12.5.1 Representation of Player Behavior

Similar to previous work by [25], the current work encodes low-level player behavior in the game environment using three attributes: *action type*, *location*, and *narrative state*.

Action type: Type of current action taken by the player such as *moving to a certain location*, *opening a door*, and *testing an object using the laboratory's testing equipment*. Our data includes 19 distinct types of player actions. The current work only considers the type (e.g., *OPEN*) of the action but does not include the associated arguments (e.g., *laboratory-door*) because adding action arguments did not offer clear benefits for the learned model, which was likely caused by a data-sparsity problem. However, action arguments in principle provide richer semantics for goal-recognition models. In future work, we plan to investigate the utility of action arguments with a larger dataset.

Location: Place in the virtual environment where a current player action is taken. This includes 39 fine-grained and nonoverlapping sublocations that decompose the 7 major camp locations in CRYSTAL ISLAND.

Narrative state: Representation of the player's progress in solving the narrative scenario. Reflecting the global task structure of CRYSTAL ISLAND, narrative state is encoded as a vector of four binary variables, each of which represents a milestone event within the narrative. The four milestone events considered are: *discuss the illness with the nurse, test the contaminated object, submit a diagnosis to the nurse,* and *submit a correct diagnosis to the nurse.* The first two are also subgoals that the player needs to achieve. If a milestone event has been accomplished, the associated variable is assigned a value of 1; otherwise, the value of the variable is 0.

12.5.2 Motivation

The data described in the previous section pose significant challenges for goal recognition. First, individual goals are not independent of one another. Goals in our data represent milestone activities players take in the course of solving the science mystery. Some of these activities naturally occur in sequential patterns driven by the game's narrative structure. The layout of the island can also impose co-occurrence patterns among goals. Thus, the previous goal can impact the probabilities associated with alternate values for the current goal. To model these associations among the milestone activities, goals should be inferred in relation to one another rather than in isolation. Second, the causality between player behavior and goals is ambiguous. In CRYSTAL ISLAND, players are not given an explicit list of goals to achieve; instead, players discover goals while interacting with the virtual environment. Thus, causality between player behavior and goals is bidirectional. In other words, a goal could influence a player's current behavior if she has a particular goal in mind and it is also possible that the player's current behavior will reveal which goal she next pursues. For instance, a player can enter a new location without a particular goal in mind and afterward can engage a character in a conversation that reveals a new goal.

To address the first challenge, the current work uses a statistical relational learning framework, which offers principled methods for collective classification in which multiple objects are jointly modeled [13]. In our case, the goal-recognition model jointly classifies successive goals. To address the second challenge, the current work, in particular, considers MLNs [30] because of the underlying semantics of undirected graphical models (see Section 12.4). In contrast to directed graphical (digraph) models, which encode explicit causality among the entities, undirected graphical models represent mutual influence among entities; this is well suited for representing ambiguous causality between player behavior and goals in our data. In addition, the first-order logic syntax of MLNs offers an intuitive interface for developers to work with data in order to construct complex Markov networks.

12.5.3 Markov Logic Network for Goal Recognition

We first defined a set of predicates as the basic building blocks to form MLN formulae for the proposed goal-recognition model. There are two types of predicates: *observed* and *hidden*. Observed predicates are those that are fully observable by the game environment while a player is performing actions. In contrast, hidden predicates are those that are not directly observable within the game environment. Instead, the groundings of the hidden predicates are predicted using MAP inference based on a learned model. In other words, hidden predicates represent the target phenomena being modeled. In our case,

Table 12.2 Observed and Hidden Predicates

	Predicate	Description
Observed	action(t, a)	Player takes action *a* at time *t*.
	loc(t, l)	Player is at location *l* at time *t*.
	state(t, s)	The narrative state at time *t* is *s*.
Hidden	goal(t, g)	Player pursues goal *g* at time *t*.

Hard Formula

$$\forall t,a : action(t,a) \Rightarrow |\exists g : goal(t,g)| = 1 \qquad \text{(F1)}$$

Soft Formulae

$$\forall t,g : goal(t,g) \qquad \text{(F2)}$$
$$\forall t,a,g : action(t,a) \Rightarrow goal(t,g) \qquad \text{(F3)}$$
$$\forall t,l,g : loc(t,l) \Rightarrow goal(t,g) \qquad \text{(F4)}$$
$$\forall t,s,g : state(t,s) \Rightarrow goal(t,g) \qquad \text{(F5)}$$
$$\forall t,a,s,g : action(t,a) \wedge state(t,s) \Rightarrow goal(t,g) \qquad \text{(F6)}$$
$$\forall t,a,g : action(t-1,a) \Rightarrow goal(t,g) \qquad \text{(F7)}$$
$$\forall t,l,g : loc(t-1,l) \Rightarrow goal(t,g) \qquad \text{(F8)}$$
$$\forall t,s,g : state(t-1,s) \Rightarrow goal(t,g) \qquad \text{(F9)}$$
$$\forall t,a,s,g : action(t-1,a) \wedge state(t-1,s) \Rightarrow goal(t,g) \qquad \text{(F10)}$$
$$\forall t,a_1,a_2,g : action(t-1,a_1) \wedge action(t,a_2) \Rightarrow goal(t,g) \qquad \text{(F11)}$$
$$\forall t,g_1,g_2 : goal(t-1,g_1) \Rightarrow goal(t,g_2) \qquad \text{(F12)}$$
$$\forall t,a_1,a_2,g_1,g_2 : action(t-1,a_1) \wedge goal(t-1,g_1) \wedge action(t,a_2) \quad \text{(F13)}$$
$$\Rightarrow goal(t,g_2)$$

FIGURE 12.5

Formulae for MLN goal-recognition model.

---

there is one hidden predicate, *goal(t, g)*, which represents the player's goal at time *t*. Three observed predicates were defined, each representing an attribute of player behavior: *action(t, a)*, *loc(t, l)*, and *state(t, s)*. Table 12.2 lists these observed and hidden predicates.

By combining the observed and the hidden predicates with logical operations, a total of 13 MLN formulae were constructed. As shown in Figure 12.5, our goal-recognition MLN consists of 1 hard formula and 12 soft formulae. A hard formula represents a constraint that needs to be satisfied at all times. For instance, Formula F1 requires that, for each action *a* at each timestep *t*, there exists a single goal *g*. In MLNs, hard formulae are assigned an arbitrarily large weight. The formulae F2 through F13 are soft formulae, which represent constraints that are allowed to be violated. Formula F2 reflects prior distribution of goals in the corpus. Formulae F3 through F11 predict a player's goal *g* at a given time *t* based on the observed player behavior.

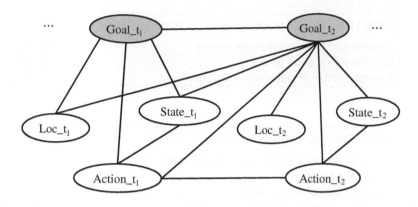

FIGURE 12.6

Graphical representation of goal-recognition MLN.

Instead of aggregating all three attributes of player behavior in a single formula, we modeled the impacts of each individual attribute separately by defining an MLN formula for each attribute. Combinations of the attributes were also considered. In contrast to F3 through F11 that predict individual goals separately from others, F12 and F13 jointly predict sequentially adjacent pairs of goals by exploiting their ordering patterns. The weights for the soft constraints were learned by using *theBeast*—an off-the-shelf tool for MLNs that employs the CPI method for MAP inference [32]. All of these formulae are included in the current goal-recognition model. Figure 12.6 illustrates a partial graphical representation of the described MLN.

12.6 **Evaluation**

To train and test the goal-recognition MLN, the data from the observation corpus was automatically preprocessed in several steps. First, all player actions that achieve goals were identified. Because the goals considered in our work are a set of milestone actions players achieved while solving the narrative scenario, they are logged in the same manner as other actions. Therefore, identification of goal-achieving actions can be performed automatically by scanning the gameplay data, without need for manually defining domain-specific knowledge such as which actions correspond to which goals. Second, all actions in the observation sequence that precede the current goal, but follow the previous goal, were labeled with the current goal. Third, actions that achieve goals were removed from the data. Removing goal-achieving actions was necessary to ensure that model training was fair because it would be trivial to predict goals from the goal-achieving actions. Finally, all actions taken after achievement of the last goal were also removed, since those actions did not lead to achieving a goal.

Table 12.3 shows summary statistics of the resulting corpus, which includes 77,182 player actions and 893 achieved goals, with an average of 86.4 player actions per goal. Table 12.4 shows the set of goals considered in this work and their frequencies in the processed corpus data. The most frequent

Table 12.3 Statistics for Observed Actions and Goals

Total number of observed player actions	77,182
Total number of goals achieved	893
Average number of player actions per goal	86.4

Table 12.4 Distribution of Goals

Running laboratory test on contaminated food	26.6%
Submitting a diagnosis	17.1%
Speaking with the camp's cook	15.2%
Speaking with the camp's bacteria expert	12.5%
Speaking with the camp's virus expert	11.2%
Speaking with a sick patient	11.0%
Speaking with the camp nurse	6.4%

goal was *running laboratory test on contaminated food*, which comprised 26.6% of the total goals in the corpus.

For evaluation, the proposed MLN model was compared to a trivial baseline system and two nontrivial baselines. The trivial baseline was the majority baseline, which always predicted the goal that appears most frequently in the training data. The nontrivial baselines were two *n*-gram models adopted from previous goal-recognition work [4,25]. Although simplistic, *n*-gram models have been shown to be effective for goal recognition in interactive narrative game environments [25] and spoken dialogue systems [4]. The following subsections provide a detailed description of the *n*-gram comparison systems and report evaluation results.

12.6.1 *n*-gram Models

Previous work [25] defined that, given an observation sequence $O_1, O_2, \ldots, O_n$, the objective of goal recognition for an interactive narrative environment is to identify the most likely goal G^*, such that:

$$G^* = \arg\max \ P\left(G \mid O_1, O_2, \ldots, O_n\right) = \arg\max \ P\left(G \mid O_{1:n}\right), \tag{12.3}$$

where O_i is an observation of player behavior at a timestep i. Applying Bayes's rule followed by the chain rule, Eq. 12.3 becomes:

$$G^* = \arg\max \ P\left(O_n \mid O_{1:n-1}, G\right) P\left(O_{n-1} \mid O_{1:n-2}, G\right) \ldots P\left(O_1 \mid G\right) P(G). \tag{12.4}$$

Since estimating these conditional probabilities is impractical, following an earlier approach [4], Mott et al. [25] defined two *n*-gram models based on a Markov assumption that an observation O_i depends only on the goal G and a limited window of preceding observations.

The unigram model states that given the goal, O_i is conditionally independent of all other observations (Eq. 12.5). Thus, the unigram model predicts a goal based on the current observation of player behavior only. Extending the window size by one timestep, the bigram model assumes that, given the goal G and a preceding observation O_{i-1}, O_i is conditionally independent of all other observations (Eq. 12.6). Therefore, the bigram model considers the previous observation of player behavior as well. An observation O_i for the n-gram models is an aggregate variable that combines all the attributes of player behavior.

$$G^* = \arg\max\ P(G)\prod_{i=1}^{n}P\left(O_i \mid G\right) \tag{12.5}$$

In spite of the simplistic approach, Mott et al. [25] found n-gram models achieved higher prediction accuracies than a more sophisticated Bayesian network model. Similar to the MLN model described in Section 12.5, their Bayesian network model used factored representation of player behavior, modeling the influence of each attribute of player behavior separately.

$$G^* = \arg\max\ P(G)\prod_{i=1}^{n}P\left(O_i \mid O_{i-1}, G\right) \tag{12.6}$$

Adopting these ideas within the MLN framework, in the work presented in this chapter we constructed a unigram and a bigram goal-recognition model as MLNs, which employed an aggregate representation of player behavior. The unigram and the bigram models were defined by a single soft Formula F14 and F15, respectively. Formula F14 predicts a goal at time t from the combination of all three attributes of player behavior observed at the same timestep. Formula F15 combines the attributes of player behavior for time t, as well as time t-1, in order to predict a goal at time t. To ensure that each player action at each timestep is assigned a single goal, the hard Formula F1 (see Figure 12.5) was also added to both the unigram and the bigram models. Without any formula that encodes relations among different goals, n-gram models predict each individual goal separately and do not take into consideration the sequential association patterns among them.

$$\forall t, a, l, s, g : action(t, a) \wedge loc(t, l) \wedge state(t, s) \Rightarrow goal(t, g) \tag{F14}$$

$$\forall t, a_1, a_2, l_1, l_2, s_1, s_2, g : action(t, a_1) \wedge loc(t, l_1) \wedge state(t, s_1)$$
$$\wedge\ action(t - 1, a_2) \wedge loc(t - 1, l_2) \wedge state(t - 1, s_2) \Rightarrow goal(t, g) \tag{F15}$$

12.6.2 Results

The two n-gram models, which employed an aggregate representation of player behavior, and the proposed MLN model, which used a factored representation, were trained using one-best Margin Infused Relaxed Algorithm [10] as the update rule. The entire dataset was partitioned into 10 nonoverlapping subsets, ensuring data from the same player did not appear in both the training and the testing data. Each subset of the data was used for testing exactly once. The three models were evaluated with 10-fold cross-validation on the entire dataset. The models' performance was measured using *F1*, which is the harmonic mean of *precision* and *recall*. In the case of multiclass classification such as ours, there are

Table 12.5 *F1* Scores for MLN and Baseline Goal-Recognition Models

	Baseline	Unigram	Bigram	Factored MLN
F1	0.266	0.396	0.330	**0.484**
Improvement over baseline	N/A	49%	24%	**82%**

multiple approaches to computing *F1*. Common approaches include computing either the micro-average or macro-average of *F1*. *Micro-average* computes *F1* by treating all objects in the testing data equally regardless of the class. *Macro-average* takes the average of *F1* scores that are separately computed for each class, by treating multiclass classification as an aggregate of binary classification.

A drawback of these approaches is entries in the confusion matrix are counted multiple times. To avoid this, an alternate approach uses the slightly different formulations of *precision* (Eq. 12.7) and *recall* (Eq. 12.8) for multiclass classification, in which the *F1* score is computed as a harmonic mean of precision and recall as for the binary classification (e.g., [23]). Our work follows this approach. It should be noted that in the current work the values of *precision*, *recall*, and *F1* are the same, because each observed player action is associated with a single goal in our data and the goal-recognition model predicts a single most likely goal for each player action; that is, the *total number of predictions made by classifier* is equal to *total number of objects*. These values again coincide with *accuracy*—another metric widely used for multiclass classification.

$$Precision = \frac{total\ number\ of\ correctly\ classified\ objects}{total\ number\ of\ predictions\ made\ by\ classifier} \tag{12.7}$$

$$Recall = \frac{total\ number\ of\ correctly\ classified\ objects}{total\ number\ of\ objects} \tag{12.8}$$

Table 12.5 shows the average performance of each compared model over 10-fold cross-validation. The factored MLN model scored 0.484 in *F1*, achieving an 82% improvement over the baseline. The unigram model performed better than the bigram model. A one-way repeated-measures ANOVA confirmed that the differences among the three compared models were statistically significant ($F(2,18) = 71.87$, $p < 0.0001$). A post hoc Tukey test revealed that the differences between all pairs of the three models were statistically significant ($p < 0.01$).

12.7 Discussion

Even though all three models performed better than the baseline, the factored-MLN model achieved the best performance, suggesting that the proposed MLN goal-recognition approach is effective in predicting player goals from observed player behavior in a complex game environment. The *F1* score of 0.484 achieved by the factored-MLN model may appear somewhat low. However, this result is encouraging given the challenges posed by the data. The chance probability of accurately recognizing the seven goals in our data was 0.143. The superiority of the factored-MLN model compared to the *n*-gram models can be partially explained by the MLN's relational learning framework, which facilitates explicit modeling of associations between goals: the factored-MLN model jointly predicts successive goals, while n-gram models predicted each individual goal separately.

Furthermore, the factored representation of player behavior enables MLNs to model richer relationships between player behavior and goals than the aggregate representation used in n-gram models. The finding that the unigram model achieved higher performance than the bigram model is consistent with the result reported [25]. Among the possible reasons for the unigram model's superiority over the bigram model is data sparsity. The bigram model considers two consecutive previous goals, which would lead to greater sparsity than in the unigram model.

The current work is a first step toward a general approach for modeling exploratory goal recognition in digital games using MLNs. The current goal-recognition model makes relatively basic use of MLNs, modeling only sequential relationships among successive goals, but MLNs provide a principled method to incorporate richer structural relations present among the goals—for example, the relations imposed by the narrative structure of the virtual world. Also, the current work is characterized as a knowledge-lean approach to goal recognition; that is, it uses only a minimal amount of domain knowledge in the model's specification. The only domain knowledge required for the proposed goal-recognition model was to identify the milestone events within the CRYSTAL ISLAND game environment.

The knowledge-lean approach offers a cost-efficient solution for devising goal-recognition models because identifying milestone events is relatively easy compared to manually annotating the data with a hand-crafted goal schema or hand-authoring the mappings between player behavior and goals. We also suspect that knowledge-lean approaches offer a more robust solution than competing approaches to goal recognition in open-ended games as a result of challenges associated with unexpected patterns in players' exploratory behavior.

Inducing accurate goal-recognition models has several prospective benefits for game-based learning environments. Goal recognizers can be used to inform player-adaptive decisions by *narrative-centered tutorial planners*; such planners comprise a particular class of software agents that simultaneously reason about interactive narrative and pedagogical issues to personalize student's game-based learning experiences. Data-driven approaches to narrative-centered tutorial planning are the subject of active research by the CRYSTAL ISLAND research team. They offer a method for dynamically tailoring events during players' game-based learning experiences in order to individualize pedagogical scaffolding and promote player engagement.

Consider the following scenario: a player begins running laboratory tests prematurely, collecting data before he has gathered enough background information about CRYSTAL ISLAND's outbreak scenario to adequately interpret the results. Goal-recognition models enable CRYSTAL ISLAND to predict that the player is attempting to find a contaminated object. However, this prediction prompts a subsequent inference that the player's goal is suboptimal for the current stage of the narrative. This realization triggers an event where a virtual character suggests that the player should instead go speak with sick patients to better understand how the disease spread through the research camp. In this manner, a narrative-centered tutorial planner can dynamically tailor events to improve students' learning outcomes and narrative experience, driven by information from goal-recognition models.

Similarly, goal-recognition models can be employed to detect situations where players attempt to solve the mystery by "gaming the system" [2]. In some cases, players may attempt to solve the mystery by guessing as they fill out the diagnosis worksheet. In this exploitative strategy, players guess responses on the worksheet, submit it to the camp nurse, receive feedback about incorrect responses, revise the worksheet, and repeat the process in hopes of stumbling upon the correct solution. A goal-recognition model could predict that the player is attempting to solve the mystery. However, if the player has not yet completed other important narrative milestones, it might be appropriate for the camp nurse to prompt the player to consider an alternate course of action. The nurse might tell the player to speak with other scientists on the island, or to collect data in the virtual laboratory, in order to obtain knowledge that will enable her to complete the diagnosis worksheet in a more deliberative fashion.

In addition to using goal-recognition models to dynamically shape events in CRYSTAL ISLAND's narrative, goal recognizers can be used during data mining to inform the analysis and design of future iterations of the CRYSTAL ISLAND software. By automatically recognizing players' goals, and identifying which actions are likely to be associated with those goals, the research team can gain insights about common types of problem-solving paths and challenges encountered by players. Furthermore, recognizing players' goals can enrich in-game assessments of player learning and problem solving, which is a critical challenge for the serious games community.

The present work has several limitations that we seek to address through continued investigation. First, the available log data did not include preexisting class labels of players' intentions. To investigate goal recognition, it was necessary to add class labels during subsequent data analysis, which necessitated single-goal assumptions that prevented consideration of concurrent or interleaving goals. In future data collections with CRYSTAL ISLAND, it may be possible to obtain class labels, or the information necessary to extract class labels, during runtime.

A common method for obtaining such data in educational research is to ask students to think aloud as they solve the problem, often with support from a researcher providing regular prompts. Although this approach provides a direct window into students' intentions, in the past we have seen considerable variability in middle-grade students' willingness to verbalize their thoughts as they play CRYSTAL ISLAND. This may be due to cognitive difficulties associated with simultaneously playing an unfamiliar game and verbalizing one's own intentions, or it may be a symptom of adolescent resistance to verbal communication. In the case of the former, it may be possible to circumvent this challenge by having students watch video recordings of their own gameplay sessions after solving the mystery, providing verbal commentary about their own play experiences in a *post hoc* manner.

An alternative approach is training human "experts" to provide judgments about player intentions by observing students as they play the game. This approach depends on humans accurately recognizing students' intentions in CRYSTAL ISLAND; in this case, goal data are not directly obtained from players. On the one hand, this method bypasses the need for students to verbalize their intentions, which is challenging in practice. On the other hand, it is resource-intense to gather human judgments for a large number of student gameplay sessions, a problem only exacerbated by the need for multiple judgments to enable interrater reliability calculations.

The preceding methods—think-alouds and expert observational protocols—also introduce opportunities for addressing another limitation of the present work: detecting nontraditional goals that are not represented in the set of seven narrative subgoals. For example, students may adopt ill-defined goals, such as "explore the virtual environment," or nonnarrative goals, such as "climb on top of the dining hall," to drive their actions. Accurately predicting these goals would substantially extend the capabilities of narrative-centered tutorial planners seeking to interpret player actions and tailor game events to individual students. However, it is necessary to obtain class labels to model these goals using the MLN-based classification approach presented in this chapter. Furthermore, plan-recognition methods that rely on inference over planning domains are unlikely to be effective for these types of intentions, as they most likely exceed the specifications typically included in most planning-domain knowledge bases.

12.8 Conclusion and Future Work

Effective goal recognition holds considerable promise for player-adaptive games. Accurately recognizing players' goals enables digital games to proactively support gameplay experiences that feature nonlinear scenarios while preserving cohesion, coherence, and believability. This chapter introduced a goal-recognition framework based on MLNs that accurately recognizes players' goals. Using model parameters learned from a corpus of player interactions in a complex, nonlinear game environment, the framework supports the automated acquisition of a goal-recognition system that outperforms three baseline models.

There are several promising directions for future work on goal-recognition models in open-ended digital games. First, the MLN model considered here deliberately leveraged minimal domain-specific knowledge. Devising systematic methods for encoding domain-specific information (e.g., interactive-narrative structure, gameplay mechanics) is a promising direction for improving the predictive accuracy of the models. Second, investigating the efficiency and convergence rate of MLN goal recognizers is an important step for eventually embedding these models in runtime settings because the real-time performance requirements of digital games demand highly efficient algorithms. Finally, integrating MLN goal-recognition models into the CRYSTAL ISLAND game-based learning environment is a key objective of this work. The models would drive narrative-centered tutorial planners that dynamically adapt game events to enhance students' learning, problem solving, and engagement outcomes. This integration will enable empirical studies involving human subjects to examine the real-world impact of goal-recognition models and player-adaptive games.

Acknowledgments

The authors wish to thank members of the IntelliMedia Group of North Carolina State University for their assistance, Omer Sturlovich and Pavel Turzo for use of their 3D model libraries, and Valve Software for access to the Source[TM] engine and SDK. This research was supported by the National Science Foundation under Grants REC-0632450, DRL-0822200, and IIS-0812291. Any opinions, findings, and conclusions or recommendations expressed here are those of the authors and do not reflect the views of the National Science Foundation. Additional support was provided by the Bill and Melinda Gates Foundation, the William and Flora Hewlett Foundation, and EDUCAUSE.

References

[1] Albrecht D, Zukerman I, Nicholson A. Bayesian models for keyhole plan recognition in an adventure game. User Model User-adap interact 1998;8(1–2):5–47.

[2] Baker RS, Corbett AT, Koedinger KR, Wagner AZ. Off-task behavior in the cognitive tutor classroom: when students game the system. In: Proceedings of the ACM Conference on Human Factors in Computing Systems; 2004. p. 383–90.

[3] Bethesda Softworks. 2011. The elder scrolls V: Skyrim. Retrieved from <www.elderscrolls.com/skyrim>.

[4] Blaylock N, Allen J. Corpus-based, statistical goal recognition. In: Proceedings of the Eighteenth International Joint Conference on Artificial Intelligence; 2003. p. 1303–8.

[5] Bui HH. A general model for online probabilistic plan recognition. In: Proceedings of the Eighteenth International Joint Conference on Artificial Intelligence; 2003. p. 1309–15.

[6] Carberry S. Techniques for plan recognition. User Model User-Adapted Interact 2001;11(1–2):31–48.

[7] Charniak E, Goldman RP. A Bayesian model of plan recognition. Artif Intell 1993;64(1):53–79.

[8] Chu Y, Song YC, Levinson R, Kautz H. Interactive activity recognition and prompting to assist people with cognitive disabilities. J Ambient Intell Smart Environ 2012;4(5):443–59.

[9] Conati C, Gertner A, VanLehn K. Using Bayesian networks to manage uncertainty in student modeling. User Model User-Adapted Interact 2002;12(4):371–417.

[10] Crammer K, Singer Y. Ultraconservative online algorithms for multiclass problems. J Mach Learn Res 2003;3:951–91.

[11] Geib CW, Goldman RP. A probabilistic plan recognition algorithm based on plan tree grammars. Artif Intell 2009;173(11):1101–32.

[12] Geib C, Goldman R. Recognizing plans with loops in a lexicalized grammar. In: Proceedings of the Twenty-Fifth National Conference on Artificial Intelligence; 2011. p. 958–63.

[13] Getoor L, Taskar B. Introduction to statistical relational learning (adaptive computation and machine learning). The MIT Press; 2007.

[14] Gold K. Training goal recognition online from low-level inputs in an action-adventure game. In: Proceedings of the Sixth International Conference on Artificial Intelligence and Interactive Digital Entertainment; 2010. p. 21–6.

[15] Hoogs A, Perera A. Video activity recognition in the real world. In: Proceedings of the Twenty-Third National Conference on Artificial Intelligence; 2008. p. 1551–4.

[16] Horvitz E, Breese J, Heckerman D, Hovel D, Koos R. The Lumiere project: Bayesian user modeling for inferring the goals and needs of software users. In: Proceedings of the Fourteenth Conference on Uncertainty in Artificial Intelligence; 1998. p. 256–65.

[17] Hu DH, Yang Q. CIGAR: concurrent and interleaving goal and activity recognition. In: Proceedings of the Twenty-Third National Conference on Artificial Intelligence; 2008. p. 1363–8.

[18] Johnson WL. Serious use of a serious game for language learning. Int J Artif Intell Educ 2010;20(2):175–95.

[19] Kabanza F, Bellefeuille P, Bisson F. Opponent behavior recognition for real-time strategy games. In: Proceedings of the AAAI-10 Workshop on Plan, Activity, and Intent Recognition; 2010.

[20] Kautz H, Allen JF. Generalized plan recognition. In: Proceedings of the Fifth National Conference on Artificial Intelligence; 1986. p. 32–7.

[21] Laviers K, Sukthankar G. A real-time opponent modeling system for rush football. In: Proceedings of the Twenty-Second International Joint Conference on Artificial Intelligence; 2011. p. 2476–81.

[22] Lee SY, Mott BW, Lester JC. Real-time narrative-centered tutorial planning for story-based learning. In: Proceedings of the 11th International Conference on Intelligent Tutoring Systems; 2012. p. 476–81.

[23] Marcu D. The rhetorical parsing of unrestricted texts: a surface-based approach. Comput Linguist 2000;26(3):395–448.

[24] Mojang. 2009. Minecraft. Retrieved from <www.minecraft.net/>.

[25] Mott B, Lee S, Lester J. Probabilistic goal recognition in interactive narrative environments. In: Proceedings of the Twenty-First National Conference on Artificial Intelligence; 2006. p. 187–92.

[26] Orkin J, Roy D. The restaurant game: learning social behavior and language from thousands of players online. J Game Devel 2007;3(1):39–60.

[27] Pietra SD, Pietra VDP, Lafferty J. Inducing features of random fields. IEEE transactions on pattern analysis and machine intelligence 1997;19(4):380–93.

[28] Pynadath DV, Wellman MP. Probabilistic state-dependent grammars for plan recognition. In: Proceedings of the Sixteenth Conference on Uncertainty in Artificial Intelligence; 2000. p. 507–14.

[29] Ramirez M, Geffner H. Probabilistic plan recognition using off-the-shelf classical planners. In: Proceedings of the Twenty-Fourth AAAI Conference on Artificial Intelligence; 2010. p. 1121–6.

[30] Richardson M, Domingos P. Markov logic networks. J Mach Learn 2006;62(1–2):107–36.

[31] Riedl MO, Saretto CJ, Young RM. Managing interaction between users and agents in a multi-agent storytelling environment. In: Proceedings of the 2nd International Conference on Autonomous Agents and Multiagent Systems; 2003. p. 741–8.

[32] Riedel S. Improving the accuracy and efficiency of MAP inference for Markov logic. In: Proceedings of the Twenty-Fourth Annual Conference on Uncertainty in Artificial Intelligence; 2008. p. 468–75.

[33] Robison J, McQuiggan S, Lester J. Evaluating the consequences of affective feedback in intelligent tutoring systems. In: Proceedings of the International Conference on Affective Computing and Intelligent Interaction; 2009. p. 37–42.

[34] Rowe J, Lester J. Modeling user knowledge with dynamic Bayesian networks in interactive narrative environments. In: Proceedings of the Sixth International Conference on Artificial Intelligence in Interactive Digital Entertainment; 2010. p. 57–62.

[35] Rowe J, Shores L, Mott B, Lester J. Integrating learning, problem solving, and engagement in narrative-centered learning environments. Int J Artif Intell Educ 2011;21(1–2):115–33.

[36] Sadilek A, Kautz H. Recognizing multi-agent activities from GPS data. In: Proceedings of the Twenty-Fourth AAAI Conference on Artificial Intelligence; 2010. p. 1134–9.

[37] Schmidt C, Sridharan N, Goodson J. The plan recognition problem: an intersection of psychology and artificial intelligence. Artif Intell 1978;11:45–83.

[38] Singla P, Mooney R. Abductive Markov logic for plan recognition. In: Proceedings of the Twenty-Fifth AAAI Conference on Artificial Intelligence; 2011. p. 1069–75.

[39] Squire K. Open-ended video games: a model for developing learning for the interactive age. In: Salen K, editor. The ecology of games: connecting youth, games, and learning. The MIT Press; 2008. p. 167–98.

[40] Yannakakis G. Game AI revisited. In: Proceedings of ACM Computing Frontier Conference; 2012.

[41] Zoeller G. Game development telemetry. In: Proceedings of the Game Developers Conference; 2010.

Using Opponent Modeling to Adapt Team Play in American Football

13

Kennard R. Laviers[a] **and Gita Sukthankar**[b]

[a]*Air Force Institute of Technology, Wright Patterson AFB, OH, USA*
[b]*University of Central Florida, Orlando, FL, USA*

13.1 Introduction

In military and athletic environments, agents must depend on coordination to perform joint actions in order to accomplish team objectives. For example, a soldier may signal another soldier to "cover" her while she attempts to relocate to another strategic location. In football, the quarterback depends on other team members to protect him while he waits for a receiver to get into position and to become "open." Because of these coordination dependencies, multiagent learning algorithms employed in these scenarios must consider each agent's actions with respect to its teammates', since even good action selections can fail solely due to teammates' choices. Team adversarial scenarios are even more complicated because opponents are actively thwarting actions. In the contest of American football, the leading causes for failures are as follows:

- An action is a poor selection for the tactical situation. *Example*: a player runs too close to a fast opponent and gets tackled.
- Good action choices are not guaranteed to succeed. *Example*: a player fumbles a well-thrown pass.
- Poor coordination between team members. *Example*: a ball handoff fails because the receiving player does not run to the correct location.
- Opponents successfully counter the planned action. *Example*: the defense overcomes the offensive line's protection scheme, leaving the quarterback unprotected.

Although reward metrics are useful for gauging the performance of a plan or policy, it is impossible to diagnose the root cause of policy failure based on the reward function alone. Moreover, often the reward metric is sparse, providing little information about intermediate stages in the plan. Even minor miscalculations in action selections among coordinating agents can be very unforgiving, yielding either no reward or a negative reward. Finally, physical agents often operate in continuous action spaces since many of the agent actions are movement-based; sampling or discretizing a large two-dimensional area can still result in a significant increase in the number of action possibilities. In summary, team adversarial problems often pose the following difficulties:

(1) Large and partially continuous search space
(2) Lack of intermediate reward information
(3) Difficulty in identifying action combinations that yield effective team coordination
(4) Constant threat of actions being thwarted by adversaries

This chapter describes a set of methods to improve search processes for planning and learning in adversarial team scenarios. American football was selected as the experimental domain for empirical testing of our work for several reasons. First, American football has a "playbook" governing the formations and conditional plans executed by the players, eliminating the necessity of an unsupervised discovery phase in which plans and templates are identified from raw data. Recognizing the play in advance definitely confers advantages on the opposing team but is not a guarantee of victory. The existence of a playbook distinguishes American football from less structured cooperative games (e.g., first-person shooters).

Additionally, football routinely punishes poor coordination, often yielding significant negative rewards for minor errors among players. It is difficult, if not impossible, to evaluate how well a play is doing until either the ball is received by a receiver or being carried up the field by a running back. We selected the Rush 2008 Football Simulator [26] for our research since it can simulate complex plays yet is sufficiently lightweight to facilitate running machine-learning experiments. It comes with an existing play library, and we developed a sketch-based interface for authoring new plays and a test environment for evaluating machine learning algorithms (shown in Figure 13.1). Our Rush Analyzer and Test Environment (RATE) is designed to facilitate reproducible research on planning and learning in a Rush 2008 football game. RATE consists of more than 40,000 lines of code and has support for separate debugging of AI subsystems, parallel search, and point-and-click configuration.

This chapter focuses on four key research areas:

- The use of opponent modeling/play recognition to guide action selection (Section 13.4)
- Automatically identifying coordination patterns from historical play data (Section 13.5)

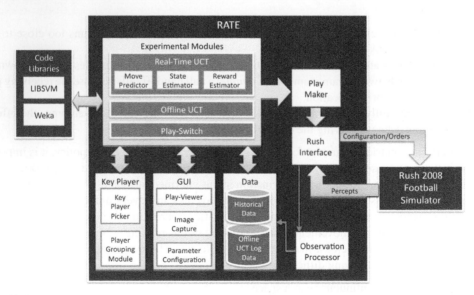

FIGURE 13.1

Rush Analyzer and Test Environment designed to facilitate reproducible research on planning and learning in a Rush 2008 football game.

- The use of play adaptation (Section 13.5.2) and Monte Carlo search to generate new plays (Section 13.6)
- Incorporating the preceding items with a set of data-driven models for move prediction and reward estimation to produce a football agent that learns in real time how to control the actions of three offensive players for a critical early stage of a play (Section 13.7).

Our system is the first autonomous football game player capable of learning team plan repairs in real time to counter predicted opponent actions.

Although effective opponent modeling is often identified as an important prerequisite for building agents in adversarial domains [42], research efforts have focused mainly on the problem of fast and accurate plan recognition [3,17] while neglecting the issues that occur post-plan recognition. Using opponent modeling to guide the play of an autonomous agent is an intuitively appealing idea for game designers, but one that poses many practical difficulties. The first issue is that many games, particularly ones that involve physical movement of the bots, are relatively unconstrained; often, there is no need for human players to consistently follow a mental playbook. This hampers plan-recognition systems that rely on pregenerated models, libraries, and templates. In contrast, the actions of a human player interacting with the Rush football system are limited since the human is only allowed to control the quarterback; the rest of the team is played autonomously according to a preexisting play library. Additionally, it is easy to segment American football plays since there are breaks in action every time a tackle occurs or the ball is fumbled, compared to soccer in which the action flows more naturally. These qualities make American football well suited for a study of the competitive benefits of play recognition; planning is crucial and accurate plan recognition is possible.

13.2 Related Work

The term "opponent modeling" has been used in a wide variety of contexts, ranging from the prediction of immediate actions to forecasting long-term strategies and intentions. Interestingly, one of the first mentions of opponent modeling in the artificial intelligence (AI) literature pertains to predicting movements in football [25]. In our work, we treat opponent modeling as a specialized version of online team behavior recognition in which our system solves a multiclass classification problem to identify the currently executing play.

Previous work on recognizing and analyzing team behaviors has been largely evaluated within athletic domains, not just in American football [15] but also basketball [5,16] and Robocup soccer [31,32,20]. In Robocup, a majority of the research on team behavior recognition has been done for the coach competition. The aim of the competitors is to create autonomous agents that can observe game play from the sidelines and provide strategy advice to a team in a specialized coaching language. Techniques have been developed to extract specific information (e.g., home areas [33], opponent positions during set plays [32], and adversarial models [31]) from logs of Robocup simulation league games. This information can be used by the coaching agent to improve the team's scoring performance. For instance, information about opponent agent home areas can be used as triggers for coaching advice and for doing "formation-based marking" in which different team members are assigned to track members of the opposing team. While the focus of the coaching agent is to improve performance of teams in future games, our system takes action immediately after recognizing the play to search for possible action improvements.

One of the other book chapters describes a new direction in Robocup research—the creation of ad hoc teams [13]. In role-based ad hoc teams, the new agent studies the behavior of its future teammates before deciding on a policy based on marginal utility calculations. Our play-adaptation system does a holistic analysis of team performance based on past yardage gained rather than disentangling the relative contributions of individual agents toward the overall success of the play.

A related line of Robocup research is the development of commentator systems that provide natural language summaries describing action on the field. For instance, the Multiagent Interactions Knowledgeably Explained (MIKE) system used a set of specialized game analysis modules for deciphering the meaning of spatiotemporal events, including a bigram module for modeling ball plays as a first-order Markov chain and a Voronoi module for analyzing defense areas [39]. MIKE was one of three similar commentator systems (along with Rocco and Byrne) that received scientific awards in Robocup 1998 [44].

While commentator systems focus on producing real-time dialog describing game play, automated team analysis assistants are used to do post hoc analysis on game logs [40]. One of the earliest systems, ISAAC, learned decision trees to characterize the outcome of plays and also possessed an interactive mode allowing the team designer to explore hypothetical modifications to the agent's parameters [28]. This style of analysis has been successfully applied to real-world NBA basketball data in the Advanced Scout system [5], which was later commercialized by VirtualGold. These data mining tools have a knowledge discovery phase where patterns in the statistics of individual players (e.g., shooting performance) are identified. Interpreted results are presented to the coaching staff in the form of text descriptions and video snippets. Our system directly channels information about past performance of plays into dynamically adapting the actions of the offensive team and also learning offline plays. The knowledge discovery phase in our work is assumed to be supervised by a knowledgeable observer who tags the plays with labels, rather than being performed in an unsupervised fashion.

One of the earliest camera-based sports analysis systems was developed for the football domain [15]. In addition to performing low-level field rectification and trajectory extraction, it recognizes football plays using belief networks to identify actions from accumulated visual evidence. Real-world football formations have been successfully extracted from snapshots of football games by Hess et al., who demonstrated the use of a pictorial structure model [14]. Kang et al. demonstrated the use of Support Vector Machines (SVM) to detect scoring events and track the ball in a soccer match [18,30]. Visual information from a post-mounted camera outside the soccer field was used to train the SVMs. For our opponent modeling, we use multiclass SVMs to classify the defensive team plays based on observation logs using a training method similar to the one of Sukthankar and Sycara [37].

Note that the use of opponent modeling to guide action selection carries the inherent risk of being "bluffed" into poor actions by a clever opponent tricking the system into learning a false behavior model. In football, running plays are more effective if the opponent can be fooled into believing that the play is actually a passing play. Smart human players often engage in recursive thinking and consider what the opponent thinks and knows as well as the observed actions [6]. The interactive partially observable Markov decision process (I-POMDP) framework explicitly models this mode of adversarial thinking (see Doshi et al.'s chapter in this book [11] for a more detailed description). In this work, we do not consider the mental factors that affect the choice of play, only post-play adaptations.

13.3 **Rush Football**

The goal is to produce a challenging and fun computer player for the Rush 2008 football game, developed by Knexus Research [26], capable of responding to a human player in novel and unexpected ways. In Rush 2008, play instructions are similar to a conditional plan and include choice points where the players can make individual decisions as well as predefined behaviors that the players execute to the best of their physical capability. Planning is accomplished before a play is enacted, and the best plays are cached in a playbook. Certain defensive plays can effectively counter specific offenses. Once the play commences, it is possible to recognize the defensive play and to anticipate the imminent failure of the offensive play.

American football is a contest of two teams played on a rectangular field. Unlike standard American football, which has 11 players on a team, Rush teams only have 8 players simultaneously on the field out of a total roster of 18 players, and the field is 100×63 yards. The game's objective is to outscore the opponent, where the offense (i.e., the team with possession of the ball) attempts to advance the ball from the line of scrimmage into the opponent's end zone. In a full game, the offensive team has four attempts to get a *first down* by moving the ball 10 yards down the field. If the ball is intercepted or fumbled and claimed by the defense, ball possession transfers to the defensive team. Stochasticity exists in many aspects of the game including throwing, catching, fumbling, blocking, running, and tackling. Our work mainly focuses on improving offensive team performance in executing passing plays.

In American football, the offensive lineup consists of the following positions:

Quarterback (QB): given the ball at the start of each play and initiates either a run or a pass.

Running back (RB): begins in the backfield, behind the line of scrimmage where the ball is placed, with the QB and FB. The running back is eligible to receive a handoff, backward pitch, or forward pass from the QB.

Fullback (FB): serves largely the same function as the RB.

Wide receiver (WR): the primary receiver for pass plays. This player initially starts near the line of scrimmage but on the far right or far left of the field.

Tight end (TE): begins on the line of scrimmage immediately to the outside of the OL and can receive passes.

Offensive lineman (OL): begins on the line of scrimmage and is primarily responsible for preventing the defense from reaching the ball carrier.

A defensive lineup has the following positions:

Defensive lineman (DL): line up across the line of scrimmage from the OL and focuses on tackling the ball handler as quickly as possible.

Linebackers (LB): line up behind the lineman and can blitz the opposing QB by quickly running toward him en masse. Often their role is to guard a particular zone of the playing field or an eligible receiver, depending on whether they are executing a zone or a man defense.

Cornerbacks (CB): typically line up across the line of scrimmage from the wide receivers. Their primary responsibility is to cover the WR.

Safety (S): lines up far behind the line of scrimmage. They typically assist with pass coverage but, like all defensive players, can also blitz and can contribute on tackling any ball handler.

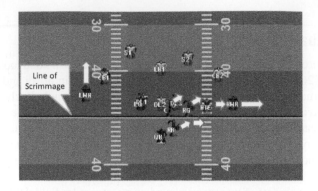

FIGURE 13.2

The Pro formation running play variant 4 against defensive formation 31 running variant 2.

A Rush play is composed of (1) a starting formation and (2) instructions for each player in that formation. A formation is a set of (x, y) offsets from the center of the line of scrimmage. By default, instructions for each player consist of (a) an offset/destination point on the field to run to and (b) a behavior to execute when they get there. Rush includes three offensive formations (**power**, **pro**, and **split**) and four defensive ones (**23**, **31**, **2222**, **2231**). Each formation has eight different plays (numbered 1-8) that can be executed from that formation. Offensive plays typically include a handoff to the running back/fullback or a pass executed by the QB to one of the receivers, along with instructions for a running pattern to be followed by all the receivers. Figure 13.2 shows an example play from the **Pro** formation:

1. The QB passes to an open receiver
2. The RB and left WR run hook routes
3. The left and right guards pass block for the ball holder
4. The other players wait

The default Rush playbook contains 24 offensive and 32 defensive plays. Playbooks for real-world football teams are limited by the ability of the players to reliably learn and execute the plays. As a rule of thumb, children's teams learn 5 to 15 plays, high school teams 80, and pro teams 120 to 250 [41]. During a single game between 50 to 70 plays will be executed, but the full season playbook for a pro team might contain as many as 800 plays [47,34].

Rush 2008 was developed as a general platform for evaluating game-playing agents and has been used in several research efforts. Prior work on play generation within Rush used a learning by demonstration approach in which the agents observed video from college football games [24]. The trained agents were evaluated on the Rush 2008 simulator and measured against hand-coded agents. A similar approach was used in the Robocup soccer domain [1]. Instead of learning from video traces, they modified the Robocup environment to allow humans to play Robocup soccer like a video game. While users play, the system engages a machine learning algorithm to train a classifier (Weka C4.5). The trained model is then used to generate dynamic C code that forms the core of a new Robocup agent. In contrast, our agents rely on two sources of information, a preconstructed playbook and reward information from historical play data: we leverage the playbook primarily as a source for rapidly generating plans for noncritical players. The behaviors of the key players can differ substantially from the playbook since they are generated through a full Monte Carlo tree search process.

Molineaux et al. [27] demonstrated the advantage of providing information gained from plan recognition to a learning agent; their system used a reinforcement learning (RL) algorithm to train a Rush football quarterback in passing behavior. In addition to the RL algorithm they used an automatic clustering algorithm to identify defensive plays and feed that information to the RL agent to significantly reduce the state space. It is important to note that while the Rush 2008 Simulator is a multiagent domain, earlier work on Rush restricted the RL to a single agent, in contrast to this work, which learns policies for multiple team members.

There are a plethora of other football simulators in the commercial market. The most popular football video game is EA Sports' Madden NFL® football game. Madden NFL football [29] was introduced in 1988 and became the third top-selling video game by 2003. The game adjusts the level of difficulty by modifying the amount of control the game engine allows the human player to assume. The novice player relies on the built-in AI to do most of the work, whereas an expert player controls a large percentage of his or her team's actions. The inherent strategies of the football teams do not appear to be a focus area in Madden football for controlling game difficulty. Our techniques enable the generation of new playbooks in an offline fashion, as well as methods for modifying plays online, to offer unexpected surprises even for those who have played the game extensively.

13.4 Play Recognition Using Support Vector Machines

We began our research by developing a play-recognition system to rapidly identify football plays. Given a series of observations, the system aims to recognize the defensive play as quickly as possible in order to maximize the offensive team's ability to intelligently respond with the best offense. In our case, when we need to determine a plan that is in play, the observation sequence grows with time unlike in standard offline activity recognition where the entire set of observations is available. We approached the problem by training a series of multiclass discriminative classifiers, each of which is designed to handle observation sequences of a particular length. In general, we expected the early classifiers would be less accurate since they are operating with a shorter observation vector and because the positions of the players have deviated little from the initial formation.

We perform this classification using support vector machines [43], which are a supervised algorithm that can be used to learn a binary classifier. They have been demonstrated to perform well on a variety of pattern classification tasks, particularly when the dimensionality of the data is high (as in our case). Intuitively an SVM projects data points into a higher dimensional space, specified by a kernel function, and computes a maximum-margin hyperplane decision surface that separates the two classes. Support vectors are those data points that lie closest to this decision surface; if these data points were removed from the training data, the decision surface would change.

More formally, given a labeled training set $\{(\mathbf{x}_1, y_1), (\mathbf{x}_2, y_2), \ldots, (\mathbf{x}_l, y_l)\}$, where $\mathbf{x}_i \in \Re^N$ is a feature vector and $y_i \in \{-1, +1\}$ is its binary class label, an SVM requires solving the following optimization problem:

$$\min_{\mathbf{w}, b, \xi} \frac{1}{2}\mathbf{w}^T\mathbf{w} + C\sum_{i=1}^{l} \xi_i$$

constrained by:

$$y_i(\mathbf{w}^T \phi(\mathbf{x}_i) + \mathbf{b}) \geq 1 - \xi_i,$$

where ξ_i is a nonnegative slack variable for penalizing misclassifications. The function $\phi(.)$ that maps data points into the higher dimensional space is not explicitly represented; rather, a *kernel* function, $K(\mathbf{x}_i, \mathbf{x}_j) \equiv \phi(\mathbf{x}_i)\phi(\mathbf{x}_j)$, is used to implicitly specify this mapping. In our application, we use the popular radial basis function (RBF) kernel:

$$K(x_i, x_j) = \exp(-\gamma ||x_i - x_j||^2), \quad \gamma > 0.$$

A standard one-vs-one voting scheme is used where all $(^k C_2)$ pairwise binary classifiers are trained and the most popular label is selected. Many efficient implementations of SVMs are publicly available; we use LIBSVM [9].

We train our classifiers using a collection of simulated games in Rush collected under controlled conditions: 40 instances of every possible combination of offense (8) and defense plays (8), from each of the 12 starting formation configurations. Since the starting configuration is known, each series of SVMs is only trained with data that could be observed starting from its given configuration. For each configuration, we create a series of training sequences that accumulates spatiotemporal traces from $t = 0$ up to $t \in \{2, \ldots, 10\}$ timesteps. A multiclass SVM (i.e., a collection of 28 binary SVMs) is trained for each of these training sequence lengths. Although the aggregate number of binary classifiers is large, each classifier only employs a small fraction of the dataset and is therefore efficient (and highly parallelizable). Cross-validation on a training set was used to tune the SVM parameters (C and σ) for all of the SVMs.

Classification at testing time is very fast and proceeds as follows. We select the multiclass SVM that is relevant to the current starting configuration and timestep. An observation vector of the correct length is generated (this can be done incrementally during game play) and fed to the multiclass SVM. The output of the play recognizer is the system's best guess (at the current timestep) about the opponent's choice of defensive play and can help us to select the most appropriate offense, as discussed next.

Table 13.1 summarizes the experimental results for different lengths of the observation vector (time from start of play), averaging classification accuracy across all starting formation choices and defense choices. We see that at the earliest timestep, our classification accuracy is at the baseline but jumps sharply to near perfect levels at $t = 3$. This definitely confirms the feasibility of accurate play recognition in Rush, even during very early stages of a play. At $t = 2$, there is insufficient information to discriminate between offense plays (perceptual aliasing); however, by $t = 3$, the positions of the offensive team are distinctive enough to be reliably recognized.

Since Rush is a simulated game, it is possible for the play recognizer to perfectly observe the environment, which may be an unrealistic assumption in the real world. To address this, we replicated the experiments under conditions where both training and test data were corrupted by observation noise. We model this noise as a Gaussian with 0 mean and $\sigma = 1$ yard. Figure 13.3 presents a more detailed look at the play-recognition accuracy for each of the 12 starting configurations, both with and without noise. Most of the curves look very similar, but we see that recognition accuracy climbs more slowly for formations where the offense has selected *power* plays; this occurs because two of the *power* plays are very similar, differing only in the fullback position.

However, reliably identifying the opponent's strategy is only one of the challenges that need to be addressed toward the creation of an adaptive football team. In the next section, we discuss the problem of avoiding coordination failures while performing runtime play adaptation.

Table 13.1 Play Recognition Results

Off	Def	t = 2	3	4	5	6	7	8	9	10
Power	23	12.5%	87.5%	87.5%	87.2%	87.3%	87.2%	87.2%	86.9%	86.8%
Pro	23	12.5%	87.5%	87.5%	87.6%	87.2%	87.7%	87.6%	87.8%	87.5%
Split	23	12.5%	87.5%	87.5%	87.4%	87.5%	87.5%	87.9%	87.2%	87.4%
Power	31	12.5%	100.0%	100.0%	100.0%	100.0%	100.0%	100.0%	100.0%	100.0%
Pro	31	12.5%	100.0%	99.9%	100.0%	100.0%	100.0%	100.0%	100.0%	100.0%
Split	31	12.5%	100.0%	100.0%	100.0%	100.0%	100.0%	99.9%	99.9%	99.9%
Power	2231	12.5%	100.0%	100.0%	100.0%	100.0%	100.0%	100.0%	100.0%	100.0%
Pro	2231	12.5%	100.0%	100.0%	100.0%	100.0%	100.0%	100.0%	100.0%	100.0%
Split	2231	12.5%	100.0%	100.0%	100.0%	100.0%	100.0%	100.0%	99.9%	99.9%
Power	2222	12.5%	100.0%	100.0%	100.0%	100.0%	100.0%	100.0%	100.0%	100.0%
Pro	2222	12.5%	100.0%	100.0%	100.0%	100.0%	100.0%	100.0%	100.0%	100.0%
Split	2222	12.50%	100.0%	100.0%	100.0%	100.0%	100.0%	100.0%	100.0%	100.0%

13.5 Team Coordination

Effective player coordination has been shown to be an important predictor of team success in adversarial games such as Robocup soccer [38]. Much work has centered on the problem of role allocation—correctly allocating players to roles that are appropriate for their capabilities and smoothly transitioning players between roles [35]. In the worst case, determining which players to group together to accomplish a task requires searching over an intractable set of potential team assignments [36]. In many cases there are simple heuristics that can guide subgroup formation; for instance, subgroups often contain agents with diverse capabilities, which limits potential assignments.

We demonstrate a novel method for discovering which agents will make effective subgroups based on an analysis of game data from successful team plays. After extracting the subgroups we implement a supervised learning mechanism to identify the *key group* of players most critical to each play.

The following are the three general types of cues that can be used for subgroup extraction:

- *Spatial*—relationships between team members that remain constant over a period of time
- *Temporal*—co-occurrence of related actions between different team members
- *Coordination*—dependencies between team members' actions

Our subgroup extraction method uses all of these to build a candidate set of subgroups. By examining mutual information between the offensive player, defensive blocker, and ball location along with the observed ball workflow, we can determine which players frequently coordinate in previously observed plays. Although automatic subgroup identification could be useful for applications (e.g., opponent modeling or game commentary), in this chapter we show how extracted subgroups can be used to limit the search space when creating new multiagent plays using two play generation methods: (1) play

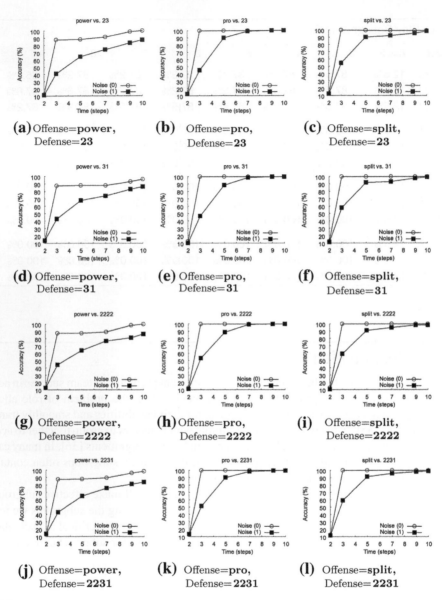

FIGURE 13.3

Classification results versus time, with and without noise for all offensive and defensive formation combinations. Observational noise is modeled on a zero mean Gaussian distribution with $\sigma = 1$ yard. For the no noise condition, there is a sharp jump in accuracy between timesteps 2 and 3, moving from chance accuracy to > 90%. Variants of the power offense are the most difficult to identify correctly; the classification is not perfect even at timestep 10 in the presence of noise. Based on these experiments, timestep 3 was selected as the best time for play adaptation, since delaying yields negligible improvements in play recognition for the no noise case.

adaptation of existing plays and (2) Monte Carlo search using Upper Confidence bounds applied to Trees (UCT).

The basic idea behind our approach is to identify subgroups of coordinated players by observing a large number of football plays. In our earlier work [23], we demonstrated that appropriately changing the behavior of a critical subgroup (e.g., QB, RB, FB) during an offensive play, in response to a recognized defensive strategy, significantly improves yardage; however, the previous work relied entirely on domain knowledge to identify the key players. In contrast, this work automatically determines the critical subgroups of players (for each play) by an analysis of spatiotemporal observations to determine all subgroups and supervised learning to learn which ones will garner the best results. Once the top-ranked candidate subgroup has been identified, we explore two different techniques for creating new plays: (1) dynamic play adaptation of existing plays and (2) a UCT search.

13.5.1 Automatic Subgroup Detection

To determine which players should be grouped together, we first must understand dependencies among the eight players for each formation. All players coordinate to some extent, but some players' actions are so tightly coupled that they form a *subgroup* during the given play. Changing the command for one athlete in a subgroup without adjusting the others causes the play to lose cohesion, potentially resulting in a yardage loss rather than a gain. We identify subgroups using a combination of two methods—the first based on a statistical analysis of player trajectories and the second based on workflow.

The mutual information between two random variables measures their statistical dependence. Inspired by this, our method for identifying subgroups attempts to quantify the degree to which the trajectories of players are coupled, based on a set of observed instances of the given play. However, the naive instantiation of this idea, which simply computes the dependence between player trajectories without considering the game state, is doomed to failure. This is because offensive players' motions are dominated by three factors: (1) its plan as specified by the playbook, (2) the current position of the ball, and (3) the current position of the defensive player assigned to block a play.

So, if we want to calculate the relationships between the offensive players, we need to place their trajectories in a context that considers these factors. Our method for doing this is straightforward. Rather than computing statistics on raw player trajectories, we derive a feature that includes these factors and compute statistics between the feature vectors as follows.

First, for each player on the offense, we determine the trajectory of the defensive player assigned to block him. Since this assigned defensive player is typically the opponent that remains closest to the player during the course of the play, we determine the assigned defender to be the one whose average distance to the given player is the least. More formally, for a given offensive player, $o \in \{o_1, \ldots, o_8\}$, the assigned defender, $d \in \{d_1, \ldots, d_8\}$, is:

$$d = \arg \min_{d_i} \sum_{t=1}^{T} |o(t) - d_i(t)|_2, \tag{13.1}$$

where $o(t)$ and $d_i(t)$ denote the 2D positions of the given players at time t. Our feature $f(t)$ is simply the centroid (average) of $o(t)$, $d(t)$, and the ball position $b(t)$:

$$f(t) = \frac{1}{3} \left[o(t) + d(t) + b(t) \right]. \tag{13.2}$$

We can now compute sets of features $\{f_i\}$ and $\{f_j\}$ from the collection of observed plays for a given pair of offensive players o_i and o_j, treating observations through time simply as independent measurements. We model the distributions F_i and F_j of each of these features as 2D Gaussian distributions with diagonal covariance.

We then quantify the independence between these feature distributions using the symmetricized Kullback-Leibler divergence [21]:

$$S(o_i, o_j) = D_{KL}(F_i\|F_j) + D_{KL}(F_j\|F_i) \tag{13.3}$$

where

$$D_{KL}(F_i\|F_j) = \sum_k F_i(k) \log \left[\frac{F_i(k)}{F_j(k)} \right]. \tag{13.4}$$

Pairs of athletes with low $S(.)$ are those whose movements during a given play are closely coupled. We compute the average $S(.)$ score over all pairs (o_i, o_j) in the team and identify as candidate subgroups those pairs with scores that falls in the lowest quartile. Figure 13.4 shows an example of connections detected using this metric.

The grouping process involves more than just finding the mutual information (MI) between players. We must also determine relationships formed based on possession of the football. When the QB hands the ball off to the RB or FB their movements are coordinated for only a brief span of time before the ball

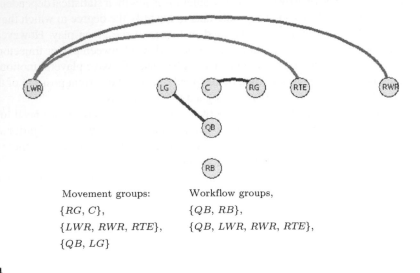

Movement groups:

$\{RG, C\}$,

$\{LWR, RWR, RTE\}$,

$\{QB, LG\}$

Workflow groups,

$\{QB, RB\}$,

$\{QB, LWR, RWR, RTE\}$,

FIGURE 13.4

Connections found by measuring D_{KL} mutual information in the Pro vs. 23 formations. These links reveal players whose movements during a play are closely coupled. Connected players are organized into a list of *movement groups*. *Workflow groups* represent how ball possession is transferred between players during a play. These lists of subgroups are used as candidates for dynamic play adaptation, since modifying the actions of these players is likely to radically influence the play's outcome. To avoid destroying these interdependencies, the play-adaptation system modifies the actions of these players as a group rather than individually.

is transferred to the next player. Because of this, the MI algorithm described before does not adequately capture this relationship. We developed another mechanism to identify such *workflows* and add them to the list of MI-based groups.

Our characterization of the workflow during a play is based on ball transitions. Given our dataset, we count transitions from one player to another. The historical data indicates that, in almost all offensive formations, the RB receives the ball the majority of the time, lessened only when the FB is in play, in which case we see the ball typically passed from the QB to either the RB or the FB. Consequently, the {QB, RB, and FB} naturally forms a group for *running plays*, termed a "key group" in Laviers and Sukthankar [23]. The same happens between the QB and the players receiving the ball in *passing plays*, which forms another workflow group {QB, LWR, RWR, and RTE}. The final list of candidates is therefore simply the union of the MI candidates and the workflow candidates (see Figure 13.4).

13.5.2 Dynamic Play Adaptation

Figure 13.5 gives an overview of the dynamic play-adaptation system; based on our estimate of the most likely defensive formation sensed early in the play (at time $t = 3$), we switch the key subgroup to an

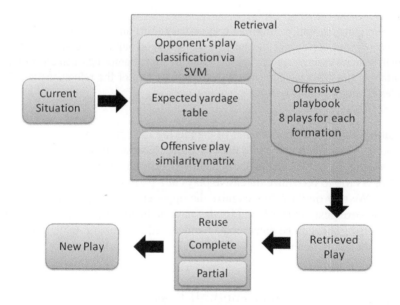

FIGURE 13.5

Overview of the dynamic play adaptation system. Shortly after the start of play, the defensive play is recognized using a set of SVM classifiers. The performance history of the currently executing offensive play versus the recognized defensive play is calculated using the expected yardage table. If it falls below an acceptable threshold, candidate offensive plays for play adaptation are identified using the offensive play similarity matrix. The aim is to find a better performing offensive play that is sufficiently similar to the currently executing one such that the transition can be made without problems. The play-adaptation system can opt for partial reuse (only modifying the actions of a subset of players) or complete reuse (switching all players to the new play).

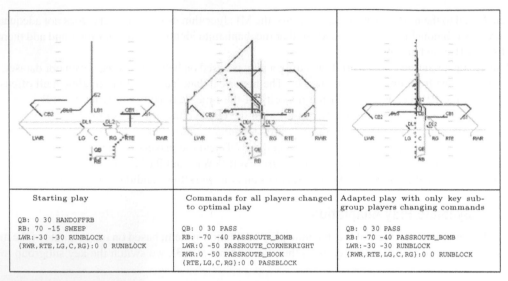

Starting play	Commands for all players changed to optimal play	Adapted play with only key sub-group players changing commands
QB: 0 30 HANDOFFRB RB: 70 -15 SWEEP LWR:-30 -30 RUNBLOCK {RWR,RTE,LG,C,RG}:0 0 RUNBLOCK	QB: 0 30 PASS RB: -70 -40 PASSROUTE_BOMB LWR:0 -50 PASSROUTE_CORNERRIGHT RWR:0 -50 PASSROUTE_HOOK {RTE,LG,C,RG}:0 0 PASSBLOCK	QB: 0 30 PASS RB: -70 -40 PASSROUTE_BOMB LWR:-30 -30 RUNBLOCK {RWR,RTE,LG,C,RG}:0 0 RUNBLOCK

FIGURE 13.6

Example of dynamic play adaptation. Given an original play (*left*) and a historically strong counter to the recognized defense (*center*), we change the behavior of a key subgroup to generate the adapted play (*right*). The bold (*green*) line shows the average yardage gained. Note that attempting a complete play switch (*center*) is inferior to switching the key subgroup (*right*). (For interpretation of the references to color in this figure legend, the reader is referred to the web version of this book.)

existing play that has the best a priori chance of countering the opponent's strategy (see Figure 13.6). Note that attempting to switch the entire play once execution has started is *less* effective than adapting the play in a limited manner by only changing the behavior of a key subgroup. As described in Section 13.4, we trained a set of SVMs to recognize defensive plays at a particular time horizon based on observed player trajectories. We rely on these to recognize the opponent's strategy at an early stage in the play and we identify the strongest counter based on the yardage history of the offensive playbook against the recognized defense. This can be precomputed and stored in a lookup table indexed by the current offensive play and the likely defense.

13.6 Offline UCT for Learning Football Plays

As an alternative to the simple one-time adaptation offered by the play-switch method, we investigated the use of UCT (Upper Confidence bounds applied to Trees) [19], a more powerful policy-generation method that performs Monte Carlo rollouts of the complete game from the current state [22]. Monte Carlo search algorithms have been successfully used in games that have large search spaces [10,8,7,45]. In UCT, an upper confidence bound, Q^+, is calculated for each node in the tree based on the reward history and the number of state visitations. This bound is used to direct the search to the branches most likely to contain the optimal plan; unlike $\alpha - \beta$ pruning, the upper-confidence bound is not used to prune actions. After the rollout budget for a level of the game tree has been exhausted, the action with the highest value of Q^+ is selected and the search commences at the next level. The output of the algorithm is a policy that governs the movement of the players.

Here we describe a method for creating customized offensive plays designed to work against a specific set of defenses. Using the top-ranked extracted subgroups to focus the investigation of actions yields significant runtime reduction over a standard UCT implementation. To search the complete tree without using our subgroup selection method would require an estimated 50 days of processing time in contrast to the 4 days required by our method.

Offensive plays in the Rush 2008 Football Simulator share the same structure across all formations. Plays typically start with a `runTo` command, which places a player at a strategic location to execute another play command. After the player arrives at this location, there is a decision point in the play structure where an offensive action can be executed. To effectively use a UCT style exploration we needed to devise a mechanism for combining these actions into a hierarchical tree structure in which the most important choices are decided first.

Because of the potentially prohibitive number of possible location points, we initially search through the possible combinations of offensive high-level commands for the key players, even though chronologically the commands occur later in the play sequence. Once the commands are picked for the players, the system employs binary search to search the `runTo` area for each of the players—see Figure 13.7(a). The system creates a bounding box around each player's historical `runTo` locations, and at Level 2 (immediately after the high-level command is selected), the bounding box is split in half. Following Monte Carlo expansion the location is initially randomly selected. At Level 3 the space is again divided in half and the process continues until Level 5 in Figure 13.7(b), where the player is provided a `runTo` location, which represents 1/16 of the bounding box area. The system takes a sample only at the leaf.

This 2D search was designed to maintain as small a sampling as possible without harming the system's chance of finding solutions that produce large yardage gains. To focus the search, the locations each player can move to are bounded to be close (within 1 yard) to the region covered by the specific player in the training data. At the leaf node, the centroid of the square is calculated and the player

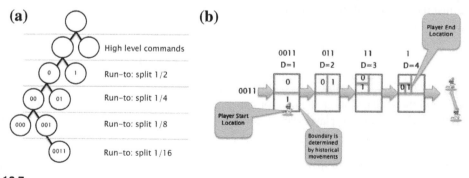

FIGURE 13.7

2D location binary search. (a) A representation of the UCT sparse tree for one player. (b) This graph shows how the binary string generated in the search tree creates a location for a player to move to in the `runTo` portion of the play.

uses that location to execute the `runTo` command. Our method effectively allows the most important features to be considered first and the least important last. For comparison, we implemented a similar algorithm that picks random points within the bounding box rather than using the binary split method to search the continuous space of `runTo` actions.

As mentioned, action modifications are limited to the players in the top-ranked subgroup identified using K*; the other players execute commands from the original play. Our system needs to determine the best plan over a wide range of opponent defensive configurations. To do this, for each rollout the system randomly samples 50% of all possible defenses (evens or odds, one for testing and the other for training) and returns the average yardage gained in the sampling. Since the UCT method provides a ranked search with the most likely solutions grouped near the start of the search, we limit the search algorithm to 2500 rollouts with the expectation that a good solution will be found in this search space.

We implemented UCT in a distributed system constructed in such a way to prevent multiple threads from sampling the same node. The update function for $n(s, a)$ was modified to increment the counter after the node is visited but before the leaf is sampled. Since sampling takes close to one second, it is imperative for the exploring threads to know when a node is touched to avoid infinite looping at a node.

After a node is sampled, the update function is called to update $Q(s, a)$.

$$Q(s, a) \leftarrow Q(s, a) + \frac{1}{n(s, a)} \left(R - Q(s, a) \right) \tag{13.5}$$

and

$$R = \frac{\sum_{i=0}^{I} \gamma_i}{I} / 15, \tag{13.6}$$

where R is the reward, I is the total number of iterations multiplied by the number of defenses sampled, and γ is the list of yards gained in each sample.

Action selection is performed using a variant of the UCT formulation, $\pi(s, a) = \text{argmax}_a(Q^+(s, a))$, where π is the policy used to choose the best action a from state s. Before revisiting a node, each unexplored node from the same branch must have already been explored; selection of unexplored nodes is accomplished randomly. Using a similar modification to the bandit as suggested in Balla and Fern [4], we adjust the upper confidence calculation

$$Q^+(s, a) = Q(s, a) + c \times \sqrt{\frac{\log n(s)}{n(s, a)}}$$

to employ $c = Q(s, a) + .\varsigma$, where $\varsigma = 0.0001$ for our domain.

We evaluated the efficacy of our method for generating passing plays, which require tightly coupled coordination between multiple players to succeed. Figure 13.8 shows the learning rate for the three proposed search procedures:

Binary Search with Key Groups: Binary search is used to identify `runTo` locations for the players and the UCT search is conducted for a subgroup of key players. The other players use the commands from the Rush playbook for the specified offensive play.

Random Placement with Key Groups: The `runTo` location is randomly selected for the players, and UCT search is conducted for a subgroup of key players.

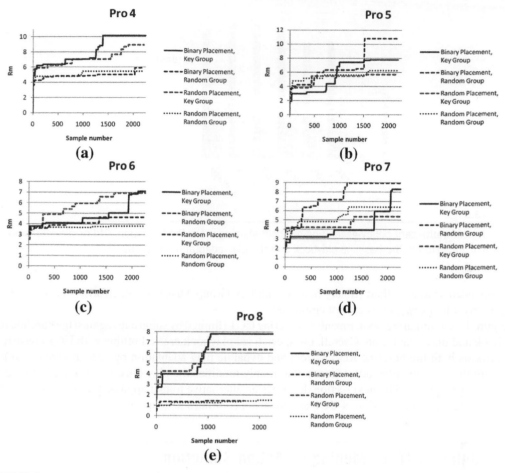

FIGURE 13.8

Binary search with key groups performs the best in most but not all of the cases. Rm is the argmax of the running average of the last ten rewards and represents a good approximation of the expected yardage gained by using the best play at that sample.

Random Placement, Random Players: We use the random group that performed the best in prior experiments, and the `runTo` location is randomly selected.

Our version of UCT was seeded with Pro formation variants (4–8). Each configuration was run for three days and accumulated 2250 samples (a total of 80 days of CPU time). The x-axis represents the sample number and the y-axis represents Rm $= \arg \max(\Gamma)$ and $\Gamma = \dfrac{1}{10} \sum_{i=0}^{10} Reward_{current-1}$. All methods perform about equivalently well with a low number of samples, but by 2000 samples, our

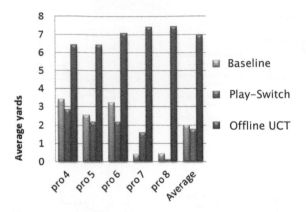

FIGURE 13.9

Comparison of multiagent policy-generation methods starting in the Pro formation. Offline play customization using UCT outperforms the baseline playbook and the play-adaptation method.

recommended search method (Binary Search with Key Groups) usually outperforms the other options, particularly when key groups are not employed.

Figure 13.9 summarizes experiments comparing UCT (limited by subgroup) against the baseline Rush playbook and play adaptation. Overall, the specialized playbook created offline with UCT consistently outperforms both the baseline Rush system and dynamic play adaptation by several yards. The main flaw with the dynamic play adaptation is that it only modifies the play once in response to the results of the play recognizer. The next section describes an alternative to that approach in which the policy is learned using an online version of UCT and the team continues to adapt in real time.

13.7 Online UCT for Multiagent Action Selection

Often in continuous-action games the information from plan recognition is used in an ad hoc way to modify the agent's response, particularly when the agent's best response is relatively obvious. In this section, we describe how coupling *plan recognition* with *plan repair* can be a powerful combination, particularly in multiagent domains where replanning from scratch is difficult to do in real time.

Paradoxically, plan repair can easily get worse over all play performance by causing miscoordinations between players; even minor timing errors can significantly compromise the efficacy of a play. Moreover, it is difficult to predict future play performance at intermediate play-execution stages since effective and ineffective plays share many superficial similarities. This section introduces an approach for learning effective plan repairs using a real-time version of UCT. Data from offline UCT searches is leveraged to learn state and reward estimators capable of making limited predictions of future actions and play outcomes. Our UCT search procedure uses these estimators to calculate successor states and rewards in real time. Experiments show that the plan repairs learned by our method offer significant improvements over the offensive plays executed by the baseline (non-AI system) and also a heuristic-based repair method. Figure 13.10 provides an overview of the key elements of our implementation.

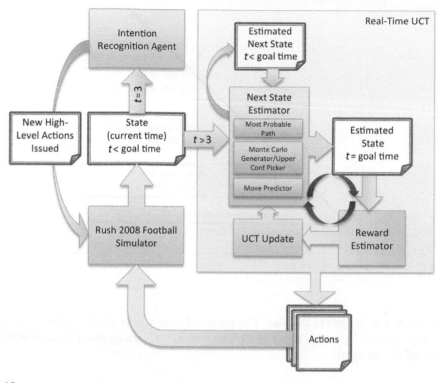

FIGURE 13.10

High-level diagram of our system. To run in real time, our variant of UCT uses a successor state estimator learned from offline traces to calculate the effects of random rollouts. The reward is estimated from the projected terminal state (just before the QB is expected to throw the ball, designated in the diagram as the goal time).

Prior work on UCT for multiagent games has either relied on hand-coded game simulations [4] or use of the actual game to evaluate rollouts (as is done in our offline UCT implementation). In this section, we describe how data from the millions of games run during the offline UCT play generation process can be used to enable online UCT. A similar approach was demonstrated by Gelly and Silver [12] in which the value function used by UCT is learned during offline training. This value function is then used during an online UCT search, significantly improving the search's performance. Their approach is to initialize Q values using previously learned Q and n values for each state visited during the offline learning process. Rather than using previously initialized Q values, we learn new Q values but use data from previous games to learn movement predictors and reward estimators.

13.7.1 Method

Each play is segmented into three parts: (1) the time period before the system can determine the defensive play, (2) the period between recognition and the time when the QB throws the ball, and (3) the time

FIGURE 13.11

The timeline of events comprising one play.

between the throw and the end of the play. The proposed system only controls players' actions in the third segment (Figure 13.11) so that $4 \leq t < 11$. Our system for learning plan repairs in real time relies on the following components.

Play recognizer: We treat the problem of play recognition as a multiclass classification problem to identify the formation and play variant currently being executed by the defense. Although recognizing the static formation is straightforward, early recognition of play variants is challenging. We achieve 90% accuracy at time $t = 3$ using a multiclass SVM. At $t = 3$ the key players are sent the high-level commands learned in the offline UCT algorithm to perform best for the specific variant in play. The players do not start executing the high-level commands until $t > 10$.

Next state estimator: To execute UCT rollouts in real time, our system must predict how defensive players will react as the offense adjusts its play. We train state and reward estimators using offline data from previous UCT searches and employ them in real time.

Reward estimator: To calculate UCT Q-values in the predicted future state, the system estimates reward (yardage) based on relative positions of the players. Because of the inherent stochasticity of the domain, it is difficult to learn a reward estimator early in the play. We focus on estimating yardage at a later stage of the play—just before we expect the QB to throw the ball.

UCT search: Using the state and reward estimators, we use the UCT search algorithm to generate a sparse tree to select actions for the key offensive players, a three-player subset of the team is automatically determined in advance. The search procedure is reexecuted at every timestep to account for unexpected actions taken by the defense.

Rush simulator: The selected player actions are issued to the Rush simulator via network sockets. The simulator returns the new locations of all offensive and defensive players to be used by the estimators.

13.7.2 **UCT Search**

After recognizing the play, UCT is employed to search for the best action available to each of the key players (Figure 13.12). Key players are a subset of three offensive players identified offline for a specific formation. As described in Section 13.6, UCT seeks to maximize the upper-confidence bound by preferentially exploring regions with the best probability of producing a high reward. The UCT search is repeatedly called for a predetermined number of rollouts; our real-time implementation sets $N = 2000$, which produced the best results while still allowing real-time execution.

We define $s \in S$, where S is in the set of locations of all players as well as the location of the ball. Action a contains the combination of actions for key players, $a = \{a_1, a_2, a_3\}$, where $a_{1,2,3} \in$ {Left, upLeft, ..., downLeft} for a total of eight possible actions.

For the online UCT algorithm, we set the upper-confidence calculation to:

$$Q^+(s, a) = Q(s, a) + c\sqrt{\frac{\log n(s)}{n(s, a)}}, \tag{13.7}$$

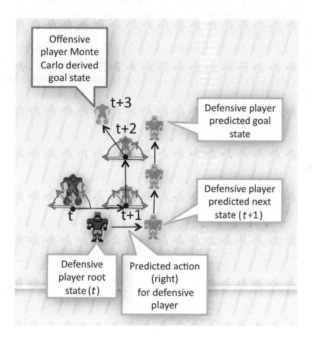

FIGURE 13.12

This image depicts one MC rollout for three timesteps starting at time $= t$. The Monte Carlo sparse tree generator determines the action and subsequent next state for the offensive key player and the move predictor uses that action and state information to predict the next action and state for the defensive player. This process is recursively called until the goal state is reached and for all defensive players and their closest offensive players. If the closest offensive player is not a key player, his actions are determined based on the most likely action he took historically.

where $c = \sqrt{2}$. We tested setting the upper confidence assuming $c = Q(s, a)$, which worked well in our offline UCT play-generation system [22]; unfortunately, this did not work as well in the real-time UCT system. Typically, c is a constant used to tune the biasing sequence to adjust exploration/exploitation of the search space. After extensive empirical evaluation, we found the original UCB1 form worked best. The quality function $Q(s, a)$, as in Section 13.6, is still the expected value of the node when taking action a from state s and ranges from 0 to 1.

After a node is sampled, the number of times the node is sampled $n(s, a)$ and $Q(s, a)$ is updated. This update occurs recursively from the leaf node to the root node and is the same as the offline UCT implementation. For this spatial-search problem, if actions are explored randomly, players will remain within a small radius of their starting positions. Even in conjunction with UCT, it is unlikely to find a good path. To eliminate circular travel, the system uses an attractive potential field [2] in the direction of the goal that guides exploration toward the correct end zone.

The path closest to the direction indicated by the potential field is selected as the primary angle. The two neighboring movement directions to the primary angle are also included in the action-search space. Assuming the potential field points up for all key players at time $= 8$, the expansion of the UCT tree would look like what is shown in Figure 13.13. Also, for every offensive formation, plan repairs are limited to a small subgroup of key players; the remaining players continue executing the original offensive play. The initial configuration of the players governs the players that are most likely to have a decisive impact on the play's success; by focusing search on a key subgroup of these three players (out of the total team of eight), we speed the search process significantly and concentrate the rollouts on higher expected reward regions. In the results section, we separately evaluate the contribution of these heuristics toward selecting effective plan repairs.

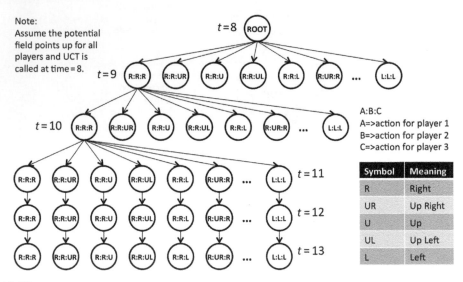

FIGURE 13.13

The real-time UCT expanded out at time $= 8$. After time $= 10$ the algorithm assumes a straight line until time $= 13$ to reduce the state space.

13.7.3 **Successor State Estimation**

To predict successor states in real time, we perform an incremental determination of where each player on the field could be at the next timestep. To accomplish this update, players are split into three groups: (1) defensive players, (2) offensive key players, and (3) offensive non-key players. The real-time UCT algorithm explores actions by the key players, and the successor state estimator seeks to predict how the defensive players will react to potential plan repairs. Locations of non-key offensive players are determined using the historical observation database to determine the most likely position each non-key offensive player will occupy, given the play variant and timestep. Rather than executing individual movement stride commands, these players are actually performing high-level behaviors built into the Rush simulator; thus, even though these players are technically under our control, we cannot predict with absolute certainty where they will be in the future.

Formally, the game state at time t can be expressed as the vector

$$\mathbf{s}(t) = (\mathbf{x}_{o1}, \ldots, \mathbf{x}_{o8}, \mathbf{x}_{d1}, \ldots, \mathbf{x}_{d8}, \mathbf{x}_b), \tag{13.8}$$

where $\mathbf{x}_{oi}$, $\mathbf{x}_{dj}$, and $\mathbf{x}_b$ denote the (x, y) positions of the offensive and defensive players and the ball, respectively. Similarly, we denote by a_{oi} and a_{dj} the actions taken by the offensive player oi and defensive player dj, respectively, and a_b denotes the action of the ball.

We predict the actions for the non-key offensive players from the historical archive of previously observed games; we simply advance the play according to the most likely action for each player and adjust the ball state accordingly. However, to determine the actions for the key offensive players (those whose actions will dramatically alter current play), we sample promising actions from the UCT tree using the Monte Carlo rollout. The goal is to alter the current play in a way that improves expected yardage.

Predicting the opponent's response to the altered play is more difficult. For this, we train a classifier to predict the next action of each defensive player dj based on its position and that of its closest offensive player:

$$o\varphi^j = \arg\min_{oi} ||\mathbf{x}_{dj} - \mathbf{x}_{oi}||^2. \tag{13.9}$$

In other words, the classifier learns the mapping:

$$(\mathbf{x}_{dj}(t), \mathbf{x}_{o\varphi}^j(t)) \mapsto a_{dj}(t + 1), \tag{13.10}$$

where $a \in A$ is selected from the discrete set of actions described before. We employ the J.48 classifier from the Weka machine learning toolkit (default parameters) for this purpose. The J.48 classifier is the Weka implementation of the C4.5 algorithm. Applying a_{dj} to the defensive player's position enables us to predict its future position, $\mathbf{x}_{dj}(t + 1)$. The classifier is trained offline using a set of observed plays and is executed online in real time to predict actions of defensive players.

We predict the play state forward up to the time τ, where we expect the QB to throw the ball. If by $t = \tau$, the QB has not thrown the ball, we continue predicting for five more timesteps. Table 13.2 shows the confusion matrix for the move predictor trained with 2000 instances and tested using 10-fold cross-validation. Note that this is an example of an unbalanced dataset in which certain actions are extremely rare.

Table 13.2 Combined Move Predictor Confusion Matrix

a	b	c	d	e	f	g	h	i	<–Predicted
5356	178	7	6	81	81	111	134	308	left
156	3975	80	0	8	11	2	30	8	upLeft
6	37	16,558	54	13	0	0	0	202	up
2	0	126	9791	1420	66	23	13	17	upRight
80	7	15	895	49,220	407	153	99	451	right
144	13	0	290	780	12,575	240	149	37	downRight
132	2	0	58	294	298	17,634	151	91	down
170	47	0	16	169	140	162	11,746	0	downLeft
181	10	150	21	285	7	63	0	23,758	stay

Note: Note that 94.13% were correctly classified.

13.7.4 Reward Estimation

The reward estimator is trained using examples of player configurations immediately preceding the QB throw. At this stage of the play, there is significantly less variability in the outcome than if we attempted to train a reward estimator based on earlier points in the play execution.

The raw training data was unbalanced, containing a disproportionate number of instances with a zero reward. To prevent the reward estimator from being biased toward predicting that none of the configurations will result in a positive reward, we rebalance the training set, discarding many of the samples with zero reward. This procedure helped reward ranges with very few samples to still influence the classifier. We started by finding the average number of instances in each reward bin and then limiting the count of instances to the average value. So if the dataset contained a mean of 100 samples of each value, after collecting 100 zero reward samples, the rest of the zeros in the sample set were discarded.

The reward estimator uses an input vector derived from the game state at the end of the prediction $s(\tau)$ consisting of a concatenation of the following attributes (Figure 13.14):

1. d_{QB}^i: distance of the QB with the ball to each key offensive player, $||\mathbf{x}_b - \mathbf{x}_{oi}||$
2. d_s^i: distance from each key offensive player to the scrimmage line
3. distance from each key offensive player to his closest opponent, $\min_{dj} ||\mathbf{x}_{oi} - \mathbf{x}_{dj}||$
4. $f_\Omega(\phi_i)$: the discretized angle from each key offensive player o_i to his closest opponent $d\rho^i$
5. sum of the angles traveled for each key offensive player k, $\sum_{w=0}^{W-1} \frac{\alpha_w^k}{W-1}$

The output is the expected yardage, quantized into seven bins. Our preliminary evaluations indicated that learning a continuous regression model for the yardage was much slower and did not improve accuracy. Therefore, we use the Weka J.48 classifier (default parameters) with the expected yardage treated as a discrete class (0–6). These bins roughly correspond to 10-yard increments (-10 to $+50$ yards gained per play).

We performed a 10-fold cross-validation to validate the effectiveness of the reward estimator. The estimator was correct in 43% of the instances and close to the correct answer 57% of the time. Since different executions from the same player positions can result in drastically different outcomes, accurately

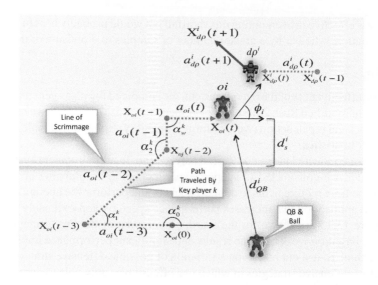

FIGURE 13.14

The features used in the reward classifier. This diagram shows one of the offensive key players oi, his closest defensive players $d\rho^i$, and the position of the QB holding the ball.

estimating reward is a nontrivial problem. Improving the classification accuracy could potentially improve the effectiveness of our system; however, even with our current reward estimator, the focused UCT search is able to identify promising plan repairs.

In Table 13.3 we show the sum of all the reward confusion matrices. This table highlights weak reward estimation results. Unfortunately, there are a significant number of instances that were classified very high and actually were very low, or classified very low and were actually high. This indicates to us that often there is very little difference in the state between a very successful play and nonsuccessful play.

Table 13.3 Combined Reward Estimation Confusion Matrix

0	1	2	3	4	5	6	←Predicted
639	5	10	14	515	637	23	0
5	12	6	0	2	0	0	1
6	11	9	1	6	2	0	2
24	0	0	5	21	16	1	3
450	1	5	18	933	282	13	4
597	0	0	22	302	775	30	5
30	0	0	1	36	46	11	6

Note: The original yardage rewards are discretized into bins ranging from 0–6. The classifier is correct 43% of the time and is close to correct in 57% of the classified instances. impressively, the online UCT algorithm does a good job of finding good actions even with imperfect reward information.

UCT in our case was effective in overcoming this shortfall but would probably benefit from improvement in the reward estimation, whether by a greater number of samples or a revision of the feature set.

13.7.5 Results

To demonstrate the effectiveness of the overall system, we compared the plans generated by the proposed method against the unmodified Rush 2008 engine (termed "baseline") and against a heuristic plan-repair system that selects a legal repair action (with uniform probability) from the available set, using potential field and key player heuristics.

Experiments were conducted using our Rush Analyzer and Test Environment system, shown earlier in Figure 13.1, which we constructed to support experimentation on planning and learning in Rush 2008. Because of the time requirements to connect sockets and perform file operations, RATE operates as a multi-threaded application that increases performance speed by approximately 500%.

Results in Figure 13.15 are shown for the fourth play variant of the Pro formation. This play was selected for testing based on weak baseline results and significant performance improvements with the offline UCT algorithm. To test our results on a variation of possible defensive strategies, we selected 10 of the most effective defensive strategies in which our offense was only able to garner 6.5 yards or less on average in the baseline tests. A two-tailed student t-test reveals that our approach (real-time UCT) outperforms both the baseline and heuristic approaches ($p < 0.01$) on total yardage gained.

In the baseline test using Rush's built-in playbook, the selected experimental offense was only able to gain on average 1.5 yards against the selected defensive strategies. Using play recognition and our

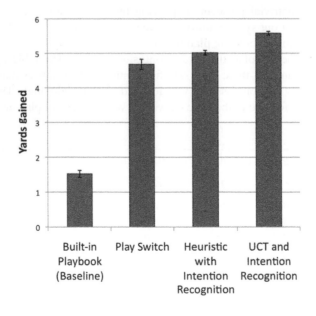

FIGURE 13.15

Relative performance of three systems compared to our real-time UCT algorithm. *Note:* Error bars mark a 95% confidence interval.

simple play-switch technique boosts performance by around 3 yards—the most significant performance increase shown. To beat that initial gain, we employ the offline UCT to learn the most effective high-level commands and real-time UCT to boost performance by another yard. In the heuristic with intention recognition condition, the system selects a legal repair action (with uniform probability) from the available set, using the potential field and key player heuristics.

13.8 Conclusion

A missing ingredient in effective opponent modeling for games is the ability to couple plan recognition with plan repair. This chapter describes a real-time method for learning plan repair policies and shows that it is possible to learn successor state and reward estimators from previous searches to do online multiagent Monte Carlo rollouts. Simultaneously predicting the movement trajectories, future reward, and play strategies of multiple players in real time is a daunting task, but we illustrate how it is possible to divide and conquer this problem with an assortment of data-driven game models. Our learned plan repair policies outperform both the baseline system and a simple heuristic-based plan repair method at improving yardage gained on each play execution. More important, our method results in a dramatic drop in the number of interceptions, which is likely to result in significantly longer ball possession periods within the context of a full game. Although the details of the learning process may differ, we believe that our techniques will generalize to other real-time, continuous, multiagent games that lack intermediate reward information (e.g., squad-based shooter games). Like American football, military operations have extensive planning and training phases, with well-rehearsed strategies for ground maneuvers, air battles between fighter jets, and naval encounters. Thus, we believe some aspects of our work will generalize well to military domains.

In future work, we plan to incorporate information about classifier error rates directly into plan repair to enable the calculation of "risk-sensitive" plan repair policies that consider the impact of prediction failures. In this particular domain, our play recognizer classifies plays with a $> 90\%$ accuracy, so this feature is not a priority. An unanswered question is the long-term effect of plan repair in computer opponents on player enjoyability. Our hypothesis is that adding plan repair increases the variability of game execution and results in an overall increase in player satisfaction based on the theory espoused by Wray and Laird [46]. However, it is possible that the plan repair algorithm needs to be tuned to provide play at the correct difficulty level rather than simply optimized to be maximally effective; studying the question of adaptive difficulty is an area of future research.

Acknowledgment

This research was partially supported by National Science Foundation award IIS-0845159. The views expressed in this document are those of the authors and do not reflect the official policy or position of the U.S. Air Force, Department of Defense, or the government.

References

[1] Aler R, Valls J, Camacho D, Lopez A. Programming Robosoccer agents by modeling human behavior. Expert Syst Appl 2009;36(2, Part 1):1850–9.

[2] Arkin R. Motor schema-based mobile robot navigation. Int J Robot Res 1989;8(4):92–112.

[3] Avrahami-Zilberbrand D, Kaminka G. Fast and complete symbolic plan recognition. In: Proceedings of International Joint Conference on Artificial Intelligence; 2005. p. 653–8.

[4] Balla R, Fern A. UCT for tactical assault planning in real-time strategy games. In: Proceedings of International Joint Conference on Artificial Intelligence; 2009. p. 40–5.

[5] Bhandari I, Colet E, Parker J, Pines Z, Pratap R, Ramanujam K. Advanced scout: data mining and knowledge discovery in NBA data. Data Min Knowl Discov 1997;1(1):121–5.

[6] Camerer C. Behavioral game theory: experiments in strategic interaction. Princeton University Press; 2003.

[7] Cazenave T. Nested Monte-Carlo search. In: Proceedings of International Joint Conference on Artificial Intelligence; 2009. p. 456–61.

[8] Cazenave T, Helmstetter B. Combining tactical search and Monte-Carlo in the game of Go. In: Processings of Computational Intelligene in Games; 2005. p. 171–5.

[9] Chang, C, Lin, C. LIBSVM: a library for support vector machines. Software available at <www.csie.ntu.edu.tw/cjlin/libsvm>; 2001.

[10] Chung M, Buro M, Schaeffer J. Monte Carlo planning in RTS games. In: Proceedings of the IEEE International Conference on Computational Intelligence in Games; 2005.

[11] Doshi P, Qu X, Goode A. Decision-theoretic planning in multiagent settings with application to modeling human strategic behavior. In: Sukthankar G, Goldman RP, Geib C, Pynadath DV, Bui HH, editors. Plan, activity, and intent recognition. Waltham, MA: Morgan Kaufmann Publishers; 2014. p. 205–26.

[12] Gelly S, Silver D. Combining online and offline knowledge in UCT. In: Proceedings of the International Conference of Machine Learning; 2007. p. 273–80.

[13] Genter K, Agmon N, Stone P. Role-based ad hoc teamwork. In: Sukthankar G, Goldman RP, Geib C, Pynadath DV, Bui HH, editors. Plan, activity, and intent recognition. Waltham, MA: Morgan Kaufmann Publishers; 2014. p. 251–72.

[14] Hess R, Fern A, Mortensen E. Mixture-of-parts pictorial structures for objects with variable part sets. In: Proceedings of International Conference on Computer Vision; 2007. p. 1–8.

[15] Intille S, Bobick A. A framework for recognizing multi-agent action from visual evidence. In: Proceedings of National Conference on Artificial Intelligence; 1999. p. 518–25.

[16] Jug M, Pers J, Dezman B, Kovacic S. Trajectory based assessment of coordinated human activity. In: Proceedings of the International Conference on Computer Vision Systems; 2003. p. 534–43.

[17] Kabanza F, Bellefeuille P, Bisson F, Benaskeur A, Irandoust H. Opponent behaviour recognition for real-time strategy games. In: Proceedings of the AAAI Workshop on Plan, Activity, and Intent Recognition; 2010.

[18] Kang Y, Lim J, Kankanhalli M, Xu C, Tian Q. Goal detection in soccer video using audio/visual keywords. In: International Conference on Information Processing; 2004. p. 1629–32.

[19] Kocsis L, Szepesvari C. Bandit based Monte-Carlo planning. In: European Conference on Machine Learning. Springer; 2006. p. 282–93.

[20] Kuhlmann G, Knox W, Stone P. Know thine enemy: a champion RoboCup coach agent. In: Proceedings of National Conference on Artificial Intelligence; 2006. p. 1463–8.

[21] Kullback S, Leibler R. On information and sufficiency. Ann Math Statist 1951;22(1):79–86.

[22] Laviers K, Sukthankar G. A Monte Carlo approach for football play generation. In: Proceedings of Artificial Intelligence for Interactive Digital Entertainment Conference; 2010. p. 150–5.

[23] Laviers K, Sukthankar G, Molineaux M, Aha D. Improving offensive performance through opponent modeling. In: Proceedings of Artificial Intelligence for Interactive Digital Entertainment Conference; 2009. p. 58–63.

[24] Li N, Stracuzzi D, Cleveland G, Langley P, Konik T, Shapiro D. Constructing game agents from video of human behavior. In: Proceedings of Conference on Artificial Intelligence and Interactive Digital Entertainment; 2009. p. 64–9.

[25] McCarthy J, Hayes P. Some philosophical problems from the standpoint of artificial intelligence. In: Machine intelligence. Edinburgh University Press; 1969. p. 463–502.

[26] Molineaux, M. Working specification for Rush 2008 interface. Technical Report Knexus Research Corp. May 2008.

[27] Molineaux M, Aha D, Sukthankar G. Beating the defense: using plan recognition to inform learning agents. In: Proceedings of Florida Artificial Intelligence Research Society; 2009. p. 337–42.

[28] Nair R, Tambe M, Marsella S, Raines T. Automated assistants for analyzing team behaviors. J Automat Agents Multi-agent Syst 2004;8(1):69–111.

[29] Nichols J, Claypool M. The effects of latency on online Madden NFL football. In: Proceedings of the International Workshop on Network and Operating Systems Support for Digital Audio and Video; 2004. p. 146–51.

[30] Pallavi V, Mukherjee J, Majumdar A, Sural S. Ball detection from broadcast soccer videos using static and dynamic features. J Vis Commun Image Represent October 2008;19(7):426–36.

[31] Riley P, Veloso M. On behavior classification in adversarial environments. In: Parker L, Bekey G, Barhen J, editors. Distributed Autonomous Robotic Systems 4. Springer-Verlag; 2000. p. 371–80.

[32] Riley P, Veloso M. Recognizing probabilistic opponent movement models. In: Birk A, Coradeschi S, Tadorokoro S, editors. RoboCup-2001: robot soccer world cup V. Springer-Verlag; 2002. p. 453–8.

[33] Riley P, Veloso M, Kaminka G. An empirical study of coaching. In: Asama H, Arai T, Fukuda T, Hasegawa T, editors. Distributed autonomous robotic systems 5. Springer-Verlag; 2002. p. 215–24.

[34] Smart Football. How do NFL players memorize all those plays? <http://smartfootball.com/grab-bag/how-do-nfl-players-memorize-all-those-plays>; 2011.

[35] Stone P, Veloso M. Task decomposition, dynamic role assignment, and low-bandwidth communication for real-time strategic teamwork. Artif Intell 1999;12:241–73.

[36] Sukthankar G, Sycara K. Simultaneous team assignment and behavior recognition from spatio-temporal agent traces. In: Proceedings of National Conference on Artificial Intelligence; July 2006. p. 716–21.

[37] Sukthankar G, Sycara K. Policy recognition for multi-player tactical scenarios. In: Proceedings of International Conference on Autonomous Agents and Multi-Agent Systems; May 2007. p. 59–65.

[38] Tambe M. Towards flexible teamwork. J Artif Intell Res 1997;7:83–124.

[39] Tanaka K, Nakashima H, Noda I, Hasida K. Mike: an automatic commentary system for soccer. In: Proceedings of the International Conference on Multi-Agent Systems; 1998. p. 285–92.

[40] Tanaka-Ishii K, Frank I, Arai K. Trying to understand Robocup. AI Mag 2000;21(3):19–24.

[41] USA Football. Let's talk football: how many plays should a playbook hold? <http://usafootball.com/news/coaches/lets-talk-football-how-many-plays-should-playbook-hold>.

[42] vanden Herik J, Donkers J, Spronck P. Opponent modeling and commercial games. In: Procceedings of the Symposium on Computational Intelligence and Games; 2005. p. 15–25.

[43] Vapnik V. Statistical learning theory. Wiley & Sons Inc; 1998.

[44] Voelz D, Andre E, Herzog G, Rist T. Rocco: a RoboCup soccer commentator system. In: Asada M, Kitano H, editors. RoboCup-98: robot soccer world cup II. Springer; 1999. p. 50–60.

[45] Ward CD, Cowling PI. Monte Carlo search applied to card selection in Magic: The Gathering. In: Proceedings of Computational Intelligence and Games; 2009. p. 9–16.

[46] Wray R, Laird J. Variability in human behavior modeling for military simulations. In: Proceedings of Behavior Representation in Modeling and Simulation Conference; 2003. p. 176–85.

[47] Yahoo! Answers. Football playbook: how many plays are usually in one? <http://answers.yahoo.com/question/index?qid=20080725053139AAX9wD7>; 2008.

Intent Recognition for Human–Robot Interaction

Richard Kelley, Alireza Tavakkoli, Christopher King, Amol Ambardekar, Liesl Wigand, Monica Nicolescu, and Mircea Nicolescu

University of Nevada, Reno, NV, USA

14.1 Introduction

For robots to operate in unstructured environments, they must be capable of interacting with humans. Although social interaction between robots and humans presently is extremely simple, one of the main goals of social robotics is to develop robots that can function in complicated settings such as homes, offices, and hospitals. To achieve this goal, robots must be capable of recognizing the intentions of the humans with whom they are designed to interact. This presents both opportunities and challenges to researchers developing intent-recognition techniques. The goal of this chapter is to provide an overview of these opportunities and challenges and to present a system we have developed that begins to address some of them.

In the context of human–robot interaction (HRI), the challenges and the opportunities for intent-recognition systems largely stem from the capabilities and constraints of the underlying robot's hardware. For instance, a modern robot may have access to fairly sophisticated sensor systems, such as a camera, that are capable of measuring the three-dimensional structure of the environment directly and in real time (as in the case of the Kinect, described in Section 14.3.1). However, the same robot may have severely limited processing capabilities that render complicated reasoning difficult to perform in real time. Or, as is increasingly likely, the robot may be operating in a networked environment in which it must offload some of its intent-recognition capabilities to other processors. In such cases, network latency adds additional challenges to real-time operation.

Although the (soft) real-time constraint has not been considered essential in many approaches to intent recognition, it is largely inescapable in the case of intent-recognition systems designed for HRI; the research that has been done on timing of actions in HRI suggests that actions must not only be correct but also must be timed to occur at interactionally significant points to have maximum effect [18]. This constraint leads to a number of design choices that are embodied in the systems we describe.

Our approach is ultimately based on psychological and neuroscientific evidence for a theory of mind [1], which suggests that the ease with which humans recognize the intentions of others is the result of an innate mechanism for representing, interpreting, and predicting other's actions. The mechanism relies on taking the perspective of others [2], which allows humans to correctly infer intentions. Although this process is innate to humans, it does not take place in a vacuum. Intuitively, it would seem that our understanding of others' intentions depends heavily on the contexts in which we find ourselves and those we observe. This intuition is supported by neuroscientific results [3], which suggest that the context of an activity plays an important and sometimes decisive role in correctly inferring underlying intentions.

Our approach to developing this ability in robots consists of two stages: *activity modeling* followed by *intent recognition*. During activity modeling, our robot performs the activities it will later be expected to understand, using data it collects to train parameters of hidden Markov models (HMMs) representing the activities. Each HMM represents a single "basic activity." The hidden states of those HMMs correspond to small-scale goals or subparts of the activities. Most important, the visible states of a model represent the way in which parameters relevant to the activity change over time. For example, a visible state *distance-to-goal* may correspond to the way in which an observed agent's distance to some activity's goal is changing—growing larger, smaller, or staying the same.

During intent recognition, the robot observes other agents interacting and performing various activities. The robot takes the perspective of the agents it is tracking and from there calculates the changes in all parameters of interest. It uses the results of the calculations as inputs to its previously trained HMMs, inferring intentions using those models in conjunction with its prior knowledge of likely intent given the robot's (previously determined) spatiotemporal context. For example, a robot meant to assist with cooking should be able to observe the actions of a person gathering eggs, milk, flour, and sugar in the kitchen, recognize the intention to bake a cake from this context, and assist, perhaps by finding a bowl.

After describing our system, we analyze its strengths and weaknesses, discuss how it can be extended and improved, and conclude with some general thoughts about the application of intent recognition to human–robot interaction.

14.2 Previous Work in Intent Recognition

This section briefly reviews some of the major work in intent recognition. Along the way, we highlight some of the limitations that make this work difficult to apply in real-time systems. We begin with a discussion of logical and Bayesian methods outside of robotics and then move on to methods that have found wider application in real-time systems.

14.2.1 Outside of Robotics

Outside of robotics, methods for plan recognition have, broadly speaking, fallen into two camps: logical and probabilistic. Some of the earliest approaches viewed plan recognition as an inverse problem to logical plan synthesis and were themselves logically based. The most notable of such approaches is that of Kautz [15]. As has been repeatedly observed in many areas of artificial intelligence (AI), purely logical methods suffer from a number of shortcomings; the most pronounced of them is their inability to account for the pervasive uncertainty found in most of the natural world [16]. In the field of plan recognition, one of the earliest arguments for the necessity of a probabilistic approach was provided by Charniak and Goldman [17]. In their paper, these authors observed a number of limitations of purely logical approaches and contend that Bayesian networks address them. They describe a system for natural-language understanding that successfully uses their approach.

14.2.2 **In Robotics and Computer Vision**

Unfortunately, both the logical and the Bayesian approaches just described are difficult to apply in human–robot interaction. There are a number of difficulties, largely dealing with resource constraints and the need to produce estimates at a rate of up to 30 hertz (Hz). We detail these issues later but here provide some discussion of methods that computer vision researchers and roboticists have used to predict intention in humans.

Previous work on intent recognition in robotics has focused on significantly simpler methods capable of working with sensor data under challenging time constraints. Much of the early work comes from the computer vision community or makes extensive use of computer vision techniques. Many of the systems that have aimed for real-time operation use fairly simple techniques (e.g., hidden Markov models).

Whenever one wants to perform statistical classification in a system that is evolving over time, HMMs may be appropriate [4]. Such models have been successfully used in problems involving speech recognition [5]. There is also some evidence that hidden Markov models may be just as useful in modeling activities and intentions. For example, HMMs have been used by robots to perform a number of manipulation tasks [6–8]. These approaches all have a crucial problem: They only allow the robot to detect that a goal has been achieved *after* the activity has been performed. To the extent that intent recognition is about prediction, these systems do not use HMMs in a way that facilitates the recognition of intentions. Moreover, there are reasons to believe (see Section 14.5.1) that without considering the disambiguation component of intent recognition, there will be unavoidable limitations on a system, regardless of whether it uses HMMs or any other classification approach.

The problem of recognizing intentions is important in situations where a robot must learn from or collaborate with a human. Previous work has shown that forms of simulation or perspective-taking can help robots work with people on joint tasks [10]. More generally, much of the work in learning by demonstration has either an implicit or an explicit component dealing with interpreting ambiguous motions or instructions. The work we present here differs from that body of research in that the focus is mostly on recognition in which the human is not actively trying to help the robot learn—ultimately, intent recognition and learning by demonstration differ in this respect.

The use of HMMs in real-time intent recognition (emphasizing the prediction element of the intent-recognition problem) was first suggested in Tavakkoli et al. [9]. That paper also elaborates on the connection between the HMM approach and theory of mind. However, the system proposed there has shortcomings that the present work seeks to overcome. Specifically, the authors show that in the absence of addition contextual information, a system that uses HMMs alone will have difficulty predicting intentions when two or more of the activities the system has been trained to recognize appear very similar. The model of perspective-taking that uses HMMs to encode low-level actions alone is insufficiently powerful to make predictions in a wide range of everyday situations.

14.3 **Intent Recognition in Human–Robot Interaction**

Performing operations with a robot places a number of constraints on an intent-recognition system. The most obvious is that the system must operate in real time, particularly if social interaction is required of the robot. However, a more crucial constraint is that the intent-recognition system must rely on the robot's sensors and actuators to obtain information about and to manipulate the world. This section introduces some of the key sensors our systems use to enable intent recognition. We also touch on actuators that may be relevant to this goal.

14.3.1 Sensors

Although humans use most of their senses to infer the intentions of others, robots are presently limited in the sensors they can use to recognize humans' intentions. In particular, the preferred sensor modality for robotic intent recognition is vision. Computer vision is a mature research area with well-established methods for performing tasks such as foreground–background segmentation, tracking, and filtering—all of which are important to intent recognition. In previous systems, we have used standard cameras to perform these tasks. With Microsoft's release of the Kinect, which provides depth information, we have moved to range images and point clouds.

In traditional camera systems, depth information has to be inferred through stereo algorithms [14]. Creating dense depth maps from conventional stereo rigs is challenging and computationally expensive. More recently, projected texture stereo has been used to improve the performance of traditional stereo [12]. Along these lines, Microsoft's Kinect provides a low-cost system that has dense, 640×480 depth maps at 30 Hz.

To process the output of these systems, there are essentially two format options: range images and point clouds. A *range image* is similar to a standard RGB image except that the value of a pixel represents the distance from the camera to the point in the scene that would have been imaged by a standard camera. A *point cloud* is simply a set of points in (usually) three-dimensional (3D) space. Given a range image and some easily estimated parameters of a camera, it is straightforward to produce a point cloud in which each point represents a sample from the scene. Both formats are useful because different methods are being developed for each. Many of the techniques of classic computer vision are applicable to range images [14]. Point clouds, however, require different techniques [13] (see Figure 14.1).

14.3.1.1 *Processing camera data*

We assume that the observer robot is stationary and observes a human interacting with various objects in a household or office setting over time. As it operates, the system takes input from a camera and performs the following steps:

Estimation of the 3D scene. In the case where the input comes from a regular camera, the system estimates three-dimensional information from the sequence of images making up the video stream. When the input comes from a Kinect, the system computes a point cloud and passes it to the next step of the processing pipeline.

Foreground–background segmentation. The system begins by segmenting out uninteresting regions from the cloud. In our office scene, this includes the floor, walls, and the table on which the objects of interest lie. This segmentation is performed using standard tools in the Point Cloud Library [13]. The output of this stage is a set of clouds corresponding to the objects of interest in the scene.

Appearance-based object recognition. Offline, we train a Gaussian mixture model for each object we want recognized. At runtime we use these models to perform classification for each segmented cloud. The output of this stage is a set of object labels and positions (centroids) computed from the

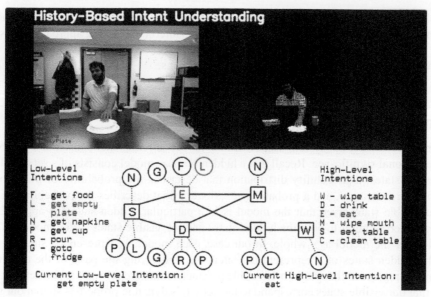

FIGURE 14.1

An example of a point cloud. Note: The image on the *left* of the display is captured from the RGB camera on a Kinect. The point cloud on the *right* is segmented so as to show only the human and the objects on the table.

classifier and the cloud information in step 1. This includes the locations of the human's head and hands.

Interaction modeling. Once the position of each object is known, the system tracks the human's motion across consecutive frames to determine whether he or she is reaching for anything. If a reaching action is detected, that information is sent to the intent-recognition system for further analysis.

At the end of the pipeline, the system produces either a classification or an action. Details regarding this further analysis appear in the next sections.

It is worth noting that in practice the preceding process is somewhat fragile. The information from the cameras is often noisy and sometimes simply wrong. We then perform symbolic reasoning on this data, which may suffer from additional modeling error (as discussed by Charniak and Goldman). Essentially, each step in the pipeline may add errors to the system.

14.3.2 Actuators

Although intent recognition relies primarily on a robot's sensors, the actuators available to a system may place some constraints on the system's ability to learn. A robot may gather data by performing the activity itself, which may be difficult or impossible. In systems that rely on theory of mind, it may be difficult for a robot to perform perspective-taking with respect to a human if the robot is not a humanoid.

For example, if a person is typing, a robot is unlikely to be able to perform that action. To address this problem on wheeled mobile robots, we have developed an alternate learning approach that is described in Section 14.4. Actuators also influence the system's ability to respond to the perceived intentions, which allows the robot to give additional feedback to humans.

14.4 HMM-Based Intent Recognition

As mentioned previously, our system uses HMMs to model activities that consist of a number of parts that have intentional significance. Recall that a hidden Markov model consists of a set of hidden states, a set of visible states, a probability distribution that describes the probability of transitioning from one hidden state to another, and a probability distribution that describes the probability of observing a particular visible state given that the model is in a particular hidden state. To apply HMMs, one must give an interpretation to both the hidden states and the visible states of the model, as well as an interpretation for the model as a whole. In our case, each model, λ, represents a single well-defined activity. The hidden states of λ represent the intentions underlying the parts of the activity, and the visible symbols represent changes in measurable parameters that are relevant to the activity. Notice, in particular, that our visible states correspond to the activity's dynamic properties so that our system can perform recognition as the observed agents are interacting.

As an example, consider the activity of meeting another person. To a first approximation, the act of meeting someone consists of approaching the person up to a point, interacting with the stationary person in some way (e.g., talking, exchanging something), and then parting. In our framework, we would model meeting using a single HMM. The hidden states would correspond to approach, halt, and part, since these correspond to the short-term intermediate goals of the meeting activity. When observing two people meeting, the two parameters of interest that we can use to characterize the activity are the distance and the angle between the two agents we are observing; in a meeting activity, we would expect that both the distance and the angle between two agents would decrease as the agents approach and face one another. With this in mind, we make the visible states represent changes in the distance and angle between two agents. Since each of these parameters is a real number, it can either be positive, negative, or (approximately) zero. There are then nine possibilities for a pair representing "change in distance" and "change in angle," and each of these possibilities represents a single visible state that our system can observe.

14.4.1 Training

We train our system in two ways. In situations in which the robot can perform the activity, we have it perform that activity. With a Pioneer robot, this approach makes sense for activities such as "follow an agent" or "pass by that person." As the robot performs the activity, it records features related to its motion (e.g., speed, direction, changes in its position relative to other agents). These are then converted to discrete symbols as described in the previous section. The symbols are then used to train HMMs representing each activity.

In situations in which the robot cannot perform the activity (in our case, this included reaching for most objects), the system observes a human performing the task. The same features of the motion are recorded as in the previous training method and are used to train an HMM.

In both cases, the topologies of the HMMs and the interpretations of the hidden and visible states are determined by hand. The number of training examples generated with either method was limited due to the fact that a human had to perform the actions. In all cases that follow, we found that, with just one or two dozen performances of the activities, the system was able to train reasonably effective HMMs.

14.4.2 Recognition

During recognition, the stationary robot observes a number of individuals interacting with one another and with stationary objects. It tracks those individuals using the visual capabilities described before and takes the perspective of the agents it is observing. Based on its perspective-taking and its prior understanding of the activities it has been trained to understand, the robot infers the intention of each agent in the scene. It does this using maximum-likelihood estimation, calculating the most probable intention given the observation sequence it has recorded up to the current time for each pair of interacting agents.

14.5 Contextual Modeling and Intent Recognition

In this section we argue for the addition of contextual information to assist in the prediction of intent. We start by exploring the distinction between activity recognition and intent recognition.

14.5.1 Activity Recognition and Intent Recognition

Although some researchers consider the problems of activity recognition and intent recognition to be essentially the same, a common claim is that intent recognition differs from activity recognition in that intent recognition has a predictive component. That is, by determining an agent's intentions, we are in effect making a judgment about what we believe are the likely actions of the agent in the immediate or near future; whereas activity recognition is recognizing what is happening now. Emphasizing the *predictive* component of intent recognition is important, but it may not reveal all the significant facets of the problem. For further discussion of intent-versus-activity recognition, see Yiannis [19].

In contrast to the more common view of intent recognition in the computer vision community, which ignores intent or considers it equivalent to action, we contend that *disambiguation* of activities based on underlying intentions is an essential task that any completely functional intent-recognition system must be capable of performing. For example, if a person's activity is reading a book, her or his intention may be homework or entertainment. In emphasizing the disambiguation component of an intent-recognition system, we recognize that there are some pairs of actions that may appear identical in all respects except for their underlying intentions.

For an example of intent recognition as disambiguation, consider an agent playing chess. When the agent reaches for a chess piece, we can observe that activity and ascribe to the agent any number of possible intentions. Before the game, an agent reaching for a chess piece may be putting the piece into its initial position; during the game, the agent may be making a move using that piece; and after the game, the agent may be cleaning up by putting the piece away. In each of these cases, it is entirely possible (if not likely) that the activity of reaching for the piece will appear identical to the other cases. It is only the intentional component of each action that distinguishes it from the others. Moreover, this component is determined by the context of the agent's activity: before, during, or after the game. Notice that we need to infer the agent's intention in this example even when we are not interested in making any predictions. Disambiguation in such circumstances is essential to even a basic understanding of the agent's actions.

14.5.2 Local and Global Intentions

In our work, we distinguish between two kinds of intentions, which we call local and global intentions. *Local* intentions exist on smaller time scales and may correspond to the individual parts of a complex activity. For example, if two agents are performing a "meeting" activity, they may approach one another, stop for some length of time, and then part ways. Each of these three components would correspond to a different local intention. In our approach, the local intentions are modeled using the hidden states of our HMMs, although, of course, there will be other ways to achieve the same result. As this modeling choice implies, though, local intentions are closely tied to particular activities, and it may not even be sensible to discuss these sorts of intentions outside of a given activity or set of activities.

In contrast, *global* intentions exist on larger time scales and correspond to complex activities in a particular context. In our chess example, "setting up the board," "making a move," and "cleaning up" would all correspond to possible global intentions of the system.

This distinction between local and global intentions may be most useful during the activity-modeling stage, if the activities being considered are sufficiently simple that they lack the internal structure that would lead to several local intentions; it may be that HMMs are not necessary for the system, so a simpler purely Bayesian approach could be used instead. In this way, the distinction between local and global intentions can be used to develop a sense of the complexity of the activities being modeled in a given application.

14.5.3 Lexical Directed Graphs

Given that context is sometimes the decisive factor enabling human intent recognition [3], it makes sense to create robot architectures that use contextual information to improve performance. While there are many sources of contextual information that may be useful to infer intentions, we chose to focus primarily on the information provided by object affordances—features that indicate the actions that one can perform with an object (e.g., a handle that allows grabbing). The problem, once this choice is made, is one of training and representation: given that we wish the system to infer intentions from contextual information provided by knowledge of object affordances, how do we learn and represent those affordances? We would like, for each object our system may encounter, to build a representation that contains the likelihood of all actions that can be performed on that object.

Although there are many possible approaches to constructing such a representation, we chose to use a representation based heavily on a graph–theoretic approach to natural language—in particular, English. Given an object, our goal is to connect it to related actions and objects. To this end, we collect sentences that contain that object and include the words in a graph that describes the relationships between them. Specifically, we construct a directed graph in which the vertices are words and a labeled, weighted edge exists between two vertices if and only if the words corresponding to the vertices exist in some kind of grammatical relationship. The label indicates the nature of the relationship, and the edge weight is proportional to the frequency with which the pair of words exists in that particular relationship.

This is a lexical-directed graph, or digraph. For example, we may have the vertices *drink* and *water*, along with the edge $((drink, water), direct\_object, 4)$, indicating that the word "water" appears as a direct object of the verb "drink" four times in the experience of the system. From this graph, we compute probabilities that provide the necessary context to interpret an activity. It is likely that spoken and written natural language is not enough (on its own) to create reasonable priors for activity and intent recognition. However, we suggest that for a wide range of problems, natural language can provide information that improves prediction over systems that do not use contextual information at all.

14.5.3.1 *Using language for context*

The use of a linguistic approach is well motivated by human experience. Natural language is a highly effective vehicle for expressing facts about the world, including object affordances. Moreover, it is often the case that such affordances can be easily inferred directly from grammatical relationships, as in the preceding example.

From a computational perspective, we would prefer time- and space efficient models, both to build and to use. If the graph we construct to represent our affordances is sufficiently sparse, then it should be space efficient. As we discuss in the following, the graph we use has a number of edges that are linear in number of vertices, which is in turn linear in the number of sentences the system "reads." We thus attain space efficiency. Moreover, we can efficiently access the neighbors of any vertex using standard graph algorithms.

In practical terms, the wide availability of texts that discuss or describe human activities and object affordances means that an approach to modeling affordances based on language can scale well beyond a system that uses another means for acquiring affordance models. For example, the use of online encyclopedias to create word graphs provides us with an immense breadth of concepts to connect to an object, as well as decent relationship estimates. The act of "reading" about the world can, with the right model, replace direct experience for the robot in many situations.

Note that this discussion makes an important assumption that, although convenient, may not be accurate in all situations. Namely, we assume that for any given action–object pair, the likelihood of the edge representing that pair in the graph is at least approximately equal to the likelihood that the action takes place in the world. Or in other words, we assume that linguistic frequency sufficiently approximates action frequency. Such an assumption is intuitively reasonable. We are more likely to read a book than we are to throw a book; as it happens, this fact is represented in our graph. However, depending on the source of the text, it may be skewed. A news website might suggest extreme situations (e.g., accidents and disasters), while a blog might focus on more mundane events. We are currently exploring the extent to which the text occurrence assumption is valid and may be safely relied on; at this point, though, it appears that the assumption is valid for a wide enough range of situations to allow for practical use in the field.

14.5.3.2 *Dependency parsing and graph representation*

To obtain our pairwise relationships between words, we use the Stanford-labeled dependency parser. The parser takes as input a sentence and produces the set of all pairs of words that are grammatically related in the sentence along with a label for each pair, as in the previous "water" example.

Using the parser, we construct a graph, $G = (V, E)$, where E is the set of all labeled pairs of words returned by the parser for all sentences and each edge is given an integer weight equal to the number of times the edge appears in the text parsed by the system. V then consists of the words that appear in the corpus processed.

14.5.3.3 Graph construction and complexity

Given a labeled dependency parser and a set of documents, graph construction is straightforward. Briefly, the steps are

1. Tokenize each document into sentences.
2. For each sentence, build the dependency parse of the sentence.
3. Add each edge of the resulting parse to the graph.

Each of these steps can be performed automatically with reasonably good results using well-known language-processing algorithms. The end result is the previously described graph that the system stores for later use.

One of the greatest strengths of the dependency-grammar approach is its space efficiency: the output of the parser is either a *tree* on the words of the input sentence or it is a graph made up of a tree plus a (small) constant number of additional edges. This means that the number of edges in our graph is a linear function of the number of nodes in the graph, which (assuming a bounded number of words per sentence in our corpus) is linear in the number of sentences the system processes. In our experience, the digraphs the system has produced have had statistics confirming this analysis, as can be seen by considering the graph used in our recognition experiments.

For our corpus, we used two sources: first, the simplified- English Wikipedia, which contains many of the same articles as the standard Wikipedia except with a smaller vocabulary and simpler grammatical structure, and second, a collection of children's stories about the objects in which we were interested [20]. In Figure 14.2, we show the number of edges in the Wikipedia graph as a function of the number of vertices at various points during the rendering of the graph. The scales on both axes are identical, and the graph shows that the number of edges for it does depend linearly on the number of vertices.

The final Wikipedia graph we used in our experiments contained 244,267 vertices and 2,074,578 edges. The children's story graph is much smaller, being built from just a few hundred sentences: it consists of 1754 vertices and 3873 edges. This graph was built to fill in gaps in the information contained in the Wikipedia graph. The stories were selected from what could be called "children's nonfiction"; the books all contained descriptions and pictures of the world and were chosen to cover the kinds of situations in which we trained our system to work. The graphs were merged to create the final graph we used by taking the union of the vertex and edge sets of them then adding the edge weights of any edges that appeared in both graphs.

14.5.3.4 Induced subgraphs and lexical "noise"

In some instances, our corpus may contain strings of characters that do not correspond to words in English. This is especially a problem if the system automatically crawls a resource, such as the worldwide Web, to find its sentences. We use the term *lexical noise* to refer to tokens that have vertices in our graph but are not in fact words in English. The extent to which such noise is a problem depends in large part on how carefully the documents are acquired, cleaned up, and tokenized into sentences before being given to the parser. Given the highly variable quality of many sources (e.g., blogs and other webpages), and the imperfect state of the art in sentence tokenization, it is necessary that we have a technique for removing lexical noise. Our current approach to such a problem is to work with induced subgraphs.

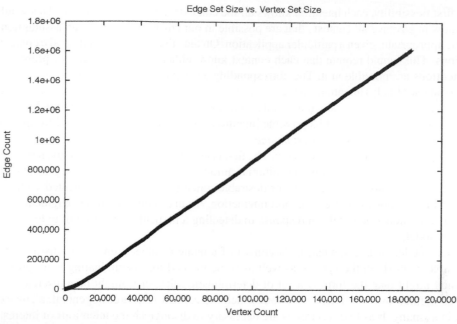

FIGURE 14.2

The number of edges in the Wikipedia graph as a function of the number of vertices during the process of graph growth.

Suppose that we have a lexical digraph, $G = (V, E)$, and a set of words, $S \subseteq V$. We assume that we do *not* care about the "words" in $V - S$ (in fact, they may not even be words in our target language). Then instead of working with the graph G, we use the graph $G' = (S, E')$, where

$$E' = \{(x, y) \mid (x, y) \in E \wedge x, y \in S\}.$$

In addition to solving the problem of lexical noise, this approach has the benefit that it is easy to limit the system's knowledge to a particular domain, if appropriate. For instance, we might make S a set of words about cars if we know we will be using the system in a context where cars are the only objects of interest. In this manner, we can carefully control the linguistic knowledge of our system and remove a source of error that is difficult to avoid in a fully automated knowledge-acquisition process.

14.5.4 Application to Intent Recognition

To use contextual information to perform intent recognition, we must decide how we want to model the relationship between intentions and contexts. This requires that we describe what intentions and contexts *are* and that we specify how they are *related*. There are at least two plausible ways to deal with the latter consideration: We could choose to make intentions "aware" of contexts, or we might make contexts "aware" of intentions.

In the first possibility, each intention knows all the contexts in which it can occur. This would imply that we know in advance all contexts that are possible in our environment. Such an assumption may or may not be appropriate, given a particular application. On the other hand, we might make contexts aware of intentions. This would require that each context know, either deterministically or probabilistically, which intentions are possible in it. The corresponding assumption is that we know in advance all the possible (or at least likely) intentions of the agents we may observe. Either of these approaches is possible and may be appropriate for a particular application. In the present work, we adopt the latter approach by making each context aware of its possible intentions. This awareness is achieved by specifying the content of *intention models* and *context models*.

An intention model consists of two parts: The first is an activity model, which is given by a particular HMM, and second a name. This is the minimal amount of information necessary to allow a robot to perform disambiguation. If necessary or desirable, intentions could be augmented with additional information that a robot could use to support interaction. As an example, we might augment an intention model to specify an action to take in response to detecting a particular sequence of hidden states from the activity model.

A context model, at a minimum, must consist of a name or other identifier to distinguish it from other possible contexts in the system, as well as some method for discriminating between intentions. This method might take the form of a set of deterministic rules, or it might be a discrete probability distribution defined over the intentions about which the context is aware. In general, a context model can contain as many or as few features as are necessary to distinguish the intentions of interest.

For our work, we focused on two kinds of information: (1) the location of the event being observed and (2) the identities of any objects being interacted with by an agent. Context of the first kind was useful for basic experiments testing the performance of our system against a system that uses no contextual information but did not use lexical digraphs at all; contexts and possible intentions we determined entirely by hand. Our other source of context, object identities, relied entirely on lexical digraphs as a way to represent object affordances. One of the major sources of information when inferring intent is contained by object affordances.

Affordances indicate the types of actions that can be performed with a particular object and through their relative probabilities constrain the possible intentions a person can have when interacting with an object. For example, one can *drink from*, *break*, *empty*, or *wash* a glass; all have different probabilities. At the same time, the state of the object can further constrain the potential intentions: It is more likely that one would drink from a full glass, while for an empty, dirty glass, the most probable intention would be to wash it. We use the system described in Section 14.5.3 to extract information about object affordances.

The goal was to build a representation that contains, for each object, the likelihood of all actions that can be performed on that object. The system produces a weighted graph linking words that are connected in a dependency parse of a sentence in the corpus. The weights count the number of times each relationship appears and must be converted to probabilities. To obtain the probability of each action given an object, O, we look at all verbs, V, in relation to O and compute the probability of V given O:

$$p(V|O) = \frac{w(O, V)}{\sum_{V' \in N(O)} w(O, V')},$$

where $N(O)$ consists of all verbs in the digraph that receive an arc from the O node and $w(O, V)$ is the weight of the arc from O to V, which we use as an approximation to the probability $p(O, V)$.

For objects that have different states (e.g., full vs. empty, open vs. closed), we infer the biased probabilities as follows:

- Merge the state vertex v_s and the object vertex v_o to obtain a new vertex v.
- Update each edge weight $w(v, v_{neighbor})$, as follows:

  - 0 if $v_{neighbor}$ was not adjacent to both v_o and v_s.
  - min $w(v_o, v_{neighbor})$, $w(v_s, v_{neighbor})$, otherwise.

- Normalize probabilities as in the stateless case.
- Return the probability distribution.

In this way, we can extract probabilities of actions for objects that are stateless as well as objects containing state.

14.5.4.1 *Inference algorithm*

Suppose that we have an activity model (i.e., an HMM) denoted by w. Let s denote an intention, let c denote a context, and let v denote a sequence of visible states from the activity model w. If we are given a context and a sequence of observations, we would like to find the intention that is the most likely. Mathematically, we want to find

$$\arg \max_s p(s \mid v, c),$$

where the probability structure is determined by the activity model w.

To find the correct s, we start by observing that by Bayes's rule we have:

$$\max_s p(s \mid v, c) = \max_s \frac{p(v \mid s, c) p(s \mid c)}{p(v \mid c)}. \tag{14.1}$$

We can further simplify matters by noting that the denominator is independent of our choice of s. Moreover, we assume without loss of generality that the possible observable symbols are independent of the current context. Based on these observations, we can write

$$\max_s p(s \mid v, c) \approx \max_s p(v \mid s) p(s \mid c). \tag{14.2}$$

This approximation suggests an algorithm for determining the most likely intention given a series of observations and a context. For each possible intention s for which $p(s \mid c) > 0$, we compute the probability $p(v \mid s) p(s \mid c)$ and choose as our intention that s has the greatest probability. The probability $p(s \mid c)$ is available, either by assumption or from our linguistic model, and if the HMM w represents the activity model associated with intention s, then we assume that $p(v \mid s) = p(v \mid w)$. This assumption may be made in the case of location-based context for simplicity, or in the case of object affordances because we focus on simple activities (e.g., reaching), where the same HMM w is used for multiple intentions s. Of course, a perfectly general system would have to choose an appropriate HMM dynamically given the context; we leave the task of designing such a system as future work for now and focus on dynamically deciding on the context to use, based on the digraph information.

14.5.4.2 *Intention-based control*

In robotics applications, simply determining an observed agent's intentions may not be enough. Once a robot knows what another's intentions are, the robot should be able to act on its knowledge to achieve a goal. With this in mind, we developed a simple method to allow a robot to dispatch a behavior based on its intent-recognition capabilities. The robot first infers the global intentions of all the agents it is tracking and, for the activity corresponding to the inferred global intention, determines the most likely local intention. If the robot determines over multiple timesteps that a certain local intention has the highest probability, it can dispatch a behavior in response to the situation it believes is taking place.

For example, consider the activity of stealing an object. The local intentions for this activity might include "approaching the object," "picking up the object," and "walking off with the object." If the robot knows that in its current context the local intention "picking up the object" is not acceptable and it infers that an agent is in fact picking up the object, it can execute a behavior—for example, stopping the thief or warning another person or robot of the theft.

14.6 Experiments on Physical Robots

This section shows how to apply the ideas described in Sections 14.4 and 14.5 to physical robots operating in unstructured environments. We provide quantitative and qualitative evaluation of several intent recognition systems in situations where service robots could be expected to operate.

14.6.1 Setup

To validate our approach, we performed experiments in two different settings: a *surveillance setting* and a *household setting*. In the surveillance setting, we performed experiments using a Pioneer 2DX mobile robot with an onboard computer, a laser range finder, and a Sony PTZ camera. In the household setting, we performed experiments using both a Pioneer robot and a humanoid Nao robot.

14.6.1.1 *Surveillance setting*

We trained our Pioneer to understand three basic activities: *following*, in which one agent trails behind another; *meeting*, in which two agents approach one another directly; and *passing*, in which two agents move past each other without otherwise directly interacting (see Figure 14.3).

FIGURE 14.3

HMM structure for the *follow* activity.

We placed our trained robot in an indoor environment and had it observe the interactions of multiple human agents with each other and with multiple static objects. In our experiments, we considered both the case where the robot acts as a passive observer and the case where the robot executes an action on the basis of the intentions it infers from the agents it is watching.

We were particularly interested in the system's performance in two cases. First we wanted to determine the performance of the system when a single activity could have different underlying intentions based on the current context. So, returning to our example in Section 14.5.1, the activity of "moving one's hand toward a chess piece" could be interpreted as "making a move" during a game or as "cleaning up" after the game is over. This case deals directly with the problem that in some situations two apparently identical activities may in fact be very different, although the difference may lie entirely in the contextually determined intentional component of the activity.

In the second case of interest, we sought to determine the performance of the system in disambiguating two activities that were in fact different but, due to environmental conditions, appeared superficially very similar. This situation represents one of the larger stumbling blocks of systems that do not incorporate contextual awareness.

In the first set of experiments, the same footage was given to the system several times, each with a different context, to determine whether the system could use context alone to disambiguate agents' intentions. We considered three pairs of scenarios: leaving the building on a normal day/evacuating the building, getting a drink from a vending machine/repairing a vending machine, and going to a movie during the day/going to clean the theater at night. We would expect our intent-recognition system to correctly disambiguate between each of these pairs using knowledge of its current context (see Figure 14.4).

The second set of experiments was performed in a lobby; it had agents meeting each other and passing each other both with and without contextual information about which of these two activities was more likely in the context of the lobby. To the extent that meeting and passing appear to be similar, we would expect that the use of context would help to disambiguate the activities.

Finally, to test our intention-based control, we set up two scenarios. In the first scenario (the "theft" scenario), a human enters his office carrying a bag. As he enters, he sets his bag down by the entrance. Another human enters the room, takes the bag, and leaves. Our robot was set up to observe these actions and send a signal to a "patrol robot" in the hall that a theft had occurred. The patrol robot is then supposed to follow the thief for as long as possible (see Figures 14.5 and 14.6).

In the second scenario, our robot is waiting in the hall and observes a human leaving the bag in the hallway. The robot is supposed to recognize this as a suspicious activity and follow the human who dropped the bag for as long as possible.

14.6.1.2 *Household setting*

In the household setting, we performed two sets of experiments that further tested the system's ability to predict intentions and perform actions based on those predictions. In the first set, we trained the Pioneer to recognize a number of household objects and activities and to disambiguate between similar activities based on contextual information. Specifically, we had the system observe three different scenarios: a homework scenario, in which a human was observed reading books and typing on a laptop; a meal scenario, in which a human was observed eating and drinking; and an emergency scenario, in which a human was observed using a fire extinguisher to put out a fire in a trash can.

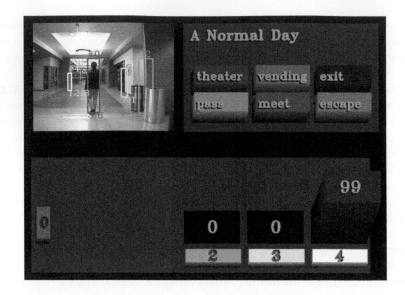

FIGURE 14.4

Using context to infer that an agent is leaving a building under normal circumstances. The human (with identifier 0 in the image) is moving toward the door (identifier 4), and the system is 99% confident that agent 0's intent is to exit the building. Agent 0 is not currently interacting with objects 2 or 3, so the system does not attempt to classify agent 0's intentions with respect to those objects.

In the second set of experiments, we trained a humanoid robot to observe a human eating or doing homework. The robot was programmed to predict the observed person's intentions and offer assistance at socially appropriate moments. We used these scenarios to evaluate the performance of the lexical digraph approach.

14.6.2 Results

In both settings, our robots were able to effectively observe the agents within their fields of view and correctly infer the intentions of the agents they observed. Videos of system performance for both the Pioneer and the humanoid robots can be found at `www.cse.unr.edu/~rkelley/robot-videos.html`.

To provide a quantitative evaluation of intent-recognition performance, we use two measures:

- *Accuracy rate* = the ratio of the number of observation sequences, of which the winning intentional state matches the ground truth, to the total number of test sequences.
- *Correct duration* = C/T, where C is the total time during which the intentional state with the highest probability matches the ground truth and T is the number of observations.

The accuracy rate of our system is 100%: The system ultimately chose the correct intention in all the scenarios on which it was tested. In practice, this means very little. Much more interesting is the correct duration. Next, we consider the correct duration measure in more detail for each of the cases in which we were interested.

14.6.2.1 *One activity, many intentions*

The first six rows of Table 14.1 indicate the system's disambiguation performance. For example, we see that in the case of the scenario *Leave building*, the intentions *normal* and *evacuation* are correctly inferred 96.2% and 96.4% of the time, respectively. We obtain similar results in two other scenarios where the only difference between the two activities in question is the intentional information represented by the robot's current context. Thus, we see that the system is able to use this contextual information to correctly disambiguate intentions.

14.6.2.2 *Similar-looking activities*

As we can see from the last four rows of Table 14.1, the system performs substantially better when using context than it does without contextual information. Because *meeting* and *passing* can, depending on the position of the observer, appear very similar, without context it may be difficult to decide what the two agents are trying to do. With the proper contextual information, though, it becomes much easier to determine the intentions of the agents in the scene.

14.6.2.3 *Intention-based control*

In both the scenarios we developed to test our intention-based control, our robot correctly inferred the ground-truth intention and correctly responded to the inferred intention. In the theft scenario, the robot correctly recognized the theft and reported it to the patrol robot in the hallway; that robot was able to track the thief. In the bag drop scenario, the robot correctly recognized that dropping a bag off in a hallway is a suspicious activity and was able to follow the suspicious agent through the hall. Both examples indicate that dispatching actions based on inferred intentions using context and hidden Markov models is a feasible approach (see Figure 14.5).

Table 14.1 Quantitative Evaluation

Scenario (with context)	Correct duration (%)
Leave building (normal)	96.2
Leave building (evacuation)	96.4
Theater (cleanup)	87.9
Theater (movie)	90.9
Vending (getting drink)	91.1
Vending (repair)	91.4
Meet (no context) - Agent 1	65.8
Meet (no context) - Agent 2	72.4
Meet (context) - Agent 1	97.8
Meet (context) - Agent 2	100.0

14.6.2.4 *Lexical-digraph-based system*

Pioneer robot experiments. To test the lexically informed system in the household setting, we considered three different scenarios. In the first, the robot observed a human during a meal, eating and drinking. In the second, the human was doing homework—reading a book and taking notes on a computer. In the last scenario, the robot observed a person sitting on a couch eating candy. A trash can in the scene then catches on fire, and the robot observes the human using a fire extinguisher to put the fire out (see Figure 14.6).

In the first set of experiments (homework scenario), the objects, their states, and the available activities were:

- Book (open): read, keep, copy, have, put, use, give, write, own, hold, study
- Book (closed): have, put, use, give, own, open, take
- Mouse: click, move, use
- Bottle (full): find, drink, squeeze, shake, have, put, take
- Laptop (open): boot, configure, break, take, leave
- Laptop (closed): boot, configure, break, take, leave

For the eating scenario, the objects, states, and activities were:

- Pitcher: find, drink, shake, have, throw, put, take, pour
- Glass (full): hold, break, drink
- Glass (empty): hold, break
- Plate (full): eat, think of, sell, give
- Plate (empty): throw

For the fire scenario, the objects and activities were:

- Snack: eat, think of, sell, give
- Extinguisher: keep, activate, use

In each scenario, the robot observed a human interacting with objects by performing some of the activities in the lists.

Defining a ground truth for these scenarios is slightly more difficult than in the previous ones since in them the observed agent performs multiple activities and the boundaries between activities in sequence are not clearly defined. However, we can report that, except on the boundary between two activities, the correct duration of the system is 100%. Performance on the boundary is more variable, but it is not clear that this is an avoidable phenomenon. We are currently working on carefully ground-truthed videos to allow us to better compute the accuracy rate and the correct duration for these sorts of scenarios.

Humanoid robot experiments. To test the system performance on another robot platform, we had our humanoid, Nao, observe a human doing homework and eating. The objects, states, and activities for these scenarios were the same as in the Pioneer experiments, with one additional object in the homework scenario: We trained the system to recognize a blank piece of paper, along with the intention of writing. We did this so that the robot could offer a pen to the human after recognizing the human's intention to write.

FIGURE 14.5

An observer robot catches an agent stealing a bag. The top *left video* is the observer's viewpoint, the top *left* bars represent possible intentions, the bottom *left bars* are the robot's inferred intentions for each agent (with corresponding probabilities), and the bottom *right video* is the patrol robot's viewpoint.

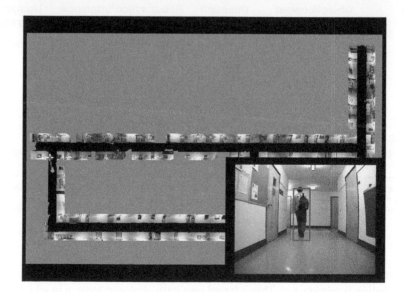

FIGURE 14.6

A patrol robot, notified that a theft has occurred, sees the thief in the hallway and follows him. Note: The video shows the patrol robot's viewpoint superimposed on a map of the building.

Table 14.2 Homework Scenario

Human action	Object/context detected	Intention	Robot action/utterance	Human utterance
reach for book	book : closed	take	"Hey, I know that book. It is about robots"	"That is right"
open book and read	book : open	read	"Are you going to read for a long time?"	"A little while"
reach for laptop	laptop : closed	take laptop	"I see you need to start your computer"	"That's right"
open laptop and type	laptop : open	type	"I will get some rest while you type"	"Thank you"
close laptop	laptop : closed	take laptop	"Oh you are done!"	
reach for paper	paper	write	"Do you need a pen for your writing?"	"Sure"

Note: This table describes the interactions that take place between the human and our humanoid robot. At the end of the scenario, the robot grabs a pen and hands it to the human.

Table 14.3 Eating Scenario

Human action	Object/context detected	Intention	Robot action/utterance	Human utterance
reach for food	paper plate : full	eat	"I see it is time for lunch. Would you like a fork?"	"Sure"
reach for bottle	bottle	pour	"Do you have a glass for your drink?"	"Yes, I have a glass"
reach for class	glass : full	drink	"Be careful - you do not want to spill"	"Yes, thank you"
reach for food on plate	paper plate : full	eat		
reach for empty plate	paper plate : empty	throw away	"Do you want me to throw that away?"	"Sure"

Note: When the human accepts the robot's offer of a fork, the robot hands the fork to the human. At the end of the scenario, the robot walks to the human, takes the plate from his hand, and throws it away.

To demonstrate that the robot detects human intentions, it takes certain actions or speaks to the person as soon as the intention is recognized. This is based on a basic dialogue system in which, for each intention, the robot has a certain repertoire of actions or utterances it can perform. Our experiments indicate that the robot correctly detects user intentions before the human's actions are finalized. Moreover, no delays or misidentified intentions occurred, ensuring that the robot's responses to the human were not inappropriate for the human's activities. Tables 14.2 and 14.3 detail the interactions between the human and the robot in these scenarios.

14.7 Discussion

The system just described illustrates a number of issues that must be dealt with to deploy an intent-recognition system on a robot intended for human interaction. In this section, we discuss a number of general concerns for future systems that may be designed for human–robot interaction. We then go on to present some of the other methods we are exploring.

14.7.1 General Concerns

The first and foremost problem that must be addressed by designers of intent-recognition systems for HRI is that they must be *fast*. Often, a robot is receiving sensor data several times per second and must integrate that data, make a prediction, and act on that prediction in a matter of a few hundred milliseconds. Even with improvements in robot hardware, it is likely that intent-recognition systems will have to be explicitly designed around time constraints.

Just as important, future systems should consider the sources of their inputs and should plan for robustness in the face of occasionally unreliable input. It is likely that probabilistic methods will continue to do well with this issue. However, explicitly planning for such inputs will likely require new techniques.

Finally, we would like to propose the following considerations for future system designs:

- *Better sensing.* As robots continue to be deployed to social situations, it will be increasingly important for designers to include more and more varied sensors to allow robots to predict intentions. The use of cameras (including depth ones) should allow robots to eventually predict intentions much in the same way that humans do, but better-than-human performance could be enabled by intelligent sensor use.
- *Better evaluation.* The preliminary system we have developed performs well on the simple tasks on which it was tested. To be deployed to real-world scenarios, further testing is required to determine the limits of this and similar systems. In particular, there are two forms of testing that would be extremely useful: (1) testing using carefully designed ground-truthed scenarios and (2) testing involving human responses to systems with and without intent-recognition systems enabled. Only with more testing will we be able to decide which systems are suitable for human interaction.
- *System integration.* With robots, intent-recognition systems rarely operate in isolation. Future research will be required to determine the best way to integrate intent recognition into larger systems that can perform useful tasks for humans.

14.7.2 Additional Approaches and Future Work

In addition to the approach outlined in this chapter, we have experimented with a few alternative methods for predicting intentions. Earlier, in Figure 14.1, we showed a history-based method for predicting intentions. In that approach, we used HMMs to recognize low-level intentions that then triggered events that led to changes in a state machine—pictured below the images in the figure. Paths through the state machine were used to identify ongoing activities. Extensions to this event-based approach are continuing and planned for future work.

Additionally, we have explored alternate methods of representing and learning contextual information. In particular, we have found that contextual information about scenes can be compactly represented using sparse autoencoders [11]. In future work, we hope to both extend the limits of this approach and combine it with our other contextual models to improve the robustness of our system.

14.8 Conclusion

Understanding intentions in context is an essential human activity, and it is highly probable that it will be just as essential in any robot that must function in social domains. The approach we propose is based on perspective-taking and experience gained by the robot using its own sensory-motor capabilities. The robot carries out inference using its previous experience and its awareness of its own spatiotemporal context. We described the visual capabilities that support our robots' intent recognition and validated our approach on a physical robot that was able to correctly determine the intentions of a number of people performing multiple activities in a variety of contexts.

References

[1] Premack D, Woodruff G. Does the chimpanzee have a theory of mind?. Behav Brain Sci 1978;1(4):515–26.

[2] Gopnick A, Moore A. Changing your views: how understanding visual perception can lead to a new theory of mind. In: Lewis C, Mitchell P, editors. Children's early understanding of mind. Lawrence Erlbaum 1994:157–81.

[3] Iacobini M, Molnar-Szakacs I, Gallese V, Buccino G, Mazziotta J, Rizzolatti G. Grasping the intentions of others with one's own mirror neuron system. PLoS Biol 2005;3(3):e79.

[4] Duda R, Hart P, Stork D. Pattern classification. Wiley-Interscience; 2000.

[5] Rabiner LR. A tutorial on hidden-Markov models and selected applications in speech recognition. Proc IEEE 1989;77(2).

[6] Pook P, Ballard D. Recognizing teleoperating manipulations. In: International Conference on Robotics and Automation; 1993. p. 578–85.

[7] Hovland G, Sikka P, McCarragher B. Skill acquisition from human demonstration using a hidden Markov model. In: International Conference on Robotics and Automation; 1996. p. 2706–11.

[8] Ogawara K, Takamatsu J, Kimura H, Ikeuchi K. Modeling manipulation interactions by hidden Markov models. In: International Conference Intelligent Robots and Systems; 2002. p. 1096–101.

[9] Tavakkoli A, Kelley R, King C, Nicolescu M, Nicolescu M, Bebis G. A vision-based architecture for intent recognition. In: Proceedings of the International Symposium on Visual Computing; 2007. p. 173–82.

[10] Gray J, Breazeal C, Berlin M, Brooks A, Lieberman J. Action parsing and goal inference using self as simulator. In: IEEE International Workshop on Robot and Human Interactive Communication; 2005.

[11] Kelley R, Wigand L, Hamilton B, Browne K, Nicolescu MN, Nicolescu M. Deep networks for predicting human intent with respect to objects. Proc HRI 2012:171–2.

[12] Konolige K. Projected texture stereo. In: ICRA; 2010.

[13] Rusu RB, Cousins S. 3D is here: Point cloud library (*pcl*). In: International Conference on Robotics and Automation; 2011.

[14] Trucco E, Verri A. Introductory techniques for 3-D computer vision. Prentice Hall PTR; 1998.

[15] Kautz H. A formal theory of plan recognition. PhD thesis, Department of Computer Science, University of Rochester, 1987 [Tech. report 215].

[16] Thrun S, Burgard W, Fox D. Probabilistic robotics. MIT Press; 2005.

[17] Charniak E, Goldman R. A Bayesian model of plan recognition. Artif Intell 1993;64:53–79.

[18] Yamazaki A, Yamazaki K, Kuno Y, Burdelski M, Kawashima M, Kuzuoka H. Precision timing in human–robot interaction: coordination of head movement and utterance. In: Proceedings of the SIGCHI Conference on Human Factors in Computing Systems; 2008.

[19] Demiris Y. Prediction of intent in robotics and multi-agent systems. Cognitive Process 2007.

[20] Wikipedia. The Free Encyclopedia; 2004.

Author Index

Subject Index

Printed and bound by CPI Group (UK) Ltd, Croydon, CR0 4YY

03/10/2024

01040322-0008